MORAL DISENGAGEMENT

Publisher: Rachel Losh
Associate Publisher: Jessica Bayne
Senior Acquisitions Editor: Christine Cardone
Assistant Editor: Catherine Michaelsen
Editorial Assistant: Melissa Rostek
Editorial Intern: Daria Kaczorowska
Executive Marketing Manager: Katherine Nurre
Director, Content Management Enhancement: Tracey Kuehn
Managing Editor: Lisa Kinne
Project Editor: Edward Dionne, MPS North America LLC
Design Manager: Vicki Tomaselli
Interior Designer: Lee McKevitt
Cover Designer: Joseph DePinho
Art Manager: Matthew McAdams
Illustrations: Electra Graphics
Photo Editor: Candice Cheesman
Production Manager: Sarah Segal
Composition: MPS Limited
Printing and Binding: RR Donnelley
Front Cover Art: *Voyager* (acrylic collage), Coxall, Margaret/Private Collection/Bridgeman Images
Back Cover Art: Albert Bandura

Library of Congress Control Number: 2015936306

ISBN-13: 978-1-4641-6005-9
ISBN-10: 1-4641-6005-8

Printed in the United States of America

First printing

Worth Publishers
One New York Plaza
Suite 4500
New York, NY 10004-1562
www.worthpublishers.com

■ ■ ■ ■ ■ ■ ■

MORAL DISENGAGEMENT

How People Do Harm and
Live With Themselves

Albert Bandura

Stanford University

worth publishers
Macmillan Learning

New York

Dedication

This book is dedicated to the memory of my wife Virginia and the fulfilling life we enjoyed. Her humanitarian commitment to the betterment of people's lives is very much in keeping with the moral issues this book addresses.

BRIEF CONTENTS

CONTENTS

PREFACE

This book addresses the moral dimension of people's lives. Societies devise policies and institutional practices that shape the quality of their members' lives and how wrongdoings are managed. Societies adopt standards of right and wrong reflecting their values and implement these standards through various legal and societal sanctions. These types of sanctions are often insufficient to curb harmful behavior because, being externally based, they are circumventable.

A humane and self-governing society is rooted in moral self-sanctions. People continuously preside over their behavior and must live with the self-evaluative consequences of what they do. Moral self-sanctions keep behavior in line with moral standards. However, even the power of moral self-sanctions can be neutralized. Social cognitive theory specifies the psychosocial mechanisms by which this neutralization is achieved. Disengagement of moral self-sanctions from detrimental behavior enables people to behave harmfully and still live in peace with themselves.

The conception of moral agency is solidly grounded in the social cognitive theory of self-regulation. The disengagement of moral agency, its social consequences, and the ways to curb it are the subject of this work.

Verification of causation in the social sciences requires converging evidence from divergent methodologies. This is especially true in the verification of theories of moral self-regulation. Because of social and ethical prohibitions, researchers are not at liberty to reproduce inhumanities under controlled laboratory conditions. Experimental studies are therefore limited to relatively minor moral transgressions and hypothetical scenarios. Because of these severe experimental constraints, researchers must investigate harmful practices under naturally occurring conditions and using a variety of methods.

This book presents a theory-based analysis of moral disengagement as it operates at the personal level under social influences that come into play in the flow of everyday life. Micro-level analysis of how people manage, both individually and collectively, the moral aspects of their lives puts a human face on moral disengagement. This level of analysis provides a deeper understanding of casual processes as they occur in natural contexts. Historical records permit longitudinal analysis of systemic moral disengagement over many years. To evaluate the generalizability of the conceptual framework, the disengagement of moral self-sanctions was assessed across radically different spheres of life. Although this book focuses heavily on micro-analysis of causal influences as they occur in natural contexts, it also addresses evidence from controlled experiments and correlational studies with multiple controls for other possible contributing factors.

This book had an unintended origin. Every five years Jeffery Zieg, the director of the Erickson Foundation, convenes a multifaceted conference on the evolution of psychotherapy. As part of this conference I usually deliver one talk, "Applications of Social Cognitive Theory for Individual and Social Change," and another talk, "Moral Disengagement in the Perpetration of Inhumanities." Jeffery kept urging me to write a book on moral disengagement on the grounds that it would address fundamental issues in moral theory and because moral disengagement is a growing social problem in all walks of life. My response was, "No way. Writing a book takes control of one's life." Besides, I had already published chapters and a set of research papers on moral disengagement viewed from the agentic perspective of social cognitive theory.

Jeffery made me an offer that I could not refuse. The Erikson Foundation would publish a volume containing a collection of the papers that I published on this topic. All I had to do, he explained, was to assemble the collection of papers and write an introductory chapter that places moral disengagement in the broader context of moral theory and provides a rich overview of key issues in the exercise of moral agency.

As I began to assemble the published items, I noticed a few conspicuous gaps that I could easily fill. The fillers ballooned to 75-page chapters! I was faced with a peculiar hybrid volume containing a couple of voluminous book chapters amid a collection of papers. Filling these gaps with chapter-length entries sparked my interest in what a book on moral disengagement, written with in-depth coverage and breadth of scope, might look like. There was no turning back. The evolved book became more suitable for a major publishing house with resources to reach both academic and lay audiences. I am profoundly grateful to Jeffery for talking me into undertaking a project I had no intention of doing. Halfway through the project my wife passed away. Engrossment in writing this book helped to lessen my loneliness and grief.

I remain ever grateful to my invaluable collaborators far and wide in diverse research projects on moral disengagement. Gian Vittorio Caprara, Claudio Barbaranelli, and Concetta Pastorelli presided over our longitudinal study at the University of Rome, La Sapienza, where we examined children's moral disengagement and its impact on their psychosocial development. Michael Osofsky, a Stanford student at the time, contributed importantly to research on the influential role of moral disengagement in executioners in several southern penitentiaries. Alfred McAlister, at the University of Texas, was a major player in the study of moral disengagement in support of the military campaigns against Iraq and terrorist sanctuaries after the 9/11 terrorist attacks. Jenny White and Lisa Bero, at the University of California San Francisco Medical Center, played a prominent role in research on moral disengagement in the corporate development and marketing of products injurious to human health.

I wish to express my indebtedness to Katie Bramlett and Priyanka Sumanadasa for their helpful assistance with early versions of this book. Special gratitude goes to Karen Saltzman for her splendid preparation of the manuscript for publication. I thank her for her forbearance with multiple revisions, collegial guidance of assistants, and assembling the huge reference sections including obscure corporate memos and other internal documents.

I am also deeply thankful for the assistance offered by a dedicated coterie of Stanford undergraduates under the enthusiastic guidance of Tommy Tobin. They include Tommy, Michael Sexton, Kelsey Mrkonic, Alexander Paraschuk, Nadia Stoufflet, and Vanna Tran. They hunted down obscure publications in unusual sources and typed the endless revisions that the book went through. Roxana Godinez was of considerable help with the references.

My two daughters had a hand in this undertaking as well. Carol kept me well supplied with wrongdoers using especially ingenious modes of moral disengagement in unusual moral predicaments. Mary was the unmerciful editor. She purged the manuscript of ambiguities, redundancies, irrelevancies, and organizational lapses. It is a much better book for her critical editing.

I had the good fortune of having Christine Cardone as the editor overseeing the publication of this book. Viewing it as a groundbreaking work, she shepherded it devotedly through every phase of the publishing process. I also wish to acknowledge my indebtedness to Barbara Curialle, who edited the manuscript meticulously.

Some of the material in this book is drawn from publications I originally authored. However, most of this material was revised, expanded, reorganized, and updated. I am deeply grateful to the following publishers for their permission to use this material. They include the American Psychological Association; the Association for Psychological Science; Annual Reviews, Inc.; Cambridge University Press; Gage Cengage Press; Kluwer Academic Publishers; Lawrence Erlbaum Associates; Oxford University Press; Prentice Hall; Sage Publications; and Springer Science + Business Media.

Chapter 1

■ ■ ■ ■ ■ ■ ■

THE NATURE OF
MORAL AGENCY

A full understanding of morality must explain not only how people come to behave morally, but also how they can behave inhumanely and still retain their self-respect and feel good about themselves. The latter part of the story on the exercise of moral agency presents the tougher explanatory challenge. Adherence to moral principles is easier to explain than is the paradox of violating one's moral principles without loss of self-respect while doing so. This violation can be achieved by selective disengagement of moral self-sanctions from harmful conduct. The disengagement of morality is typically cited in weighty moral predicaments and large-scale inhumanities. In point of fact, it is common in all types of moral predicaments managed by ordinary people in all walks of everyday life.

In the development of a moral self, individuals adopt standards of right and wrong that are guides and deterrents for conduct. They do things that give them satisfaction and a sense of self-worth. They refrain from behaving in ways that violate their moral standards because such conduct will bring self-condemnation. Moral agency is thus exercised through the constraint of negative self-sanctions for conduct that violates one's moral standards and the support of positive self-sanctions for conduct faithful to personal moral standards. In the face of situational inducements to behave inhumanely, people can choose to behave otherwise by exerting self-influence or learn how to do so. Self-sanctions keep conduct in accordance with internal standards.

The exercise of moral agency has dual aspects—*inhibitive* and *proactive*. The inhibitive form is manifested in the ability to refrain from behaving inhumanely. The proactive form, grounded in a humanitarian ethic, is manifested in compassion for the plight of others and efforts to further their well-being, often at personal costs (Rorty, 1993). In cases of proactive moral courage, individuals prevail as moral agents over entrenched social practices that are unjust and inhumane. An all-embracing morality includes doing good things, not just refraining from bad ones. However, theories of morality focus on the inhibitive form more intensively than on the proactive one.

Most of the theorizing and research on morality focuses heavily on the acquisition of moral standards and moral reasoning, often detached from moral conduct. However, the acquisition of moral standards is only half the story in the exercise of moral agency. Moral standards, whether characterized as conscience, moral prescripts, or principles, do not function as unceasing internal regulators of conduct. People often face pressures to engage in harmful activities that provide desired benefits but violate their moral standards. To engage in those activities and live with themselves, they have to strip morality from their actions or invest them with worthy purposes. Disengagement of moral self-sanctions enables people to compromise their moral standards and still retain their sense of moral integrity.

Self-regulatory mechanisms do not come into play unless they are activated. Many psychosocial maneuvers can be used to disengage moral self-sanctions from inhumane conduct. Selective activation and disengagement of self-sanctions permits different types of conduct by persons with the same moral standards. Indeed, large-scale inhumanities are typically perpetrated by people who can be considerate and compassionate in other areas of their lives. They can even be ruthless and humane simultaneously toward different individuals, depending on whom they include and exclude from their category of humanity. This selectivity of moral engagement was strikingly illustrated by Amon Goeth, the notorious Nazi commandant of a concentration camp. While dictating a letter replete with empathy and compassion for his ailing father, he saw a prisoner on the grounds who he thought was not working hard enough. He whipped out his revolver and callously shot the prisoner. The commandant was both overcome with compassion and savagely cruel at the same time.

Figure 1.1 presents schematically eight psychosocial mechanisms by which people selectively disengage moral self-regulation from their harmful conduct. These mechanisms operate at four sites in the process of moral self-regulation. At the *behavior locus*, people sanctify harmful means by investing them with worthy social and moral purposes. The righteous ends are used to justify harmful means. Harmful conduct is also rendered benign or even altruistic through advantageous comparison. Belief that one's harmful actions will prevent more human suffering than they cause makes the behavior look altruistic. Euphemistic language in its sanitizing and convoluted forms cloaks harmful behavior in innocuous language and removes humanity from it. These three mechanisms at the behavior locus are especially powerful because they serve a dual function: They engage morality in

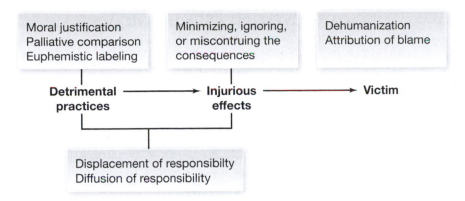

Figure 1.1 Eight mechanisms through which moral self-sanctions are selectively disengaged from harmful behavior at four points in moral self-regulation. From A. Bandura, 1986, *Social foundations of thought and action: A social cognitive theory*, 1st edition, © 1986. Reprinted by permission of Pearson Education, Inc., Upper Saddle River, NJ.

the harmful mission but disengage morality in its execution. For example, in instances of military force, leaders morally justify the military mission as serving humane purposes. However, the soldiers who have to do the fighting strip morality from their lethal activities to enable themselves to kill the enemy without being tormented by the slayings.

At the *agency locus*, people evade personal accountability for harmful conduct by displacing responsibility to others and by dispersing it widely so that no one bears responsibility. This absolves them of blame for the harm they cause. At the *outcome locus*, perpetrators disregard, minimize, distort, or even dispute the injurious effects of their actions. As long as harmful effects are out of sight and out of mind there is no moral issue to contend with because no perceived harm has been done. At the *victim locus*, perpetrators exclude those they maltreat from their category of humanity by divesting them of human qualities or attributing animalistic qualities to them. Rendering their victims subhuman weakens moral qualms over treating them harshly. The additional moral disengagement at the victim locus blames the victims for bringing the maltreatment on themselves or attributes it to compelling circumstances. In this mode of self-exoneration, perpetrators view themselves as victims forced to behave injuriously by wrongdoers' offensive behavior or by force of circumstances. By viewing themselves as victims, they may feel self-righteous in their retaliatory actions. This set of mechanisms either weakens or eliminates the regulatory power of moral self-sanctions over harmful practices.

Moral disengagement does not alter moral standards. Rather, it provides the means for those who morally disengage to circumvent moral standards in ways that strip morality from harmful behavior and their responsibility for it. However, in other aspects of their lives, they adhere to their moral standards. It is the selective suspension of morality for harmful activities that enables people to retain their positive self-regard while doing harm.

SOCIAL COGNITIVE THEORY

The conception of the nature and function of morality is embedded in a broader social cognitive theory of human agency (Bandura, 2006c, 2008). Before we address issues regarding moral agency and its selective disengagement, a brief review of the agentic conceptual framework of social cognitive theory is presented. To be an agent is to exert intentional influence over one's functioning and over the course of events by one's actions. The capacity for self-influence gives meaning to the exercise of morality. If human behavior were controlled solely by external forces, it would be pointless to hold individuals responsible for their behavior.

Human agency is manifested through forethought, self-reaction, and self-reflection. In *forethought*, people motivate and guide themselves by creating action plans, adopting goals and challenges, and visualizing the likely outcomes of their efforts. A future state has no material existence, so it cannot be a cause of current behavior acting purposefully for its own realization. But through cognitive representation, visualized futures are brought into the present as current guides and motivators of behavior. In this form of anticipatory self-guidance, behavior is governed by visualized goals and anticipated outcomes rather than being pulled by an unrealized future state. The ability to bring goals and anticipated consequences to bear on current activities promotes purposeful and foresightful behavior. Forethought enables people to transcend the dictates of their immediate environment and to shape and regulate the present to realize a desired future. When projected over a long-term course on matters of value, a forethoughtful perspective provides direction, coherence, and meaning to one's life.

Regulation of transgressive behavior by outcome expectations operates through three types of sanctions: legal, social, and self-evaluative. These regulatory sanctions are based on anticipation of consequences. In the legal form, people refrain from behaving transgressively for fear that they will get caught and suffer legal penalties. In the social form, people refrain from transgressive behavior for fear of social censure and other aversive social consequences. In self-regulation based on self-sanctions, self-censure deters people from behaving transgressively. Legal and social systems of control, which are rooted in external sanctions, are called fear controls. The control rooted in self-sanctions is called guilt control.

Self-regulation via self-sanctions is manifested in two ways. The first involves the exercise of restraint over behavior that violates one's standards, even when it is unlikely to be detected. The second is experienced as guilt, remorse, self-criticism, and attempts at restitution for having behaved transgressively. Successful socialization aims to substitute self-control for external social control. As will be amply demonstrated in subsequent chapters, when morality is stripped from profitable transgressive activities, wrongdoers find creative ways of circumventing legal penalties. If social norms regarding the reprehensibility of transgressive activities have eroded, social sanctions carry little weight as deterrents. Despite the centrality of self-sanctions in the regulation of behavior, they typically are unacknowledged or never measured in psychosocial and economic theories. Regardless of whether individuals are "good" or "bad," they have to live with themselves, with the choices they make, and how they behave in their daily lives. A civil society cannot be run on fear control alone. It requires massive social surveillance and an extensive system of punitive sanctions to stifle noncompliance. A civil society is largely a self-governing one.

The second agentic property is *self-reactiveness*. Agents are not only planners and forethinkers: They are also self-regulators. As Searle (2003) notes, having adopted an intention and action plan, one cannot simply sit back and wait for the appropriate performances to appear. Agency thus involves not only the deliberative ability to make choices and action plans but also the ability to construct appropriate courses of action and to motivate and regulate their execution. In the self-regulation process, individuals adopt evaluative standards of conduct, judge their behavior relative to those standards, and respond with self-approval or self-censure, depending on whether the behavior measures up to adopted standards (Bandura, 1991a). In instances of moral failure, moral standards are disengaged from detrimental behavior.

The third agentic property is *self-reflectiveness*. People are not only agents of action: They are also self-examiners of their own functioning. They reflect on their personal efficacy, the soundness of their thoughts and actions, their values, and the meaning and morality of their pursuits. It is at this higher level of self-reflectiveness that individuals address conflicts in alternative courses of action and competing values and favor one course over another. The metacognitive capability to reflect on the nature of oneself and the adequacy of one's thoughts and actions is the most distinctly human core property of agency. It is primarily at the level of self-reflectiveness that individuals confront moral predicaments and distance and exonerate themselves from their detrimental conduct should they choose transgressive courses of action.

These agentic functions are rooted in the belief in one's causative capabilities. This core self-belief, called *self-efficacy*, is the foundation of human aspirations, motivation, and accomplishments (Bandura, 1997). Unless people believe they can produce desired effects by their actions, they have little incentive to act or to persevere in the face of difficulties. Whatever other factors serve as guides and motivators, they are rooted in people's core belief that they can affect the course of events by their actions.

Self-efficacy beliefs affect the quality of human functioning through cognitive, motivational, emotional, and decisional processes—specifically, whether people think optimistically or pessimistically, in self-enabling or self-debilitating ways. These beliefs play a role in the self-regulation of motivation by influencing the goals and challenges people set for themselves, their commitment to those goals, the effort they invest in activities they undertake, and their perseverance in the face of adversity.

Efficacy beliefs also shape people's outcome expectations—whether they expect their efforts to produce favorable outcomes or adverse ones. In addition, efficacy beliefs determine how people view opportunities and impediments. People with low self-efficacy beliefs are easily convinced of the futility of their effort in the face of difficulties. They quickly give up trying. Those with high self-efficacy beliefs view impediments as surmountable by the improvement of self-regulatory skills and perseverant effort. They stay the course in the face of difficulties. People's beliefs in their coping efficacy also play a pivotal role in the quality of their emotional life and their vulnerability to stress and depression. The final way in which self-efficacy beliefs shape people's lives is through their choice of activities and environments at important decision points. By their choices people influence what they become and set the course their lives take.

Resilient belief in one's causative capabilities is a highly adaptive resource in self-development, adaptation, and change. Agentic capability, however, does not come with a built-in value system. It can be used for humane or inhumane purposes. Wrongdoers with an unshakable sense of efficacy can do a lot of harm. For example, an exaggerated collective belief in the power of military might got the United States entangled in what the upper echelon considered to be morally justified wars that became disastrous (Halberstam, 1972; Purdam, 2003).

Triadic Codetermination

Over the years, theorists have engaged in fruitless debates on whether the causes of human behavior reside in the individual, as the dispositionalists claim, or in the environment, as the situationists claim. Social cognitive theory rejects such unidirectional causation in favor of a three-way, interactive causation (Bandura, 1986). In this *triadic codetermination*, as shown in Figure 1.2, human functioning is a product of the interplay of personal influences, the behavior individuals engage in, and the environmental forces that impinge on them. The personal determinants include biological endowment and intrapsychic influences in the form of competencies, belief systems, self-conceptions, emotional states, goals, attitudes, and values. These intrapersonal factors influence how individuals perceive the environment and how they behave. The second contributor is the nature of the behavior that is performed. It can take physical, social, and emotional forms. In the transactions of everyday life, behavior alters environmental conditions, and it is, in turn, altered by the very conditions it creates (Patterson, 1976). Individuals can evoke stereotypic reactions from their

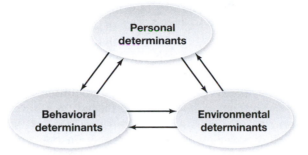

Figure 1.2 Interplay of personal, behavioral, and environmental influences in the motivation and regulation of behavior (Bandura, 2008).

social environment independent of what they say or do on the basis of their race, ethnicity, gender, age, and physical characteristics. In addition, they evoke different social reactions depending on their socially conferred roles and status.

The third contributor in the three-way interplay of determinants is the profusion of environmental influences. The environment is not a monolithic force acting unidirectionally on organisms. Social cognitive theory distinguishes among three types of environments: imposed, selected, and created. The imposed physical and sociocultural environment impinges on people whether they like it or not. They have little control over its presence, but they have some latitude in how they construe it and react to it. However, for the most part, the environment is only a potentiality that does not come into being until it is selected and actualized by the actions that people take. This constitutes the selected lived environment. For example, although college students all inhabit the same campus milieu, they experience different lived environments depending on the courses they select, the extracurricular events they engage in, and the friends they choose. Within the same potential environment, some people take advantage of the opportunities it provides and its enabling and rewarding aspects. Others get themselves intricately enmeshed in its debilitating and aversive aspects. These choices will affect the types of moral predicaments they face. People also construct new physical, technological, and social environments to improve their life conditions. By constructing environments to their liking that previously did not exist, they exercise better control over their lives. Life conditions that provide a wide range of options and opportunities for modifying existing environments and creating new ones require increasing levels of personal agency.

The environment is not confined to physically proximate influences. Integration of social cognitive theory with social network theory specifies the sources and patterns of social influences across broad social networks (Bandura, 2006b). Moreover, recent revolutionary advances in electronic technologies, which enable instant communication worldwide, have transformed the nature, reach, speed, and loci of human influence (Bandura, 2002d). People now spend a good share of their waking life in the symbolic environment of the cyberworld. Life in the cyberworld transcends time, distance, place, and national borders and alters our conceptions of them. This transformative technology has vastly expanded the exercise of personal agency and people's ability to create personalized environments. Through the global Internet, individuals now have at their fingertips the means to convey information and personal views worldwide, independent of time and place. The ability to bypass gatekeepers provides considerable freedom to select and create symbolic environments that can be transmitted via the Internet to vast populations. Moreover, people can now transcend their proximate environment by way of miniaturized wireless devices that make the vast symbolic environment portable, able to be actualized anytime, anyplace. Agentic capability, however, does not come with a built-in value system. It can be used for humane or inhumane purposes.

Traditional psychological theories were formulated long before these revolutionary advances in information technologies. People live in a much different world in the contemporary electronic era. Moral battles are now being waged transnationally by Internet-savvy participants sharing morally relevant information via blogging, podcasting, and texting with unfettered, wireless devices. These globalized modes of influence are being used both in the service of moral disengagement and to expose the use of such practices.

Freedom Within the Triadic Interplay of Influences

The exercise of moral agency raises issues of freedom and determinism. Views on this issue affect judgments about the extent to which individuals can be held accountable for their actions. Humans do not simply react to external inputs in a preprogrammed, robotic way. In the triadic interplay, intrapersonal determinants are part of the causal mix. Hence, individuals are contributors to the conditions that affect them. An agentic conception is at odds with the radical view of causal determinism, which contends that human behavior is completely and inevitably controlled by antecedent, external forces. Murray Gell-Mann, who was awarded the Nobel Prize in physics, insightfully acknowledged the causal complexity of human behavior due to the intervention of thought in the causal chain when he commented, "Imagine how hard physics would be if particles could think" (Gruman, 2006).

Because intrapersonal influences are part of the determining conditions, freedom is not incompatible with people's actions being determined. Through their contributing influence, people have a hand in shaping events and the courses their lives take. In her philosophical analysis of causation, Ismael (2006, 2007) builds a strong case that deliberative and self-referent thought brings into play a variety of intrapersonal influences that can break the chain of determination from environmental influences to action. Deliberative thought not only affects reactions to the environment but also is a means of creating and altering physical and social environments.

When viewed from a social cognitive perspective, freedom is not construed merely passively as the absence of constraints and coercion in choice of action. Rather, it is viewed proactively as the exercise of self-influence in the service of selected goals and desired futures. For example, people have the freedom to vote, but whether they persuade themselves to vote and the level and form of their political engagement depends, in large part, on the self-influence they bring to bear. Through the social influence of collective action, they change political and other social systems. In addition to regulating their actions, people also live in a psychic environment largely of their own making. In this environment, the self-management of their inner lives frees them from unwanted trains of thought (Bandura, 1997).

The development of agentic capabilities adds concrete substance to abstract discourses about freedom and determinism. People who develop their competencies, self-regulatory skills, and enabling self-beliefs create and pursue a wider array of options that expand their freedom of action (Bandura, 1986). They are also more successful in realizing desired futures than those with less-developed agentic resources. The development of strategies for exercising control over perturbing and self-debilitating thinking is also intrapsychically liberating.

There is no absolute freedom. Paradoxically, to gain freedom, individuals have to negotiate rules of behavior for certain activities that require them to relinquish some autonomy. Without traffic laws, for example, driving would be chaotic, perilous, unpredictable, and uncontrollable for everyone. Sensible traffic rules provide predictability and an increased measure of control over getting safely to one's destination and knowing how long it will take.

The exercise of freedom involves rights as well as options and the means to pursue them. At the societal level, people institute, by collective action, sanctions against unauthorized forms of societal control (Bandura, 1986). The less social jurisdiction there is over given activities, the greater the freedom of action in those domains. Once protective laws are built into social systems, there are certain things that a society may not do to individuals who challenge conventional values or vested interests, however much it might like to. Legal prohibitions against unauthorized societal control create personal freedoms that are realities, not illusory abstractions.

Societies differ in their institutions of freedom and in the number and type of activities that are officially exempted from institutional control. For example, societies that decriminalize dissent and social systems that protect journalists from criminal penalties for criticizing government officials and policies are freer than those that allow authoritative power to be used to silence critics or their means of expression. Societies that possess a judiciary independent of other government institutions ensure greater social freedom than those that do not.

Interplay of Social and Self-Influences

People do not operate as autonomous moral agents, impervious to the social realities in which they are enmeshed. In keeping with the socially situated causal structure, social cognitive theory adopts an interactionist perspective on morality. After moral standards are adopted, behavior usually produces two sets of consequences: social outcomes and self-evaluative reactions. These effects may operate as complementary or opposing influences on behavior (Bandura, 1986). Under conditions of shared moral standards, self-regulation of moral conduct creates the fewest strains. This is because socially approved conduct is a source of self-satisfaction and self-pride, and socially punishable conduct is self-censured.

Under social variation in moral standards, individuals generally select like-minded associates who share similar values and moral standards. Compatible associates ensure social support for one's own system of self-evaluation. Selective association reduces personal conflict within social diversity. Behavior is especially susceptible to external influences in the absence of countervailing internal standards. People with weak commitment to personal standards tailor their behavior to fit whatever a situation seems to call for or whatever is most expedient (Snyder & Campbell, 1982).

In conflicts of greater moral weight, there is no more devastating consequence than self-contempt. If the allure of rewards or social pressures outweigh self-censure for personally devalued actions, the result can be cheerless accommodation or disillusionment and cynicism about one's activities. However, people figure out ways to mitigate the costs of self-devaluation. As already noted, people are skilled at reconciling perturbing disparities between personal standards and dissonant conduct by selectively disengaging their moral self-sanctions.

A telling case of selective suspension of morality under forceful political pressure occurred during the earliest days of the United States. The Declaration of Independence proclaims that "all men are created equal" with "unalienable rights." However, in drafting the Constitution the founders were forced to compromise their moral principles over slave ownership because the economies of the southern states relied heavily on slave labor. This bloc of states used its considerable political leverage to maintain slave ownership, whereas northern states had already begun a process of gradual emancipation. The northern states did not want to count the slaves as part of the population, considering them the property of their owners and fearing that the South would have more representatives in the House. Southern states, with a smaller White population than the North, wanted the slaves counted, fearing that otherwise they would be outnumbered in the House of Representatives. In a compromise, the delegates to the Constitutional Convention decided to count five slaves as three Whites. In the mistaken belief that slavery would die out over the next two or three decades, the founders based the Union on racial exclusion, leaving a grievous legacy for future generations to correct (Urofsky, 1988; Wood, 2009). The founders justified their moral compromise as establishing the institutional mechanisms for the eventual abolition of slavery, which they lacked the political power to achieve. However well meaning the intent, subhumanizing an entire group of people as a political strategy officially instills a morally reprehensible public view of that group.

Some of the signers of the Declaration of Independence were slave owners and had to justify to themselves their holding of Black people in servitude as property. In his original draft of the Declaration of Independence, Thomas Jefferson blamed British slave traders for bringing enslaved Blacks to America but tacitly absolved Americans of responsibility for owning them. Some slave owners had the toughest time justifying the very behavior they regarded as "disgraceful to mankind," as George Mason, one of the "fathers of the bill of rights [sic]" called the slave trade (Pavao, 2014). They viewed themselves as compassionate owners who provided a better life for their slaves under the circumstances. Some, such as George Washington, left instructions in their wills freeing their slaves. Patrick Henry, who declared, "Give me liberty, or give me death," acknowledged the power of the convenience of slave ownership: "I am drawn along by the general inconvenience of living without them." He decided to live with the moral compromise without attempting to justify the servitude: "I will not—I cannot justify it, however culpable my conduct" (Pavao, 2014). Vigorously condemning the practice of slavery verified their self-view as compassionate and apparently gave license to own them. The Founding Fathers were not the semi-gods that they are often made out to be.

The struggle for equality continued for a long time before the enslaved were legally freed. The legislative and legal systems the founders created laid the groundwork for Abraham Lincoln to persuade Congress to ratify the Thirteenth Amendment, which abolished slavery, over half a century later. The president faced formidable challenges. Much of the public was unsympathetic to the initiative. His own party was deeply divided on the issue, which threatened to prolong the horrendous Civil War. Lincoln was a resolute moralist on the core principle of racial equality but a pragmatist on the means to achieve it. He used his considerable influence, along with the forceful political maneuvering of Thaddeus Stevens, a powerful House member, to sway reluctant congressmen. The maneuvering included arm-twisting, promises of patronage jobs, and even political bribery. In his review of the movie *Lincoln* commenting on these coercive tactics, A. O. Scott (2012) noted, "The better angels of our nature sometimes need earthly inducements to emerge."

Although the Thirteenth Amendment abolished slavery, the fight for legal equality and justice continued. Many moral compromises were made along the way that impeded the realization of basic human rights. Another century later, in the wake of a monumental civil rights protest movement, President Lyndon Johnson muscled through Congress and signed the Civil Rights Act of 1964, which prohibited racial segregation. In reflecting on this legislative action, he predicted that "we just delivered the South to the Republican Party for a long time to come" (Germany, 2010). The pace of social change is exceedingly slow when heavy political costs make it hard to be morally courageous.

Another type of conflict between social and self-outcomes arises when individuals are punished for activities they value highly. Principled dissenters and nonconformists often find themselves in such predicaments. The relative strengths of self-approval and external censure determine whether a course of action will be pursued or abandoned. There are individuals, however, who sacrifice their lives for their principles. As an adolescent, Alexander Hamilton, who became one of the founders of the United States, explained that he would rather risk death than lose his honor (Freeman, 2001). In a duel with his political rival Aaron Burr, whom he condemned as a conniving politician, Hamilton received a mortal wound defending his honor and died the next day.

Modes of Agency

Theories of human agency focus almost exclusively on agency exercised at the individual level. Social cognitive theory distinguishes among three modes of agency, each of which is founded on the belief in one's ability to affect the course of events by one's actions (Bandura, 1997). These modes of agency include individual, proxy, and collective agency.

In personal agency exercised individually, people bring their influence to bear on activities over which they can exercise direct control. In many spheres of functioning, however, people do not have direct control over conditions that affect their lives. They rely on socially mediated proxy agency by influencing others who have the resources, knowledge, and means to act on their behalf to gain the outcomes they desire. Children work through parents to get what they want, marital partners through spouses, employees through labor unions, companies through outsources, and the general public through elected officials. However, people often turn to proxy agents even in realms of life where they can exercise direct control. They choose not to for a number of reasons. Perhaps they have failed to develop the required competencies to manage certain activities on their own. They believe others can do it better. They do not want to saddle themselves with heavy task demands and stressors. Or they do not want to bear the moral responsibility for harmful activities they perform.

Many of the things that people seek are achievable only by working together through interdependent effort. In the exercise of collective agency, they pool their knowledge, skills, and resources and act in concert to shape their future (Bandura, 2000; Stajkovic, Lee, & Nyberg, 2009). In this multiagent mode of collective agency, participants achieve unity of effort for common cause. They have to coordinate distributed subfunctions across a variety of individuals. The distinctive blend of individual, proxy, and collective agency varies across cultures. But people need all three forms of agency to make it through the day, wherever they live (Bandura, 2002d). Expanding the scope of agency enhances the generalizability of social cognitive theory to collectivistically oriented societies.

There is no such thing as a disembodied group mind that does the reasoning, the morally disengaging, and the acting. A group operates through the behavior of its members. However, a group's belief is not simply the sum of the individual members' beliefs. Interactivity produces emergent effects. It is people who make up a group acting coordinately on shared belief. Emergence is captured in the saying that the "whole is greater than the sum of its parts." In emergence, constituent elements are transformed into new physical and functional properties that are not reducible to those elements. For example, the novel emergent properties of water, such as fluidity and viscosity, are not simply the combined properties of its hydrogen and oxygen microcomponents (Bunge, 1977). Through their interactive effects, the constituents are transformed into new phenomena. Thus, for example, members of a group may not be all that impressive as individuals, but collectively they work in ways that bring out the best in each of them to great effect. A transformative leader can turn a failing group into a successful one. However, the emergent collective agency is not always better. It is not uncommon for groups with members who are highly talented individually to perform poorly collectively because the members cannot work well together as a unit. In such a case, the whole is less than the sum of its parts.

Moral disengagement operates at each of the three types of agency. In moral disengagement at the individual level of agency, individuals try to sanitize and sanctify detrimental activities that are within their sphere of control and shift the responsibility for the activities elsewhere in the chain of command. Proxy agency is widely used by organizations to shield themselves from controversial policies they promote, usually through proxy front groups masquerading as the independent, grassroots voice of the general public. Their mission is disguised under a misleading title with no disclosure of their sponsors. Critics call such pseudo grassroots Astroturf and refer to stealth industry proxies as Astroturfers.

Not all proxy agents operate surreptitiously. Freelancing scientists and those in research institutes set up and funded by sponsor industries challenge the reliability of scientific evidence unsympathetic to their sponsors. They also promote their sponsors' interests at conferences, in the scientific literature, and in testimony before government agencies. Think tanks are the elite proxy agents. Their members analyze data and write policy papers favoring their donors' interests and ideological perspectives. They are the ones who appear regularly in the mass media.

A large-scale form of proxy agency that is heatedly debated concerns outsourcing, especially the offshoring of manufacturing and customer services abroad to reduce labor costs. The proxies include contract factories, vendors, and freelancers. These business practices have been accelerated by globalization and the Internet. Protectionists and free traders fight vigorous battles over the ethics of offshoring. Protectionists focus on the harm these practices cause, arguing that they put people out of work at home, shrink investment in domestic manufacturing, and foster sweatshop working conditions abroad with little respect for human and labor rights. Moreover, such practices degrade local environments in countries that often lack regulatory safeguards. In the protectionists' view, offshoring is exploitative economic colonialism. Free traders, in contrast, accent the benefits of offshoring. They claim that without offshoring, their businesses cannot survive in the severely competitive marketplace, creating even greater job losses at home. A free-trade system, they argue, promotes mutual benefits for the societies involved. It spurs economic growth, which raises living standards. On the negative side, free traders argue that trade barriers and other protectionist policies distort and stifle the free-market system, which hurts everyone. Among the ethical issues linked to offshoring, inhumane and abusive workplace conditions are of special concern. Ethical outsourcers and offshorers should set workplace standards, monitor their enforcement, and apply penalties for violations of those standards.

There is a growing trend in warfare to outsource risky security and military services to private contractors as the proxy agents. The contractual delegation of responsibility raises complex issues: Who are the authorizers? Who is accountable for the conduct of private employees conducting risky operations in harm's way (Francioni & Ronzitti, 2011)? These employees' actions are those of a private company, not of a nation-state. Moreover, they perform their operations abroad, beyond national jurisdiction, so they are not bound by domestic law. It remains uncertain how private employees can be held accountable for abuses and human rights violations under international and humanitarian laws. The outsourced operations include ambiguous chains of command, spotty oversight, weak regulatory and enforcement systems, and a code of silence regarding transgressive conduct. These conditions provide a fertile ground for corruption and abuse.

Sometimes the outsourcing of a controversial product to a foreign proxy is disallowed by government officials in the host country (Eckholm & Zezima, 2011). The only American manufacturer of sodium thiopental, which is used in state executions, farmed out its production to an Italian plant, but the Italian government prohibited its export for executions. Great Britain had done so earlier, and the European Union collectively banned export. Prohibition of the offshore proxy arrangement upended execution schedules. In an ironic twist, the Drug Enforcement Administration seized a supply of thiopental imported illegally from an unlicensed British supplier by the state of Georgia to conduct its executions (Savage, 2011).

In collective agency in the service of detrimental pursuits, moral disengagement operates throughout a social system in ways designed to exonerate the system as a whole. Collective agency involves many participants doing their part as best they can in the larger scheme of things. Moreover, large-scale inhumanities require the contributions of different types of professionals in diverse social systems acting in concert in morally disengaged ways. For example, the tobacco industry, whose products kill almost half a million people annually in the United States alone, relies on a large network of collaborators who have no qualms about the production and sale of this toxic product. Much of the suspension of morality in the harmful practices reviewed in the following chapters occurs collectively at the level of social systems.

Fortuitous Determinants of Life Paths

People do many things planfully to shape the course their lives take. But chance events often influence their life paths. Indeed, some of the most important determinants of life paths occur through happenstance (Bandura, 1982; Merton & Barber, 2004). A book editor enters a hall as it rapidly fills up for a talk on the psychology of chance encounters and life paths. He seizes an empty chair near the entrance and ends up marrying the woman he happens to sit next to. With only a momentary change in time of entry seating, the arrangements would have changed, and their lives would have taken different courses. By chance, Diana, a compassionate and caring Voluntary International Service Assignments (VISA) volunteer, meets Howard, a cynical visiting American scholar, at a café in Guatemala City. Over conversations about the need for radical social change, he sets her on a path that leads to the Weather Underground. In a Greenwich Village townhouse, the explosion of a bomb she is making takes her life (Franks & Powers, 1970). Were it not for this chance meeting, Diana's life would most likely have continued on a peaceful course. Later, in an analysis of moral disengagement in terrorism, we will examine the process of moral disengagement in this compassionate person. In these cases, a seemingly trivial, fortuitous event sets in motion constellations of influences that shape the direction of people's life courses for better or worse.

A fortuitous social encounter is an unintended meeting of persons unfamiliar with each other. Their separate paths have their own determinants, but they are causally unconnected until they intersect, at which point the encounter creates a unique confluence of influences that can alter life courses. The profusion of separate chains of events in everyday life provides myriad opportunities for such fortuitous intersects. Even if we knew all the determinate conditions for particular individuals, we cannot know in advance the intersection of socially unconnected events. The physical sciences acknowledge indeterminacy at the quantum mechanical level in the natural world. Fortuitous events introduce an element of indeterminacy in the behavioral sciences.

Most fortuitous events leave people untouched, others have some lasting effects, and still others send them into new trajectories of life. A science of psychology cannot foretell the occurrence of fortuitous intersects, except that personal proclivities, the types of settings in which one travels, and the types of people who populate those settings make some types of intersects more probable than others.

Fortuity does not imply uncontrollability of its effects. Fortuitous occurrences may be unforeseeable, but once they have happened, the conditions they create operate as influential factors in causal processes in the same way as do intentionally designed ones. Hence, psychology can advance knowledge on the effects of fortuitous events on life paths. Different lines of research identify personal attributes and the properties of the environments into which individuals are fortuitously inaugurated as interacting predictors of the nature, scope, and strength of impact that chance encounters are likely to have on personal lives (Bandura, 1982, 1986). These investigatory efforts are designed to bring science to bear on the fortuitous character of life.

THE NATURE OF HUMAN NATURE

Conceptions of human nature are not just a philosophical issue. When acted on, they are socially and morally consequential. In the moral domain, they can influence whether people believe they have some measure of control over what they do, the types of causal attributions they make, and their sense of moral responsibility for their conduct. In ancient theology, human nature was ordained by original divine design. Having been divinely granted the power of free will, individuals were free to choose how to behave in the likeness of absolute agency. Free will is an enigmatic, autonomous force that is self-negating in function. If individuals have the power of free choice, why do they choose the wrong course while under evil influences? An autonomous free will that succumbs to pernicious influences is a contradiction in terms. Over the years, many lively debates have been devoted to this misnomer.

Evolutionism transformed the conception of human nature to one in which it is shaped by environmental pressures acting on random gene mutations and reproductive recombinations. This nonteleological process is devoid of deliberate plans or purposes. In this view, human nature is shaped by brute environmental forces. However, the evolution of the brain provided the neuronal structures for supplanting aimless environmental selection with cognitive agency. The emergence of language and the symbolic ability to comprehend, predict, and alter the course of events confers considerable functional advantages. With the power of forethought, human ancestors developed into a sentient, agentic species.

Their advanced symbolizing capacity enabled humans to transcend the dictates of their immediate environment and made them unique in their power to shape their environment and life courses. Through cognitive self-regulation, humans can visualize futures that act as present guides and motivators for purposeful behavior; order preferences rooted in personal values; construct, evaluate, and modify alternative courses of action to secure valued outcomes; and override environmental influences if necessary. We analyzed earlier how individuals contribute to the quality of their functioning and life circumstances within the reciprocal interplay of personal and environmental influences.

Nature as Determinist or Potentialist

Biological evolution provides bodily structures, information-processing systems, and other physical potentialities. Psychosocial influences operate through these biological endowments to promote self-development, adaptation and change. In an insightful analysis, Stephen Jay Gould (1987) notes that the major explanatory battle is not between nature and nurture as commonly framed. Rather, it is whether nature operates as a determinist that has culture on a "tight leash," as Edward Wilson (1998) argues, or as a potentialist that has culture on a "loose leash," as Gould (1987) contends. Evidence supports the potentialist view. Humans have created societies with diverse natures: aggressive and pacific ones, egalitarian and despotic ones, altruistic and selfish ones, individualistic and collectivistic ones, enlightened and backward ones.

Many inhumanities are perpetrated through aggressive behavior. Because aggression figures prominently in the disengagement of moral self-sanctions, the evaluation of its nature is especially relevant. Aggression is typically cited as the prime example of an inbred, universal trait. This view argues for a strong genetic basis for people's inhumanities toward each other. In evaluating the role played by biological factors in aggression, it is important to distinguish between the proximate hormonal and neuronal regulators of aggressive behavior and the cognitive and social influences that preside over these biological mechanisms. The difference between biological and sociostructural levels of control is strikingly illustrated in studies of primate aggression in social contexts that add ecological validity to the research.

Electrical stimulation of the hypothalamus in the vicinity of the ventro-medial nucleus generally evokes attack behavior in animals. In an ingenious study, Delgado (1967) included a social determinant in research that threw new light on hypothalamic control of aggression. He recorded the social behavior of a colony of monkeys at normal times and when selected members with brain-implanted electrodes were electrically stimulated through radio transmission. Hypothalamic stimulation of a monkey who held a dominant rank in the colony instigated him to attack other males, but the stimulated boss monkey did not assault the females. Nor did he attack his immediate male subordinate, with whom he was on friendly terms.

More impressive is evidence that electrical stimulation of the same specialized brain region can evoke markedly different behavior in the same animal when its social rank is modified merely by changing the membership of the colony. Hypothalamic stimulation of a female at the bottom of the power structure elicited cowering and submissiveness rather than aggression. However, when she was elevated in rank, simply by replacing the more dominant members with subordinate ones, she beat them up during hypothalamic stimulation. Thus, stimulating the same brain site activated aggression or submissiveness, depending on the animal's level of social power. Power relations similarly determine drug effects on aggression (Martin, Smith, & Byrd, 1990). Amphetamine in a dominant monkey in the social hierarchy increased aggression at higher doses, whereas amphetamines given to a subordinate monkey reduced aggressive behavior. The findings of these studies underscore the importance of situating research on biochemical and neuronal regulation of aggression in the context of power relations and other social determinants of aggression.

The powerful role of sociocultural influences in human aggression is strikingly revealed in ethnographic studies of cross-cultural diversity. These variations, which challenge the view that aggression is inbred, take three forms: cross-cultural diversity, intracultural diversity, and transformative societal change. Certain fighting cultures breed aggression by modeling it pervasively; attaching prestige to it; and according it functional value for gaining social status, material benefits, and social control. In other, pacific cultures, interpersonal aggression is a rarity because it is devalued and rarely modeled and has no functional value (Alland, 1972; Bandura, 1973).

The Dugum Dani, who live in the New Guinea highlands, exemplify a warrior society (Gardner & Heider, 1969). In traditional Dani culture, men from villages separated by agricultural gardens regularly engaged in intertribal warfare, one of the most socially valued activities in Dani life. The Dani did not fight for land, food, resources, mates, or the conquest of opponents. Rather, fighting served social and spiritual purposes. Dani warfare, which was highly stylized, took place in designated battlefields adjacent to the villages. Sentries maintained continuous surveillance from high watchtowers to safeguard against enemy ambushes. Much of Dani life was organized around warfare, including such activities as extended guard duty, making weapons, cutting grass to prevent ambushes, and performing magical rituals to strengthen defense systems. Formal battles were initiated by shouted challenges across the no-man's-land. After ritualistic confrontations between advance bands of warriors, the combatants, armed with spears and bows and arrows, engaged in repeated brief clashes of deadly fighting throughout the day.

Though the origin of this institutionalized warfare remains unknown, fighting was instigated and perpetrated largely by fear of reprisal by unavenged spirits. Spiritual agents wielding severe sanctions demanded it. The Dani believed that when a dead warrior was cremated, a ghost was released that had the power to cause accidents, sickness, crop damage, and other misfortunes for living relatives until it was avenged by the taking of an enemy's life. Another method of placating malicious ghosts involved the amputation and burning of a finger of a little girl. In addition to the threats of unavenged ghosts, goading by women who sought retaliation for family deaths and the status rewards bestowed on adept fighters also motivated fighting.

Boys of the Dani underwent a graduated training program in learning how to be warriors that was remarkably close to the best of guided mastery programs for cultivating competencies (Bandura, 1997). The training included instructive modeling, skill perfection under simulated conditions, and a graduated transfer program in which youths exercised their newly acquired skills in progressively tougher scenarios.

The traditional Polynesians of the Society Islands, which include Tahiti, presented a marked contrast to the Dani in the socialization of aggression (Levy, 1969). In Tahitian society, aggressive behavior was rarely modeled but rather devalued. Unlike in the belief system of the Dani, ancestral spirits were punishers rather than inciters of aggression. Tahitians characterized themselves as affable people who were slow to anger, who quickly got over any ill feelings, and who lacked vengefulness and hostile aggressiveness. They were disinclined to create anger-provoking situations, and when they showed aggression, it generally was expressed in words rather than by physical fights. On the infrequent occasions when they aggressed physically, they did so in relatively harmless and intentionally inept ways.

From an early age, Tahitians were taught to fear the consequences of anger arousal and aggressive actions. They claimed that anger had toxic effects on the body and therefore was best avoided. If provoked, Tahitians believed that their spoken threats aroused ancestral spirits who could hurt the provocateur. Anticipated adverse consequences fostered conciliatory behavior, even in highly irritating situations. Although parents initially permitted mock aggressiveness in young children, they strongly discouraged hurtful actions and prolonged anger. Control of aggression was largely achieved by threats of punishment, especially through the action of spirits who punished aggressors by causing illnesses and other harmful outcomes. Because Tahitian culture provided few opportunities to learn aggressive behavior and stripped it of its functional value, aggression played a minor role in the traditional Tahitian way of life.

Numerous other examples can be cited of different societies that create different natures. In cultural settings where interpersonal aggression is discouraged and devalued and amicableness and cooperativeness are the functional behavior, people live peaceably (Alland, 1972; Lantis, 1959; Mead, 1935; Turnbull, 1961). In other societies that provide extensive training in aggression and invest it with functional value, people spend a great deal of time threatening, fighting, maiming, and killing each other (Bateson, 1941; Chagnon, 1968; Whiting, 1941).

That divergent cultural practices produce different human natures is further shown in contrasting lifestyles of people coexisting for centuries in different regions of the same nation. Dissimilar socialization practices produced markedly different characteristics in different Native American peoples. The Apache and Comanche peoples raised their children to be valiant warriors (Goodwin, 1942; Linton, 1945), whereas the Hopi and the Zuni, who embraced peaceful lifestyles, reared children with gentle dispositions (Goldfrank, 1945).

There are marked cross-cultural differences in sexual violence. In her cross-cultural study of the prevalence of rape, Sanday (1997) found that sexual violence is an expression of a cultural ideology of male dominance. Rape is prevalent in societies where violence is a way of life, male supremacy is enshrined, women are treated like property, and aggressive sexuality is a valued sign of manliness. In rape-prone cultures, rape is socially condoned; in some societies, it is even morally revered as an act of honor to restore the dignity of an offended family. Rape is rare in societies that repudiate aggression, endorse gender equality, and treat women respectfully. In contrast, both rapists and men who acknowledge they would rape if they were certain they would not get caught believe in rape myths (Burt, 1980; Check & Malamuth, 1986). These myths embrace several of the mechanisms of moral disengagement. Victims are blamed for enticing rape by seductive dress and provocative behavior, derogated as promiscuous or depraved, and believed to invite rape unconsciously because they supposedly experience being roughed up as sexually stimulating.

Intracultural diversity also calls into question the view of aggression as innate in human nature. Although the United States has its share of violence, the Quakers, who are fully immersed in the mainstream culture, embrace nonviolence as a way of life. The strongest evidence against an innate trait of aggression is the transformation of entire nations from warring societies to pacific ones. The Swiss once were the main suppliers of mercenary fighters in Europe. After they transformed into a pacific society, they still maintain a standing army but deploy it for peacekeeping and lifesaving missions (Swiss Armed Forces, n.d.). Perhaps the most familiar aspect of their more militant past is the colorful uniforms of the Swiss-born Vatican guards.

For centuries, the Swedes plundered other nations. People prayed for protection: "Deliver us, O Lord, from the fury of the Norsemen." After a prolonged war with Russia that exhausted their resources, the Swedish populace rose up and forced a constitutional change, with kings prohibited from initiating military adventures (Moerk, 1995). This political act transformed a militaristic society into a peaceful one. Sweden is now a mediator for peace among warring nations. In keeping with Sweden's pacific ethos, there is little violence in society. Cultural diversity and rapid transformative societal change lend support to the view that the answer to human aggression lies more in ideology than in biology.

The rapid pace of social change causes even thornier problems for the biologically deterministic view. People have changed little genetically over the past millennium, but they have changed markedly in their beliefs, mores, social and occupational roles, cohabitating arrangements, family practices, and styles of behavior even within the past decades through rapid cultural and technological evolution. Dobzhansky (1972) has argued eloquently over the years that humans are a generalist species that was selected for learnability and malleability of behavior, not for behavioral fixedness. Although not limitless, changeability and agentic capability are the hallmarks of human nature. Because of limited innate programming, humans require a prolonged period of development to master essential competencies. Moreover, different periods of life present new competency demands that require self-renewal over the life course if the challenges of changing life circumstances are to be met (Bandura, 1997). Adding to the necessity of changeability, the eras in which people live usher in major technological innovations, shifts in socioeconomic conditions, cultural upheavals, and political changes that make life markedly different and call for new, advantageous adaptations (Elder, 1994). These diverse adaptational changes are cultivated by psychosocial means.

The alternative conceptions of human nature have important policy implications. Biological determinists support a conservative view of society that emphasizes the rule of nature, inherent constraints, and limitations. They contend that people should not try to remake themselves and their societies against the rule of nature, however the determinists construe it. Biological potentialists give greater weight to establishing social conditions that promote personal development and societal change. They emphasize human possibilities and how to realize them.

In Gould's (1987) view, biological determinism is often clothed by its proponents in the language of interactionism to make it more palatable. The bidirectional biology–culture coevolution is acknowledged, but then biological endowment is treated as the ruling force. The cultural side of this two-way causation receives little notice. Gould further maintains that biological determinism is also often clothed in language of changeability. The malleability of evolved dispositions is acknowledged, but determinative potency is then ascribed to them with caution against efforts to change existing sociostructural arrangements and practices allegedly ruled by these evolved dispositions. In contrast, social cognitive theory is rooted in an agentic conception of human nature. As such, it is in keeping with the potentionialist view of biological endowment.

Growing Primacy of Human Agency in Coevolution Process

People are not merely reactive products of selection by environmental pressures served up by a one-sided evolutionism. They not only are prime players in the coevolution process but gain ascendancy in the codetermination process by altering their life conditions at a dizzying pace. Other species are heavily innately programmed as specialists in a stereotypic behavioral repertoire suited to survival in a particular habitat. In contrast, through agentic action, humans devise ways of adapting flexibly to remarkably diverse geographic, climatic, and social environments. They even live in uninhabitable environments by transporting habitable ones—for example, spacecraft and submarines—with them. They devise ways to transcend their biological limitations. For example, humans have not evolved morphologically to fly, but they can soar through the air and even in the airless environment of space at breakneck speeds. To become airborne and fly vast distances, humans have called on their agentic inventiveness in applying aerodynamic principles to trump biological design.

People use their ingenuity to circumvent and insulate themselves from environmental selection pressures. They create technologies that compensate immensely for their limited sensory and physical capabilities. To cite an example, they cannot lift much weight with their bodies, but they can lift tons with gigantic forklifts. They construct and redesign complex environments to fit their desires, many of which are fads and fashions that are socially created by alluring marketing practices. They create intricate styles of behavior necessary to thrive in sophisticated social systems. Through social modeling and other forms of social guidance, they transmit to subsequent generations their own accumulated knowledge and effective practices. They transcend time, place, and distance as they interact worldwide with the virtual environment of the cyberworld. By these inventive means, people improve their odds in the fitness biopsychosocial game.

The growth of knowledge is increasingly enhancing human power to control, transform, and create environments of increasing complexity and consequence. This creative power is even being extended to the modification of biological features. Through ingenious contraceptive methods that disconnected sex from procreation, humans have outwitted and taken control over their evolved reproductive systems to prevent impregnation. They are developing reproductive technologies to separate sex even from fertilization.

Through genetic engineering, humans are creating biological natures, rather than waiting for the slow process of natural evolution. They are now replacing defective genes with modified ones and changing the genetic makeup of plants and animals by implanting genes from other sources. Unique native plants that have evolved over eons are disappearing as agribusiness supplants them with genetically uniform hybrids and clones. Not only are humans cutting and splicing nature's genetic material, but through synthetic biology they are also creating new types of genomes. In a budding biotechnology that is forging ahead to bypass evolutionary genetic processes, humans are even toying with the prospect of fashioning some aspects of their own biological nature by genetic design. In short, humans are an agentic species that can alter evolutionary heritages and shape the future. Were Darwin writing today, he would be documenting the overwhelming human domination of the environment for better or worse.

If something is technologically possible, it is likely to be attempted by someone. We face the prospect of increasing effort directed toward social construction of our biological nature through genetic engineering. These developments present an enormous challenge on how to curb unbounded genetic manipulation (Baylis & Robert, 2004). The values and moral standards to which people subscribe, and the social systems they devise to oversee the uses to which their technological power is put, will play a vital role in what people become and how they shape their destiny.

The conception of humans as an agentic, malleable species does not mean that they have no nature (Midgley, 1978) or that they come structureless and biologically limitless. Quite the opposite is true. Changeability, which is intrinsic to the nature of humans, depends on specialized neurophysiological structures and mechanisms that have evolved over time. These advanced neural systems are specialized for channeling attention, detecting causal structures in the outside world, transforming information into abstract representations, and integrating and using knowledge for adaptive purposes. These evolved information-processing systems provide the capacity for the very agentic characteristics that are distinctly human—generative symbolization, symbolic communication, forethought, self-regulation, and reflective self-consciousness. Neither the agentic human ascendancy in the coevolution process nor the rapid transformational societal changes we see today would be possible without the biological endowment of abstract cognitive capabilities.

Social cognitive theory highlights the forward-looking impact of our biological endowment, rather than post hoc speculations about how prehistoric humans adapted to primitive conditions that remain unknown. The study of how humans cultivate endowed potentialities, circumvent biological constraints, and shape their future through social and technological evolution provides an alternative conceptual framework for clarifying the interplay of biological and psychosocial factors in human self-development, adaption, and change. Social cognitive theory also provides a conceptual framework for analyzing how moral considerations influence the purposes to which these transformative biological technologies are put.

SOCIAL COGNITIVE THEORY OF MORALITY

A variety of moral theories, rooted in different moral principles, have been proposed for judging the rightness and wrongness of conduct. This moral pluralism includes, among other principles, social justice, duty, benevolence, and equality as well as composites of them. There is no consensus among scholars of grand moral theories on a universal principle that governs the moral behavior of all persons, in all cultures, under all conditions. In actuality, people live moral lives based on a variety of moral principles.

Most of the traditional moral theories tell only half the story in the regulation of moral behavior. They focus almost entirely on the cognitive aspect of morality and invest moral thought with overruling power. For example, proponents of rationalism usually have little to say about the mechanisms by which moral standards are converted to moral conduct. This is because rationalists assume that people do what they believe they are obliged to do. According to deontological theory, for example, moral conduct is governed by duty to adopted moral principles regardless of circumstances and behavioral consequences. Given the extensive moral disengagement richly documented in this volume, individuals are not as intractably duty-bound to their moral principles as claimed. It is not uncommon for individuals to use various psychosocial means to circumvent them.

Immanuel Kant was the foremost proponent of the rationalism method as the means of discovering ultimate rightness (Guyer, 1998). As an advocate of a strong form of cognitive determinism, Kant argued that only rational analysis of moral concepts is the method for discovering the core principles of morality. Once a cardinal moral principle is revealed by reason, a rational, autonomous will ordains it as a commandment that must be accepted universally and applies it unconditionally. In this moral absolutism, what one is obliged to do out of a sense of duty to the moral rule overrides all other influences. For example, "You should not lie" is a universal moral rule that must be followed for the sake of reason alone and under all circumstances, whatever the consequences might be.

A theory of absolute moral rationalism is at variance with the exercise of morality in everyday life. There is no such thing as autonomous agency that is impervious to environmental influences. Autonomous agency is an illusion. In managing moral predicaments, people do not unyieldingly adhere to their moral principles regardless of circumstances. Recall the Nazi commandant's compassion for his father and his callous barbarity toward the captive, a vivid example of the conditionality of morality based on selective inclusion and exclusion from the category of humanity. In moral disengagement, people use reasoning to sanctify harmful activities and to dismiss personal responsibility for them.

Kohlberg (1984) adopted the rationalism model of morality in a developmental-stage theory rooted in Piaget's theory of cognitive development. It dominated developmental research on morality during the period when Piagetian theory was very much in vogue. Eventually, Kohlberg's theory came under increasing criticism for contending that reason alone determines moral conduct, restricting morality to social justice, and failing to test the link between moral reasoning and moral action. In actuality, moral conduct is too diverse, determined by too many factors, too situationally variable, and too selectively inextricable from self-sanctions to be adequately explained in terms of hierarchically categorized forms of reasoning. The stage progression in moral reasoning essentially marks increasingly sophisticated justifications for behavior in various moral predicaments. Higher levels of moral "maturity" do not necessarily foretell stronger commitment to humane conduct. This is because justifications, whatever their level, can be applied in the service of harmful activities as well as benevolent ones. Indeed, in moral disengagement, justice is often used righteously to justify harmful means. In his book *The Best and the Brightest*, David Halberstam (1972) reports how highly principled presidential advisors, schooled in cardinal values at elite universities, got the nation deeply entangled in the disastrous Vietnam War. The metaphoric domino theory, which predicted successive communist takeovers of neighboring weak countries, provided the justification for the ill-fated action.

Some conceptions of morality are based on virtue ethics (Hursthouse, 2012). This approach focuses on the character of the person rather than on moral principles. The virtues that are embodied in the character may include fairness, honesty, integrity, loyalty, generosity, and the like. In virtue ethics, one's character is deeply ingrained in a generalized disposition. Hence, in this view, individuals of virtuous character adhere to moral conduct in varying circumstances. In virtue ethics, good behavior naturally follows from moral virtues. If only it were that simple. Attribution of causation to moral character is more descriptive than explanatory. Virtue ethicists must explain the mechanisms by which what one *is* motivates and regulates what one *does*. That is an explanatory gap that needs to be filled.

Virtue ethics is essentially a dispositional trait theory of morality. Theories that invest dispositions with overruling power predict higher consistency in moral behavior across situations and areas of life than is observed (Bandura, 1999). In practice, virtuous individuals can behave harmfully under social inducements and even enlist their virtues in the service of violent means for ideological and religious purposes. When bad means are used for good ends, virtues conflict. Inflicting harm is morally reprehensible but improving peoples' well-being is morally laudatory. The theory of moral disengagement resolves the conflict between virtue and harm through the variety of psychosocial mechanisms that enable virtuous individuals to behave in harmful ways but still retain a self-view as virtuous.

Although virtues are considered to be influential determinants of behavior across situations, virtue ethicists acknowledge that virtuous individuals are not infallible. Proponents of this view attribute harmful conduct with virtuous character to lack of knowledge and practical wisdom, which come with life experiences. These conditional factors are called "situational appreciation" (Hursthouse, 2012). If the practical wisdom and knowledge include likely consequences for given courses of action, then virtue ethics adopts some aspects of consequentialism, in which the rightness of an act is judged by the good it produces.

Virtues are a varied lot. Without agreement on which virtues are morally relevant and valid measures of practical wisdom and outcome expectations, the theory does not lend itself to empirical verification. Also, the problem of causal circularity arises if virtuous dispositions and motives are inferred from virtuous habits and then treated as the causes of such habits.

Moral disengagement is not a dispositional trait that can be assessed by a one-size-fits-all measure. Disengagement mechanisms operate across different aspects of life, but they are manifested differently depending on the sphere of activity (Bandura, 2006). For example, justifications for the death penalty focus on retribution, public safety, and preservation of the social order. The tobacco industry justifies advertising campaigns designed to get youngsters hooked on smoking in terms of freedom of speech. Both examples use the justification mechanism, but they differ markedly in its form: capital punishment in terms of retribution, tobacco advertising in terms of free speech. Measures of moral disengagement must, therefore, be tailored to activity domains. Development of valid measures requires thorough understanding of how disengagement mechanisms are manifested in given spheres of activity.

Moral philosophy cannot be severed from moral psychology. This is because moral philosophy makes empirical claims. We saw earlier that human functioning is the product of a complex interplay of intrapersonal, behavioral, and environmental influences. Hence, morality is not solely an intrapsychic matter but is deeply embedded in human relationships, with rights, obligations, emotional involvements, and societal networks of normative codes backed up with social sanctions. The moral principles discovered by intuitionists through rational analysis therefore require empirical verification. In actuality, empirical findings reveal that the absolute form of rationalism is at odds in many respects with how people actually regulate their moral conduct.

Self-regulation of morality is not achieved by moral thought alone or by a feat of autonomous willpower that overrides all other influences. In fact, moral mandates are often overridden by emotions, enticing incentives, and coercive social pressures. Kant's contemporary David Hume, who emphasized the acquisition of morality through experience rather than intuition, downgraded the power of reason, which he argued is often the "slave to the passions" (Denis, 2012). He grounded his theory of morality in benevolence. Nor do people everywhere adopt the same core moral standards or always adhere to the moral standards they have adopted. In navigating troublesome social realities involving moral predicaments, individuals are vulnerable to compromising their moral standards and even disengaging morality entirely from their harmful conduct.

A comprehensive theory of morality must address its dual aspects. The first aspect, which centers on the acquisition of moral standards and moral reasoning, constitutes mainly the cognitive side of morality. The second aspect of a theory of morality addresses the motivational and self-regulatory mechanisms whereby moral thought gets translated into moral action. Specification of the mechanisms that link thought to action is a vital feature of a comprehensive theory of morality because it focuses on the locus where moral agency is exercised. However, moral theorists usually ignore the gap in moral theorizing, leaving the impression that moral thought automatically begets moral action. In the agentic theory, as will be explained shortly, affective self-sanctions are the major mechanism by which people come to live in accordance with their moral standards.

The self-regulatory mechanisms governing morality operate through several major subfunctions (Bandura, 1991b). These subfunctions include self-monitoring of morally relevant behavior, judging it in relation to personal standards and environmental circumstances, and affective self-evaluative reactions to the judged behavior. Next, we review these subfunctions briefly.

To exercise self-influence, people have to attend to and reflect on what they are doing and the conditions under which they act. The process of self-monitoring is not simply a mechanical audit of one's performances and social influences. Beliefs, values, attitudes, situational conditions, emotional proclivities, and the effects of one's activities influence how one's actions and social contributors to it are perceived and cognitively processed.

An especially important issue in the self-monitoring of behavior concerns the types of activities that get assigned to the moral domain. Social convention is traditionally distinguished from morality (Turiel, 1983). Conventions encompass social rules of acceptable conduct established by consensus in a given group. Conventional standards vary across time, place, and cultural milieu. Morality encompasses behavior that can be physically and psychologically injurious, behavior that inflicts harm on others, degrades them, and violates their human rights. However, a variety of social factors influence which harmful activities are assigned to the moral domain and which are excluded (Bandura, 1991b). In moral disengagement, self-monitoring is the locus for reconstrual of harmful behavior, minimizing its wrongfulness and disputing its harmfulness.

Attending to what one is doing is the first step toward exercising influence over one's behavior. But such information in itself provides little basis for self-directed reactions. The behavioral impact of self-monitoring depends on the moral standards against which it is compared. Moral standards influence whether actions are judged to be right or wrong. Individuals draw on a variety of sources in constructing their standards of morality (Bandura, 1986), partly from how significant people in their lives have reacted to the rightness and wrongness of their behavior. They are especially influenced by the evaluative reactions of those to whom they are emotionally attached and whose views they value.

The construction of personal standards can also be influenced by values that are taught directly or symbolically. In this form of influence, moral standards are drawn from the tutelage of persons in one's social environment as well as standards depicted in the writings of influential figures. Moreover, significant others model moral standards by their reactions to their own behavior. They respond self-approvingly when they fulfill their personal standards but self-critically when they violate those standards. It should be noted that people do not passively absorb ready-made moral standards from whatever social influences happen to impinge on them. Rather, they construct their own standards by reflecting on multiple sources of direct and vicarious influences (Bandura, 1986).

The self-construction of standards is complicated, with so much diversity and inconsistency in the standards being socially prescribed and modeled. Different people adopt different standards and often do not practice what they preach. The exercise of morality involves a fair amount of selectivity and hypocrisy. Even the same individuals may adhere to different moral standards in different settings and domains of activity. For example, they may behave morally in their social relationships but transgressively on their income tax returns. In short, the standards people adopt are not merely facsimiles of what they have been taught or prescribed or have seen modeled. Rather, they are constructions based on reflections on diverse sources of morally relevant information.

Situations with moral implications contain many judgmental ingredients that not only vary in importance but may be given lesser or greater weight, depending on the particular constellation of events in a given moral predicament. In the process of moral reasoning, individuals extract, weight, and integrate morally relevant information in the situations confronting them (Bandura, 1991b; Leon, 1980). Factors that are weighted heavily under some circumstances may be disregarded or considered less important under other circumstances. In the perpetration of inhumanities, moral predicaments usually contain enough ambiguity to provide interpretive leeway for disavowing responsibility, attributing blame to victims, and marshaling extenuating circumstances.

Moral judgment sets the standard for reactions to one's own behavior. Social cognitive theory grounds the behavioral exercise of morality in the self-sanction component of the self-regulatory mechanism. These self-reactions can take self-evaluative, affective, and behavioral forms. Self-approval and self-respect for behaving in accordance with one's moral standards and self-condemnation for violating them constitutes the self-evaluation aspect. Feelings of guilt and remorse are the affective aspect. In the behavioral form, individuals treat themselves self-rewardingly with activities they value and enjoy or self-punitively by withholding desired activities or imposing aversive ones. Restitution is a common behavioral effect of harm caused by moral violations. It is not the moral principles or standards per se but the investment of one's self-regard in how one lives up to those standards that governs the motivation and self-regulation of moral conduct. Fulfilling moral standards affirms one's positive self-view. Violating them causes self-chastisement. Affective self-reactions to one's actions underscores the agentic aspect in the management of one's moral life. These multiple anticipatory consequences are strong motivating and self-regulatory influences on moral behavior.

Because individuals have to live with themselves, they strive to preserve a self-view as decent, self-respecting people. There is no self-view more personally devastating than self-loathing. Consider the powerful sway of self-respect in the following examples. An individual goes to great lengths to return a lost wallet containing $34,000. His self-respect trumps material gain: "The money is something, but the feeling inside is worth a heck of a lot more than the money." Gil Meche, a pitcher for the Kansas City Royals, provides an even more striking example of the extraordinary power that self-respect can exert over one's behavior (Kepner, 2011). Because of shoulder injuries, Meche was unable to pitch but was guaranteed the remaining $12 million in his contract. In an astonishing decision, he declined the money. As he explained, it was the right thing to do, "Once I started to realize I wasn't earning my money, I felt bad." He went on to explain that his self-respect meant more to him than the money. "I didn't feel like I deserved it. I didn't want to have those feelings again."

It is not uncommon for individuals to find themselves in situations in which they are overtly or subtly punished for beliefs and activities they value highly. Principled dissenters and nonconformists often find themselves in such predicaments. The relative strength of self-approval for adhering to one's moral standards and social censure for acting on them determines whether a morally valued course of action is pursued or forsaken. Under severe social threats, individuals often hold in check personally valued but socially chastised behavior in risky situations.

There are some individuals, however, whose sense of self-worth is so strongly invested in certain convictions that they submit to prolonged maltreatment rather than accede to what they regard as unjust or immoral. Thomas More, who was beheaded for refusing to compromise his resolute religious convictions, is a notable example from history. Social reformers often endure untold hardships for unyielding adherence to ideological and moral principles. Mahatma Gandhi, Martin Luther King, and Nelson Mandela are but a few reformers who sacrificed their well-being and even their lives for their principles. Moral heroism is not confined to phenomenal reformers, however. In later analyses, we cite examples of extraordinary moral courage by common individuals and address the psychosocial factors that motivated them.

Adept moral disengagement removes both restraints on harmful conduct and condemnatory self-reactions to it. Harmful conduct can even be exhilarating when perpetrators invest it with high moral purpose, sanitize it, and strip humanity from it. When wrongdoing results in achieving a goal and morality is thoroughly disengaged from the means used to get it, individuals are not bothered about what they are doing. However, morality is not always so easily disengageable, and moral disengagement is not always sustainable. Someone once described a "scotch conscience" as one that is too weak to deter wrongdoing but strong enough to make one feel miserable about it. The tormented life of Emma O'Reilly, a *soigneur* for the famed but later discredited cyclist Lance Armstrong, illustrates the heavy social and personal costs of engaging in an illicit activity while acknowledging that it is shameful (Ranieri, 2012).

Although O'Reilly began as *soigneur* for the U.S. Postal Service team when Armstrong was competing in the Tour de France, before long she was a conflicted participant in an elaborate doping scheme, obtaining drugs, disposing of syringes, covering up needle marks with makeup, distributing doping products to other team members, and helping to conceal the doping operation. She became enmeshed in this sophisticated conspiracy through her emotional attachment and loyalty to Armstrong: "I was incredibly fond of Lance." She even felt remorseful for not being more helpful: "I was feeling bad that I was not helping him as much as I could" ("Lance Armstrong 'Sold,'" 2012). To blunt self-condemnation of what she was doing, O'Reilly focused on the methodical efficiency and concealment of the doping rather than the morality of it: "It was just part and parcel of the team's needs at the time. You don't question and analyze it" (Ranieri, 2012). Doping was linguistically sanitized as being on the "medical program," with the drug taking the "recovery." Because of its prevalence in cycling, doping was regarded as a competitive, normative practice rather than an issue of morality. Nondoping cyclists were portrayed amusingly as pedaling on bread and water.

Although a dutiful functionary, O'Reilly was haunted by self-devaluative reactions to her role in the doping scheme. When she was persuaded once to smuggle pills across a national border, she "felt no better than a drugs runner" (Rankin, 2013). At other times, "some of it made me ashamed." She was caught between loyalty and self-censure. Loyalty overruled morality.

"I felt bound by a sense of loyalty to do it, even though I knew it was wrong." Eventually, despite feelings of disloyalty, in a restitutive act she went public to expose the doping practices because of her growing concern that the drug culture was corrupting professional cycling.

Armstrong vehemently denied the charges, disparaged O'Reilly as a "prostitute" and a "drunkard," and filed a defamation lawsuit against her. Nothing much happened until, one by one, Armstrong's teammates corroborated her charges. Eventually he was stripped of his seven Tour de France titles and banned for life from competitive sports. In reflecting on her "living hell," O'Reilly acknowledged that "by not saying anything, you're part of the problem" (Pilon, 2012). She took comfort in helping to clean up cycling.

Lance Armstrong granted Oprah Winfrey a lengthy televised interview that addressed his sophisticated doping operation (Armstrong & Winfrey, 2012). These interviews shed some light on how a phenomenal athlete can cheat in an elaborate scheme to win seven prestigious titles; elude antidoping officials and enforcers; proclaim his innocence in many mass media appearances; disparage his teammates as liars, knowing that they were telling the truth about the doping operation; win a lawsuit against O'Reilly, knowing that her allegations were true; betray his highly regarded cancer foundation; and still evidently feel good about himself.

To begin with, Armstrong did not construe his doping behavior as ethically transgressive. "Did it feel wrong?" Oprah asked. "No," Armstrong replied. "Did you feel bad about it?" "No." He regarded the use of performance-enhancing substances as a normative practice in the fiercely competitive culture of professional sports. Viewing one's behavior as a product of the time and place reduces a sense of personal responsibility for it. With increasing allegations that he was a cheater, Armstrong consulted a dictionary: "So I looked up the definition of 'cheat.' And the definition of 'cheat' is 'to gain an advantage on a rival or foe that they didn't have.'" He concluded that he did not fit the description. "I didn't view it that way; I viewed it as a level playing field." He was equalizing the competitive baseline, he reasoned, rather than gaining a competitive edge. One has to cheat to win. What he failed to acknowledge is that the doping culture is partly of his own making. He was the masterful operator, not just a victim.

Armstrong trivialized doping metaphorically as no different from "putting air in the tires and water in the bottle." Doping substances were linguistically sanitized as his "cocktail." In commenting on the comparative unjustness of his penalty, Armstrong complained that his teammates received six-month suspensions, whereas he received the "death penalty," a lifetime ban from competitive sports.

Critics judged Armstrong's admission of doping harshly as nothing new (WFAA Staff, 2013). They dismissed it as a ploy for redemption and for getting a reduction in his ban that would allow him to compete again. The problem, from his perspective, was getting caught in a pervasive practice, not an ethical violation occasioning remorse and self-censure. His unmerciful abuse of his teammates and O'Reilly was quite a different matter. In Armstrong's management of the abuse problem, his self-exoneration took a unique form, a dissociative third-person scenario. Armstrong attributed his abusive behavior to a character flaw to which he reacted like a disembodied self evaluating its own behavior: "And it's a guy who expected to get whatever he wanted and control every outcome." He went on to disapprove of the behavior of this "guy": "And it's inexcusable." He evaded his cruelty to O'Reilly with the dissociated third-person scenario as well. After acknowledging that his brutal attack on O'Reilly was "embarrassing" and "humiliating" for her, he slipped into the third-person role of the condemning observer: "[I]f I saw my son do that, there would be a fucking war in our house" ("Lance Armstrong Comes Face to Face," 2013).

Armstrong describes his personal flaw as a "relentless desire to win at all costs." However, he does not regard the flaw as a defect, rather as a powerful asset that enables him to do extraordinary things. Any accompanying harm is an unavoidable side effect. This was the driving force, he explained, that enabled him to triumph over his metastasized cancer and to defeat his cycling challengers. These two benefits demonstrate that the flaw can result in good things as well as detrimental ones. Armstrong could also take pride in the good work done by his cancer foundation, for which he raised millions of dollars.

In a BBC interview Armstrong continued to portray himself as a victim of an overpowering doping culture (Roan & Slater, 2015). He felt sorry, not about the doping operation and its hurtful interpersonal costs, but for being forced to do it by the pernicious culture at the time. "And do you know what we're sorry for? We're sorry that we were put in that place. None of us wanted to be in that place. We all would have loved to have competed man on man, bread, water, naturally clean, whatever you want [to] call it" (Roan & Slater, 2015).When asked about making amends to those he hurt, he slipped into the third-person mode: "I would want to change the man that did those things, maybe not the decision, but the way he acted."

Armstrong plans to make amends to those whose lives he harmed, although he emphasizes that he has just "started the process." Pledged amends can fend off criticism of wrongdoing. At the outset of a reparations process, one should not expect restitutive action from the offender beyond acknowledging that one is sorry. However, a hard-driving flaw does not lend itself readily to moral self-censure or repentance. Given Armstrong's history of falsehoods, people are likely to distrust the sincerity of his redemption. He arranged a meeting with O'Reilly, which turned out to be a "stilted" chat about acquaintances and families. In reflecting on the meeting O'Reilly remarked, "I was thinking, he never actually used the word sorry" ("Lance Armstrong Comes Face to Face," 2013).

With new advances in biological technology, clean athletic contests are a thing of the past. Whatever officials and enforcers ban, some enterprising athletes will not only devise a way around it but will find even more sophis-ticated biochemical enhancers that are better at eluding detection. Sports are deeply rooted in the corporate culture. They bring in profits from the games and supporting services. They also are an important vehicle for advertising countless services and products that are unrelated to athletics. Athletes have powerful incentives to strive to make it into the upper ranks: huge salaries, celebrity status, lucrative sponsorships, and postcareer business and employ-ment opportunities. Armstrong reported that his public confession cost him $75 million in sponsorships alone. It takes robust moral self-regulation to resist such enticements that are achievable by morally compromised means.

Developmental Aspects of Moral Disengagement

We are beginning to gain understanding of children's development of moral disengagement and the processes through which it shapes their life course. In the developmental study of moral disengagement, the various mechanisms are measured in the concrete language they take in childhood (Bandura, Barbaranelli, Caprara, & Pastorelli, 1996). Children's moral justifications ab-solve fighting and lying as a social obligation to protect their friends and to preserve the respect of their peer group or family. Advantageous com-parisons absolve thefts, assaults, and property destruction by contrasting them with worse offenses in the society at large. Maltreatment is sanitized as simply teaching the victim "a lesson." In displacing responsibility, children contend that they should not be blamed for transgressive conduct if they were pressured into it by others or by bad circumstances. In the diffusion of responsibility, they argue that a single child should not be blamed for the trouble caused by a group. In minimizing and distorting consequences, children claim that physical provocation, insults, and harassment are harm-less or just a way of joking. In attribution of blame, victims are said to bring maltreatment on themselves by their witless behavior. In dehumanization, children claim that certain others must be treated harshly because they lack the usual sensitivities or deserve to be treated as subhuman.

Persuasive moral disengagement has functional value for perpetrators. By exonerating themselves from the harm they cause, they can ward off so-cial censure. Indeed, children learn at an early age that they can reduce, and even escape, social reprimands for their misdeeds by shifting the blame to others and invoking extenuating circumstances (Bandura & Walters, 1959; Darley, Klosson, & Zanna, 1978; Sears, Maccoby, & Levin, 1957). However, with the development of moral standards, children learn that they have to live with themselves, not just with the evaluations by others. This marks the developmental shift in the regulation of behavior from social sanctions to self-sanctions (Bussey & Bandura, 1992). They have to convince themselves of their self-exonerations to neutralize their own negative self-sanctions, not just to persuade others. If they intentionally use the exonerative means manipulatively, they have the dual problem of being cynical deceivers as well as wrongdoers.

Although the various disengagement mechanisms operate in concert in the self-regulatory process, they vary developmentally in the extent to which children enlist them (Bandura et al., 1996). Construing injurious behavior as serving worthy purposes, disowning responsibility for harmful effects by fixing the blame on others, and devaluing those who are maltreated are the most widely used modes of self-exoneration. Disguising censurable activities in sanitizing and convoluted language or rendering them benign by favorable comparison with worse conduct requires higher cognitive skills. Hence, children use these strategies less often. By late adolescence, children have learned the full array of disengagement practices. As noted, the developmental progression proceeds from neutralizing social censure to neutralizing self-censure, with the variety and complexity of moral disengagement increasing with social and cognitive development.

Gender differences are not present in the early years, but before long, boys become more facile than girls at all of the forms of moral disengagement. The differential gender proneness for moral disengagement may arise, in large part, from the gendered socialization of aggression. For males, aggressive styles of behavior are more extensively modeled, socially condoned, and invested with functional value (Bandura, 1973; Bussey & Bandura, 1999). This makes it easier for males to morally legitimize injurious means. Moreover, males engage more often in transgressive behavior that inflicts harm, so they have a greater need to perfect exonerative justifications.

When the various mechanisms are grouped by locus of moral disengagement, the reconstrual of injurious behavior as serving a good purpose at the behavior locus and vilifying the victims by blaming and devaluating them at the victim locus were the strongest predictors (Bandura et al., 1996). It is easy to hurt others under these circumstances. Obscuring responsibly and minimizing harmful effects were also significant predictors but at a lower level. The greater the moral disengagement, the greater the involvement in aggressive and antisocial behavior (Bandura et al., 1996; Kwak & Bandura, 1998).

Moral disengagement retains its predictiveness of delinquency after we control for past unlawful behavior and other factors that can contribute to transgressive activities, such as perceived academic efficacy, social efficacy, and efficacy in resisting peer pressure to engage in transgressive activities (Bandura, Caprara, Barbaranelli, Pastorelli, & Regalia, 2001). The finding that moral disengagement is unrelated to socioeconomic status indicates that both the advantaged and disadvantaged do it. Correlational evidence shows that such practices are plied regardless of age, gender, race, social class, level of transgressiveness, and religious affiliation (Elliott & Rhinehart, 1995). They also operate cross-culturally (Bandura, 1997; Kwak & Bandura, 1998; Pastorelli, Caprara, Barbaranelli, Rola, Rozsa, & Bandura, 2001). These

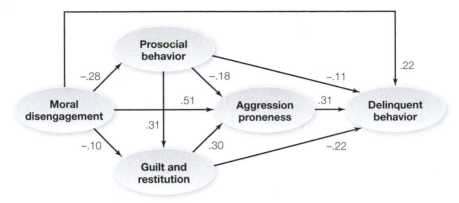

Figure 1.3 Contribution of moral disengagement to delinquent behavior both directly and through its influence on low guilt, low prosocialness, and vengeful rumination (Bandura, Barbaranelli, Caprara & Pastorelli, 1996). © 1996 American Psychological Association. Reprinted with permission.

findings underscore the pervasiveness and centrality of moral disengagement in the management of moral predicaments during the formative years.

Developmental research has also begun to clarify some of the processes through which moral disengagement works. These are shown in Figure 1.3 (Bandura et al., 1996). Reduction of anticipatory guilt over harmful behavior is one such disinhibitory process. *Disinhibitory* refers to the weakening of restraints over harmful behavior. When harmful means are sanctified as serving worthy purposes, wrongdoers have no reason to be troubled by guilt or to feel the need to make amends. Quite the contrary: They take pride in doing even harm well, and when that harm is ignored or minimized, there is no moral predicament calling for self-sanctions.

The second disinhibitory process operates through the effects of moral disengagement on prosocial behavior and the emotional and social climate it creates. Prosocialness is characterized by cooperativeness, helpfulness, and sharing. It also arouses empathy for the plight of others and moves us to console them in difficult times. Individuals who behave prosocially create amicable social environments, whereas those who behave aggressively are quick to attribute hostile intent to others and to produce hostile environments wherever they go (Raush, Barry, Hertel, & Swain, 1974). Discordant relationships in the early formative years are likely to lead a child down dissocial paths. In their research on the development of deviancy, Patterson and Bank (1989) have shown that discordant behavior provokes peer rejection, which in turn increases the likelihood of gravitation to antisocial associates.

If people in conflictual situations absolve themselves of responsibility and shift the blame to the maltreated, they gain a sense of social rectitude and self-righteousness. This mind-set breeds ruminative hostility and retaliatory thoughts about perceived grievances. People often ruminate hostilely but do not act on their feelings. However, when freed from the restraint of moral self-sanctions, they are more likely to act out their resentments. Dehumanization weakens moral self-restraints by undermining prosocialness, blunting empathy for others' suffering, and excluding devalued individuals from the concept of common humanity. Perceived self-efficacy for empathy not only curtails inhumane behavior but fosters prosocial humane behavior as well (Bandura, Caprara, Barbaranelli, Gerbino, & Pastorelli, 2003).

Empirical support for the processes through which moral disengagement works is provided in research on the role of moral disengagement in children's delinquent behavior (Bandura et al., 1996). The findings are summarized in Figure 1.3. Compared with low moral disengagers, high moral disengagers express less anticipatory guilt over delinquent conduct and are less prosocial in their interpersonal relationships, more prone to ruminate over perceived grievances, and more easily angered. Moral disengagement contributes to level of delinquency both directly and mediationally through its influence on the disinhibitory processes described above. In tests of alternative causal paths, the theory that moral disengagement drives the disinhibitory processes fits well with the empirical findings. The alternative theory—that weak prosocialness, low guilt, moral disengagement, and delinquent behavior are simply effects of proneness to aggression—is not supported by the findings. Nor do the findings support the theory that proneness to aggression affects delinquent behavior both directly and through the mediation of prosocialness, guilt reactions, and moral disengagement.

The unique predictiveness of moral disengagement and some of its accompanying disinhibitory processes is replicated longitudinally in serious offenses requiring enlistment of moral disengagement to maintain positive self-regard (Bandura et al., 2001). The level of moral disengagement contributes to delinquent conduct directly by reducing prosocialness and fueling vengeful emotive rumination. In path analysis of the theoretical model, moral disengagement retains its predictiveness of subsequent engagement in delinquent activities after researchers controlled for prior delinquent conduct and perceived academic self-efficacy, social self-efficacy, and self-efficacy to resist peer pressure. A number of alterative causal models were also tested. In one model, prior transgressiveness was assigned causal primacy affecting subsequent transgressiveness directly and through its impact on perceived self-efficacy, moral disengagement, prosocialness, and ruminative affectivity. The second model conferred causal primacy on ruminative affectivity, which contributes to subsequent delinquency directly and through its influence on the set of factors described earlier. These alternative causal models provided a poorer fit to the empirical findings.

Longitudinal analysis of developmental changes in moral disengagement reveals four developmental trajectories accompanied by different levels of aggressive behavior (Paciello, Fida, Tramontano, Lupinetti, & Caprara, 2008). Adolescents who repudiated moral-disengagement practices when younger and continued to do so into early adulthood refrained from harmful behavior.

By contrast, those who began as high moral disengagers and continued to suspend self-sanctions for wrongdoing experienced little guilt about it and were prone to aggressive and violent conduct. Their counterparts, who began as moral disengagers but later renounced such practices, were less inclined to behave aggressively as young adults.

Moral development has typically been studied in terms of abstract principles of morality. Elliott and Rhinehart (1995) report that adolescents who differ in delinquent conduct do not differ in abstract moral values. Almost everyone is virtuous in the abstract. Rather, the differences lie in the ease of moral disengagement under the conditional circumstances of everyday life. For example, through inventive exonerative reasoning, transgressive adolescents convert theft to an act of altruism. It's all right to steal school equipment, they say, because it is insured and will be replaced with newer equipment. They can even feel righteous about their thievery because, as they justify it, merchants raise the prices for their goods to cover expected losses through theft and thus overcharge their customers.

Children can be taught to judge morality in terms of social justice and espouse it in the abstract, but in actual practice they find conditional justifications for violating that principle. The discordance between high morality in the abstract and low observance in practice is by no means confined to youngsters. The present volume richly documents that it is common in adulthood for individuals to embrace high moral principles but to find self-persuasive justifications to compromise them.

Bullying and Cyberbullying

Bullying is a prevalent problem that ranks high among children's fears and parental concerns. These fears are heightened by publicized cases of children driven to suicide by bullying. Bullying encompasses repeated physical and verbal abuse, disparaging rumors, and hurtful social exclusion in the exercise of power over weak and vulnerable victims. Bullying not only harms children's lives but also has repercussions in a troubled adulthood for the abusers (Olweus, 1991). A major share of child bullies end up with court convictions as young adults, whereas children who were nonabusive in their early years rarely do.

We saw earlier that moral disengagers are prone to aggressiveness and antisocial pursuits (Bandura et al., 1996). They do so with little guilt or socially sympathetic behavior. In a comprehensive review of research on bullying, Hymel and her collaborators report consistent evidence that bullies strip morality from their abusive conduct (Hymel, Schonert-Reichl, Bonanno, Vaillancourt, & Rocke Henderson, 2010). The higher the moral disengagement, the more abusively bullies behave (Gini, Pozzoli, & Hymel, 2014). Freed from moral restraints, belief in one's efficacy to exercise control by abusive behavior fosters bullying (Barchia & Bussey, 2011). Bullying occurs in the social climate of schools that vary in their prohibition of it. Some bullying is carried out by groups of friends as well as by individuals. In collective moral disengagement, classmates influence one another such that their group moral disengagement is usually greater than the sum of their individual mind-sets. Hence, the level of classroom moral disengagement accounts for the amount of bullying in schools over and above the predictiveness of individual moral disengagement (Gini, Pozzoli, & Bussey, 2013).

Bullying is socially situated, with bystanders witnessing victims being physically and verbally abused. For the most part, bystanders are reluctant to interfere in bullying episodes. Many simply distance themselves from the problem by viewing it as none of their business. Bystanders, however, face the moral predicament of allowing the abuse of defenseless classmates to continue. They can gain relief from self-censure for tolerating inflicted suffering by moral disengagement. They can minimize bullying as a normal part of growing up; invest it with worthy purpose, such as toughening up victims, teaching them a lesson, and upholding social norms; distance themselves from any responsibility for the problem; and disparage victims as losers and blame them for bringing maltreatment on themselves by not fighting back (Hymel et al., 2010).

Bystanders are not a homogeneous group. Their level of moral disengagement influences how they respond to witnessed abuse. Thornberg and Jungert (2013) found that high moral disengagers cheer bullies on in their maltreatment of victims. In contrast, bystanders who see the moral wrongness of the abusive conduct are prone to come to victims' defense. However, intervening carries the risk of also becoming a target of bullies. It is the bystanders with a high sense of efficacy in mediating conflicts and subduing bullies who act on their moral disquiet.

Obermann (2011) also found that bystander tolerators of abuse exhibit higher moral disengagement than guilty bystanders and those who come to the defense of victims. The guilty ones see the moral wrongness of bullying but apparently are deterred from intervening. However, empathy for the suffering of others combined with self-efficacy at managing difficult social relationships increases bystanders' willingness to come to the defense of victims (Gini, Albiero, Benelli, & Altoè, 2008).

Outcome expectations, which also influence the self-regulation of behavior, can affect whether bystanders exhibit moral courage. Bystanders may doubt that they have what it takes to stop abuse on their own but are emboldened if others join in the effort. In joint intervention, the power of collective efficacy comes into play (Bandura, 2000). Barchia and Bussey (2011) verify the role played by collective efficacy in a prospective study of changes in peer aggression over the course of an academic year. The higher the childrens' and teachers' collective efficacy in working collaboratively to reduce aggression the lower the peer aggression at the end of the school year. Collective efficacy retains its pacifying influence after controlling for aggressiveness at the beginning of the school year.

Eradicating the scourge of bullying cannot be placed solely on the shoulders of a few children who are morally heroic bystanders. It requires systemic changes in the school culture involving key constituencies at all levels of influence. A nationwide program in Norway, designed by the pioneer of bullying research Dan Olweus (1991) is the most ambitious effort to eliminate it. It was launched by public concern over news of several children driven to suicide on the same day by relentless bullying. The mass media publicized the seriousness of the social problem. The nationwide intervention was aimed at teachers, parents, and students alike.

At the school level, a school conference was held on bullying and the process of victimization. Explicit standards were issued, affirming that bullying is unacceptable. Guidelines were provided for all school personnel on how to manage bullying to promote a sense of collective responsibility. At the class level, rules and sanctions against bullying were specified. Students were taught through role-playing how to defuse conflicts so they do not escalate into physical violence. Cooperative classroom activities were adopted to promote a sense of interdependence among classmates. At the parental level, staff–parent meetings were conducted on how to foster a favorable school climate. At the individual parental level, serious talks were held with bullies, victims, and their parents. In sum, this was a comprehensive collective enablement program with shared responsibility to eradicate bullying.

A stringent evaluation found that the program markedly reduced bullying at each age level (Olweus, 1991). Interventions to reduce aggression must also test for possible displacement effects, but there was no shift of bullying from school to non-school settings. The program has had additional positive generalized effects. It reduced truancy and antisocial behavior and increased satisfaction with school life. Applications in which the diverse elements of the program were faithfully implemented testify to its effectiveness in curbing bullying (Olweus & Limber, 2010).

Cyberbullying has become the most pervasive and devastating form of peer malevolence as it moves beyond schools to children's online life. Mobile phones are handy vehicles for sending mean and threatening messages via e-mail, texts and posts of malicious rumors, gossip, and embarrassing photos on social networking sites. These assaults are designed to damage the victims' reputation and undermine their well-being. The humiliation can be perpetrated anonymously, anywhere, anytime, and publicized for all to see. Cyberbullies are difficult to study because they go to great lengths to remain unknown. Studies based on self-reported cyberbullies, therefore, include a self-selection bias of unknown degree.

Cloaked in the anonymity afforded by the Internet, people say cruel things that they would never dare say publicly. In a particularly tragic example, a vindictive mother used a deceptive Facebook profile to launch a hateful campaign against her neighbor's daughter, Megan Meier. Hiding behind the mask of anonymity and a fake identity as a teenage boy, the mother befriended Megan with flirtatious messages, then turned against her, calling her a mean person and a slut. At the height of Megan's emotional distress over the hideous turn of events, the mother posted an especially hateful message: "Everybody in O'Fallon knows who you are. You are a bad person and everybody hates you. Have a shitty rest of your life. The world would be a better place without you" (Pokin, 2007). A few minutes later, Megan hanged herself. Because of the vagueness of the law regarding verbal abuse in the cyberworld, the lawsuit against the perpetrator of this tragedy was dismissed. In some of the cruelest forms of child cyberbullying, kids vote for the ugliest or most unpopular one among their peers, sometimes with photos. Cyberbullying is not confined to children, however. Adults engage in it as well, especially in the workplace.

Several features of cyberbullying make it especially devastating. It is boundless in scope. Verbal abuse posted online can remain there permanently, to be viewed anywhere, anytime, by anyone. There is no way to escape from it physically or to know how to deal with a faceless attacker. The unpredictability and uncontrollability of such threats arouse generalized anxiety (Bandura, 1986; Miller, 1981). Not knowing the identity of one's attacker leaves the victim in a heightened state of apprehension about who is friend and who is foe. Victims can, of course, avoid the postings, but if the disparaging online portrayals turn peers against them, they have few places of refuge.

NEUROETHICS

The role of neuroethics in a theory of morality should be distinguished from the role of bioethics. The latter is primarily concerned with diverse biologically oriented ethical issues such as the use of drugs to enhance performance, genetic counseling about birth defects, genetic engineering and reproductive cloning, use of human stem cells, the moral status of the fetus, informed consent for medical practices and research, use of animals in biomedical research, and the like (Arras, 2010). Neuroethics addresses fundamental issues on the locus of causation in agentic and subpersonal theories of human behavior. These theories have different implications for moral responsibility for one's actions.

Agentic and Subpersonal Theories of Morality

Neuroscientists who favor the philosophical theory of epiphenomenalism regard mental events, such as thoughts, consciousness, and cognitive activities, as simply nonfunctional by-products of low-level physical states. This is a peculiar status for consciousness and mental events, given that they occupy people's entire waking psychic life and determine, in large part, whether it is pleasant or disconcerting. The behavioral sciences continue to be plagued by the consciousness problem. Consciousness is a major vehicle for cognitive activities, but its nature defies explanation. Epiphenomenalists evade the problem of consciousness by dismissing it outright as serving no purpose. From an evolutionary perspective, if consciousness and cognitive activities were functionless, they should have extinguished eons ago.

Epiphenomenalists argue that behavior is regulated by neural networks that operate outside one's awareness and control. Hence, thoughts are epiphenomenal events that create an illusion of control but actually have no effect on how one behaves. This subpersonal view strips humans of personal identity, agentic capabilities, and functional consciousness. It is not thinking individuals but their subpersonal parts that unconsciously orchestrate activities. A detailed critique of epiphenomenalism and the evidence that proponents use in support of it is presented elsewhere (Bandura, 2008). In this view, individuals should not be held responsible for what they inherently cannot control.

Humans come equipped with brain systems and a functional consciousness that enables them to engage in complex cognitive activities. It is at the level of working consciousness that so-called mental work is done: manipulating information in reasoning, decision making, self-evaluation, and the like. In this electronic era, immense amounts of information on virtually any topic are instantly retrievable with the click of a mouse.

Social cognitive theory adopts a physicalistic conception of human agency (Bandura, 2008). In this view, the mind is considered the embodiment of higher-level cerebral processes rather than a disembodied immaterial entity. Thoughts are internally generated neural events in a top-down regulation of behavior. Advanced symbolizing capacity, neuronally distributed and richly interconnected to diverse sensory and motor systems, enables humans to function as mindful agents.

Social cognitive theory posits that epiphenomenalists address the issue of personal control in the wrong terms and at the wrong level of control. There is a difference between first-order control of biological micromechanics and second-order agentic control of biological systems that subserve given purposes. For example, individuals obviously are neither aware of nor can they intentionally direct their atrial and ventricular cardiac muscle fibers to fire or their aortic and pulmonary valves to open and close. This biomechanical microregulation, which evolved over millennia, operates at the first-order level of control. However, at the agentic second-order level of control, individuals can intentionally speed up and slow down their heart rate with physical activity and emotionally arousing or tranquilizing thoughts without having the foggiest idea of how the subserving neurophysiological mechanisms they have enlisted work mechanically. Moreover, by endurance training at the level of second-order control, they can increase their cardiovascular capacity with a host of accompanying health benefits.

To further illustrate the difference between the two levels of control, consider the following analogy. In driving an automobile, the driver engages in coordinated acts of shifting gears, steering, regulating the gas pedal, and applying the brakes. The assemblage of auto subsystems makes up the intricate operational machinery. However, driving requires higher-order activation and regulation. The actions involved in driving, which the driver controls directly, regulate the mechanical assemblage to arrive safely at where the driver wants to go. But the driver neither has awareness of the chemical combustion processes in the automobile engine nor directly controls the chemical reactions that power the car. To act agentically, the driver does not have to understand the correlative mechanics whereby pressing the gas pedal gets the car to move. Knowledge of the functional relation between action and desired outcomes is sufficient.

The deliberate planning of where to go on a vacation, what route to choose, what to take along, what to do when one gets there, and how to make reservations far in advance requires considerable proactive, top-down cognitive regulation over an extended time. The proactive temporal structuring of behavior sets the course for the individual's activities. Having constructed a vacation plan, travelers cannot sit back and wait for lower-level sensorimotor activity to consummate the vacation arrangements unconsciously. Proximal self-regulation of what needs to be done and when to do it provides the guides, strategies, and motivators in the here and now to prepare for the future trip (Bandura, 1991a). Moreover, it requires flexibility in execution. An action plan is rarely specified in full detail at the outset (Bratman, 1999). Rather, it is filled in, adjusted, revised, and even reconsidered in the face of new information along the way.

We are currently witnessing pervasive biological reductionism. Knowing where things happen in the brain does not tell you how to make them happen. For example, knowing the locality and brain circuitry that subserve learning can say little about how to devise learning conditions in terms of level of challenge; how to get people to study particular subjects; and whether learning is best achieved independently, cooperatively, or competitively. These factors have no conceptual counterpart in neurobiological theory. Hence, they are not derivable from biological theory. How to make things happen is among the leading principles of psychological and social-structural theories.

In sum, people are contributors to their activities, not merely onlooking hosts of subpersonal networks autonomously creating and regulating their performances. People conceive of ends and work purposefully to achieve them. They are agents of experiences, not just passive undergoers of experiences. In their transactions with the environment, as mindful agents they are generative, creative, proactive, and reflective, not simply reactive to external input. The sensory, motor, and cerebral systems are tools people use to accomplish the tasks and goals that give meaning, direction and satisfaction to their lives (Bandura, 1997; Harré & Gillett, 1994). These biological tools do not come fully prestructured for complex skills. For example, to master the pyrotechnics of a violin concerto, an aspiring violinist has to spend endless hours training the remarkably versatile brain to remember and execute the profusion of notes, build muscular strength and dexterity, and hone sensory acuity. Epiphenomenalists use the lack of first-order control of biological micromechanics to negate psychosocial theories that are based on second-order cognitive control.

A Neuroethics Conundrum

Some of the more radical forms of neuroscience theorizing, which exclude self-influence as part of the determining conditions of behavior, dismiss the exercise of moral self-regulation. Environmental inputs are said to activate subpersonal modules that cause the actions below the level of awareness and control. If people's actions are the product of the unconscious workings of their neuronal machinery, and their conscious states are simply the epiphenomenal outputs of lower-level brain processes, it is pointless to hold anyone responsible for the choices they make and what they do. Transgressors should not be held personally accountable for their crimes, nor police for abusive enforcement practices, jurors for biased sentencing, jailers for maltreatment of inmates, and the citizenry for harmful social conditions that their public policies and practices breed. They can all disclaim moral responsibility for their harmful actions: Their neural networks made them do it.

Neural networks are nonethical. The unconscious neural processes have neither a sense of personal responsibility nor morality. The issue of morality arises in the purposes to which behavior is put, the means that are used, and the human consequences of the actions. A deterministic thesis that humans have no conscious control over what they do, in fact, is a position on morality—it is one of moral nonaccountability. Such a view is socially consequential. Does a nonagentic conception of human nature erode the personal and social ethics that undergird a civil society? How would people create and maintain a civil society if its members were divested of any conscious regulation for their actions?

The functional impossibility of nonethical neuronal processes producing ethical and socially responsible conduct poses a formidable challenge for nonagentic theories of human behavior. The proposed solutions usually invoke a disputable selective allowance for conscious regulation in the moral domain. In this way one can have automatonization of behavior with moral accountability. Libet (1985) conducted research reporting that a voluntary movement of a finger was initiated by unconscious neural events before the conscious intention to do so. This study is widely cited as evidence that human behavior is orchestrated unconsciously; hence, the exercise of thought control is illusory. However, a variety of methodological deficiencies have called into question the validity of these findings (Bandura, 2008; Gomez, 2002; Klein, 2002; Libet, 1999).

Libet (1999) voiced concern over the automaton view of human nature and the characterization of humans as blissful illusionists. He proposed a dual-control system in which individuals do not control the neural forerunner of a voluntary act, but they can consciously control whether to enact it or veto it. Given this "conscience veto," people can be held morally responsible for their conduct. Libet's critics vetoed his conscious-control function with the regress argument that the conscience veto is itself the product of preceding unconscious neural events. Thus, individuals cannot be held accountable for what they cannot consciously control. This view strips humans of any capacity for conscious control of behavior.

Wegner (2002) also proposed a selective-controllability solution for the pesky morality problem in terms of his conceptual model that Nahmias (2002) calls "modular epiphenomenalism." In this view, environmental inputs subconsciously activate both the action system and an epiphenomenal interpretive module that creates post hoc explanations of behavior. This module cannot affect how one behaves because it is disconnected from the action system. Wagner calls this noncausal module a "loose end" that concocts post hoc, spurious explanations for one's actions under the illusion that one caused them.

Why should an epiphenomenal factor that cannot affect behavior be held morally responsible for it? Faced with this functional impossibility, Wegner (2004) invested the illusory epiphenomenon with powerful casual properties that "can have influences galore." The illusory self-view as a wrongdoer allegedly makes one feel guilty, prompts restitutive acts for the harm one has caused, and gets one to behave responsibly on future occasions. In Wegner's conceptual model, the epiphenomenal self-view cannot do any of these moral things because it is structurally disconnected from the behavior system. The contradictory structural connection to the behavior system invests the nonfunctional epiphenomena with causal properties. Wegner's selective abandonment of epiphenomenalism restores accountability for harmful behavior but raises thorny conceptual issues about why the causative self-view is restricted to moral behavior but remains disconnected from the behavior system in all other activity domains. As with Libet's conscience veto, the effort to carve out an exception in epiphenomenal theory in which it operates causally in morality creates theoretical contradictions. So after Libet's conscience veto and Wegner's causal epiphenomenalism, it is back to the conceptual drawing board on how to make a conscious automaton morally accountable for its conduct.

The prominent cognitive neuroscientist Michael Gazzaniga (2005) is skeptical of the relevance of neuroscience to morality. He is not of one mind on this issue, however (Carey, 2011). On one hand, he argues that neuroscientific data cannot tell us whether a given behavior is right or wrong or determine responsibility for it. Judgments of rightness and responsibility, he contends, are explained at the psychological and sociostructual levels of causation. On the other hand, he is an exponent of the view that behavior is automatically controlled at the subpersonal micromechanical level: "[T]he brain runs largely on autopilot; it acts first and asks questions later" (Carey, 2011). In this view, thought processes are, for the most part, concocted accounts rather than genuine determinants of behavior. An autopilot that operates below the level of consciousness cannot be held responsible for the behavior it spawns. Stripping conscious thought of causal influence renders both neuroscience and behavioral science irrelevant to morality. It is left bereft of a theory.

Roskies (2006) reassures readers that they need not fear that neuroscience will undermine people's view of themselves as responsible agents. Roskies explains that this is because people's judgments of responsibility are unaffected by whether they subscribe to a deterministic or indeterministic view of the world. However, the case is quite the contrary. In point of fact, individuals who believe they are simply powerless cogs in a system feel no responsibility for their actions, whereas those who believe they have some influence over what they do hold themselves at least partially accountable. These alternative views are personally and socially consequential. For this reason, moral disengagers devise intricate ways of absolving themselves of responsibility for the harm they cause.

Roskies goes on to explain that, given the profusion of interacting neurons, whether a neuron will fire and the type of action potential it generates is probabilistic rather than deterministically inevitable. Hence, Roskies contends that neuroscience cannot undermine freedom and moral responsibility because, at the present state of knowledge, it cannot tell us whether the brain is a deterministic machine. Whether this variability reflects indeterministic processes or complex deterministic ones, she concludes, has to be resolved by physical theory rather than at the level of neurons. For these reasons, in Roskies's view, the ostensible moral problem is the perception of a problem, which she regards as misguided. Neuroethicists and metaphysicists are not the only ones who have addressed the ethical implications of a neuroscientfic view of human nature. Some insightful writers outside the field, such as Tom Wolfe (1996), also have weighed in with thought-provoking perspectives on this matter.

All too often, disputes about personal control are framed in dichotomous, absolute terms, especially in philosophical disputes. Either one can exercise control at will or one is a conscious automaton driven by conditions beyond one's control. In moral agency, individuals can exercise some measure of control over how situations influence them and how they shape their situations. In the triadic interplay of intrapersonal, behavioral, and environmental events, individuals insert personal influence into the cycle of causation by their choices and actions. Activities, of course, vary in controllability. Self-regulatory capabilities, which are learnable, can make difficult attainments more doable. Moreover, loss of control is the end result of a chain of events that vary in controllability along the way. In the sequential gradient of controllability, it is easier to exercise control at incipient phases of an activity than after finding oneself forced by compelling circumstances to behave otherwise. For example, a heavy drinker has a good chance of arriving home sober after an evening meeting by picking a barless route home rather than a route with inviting bars that present the challenge of having to resist a brief stopover and the even tougher task of controlling the amount drunk, should the drinker choose to go in. What is seemingly uncontrollable under compelling circumstances is controllable at its incipient points. Visualizing the likely aversive consequences of a drinking stopover would help steer the drinker toward the barless route.

People's belief in their self-regulatory efficacy is also a contributor to controllability. Those with high perceived self-regulatory efficacy mount stronger control efforts, persevere in the face of difficulties, and are likely to attribute setbacks to external conditions that are changeable rather than to inherent personal deficiencies that render one powerless in difficult circumstances (Bandura, 1997). The higher the perceived self-regulatory efficacy in resisting social pressures to behave transgressively, the lower the engagement in antisocial activities (Caprara, Regalia, & Bandura, 2002).

Personal control is not practiced in social isolation. In the exercise of proxy agency, individuals maintain self-control by enlisting the help of others. Social support buttresses self-control in taxing situations. In this electronic era, social media can provide instant proxies. In the exercise of collective agency, control is enabled and practiced at the group level. The conception of controllability as a gradation in social context is more in keeping with the everyday realities of self-management than the dichotomous view that behavior is either controllable or uncontrollable. In the case of moral disengagement, personal and social influences are used to remove restraints over detrimental conduct rather than to buttress them.

Whether or not a neuroscientific view will erode moral responsibility depends on the scope of the theorizing and the types of experimentation it spawns. In a stimulus-driven, bottom-up view, human behavior is automatically activated by neuronal processes outside one's awareness and control, with thoughts being functionless by-products. In this line of theorizing, it is pointless to hold people responsible for what is beyond their awareness and control. Recall the distinction between understanding how biological machinery works in producing behavior and how biological machinery is orchestrated agentically for diverse purposes. To use an analogy, knowing how the laws of chemistry and physics apply to how a television set produces images does not explain the endless variety of programs it transmits. Human creative neuronal activities must be distinguished from the biomechanical production of dramatic images in the brain. Viewed from an agentic metatheory (Bandura, 2008; Sperry, 1993), cognitive activities, operating primarily at higher-level brain structures, have a downward regulatory function over lower-level brain processes that beget actions.

Early in life individuals acquire a sense of selfhood with a distinct identity and personal features that comprise their individuality. They process most of their everyday experiences through their self-representation. Based on experiences in which individuals produce effects by their actions they also develop a sense of agency. The exercise of moral agency is brain-based in moral reasoning and self-regulatory influence rooted in moral standards and evaluative self-sanctions. As explained earlier, in the triadic interplay of influences individuals are part of the determinants governing the course of events. With exercise of agency comes some measure of responsibility. In a cognitive and affective neuroscience that recognizes second-order control exercised through moral self-sanctions people can be held partly accountable for what they do.

This prefatory chapter presented the conception of human nature on which the exercise of moral agency is founded. The next chapter reviews in considerable detail the various mechanisms of moral disengagement and how they operate in concert at both the individual and social system levels in the service of inhumane practices. The subsequent chapters document how this occurs in diverse spheres of life.

Chapter 2

■ ■ ■ ■ ■ ■ ■

MECHANISMS OF
MORAL DISENGAGEMENT

The preceding chapter presents moral disengagement as grounded in the agentic perspective of social cognitive theory, and more specifically in the exercise of moral agency. This chapter analyzes in detail the various mechanisms of moral disengagement and how they operate in concert at both the individual and social systems levels. The analysis draws on diverse spheres of activities in which people do harmful things. The diversity attests to the pervasiveness of the various ways people absolve themselves of moral self-sanctions. The transgressions are not just brief ethical lapses. For the most part, selective disengagement of morality requires construction of persuasive self-exonerations, some of which are built into the structure and operating practices of social systems.

We should note that analyses of the disengagement of morality in the perpetration of inhumanities are not always welcome, for fear that any explanation of cruel conduct excuses it. This is especially true if the personifiers of cruelty are detested evildoers. There is a marked difference between scientific explanations of how moral self-sanctions are disengaged from inhumane conduct and evaluative judgments of that conduct. Elucidating the psychosocial mechanisms of moral disengagement does not excuse or condone the conduct being analyzed. Rather, scientific knowledge informs us on how to prevent and counteract the suspension of morality in the perpetration of inhumanities.

THE BEHAVIORAL LOCUS

At the behavioral locus of moral agency, harmful behavior is turned into good behavior. It takes a lot of self-persuasive machination to sanctify harmful means of achieving worthy ends, to further legitimize them by self-exonerating advantageous comparison, and to cloak them in sanitizing or convoluted language. The sections that follow explain how harmful behavior is transformed into good behavior by these three mechanisms, which operate at the behavioral locus.

Moral, Social, and Economic Justification

People do not usually engage in harmful conduct until they have justified to themselves the morality of their actions. Social and moral justifications sanctify harmful practices by investing them with honorable purposes. Righteous and worthy ends are used to justify harmful means. The moral imperative enables people to preserve their sense of self-worth even as they inflict harm on others. *Sanctify* is used as a generic term for diverse ways of justifying the rightness of harmful practices. It includes not only religious justifications but also ideological, social, economic, and constitutional forms.

Rapid radical shifts in destructive behavior through moral justification are most strikingly revealed in the military. The conversion of socialized individuals into dedicated fighters is achieved not by altering their personalities, aggressive drives, or moral standards but by cognitively reconstruing the morality of killing so that soldiers can do it free from self-censure. In this new context of moral obligation, soldiers see themselves as fighting ruthless oppressors, protecting cherished values, honoring their country's obligations, preserving world peace, and saving humanity from subjugation. With commitment to the justness of the cause, killing becomes an act of heroism. Soldiers are returned to civilian life without going through a moral resocialization process. On discharge, moral standards are reengaged so that violent conduct is again deterred by self-sanctions.

The moral reconstrual of killing is nowhere more dramatically illustrated than in the case of Sergeant Alvin York, one of the most phenomenal fighters in the history of modern warfare, who with only a handful of men overpowered a much larger enemy force (York & Skeyhill, 1928). Because of his deep religious convictions and despite being an expert marksman, York registered as a conscientious objector, but his numerous appeals to be exempted from military service were rejected. His battalion commander quoted chapter and verse from the Bible to persuade him that under certain conditions it was a Christian duty to fight and kill. A marathon mountainside prayer vigil finally convinced him that he could serve both God and country by becoming a dedicated combatant. He fought heroically in the service of his faith.

Just-war principles were devised that specify when the use of violent force is morally justified. However, given people's dexterous facility for justifying violent means, all kinds of inhumanities are clothed in moral trappings. When soldiers are sent into battle with questionable justification or in the context of national discord over the morality of the cause, they pay a heavy social and psychological price. They are viewed by many as having fought for an illegitimate rather than a noble cause. Some return haunted by their combat experiences and guilt ridden over moral breaches that led to some of their military actions (Wood, 2014).

Voltaire put it well when he said, "Those who can make you believe absurdities can make you commit atrocities." Over the centuries, much destructive conduct has been perpetrated by ordinary, decent people in the name of righteous ideologies, religious principles, sociopolitical doctrines, and nationalistic imperatives (Kramer, 1990; Rapoport & Alexander, 1982; Reich, 1990). True believers sacrifice themselves to their principles.

The politicization of religion has a long and bloody history. In holy terror, perpetrators twist theology and see themselves as doing God's will. In 1095, Pope Urban II launched the Crusades with the following impassioned moral proclamation: "I address those present, I proclaim it to those absent; moreover, Christ commands it. For all those going thither there will be remission of sins if they come to the end of this fettered life." He then dehumanized and bestialized the Muslim enemy: "Oh what a disgrace if a race so despicable, degenerate, and enslaved by demons, should overcome a people endowed with faith in Almighty God and resplendent in the name of Christ!" He then commands the faithful to vanquish the "barbarians": "Let those who once fought against brothers and relatives now rightfully fight against the barbarians under the guidance of the Lord" (Geary, 2010).

Similarly, Islamic extremists construe their jihad as an armed struggle in self-defense against tyrannical, decadent infidels who seek to enslave the Muslim world. Osama bin Laden claimed nobility for his global terrorism as serving a holy imperative (Borger, 2001; Ludlow, 2001). Because of the diverse ways in which bin Laden used morality to sanctify terrorism, his case provides an informative example of how the full set of moral disengagement mechanisms operate in concert. He justified killing in the name of Allah by making it honorable to kill without guilt: "We will continue this course because it is part of our religion and because Allah, praise and glory be to him, ordered us to carry out jihad so that the word of Allah may remain exalted to the heights" (Ludlow, 2001). Islamic extremists believe that they are carrying out Allah's will as a religious duty. The prime agency for the holy terror is thus displaced to Allah.

By attributing blame elsewhere, terrorists construe their strikes as morally justifiable, defensive response to humiliation and atrocities perpetrated by atheistic forces: "We are only defending ourselves. This is defensive jihad" (bin Laden interview, 2001). Through advantageous comparison with the nuclear bombing of Japan at the end of World War II and the toll of sanctions on Iraqi children's well-being, jihad takes on an altruistic appearance: "When people at the ends of the earth, Japan, were killed by their hundreds of thousands, young and old, it was not considered a war crime, it is something that has justification. Millions of children in Iraq are something that has justification" (Associated Press, 2001). Bin Laden also enlisted historical comparison by likening the war in Iraq to the Crusades and characterizing the Allied forces as crusaders. He bestialized the American enemy as lowly people perpetrating acts that "the most ravenous of animals would not descend to" (Ludlow, 2001). Terrorism is sanitized metaphorically: "The winds of faith have come" to eradicate the "debauched" oppressors" (Associated Press, 2001). Islamic extremists see themselves as holy warriors who gain blessed eternal life through martyrdom. Each side in holy warfare claims that it alone is doing God's bidding. The warring parties solve the disconcerting problem of two-sided divine authorization of deathly combat by characterizing their foes as demonic infidels.

Yigal Amir, who assassinated the Israeli prime minister Yitzhak Rabin, similarly claimed to be acting on a divine mandate, using the rabbinical pursuer's decree as moral justification. The religious right was alarmed by the Oslo accords. The second Oslo Accord of 1995 mandated that parts of the West Bank would be transferred to Palestinian control. The right viewed this land as part of Israel's biblical heritage and the giveaway as a betrayal. For Amir the accords provided a moral imperative to assassinate Rabin, the betrayer. As Amir put it, "Maybe physically, I acted alone but what pulled the trigger was not only my finger but the finger of this whole nation which, for 2,000 years, yearned for this land and dreamed of it." He further proclaimed that he acted for "all those thousands who had shed their blood for this country" (Greenberg, 1995). He, too, was doing God's bidding. He felt no remorse over his perceived martyrdom: "I have no regrets. Everything I did was for the sake of God."

Paul Hill, a former Presbyterian minister, also justified the killing of a doctor and his assistant outside an abortion clinic as carrying out God's will: "God's law positively requires us to defend helpless people. God has used people, who are willing to die for their cause to save human life. I'm willing to do that." In defending a previous slayer of a doctor at an abortion clinic, Hill not only used biblical justifications, but advantageous comparison as well. The action was as moral he contended, as killing Hitler or someone who was murdering children on a playground (Dahlburg, 2003). Hill's spiritual advisor commended him for his moral courage in "saving the lives of unborn children." After receiving the death sentence, Hill remarked that he was at peace with himself.

Vigorous disputes arise over the morality of militant actions directed against institutional practices that are socially harmful. The African American civil rights movement is a notable example of this type of challenge. Power holders and those in privileged positions resist pressure to make needed social changes when those changes jeopardize their self-interests. Challengers consider their militant actions to be morally justifiable because their goal is to eradicate harmful social practices. Those who run the institutional systems condemn coercive means as unjustified and unnecessary, because lawful means exist to effect social change. Anarchy would flourish, they argue, in a climate in which individuals act on their particular moral imperatives and consider militant means acceptable when they find majority decisions objectionable. Some observers argue for a high threshold of justifiability of unlawful means (Bickel, 1974). In this view, civil disobedience is justified only if legitimate means have failed, and those who break the law do so publicly and willingly accept the consequences of their actions. In this way, unjust practices can be challenged while respect for the judicial process is maintained.

Challengers refute such moral arguments by appealing to what they regard as a higher level of morality derived from communal concerns. They see their constituencies as comprising entire classes of people who are harmed either directly or indirectly by injurious institutional practices. Challengers argue that, when many people benefit from a system that has adverse effects on marginalized or devalued segments of society, harmful social practices receive widespread public support. As the challengers see it, they are acting under a moral imperative to stop the maltreatment of people who have no way of modifying injurious social policies because they are either outside the system that harms them or they lack the resources to effect changes from within by peaceable means. Their defenders regard militant action as the only recourse available to them to redress the injustice.

In the clash between moral imperative and legal order, institutional officials marshal moral reasons for the use of aggressive means of social control, whereas challengers marshal moral reasons for militant action for social change. The public is more supportive of the use of aggression for social control than for social change (Blumenthal, 1972). It is likely to view dissent and protests as violent acts but is more forgiving of police abuses and denial of civil rights.

Harmful practices by some industries rely on economic justifications based on a belief in unfettered free-market forces. Examples include some companies in the finance industry and others that produce products that have injurious effects. Exonerative justifications keep those who engage in harmful activities from being morally troubled by the harm they cause. The customary justification in the finance industry—and indeed, industry as a whole—takes the following form: Unfettered by intrusive regulations, commercial innovations flourish, and productive industries fuel economic growth. The finance industry promotes and sustains economic viability for the nation. In doing so it contributes to the livelihood of the nation's citizenry and raises the standard of living. Market forces are alleged to be governed by rational decision making. The free market rewards good financial practices with success and punishes bad ones with failure, Thus, when left to its own devices, the free market is self-correcting. Thus, the finance industry makes life better for everyone. By vigorously pursuing their self-interests, financiers are advancing the common good.

The production and marketing of products that cause harm are often jus-tified on constitutional grounds. The use of such products is regarded as an exercise of people's freedom of choice; regulations are considered an intru-sion of big government into people's private lives. Shielding faulty products from regulatory efforts protects democratic values. Disputes over justifica-tions of this type are most heated when the public ends up bearing the cost of laissez-faire financial practices and dealing with the personal and environ-mental harm of the choices that are made.

Euphemistic Language

Language shapes the perception of events and the thought patterns on which people base many of their actions. The personal and social acceptability of given activities, therefore, can differ markedly depending on what those activities are called. Euphemistic machinations are used widely to detach and depersonalize doers from harmful activities (Lutz, 1987). Cloaking det-rimental activities in euphemisms can be a powerful weapon. For example, people behave much more cruelly when assaultive actions are given a sani-tized label than when they are called *aggression* (Diener, Dineen, Endresen, Beaman, & Fraser, 1975).

In an insightful analysis of the language of nonresponsibility, Gambino (1973) identified the different varieties of euphemisms. They include sanitiz-ing and convoluted language, the agentless passive form, and the borrowing of specialized jargon from a respectable enterprise. In the sanitizing form, for example, military combatants have to sanitize killing to override restraints against the taking of human life. Through the power of sanitized language, killing a human being loses much of its repugnance. Soldiers "waste" peo-ple rather than kill them. Death tolls are reported with the acronym KIA, for "killed in action." Bombing is called "coercive diplomacy." The bombs are "force packages," as if they were propelled nonagentically. In borrowed jargon, bombing missions are described as "servicing the target" as a public utility or as "visiting a sight" as if going on a recreational outing. The attacks become "clean, surgical strikes," eliciting imagery of curative activities. The civilians the bombs kill are linguistically converted to "collateral damage," often the victims of bombs that were "outside current accuracy require-ments." Soldiers killed by misdirected missiles fired by their own forces are the tragic recipients of "friendly fire."

Thorough linguistic cleansing extracts every ounce of humanity. Who would know from NASA's account that the "recovered components" in "crew transfer containers" were the remains of the astronauts killed in the 1986 explosion of the space shuttle *Challenger*? Oftentimes the linguistic masking of detrimental activities takes the form of convoluted language. Doublespeak disguises by piling on inflated words and opaque professional jargon (Lutz, 1987). Who could translate "vertically deployed anti-personnel devices" as bombs, or "atmosphere deposition of anthropogenically derived acidic substances" as acid rain. In his book *Telling It Like It Isn't*, J. Dan Rothwell (1982) characterizes sanitizing euphemisms as "linguistic Novocain" for the conscience and convoluted language as "semantic fog" that obscures and conceals detrimental practices. Such language numbs us to unpleasant and harmful realities.

Professor Gerald Grow (2012) has written brief guidelines called "How to Write 'Official,'" which provides a set of rules on how to communicate opaquely and misinformatively. These rules, which specify the nine top features of good euphemistic writing, include: Put it in the passive voice and delete the agent of the actions; inflate with terminology that does not add meaning; build in noun strings; add a qualifier of uncertain relation to the original statement; add noun strings and terminology to the qualifier; separate related words; equivocate and obfuscate; cover your tracks and make yourself look good.

Verbal camouflage disguises all types of activities that raise moral concerns. The *Quarterly Review of Doublespeak* (National Council of Teachers of English, 1988) organizes sanitizing and obfuscating linguistic packaging by occupations. Consider the business world as but one example. An "equity retreat" is a stock market crash. Financial market traders who produced the global economic meltdown portrayed themselves as the victims of a metaphoric "tsunami." People treasure their privacy, yet AOL is selling their private online behavior as a "transferable business asset." A business course on "competitive decision making" includes instruction in "strategic misrepresentation" that teaches students how to lie when making vulnerable transactions. A Gas Research Institute memo recommended discarding the phrase "low-cost gas," and instead referring to marketing it as making marginally priced resources more cost-competitive. Slow sales in a high-tech business were attributed to an "undersupply of market demand." The communal-sounding announcement that "there are some places we will be exiting together" means that the company is shutting down some of its units. A proposal is not rejected; it is "selected down." Firing or laying off workers, especially those who have been with the company for a long time, is a tough task. Dismissals are clothed in softened or even promotive terms. The hapless workers are recipients of a "career alternative enhancement" or are placed in "non-duty, non-pay status." Jobs that are socially devalued and underpaid are given convoluted, fancy names. A garbage worker is a "collector of surplus commodities." A janitor is a "particulate matter remover."

As documented by Gambino (1973), the Watergate burglary, which brought down the Nixon presidency, was masked in benign and innocuous jargon. This politically motivated burglary was called a "surreptitious entry." Casing the Watergate building was a "vulnerability and feasibility study." Illegal wiretapping was "electronic surveillance." Spying on people was "visual surveillance." Lying was a "different version of the facts."

The agentless passive form is a linguistic device for creating the appearance that harmful acts are the work of nameless forces rather than of individuals (Bolinger, 1980). It is as though people are moved mechanically but are not really the agents of their own acts. Gambino describes how the passive voice is used to "create an illusory animistic world where events have lives, wills, motives and actions of their own without any human being responsible for them" (Gambino, 1973). In his 1987 testimony on misinforming Congress about illegal arms shipments in the Iran–Contra affair, National Security Advisor John Poindexter recounted, with mechanical detachment, how millions of dollars could be transferred illegally by a "technical implementation" without making a "substantive decision." When someone at Kodak botched the development of twelve rolls of prized film, the photographer was informed that "the films were involved in an unusual laboratory experience." Even inanimate objects are sometimes turned into agents. Here is a driver explaining to police how he managed to demolish a telephone pole: "The telephone pole was approaching. I was attempting to swerve out of its way when it struck my front end." And crimes are erased by construing them as things one did not do, as former New York mayor David Dinkins explained his failure to pay taxes: "I haven't committed a crime. What I did was fail to comply with the law."

People speak extensively in metaphors. When persons, ideas, and activities are likened to something else, even though they are not literally the same, people think and behave in terms of the resembled one. For example, corporate wrongdoers are likened to isolated "bad apples" within the organizational barrel. Portraying an entire group with a single word that compares them with "animals" heightens a punitive attitude toward them (Bandura, Underwood, & Fromson, 1975). Thibodeau and Boroditsky (2011) illustrate how even a single word can markedly affect the type of social policies people favor to ameliorate societal problems. When a soaring crime wave was metaphorically likened to a spreading "virus," individuals favored social policies that address root causes and promote preventive measures. In contrast, when the same crime wave was metaphorically likened to a "beast" preying on the public, individuals favored tougher laws for catching and jailing offenders.

The specialized jargon of a legitimate enterprise can be misused to lend an aura of respectability to an illegitimate one. To add cover to their criminal activities, the Watergate burglars cloaked them in metaphors of admirable teamwork and sportsmanship. In Watergate jargon, criminal conspiracy became a "game plan," and the conspirators were "team players" with qualities befitting the best sportsmen. Their domestic spying operation was called a "new intelligence unit" in the likeness of a legitimate information-gathering agency. Like dutiful seamen, the burglars were "deep-sixing" incriminating documents, not destroying them illegally. Seeing oneself as a team player faithfully executing a game plan against a political foe will rouse weaker self-restraint of transgressive conduct than seeing oneself as a common burglar committing criminal acts.

The chapters that follow illustrate how wordsmiths in all walks of life use sanitizing and obfuscating language in the service of harmful purposes. Each year the National Council of Teachers of English selects winners for both the NCTE Doublespeak Award and the Orwell Award. The National Council of Teachers of English bestows its uncoveted Doublespeak award on "public figures who have perpetuated language that is grossly deceptive, evasive, euphemistic, confusing, or self-centered" (National Council of Teachers of English, 1988). The National Council of Teachers of English awarded third place to Senator Orrin Hatch of Utah, who declared, "Capital punishment is our society's recognition of the sanctity of human life." The Orwell Award "honors an author, editor, or producer of a print or nonprint work that contributes to honesty and clarity in public language."

Advantageous Comparison

How the self and others view human behavior is colored by what it is compared against. Self-exoneration by advantageous comparison with more flagrant inhumanities is a third mechanism for cloaking behavior in an aura of benevolence. Exploiting the contrast principle can make even highly detrimental activities seem righteous. Skillful framing of an issue in an advantageous comparison can make the lesser of two evils not only acceptable but even morally right. As we have seen, terrorists depict their deeds as acts of selfless martyrdom by comparing them with cruelties that others have inflicted on the people with whom they identify. The more flagrantly the inhumanities are contrasted, the more likely it is that one's own destructive conduct will appear benevolent and righteous.

Expedient historical comparison also serves self-exonerating purposes. For example, apologists for the lawlessness of political figures they support cite transgressions by past rival administrations as vindication. In civic and international conflicts, aggressors are quick to point out that some nations, such as France and the United States, became democracies through violent rebellion against oppressive rule. Historical comparative exoneration also is illustrated in a radio address by Ronald Reagan about restoring aid to the contra guerrilla forces in Nicaragua. The aid had been cut off by Congress in response to the CIA's mining of a Nicaraguan harbor in violation of international law. Employing historical justification, Reagan cited the French military provided by the marquis de Lafayette, which helped defeat the British oppressors during the American Revolution. Reagan went on to explain that the system of constitutional democracy, born of that revolution, serves as the governmental model for freedom worldwide (Skelton, 1985). Jeane Kirkpatrick, then the U.S. ambassador to the United Nations, provided further justification for the covert CIA operation: "Those who wield swords against their own people and their neighbors risk having swords turned against them" (Bernstein, 1984).

Exonerating comparison relies heavily on moral justification by utilitarian standards. Making violence morally acceptable from a utilitarian perspective is facilitated by two sets of judgments. First, nonviolent options are depicted as ineffective for achieving desired changes, thus removing them from consideration. Second, utilitarian analyses using advantageous comparisons affirm that one's injurious actions will prevent more human suffering than they cause. The utilitarian cost-benefit calculus, however, can be quite slippery in specific applications. Estimates of future harm contain many uncertainties and ambiguities. Predictive judgment is, therefore, subject to many biases (Nisbett & Ross, 1980). As a result, calculations of long-term human costs and benefits are often suspect. Estimating the gravity of potential threats also is fraught with subjectivity. Moreover, violence is often used as a weapon against minor threats on the grounds that if left unchecked, they will escalate and spread to cause far more human suffering. The frequently invoked domino theory reflects this type of escalative projection error concerning a likely course of events. Estimate of the gravity of a situation justifies choice of options. But preference for violent options often biases estimates of gravity.

Assessing the future course of violence and the best means of dealing with it can be flawed by bias-based social as well judgmental errors from uncertain information. The information on which judgments are made may be tainted by the policy biases of those gathering and interpreting it (March, 1982). For example, the justification for the second Iraq war was based on flawed and fabricated information that Iraq had at least the potential to build nuclear weapons and that Saddam Hussein possessed weapons of mass destruction and was linked to al Qaeda. The use of superficial similarities in the framing of issues can also distort judgment of the justification of violent means (Gilovich, 1981). For example, in judging how the United States should respond to a threat by a totalitarian regime against a small nation, people were more supportive of military intervention if the international crisis was likened to the 1938 Munich agreement with Nazi Germany, an example of appeasement, than when it was likened to another Vietnam, an example of a disastrous military entanglement. Gilovich adds a new twist to George Santayana's adage that those who cannot remember the past are condemned to repeat it: Those who see an unwarranted likeness to the past are disposed to misapply its lessons.

In the preceding analysis, we framed the exonerative maneuver comparatively in terms of good achieved by the lesser of two evils. In moral disengagement in the corporate world, some organizations use uplifting comparisons that cloak potentially harmful products in an aura of high principle. The gun industry is a case in point. In response to sagging gun sales, the gun industry introduced semiautomatic pistols of escalating lethality, with larger magazines holding bullets of higher caliber, with the pistols made smaller for easy concealment. The gun lobby fights virtually every gun regulation on the grounds that even sensible restrictions are the first step toward banning guns altogether, violating the Second Amendment to the Constitution.

In the uplifting comparative exoneration for creating these lethal wares, guns are equated semantically with freedom of speech and linked to just causes fought for by revered social reformers. President of the National Rifle Association Sandra Froman (2007) compared the fight for One time "gun freedom" with George Mason and Patrick Henry's campaign for a Bill of Rights, Susan B. Anthony's fight for women's voting rights, Pasteur's and Einstein's defenses of their theories, and Rosa Parks and Martin Luther King Jr.'s struggle for civil rights. She added the Greek dramatist Euripides and President Kennedy as defenders of free speech. Charlton Heston weighed in with the claim that the Nazi Gestapo were able to persecute the Jews because the Jews lacked gun freedom ("Charlton Heston's Speech," 1999). Uplifting comparison bears some likeness to moral justification but differs in how justifications are used. In moral justification, rightness is used directly to turn harmful behavior into good behavior. In uplifting comparisons, the harmful behavior is made worthy indirectly by associating it with revered persons exhibiting moral courage.

Before examining the other mechanisms of moral disengagement, we should recall that the triad of moral and social justification, advantageous comparison, and sanitizing and uplifting language convert harmful conduct into humane conduct. Moral justifications serve dual functions. They engage morality in the worthy mission but disengage morality in its deadly execution. Hence, moral justifications are the most powerful set of psychological mechanisms for promoting detrimental activities. Belief in the morality of a cause not only eliminates self-censure but also engages self-approval in the service of destructive exploits. What was once morally reprehensible becomes a source of positive self-valuation. Functionaries work hard to become proficient in harmful activities and take pride in their destructive accomplishments.

THE AGENCY LOCUS

Displacement of Responsibility

Moral control operates most strongly when people acknowledge that they have caused harm by their detrimental actions. The second set of disengagement practices—displacement of responsibility—operates by obscuring or minimizing one's agentive role in causing harm. People will behave in ways they would normally repudiate if a legitimate authority accepts responsibility for the effects of their conduct (Kelman & Hamilton, 1989; Milgram, 1974). With displaced responsibility, they view their actions as arising from the dictates of authorities. Because they are not the actual agents of their actions, they are spared self-condemning reactions.

Self-exemption from inhumane acts via displacement of responsibility is most gruesomely revealed in institutionally sanctioned genocide. Nazi concentration-camp commandants and their functionaries absolved them-selves of personal responsibility for their unprecedented atrocities (Andrus, 1969). They claimed they were simply carrying out orders. In his memoirs, Adolf Eichmann, who managed the mass deportation of Jews to the exter-mination camps, portrayed himself as a mere functionary obeying orders: "It is normal that I who was not responsible, was not the master planner, the initiator or the one giving orders, should set out to defend myself against these accusations" (Greenberg, 2000). He not only excluded Jews from his view of shared humanity but also took pride in their mass annihilation: "I will leap into my grave laughing," he boasted, "because the feeling that I have five million human beings on my conscience is for me a source of extraordinary satisfaction" (Cullen, 1961).

Self-exonerating obedience to horrific orders is similarly evident in mili-tary atrocities, such as the My Lai massacre (Kelman, 1973). The incidence of genocidal violence testifies to the writer C. P. Snow's insightful observation that "more hideous crimes have been committed in the name of obedience than in the name of rebellion." In an effort to deter institutionally sanctioned atrocities, the Nuremberg Principles declared that obedience to inhumane orders, even orders from the highest authorities, does not relieve subor-dinates of responsibility for their actions. However, victors rarely try their upper-echelon authorities as criminals.

In the oft-cited psychological studies by Stanley Milgram (1974) of dis-engagement of moral control by displacement of responsibility, authorities explicitly sanctioned injurious actions and held themselves responsible for any harm caused by their followers. The experimenter got participants to escalate their level of aggression by commanding them to do so, pressur-ing them when they resisted, and telling them he took full responsibility for the consequences of the participants' actions. As shown in Figure 2.1, the greater the legitimacy and proximity of the authority issuing injurious commands, the higher the level of obedient aggression. However, the par-ticipants disregarded demands to escalate the punishments when the com-mands were issued remotely, when their peers disobeyed, or when different authorities issued conflicting commands.

The sanctioning of harmful conduct in everyday life differs in two im-portant ways from the direct-authorization system examined by Milgram (1974). They include surreptitious sanctioning systems and obliging func-tionaries. Responsibility is rarely assumed openly. Only obtuse authorities would leave themselves open to accusations of authorizing harmful acts. They usually invite and support harmful conduct surreptitiously for social and personal reasons. Surreptitious sanctioning shields higher echelons from social condemnation should an authorized course of action go awry. Because of the lack of direct evidence, they can argue that they are blame-less. However, the greater concern is that they have to live with themselves. Sanctioning by indirection enables them to protect themselves against the

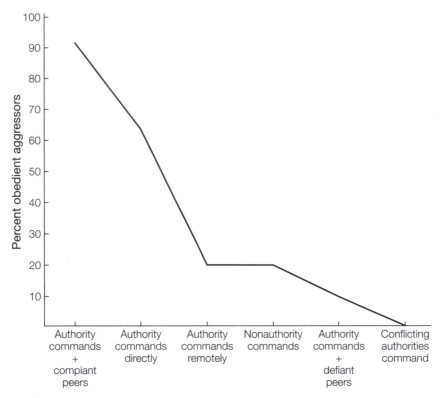

Figure 2.1 Percentage of people fully obedient to injurious commands. From "Moral Disengagement in the Perpetration of Inhumanities," by A. Bandura, 1999, *Personality and Social Psychology Review, 3,* 193–209, Figure 2. This figure is plotted from data from Experiments 5, 7, 13, 15, 17, and 18 from *Obedience to Authority: An Experimental View,* by S. Milgram, 1974, New York: Harper & Row. Copyright 1974 by Harper Collins, Publishers.

loss of self-respect that would result from the judgment that they were the authorizers of the human cruelty.

In detrimental schemes, authorities act to keep themselves uninformed. The Iran–Contra affair is a good case in point. Deceiving and defying Congress, officials in the Reagan administration diverted money from covert, illegal weapons sales to Iran to fund Nicaraguan rebels. The major players in this surreptitious scheme went to great lengths to keep themselves uninformed, instructing their aides and advisors to create a system of "plausible deniability." For example, when testifying before Congress, National Security Advisor John Poindexter explained that he insulated the president to "provide some future deniability" in case information about the clandestine operation leaked out (Rosenbaum, 1987). He reported that Secretary of State George Shultz also wanted to be kept uninformed about what was going on: "He indicated he didn't particularly want to know the details. He said, just tell me what I need to know." Schultz did not agree with this accusation. In congressional testimony, Robert Gates, the deputy director of central intelligence in the CIA, admitted that he did not pursue information about the covert operation because he did not want to know about it. What made this system of collective willful uninformedness so unusual was that it extended throughout the chain of command, with the top overseers of the nation's international affairs evading accountability for illegal international arms sales to fund a rebel uprising.

Authorities do not go looking for evidence of wrongdoing. Obvious questions that would reveal incriminating information remain unasked, so officials do not find out what they do not want to know. Implicit agreements, insulating social arrangements, and authorization by indirection ensure that the higher echelons are unaccountable. When harmful practices are publicized, they are officially dismissed as only isolated incidents arising from misunderstandings of what had been authorized. Or blame is shifted to subordinates, who are portrayed as misguided or overzealous. Investigators who go looking for incriminating records of authorization display naiveté about the insidious ways that pernicious practices are usually sanctioned and carried out. A cursory investigation might usually reveal only decisional arrangements of foggy nonresponsibility rather than incriminating traces of smoking guns.

Officials can issue orders in ways that invite illegal activities but provide deniability for the authorizers. In her book *Willful Blindness*, Margaret Heffernan (2011) reports a case that typifies this process. The telecommunications company MCI persuaded unsuspecting customers who ran up high telephone bills to sign promissory notes that committed them legally to pay what they owed. The top official ordered subordinates to remove the bad debts from the books. They did so by misrepresenting the outstanding debts as assets. Walter Pavlo, who served prison time for cooking the books, described the surreptitious authorization and collective willful evasion of how the debt mysteriously disappeared: "Of course there was never a direct order to cook the books, instead it was just a kind of willful neglect. No one would ever ask how the debt disappeared. So since nobody told you to stop, you kept going. The only order we had was just: make the debt vanish. Don't bring me problems, bring me solutions" (Heffernan, 2011). In his self-exoneration, Pavlo trivialized the criminal activity as harmless: "Where was the harm? You couldn't see any." He shifted the blame to corporate pressure: "MCI is making me smoke and drink and write these notes. It's not me, it's them" (Heffernan, 2011).

The other basic difference from the direct authorization system in Milgram's study centers on the implementation of the actionable policies, however they are conveyed. Displacement of responsibility requires obliging functionaries. If they cast off all responsibility, they would perform their duties only when told to do so and only when the authorizers were present. It requires a strong sense of responsibility, rooted in ideology, to be a good functionary. It is therefore important to distinguish between two levels of responsibility: duty to one's superiors and accountability for the effects of one's actions. In a system of wrongdoing, the best functionaries are those who honor their obligations to authority but feel no personal responsibility for the harm they cause. They work dutifully to be good at their evildoing. Followers who disowned responsibility, without being bound by a sense of duty, would be quite unreliable in performing their duties when the authorities were not present.

Diffusion of Responsibility

The exercise of moral control is also weakened when personal agency is obscured by diffusing responsibility for detrimental behavior. Any harm done by a group can always be attributed largely to the behavior of others. Figure 2.2 shows the level of harm inflicted on others on repeated occasions depending on whether the harm was done by a group or by individuals (Bandura et al., 1975). People act more cruelly under group responsibility than when they hold themselves personally accountable for their actions.

Kelman (1973) describes the different ways in which personal accountability is dispersed. Group decision making is a common practice that can result in otherwise considerate people behaving inhumanely. The faceless group becomes the agent that does the deciding and the authorizing. Members can discount their contribution to the policies and practices arrived at collectively so they are not really responsible. When everyone is responsible, no one really feels responsible. Napoleon put it well when he noted that

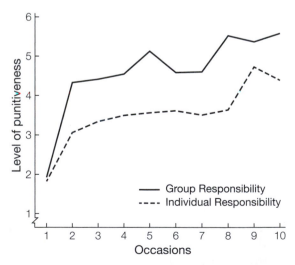

Figure 2.2 Level of punitiveness by individuals. From "Disinhibition of Aggression Through Diffusion of Responsibility and Dehumanization of Victims," by A. Bandura, B. Underwood, & M. E. Fromson, 1975, *Journal of Research in Personality, 9*, 253–269, Figure 4. Reprinted with permission from Elsevier.

"collective crimes incriminate no one." Social systems go to great lengths to devise social arrangements for diffusing responsibility for decisions that affect outsiders adversely.

A division of labor also diffuses, and thereby diminishes, a sense of responsibility. Most undertakings require the services of many people, each performing subdivided jobs that seem harmless in themselves. Departmentalization of subfunctions into isolated units within a system creates a further sense of detachment from the production of tools of destruction. After activities become routinized into detached subfunctions, people shift their attention from the morality of what they are doing to the operational details of the fragmented activity and efficiency in performing their specific job (Kelman, 1973). The implementers strive to be good at their particular piecework.

The most graphic example of moral self-exoneration through diffusion of responsibility occurs within the act of intentionally putting a human being to death. Executing a person requires subdivision of the task to get individuals to do it. In execution by lethal injection, the drug subfunctions are spread across the team of drug technicians. Some members insert the intravenous lines for the syringes into the inmate's veins; others attach the electrocardiogram electrodes to monitor the inmate's heart rate. In the semiautomated drug delivery system, still others push the plungers. Responsibility is similarity diffused in the strap-down teams. Each member straps an isolated part of the body. The power of diffusion to erase a sense of personal responsibility is revealed in the remarks of a guard in San Quentin whose role was limited to strapping down an inmate's leg to the electric chair in 126 executions (Marine, 1990). This spared him the appearance of executioner. "I never pulled the trigger," he said. "I wasn't the executioner." He goes on to describe how, over time, an execution becomes a routinized task performed perfunctorily. "But after I'd get home I'd think about it a little bit. But then it would go away. And then, at last, it was just another job."

Collective action is the third form of moral disinhibition through diffused responsibility. Several psychosocial processes are at work. Collective action adds legitimacy to harmful means, especially if supported by principled justifications (Bandura, 1973). Enmeshment in group action fueled by mounting emotional arousal can override cognitive control. In highly aroused states, individuals are prone to act impulsively with little thought about the consequences of their actions. Group actions also provide a sense of anonymity (Zimbardo, 1969). As long as one remains personally unrecognizable, one need have little concern for adverse social evaluation.

The preceding disinhibitory processes are rooted in a reduction of perceived social sanctions. Amid many players acting together, one easily can discount one's contribution to the harm perpetrated by the group. As a consequence, people act more cruelly when responsibility is diffused than when they hold themselves accountable for the effects of their actions. However, enmeshment in group action does not completely eliminate self-awareness: Individuals still have to contend with their self-evaluation.

Egregious systemic transgressions fostered surreptitiously from above make it hard to believe that the upper echelon is entirely blameless. In a common scenario, top officials evade accountability by stepping forward with a ritualized public apology. They announce that they accept ultimate responsibility because the transgressions occurred "under their watch." However, the scenario frames the issue as a lapse in oversight of wrongdoers rather than the culpability of those in charge. This sleight of hand quickly shifts responsibility to rogue underlings who are charged with violating the organization's policies and values. Expressing hurt feelings over a wrong-doer's betrayal can arouse empathy in others for the officials' plight. If skill-fully orchestrated, apologetic admission of ultimate responsibility can bring forgiveness and even sympathy for officials portrayed as victims of subordinate wrongdoers. The public apology typically closes with a forward-looking statement aimed at curbing further probing. It is time to put the problem behind us, the officials announce, and quickly move on to right the wrongs and restore public trust. Admissions of ultimate responsibility are usually devoid of consequences. The officials are not chastised, demoted, dismissed, docked pay, or penalized in other ways.

THE EFFECTS LOCUS

Disregard, Distortion, and Denial of Harmful Effects

Other ways of disengaging moral control operate by minimizing, disregarding, or even disputing the harmful effects of one's actions. When people pursue activities that harm others, they avoid facing the harm they cause or minimize it. They are especially prone to minimize the harm they cause when they act alone and thus cannot easily evade responsibility (Mynatt & Herman, 1975). If minimization does not work, the evidence of harm can be discredited. As long as the harmful results of one's conduct are ignored, minimized, or disputed, there is little or no reason for self-censure to be activated. Vigorous battles are therefore fought over the credibility of evidence of detrimental effects. Witness the heated dispute over the existence of global warming and whether it is caused by human activity.

It is easier to harm others when their suffering is not visible and when destructive actions are physically and temporally remote from their effects. When people can see and hear the suffering they cause, vicariously aroused distress and self-censure become self-restraining influences (Bandura, 1992). As shown in Figure 2.3, people are less likely to comply with the commands of authorities to carry out injurious actions when the victims' pain becomes more evident and personalized (Milgram, 1974). Even a high sense

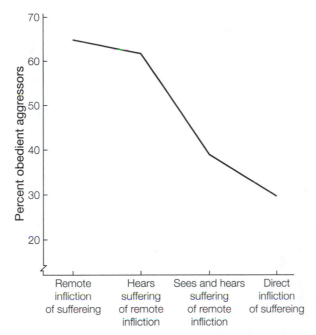

Figure 2.3 Percentage of people fully obedient to injurious commands issued by an authority. From "Moral Disengagement in the Perpetration of Inhumanities," by A. Bandura, 1999, *Personality and Social Psychology Review, 3*, 193–209, Figure 4. This figure is plotted from data from Experiments 1 through 4 from *Obedience to Authority: An Experimental View*, by S. Milgram, 1974, New York: Harper & Row. Copyright 1974 by Harper Collins, Publishers.

of personal responsibility for the effects of one's actions is a weak restraint on conduct when the perpetrators do not see the harm they inflict on their victims (Tilker, 1970).

A Pulitzer Prize was awarded for a powerful photograph that captured the anguished cries of a girl whose clothes were burned off by the napalm bombing of her village in Vietnam. This single humanization of inflicted destruction probably did more to turn the American public against the war than the countless reports filed by journalists. The military subsequently banned cameras and journalists from battlefield areas to block the publication of images of death and destruction.

Most organizations involve hierarchical chains of command in which superiors formulate plans and intermediaries transmit them to functionaries, who then carry them out. The further removed individuals are from the destructive end results, the weaker the restraining power of injurious effects. Disengagement of moral control is easiest for the intermediaries in a hierarchical system. They neither bear responsibility for the decisions nor do they carry them out and face the harm being inflicted (Kilham & Mann, 1974).

In addition to keeping harmful effects out of sight by avoiding them physically, people can bring intrapsychic processes into play to diminish the perceived extent and severity of the harm done. These cognitive processes include selective inattention to harmful effects, construing them in ways that make them look less harmful, and not remembering them. Memory is a reconstruction rather than a replay of recorded experiences, so there is a lot of leeway for memory distortion. For example, in the mix of doing good and bad things, people remember the good things they have done but recall less of the harmful ones (Brock & Buss, 1964). When people are socially influenced to behave punitively, their recollection is that the harm done was less severe than actually was the case (Larsen, Coleman, Forbes, & Johnson, 1972). An interesting finding of this study was that the minimization of harm is greater when participants' punitiveness was increased by exposure to aggressive models than by social pressures. In the latter case, the pressure of others provides a clear external source to blame in self-exoneration. Females have a harder time forgetting the harm they have caused than do males.

We shall revisit later how modern warfare requires fighting two battles—the military one and the public relations one in the global media. We are now in the era of satellite and laser-guided warfare. These technologies have become highly lethal and depersonalized, delivering mass destruction remotely via satellite-guided systems, without any direct human contact. For example, military personnel operate pilotless drones equipped with bombs and missiles from a control center in Nevada. The cameras aboard the drones identify possible suspects in Iraq, Afghanistan, Pakistan, and other countries. The pilot fires the rockets that blow up the people being targeted. The trigger is pulled in Nevada, but the deadly effects occur on another continent thousands of miles away. The military's euphemistic language deletes the human operators of the drones, which are referred to as "unmanned aerial vehicles" or "uninhabited aerial vehicles."

Remotely implemented, faceless warfare underscores the extraordinary flexibility of moral self-regulation of conduct. The drone pilots switch their moral control off and on in daily shifts between their working hours and their off-duty family and social lives. Drone warfare does not require brawn. Female as well as male officers conduct the remote-controlled killing missions. Indeed, one of the women pilots was so adept at flying the remote-controlled Predator drones that she was chosen to fly supersecret CIA missions (Purdam, 2003). Women's adoption of a killer role is a product of the evolution of military technology, not biological evolution.

Although they are physically isolated from harrowing combat experiences, nearly half of the drone operators experience high levels of stress (Bumiller, 2011). The air force attributed the emotional distress to heavy workload demands. A more likely explanation is that drone bombers see the people they are killing and the resulting carnage. Here is a drone pilot reassuring himself that he made the right decisions: "There was good reason for killing the people that I did." However, the drone strikes continued to intrude into his mental life: "I go though it in my head over and over and over....But you never forget about it, it never just fades away" (Bumiller, 2012). Morally based anguish, which is distinguished from stress disorders arising from traumatic battle experiences, is called "moral injury."

Abrupt daily shifts between moral engagement and disengagement are undoubtedly another major stressor. Having to turn one's morality off and on, day in and day out, between lethal air strikes and prosocial home life makes it difficult to maintain a sense of moral integrity. To complicate matters, the actionable ground intelligence guiding the air strikes is not always trustworthy. The difficulty in distinguishing combatants from civilians can result in a heavy toll on innocent victims. Video closeups of women, children, and other civilian casualties of air strikes are a source of posttraumatic stress disorder in some drone pilots. As the neuropsychiatrist Colonel Kent McDonald put it, "collateral damage is unnerving or unsettling to these guys" (Bumiller, 2014). Self-forgiveness and peace of mind are especially difficult to achieve when one has killed for a cause that turned out to lack moral legitimacy.

Drone warfare is the new source of "collateral damage" in the war on terrorism. The legality and morality of U.S. drone strikes in targeted killings of al Qaeda leaders and their associates are hotly debated. Some justify the drone strikes as national self-defense against imminent threats by terrorist groups. Drone strikes are also justified by savings in costs and soldiers' lives compared with the rooting out of militant groups by ground operations (Shane, 2013a). The threats to national security are real. For example, one bomber attempted to detonate a bomb in his sneakers in a flight from Paris to Miami but was subdued by the passengers. In a Christmas flight over Detroit, a bomber tried to detonate a bomb hidden in his underwear, but it failed to go off. At his sentencing, he proclaimed that he was "proud to kill in the name of God" (ABC News, 2012).

Although the threats to the United States are real, there is no clear legal framework governing national protection against foreign terrorists groups. They are nonstate actors with no national borders. Nor are they controllable when they enjoy safe haven in failed states or in sovereign nations with tribal regions sympathetic to their ideology. The targeted killings abroad of American citizens turned jihadists raises serious questions about the constitutionality of such actions. Because the rules governing targeted killings were cloaked in classified secrecy, under what review they were carried out is unclear.

The constitutional and moral issues of drone strikes were highlighted with the controversial drone killing of Anwar al-Awlaki and his teenage son in Yemen. Al-Awlaki was an American Muslim cleric who became a firebrand radicalizer through his widely read blog. He was charged with inspiring some of the attempted terrorist attacks against the United States. Before his shooting rampage at Fort Hood, the army psychiatrist Nidal Hasan consulted al-Awlaki on the religious legitimacy of killing American soldiers. Hasan killed 13 soldiers and wounded 30 others while shouting, "God is great" (Kenber, 2013). After the attack, al-Awlaki posted a prayer for this "heroic man of conscience" for striking a blow against the American enemy conducting a "war against Islam."

Pilotless drones are being heralded as the weapons system of the 21st century. The military is already experimenting with robotic weapons systems in ground warfare to keep personnel out of harm's way under especially hazardous circumstances. Some countries are developing autonomous robotic systems in which armed robots select and demolish targets without human control. In this new phase of robotic technology, autonomous combat drones are programmed to take off, perform a mission, and fly back without requiring any human guidance (Parker, 2013). This is a relatively cheap and safe way of conducting some military missions.

Borenstein (2008) raises legal and ethical concerns about robotic systems. If they become more reliable than foot soldiers in reading and responding to combat situations, human oversight could be phased out. If a robotic system mistakes civilians for combatants, who would be held accountable for the actions of the robotic system? Christof Heyns, a UN expert on extrajudicial executions, declared that production and use of armed robots should be banned, saying, "War without reflection is mechanical slaughter" (Cumming-Bruce, 2013).

The advent of the Internet ushered in a ubiquitous vehicle for disengaging moral self-sanctions from transgressive conduct. The Internet was designed as a highly decentralized system that defies regulation. Anybody can get into the act, and nobody is in charge. Internet trolls can readily use this unfettered vehicle for destructive purposes. Rubin (1994) describes certain characteristics of electronic technologies that can increase the propensity for moral disengagement. Transgressive acts can be performed privately and anonymously against depersonalized or faceless victims located thousands of miles away. Breaking into an office to steal paper files is difficult to execute, as is escaping detection. But with the right malware, hackers can break into web sites with minimal effort and without leaving tracks or displacing of the owner's property. The notions of breaking and entering and burglary in the cyberworld are more likely to be viewed by computer hackers as metaphorical rather than criminal.

By weakening moral restraints, other aspects of Internet transactions make it easy to behave transgressively in the cyberworld. In personal transactions, there is a close connection between actions and outcomes. In the cyberworld, a hacker's actions can affect a multitude of interconnected networks in diverse distant places that, in turn, determine the outcomes via their functional properties. The hacker is the initiator rather than the sole author of the outcomes. This complex mediation blurs the link between actions and outcomes. If the computer crimes are not widely publicized, the hacker may not know the nature and full extent of the damage done. The sight of human pain and suffering makes personal crimes more morally unsettling than property crimes. Many computer crimes are directed at faceless corporate and governmental systems. These types of impersonal transgressions are more likely to be viewed as legal threats than as moral violations.

Additional unique features of electronic communication technologies make them perilous if used for harmful purposes. They are readily accessible, portable, easily implementable remotely by clicks, connected worldwide for far-reaching consequences, and exceedingly difficult to control as institutions. Transgressive actions that produce diffuse outcomes via circuitous paths are also less amenable to personal control than actions that beget direct, tightly contingent outcomes. Societal vulnerabilities are enormously magnified because virtually all of the systems on which people depend in their everyday life are interdependently run by computer network systems. These can be easily knocked out, as shown by the computer student in the Philippines who wreaked havoc worldwide by crippling e-mail systems, costing billions of dollars. Smart hackers can do much more serious damage. Cybercrime and cyberterrorism, committed through the Internet, form the dark side of the cyberworld that increasingly commands societal attention.

The preceding analyses centered mainly on moral disengagement from behavior that has destructive and physically injurious effects. The moral neutralizing strategies at the outcome locus of moral control are designed to keep detrimental effects out of sight and mind, minimize them, or dispute their very existence. Without perceived adverse effects there can be no moral predicament. Verbal abuse, in the form of hateful comments, vicious rumors and cruel disparagement and humiliation, has detrimental effects of a different sort. Unlike physically destructive conduct, verbal abuse leaves no evident bruises, open wounds, spurting blood, anguished cries, or death. Although verbal abuse has few immediate tangible effects, its psychological and social effects can be devastating. Destroyed structures can be rebuilt and physical wounds heal, but destroying people's sense of self-worth and social reputation results in psychic wounds that endure. Moreover, such wounds can be exacerbated or even extended by the changes in interpersonal relationships the hateful postings cause. To the extent that a falsely tainted reputation colors how others treat the victim, it can create a self-confirming social reality (Snyder, 1980). In this instance, the adage "Sticks and stones may break my bones, but words will never hurt me" is wrong.

The social effects of cyberviolence are somewhat ambiguous. Perpetrators lack firsthand information on how their victims are affected intrapsychically by verbal abuse. Nor do they know who reads their postings, whether those readers have had any contact with the victim, and how they behaved toward the victim. These unknowns make it easy to persuade oneself that one's conduct caused little or no harm and that one is merely exercising the constitutionally protected right of free speech.

Moral Disengagement by Observers of Harmful Practices

The preceding analyses have largely focused on the lengths to which perpetrators go to avoid seeing the harm they cause. The world of work presents another type of moral predicament in which associates and supervisors are witness to institutional wrongdoings. Out of fear of retaliation and being ostracized as informers or troublemakers, they collectively turn a blind eye to what is going on (Heffernan, 2011). Compliant accommodation to institutional wrongdoing is self-devaluing unless morally justified.

In the workplace, some employees troubled by organizational wrongdoing voice their concerns internally. Others report detrimental organizational practices to regulatory agencies and influential mass media. The search in personality traits and organizational characteristics for predictors of whistle-blowers has not yielded much reliable information. The frequent focus of research on whistle-blowers' intentions rather than their actual behavior also limits the generalizability of the research findings (McGinnis & Foege, 1993; Mesmer-Magnus & Viswesvaran, 2005). Intrapersonal determinants of whistle-blowing are more fruitfully explored in terms of self-regulatory processes than decontextualized personality traits.

The personal accounts of whistle-blowers indicate that they tied their moral integrity to taking action against institutional wrongdoing (Heffernan, 2011). Most pay a heavy social and emotional price for their actions. Whistle-blowers are legally safeguarded against retaliation. However, if they remain on the job they are likely to find themselves marginalized in an inhospitable workplace. If they leave, other companies are not about to hire whistle-blowers, so they are probably unemployable in their particular line of work. This trying experience upends their occupational and social life and changes their outlook on life.

Research on the self-management of morality holds the promise of clarifying the role of moral disengagement in accommodating institutional wrongdoing and moral engagement in exposing it. Challenging transgressive powers requires robust belief in one's own ability to effect change by one's actions (Bandura, 1997). Those beset by doubts over their causative capabilities respond resignedly to wrongdoing, but those imbued with a strong sense of efficacy are willing to take on the challenge of unmasking institutional practices that do social harm (MacNab & Worthley, 2008). Whistle-blowers often feel liberated by doing the right thing and preserving their self-regard. It takes a lot of moral courage and perceived self-efficacy to blow the whistle.

The Catholic Church

For decades, Roman Catholic bishops knew of transgressions by rogue clergy who sexually abused children. The children's trauma included not only sexual assault but also sometimes frightening threats that forced the victims into silence. For example, while brandishing a gun a molesting priest threatened to hurt the child's family if he told anyone about the assault. Given the prevalence, scope, and duration of the crimes, church officials invested a great deal of collective effort in not knowing what was going on. The bishops used several mechanisms of moral disengagement at the diocesan level to cover up the abuse and the harm inflicted on children. They withheld information about the abuse and resisted reporting the allegations to law enforcement authorities (Robinson, 2002). Victims who filed complaints were compensated secretly to silence them. These efforts to conceal the sexual abuse operated mainly at the effects locus of moral disengagement. The bishops not only maintained secrecy among themselves about what was going on but also provided deniability at higher levels of the church hierarchy. One organization for victims of abuse summarized an Irish governmental report on the child molestations as documenting how "senior churchmen conspir[ed] to cover up the abuse with an astounding indifference to the safety of children" (Dalby & Donadio, 2011). Moral disengagement in the cover-up of these sex crimes is analyzed in some detail because litigation yielded a large body of church documents for analysis. Moreover, moral disengagement by major religious institutions that are considered arbiters of morality is an astonishing paradox that defies explanation. The widespread sexual transgressions by clergy testify to the power of moral disengagement to override the sanctions of conscience.

Sexual molestation of children has no justification. Nor can it be sanitized linguistically. However, the cover-up by the bishops required justification. The bishops' actions indicated that their justification was based on utilitarian grounds: The harm to the moral authority of the church from disclosing the sexual abuse outweighed the harm inflicted on children. In the cover-up, which went on for years in the United States and Europe, some of the offending priests were relocated to other parishes. Many were assigned to mainly nonparish duties and referred for spiritual counseling. Families of victims who filed charges received sizable settlements. The lawyers representing the families referred to the payments as "hush money."

The Reverend Andrew Greeley, an outspoken critic of the Catholic hierarchy, warned church officials about the molestation of children. He described the form the cover-up took in response to parental complaints: "Parents complain first to the church and are rebuffed. Then they go to the police and are given the runaround. They return to the church and are told in effect that the church thinks their child is lying. Reluctantly, they sue" (Editorial: Father Greeley, 2013). His early warnings were not well received. Fellow priests blamed the victims, claiming that the children were lying. They told him, "Don't air our dirty linen in public." The sexual abuse was concealed.

Faced with disturbing revelations, various countries took steps to impose legal liabilities for child molestation by priests. For example, Ireland drafted a law requiring church officials to report suspected child sexual abuse to civil authorities. In a landmark case in the United States, Monsignor William Lynn, a supervisory priest in Philadelphia, was charged with conspiracy to conceal sexual molestation of minors by priests and exposing children to sexual abuse. Testimony from his trial provides a glimpse of how morality was put on hold at the archdiocesan level to cover up the abuse (Eckholm & Hurdle, 2012). Concealing and minimizing the crimes, displacement and diffusion of responsibility, discrediting informers, disparaging victims, and indifference to them all contributed to the self-exoneration. Lynn, who was responsible for investigating allegations and overseeing priest assign-ments, reported the offenses to his superiors but felt it was the responsibil-ity of the Philadelphia archdiocese to deal with the problems. Rather than being removed, some offending priests were reassigned to active ministry in other parishes where they could continue the sexual abuse. On orders from his superior, Lynn did not explain to parishioners, why priests were re-moved and reassigned. "I was given the directions what to do," he explained (Warner, 2012a). A nun working in one of the parishes reported concern that a priest was receiving child pornography in the mail. She was branded a troublemaker who was trying "to stir up conflict" and accused of having suspect motives.

The head of the archdiocese, Cardinal Anthony Bevilacqua, ordered the shredding of a list of credibly charged priests. Lynn, along with other church officials, discussed how to withhold such information in future lawsuits against the church. In other litigation, church officials shifted their strategy from legal settlements to adversarial legal challenges of alleged clergy abuse (Goodstein, 2012). William Donohue, president of a Catholic advocacy group called Catholic League, is the public face of staunch defense of the Vatican. He criticized one advocacy network for abuse victims as "a menace to the Catholic Church." Church officials subpoenaed the advocacy group to turn over all documents regarding the plaintiffs that they had collected over the years. The founder claimed that the purpose of the subpoena and deposition was to harass, discredit, and bankrupt the group, which is run mostly by volunteers, in an effort to deter suits against the church (Goodstein, 2012).

When questioned about why a priest who forced an altar boy to have oral and anal sex was not removed from the parish ministry, Lynn displayed striking indifference to the abused child (Warner, 2012a). He provided the odd justification that the abusing priest was also having sex with a woman, so he was "not a pure pedophile" (Warner, 2012b). The willful disregard for victimized minors in this tragedy is further shown in priests' justifications for not reporting the sexual crimes to law-enforcement officials. Church law-yers told them they did not have to because they were not legally obligated to do so or because the statute of limitations had expired (Rogers, 2012).

The Catholic Church launched a vigorous campaign, hiring lobbying and public relations firms and pressuring churchgoers, to get state legislators to shorten the deadline for bringing charges of child sexual abuse (Goodstein &

Eckholm, 2012). Patrick Brannigan, the director of a New Jersey Catholic advocacy group, argued that long deadlines produce less reliable evidence due to fading memories and deaths. What he failed to mention were cases in which the church acknowledged the sexual abuse and the priests confessed, but nothing could be done about the crimes because the statute of limitations had expired. Shorter deadlines would increase the number of cases that could not be tried. Joan Fitz-Gerald, who presided over the Colorado Senate, reported being stunned by the harshness of the onslaught against proposed legislation regarding deadlines for filing charges of child sexual abuse and the indifference to the victimized. "It was the most brutal thing I've ever been through. The politics, the deception and lack of concern for not only children in the past, but for children today" (Goodstein & Eckholm, 2012).

The leader of the Catholic Church in Ireland, Cardinal Sean Brady, was under growing public pressure to resign for his failure to protect children against sexual molestation in his prior role as secretariat. Like Monsignor Lynn in Philadelphia, Cardinal Brady used displacement of responsibility as the principal mode of self-exoneration. Having passed the evidence of molestation on to his superiors, he felt that he had fulfilled his responsibility. The superiors took no protective action. Rather, they reassigned a notorious child molester to Irish and American parishes to prevent attachments to particular children. Nonetheless, he continued to molest and rape countless minors. Cardinal Brady claimed that he was just a "note taker" in the internal church investigation and "felt betrayed" on learning, twenty years later, that his superiors ignored his report. Both Monsignor Lynn and Cardinal Brady showed an unusual lack of interest in the outcome of the evidence they submitted. When asked whether he checked on the outcome of his report, he restated his limited responsibility: "I don't think it was my role to follow through" (Pogatchnik, 2012). One of the victims disputed Cardinal Brady's exonerative self-portrayal by explaining that, as a holder of a doctorate in church law, Brady was widely consulted as a highly skilled canon lawyer. He was instrumental, for example, in getting a child to sign a pledge of secrecy, in the absence of his parents, regarding sexual abuse by a priest.

Denial and minimization of criminal offences also blinded religious officials to what they did not want to hear. Cardinal Edward Egan, the late archbishop of New York, treated abuse allegations with skepticism and regarded the incidence rate as "marvelous" in that only a few priests were accused of sexually molesting children (Christofferson, 2012). It is true that reported cases of abuse involve only a small percentage of priests, but the number of occurrences is high. Contrary to the claimed rare incidence, a report commissioned by the National Conference of Catholic Bishops revealed that, during a 50-year period, over 10,000 allegations of molestation of minors were brought against priests in the United States alone (Warner, 2012b).

Monsignor Lynn was sentenced to a six-year prison term for priest reassignments that endangered children and for lying to unwary parishioners about why those priests were being relocated. He was acquitted of conspiracy. His trial set an important precedent because a higher church official was convicted, not because he himself committed a sexual crime but because he enabled predatory priests to do so. The court ruling affirmed that clergy are not exempt from civil laws as an exercise of religious freedom and that upper-level clergy cannot absolve themselves of responsibility for crimes committed by transgressors under their supervision. Daniel Maguire (2012), a professor of theology at Marquette University, argued that because the church neither rescinded Lynn's honorific title nor suspended him from the priestly ministry, "the church has not risen to the standards of the state when it comes to protecting children."

When the verdict was handed down, William Donohue issued an unabashedly exonerative press release that drew on the various modes of moral disengagement (Donohue, 2012b). He shifted the blame to the alleged "witch-hunt" against the Catholic Church and "church-chasing" attorneys. In a diversionary use of advantageous comparison, Donohue sent a letter to the prosecutor requesting her to identify which religious denominations, other than the Roman Catholic Church, she pursued for sexual crimes by clergy. By selectively disregarding the conviction of child endangerment, Donohue claimed that the litigants were the losers because the conspiracy charge was dismissed. "Those who have been clamoring for blood," he declared, "lost big time." In the most callous indifference to the enduring suffering inflicted on children by the predatory priests, Donohue disparaged the child victims as a "pitiful bunch of malcontents" (Donohue, 2012a). Following the dictum that offense is the best defense, dutiful efforts at damage control by disparaging sexually abused children requires the sacrifice of moral principles.

Monsignor Lynn's conviction was overturned on the technical grounds that the child welfare law under which he was tried at the time applied only to parents and guardians (Hurdle, 2013). However, in April 2015, the Pennsylvania Supreme Court reinstated the conviction of Monsignor Lynn on a charge of endangering the welfare of a child. He was then sent back to prison. His conviction is on appeal. Judy Miller, the leader of a network representing children sexually abused by priests, objected to his release: "They have protected criminals and their reputation, and not protected children that were placed in their care" (Hurdle, 2013).

In a rare case further up in the church hierarchy, Bishop Robert W. Finn of Kansas City was convicted of shielding a priest who took thousands of pornographic photos of young girls (Goodstein & Eligon, 2012). Despite alarming reports by families and warnings by staff members, Finn euphemistically minimized the offenses as simply "boundary violations" between an adult and a child. He reassigned the offending priest to another parish where, unsupervised, he continued his pornographic photography. The offending priest photographed close-ups of girl's genitals. At a parishioner's dinner in the new parish the priest was caught photographing under their daughter's skirt under the table (Hurdle, 2013). The priest was convicted on federal charges of child pornography and is serving a 50-year prison sentence. In the end, Finn pleaded guilty to a misdemeanor and was sentenced to two years' probation.

Once again Donohue came to the rescue (Donohue, 2012d). He argued that no crime had been committed: "The case did not involve child sexual abuse—no child was ever abused, or touched....Nor did this case involve child pornography." He attributed the trial to an anti-Catholic conspiracy: "[W]e find the chorus of condemnations targeting Bishop Finn to be as unfair as they are contrived" (Donohue, 2012d). By denying the offenses and blaming conspirators for the alleged unfair trial, Donohue stripped the immorality from pornographic abuse of young children. In 2015, Finn resigned from the Church and Pope Francis accepted his resignation.

The veil of secrecy and moral compromise operated throughout the church hierarchy. Although the problem was systemic, as is usually the case, it was the underlings in the hierarchy who were indicted and who served prison time. The leaders of the archdiocese of Kansas City, where the abuse occurred, claimed no recollection of previous charges of abuse. Although the sexual crimes violated civil law, not a single clergyman broke rank and reported the crimes to civil authorities.

In an interview, the Reverend Benedict Groeschel, well known as an author and the host of a weekly show on a Catholic television network, blamed children for priests' sexual abuse. He claimed that in a "lot of cases, the... youngster is the seducer" (Otterman, 2012). He went on to express sympathy for a football coach convicted of child molestation. Father Groeschel was not new to the problem of predator priests. For years he was in charge of screening candidates for the priesthood, searching for potential pedophiles. In a prompt response to public outrage, he retracted his remarks and expressed regret for them. Church authorities repudiated the claim that children seduce priests, attributing Father Groeschel's remarks to failing health and advancing age. Ever protective of the church, Donohue (2012c) came to his defense. The sympathy for the offending coach (Jerry Sandusky), Donohue argued, was for Sandusky's "maladies," not vindication of his behavior. Critics viewed the incident as further evidence of the moral failing of church officials.

Church records from a court settlement by the Los Angeles archdiocese revealed a child-abuse scandal. The cover-up of the scandal was presided over by Cardinal Roger Mahony, the archbishop, and other high-echelon clergymen. The scandal involved over 100 priests and over 500 abused children, in cases spanning four decades (Lovett, 2013). In an elaborate scheme to protect offenders from law officials, the molesting priests were sent for treatment to New Mexico, which lacked a legal requirement to report evidence of child abuse. One of the priests preyed on young Hispanic boys from families of illegal immigrants, knowing that they would be fearful of filing lawsuits. He tied up and raped one boy, then threatened him with deportation if he mentioned it to anyone. The priest was urged by Mahoney not to return to California because he could be subject to criminal prosecution. Another priest molested 20 altar boys. Cardinal Mahoney concurred with Monsignor Thomas Curry in not sending the list to the police: "We cannot give such a list for no [sic] cause whatsoever" (Flaccus, 2014). Mahoney also signed off on the referral of an egregious molester to a psychiatrist who, because he was a lawyer as well, was not required to report the offender to law authorities (Medina, 2013).

These practices came to light after years of obstructive litigation because the state of California temporarily lifted the statute of limitations for one year to permit families to file lawsuits. The archdiocese continued to fight in court against releasing church documents but was forced to do so because their release was part of the settlement with the abused victims.

Cardinal Mahony (2013) minimized the harmfulness of the sexual abuse, calling it "misconduct," as though it were mere misbehavior rather than a sex crime. He minimized the scope of the sex scandal as well: "During these intervening years a small number of cases did arise." In a statement reflecting a bewildering lack of compassion and sensitivity to the enduring harm caused by sexual abuse in childhood, Mahony attributed his actions to naiveté: "I remained naïve myself about the full and lasting impact these horrible acts would have on the lives of those who were abused by men who were supposed to be their spiritual guides" (Lovett, 2013). Even his early training in social work, he explained, did not prepare him for dealing with child molestation: "Nothing in my own background or education equipped me to deal with this grave problem...no textbook and no lecture ever referred to the sexual abuse of children" (Mahony, 2013). It was not until he met with 90 abused victims, he said, that he had come to understand the harm inflicted on the children. This is an example of genuine self-deception. One remains uninformed about what one does not want to know by not doing what would reveal it. It took hundreds of molested children before the cardinal decided to find out whether being sexually abused by a priest is enduringly harmful to young children (Lovett, 2013).

Cardinal Mahony's direct involvement in the deception precluded the oft-used downward displacement of responsibility by claiming he wasn't informed about what was going on. However, the cover-up methods that were used did involve extensive displacement and diffusion of responsibility. He consulted with other bishops throughout the country, who recommended referring the predator priests for residential treatment. He viewed the referral approach as the standard church procedure, not his own: "This procedure was standard across the country to all Arch/Dioceses" (Mahony, 2013). However, illegally concealing sex crimes, sending offending priests to places that do not require therapists to report child abuse, and offering advice on avoiding criminal prosecution were violations beyond evasive therapeutic referrals. To reduce his personal responsibility further, Cardinal Mahony complained that bishops were never informed that the treatments were ineffective, which would have meant that molesting priests could not "safely pursue priestly ministry."

In broadening the supervisory responsibility, Mahony created advisory and oversight boards to superintend the protection of children. However, resistance to litigation over the release of church documents continued. The archdiocese was accused of withholding many documents and removing the names of church officials who had supervisory responsibility (Goodstein & Medina, 2013). The church lawyers resisted the release, arguing that they would have to reexamine thousands of redacted documents.

Archbishop José Gomez, who succeeded Mahony, stripped him of public duties. Cardinal Mahony concluded a letter of self-defense to Archbishop Gomez with a bitter remark suggestive of hypocrisy: "Not once over the past years did you ever raise any questions about our policies, practices, or procedures in dealing with problems of clergy sexual misconduct involving minors" (Mahony, 2013). Archbishop Gomez explained the reason for his actions: "The behavior described in these files is terribly sad and evil. There is no excuse, no explaining away what happened to these children" (Flaccus, 2013).

In the insightful words of one of the parishioners, a person is neither "entirely good" nor "entirely bad" (Medina & Lovett, 2013). Indeed, with selective moral disengagement, the same person can be both good and bad simultaneously and even preserve a sense of moral integrity while behaving inhumanely. On one hand, Cardinal Mahony marched with César Chávez for the rights of Hispanic farm workers and championed other Hispanic causes (Goodstein, 2013b). On the other hand, he betrayed the Hispanic community by allowing the sexual abuse of children.

With priest relocations, counseling referrals, and sizable financial settlements, it is difficult to believe that the upper echelons had no inkling of what was going on in the parishes. Nonetheless, once the sex scandal was publicized, the Vatican had to deal with it. In its early attempts at damage control, the Vatican employed even more of the mechanisms of moral disengagement than did the bishops. Neutralization by advantageous comparison was the favorite exonerative means. Speaking at a Good Friday service, a senior Vatican priest likened the criticism of the Catholic Church to the persecution of the Jews (Wakin & Donadio, 2010). This self-commiserating equivalency made the church the victim of outside critics. The director of the Anti-Defamation League called the exoneration a "hideous comparison." Vatican officials criticized governmental reports of sexual abuse as a "deceitful" and "defamatory campaign" designed to undermine the church.

In a contentious response to early charges that the sexual abuse violated the human rights of children, Pope Benedict XVI contended that the sexual abusers were homosexuals, not pedophiles, thereby stereotyping individuals who are homosexually oriented as child predators (Butt & Asthana, 2009). In the effort at comparative neutralization of clergy sexual abuse, the pope reported that sexual abuse of minors was common among the Protestant and Jewish communities as well. The head of the New York Board of Rabbis cautioned the pope that "comparative tragedy is a dangerous path on which to travel. All of us need to look within our own communities" (Butt & Asthana, 2009). In a further comparative exoneration, the pope added that children are more likely to be sexually abused by family members, babysitters, friends, relatives or neighbors (Butt & Asthana, 2009). As the old saying goes, two wrongs do not make a right.

In the attribution of blame, Father Gabriele Amorth, the chief exorcist for the Vatican, claimed that the priests' sexual molestations were "prompted by the Devil" (Owen, 2010). Moreover, he saw evidence that the Devil had also infiltrated the Vatican itself and was waging war with the pope: "Because he is a marvelous Pope and worthy successor to John Paul II, it is clear that the Devil wants to grab hold of him."

In reforming child-protection guidelines, the Irish bishops made it mandatory for clergy to report sexual molestation of children to civil authorities. A Vatican letter warned church officials that the reporting guidelines violated canon law and should therefore be regarded as "merely a study document" (Donadio, 2012). An Irish government report severely criticized the Vatican for discouraging implementation of the reporting protection policy. The Vatican responded by withdrawing its ambassador to Ireland.

A study commissioned by the American bishops attributed the clergy sexual abuse, in addition to ill-prepared and inadequately monitored priests, to the sexual revolution of the 1960s and 1970s, a conclusion dubbed the "blame Woodstock" explanation (Goodstein, 2011). Critics questioned the reliability of this study on the grounds that it was based on anecdotal data provided by the bishops, which are lower than the rates reported by prosecutors.

In response to the scandal, the Vatican issued guidelines for internally reporting cases of suspected abuse. However, Maeve Lewis, the director of an Irish charity representing child-abuse victims, criticized the Vatican because it "still did not accept responsibility for its role in creating the culture that facilitated cover-ups" (Donadio, 2012). Lewis also reports cases suggesting a more assertive legal approach toward complainants. In these cases, senior churchmen expressed remorse to the victims for the abuse and asked for forgiveness while instructing their lawyers to fight the civil compensation suits.

When Cardinal Timothy Dolan was archbishop of the Milwaukee archdiocese, he requested permission from the Vatican to transfer millions of dollars to a trust that would shield the money from damage suits by victims: "I foresee an improved protection of these funds from any legal claim and liability," he wrote (Goodstein, 2013a). The Vatican approved the request.

What is disconcertingly ironic about the church's response to the sexual-abuse cases is the extent to which efforts to keep the crimes from being made public superseded attention to the harm inflicted on children, as well as the lack of consequential accountability for the bishops who protected predator priests, covered up the abuse, negotiated secret compensation, and failed to report the cases to higher church officials and civil authorities. The many instances of shirking of responsibility in the face of grave harm to defenseless children were wrongs of omission. The efforts to protect the church at all costs ended up seriously harming the church and undermining its moral authority. What is even more disconcerting is the morally disengaged damage control by the Vatican.

In February 2014, a UN panel on the human rights of children issued a scathing indictment of the church hierarchy for shielding molesting priests, imposing a "code of silence" regarding their crimes and covering up a widespread scandal. The panel demanded that the Vatican remove molesters, open up files on offending priests and cardinals and bishops who covered up their sexual crimes and to observe civil law requiring report of child abuses to law officials. The panel rejected the Vatican claim that their accountability is limited to the people who live in Vatican City. Given the tight church hierarchy the professed truncated responsibility strains credibility. The UN panel underlined the force of its indictment and prescribed reforms by urging the Vatican to change its position on same-sex marriage, contraception, premarital sex and abortion (Winfield, 2014).

A Vatican spokesman promptly shifted the debate from the moral failings of the church on child sexual abuse to the ideology of the panel with a righteous statement that the Vatican will not compromise its moral teachings on sexuality and abortion. It further accused the UN panel of infringing on the church's "exercise of religious freedom" (Goodstein, Cumming-Bruce, & Yardley, 2014).

The Vatican continued to evade responsibility for the sexual abuse of children. In representing the Vatican, Archbishop Silvano Tomasi answered questions at a UN panel reviewing the Vatican's compliance with the international covenant prohibiting torture (Cumming-Bruce, 2014). One can debate the legality of whether the rape of a young child by a priest is an act of torture. However, this is a separate issue. The present analysis focuses on the morality of how the sexual abuses were handled. Tomasi repeated the exonerations that the pope's jurisdiction is confined to Vatican City and that the sex crimes are a product of a permissive culture. What was new was the complete silence on the legal and moral failings of the upper echelon of the church hierarchy. The bishops and archbishops presided over the cover-up, reassigned predatory priests to unwitting parishes, and broke the law by not reporting the sex crimes to civil authorities. The hierarchy continued to be shielded from accountability for their actions until Pope Francis approved a Vatican tribunal in June 2015 to hold bishops who failed to report abuse accountable for their actions. At the civil level, they incurred no penalties for breaking the law.

The British Broadcasting Corporation

Another moral failing of vast systemic proportions concerns the collective willful blindness by the venerated BBC and a host of societal systems toward a sexual predator who preyed on hundreds of young girls for over four decades, a situation that was not fully revealed until after his death in 2011. Jimmy Savile gained celebrity status and power early in his media career (Burns & Somaiya, 2012). He did so in a variety of ways. He hosted a hugely popular children's program called *Jim'll Fix It*, centered on children's wishes, and *Top of the Pops*, a musical countdown of hits that attracted millions of young viewers. These programs, along with post-*Pops* parties with rock stars, gave him ready access to admiring young girls. In addition, Savile raised millions of dollars for schools, hospitals, and centers for emotionally disturbed children. His charity work throughout the country linked him to wealthy patrons and individuals of high standing. It also expanded his access to vulnerable young girls. For his philanthropic work, Savile was knighted by both Queen Elizabeth II and Pope John Paul II. He had become an adored national treasure.

To increase his social power, Savile cultivated influential friends in high places. The weekly "breakfast club" meetings in his luxurious penthouse included local police officers and influential friends. Even if they were not co-opted, both police and prosecutors were reluctant to scrutinize allegations of Savile's molestations. "Really, it came down to this: do we really want to take on this man, Saint Jimmy, who does all of this fund-raising and knows all of these people?" a police officer asked (Burns & Somaiya, 2012). The charges included groping, forced oral sex and rape. "This is what happens," a Scotland Yard commander remarked, "when vulnerability collides with power" (Burns & Cowell, 2013).

Through his celebrity status, philanthropy, and social power, Savile was able to elude legal investigation of his sexually abusive behavior for decades. Many complaints of sexual abuse were filed with local police, but they were ignored or dismissed for insufficient evidence. The word of a child against a denial by a knighted celebrity did not have much chance of being taken seriously. A national crime database, which did not exist at the time, would have cast a pattern of local allegations in a more believable light. Early on, the BBC investigated some complaints. They absolved Savile of any wrongdoing. With strict libel laws, newspapers were leery of investigating allegations that Savile was sexually abusing children for fear of defamation lawsuits. "It's too controversial—we can't touch it" (Lyall & Turner, 2012). Paul Gambaccini, a radio host, claimed that Savile warned newspapers that publishing allegations would destroy his important charity work (Alleyne, 2012).

The recipients of the charitable funds were confronted with legal and moral issues when sexual transgressions occurred in their facilities. Duncroft, a private reform school, is a good case in point. "Jimmy treated Duncroft like a pedophile sweet shop," according to Toni Townsend, a former student

(Pettifor, 2012). "He used to take the pick of the mix," she said when he stayed overnight at the residential school. The school officials felt they had to choose between protecting the children or Savile. He came out the winner. Deborah Cogger, another former student at the school, shed some light on how the staff eluded the morality of their inactions. They denied the molestation: "Don't be wicked, he would never do that" (Lyall & Turner, 2012). They trivialized the groping as just his whimsical self: "Oh, that's just Jimmy, that's his way; he loves you girls" (Lyall & Turner, 2012). The children were accused of lying by a social worker. If they continued to complain they were stripped of privileges. The former headmistress who denied knowing about the abuse disparaged the children as "delinquents" making "wild accusations." As one of the abused children put it, "They just didn't want to know" (Lyall & Turner, 2012). Police investigated the complaints but did not charge him with any offenses.

Savile was not especially cautious in his sexual encounters. For example, at one time he was shown groping a young girl during a live telecast! A former BBC producer, Wilfred De'Ath, warned Savile that he was "living dangerously" when he spent a night in a seedy hotel with a 12-year-old girl (Alleyne, 2012). Savile replied that he was invulnerable: "Oh no no no no. I'm much too valuable to the BBC for them to do anything to me" (Alleyne, 2012). He was not boasting. De'Ath went on to say that Savile's sexual activities were widely known among his colleagues, but no one intervened: "Nobody grassed [informed the police] on him in any way, although we all knew" (Alleyne, 2012). Another former BBC producer, Esther Rantzen, described him as "untouchable." She said, "We all blocked our ears to the gossip."

Savile's alleged sexual abuses were brought to light in a documentary exposé aired by a rival television network. In a 2006 interview, Savile denied the allegations with terse objection: "I don't do underage sex" (Cowell, 2012). The interviewer seemed too intimidated to follow-up on his inquiry: "[H]e was saying he didn't do these things. I could hardly call him a liar, could I?" (Cowell, 2012).

Savile died in October 2011. As the open secret of his sexual abuses became public, hundreds of women who claimed that they were molested as children were no longer afraid to speak out.

BBC officials had to deal with the compromised morality of shielding a child sexual abuser for decades. They used both structural and psychosocial means of evading responsibility. They instituted an insulated hierarchical system of bureaucratic layers of management that was better suited to passing the buck than for decision making within a clear chain of responsibility (Kulish, 2012). There was little informative communication among the compartmentalized bureaucratic levels.

With rumors of sexual abuse floating around, it is difficult not to entertain the suspicion that there might be some truth to them. If the rumors are confirmed, one has to deal with the morality of children being harmed. The concluding section of this chapter explains how self-deceptive avoidance provides a means of distancing oneself from any responsibility for detrimental actions. This process keeps one uninformed and guilt free, because one avoids actions that would reveal what one does not want to know. David Elstein, a former executive at BBC, regards "the deliberate incuriosity of the senior executives" as a big internal failure of the BBC (Kulish, 2012). "There is a culture of avoiding knowledge so as to evade responsibility," he said.

Mark Thompson, then the BBC director, claimed he knew nothing about the allegations concerning Savile's sexual exploitation of children. The BBC was about to air a documentary on its *Newsnight* program investigating the charges against Savile, including interviews with some of his accusers. The program was canceled, allegedly because it did not meet journalistic standards. Thompson claimed that he knew nothing about the cancellation of the documentary either (Purdy & Haughney, 2012). He issued a clarification distinguishing between knowing about the canceled documentary and knowing its content, seemingly an odd lack of interest in the content of a highly controversial documentary about the sexual misconduct of the BBC's star performer.

Savile exploited his celebrity, philanthropy, and social connections in high circles, as documented earlier, to enable his sexual abuses to go unchecked for over four decades under a succession of BBC presidents. They all professed unawareness of his unlawful conduct, even though it was widely known among their colleagues. Despite the seriousness of the harm inflicted on vulnerable children, widespread suspicion and rumors of sexual misconduct and hundreds of charges filed with police department, BBC officials made no serious efforts to investigate Savile's behavior. Commander Peter Spindler of Scotland Yard summarized the tragic state of affairs: "He was hiding in plain sight, and none of us was able to do anything about it" (Burns & Cowell, 2013).

Pennsylvania State University

The systematic moral failings in this third case occurred in an academic institution where top officials shielded a child molester, Jerry Sandusky, an assistant football coach at Penn State University. He invited young boys as his guests to football games, then lured them to a locker room where he raped them in the showers (Belson, 2012). After witnessing one assault, in a history of child sexual assaults, a student reported it to the football coach, Joe Paterno. Earlier, a mother had filed a complaint with the university police that her son was molested by Sandusky. The handling of this allegation was another exercise in collective self-deception. Vice President Gary Schultz, who was in charge of the campus police, had an inkling that the complaint might signify a broader abuse problem. In a note he wrote to himself, "[I]s this opening of Pandora's box? Other children?" (Belson, 2012). However, the university police chief decided not to pursue the case because he saw no evidence of a crime. Thus, exoneration justified the university police chief's inaction.

With eyewitness evidence of a child rape, the university officials faced a choice of protecting children or safeguarding the reputation of the university and its renowned football program. They chose to shelter the university image. President Graham Spanier, Vice President Gary Schultz, and Athletic Director Tim Curley decided to report the incident to the Department of Public Welfare rather than to law-enforcement officials. However, Tim Curley announced that he had changed his mind after talking to Paterno: "After giving it more thought and talking it over with Joe yesterday—I am uncomfortable with what we agreed were the next steps" (Belson, 2012). Apparently shielding the football program superseded child safety. Curley recommended that the incident be handled secretly by urging Sandusky to seek professional help and to refrain from bringing "guests" to the football locker room. President Spanier signed off on this plan, reasoning that it was the "humane" thing to do. However, he had legal misgivings. "The only downside for us is if the message isn't 'heard' and acted upon, and we then become vulnerable for not having reported it" (Belson, 2012). A few months later Sandusky raped another child in the shower and was arrested. The board of trustees hired Louis Freeh, the former director of the FBI, to investigate the sexual scandal (Bazelon & Levin, 2012). Freeh submitted a scathing report on how the highest officials of the university worked together to conceal the sexual assaults with passive oversight by the board of trustees. What surprised him was the "striking lack of empathy" for the children who were sexually abused.

As a result of the report, Paterno was fired (he died not long after), and Spanier was forced out of the presidency. Sandusky was tried and convicted of sexual abuse and sentenced to what amounted to life in prison. The National College Athletic Association (NCAA) imposed severe penalties on Penn State and its football program (Drape, 2012). The governor of the state, Tom Corbett, filed a federal lawsuit to compel the NCAA to rescind the sanctions levied against Penn State and the football program (Thamel, 2012). He argued that it was unfair to punish the entire university for the actions of a few. He also objected to the harsh penalties because they would harm the university and the local economy. He further argued that sexual abuse is a criminal matter over which the NCAA has no jurisdiction. The NCAA called the lawsuit an "affront" to the victimized children (Eder, 2013).

In an interview with the *New York Times*, Graham Spanier reported that he was never told that Sandusky committed a sexual offense in the shower: "If Gary Schultz or Tim Curley has said to me anything about child abuse, sexual abuse, anything criminal, even had hinted about that possibility, of course we would have said something" (Sokolove, 2014). Instead he says the encounter was described to him as boisterous "horseplay." It strains credibility that Spanier and his two colleagues decided to report Sandusky to child welfare authorities for horseplay. Nor did it make sense to urge Sandusky to seek professional help for boisterous play. Their considered actions clearly reflected something more serious. In a common form of self-deception and willful ignorance, Spanier never talked to McQueary, who witnessed the sexual attack, to learn what happened, nor did he call for a formal investigation. Instead, he relied on a second-hand account that trivialized the encounter as a playful event.

Spanier's concern about legal liability was justified. He, Curley, and Schultz were charged with perjury, obstruction of justice, and endangering the welfare of children (Wetzel, 2011). They pleaded not guilty to these charges. The trial is on hold while a ruling is being appealed. Why would a respected university president compromise his moral standards, bring harm on the university he was entrusted to guide, and ruin his reputation and career by knowingly violating a federal law designed to protect children from abuse? The Freeh report placed much of the blame on Paterno, a legendary coach who presided over a dominant football culture with its own set of rules to which the university often accommodated when they conflicted.

THE VICTIM LOCUS

Dehumanization

The final set of disengagement practices operates on the victims of detrimental practices. The strength of moral self-censure for harmful practices depends on how the perpetrators regard the people they mistreat. To perceive another as a sentient human being with the same basic needs as one's own arouses empathy and compassion for the plight of others through a sense of common humanity (Bandura, 1992). This makes it difficult to abuse them. The development of empathy and compassion will be addressed in some detail later. The joys and suffering of those with whom one has a sense of kinship are more vicariously arousing than are those of strangers or those divested of human qualities. It is difficult to inflict suffering on humanized persons without experiencing distress and self-condemnation. But it is easy to do so without guilt if they are diminished to subhuman beings.

Self-censure for cruel conduct can be disengaged or blunted by stripping others of human qualities. After they are subhumanized, they are no longer viewed as persons with feelings, hopes, and concerns. They are portrayed as mindless "savages," "degenerates" and other despicable wretches. If stripping one's foes of humanness does not weaken self-censure, it can be eliminated by attributing demonic or bestial qualities to them. They become "satanic fiends," "rats," and other bestial creatures. It is easier to brutalize

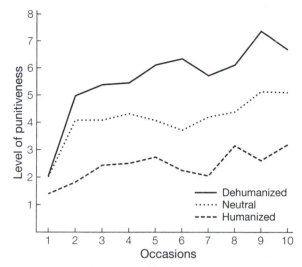

Figure 2.4 Level of punitiveness on repeated occasions toward people characterized in humanized terms. From "Disinhibition of Aggression Through Diffusion of Responsibility and Dehumanization of Victims," by A. Bandura, B. Underwood, & M. E. Fromson, 1975, *Journal of Research in Personality, 9,* 253–269, Figure 3. Reprinted with permission from Elsevier.

people when they are viewed as lower life forms, as when during the Greek military regime (1967–1974), the regime's torturers called their victims "worms" (Gibson & Haritos-Fatouros, 1986).

In experimental studies, when otherwise considerate people are given punitive power, they treat dehumanized individuals more harshly than those who are personalized or are invested with human qualities (Bandura et al., 1975). These marked differences in punitiveness are shown in Figure 2.4. Individuals cannot get themselves to treat the humanized ones harshly. Combining diffused responsibility with dehumanization greatly escalates the level of punitiveness (Figure 2.5).

In contrast, the personalization of responsibility and the humanization of others together have a powerful self-restraining effect. The power holders in the study differed markedly in their self-evaluative reactions to their punitive role, depending on how conducive the environmental conditions were to disengaging moral self-sanctions. Those power holders who assumed personal responsibility for their actions with humanized individuals rarely expressed self-exonerative justifications and uniformly disavowed punitive behavior. In contrast, when individuals were divested of humanness and punished collectively, the power holders voiced exonerative justifications for punitive behavior and were disinclined to condemn its use. This was especially the case when punitive sanctions were dysfunctionally applied in increasing intensities that impaired rather than improved the victim's performance. Self-exonerators behaved more harshly than did self-disapprovers of punitive actions.

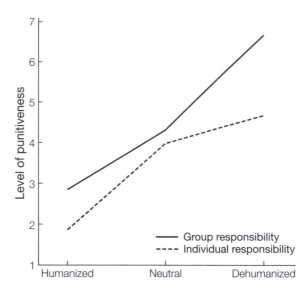

Figure 2.5 Level of punitiveness as a function of diffusion or responsibility and dehumanization of the recipients. From "Disinhibition of Aggression Through Diffusion of Responsibility and Dehumanization of Victims," by A. Bandura, B. Underwood, & M. E. Fromson, 1975, *Journal of Research in Personality*, *9*, 253–269, Figure 2. Reprinted with permission from Elsevier.

The shocking photographs of Abu Ghraib guards smilingly abusing and humiliating Iraqi detainees provided a treasure trove of degradation and dehumanization that incited international outrage. Naked detainees were forced to wear leashes and crawl for hours like dogs, to bark to the sound of a whistle, to crawl with guards mounted on their backs like jockeys, to wear women's underwear, to remain stacked naked with bags over their heads, and to engage in humiliating sexual acts with bestial attributions for the very behavior the guards coerced: "Look what these animals do when you leave them alone for two seconds" (Hersh, 2004). These abuses became a source of amusement in the guards' otherwise boring prison routines.

Private Lynndie England, a friendly young woman who always aimed to please others, became the public face of the prisoner abuse scandal because she posed for many of the photographs. Her family and friends were shocked by the sight of what England had become: "It's so not her. It's not in her nature to do something like that. There's not a malicious bone in her body" (Dao, 2004). In an interview with a German news magazine, she said she was initially disturbed by the abuse, but with no one saying anything against it, she assumed that the practices were officially authorized: "One does not question orders when you're in the military you automatically do what they say. It's always, 'Yes Sir, No Sir.' You don't question it" (Streck & Wiechmann, 2008). She went on to explain how displaced responsibility absolved her of any feelings of guilt over the degrading activities. "To be honest, the whole time I never really felt guilty because I was following orders and I was doing what I was supposed to do" (Streck & Wiechmann, 2008). After a while, she too came to view the humiliating abuses as amusing but not out of bounds. "We thought it looked funny, so pictures were taken" (Zernike, 2004). She initially resisted posing for the photos but was pressured by her lover, Charles Graner, into doing so: "I did everything he wanted me to do. I didn't want to lose him" (Zernike, 2004). As she reflected on her experience in those brutally bizarre cellblocks, she characterized it succinctly as a "sad love story."

When institutional harmful practices go awry, the political damage is typically contained by shifting the blame to bad attributes of isolated subordinates in the social system. This is the all-too-familiar metaphoric "bad apples" vindication. The Abu Ghraib scandal provides a telling example. The Bush administration attributed the degrading abuse to "a few bad apples" acting entirely on their own. In fact, the abuses at Abu Ghraib were the product of a dangerous mix of multilevel influences operating in concert explicitly and tacitly at the individual, institutional, and social structural levels. In the military intelligence unit, where the abuses took place, recruits were cast in the role of guards with no adequate training. They received virtually no supervision while on the job. A ringleader of the group concocted demeaning stunts so that the guards could amuse themselves with detested foes at their mercy. These were the immediate local conditions, but they were only a small part of the story of how intelligence information seeking turned into bizarre abuse.

Moving up the chain of command, we find a detached military overseer of the prison system who rarely checked what was going on. Brig. Gen. Janis Karpenski, who oversaw three Iraqi prisons, rarely checked what was going on in Abu Ghraib. She was suspended and demoted. Released memos, she maintains, show that she was following orders to use harsher interrogation methods approved by "top brass". "The outrage was over the photographs, because the photographs were living color of what those top-secret memorandums authorized," (Simone, 2009). There were conflicts over who was in charge of the intelligence unit between prison guards and the intelligence officers who were pressured to use more painful interrogation procedures. Noncommissioned officers ignored complaints from soldiers that the abuse was getting out of control.

At the uppermost level, detainees were dubbed "unlawful combatants," which exempted them from the Geneva Conventions, which afford protection from abuse to prisoners of war. Administration lawyers prepared controversial memoranda laying the groundwork for legalizing tortuous interrogation methods. Adding to the condoning climate for brutal interrogation, the White House Counsel at that time, Alberto Gonzales, dismissed international laws prohibiting the torture of war prisoners as "quaint" (Branigin, 2005). Defense Secretary Donald Rumsfeld approved aggressive techniques at the Guantánamo Bay prison and in Iraq to force detainees to divulge information about al Qaeda and insurgents. The list of acceptable physical and mental abuse kept changing. Rumsfeld also trivialized the infliction of pain in a penned postscript on a memorandum limiting the use of stress standing to four hours. "I stand for 8-10 hours a day. Why is standing limited to 4 hours?" (Jehl, 2004). In a military investigation to determine the scope and sources of abusive practices, the army's inspector general reported that their investigation revealed no "systemic" problems. "These abuses should be viewed as what they are—unauthorized actions taken by a few individuals" (White & Higham, 2004). Ironically, the exonerative report only further exemplified the systemic problem.

During wartime, nations cast their enemies in the most dehumanized, demonic, and bestial light to make it easier to kill them (Ivie, 1980). The process of dehumanization is an essential ingredient in the perpetration of massive inhumanities. Levi (1987) reported an incident in which a Nazi camp commandant was asked why the Nazis went to such extreme lengths to degrade their victims, whom they were going to kill anyway. The commandant chillingly explained that it was not a matter of purposeless cruelty. Rather, the victims had to be degraded to the level of subhuman objects so that those who operated the gas chambers would be less burdened by distress.

Dehumanization has a long bloody history. In the holy terror of the Crusades, Pope Urban II portrayed Muslims as "despicable, degenerate, and enslaved by demons." In his contemporary jihad, Osama bin Laden portrayed the American "decadent infidels" as "the most ravenous of animals." The Holocaust, genocides, mass killings, and military atrocities are fueled by institutionally orchestrated campaigns of dehumanization. Once entire classes of people are rendered less than human, their stigmatization, persecution, and exclusion from the most basic human rights becomes personally and socially acceptable. If the justifications are crafted skillfully, the degrading treatment can be made morally acceptable as well.

Under certain conditions, wielding institutional power changes the power holders in ways that are conducive to dehumanization. This happens when persons in positions of authority have coercive power over others but with few safeguards to constrain their behavior. In such situations, those in power come to devalue those over whom they wield control. In Zimbardo's (2007) classic simulated prison experiment, college students were randomly assigned roles as either inmates or guards. Given unilateral power, the guards quickly began treating their inmate charges in degrading, tyrannical ways. Kipnis (1974) documents the devaluing effects of unilateral power even when it involves the use of reward as the mode of influence. Compared with supervisors who had to rely on their persuasive skills to improve workers' performance, those who influenced workers' behavior through money rewards thought less of their ability and performances, viewed them as objects to be manipulated to get things done, and had less desire to associate with them.

Many conditions of contemporary life are conducive to depersonalization and dehumanization. Bureaucratization, automation, urbanization, and high mobility lead people to relate to each other in anonymous, impersonal ways (Bernard, Ottenberg, & Redl, 1965). Strangers can be more easily dehumanized than can acquaintances. In addition, social and political practices that divide people into in-group and out-group members result in estrangement that fosters dehumanization. Perpetrators group, divide, devalue, and dehumanize those they disfavor. Once people are typecast, they are treated in terms of the group stereotype rather than their personal attributes.

In this electronic era, which fosters estrangement in service and institutional transactions, much of the depersonalization occurs through digitization. In their everyday activities, people are prompted through anonymous and impersonal electronic menus. When phoning a help line, rather than eventually reaching an actual human being, callers are likely to end up with an automated reply in convoluted language that leaves them more confused. People now shop and conduct many of their daily affairs impersonally online rather than face-to-face. Anonymity and lack of social contact with individual diversity are conducive to stereotyping.

Depersonalization should be distinguished from dehumanization. In the latter, others are stripped of human qualities or invested with demonic or bestial ones, whereas in the former, others are treated with emotional detachment and little regard for them as persons. Under certain conditions, some emotional detachment can serve constructive purposes. Members of the helping professions must deal day in and day out with people whose lives are full of suffering and hardships that do not lend themselves to easy solutions. For example, those who staff social welfare programs see endless lines of people ravaged by poverty, disease, and years of maltreatment and neglect. Were they to empathize fully with the suffering of their clients, they would be too overwhelmed emotionally to be able to help them. Emotionally moderated concern for other people's suffering spares them impairing personal distress.

In other lines of work that get reduced to wearisome routines, it is all too easy to slip into an indifferent, depersonalized mode to the point where people are treated like objects. Maslach (1982) identified burnout syndrome, which includes depersonalization, emotional exhaustion, a low sense of accomplishment in one's work, and cynicism about the prospect of effecting changes. Individuals who have a low sense of efficacy in helping others make needed changes are prone to blame and disparage them for their difficulties and their failure to do the things that can improve their lives. It is a small step from depersonalization to dehumanization.

Attribution of Blame

Blaming those who are maltreated is another means operating within the victim locus that can serve self-exonerative purposes. Conflictful transactions typically involve reciprocally escalative acts. One can select from the chain of events a defensive act by one's adversaries and portray it as the initiating provocation. One then blames the adversaries for bringing suffering on themselves by their instigative belligerent behavior. Hence, they deserve to be punished. Self-exoneration is also achievable by viewing one's harmful conduct as forced by compelling circumstances rather than as a personal decision. External attribution of blame turns the perpetrator self into a victim, perceived as faultless and driven to injurious actions by forcible provocation. Fixing the blame on others or on compelling circumstances not only excuses one's injurious actions but can even make retaliation seem self-righteous. For example, Osama bin Laden characterized his terrorist activities as "defensive jihad," compelled by "debauched infidels" bent on enslaving the Muslim world.

Attribution of blame differs from displacement of responsibility in terms of who is responsible for the harm and where moral disengagement occurs in the process of moral control. In attribution of blame, victims are faulted for bringing maltreatment on themselves. This mode of self-exoneration makes the victims the blameworthy ones. In displacement of responsibility, perpetrators shift blame for their detrimental behavior to those in the chain of command who authorized it. The authorizers are the blameworthy ones.

Maltreatment that is blamed on the victim can have more devastating human consequences than the cruelty that the perpetrator acknowledges. Mistreatment that is not clothed in righteousness makes the perpetrator rather than the victim blameworthy. But when victims are convincingly blamed for their plight, they may eventually come to believe the degrading characterizations of themselves. Exonerated inhumanity is more likely to instill self-dislike in victims than inhumanity that does not attempt to justify itself. Seeing victims suffer maltreatment for which they are held responsible also leads observers to derogate them (Lerner & Miller, 1978). The devaluation and indignation aroused by ascribed culpability provide further moral justification for even greater maltreatment.

All too often, marginalized and negatively stereotyped groups are viewed as inherently deficient and flawed human beings. Some individuals living under disadvantaged and prejudicial conditions do not turn out well. In the mix of determinants contributing to personal shortcomings and troublesome conditions, social conditions typically get ignored in favor of dispositional attributions to innate bad natures. People's social identity gets linked to group membership. This makes them vulnerable to negative social stereotyping. Stereotypes can be based on a variety of social classifications including social, ethnic, religious, and socioeconomic status, just to mention a few. Once negatively typecast, perceived members of a stereotype are treated as though they share all the attributes and behave in the same way as the stereotype.

In moral disengagement in the corporate world, some products and production processes are injurious to the health of consumers and workers. Blaming them for related health problems is a common exonerative practice. The chapters that follow richly document the ways in which industries absolve themselves of any responsibility. To cite a few examples, the tobacco industry argues that, because not every smoker develops cancer, the causes lie in smokers' faulty biological makeup and unhealthful lifestyle habits. Besides, given the warning labels, if individuals choose to smoke, it is their fault if they develop health problems. The mantra of the gun industry is that it is people, not guns, that kill. Therefore, people are solely to blame for killing each other with firearms. For shipping convenience, Union Carbide located their chemical plant in Bhopal, India, a densely populated area near the closest railway station. When an industrial accident released toxic gases, thousands of people lost their lives, and even more suffered permanent physical injuries. Union Carbide blamed city officials for allowing people to live nearby even though they had lived there before the chemical factory was placed in their midst.

The Power of Humanization

Psychological research tends to emphasize how easy it is to bring out the worst in people through dehumanization and other forms of self-exoneration. Sensational perniciousness receives major attention. For example, Milgram's (1974) research on obedient aggression is widely cited as evidence that good people can be talked into performing cruel deeds. What is rarely noted, however, is the equally striking evidence that most people refuse to behave cruelly toward humanized others under strong authoritarian commands, and when they have to inflict pain directly rather than remotely.

When power holders have only punitive sanctions to exert influence over others they increase their punitiveness toward those who are dehumanized even when it does not work and only makes things worse (see Figure 2.6). Under conditions combining dehumanization with group decision making that masks personal accountability, the level of punitiveness escalates markedly (Bandura et al., 1975). In contrast, power holders with the same sanctions cannot make themselves behave punitively toward those who are humanized and when they have to take personal responsibility for their punitive conduct. The emphasis on obedient aggression is understandable, considering the prevalence of people's inhumanities toward one another. But the power of humanization to counteract cruel conduct also has important social implications. The affirmation of common humanity can bring out the best in others. The following section addresses how moral engagement promotes humaneness through a sense of common humanity.

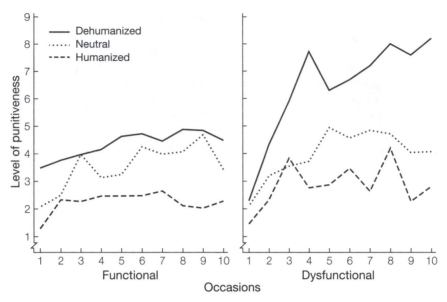

Figure 2.6 Level of punitive sanctions imposed on repeated occasions as a result of dehumanization. Under the functional condition, punishment consistently produced improved performances; under the dysfunctional condition, punishment usually diminished performance. From "Disinhibition of Aggression Through Diffusion of Responsibility and Dehumanization of Victims," by A. Bandura, B. Underwood, & M. E. Fromson, 1975, *Journal of Research in Personality, 9*, 253–269, Figure 5. Reprinted with permission from Elsevier.

The Development of Compassion

The capacity for vicarious arousal to the plight of others plays a vital role in the development of compassion. Empathy is the emotional reaction to the experiences of others. Compassion is the desire and effort to alleviate the perceived suffering of others. Some theorists have argued that organisms have evolved to respond automatically to the emotional states of others (Preston & de Waal, 2002). However, empirical evidence across species calls into question hard-wired reflexive empathy. If people's emotional lives were automatically triggered by others' emotional experiences, they would be emotionally exhausted and functionally debilitated by the expressions of pain, grief, fear, anger, sadness, frustration, disgust, and suffering by anyone and everyone in sight. Even informal observation reveals that people are hardly consumed by empathy. All too often they respond indifferently or even callously to the suffering of others.

People are innately equipped with the expressive and receptive biological structures for vicarious activation of emotion. Although they are endowed with the capacity for vicarious arousal, learning experiences largely determine the level and pattern of empathic reactions. Through cognitive regulation, empathy can be elevated, eliminated, and selectively altered according to whose emotional experiences are vicariously arousing for given individuals.

If the emotional experiences of others aroused observers only fleetingly, it would be of some interest but of limited psychological import. What gives significance to vicarious influence is that observers can acquire lasting attitudes, emotional reactions, and behavioral proclivities toward persons, places, or things that have been associated with the emotional experiences of others. They learn to fear the things that frighten others, to dislike what repulses them, and to like what gratifies them (Bandura, 1986; Duncker, 1938).

Correlated shared experiences heighten vicarious arousal because they make what happens to others predictive of what might happen to oneself. That is, when individuals are in high spirits, they treat others amiably, which generates positive feelings for those around them. Through correlated experiences, the happiness of others comes to signify positive experiences for oneself. Conversely, when individuals are dejected, ailing, distressed, or angry, the people around them are likely to suffer in one way or another. Signs of anger or despondency in significant others forebode aversive experiences for oneself. This is why the injuries and delights of strangers are less vicariously arousing than the suffering and joy of close associates or those who are similar to oneself. The more one's well-being depends on others, the stronger the signaling power of others' emotional plight. Research that varies the degree of social connectedness highlights the centrality of correlated experience in the development of the capability for vicarious arousal. Church (1959) found that cries of pain by an animal evoked strong emotional arousal in animals that had suffered painful experiences together. The cries of another animal were less emotionally distressing to animals who had undergone equally painful experiences but separately. Cries of pain left unmoved those animals who had never been subjected to painful treatment.

That sensitivity to emotional displays of others grows out of shared experiences receives further support from Miller, Caul, and Mirsky (1967). They found that monkeys reared in social isolation during their infancy were unresponsive to the facial expressions of emotion by other monkeys. Thus, even primates require correlative social experiences to develop vicarious affective responsiveness. Sackett (1966) similarly found no innate fear response to fear displays in monkeys reared in isolation where they could hear but not see other monkeys. Little in these findings supports the view that emotional expressions are innate vicarious instigators of emotion.

People who experience their welfare as linked to the well-being of others respond empathetically to the joys and sufferings of others (Englis, Vaughan, & Lanzetta, 1982; Lanzetta & Englis, 1989). Conversely, competitive experiences, in which another's gains bring suffering to oneself, generate counter empathy. Displays of joy by competitors distress their rivals, whereas displays of distress by competitors comfort their rivals. Even the belief that others will be cooperative or competitive elicit empathetic or counterempathetic reactions, respectively, to those others' emotional experiences. Much of people's perceived connectedness is linked to membership in groups of people like oneself. Thus, individuals respond empathetically to the emotional experiences of others who are merely portrayed as in-group members but counterempathically to those portrayed as out-group members without having shared any experiences with them (McHugo, Smith, & Lanzetta, 1982). If a sense of social connectedness is created, so that the joys and distresses of an outsider foretell similar experiences for oneself, counter empathy is transformed into empathy. Together these findings underscore the power of beliefs about others and whether they are included or excluded from one's communal category in regulating empathy to the plight of others.

Research comparing the early familial socialization practices of antisocially aggressive sons with those of prosocial sons sheds some light on the development of empathy and its role as a restrainer of aggression (Bandura & Walters, 1959). In their early child rearing, parents of aggressive sons relied heavily on fear-based control. They sought to curtail or discourage their sons' aggressive conduct by emphasizing the external punishment it would bring upon them. In contrast, the parents of prosocial sons cultivated empathic-based control, portraying the consequences of aggressive conduct in terms of the injury and suffering it brings to others. In handling problems of misconduct, parental socialization practices that direct attention to the suffering inflicted on others foster development of empathic perspective taking and prosocial behavior (Bandura & Walters, 1959; Hoffman, 2001; Mussen & Eisenberg, 2001). A sense of empathic self-efficacy at involving oneself in the plight of others both promotes prosocialness in the form of helpfulness, sharing, consoling, and supportiveness and curbs socially injurious conduct (Bandura, Caprara, Barbaranelli, Gerbino, & Pastorelli, 2003). The Delancey Street Foundation model of change, which transforms hard-core criminals and multiple-drug users into considerate, prosocial individuals, is founded on an interdependent ethos in which participants derive their self-regard and well-being from improving each other's lives (Silbert, 1984). They extend this ethos to the social level by working toward improving the conditions of life in society at large.

Morality can also be fostered by restoring humanity to harmful conduct that has been freed from the restraints of moral self-sanctions. McAlister and his colleagues fostered moral reengagement as an alternative to resorting to violent means. They did so by peer modeling of prosocial solutions to conflicts and exposure to communications that unmasked the various self-exonerative methods of moral disengagement (McAlister, Ama, Barroso, Peters, & Kelder, 2000). Moral engagement reduced support of violent means, whereas boosting self-exonerative vindications raised endorsement of violent means.

The transformative power of humanization is graphically illustrated by the actions of one man during a military massacre in 1968, at the height of the Vietnam War (Zganjar, 1998). An American platoon led by Lieutenant William Calley had killed about 500 Vietnamese women, children, and elderly men in the village of My Lai. Detailed analyses of this event have documented how members of the platoon disengaged their moral self-sanctions (Kelman & Hamilton, 1989). Hugh Thompson, a young helicopter pilot, had swooped down over the village on a search-and-destroy mission. He spotted an injured girl, marked her location with a smoke signal, and radioed for help. To his horror, he saw a soldier flip her over and spray her with a burst of machine-gun fire. When he saw bodies of the villagers heaped in an irrigation ditch and soldiers firing into them, he realized that he was watching a massacre.

Thompson was moved to moral action by the sight of a terrified woman with a baby in her arms and a frightened child clinging to her leg. He described his sense of common humanity: "These people were looking at me for help and there was no way I could turn my back on them." He told a platoon officer to help him remove the remaining villagers. The officer replied, "The only help they'll get is a hand grenade." Thompson lowered his helicopter into the line of fire and commanded his gunner to fire on his approaching countrymen if they tried to harm the family. He radioed the accompanying gunships for help, and together they airlifted the remaining dozen villagers to safety. He flew back to the irrigation ditch, where they found and rescued a two-year-old boy still clinging to his dead mother. Thompson described his empathetic human linkage: "I had a son at home about the same age."

Thompson's killing mission abruptly had turned into a humanitarian one. He did not stop there, however. On returning to base, he reported the carnage to his commander, only to be told to keep quiet and that pursuing it further could get him into trouble. Undeterred, he contacted members of his battalion until he found one who was willing to corroborate his story. Thompson filed a formal report that ultimately resulted in the court-martial of Lieutenant Calley. The moral power of one had triumphed over the antagonistic force of many, but Thompson received no military commendation for his heroic actions at the time. Thirty years later, a ceremony was held at the Vietnam Veterans Memorial honoring the extraordinary heroism of Thompson's prosocial morality (Zganjar, 1998).

The extraordinary power of humanization to curb violence is poignantly documented in a remarkable event on a battlefield in Flanders in 1914, early in World War I (Weintraub, 2001). It is Christmas Eve. The Allied and German forces are poised in their trenches for the bloody assault. In the eerie silence, the Allied soldiers witnessed the surreal spectacle of German soldiers adorning their parapet with candle-lit Christmas trees and singing the Christmas carol "Silent Night." The soldiers exchanged friendly banter across enemy lines, and sang Yuletide carols and folk songs as initial peace gestures. To further convey their peaceful intentions, the soldiers created placards: You no fight. We no fight, by the Germans, and Merry Christmas, by the Allied soldiers. A few Germans emerged from their trenches unarmed. The field officers from both sides negotiated an impromptu truce, during which they personalized their lives. The combatants climbed out of their trenches and joined in a host of social activities in festive comradeship. They shared their rations, cigarettes, and "liberated cognac" from the local chateau and swapped uniform accessories and souvenirs. They shared photos of their girlfriends and wives and children. They also organized communal events, preparing meals with ingredients from farms behind enemy lines, staged concerts with a makeshift orchestra, and even arranged soccer matches in their no-man's-land. As night fell, they returned to their respective trenches as humanized foes rather than faceless enemy combatants.

Both the Allied (British and French) and German high commands had a major problem on their hands. The military feared that fraternization had humanized the combatants on both sides. Some of the field officers warned the soldiers in the opposing trenches to stay low when hostilities resumed. They refused to obey orders to start shooting. "We can't—they are good fellows—we can't" (Weintraub, 2001). As one of the soldiers explained to his military foe during the prior festive gathering, "We do not want to kill you and we don't want you to kill us. So why shoot?" (Weintraub, 2001). To avoid killing each other, they shot high above the trenches. In a letter home, one of the soldiers described the untargeted shooting: "We spent that day and the next morning wasting ammunition in trying to shoot the stars from the sky" (Weintraub, 2001).

There was no way that the spontaneous truce amid the abysmal trenches of Flanders could survive for long in the face of overwhelming military force. Newly arrived troop replacements had no personalized restraint to killing the faceless foe. Moreover, some of the Allied national units rejected the peace gestures and continued the fighting in their sectors. Such internal dissent can easily jeopardize maintenance of a truce. It remains unknown how the humanized combatants continued to deal with their moral predicament during the military war and its aftermath. If, under military coercion, they ended up killing their humanized foes, they would likely carry a burden of guilt. They could seek vindication in the fact that they were forced to do it, but unless it provided complete self-exoneration, they could be haunted by flashbacks of their combat activities in the trenches.

The transforming effect of perceived common humanity is further illustrated in a daughter's mission of vengeance (Blumenfeld, 2002). Her father, a New York rabbi, was shot and wounded in Jerusalem by Omar Khatib, a Palestinian militant. Twelve years later, the daughter set out to exact revenge by forcing Khatib to confront his victim's humanity. Concealing her identity, she exchanged letters with the jailed gunman. The militant gunman, the victim, and the filial avenger were humanized through this process. In a dramatic courtroom parole hearing, the daughter identified herself to Khatib as she pleaded for his release from prison, vowing he would never hurt anyone again. He wrote a letter to her father, likening his daughter to "the mirror that made me see your face as a human person [who] deserved to be admired and respected." In this case, hatred resulting in escalative cycles of violence turned into mutual compassion. At a national level, Nelson Mandela singularly displaced hatred of apartheid with reconciliation by affirming people's common humanity.

The preceding psychosocial analyses illustrate how individuals can shift rapidly from being moral disengagers to moral engagers through the transformative power of humanization. Social psychology often emphasizes the power of environmental forces over individuals. In the case of proactive moral courage, individuals triumph as moral agents over compelling environmental pressures to behave otherwise. Such moral heroism is most tellingly documented in rescuers who saved persecuted Jews from the death camps during the Nazi Holocaust (Oliner & Oliner, 1988). They did so at great risk to themselves and their families, with a heavy burden of extended protective care. The rescuers had no prior acquaintance with those they sheltered and had nothing material or social to gain by doing so. Such moral commitments involved courageous humaneness amid overwhelming evil. As previously noted, humanization can rouse empathic sentiments and a strong sense of social obligation that enlists self-evaluative reactions that motivate humane actions on others' behalf at the sacrifice of one's self-interest or even at personal danger. The rescuers viewed their actions as a human duty rather than as extraordinary examples of moral heroism. After the protective relationship was established between rescuers and rescued, the development of social bonds heightened the force of empathic concern and moral obligation.

In the arena of social change, the model of nonviolent collective protest to eradicate institutionalized injustice and detrimental social practices relies heavily on appeals to common humanity. Mahatma Gandhi model of active nonviolent resistance (Gandhi, Desai, & Nayyars, 1942) inspired others to use this means in the fight for civil rights (King, 1958). To the extent that publicizing the suffering endured by the aggrieved shakes the moral complacency of citizens, they lend the support needed to force warranted reforms.

RELATED FACETS OF MORAL DISENGAGEMENT

The Transformative Power of Progressive Moral Disengagement

Conditions conducive to moral disengagement will not instantly transform considerate individuals into cruel ones. Rather, the personal change occurs through progressive disengagement of self-censure for acts of cruelty. Initially, individuals perform mildly harmful acts they can tolerate with some twinges of guilt. After their self-reproof has been diminished through repeated enactments, the level of ruthlessness increases until eventually acts they originally regarded as abhorrent can be performed with little anguish or self-censure. At this point, inhumane practices become thoughtlessly routinized. Because of the gradualness of the transformation, individuals may not even recognize the changes their moral selves have undergone.

Haritos-Fatouros (2003) provides a revealing account of the most sweeping transformative changes in which the Greek military junta of 1967 to 1974 trained ordinary youths to be ruthless torturers. The junta justified its reign of terror by invoking national security. The military police, who did the training in torture for their special interrogation unit, selected ordinary young men from conservative families in rural areas. They first put them through brutal initiation rites in which they were isolated from all outside influence, forced to perform exhausting physical activities for hours on end that left little time for thought, indoctrinated in the ideology of the dictatorship, and subjected to arbitrarily degrading obedience training. This abusive treatment served two purposes. It taught unquestioning obedience even to the most outrageous demands and modeled how to torture without any qualms. In the more formal training that followed, the recruits practiced progressively more brutal ways of inflicting pain. At first they watched the more seasoned torturers do it. Then they participated in torturing prisoners as part of a group but performed the milder forms of torture. With further habituation to cruelty, they carried out beatings callously with only one other peer, using the most excruciating methods. For convenience, the methods of torture were numbered according to severity, with sanitized labels such as "tea party with toast." The torturers used only assigned nicknames to hide their identities. The beatings went on for hours, sometimes to the point where the prisoners, mainly opponents to the military dictatorship, became delirious or passed out, whereupon they would be revived and continue to be beaten until they signed confessions to trumped-up charges or revealed information about opponents of the regime.

During the training, the recruits were punished with beatings for any signs of compassion or empathy and rewarded for skill in forcing confessions. They not only began to take pride in their brutality but also competed among themselves to see who was the best torturer. Some reported that the exercise of complete domination over their prisoners made them feel like "supermen." When they had completed the torture training, the onerous rules were relaxed. The graduates were granted control over junior recruits who catered to their wishes. The graduates also were provided with a host of special privileges such as fancy clothes, free use of cars, free travel, and tickets to entertainment events. They now enjoyed the many benefits of having endured the torturous training. This heady life of power and privilege was a stark contrast to their former prosaic life in the rural villages, many of which were poverty ridden. In this brutal transformation, the military junta took ordinary farm boys and turned them into extraordinary torturers. Having embraced the ideology of the junta, the newly fledged torturers viewed themselves as an elite corps promoting the rightness of the military takeover.

The making of torturers testifies to how, given appropriate social conditions, decent, ordinary people can be led to do extraordinarily cruel things. Other studies further underscore that it requires conducive social conditions rather than monstrous people to produce atrocious deeds. In a laboratory experiment, Larsen and his collaborators compared the relative influence of personality traits and situational influence on aggressive behavior (Larsen et al., 1972). The set of personality traits, which included hostile disposition, Machiavellian cynical manipulation, and orientation toward the exercise of power, had little effect on aggression. In contrast, exposure to aggressive models heightened level of aggression (35%) and its intensity (23%). Conformity pressure, in which others escalated their collective aggression, produced even higher increases in level (79%) and intensity (55%) of aggression. Displacement of responsibility was the favorite mode of self-exoneration. It took two forms. In the socially explicit form, participants said they were merely doing what they had been told to do. In the more passive form, participants said they were following orders because the authorities know what they were doing. They also blamed those who performed the activity for not doing it better. Justification in terms of contribution to science also figured prominently.

In his landmark simulated-prison experiment, Philip Zimbardo randomly assigned healthy, normal college students to be prisoners or prison guards (Haney, Banks, & Zimbardo, 1973; Zimbardo, 2007). The role-playing quickly turned into a harsh reality. The guards began to harass and humiliate the prisoners and punish them severely for the slightest disobedience. As further testimony to the transformative power of the simulated prison environment, Zimbardo recounted how he found himself crossing the line from observant researcher to authoritarian prison warden. With guards escalating their abuse and inmates exhibiting increasing physical and emotional distress and a growing sense of helplessness, the simulated prison had spun out of control and had to be terminated prematurely. In his book *The Lucifer Effect*, Zimbardo provides an insightful analysis of the social forces that were at play in turning American military prison guards into callous perpetrators who humiliated, debased, and physically abused detainees in Iraq's Abu Ghraib prison (Zimbardo, 2007). Demonstrating that local situations have their basis in higher-level social systems, Zimbardo deepens the causal analysis by embedding the influences operating at the local prison situation within higher-level pressure from governmental officials to use physically painful methods of interrogation to extract information from the detainees.

Transformative change is also evident in the evolution of domestic terrorist groups. Sprinzak (1990) has shown that terrorists, whether on the political left or right, evolve gradually rather than setting out to be radicals. The process of radicalization involves a gradual disengagement of moral self-sanctions from violent conduct. It begins with prosocial efforts to change particular social policies deemed detrimental or contrary to the common good, coupled with opposition to the forces of influence and power who have a vested interest in keeping things as they are. Embittering failures to accomplish the hoped-for social changes and hostile confrontations with authorities and police lead to growing disillusionment and alienation from the whole system. Escalative battles culminate in the terrorists' efforts to destroy the system and its power holders.

Moral Disengagement at the Social Systems Level

As evident from the preceding examples, moral disengagement is not confined to individuals acting independently. Quite the contrary. It often operates on a large scale within multiple interdependent social systems. Collective moral disengagement at the social system level requires a network of participants vindicating their harmful practices. As explained earlier, there is no group mind doing the moral disengaging independent of the behavior of its members (Bandura, 2004). Rather, members act together on their shared beliefs. With collective moral disengagement, members do not have to concoct their own individual exonerations. Instead, the different players in the system have to neutralize the moral implications of their role in their organizational activities. In doing so, they provide exonerations for each other. Therefore, collective moral disengagement is not simply the aggregation of the moral exonerations of its individual members operating in isolation. It is an emergent group-level property arising from interactive, coordinative, and synergistic group dynamics (Bandura, 2000).

Consider, by way of example, the widespread moral compromises across multiple social systems in the tobacco industry, which we discuss further in Chapter 5. Tobacco products take the lives of over half a million people annually in the United States alone. As smoking rates declined in developed countries, the tobacco industry shifted promotion of the smoking habit to developing countries as the lucrative growing market. High smoking rates worldwide will usher in a global cancer epidemic.

Promotion of this deadly product depends heavily on a vast network of otherwise considerate people engaged in a bewildering array of occupations. The moral compromise begins at the heart of the tobacco industry, with top executives denying that tobacco products have harmful health effects. In sworn testimony before a congressional subcommittee, all seven chief executive officers of the leading tobacco companies declared that nicotine is not addictive (Hilts, 1994).

The contributors include the following:

Chemists who discovered that ammonia increases the nicotine "kick" by speeding the body's absorption of nicotine

Biotech researchers who genetically engineered a tobacco seed that doubles the addictive nicotine content of tobacco plants, cultivated it abroad and imported tons of it surreptitiously

Scientists hired to obfuscate well-founded evidence of harmful health effects

Lobbyists who seek to persuade lawmakers to protect the industry from governmental regulation of tobacco products

Advertisers who target young people with merchandising and advertising campaigns.

Movie actors who agreed to smoke in their movies for a hefty fee

Historians who sanitized the history of the tobacco industry

Pharmacists who sell cigarettes within their health-promotion mission

Farmers who defend their livelihood

Investors and shareholders who seek profits from this deadly product

Lawyers who fend off liability suits against the tobacco industry

Legislators with campaign contributions who exempted nicotine from drug legislation and passed preemption laws that block states from regulating tobacco products and their advertising

The U.S. Department of Agriculture, which essentially banned low-nicotine tobacco by making farmers ineligible for government price supports if they grow low-nicotine varieties

Trade representatives who threatened sanctions against countries that erect barriers against the importation of American cigarettes

The U.S. government, which opposed a worldwide ban on cigarette advertising and sponsorship of entertainment and sports events, even though the ban exempted countries if it violated their constitutions.

This is a remarkable array of governmental, research, entertainment, and tobacco-industry systems promoting, both domestically and internationally, a deadly product that sickens and kills people when used as intended. It is an extraordinary feat of widespread moral sanitization of one of the most destructive products. Analyses in Chapter 5, based on documents from the tobacco industry and those of tobacco litigators, testify to the pervasiveness of this moral disengagement. By these exonerative means, employees of the tobacco industry see themselves as victimized defenders of human rights, fighting off zealous health posses bent on depriving people of the pleasures of smoking.

Moral Disengagement and Self-Deception

The issue arises as to whether disengagement of moral self-sanctions involves self-deception. One cannot deceive oneself into believing something while simultaneously knowing it to be false. Hence, literal self-deception cannot exist (Bok, 1980; Champlin, 1977; Haight, 1980). Attempts to resolve the paradox of how one can be a deceiver fooling oneself while knowing the falsehood have met with little success (Bandura, 1986). These efforts usually involve creating split selves and rendering one of them unconscious. A theory of self-deception cast in terms of multiple selves plunges one into deep philosophical and unfriendly empirical waters (Bandura, 2011).

In genuine self-deception, people avoid doing things that they have an inkling might reveal what they do not want to know. However, suspecting something is not the same as knowing it to be true. As long as one does not find out the truth, what one believes is not known to be false. Keeping oneself willfully uninformed about an unwanted truth is the main vehicle of genuine self-deception. This is a common self-deceiving way of evading responsibility, as we illustrate in ensuing chapters. By not pursuing courses of action that would reveal the actual state of affairs, individuals keep the knowable unknown (Haight, 1980). Acting in ways that keep one uninformed about unwanted information is self-deception. Acting in prejudicial and mistaken ways is self-biasing. These are different phenomena (Bandura, 2011).

Both Haight (1980) and Fingarette (1969) give considerable attention to processes whereby people avoid facing an incriminating truth, either by not taking actions that would reveal it or by not spelling out fully what they are doing or undergoing that would make it known. They act in ways that keep themselves intentionally uninformed. They do not go looking for evidence of their culpability or the harmful effects of their actions. We saw earlier how obvious questions that would reveal blameworthy information went unasked so that individuals would not find out what they did not want to know. Not all genuine self-deception is entirely intrapsychic. It can be aided by the way social systems are structured. Recall the examples in which upper-echelon officials were surreptitiously kept uninformed by building deniability into the chain of responsibility. As we have seen, implicit agreements and complex social arrangements are created to keep officials uninformed about what functionaries are doing. These types of self-shielding maneuvers leave the foreseeable unforeseen and the knowable unknown.

In addition to contending with their own self-censure, people are concerned with how they appear in the eyes of others and the threat of social sanctions for engaging in conduct that is morally suspect. This adds social incentives for self-exoneration. Haight (1980) argues that in much of what is called self-deception, individuals are aware of the reality they are trying to deny, but they create the public appearance that they naively misjudged what was going on. Others are thus left uncertain about how to judge and treat persons who seem sincerely to have misled themselves. The public pretense is designed to head off social reproof. When people are caught up in the same moral predicament, the result may be a lot of collective pretense.

The mechanisms of moral disengagement operate through cognitive and social machinations, but only a few of them involve literal self-deception. In moral justification, for example, people may be misled by those they trust into believing that harmful means are morally right because the means will reduce human suffering and promote the common good. The persuasive portrayals of the likely perils and benefits may be accurate, exaggerated, or just pious rhetoric masking less honorable purposes. The same precursory process applies to weakening of self-censure by dehumanizing and blaming adversaries. In the rhetoric of conflict, opinion shapers ascribe to their foes irrationalities, barbarities, and culpabilities that color public beliefs (Ivie, 1980). In these different instances, those who have been persuaded are not lying to themselves. The misleaders and the misled are different persons. When the misleaders are themselves operating under erroneous beliefs, the views they voice are not intentional deceptions. They seek to persuade others into believing what they themselves believe. In social deception, public declarations by promoters may belie their private beliefs, which they conceal from those being deceived.

Two of the mechanisms of moral disengagement play an influential role in supporting genuine self-deception. By keeping the adverse effects of one's actions out of sight, one can continue to believe that one has done no harm. The second means of support for self-deception relies on mazy social systems of nonresponsibility that enable individuals to distance themselves from harmful practices to which they are parties. This permits them to believe that they are blameless. Culpable individuals can maintain a self-deceptive belief in their innocence as long as they remain uninformed about the adverse outcomes of their activities and have the benefit of social arrangements that obscure any sense of personal responsibility.

Chapter 3

■ ■ ■ ■ ■ ■ ■

THE ENTERTAINMENT
INDUSTRY

There are two basic modes of learning: through direct experience and through the power of social modeling. Direct experience is a laborious and tough teacher. Fortunately, humans have evolved an advanced capacity for observational learning through social modeling, which shortcuts this tedious process. The traditional psychological theories were formulated long before the revolutionary advance in information technologies. As a result, these theories focused mainly on learning by direct experience in the immediate physical and social environment. Unlike in learning by doing, whereby individuals alter their actions through repeated trial-and-error experiences, in observational learning a single model can transmit new ways of thinking and behaving simultaneously to vast populations in widely dispersed locales. In this electronic era, the nature of the environment has changed radically and altered the functional value of different modes of learning. The symbolic environment of the Internet, in which people exchange information and knowledge that is stored on servers, is gaining growing influence in human self-development, adaptation, and change. New ideas, attitudes, values, and styles of conduct are now being spread rapidly worldwide by modeling via the symbolic environment (Bandura, 2002b).

Another aspect of symbolic modeling amplifies its power. During the course of their daily lives, people have direct contact with only a small sector of the physical and social environment. They work in the same setting, travel the same routes, visit the same places, and see the same set of friends and associates. Consequently, their conceptions of social reality are greatly influenced by observational experiences—by what they see, hear, and read—rather than through direct experience. To a large extent, people act on their images of reality. The more people's view of reality depends on the mass media's symbolic environment, the greater is its social impact (Ball-Rokeach & DeFleur, 1976).

The advent of television enabled people to transcend their environment and vastly expanded the range of models available to them. People spend a major share of their free time in the televised world and the cyberworld. In its entertainment offerings, the commercial broadcast industry trades heavily on gratuitous violence in the belief that violence sells (Bandura, 1973; Gerbner, Gross, Morgan, & Signorielli, 1980). Television provides viewers with unlimited opportunities, day in and day out, to learn the whole gamut of homicidal conduct within the comfort of their homes. Public concern has grown about the possible harmful effects of televised violence on viewers. It is not violence per se but the heavy commercialization of gratuitous violence and the way in which the broadcast industry circumvents accountability for it that have raised concerns about issues of morality.

The empirical findings of diverse lines of research demonstrate that exposure to televised violence has four separable effects. It can teach novel styles of aggressive behavior; weaken restraints on the performance of preexisting styles of aggressive behavior; desensitize and habituate viewers to human cruelty; and shape public images of reality. These diverse effects are analyzed in some detail later. Verifying the determinants and mechanisms through which the televised mode of influence produces each of these effects requires diverse methodologies, because the acquisition, motivation, and regulation of behavior are governed by different processes. Moreover, no single method can provide a full explanation of human behavior. The four major research strategies include controlled laboratory experiments, correlational studies, controlled field studies, and naturalistic studies. These various methods complement each other by providing evidence for different facets of causal processes. To advance our understanding of how media influences operate, we need converging evidence from complementary methodologies. Before we analyze the nature and scope of moral disengagement in the broadcast industry, we will summarize evidence for the psychosocial effects of exposure to media violence and the mechanism through which such influences operate.

Research Strategies

Controlled experimentation is well suited to verifying the nature and direction of causation by systematically varying specified determinants and assessing their effects after controlling for other possible factors. Experimental approaches are often mistakenly dismissed as "artificial"—but that is, in fact, their explanatory power. They address basic processes governing a given phenomenon and would lose their informative value if they mimicked surface similarities to the natural forms. For example, aerodynamic principles, verified in wind tunnels, got us airborne in gigantic airliners. Airplanes do not flap their wings as do flying creatures in nature.

The early inventors who tried to fly with flapping wings ended up in orthopedic wards.

The scope of *controlled experiments* is limited, however. They cannot be used to produce types of aggressive behavior that are prohibited socially and ethically. Moreover, some forms of aggression are not reproducible in laboratory situations because they require a lengthy period of development or are the products of complex constellations of influences from different social systems operating interactively. A second way of studying media effects is to examine correlations between natural occurrences. *Correlational studies* establish whether viewing violence is related to aggressive conduct in everyday life. But as the analytic mantra reminds us, correlation does not prove causation. For example, frequency of doctor visits correlates with patient deaths, but this does not mean that doctors are killing their patients. Correlations involving televised violence can arise through four different paths of influence. Viewing violence fosters aggression. Aggressive viewers are attracted to violent programs. The influence is a bidirectional one: Viewing violence fosters aggression; in turn, an aggressive proclivity increases the attraction to violent programs. In the fourth path of influence, a third factor may influence both aggression and viewing violence, creating a spurious causal relation between the two other factors. They are co-effects of the third factor rather than causally related. The third factor has no fixed content. It could be socioeconomic status, ethnicity, or intelligence. Multiple controls, therefore, must be applied to rule out third-factor causation.

The *controlled field study* is the third method used to clarify the direction of causation. The level of exposure to media violence is systematically varied in the natural setting over a long period, and the level of interpersonal aggression is measured as it occurs spontaneously in everyday transactions. This approach combines the strength of the experimental method with the natural functional relations provided by the correlational method. However, controlled field studies have certain limitations as well. Social systems impose limits on the types of interventions they allow. Moreover, no one can ever impose full control over naturally occurring events. Experimental exposure to violent programs may spill over to viewers in control conditions if they happen to see some of the violent fare or are influenced by modeled aggressive behavior of those in the experimental condition. It is also difficult to maintain experimental conditions over a lengthy period.

Many forms of aggression do not lend themselves to controlled variation because of their severity, antisocial nature, and rare occurrence. The fourth complementary method relies on highly informative *naturalistic events*. Some natural occurrences have characteristics that provide persuasive evidence of causality. They fit three of the criteria of a causative modeling relation (Phillips, 1985). A highly novel style of behavior is modeled so there is no ambiguity about the source of behavior. There is a temporal conjunction in which viewers exhibit the same style of behavior after the exposure. The behavioral matching occurs in the broadcast region but not in nonbroadcast regions.

Because of the social and ethical constraints listed above, the challenge to verifying causality is endemic to the social sciences rather than unique to media influences. Verification of causation in the social sciences therefore requires converging evidence from these diverse methodologies. Establishing the causal role that mass media play in people's lives requires considerable methodological ingenuity. Hence, this review of the evidence for each of the major four effects of exposure to televised violence is based on diverse methodologies. Further complicating evaluation of the effects of broadcast violence is the need to tailor investigative methodologies to four major types of media effects.

THE FOUR TYPES OF MEDIA EFFECTS

The Instructional Effect

People are not born with aggressive skills. They have to learn them. Direct experience can be an unmercifully hazardous teacher in the case of aggression, because mistakes in aggressive transactions are not only injurious but potentially lethal in their more perilous forms. Observational learning, therefore, plays a key role in the development of aggressive styles of behavior. Most people rarely have direct experience with extreme violence. Rather, the mass media continuously provide images of every possible form of inhumanity. Indeed, by the time they reach their teens, children will have witnessed thousands of ways to abuse, injure, and kill people. Broadcast modeling is an excellent teacher of aggressive styles of conduct.

Laboratory studies have increased our understanding of the psychological mechanisms through which media influences produce their effects (Bandura, 1986). This mode of learning is governed by four psychological subfunctions. *Attentional processes* determine what people observe in the profusion of modeling influences and what information they extract from ongoing modeled events. Depicted activities are fleeting. Viewers cannot be much influenced by modeled events if they do not remember them. The second subfunction in modeling involves *representational processes*, whereby observed events are converted into symbolic representations that are available for future recall. In the third subfunction, which involves *translational production processes*, symbolic representations are translated into corresponding courses of action. People do not perform everything they have learned through observation. *Motivational processes* determine whether people will act on what they have learned. In short, laboratory studies verify the inner workings of the cognitive processing of modeled events and the functional use of that information.

Albert Bandura

Figure 3.1 Photos of the Bobo doll experiment.

Through observational learning, people acquire attitudes, values, emotional proclivities, and new styles of thinking and behaving from the activities exemplified by models (Bandura, 1986). The widely cited Bobo doll laboratory experiments examined the acquisition of novel forms of aggression through simulated televised modeling (Bandura, 2014). In this program of research, children observed an adult assault an inflated Bobo doll in novel ways such as pummeling it with a mallet, kicking it, hurling it aggressively, and throwing it down and beating it on the face (Bandura, Ross, & Ross, 1963). The physical assault was accompanied by neologistic hostile expressions, such as "sockeroo." To remove any social demand and to permit a rich array of behavioral options, the environmental setting in which the children's behavior was measured was stocked with an abundant array of toys that boys and girls traditionally would play with, not just a Bobo doll.

The theory in vogue at the time contended that exposure to modeled aggression is cathartic, allegedly reducing aggression by draining aggressive impulses. The modeling experiments demonstrated otherwise. Children who had observed the modeled aggression readily adopted the unique verbal and physical aggressive style of behavior, as illustrated in Figure 3.1. Some of the children also improvised on the novel modeled aggression. For example, in creative improvisation one of the girls pummeled Bobo with a doll as well as with the mallet! In contrast, children who had no exposure to the televised modeling never exhibited the novel forms of aggression.

Children learned the modeled behavior equally well regardless of whether it was rewarded or punished (Bandura, 1973). Seeing modeled aggression punished discouraged them from performing it. However, the observed consequences did not wipe out the learning, thus leaving it available for future use, given sufficient incentive to do so. As previously noted, these experimental studies were designed to clarify the process of observational learning. The methodology for measuring learning effects requires conditions in which the observers feel free to reveal all they have learned. In the case of aggression, this requires simulated targets rather than retaliative ones. Using human targets to assess the instructional function of media influence would be as absurd as requiring pilots to bomb San Francisco, New York, or other inhabited locations to test their level of acquisition of bombing skills.

Sometimes the broadcast industry creates an unintended natural experiment that provides evidence that televised aggressive modeling is causative (Bandura, 1978). The made-for-TV film *The Doomsday Flight* (Price & Graham, 1966) was a notable example. In the film, written by Rod Serling, an extortionist warns airline officials that an altitude-sensitive bomb hidden on a transcontinental airliner will explode as the plane descends below 5,000 feet when landing. In the end, the pilot outwits the extortionist by selecting an airport above the critical altitude.

According to data collected by the Federal Aviation Agency, for two months following the broadcast, there was an eightfold increase in attempted extortions using an identical scenario. Requests by the airline industry to remove this hazardous drama from the airwaves were rebuffed. Airlines continued to be subjected to extortion threats a day or two after the program was shown as a rerun in different cities in the United States and abroad. Western Airlines paid $25,000 to an extortionist in Anchorage the day after the rerun was shown. A San Francisco rerun was followed by an extortion threat to a United Airlines flight to Hawaii. The extortionist was apprehended as he picked up the money package dropped from a helicopter. National Airlines experienced an extortion attempt the day after the rerun in Miami, but the extortionist did not show up to collect the $200,000 he had demanded. The day after the program was shown in Sydney, Australia, an extortionist informed Qantas officials that he had placed an altitude-sensitive bomb on a flight in progress to Hong Kong. He also directed the officials to a locker containing such a bomb to prove he was not bluffing. Qantas paid $500,000— only to learn that the airliner contained no bomb (Schulz & Aitken, 2014). Following a showing of *The Doomsday Flight* on Montréal television, an extortionist attempted to force British Overseas Airways to give him a quarter of a million dollars by warning that a barometric bomb was set to explode on a jet bound for London when it descended below 5,000 feet. The hoax was unsuccessful because the airline officials, familiar with the oft-repeated scenario, diverted the plane to Denver, whose airport is at 5,339 feet. A TWA flight bound for New York from Madrid was rerouted to an air force base in South Dakota when a Madrid viewer phoned in a threat that turned out to be a hoax. A rerun in Paris resulted in the same extortion scenario, but the extortionist was apprehended.

Modeling novel ways to blow up airliners was irresponsible, but so was the apparent indifference of the broadcast system. Broadcasters not only rejected requests by the airline industry to remove the program but included it in a package of programs for reruns. As passengers' frightening experiences and financial costs to the airline industry increased, Rod Serling expressed regrets for writing the script: "I wish...I had written a stage coach drama starring John Wayne instead. I wish I'd never been born" ("Doomsday Flight: Serling," 1971).

Some studies cost little but are highly informative. To increase authenticity, crime shows convey a lot of useful information about criminal techniques, security systems, and police procedures. A study of inmates in a maximum-security prison revealed that they improve their criminal skills by watching crime programs (Hendricks, 1977). Forty percent of the inmates reported that they modeled crimes they saw on television. For inmates, crime shows are educational TV. They take notes. They learn how to break into homes, how to hot-wire cars, and how to pull off scams. They also learn how the police work in apprehending transgressors and how alarm systems operate. Crime shows also bring them up to date on modern police procedures. Novel strategies modeled after televised programs, such as using an ambulance to break through a roadblock, were verified independently through checks of police records.

News stories about novel crimes can inadvertently spread what they report if they provide details on how to do the crimes (Bandura, 1973). Although the print media disseminate information about violent events, televised newscasts are more influential. Not only do they portray events more informatively and vividly but most people learn about violent incidents from watching television rather than from reading newspapers.

A man calling himself Dan Cooper, but who became known as D. B. Cooper, was a notable example of modeled instruction in novel aggression strategies. Cooper devised a clever extortion technique. He hijacked a Boeing 727 and exchanged the passengers on the flight for four parachutes and $200,000 when the plane landed in Seattle. He then ordered the flight crew to fly the plane to Mexico City. As the plane flew into the night, he parachuted from the tail exit to avoid entangling the parachute lines on the tail or the stabilizers. Although massive searches were conducted, no trace of Cooper has ever been found, except for some money whose serial numbers matched those on the bills given to Cooper (Gray, 2007). Within a few months there were 18 hijackings on Boeing 727s modeled on the parachute-extortion technique. They continued until a mechanical door lock was installed on 727s so that the rear exit could be opened only from the outside. Cooper became a folk hero for eluding the FBI, celebrated in songs, on T-shirts, and in fan clubs.

The example of punishment is intended as a deterrent, but it is also informative. Publicized failures can promote innovations in antisocial behavior. The first imitator of Cooper's extortion strategy was apprehended as he parachuted over Colorado because, unknown to him, the air force had

planted an electronic signal device on the parachute. A welcoming committee awaited his descent. The air force announced publicly that the failure
should be a lesson to others. It was. The next hijacker brought his own parachute aboard the plane and tossed out the bugged air force one. This sent
the pursuit planes astray as he descended serenely on the sweeping plains
of Utah, only to be apprehended after he boasted about his feat to a man
at a bar who happened to be an off-duty policeman. Another extortionist
parachuted with a large bundle of money over the Honduras jungle, thereby
eluding both pursuit planes and ground forces.

This extortion strategy also gave rise to a creative synthesis. Modeling
plays an especially significant role in the rapid spread of aggressive tactics under conditions of civil strife. Airline hijacking is a striking example. Air piracy
was unheard of in the United States until an airliner was hijacked to Havana
in 1961. Prior to that incident, Cubans had been hijacking planes to Miami.
These incidents were followed by a wave of hijackings, both in the United
States and abroad, eventually including over 70 nations (Bandura, 1976).
The international modeling of the hijacking strategy is shown in Figure 3.2.

Hijackings were brought under control by an international agreement
to suspend commercial flights to countries that permitted safe landings to
terrorists. As Figure 3.2 shows, Cooper temporarily revived a declining phenomenon in the United States as others became inspired by his successful example. The Cooper modus operandi was employed in international

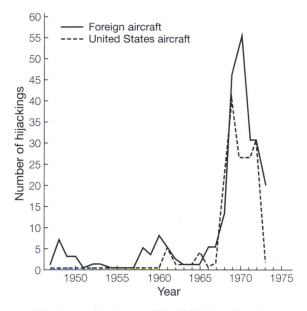

Figure 3.2 Incidence of hijackings of airplanes, 1950–1975. From "New Perspectives on Violence,"
by A. Bandura, in T. B. Brazelton & V. C. Vaughan III (Eds.), *The Family*, 1976, pp. 41–55, Figure 3.3
(Chicago: Year Book Medical Publishers).

hijackings. The first hijacker to try it was overpowered by the money courier, who was an FBI agent. This led to further refinements of the hijacking-extortion procedure. Hijackers insisted that the money couriers be nude!

These unintended powerful natural experiments, with fictional dramas and authentic newscasts as the vehicle, provide insights into the role of the media in the social transmission of forms of aggression that cannot be studied by other means. The causal relations revealed in the modeling of novel styles of aggression under naturally occurring conditions complement those verified in laboratory experiments. Once a novel idea is planted, some time must pass before it fades from public consciousness. Highly publicized novel modes of aggression typically trigger copycat events.

Motivational and Self-Regulatory Effects

Acquisition of aggressive styles of conduct enables individuals to behave aggressively. However, self-regulatory factors, operating as motivators, inhibitors, and disinhibitors, play an influential role in whether individuals will put into practice what they have learned. In addition to cultivating competencies, modeling influences have strong motivational effects. They operate through depictions of the functional value of the exhibited conduct (Bandura, 1986). Vicarious motivators are rooted in outcome expectations formed from information conveyed by the rewarding and punishing outcomes of modeled courses of action. Seeing others gain desired outcomes through their actions can create outcome expectancies that function as positive incentives; observed punishing outcomes can create negative outcome expectancies that function as disincentives. When aggressive behavior that is ordinarily disapproved of elicits no evident consequences, the implied permissiveness for it increases such behavior. These motivational effects are governed by observers' belief in their ability to perform the modeled behavior, their perception of the modeled actions as producing favorable or adverse consequences, and their judgment that similar or unlike consequences would result if they themselves were to engage in similar activities.

Media portrayals alter perceived social sanctions by the way in which the consequences of different styles of conduct are portrayed. Televised violence is often exemplified in ways that weaken restraints on aggressive conduct (Bandura, 1973; Goranson, 1970; Halloran & Croll, 1972; Larsen, Gray, & Fortis, 1968). In televised representations of human discord, physical aggression is often the preferred solution. It is acceptable, usually successful, and relatively clean. The societal protectors of the social order do most of the killing. When good triumphs over evil through violent means, viewers are more favorably disposed to such means than if they are not socially sanctioned by admired characters. Televised depictions legitimize, glamorize, sanitize, and trivialize human violence. Televised violence not only glamorizes gun violence, it even boosts sales of the types of gun that TV heroes favor (Diaz,

1999). Media portrayals influence the exercise of moral agency by altering moral standards and disengaging self-sanctions from harmful conduct.

As in the research on the instructional function of modeling, a variety of methodologies have been used to assess the effect of exposure to televised violence on the self-regulation of aggression. In controlled laboratory experiments, adults behave more punitively after they have seen others act aggressively than if they have not been exposed to aggressive modeling. The disinhibitory power of aggressive modeling is enhanced if the perpetrators are admired figures and if the violence is socially or morally justified, it is rewarded or goes unpunished, and is portrayed in a sanitized way free of gore and suffering in its wake (Bandura, 1973; Berkowitz, 1990).

Of the many correlational studies that have been conducted, those that examine long-term effects with multiple controls for other potentially relevant factors are most informative. In an extended longitudinal project, Huesmann and collaborators found that the amount of televised violence children watched as youngsters predicted their aggressiveness decades later (Huesmann, Moise, Podolski, & Eron, 2003). The more strongly the children identified with the aggressive models, tried to act like them, and saw the programs as portraying what life is really like, the higher their aggressiveness as young adults. The positive relation between watching violent programs and later aggressiveness remains after controlling for childhood aggressiveness, academic achievement, and familial socioeconomic status.

A distant cause can be reflected in behavior years later through the conjoining processes it sets in motion that shape the future. To the extent that heavy viewing of televised violence fosters aggressive styles of behavior, it influences how individuals construe troublesome events, the quality of their interpersonal relationships, and the types of social environments they construct. Behaving aggressively generally draws rejective or hostile reactions from others (Dodge, 1991; Patterson, 1986; Raush, 1965; Raush, Barry, Hertel, & Swain, 1974). Through such transactional processes aggressive individuals create hostile environments, whereas those who behave in a friendlier manner create amiable social milieus. Thus, by fostering aggressive proclivities, televised influence can leave its mark in the courses lives take.

The disinhibitory power of aggressive modeling is further replicated in controlled field studies in which adolescent boys were exposed for several weeks to either violent movies or prosocial ones (Berkowitz, Leyens, Parke, Sebastian, & West, 1977; Leyens, Camino, Parke, & Berkowitz, 1975). A diet of violent modeling increased physical aggression in everyday interactions by both high- and low-aggressive boys. Violent modeling also heightened hostile reactions to provocation. In contrast, prosocial modeling reduced aggressive behavior in aggression-prone adolescents.

Television was adopted at such a rapid pace that, by the time researchers got around to examining its effects, virtually everyone was glued to their TV sets. A critical opportunity was lost to evaluate the psychosocial impact of television at the outset. With anticipatory ingenuity, Williams (1986) conducted a quasi-experiment that shed highly informative light on how the introduction of television alters the life of a community. Williams studied three towns in the Canadian Rockies before they received television reception via cable at staggered times and over a two-year period thereafter. Changes in level of aggression were measured as one of the many social effects. Children's physical and verbal aggression were measured during free-play periods in school and by teacher and peer ratings. The introduction of television substantially increased the children's level of aggression over the two-year period. The effects were not confined to a subset of children. Both boys and girls behaved more aggressively. Those initially low and high in aggressiveness exhibited the increases as well. There was also a dose of exposure effect. Higher viewing was accompanied by higher aggressiveness. The introduction of television also changed community life. The residents reduced their participation in community activities, especially the younger and older age groups. During free time they stayed at home watching television.

The traditional method used to study performance effects assesses the psychosocial changes resulting from exposure to increased levels of media violence. In a creative alternative to this method, Robinson and colleagues studied the effects of reducing the amount of time children were exposed to media violence (Robinson, Wilde, Navracruz, Haydel, & Varady, 2001). Elementary schools were randomly assigned to conditions in which teachers taught children how to spend less time watching television and playing violent computer games, or to control schools in which they received no such guidance. The children's level of aggression was measured before and after the intervention by behavior observation during recess periods and by peer ratings. Children in the experimental schools spent about a third less time watching TV. They showed a 50% reduction in verbal aggression and a 25% reduction in physical aggression. The most aggressive children showed the greatest decline. Both boys and girls were less aggressive when they spent less time watching television.

Taken together, these studies, through diverse methodologies, verify the relation of televised violence to children's aggressiveness by evaluating the effects of increasing or decreasing the level of media exposure. In Williams's study, increased exposure with the introduction of television in the community raised children's level of aggression. In Robinson's study, decreased exposure reduced children's aggression.

Desensitization and Habituation Effects

People who devote appreciable time to television viewing experience a heavy dose of modeled cruelty. They are easily aroused by the emotional experiences of others. However, repeated exposure to aversive events erodes emotional reactions to them (Bandura, 1986). The emotional blunting by exposure to violent events takes two forms. In emotional desensitization to violence, people are no longer upset by it. In behavioral habituation, they no longer care to take action against it.

In tests for desensitization effects, individuals repeatedly watch violent events while their subjective and physiological reactions to those events are recorded. The research by Cline and colleagues typifies this approach (Cline, Croft, & Courrier, 1973). They compared the physiological reactions of light and heavy TV viewers to brutal boxing scenes alternating with nonviolent but emotive crowd scenes between rounds. The two groups did not differ in their emotional reactivity at baseline, to a daring ski run, or to the animated but nonviolent crowd scenes between rounds. However, the brutal beating was less physiologically upsetting for heavy viewers of television than for light viewers. That exposure to fictional violence blunts emotional upsetness to observed actual violence is verified in studies in which level of exposure to fictional violence is varied experimentally (Thomas, Horton, Lippincott, & Drabman, 1977).

Research on habituation effects examines people's willingness to take action against aggressive mistreatment of others as a function of prior exposure to televised violence. This approach is well illustrated in the program of research conducted by Thomas and colleagues. In the prototypic research design, children were given the responsibility of overseeing, on a TV monitor, the actions of children in another room. The overseers were told to get the experimenter if the children "get into any trouble". They saw a prerecorded video of escalating aggression in which children played quietly, then started arguing, dismantled their construction projects, and started fighting. Then the monitor went blank, suggesting that the children being observed had wrecked the camera, but the audio of the fight continued until it, too, stopped. Before the experiment, half the children had been randomly exposed to a Western strewn with shootings, gun battles, and fistfights. The other half had no such exposure. In tests of tolerance of aggression, children exposed to fictional violence were slower to seek help to stop the altercation and 35% did not intervene at all. In contrast, those in the control condition not only intervened faster, but only 5% of them failed to take action to stop the aggression (Thomas & Drabman, 1975).

Although exposure to modeled violence is shown to habituate viewers to it, how it does so remains to be verified. One possible explanation is that emotional blunting reduces the impetus to action. An alternative explanation is that frequent exposure to violence establishes aggression as normative behavior, which does not call for intervention. A third possibility is that indifference to violent conduct reflects the contrast principle at work. The importance of common real-life aggression pales when compared with the more egregious fictional forms. Habituation to human cruelty is not just an individual matter. It is also socially consequential. Desensitization can erode empathy to the plight of others. Widespread indifference to inhumanities gives free reign to such practices. Recall Edmund Burke's aphorism: "The only thing necessary for the triumph of evil is for good men to do nothing."

Social Construction of Reality

Media representations of society reflect ideological orientations by their portrayals of human nature, social and power relations, and the norms and structure of social systems (Adoni & Mane, 1984; Gerbner, 1972a, 1972b). These representations shape people's images of reality, on which they base many of their actions. This fourth type of media influence, which is the most pervasive one, concerns the shaping of public consciousness and the legitimization of violence in a society.

In the case of televised violence, the basic messages portray power relations and subordinate status in human affairs. These messages are conveyed by choice of aggressors, victims, driving motivators, and the depicted functional value of coercive and aggressive means. For example, in the televised world, most violent crimes are offenses of power and greed motivated by personal failings (Dominick, 1973). In the real world, most crimes are largely the product of poverty, reflecting, in large part, the failings of society rather than just troublesome personal attributes. Human failings have much greater dramatic appeal, so societal failings are rarely shown. People's images of crime influence the types of public policies they favor. The personal failings view of crime is likely to enlist support for social control. The societal failings view favors social policies that enable those living under adverse conditions to escape from poverty and crime.

The world of television is heavily populated with villainous and violent characters. In reality, only about 10% of crimes are violent, whereas about 66% of the crimes committed on television are violent ones (Gerbner, 1972b). This distorted portrayal of crime can breed frightful public images. In a test of this cultivation effect, Gerbner and Gross (1976) found that, indeed, compared with light television viewers, heavy viewers were more fearful of being criminally victimized and were more distrustful of others. A limitation of this research is that it included a crude measure of televised influence—the amount of TV viewing rather than what types of programs people were watching. Hawkins and Pingree (1982) improved on the design by comparing heavy and light viewers of violent programs. The findings confirmed that a heavy dose of violent fare fosters fearfulness and social distrustfulness. These effects remained when differences between light and heavy viewers on a variety of other relevant factors were controlled.

Vicarious cultivation of public images of reality is most clearly revealed in studies that verify the direction of causality by varying experimentally the nature and amount of exposure to media influences. Bryant, Carveth, and Brown (1981) had individuals watch television programs over a long period of time that contained either light or heavy doses of violence. This controlled experimental research further verified that heavy doses of televised violence increase fear of becoming a victim of a violent assault. The extensive overreporting of violent crimes in daily newscasts further reinforces the fear of criminal assault. Fear of criminal victimization has widespread social consequences. Recent decades have witnessed contradictory trends. The nation's murder rate has declined, but the number of murder stories in newscasts has soared. Fear of violence has risen.

To sum up, the diverse psychosocial effects of exposure to televised violence have now been amply documented by converging evidence from diverse methodologies. Meta-analysis summarizes the size of influence of a given factor based on a large set of empirical studies. Anderson and Bushman (2001) report a cumulative meta-analysis that combines the studies included in four meta-analyses. The findings confirm that aggressive behavior is positively related to exposure to media violence. As previously documented, televised violence is a first-rate instructor in aggressive styles of conduct, a disinhibitor and motivator of preexisting forms of aggression, a desensitizer and habituator to human cruelty, and a shaper of public consciousness. Additional meta-analyses are needed to determine the effect size for each of these types of media effects. Given that individuals do not put into practice everything they have learned, the learning effect, which creates the potential for aggression, is considerably stronger than the performance effect (Bandura, 1965).

There is a striking paradox in how the body of empirical evidence regarding media effects is presented to the general public (Anderson & Bushman, 2001). The evidence linking media violence to aggression has increased over time, whereas news coverage presents the relation over recent decades as growing weaker. The stronger the empirical effect, the weaker the effect portrayed in the news coverage: $r = -.68$. We shall revisit this issue in an analysis of the obfuscation of scientific evidence regarding media effects. Not surprisingly, the broadcast industry is not especially keen on publicizing the negative effects of some of its practices. A Senate hearing revealed the control exercised by the industry over the surgeon general's report on the effects of televised violence is a good case in point. Neither the television nor print media mentioned the findings of the Senate proceedings regarding media effects on aggression. American televised violence spills over into Canadian audiences. To inform the Canadian public, the National Film Board of Canada (Chatwin & Low, 1972) filmed the full Senate hearings. This documentary provides a revealing glimpse into the power politics of media effects. The American public was kept uninformed about the political machinations regarding media effects.

Journalists who cover newsworthy scientific evidence may be reluctant to report negative effects of televised violence for fear of providing support for crusaders bent on banning televised content they find objectionable. As will be explained later, censorship is not the remedy for harmful media effects. In fact, television content enjoys broad constitutional protection under the First Amendment. This is well illustrated in a lawsuit filed against NBC for dramatizing the rape of a young girl with the handle of a toilet plunger in the TV movie *Born Innocent* (Zane, 1981). Four days after the film was aired, four adolescents—one of whom had watched the program and three others who had heard about it—raped two young girls with a glass bottle on a San Francisco beach. The attorney representing the family of one of the victims argued that the case should be tried on issues of negligence and recklessness rather than on constitutional grounds. He argued further that the lawsuit did not object to the airing of the rape scene, rather that the network was negligent and reckless in airing it during prime-time hours when children would be watching. He cited the precedent of a successful lawsuit against a radio station. A listener who followed the final clues in a treasure hunt the station was broadcasting was speeding to the location and slammed into another car, killing the driver.

The law does not have much to say about influence through social modeling. Proving intentional incitement via a vicarious mode of influence is a formidable legal challenge. The rape lawsuit was dismissed at all appellate levels, not only on free-speech protection but also on the grounds that subjecting networks to negligence liability would have a self-censoring, chilling effect that would stifle expression of varied views. The appellate judges further argued that TV stations would be legally liable if children imitated events portrayed in newscasts and documentaries. Hence, negligence liability "could reduce the U.S. population to viewing only what is fit for children" (Zane, 1981). When the U.S. Supreme Court ruled that the case had to be tried on constitutional rather than negligence grounds, the family dropped the lawsuit. Years later, the Supreme Court struck down as an infringement on free speech a California law prohibiting children from buying violent video games.

Television can, of course, also be a force for good. For example, prosocial modeling can bring out the best in others (Johnston & Ettema, 1986). At the broader social level, enabling televised dramas are being used worldwide to promote personal and social changes that improve people's lives (Bandura, 2006; Singhal, Cody, Rogers, & Sabido, 2003). These productions, which reflect people's everyday struggles, help them see a better future and enable and guide them to take realistic steps to realize their hopes. This use of the media in compassionate, enabling ways is addressed in detail later.

SYSTEMIC MORAL DISENGAGEMENT

Various survey studies have shown that the American televised world is a rich source of violence. Gerbner (1972b), who has conducted the most comprehensive yearly analyses of televised violence, reports a stable violence rate of eight assaults per hour, with approximately 66% of dramatic programs containing violent activity involving either commiters or victims of violence.

Violence rates fluctuate somewhat for different networks and program categories, but there is no overall decline in this figure. The patterns of victimization are also quite stable over time. Children's programming, which consists mainly of cartoon heroes beating up evildoers, has the highest concentration of violent activity. American viewers overdose on gratuitous violence, but much of it is deleted when the shows are exported to other nations.

Viewers of hefty doses of media violence have been studied extensively, but the broadcast system producing the violent fare has received surprisingly little analysis. The issue in contention is not the appropriateness of violence in dramatic plotlines but the widespread use of gratuitous violence for commercial purposes. Gratuitous violence is violence that is injected into programs for extraneous reasons rather than being dramatically necessary for plot development and character designation. It is also excessive in amount, duration, and intensity. A script writer described how gratuitous violence was added, for ratings' sake, to a script about a battle between the French and the British: "I was told, 'Here's a good place where they can jump each other.' So they've added a scene where Lafayette fights with the British officer and one of them falls in the river. They can do that, since their company owns the material outright" (Baldwin & Lewis, 1972). Broadcasters would argue that the excessive violence was necessitated by the story line. However, we shall see later that the use of violence is dictated more by the economics of the system than by dramatic necessity or viewer preference.

With the evidence that modeled violence is socially consequential, its gratuitous use creates a moral predicament for the producers of it. How does one preserve one's self-regard under such conditions? The sections that follow document how each of the eight mechanisms of moral disengagement is enlisted in the management of the moral dilemma regarding gratuitous violence in television programming at the industry level. The data for this analysis were drawn from a variety of public documents. Some sources include testimony by broadcast executives and other media personnel at Senate hearings concerning media practices and their possible social effects. The hearings were conducted by the Subcommittee of the *Committee on the Judiciary United States Senate. Part 10. Effects on young people of violence and crime portrayed on television* (1962). In the interest of citation brevity it will be cited as (Senate Hearings, 1962). Another source is *Violence and the Media: A Staff Report to the National Commission on the Causes and Prevention of Violence*, edited by Robert Baker and Sandra Ball (1969).

A highly informative source of moral disengagement practices in the broadcast industry is the volume edited by Comstock and Rubinstein (1972). This volume, which is a technical report to the Surgeon General's Scientific Advisory Committee on Television and Social Behavior, includes an in-depth analysis by Baldwin and Lewis (1972) of televised violence from the broadcast industry's point of view. The data were provided by producers, writers, and directors who put the violence in the programs and by enforcers of the broadcast standards who set the limits. The industry's view of the possible effects of media violence on children was also examined. A Senate hearing filmed by the National Film Board of Canada (Chatwin & Low, 1972), prompted by scientists' objections to misrepresentations of their research findings in the surgeon general's report on media effects, was an additional source. Statements in newscasts and press reports by representatives of the broadcast media provided further data.

In the Senate hearings, creators of dramatic series described pressure from broadcasters to inject more violence into their programs (Senate Hearings, 1962). Ivor Tors, a creative producer with a track record of highly rated shows, structured his programs to entertain viewers in informative and inspiring ways without gratuitous violence. His popular series *Sea Hunt* had only five violent incidents in 155 episodes. After loss of control of a show he produced for CBS, Tors added a clause in his contract stipulating that if the network or sponsors inserted anything in a show that could adversely affect youth, his name should be removed and he would be free to leave the show. He began production for an NBC series, *Man and the Challenge*, in which a doctor explores human capabilities in ways that dramatized how interesting science can be. In a directive conveyed by a media subordinate, Tors was told that he could have a prime-time slot: "But the price was that we cannot call our doctor a doctor or scientist, and we have to put a great deal of sex and violence into the show" (Senate Hearings, 1962). When he objected, he was reminded that violence was required for competitive purposes. "We are against a show which is 'Wanted Dead or Alive,' and in that show he said the hotrod cowboy kills a man a minute. This is what you have to remember." Faced with Tors's continued resistance to its demands, NBC informed him that given the exciting quality of his shows, they would back off, but "[a]pparently New York prefers this to be an exception rather than the rule" (Senate Hearings, 1962). Tors's resolute moral engagement in the face of stiff pressure to compromise his standards was remarkable. It took even more moral courage, at the risk of financial loss and the resentment of the broadcast establishment, for Tors to testify publicly about the industry's exploitation of gratuitous violence.

Norman Retchin, the producer of the series *The Untouchables*, experienced a similar conflict of values. His overseers at ABC complained that his programs were too "talky" and instructed him to replace the "New York fink writers" and inject more violence into the program. He described his conflict with Quinn Martin, the executive producer of the series, who was characterized by a Hollywood liaison as a "blood and guts" producer. Retchin said of Martin, "He feels that it isn't worth the effort to go for these quality writers. He wants to get out a batch of scripts fast: to do this he has hired some slick, quick Hollywood TV writers who will turn in a shooting script full of plot and violence and damn little character. I go for character. Let the violence come honestly out of that character" (Senate Hearings, 1962). Retchin explained the demand for more violent content: "It now develops that Martin wants to concentrate on the slam-bang stuff and that isn't my cup of tea" (Senate Hearings, 1962). Retchin was summarily fired for "insubordination and inability to deliver the necessary material."

Repeated exposure to redundant brutality breeds boredom. As a consequence, institutional demands for gratuitous violence call for new forms of cruelty. In a memo to a script writer, an executive producer suggested the following revision: "I wish we could come up with a different device than running the man down with the car as we have done this now in three different shows. I like the idea of the sadism, but I hope we can come up with another approach for it" (Senate Hearings, 1962). Habituation through massive exposure also shifts preferences for more extreme forms of detrimental behavior (Zillmann & Bryant, 1984). "Last week you killed three men. What are you going to do this week?" (Senate Hearings, 1962).

Broadcast companies have continuity acceptance departments, which review scripts for objectionable material. Some of the revisions suggested by the gatekeepers at ABC's continuity acceptance department seemed to suggest a rather low standard: "Cut down on the lashes—the blood, the 'raw and bloody face,' the fall downstairs, etc. All this—plus the number of people killed in the closing scene makes this a pretty horrible 10 minutes" (Senate Hearings, 1962). One suggests a lower body count: "I think killing five people in this last scene would be deemed unnecessary violence" (Senate Hearings, 1962). The violence shown in promotionals for programs of yesteryear pales in comparison to the wanton destruction and carnage in the promotionals of today.

Social and Moral Justifications

Justifications of media violence take varied forms. Constitutional protection of free speech is, of course, a forceful vindication. It is often paired with alarming scenarios of governmental regulators dictating what people can watch. The rape lawsuit cited earlier is testimony that any civil or governmental efforts to regulate violent content would not survive a constitutional challenge. Despite this empty threat, broadcasters portray themselves as protectors of the public against big government. Framing justifications of harmful practices as protection against big government is a recurrent strategy used across diverse industries. For example, as we will see in Chapter 5, the tobacco industry used the same strategy to diffuse public protests against its marketing campaigns that get teenagers hooked on nicotine. With the help of a clever wordsmith, the tobacco industry successfully reframed the public debate from children against big tobacco to tobacco against big government.

In the justification of gratuitous violence there is much talk about freedom of speech, but silence about public access to the media. With the broadcast media in the hands of a few corporate owners, network officials exercise tight control over what people will view. An antitrust lawsuit to increase access to television time for public expression of diverse views was rejected by the U.S. Supreme Court on the grounds that it would threaten free speech. In the National Film Board of Canada documentary, Nicholas Johnson, a former commissioner on the Federal Communications Commission, characterized much of the debate on this issue as concerned more with profitable speech than free speech (Chatwin & Low, 1972).

Another justification is that curtailing violence will stifle creativity, leaving bland fare in its place. As noted earlier, it is not portrayal of conflict that people object to. Rather, it is the unrelenting use of physical violence to portray human conflict and fixation on violent solutions to it. Plot development is often sacrificed for gratuitous redundant brutality. Concerned writers expressed their indignation at being instructed to devise more interesting ways of killing people, and at finding violence added to their scripts without their knowledge. Scenes were rearranged to begin the program with violent teasers highlighting the most brutal actions, which are repeated in the body of the programs.

Rather than stifling creativity, lifting network directives for gratuitous violence is liberating. Producers generally prefer to create programs that portray nonviolent conflict to those oriented around violence. Some acknowledge that not substituting gratuitous violence for engrossing drama prods creativity rather than curtailing it. A producer describes the freeing creative effect: "The antiviolence thing has done some good in one way: in order to get attention, you have to have a better story.... Sometimes these restrictions are challenging. How can I show tension in a fresh way without a punch in the gut?" (Baldwin & Lewis, 1972). Inventive producers welcome and enjoy the creative challenge. Screen writers find their work more enjoyable when creativity replaces gratuitous violence: "Now we are using our brains coming up with ways of doing things that do not rely on smashing, hitting, and banging. Now we are enjoying our work" (Cantor, 1972).

Children's programming consisted mainly of Saturday morning violent cartoons in which "superheroes" beat up "supervillains." Violent cartoons were replaced by "morally repellent pseudoscientific space fantasies" (Cantor, 1972). However, the success of *Sesame Street* changed commercial children's programming. The industry opted for nonviolent content with some educational value for children, much to the relief of writers: "You get sick doing that crap. We *had* to do it for two years because that is what the network wanted. For a while, from every studio, all programs were the superhero variety. We were glad when this phase ended because it had created a penetrance of violence.... We are now using our brains coming up with ways of doing things that do not rely on smashing, hitting, and banging.... Now we are enjoying our work" (Cantor, 1972).

The use of gratuitous violence eventually became an occupational norm that no longer required explicit orders. Like other commodities, its production required efficient routinization. Writers and producers who find the artistic constraints and exploitation of violence objectionable are selectively eliminated. Those who remain as regular contributors become socialized into the practices of the system to use violence in amounts and forms that are institutionally expected.

Other justifications extol the personal and social benefits of modeled violence. A high moral purpose, in the form of a national character-building service, is sometimes assigned to human brutality: "The government wants kids to think that there are values worth fighting for, and that's basically what the leads on our show are doing." Violent enforcement allegedly helps to codify societal values: "If people who break the society's code resist the law, we have to use violence to suppress them. In doing so we are in the mainstream of American morality" (Baldwin & Lewis, 1972). In this form of justification, modeling violent solutions to human discord builds character, establishes the measure of man, and articulates the moral values and aspirations of the society.

In the view of William Orr, the executive producer of television films at Warner Brothers, slaying evildoers not only builds character but also instills moral standards that undergird a civil society. Orr was the producer of the hit Western series *Cheyenne*: "As a matter of fact, I believe that a certain amount of violence, as it is portrayed on 'Cheyenne,' has a good moral effect." Orr justified excess violence in television programming with a historical myth created by Hollywood. "The winning of the West was a victory for law and order. Such violence that is shown occurred because law and order were absent. With the coming of the sheriffs and the marshals and the growth of their influence, the West became a respectable part of our community" (Senate Hearings, 1962).

Contrary to this mythical frontier ethos, according to historians of the West, "prohibitions against carrying guns were strictly enforced, and there were few homicides" (Spitzer, 1995). When people entered a frontier town they were legally required to turn in their guns to the sheriff. "The Carrying of Firearms Strictly Prohibited" read a huge sign in Dodge City (Winkler, 2011). Next to disorderly conduct, carrying a firearm was the most common cause of arrest. The glorified Western-style shootouts have no historical roots. After seeing a scene strewn with dead bodies in a Western drama shown at a Senate hearing, Senator Thomas Dodd, who chaired the subcommittee on media effects, had this to say about the trek west and the region's taming: "I do not know about this winning of the West, but I do know that in watching these films, I marveled that anybody ever got West" (Senate Hearings, 1962).

Some television executives also claim that media violence serves a national cathartic function. According to catharsis theory, viewing displays of aggression drains aggressive impulses, thereby reducing the likelihood of aggressive behavior. Catharsis theory is founded on a hydraulic model in which aroused aggressive impulses remain active unless discharged by vicarious or enacted aggression. Actually, anger arousal dissipates over time but is easily regenerated on later occasions if the person ruminates about anger-provoking incidents. Indeed, people can work themselves into a rage long after their anger has subsided. Persisting anger has more to do with ruminative self-arousal than with an undischarged reservoir of aggressive impulses pressing for release.

The hydraulic metaphor of pent-up aggressive impulses pressing for discharge offers misleading causes and remedies for human violence. Individuals are helped more by learning to develop skills in anger management and better ways of coping with conflicts than by immersion in media violence or venting aggression. Contrary to predictions from catharsis theory, for reasons given earlier, exposure to televised violence increases rather than reduces the likelihood of aggressive behavior (Anderson et al., 2003; Anderson & Bushman, 2001; Bandura, 1973). However, in the view of the broadcast industry, "Violence is a catharsis for kids" (Baldwin & Lewis, 1972). Moreover, the broadcast industry claims it is therapeutic as well for adults burdened with the frustrations and conflicts of everyday life: "Human culture is a thin shield superimposed over a violent core. It's better to crack it fictionally than to see it explode in the streets" (Baldwin & Lewis, 1972). The producer confidently proclaims a cathartic therapeutic effect that has no foundation in fact. "Exposure to properly presented conflict which results in violence acts as a therapeutic release for anger and self-hatred" (Baldwin & Lewis, 1972). A TV producer further claimed that if pent-up anger is not vicariously discharged by televised violence, it will spawn aggression in real life: "People need to watch a certain amount of aggressive action to get release and escape" (Baldwin & Lewis, 1972). According to the hydraulic theory, if violence is curtailed on television, it will discharge elsewhere: "Note that, now violence has been soft-pedaled in television drama, it has come out more strongly in films for theatre showing" (Baldwin & Lewis, 1972). If TV producers believe that exposure to televised violence is therapeutic despite evidence to the contrary, they have no need for moral concern.

Advantageous Comparison

The contrast principle is enlisted in whitewashing televised violence. One form of comparative vindication is to sanctify brutalizing excesses on television by pointing to violent episodes in literary classics and the Bible: "There is in Oedipus, Hamlet, and it permeates in [sic] the Bible." The TV film producer William Orr added the *Iliad* and the *Odyssey* to the list for good measure, with the claim that literary classics demonstrate that violence is a key dramatic principle for masterpiece work: "There is hardly a book or a play that would be considered a classic—or even worthwhile reading—that doesn't extend human emotion to the point of violence on the part of its important characters" (Senate Hearings, 1962). Orr frames the issue in terms of the necessity of conflict for captivating drama but adds the inevitability of violence as the resolution. As shown in the memoranda and Senate testimony concerning demands to inject gratuitous violence in plotlines, the heavy use of violence ain't in the service of Shakespearian character elucidation.

In *The Storyteller*, a television movie directed by Robert Markowitz that was designed to vindicate televised violence, a father reminds his married daughter, who is concerned about televised fare, that classic children's stories are of violence: "Little Red Riding Hood" and "Hansel and Gretel" are much worse (Levinson & Link, 1977). Other media personnel point to the knights of yore in the tales of King Arthur as a mighty violent lot. The violence on television is said to pale in comparison to that in comic books. Why pick on television, the scapegoat disclaimer goes, when the government is wreaking havoc through societal violence? "To examine violence where the end result is a dead body on television glosses over the point. This evades the culpability of a whole society which permits wars.... Television and motion pictures are fall guys for a sick society" (Baldwin & Lewis, 1972). Even the death toll caused by the tobacco industry is recruited in the service of comparative exoneration: "Exploring the effects of violence on my program is a sliver as compared with manifestations of violence in the total society. My program is fitted between cigarette advertisements, which are murder weapons and other commercials which ask, 'Madam, are you attractive in bed?'" (Baldwin & Lewis, 1972). Aggression in literary works and wars, and harmful corporate products, presumably absolve the saturated overkill delivered daily to households throughout society, year after year.

Euphemistic Language

The television industry cloaks violence in innocuous language. The term *violence* rarely appears in the vocabularies of media personnel. Rather, sanitized labels such as "action and adventure" programming are used in its place. This shifts the focus from the violent substance to generic program packaging devoid of humanity. Requests for more violence are camouflaged in inoffensive code words such as *excitement*. Here is the sanitized call for more violence: "Put in more excitement."

Much of the brutality on television is not easily sanitizable. "Context" came to the rescue. Congressional hearings on the effects of televised violence often include excerpts of human cruelty. The broadcast industry voiced complaints that the excerpts are misleading because they are stripped of their context. This proved to be an ill-advised exoneration because the industry itself makes heavy use of violent excerpts. These include "teasers" that highlight the violence that will appear in the program, "trailers" that feature the violence in next week's episode, and "promotionals" that show the excerpted violence throughout the broadcast day. The Senate committee put together a collection of teasers, trailers, and promotionals which provided a grisly archive of human atrocities. People were bludgeoned to death; attacked with knives, meat cleavers, pitchforks, and stilettos; machine-gunned, drowned, burned, stomped, whipped, viciously beaten, and ruthlessly tortured.

A committee member asked Oliver Treyz, president of ABC, whether the broadcast excerpts were scenes of violence. To the astonishment of his questioners, Treyz staunchly maintained that they were just scenes of "physical activity" (Senate Hearings, 1962). When pressed further by Senator Dodd on whether "machine gunning of people" is a scene of violence, Treyz explained that he could not "evaluate those particular scenes out of context of the program with which they were shot" (Senate Hearings, 1962). To further preclude judgment of the depicted brutality, "the definition of violence is a subjective one on the part of the person who views the film" (Senate Hearings, 1962). As Treyz described it, given competing versions of reality in which one person's view is just as good as another's, violence is essentially unidentifiable. The hearing continued in this vein, with quibbling about the definitions of violence and arbitrary categorization of programs. In the interchange, the investigation of the exploitation of violence got submerged in a linguistic quagmire (Senate Hearings, 1962). The testimony of producers, supplemented with industry memos calling for violence in shows, could not be dismissed semantically.

Displacement and Diffusion of Responsibility

The creation, funding, production, and broadcasting of television programs are widely distributed across a diverse network of players in a multiplicity of social systems. They include television networks, Hollywood studios, independent producers, production companies, network programming departments, sponsors, advertisers, freelance writers, directors, overseers of broadcast standards, editors, and others as well. Systems in which activities are fractionated and carried out under obfuscating authorization provide a fertile ground for vindicating personal responsibility by structural means. Testifying before the Senate, the producer Ivor Tors described his frustration at trying to pin down who authorized a network directive to inject more sex and violence into his programs: "Mr. Daly said that this came from Mr. Levy, but Mr. Levy at that time received instructions from Mr. Kintner. Again I have no firsthand knowledge whose suggestions it was. I knew only that I was told to put sex and violence in my show" (Senate Hearings, 1962).

Sometimes a faceless executive entity located in another city is the authorizer. Here is a liaison person from NBC conveying the directive to Tors to inject sex into his plotlines: "New York has indicated to me recently their concern over the absence of sex in the following outlines" (Senate Hearings, 1962). Tors called for transparency of authorization to curb network pressures of this sort.

Multiple contributors make it easy to fix the blame for excessive violence on others. For example, here is a writer blaming advertisers for the prevalence of violence on television: "We aren't going to get rid of violence until we get rid of advertisers. The advertiser wants something exciting with which to get the audience. Violence equals excitement equals ratings" (Baldwin & Lewis, 1972). Diffusion of the creation and production process further reduces a sense of personal accountability for the final product. Writers produce scripts, rewriters alter them, directors fill in the details of the scenarios, and editors have a part in how filmed events are depicted by what they select from the lengthy footage. If the original writers are offended by alterations of their scripts, they can use their registered pseudonyms to dissociate themselves from the product and spare themselves personal embarrassment.

Displacement of responsibility for televised gratuitous violence includes a unique form of agentic self-exoneration. The dramatic form is construed as the agent of its violent self, as though it had a life of its own. This novel displacement of agency takes a variety of forms. At the general level, drama allegedly dictates violence. A producer voices this view unequivocally: "Good drama is based on conflict which erupts in violent emotions" (Baldwin & Lewis, 1972). Another producer underscores the inevitability of violence in a long-running series: "Violence and drama are almost synonymous.... I defy anyone to produce a twenty-six drama a year [sic] without a good deal of violence" (Senate Hearings, 1962). As reported earlier, Ivor Tors had no problem in producing a highly rated serial drama with 155 programs that included only a few violent episodes.

Engrossing drama requires conflict and suspense, but violence is not inherently linked to conflict and its resolution. Suspenseful conflict can be resolved nonviolently. The dramas that command attention without resorting to chase scenes, explosions, and killings focus on character study. They go beneath surface actions to the psychosocial forces governing those actions. However, in the view of television storytellers, nonviolent resolutions are unthinkable, especially in the Western genre. In point of fact, such conflict resolutions are not only conceivable. They are doable. For example, the Western series *Wyatt Earp*, which enjoyed a six-year run at the top of its time slot, included only one shooting, which was a reenactment of the historic fight at the OK Corral (Senate Hearings, 1962). Consistent with the historical character, Wyatt Earp was portrayed as a police officer on the Western frontier who dealt with troublemakers in a mindful way.

Another long-running Western, *Bonanza*, was a dominant television show that ran for 14 seasons. David Dortort, who wrote and produced this series, refuted the myth of frontier lawlessness combated by a gunslinging sheriff. The program favored character-driven plotlines rather than physical violence.

In the series, the Cartwright pioneer family fought injustice, bigotry, and oppression and protected human rights rather than nonchalantly killing off evildoers. Dortort, who was a student of American history, maintained that "[t]he true history of the West is about family, pioneers" (Weber, 2010). As Dortort explained, contrary to the centrality of gunfighters in typical Western plotlines, "[t]he gunfighter played a small, inconsequential role in the story of the West." Network executives tried to inject gratuitous violence into the series at the request of a sponsor but retreated when viewers protested. Storytelling that addresses fundamental societal problems in constructive, nonviolent ways does not make a program bland or diminish its attraction.

Another variant on the theme of nonresponsibility for televised violence is that the script, in the likeness of an impersonal agentic force, prescribes it. As one producer put it, "The director is tightly bound by the script" (Baldwin & Lewis, 1972). Scripts do not, in fact, strip directors of all creative freedom. They can request revisions of elements they find objectionable. Moreover, scripts provide guidelines, but directors have to fill in the details. This gives them some leeway in how they portray violent episodes. Writers and producers who remain in the broadcast system accept network directives regarding the use of violence and work within that framework. Those who are unwilling to compromise their standards leave. If they have a talent for producing highly rated shows, the issuers of the directives grudgingly back down.

Not only do the dramatic format and script allegedly mandate violence, the nature of the characters also allegedly dictate it. Virtually all producers disclaim using violence unnecessary to the plot by attributing evident excesses to the characters they create. Their conduct must conform to their natures. Ruthless evildoers and even peaceful folks confronted with mortal jeopardy demand acts of violence. The violence is portrayed as dispositional in the evildoers but situational in the righteous doers. The former are driven by inherent evilness; the latter are forced to violent means by the wanton cruelty of super villains. An executive of one of the Networks blamed the story for the violence as though the story was the agent dictating the action: "I think that violence is a function of the story that was being told" (Senate Hearings, 1962). One of the more candid script writers dismissed the asserted dramatic necessity for violence as analogous to saying, "I never put cotton in a wagon that's not prepared for cotton but I never use anything but a cotton wagon" (Baldwin & Lewis, 1972).

Leading performers, not just the scripted characters, can also be blamed for the violence. In efforts to protect their image, some actors seek revisions in their scripts to portray more aggressive, sexier versions of themselves. This is not always unwelcome. Some producers use such requests as leverage with production departments to raise the amount of violence they can use. In sum, given the multitude of players doing their bit in widely dispersed systems under veiled authorization, the capacity for self-exoneration by shifting blame elsewhere is almost boundless.

Denial and Dispute of Negative Media Effects

The role of televised violence in the transmission, legitimization, and promotion of aggressive styles of behavior was reviewed earlier. The present section is devoted to analysis of how moral self-sanctions can be disengaged from the effects of the product one is creating by denial, distortion, and minimization of its negative effects. Moral self-sanctions are contingent on evidence that one's activities cause harm. Neutralizing the moral predicament roused by reported adverse effects requires challenging scientific findings and managing how those findings are interpreted and presented to the general public. Recall from the earlier analyses that members of the broadcast industry construe violent programming as a force for good. As morality plays, in which good triumphs over evil, these shows allegedly strengthen societal standards of law-abiding conduct. In addition, the industry claims that these programs cathartically relieve viewers of frustrations in their everyday life and entertain them without any demonstrable ill effects.

Those who run the networks and their social scientists vigorously dispute the notion that modeled violence has any harmful effects. The disputations often take contradictory forms. On the one hand, they argue that media effects are unknowable, because media influences can never be disentangled from the multitude of other determinants in the causation of human behavior. On the other hand, they claim that such programs have good effects. They allegedly are causative for good but unknowable for ill. Writers and producers are disconnected from the psychosocial effects of the programs they create. Disconnectedness precludes reality testing. Most of them report that they are unaware of existing research findings, they are not especially eager to see them, they doubt the effects can ever be convincingly demonstrated, and network social scientists reassure them that there is no reason for concern.

Joseph Klapper, director of the Office of Social Research at CBS, was the point man for the broadcast industry in criticizing research in the field and testifying before congressional committees and commissions. In testimony before the National Commission on the Causes and Prevention of Violence, Klapper reported that the effects of television violence are unknown: "I don't know what effect the depictions of violence have" (Baldwin & Lewis, 1972; Baker & Ball, 1969). And they are likely to remain unknowable for a long time: "I would say our ignorance is abysmal and unfortunate, but very difficult to ameliorate." When asked whether there was anything the media could do to reduce youth aggression, he expressed skepticism they could do so, arguing by an odd religious analogy, "I think it would be virtually impossible for the mass media to effect a revolution in people's religious beliefs" (Baker & Ball, 1969). In point of fact, prosocial modeling on *Sesame Street* and *Mister Rogers' Neighborhood* not only reduces aggression in young children but fosters cooperativeness and sharing (Johnston & Ettema, 1986). Prosocial modeling likewise reduces aggressiveness in aggressive delinquents (Leyens et al., 1975).

There was no uncertainty about the innocence of the media in Oliver Treyz's mind; he repudiated any adverse effects: "I have no feeling about any ABC programs having an ill effect on members of our society"(Senate Hearings, 1962). Under the mistaken idea that studies of televised violence are devoid of control groups, some producers dismissed reported empirical findings as unfounded and lambasted the supposedly flawed methodology. "Nobody has been able to make a definite statement about the effects of televised violence. I'd assume the matter has reached a dead end. I'm surprised that there haven't been control groups and controlled scientific studies of it.... To investigate a hypothetical, psychological action without a control group is absolutely insane" (Baldwin & Lewis, 1972). This characterization of experimental studies as lacking control groups is unfounded. Control groups are routinely used in experimental studies. Moreover, well-designed studies use multiple statistical controls to exclude the influence of other possible covarying factors.

Another way of exonerating televised violence of any adverse effects is to invoke a single-cause theory and then disparage it as a fallacious view that makes television the scapegoat for other actual causes. No one has claimed that television is the sole cause of aggression. The same can be said of any other social influence. Human behavior is always the product of multiple determinants operating in concert. In a televised ad, for example, an ordinary guy draws admiring glances from comely blondes for driving a particular brand of automobile. The commercial vendors obviously do not expect every viewer to dash off immediately to the nearest dealer selling that brand. Most will not act on what they have learned because they do not need a car, are satisfied with the one they have, lack the money to buy a new one, or have other priorities at the moment. The idea has been planted, however, and given appropriate conditions some of the viewers will return to it on a later occasion.

A combination of influences is required to produce a violent act that otherwise would not have occurred if any of the key contributing elements were missing. When behavior is activated only by a particular constellation of determinants, those factors that prove ineffective alone or even in partial combination may play a decisive role in the unique constellation. In the bomb-extortion incidents triggered by the airing of *The Doomsday Flight*, the televised influence was an essential but insufficient cause alone. In a medical example that further illustrates the conditional nature of causation, not everyone who smokes develops lung cancer, but given other biological factors it is a key contributor to this disease.

The foregoing comments focus on moral disengagement by contesting harmful media effects. Moral disengagement can also be achieved by willful negligence in the evaluation of effects. As long as the effects of one's products remain unknown, one has no evidential basis for moral self-evaluation.

Industries bear the responsibility of measuring the effects of their products. Presiding over a huge, profitable industry, broadcasters spend vast sums on increasing their market share of viewership in numbers and desired makeup. However, during congressional hearings, efforts to determine the size of the budget for research on the effects of exposure to televised violence drew a blank. Oliver Treyz was unaware of any such studies at ABC: "We have not, to my knowledge, expended any funds on the specific reaction of children to action-adventure shows" (Senate Hearings, 1962). Joseph Klapper spoke in hypothetical terms about the willingness of CBS to do so (Baker & Ball, 1969). Neither respondent showed much in the way of concerned curiosity or a sense of obligation to find out how their programs were affecting viewers. Keeping the knowable unknown is the genuine protective form that self-deception takes.

It is widely assumed that displays of violence may affect children because they are less able to foresee the full consequences of their actions but that adults, who possess a greater reality sense, are relatively immune to such influences. However, the television industry exonerates media influences by minimizing adverse effects, even for children, on the grounds that they know the difference between fantasy and reality: "Children know about violence from their own experience and are able to distinguish television dramatized violence as make-believe" (Baldwin & Lewis, 1972). Because the portrayals are make-believe, viewers supposedly do not model their behavior after fictional characters who are aggressing in atypical situations. Quite the contrary. When exposed to televised violence, viewers learn a style of behavior and its valuation, not just an isolated aggressive act. Some studies use violent cartoons to verify the impact of viewing violence on aggression in young children. In studies with adults, researchers find that viewers behave more aggressively after exposure to fictional aggressors as well as real-life ones. Indeed, justified violence by fictional characters can be just as effective in weakening restraints on aggression as justified real-life violence (Meyer, 1972). Even intelligent and otherwise considerate college students behave more punitively after seeing others act aggressively than if they have had no exposure to such modeling. The problem is not the failure to distinguish between fantasy and reality but the media's construction of a reality in which the exercise of control by aggressive means is morally justified and glamorized. Investing aggression with moral and functional value increases viewers' willingness to adopt it.

My Baptism in Public Policy

The battle over media effects was carried over into the public arena. Network representatives personalized their critiques and used their influence to control what the public would be told in the surgeon general's report on the effects of televised violence. Some of the critiques were directed at me personally and at my studies of observational learning. My program of research sought to clarify the nature of observational learning and the mechanisms governing the acquisition of attitudes, values, and new forms of behavior by this means. Much of the controversy arose from failure to distinguish between research on how viewers learn by social modeling and whether they put into practice what they have learned. For reasons given earlier, tests for observational learning use simulated targets.

I was invited to testify before the Senate Communications Committee on the effects of televised violence, the Federal Trade Commission on advertisements, and the National Commission on the Causes and Prevention of Violence in hearings prompted by the assassination of Senator Robert F. Kennedy. The Federal Trade Commission was troubled by increasing reports of serious injuries suffered by children who modeled hazardous activities in televised advertisements. The commission used our research findings on modeling to get advertisers to alter ads depicting injurious feats by children on bicycles and dune buggies, ads for headache remedies in which the characters induce splitting headaches by pounding each other on the head with mallets, and other types of ads showing children performing activities that risk serious injury.

This excursion into the public policy arena provided a sobering glimpse into the power of the broadcast industry. *Look* magazine invited me to write a piece on the social influence of television for a special issue they were publishing on Youth. When it appeared, the Television Information Office, a subsidiary of the National Association of Broadcasters, sent a large packet to its sponsor stations explaining why my research on social modeling and testimony at a Senate hearing should be disregarded. This was just the beginning of a multipronged offensive. The psychologist Ruth Hartley prepared a document, commissioned by CBS (1964), in which she criticized my studies on the power of social modeling and the relevance of other experimental studies demonstrating social modeling of televised styles of aggression.

Edith Efron, the senior editor of *TV Guide*, published a series of six lengthy editorials on the influence of television on children. Two of the editorials addressed my research on social modeling. In one of these editorials, "A Child Is Not a Rat" (1969a), Efron likened experimental studies of children learning to rat studies and concluded that humans "do not behave like laboratory rats." She misrepresented social modeling as "conditioning." This misunderstanding was the height of irony, because the theory of social modeling fundamentally disagrees with conditioning theory. As part of social cognitive theory, social modeling relies on symbolizing capabilities, but radical behaviorists dismiss them (Bandura, 1986, 1997). Efron cited Ruth Hartley, whom she dubbed the "best-known attacker," as the authoritative critic of experimental research on the effects of televised violence. In an expanded indictment, Efron not only took issue with my studies but also included "virtually all of his colleagues" in the critique of experimental studies of aggressive modeling. In a concluding statement, Efron enlightened the viewing public with the following statement regarding research on television effects: "There is no proof that the human child or adult sitting in a living room looking at TV is psychologically similar to a rat sitting in a cage staring at a blinking light" (Efron, 1969a).

In a second editorial in *TV Guide* under the title "The Man in the Eye of the Hurricane," Efron (1969b) further dismissed the modeling studies, complained that the research by members of the "Bandura school...won them center stage in Washington," and criticized the surgeon general's office for acting "as if Rome were burning and Dr. Bandura were a fire extinguisher."

One evening I received a call from one of my graduate students, who told me to turn on my television set to the TV movie *The Storyteller* in which a harried researcher underwent a blistering cross-examination concerning modeling studies (Levinson & Link, 1977). He was not doing well. Professor George Gerbner (1972b) of the University of Pennsylvania was tracking the prevalence of televised violence, its forms, those who commit it, and those who are the victims. In a further segment devoted to a thinly veiled disparagement of this program of research, the executive tells the reporters there is a professor who counts a pie in the face as a violent act.

It was remarkable to see an entire movie exonerating televised violence inadvertently built on the mechanisms of moral disengagement. In the story line, a screenwriter's TV movie is held responsible for triggering an imitative arson that killed a youngster. In justifying the reliance on violence, the broadcast industry was portrayed as fending off censorship that threatened to kill creativity. In a scene devoted to exoneration by advantageous comparison, the screenwriter confronts his married daughter, who allows her daughter to read the violence in "Little Red Riding Hood" but restricts what her daughter can watch on television. In a tranquil scene in which the screenwriter builds sand castles on the beach with his granddaughter, he tells a metaphoric story about protection against an attack in which seagulls bring grains of sand to protect the sand castle from the tidal onslaught. He asks his granddaughter whether she is ever scared by what she sees on television. Voicing the industry's erroneous claim that children are not frightened by menacing scenes, she replies, "No, it's only make-believe."

The plot continues with the negation of adverse effects. A television executive is asked by reporters whether he is aware of research showing that exposure to televised violence can have adverse effects. The executive replies that he is also aware of research disputing that claim. This encounter with the press includes a cut to a scene in which callous reporters press for comments from an anguished wife standing beside the body of her husband, who was crushed to death in a car accident.

The mother whose son died in the fire is disparaged and psychopathologized. She is depicted as a vindictive, deranged woman bent on making life miserable for the screenwriter's family with telephone calls at odd hours

and mailings of photos of her deceased son. Through a morally disengaged sleight of hand, the industry is exonerated and made the victim of unjust attacks. In this cinematic production, the intersecting moral disengagement plotlines are a sight to behold. Ironically, this movie was nominated for an Emmy for "outstanding writing."

As I was being pummeled by media-commissioned critiques, sponsored studies, paid consultants, the *TV Guide* editor, and the movie exonerating the broadcast industry, I began to feel a kinship with the battered Bobo doll!

The television industry tried its hand with research of its own by sponsoring several field studies. The findings of one such study by Feshbach and Singer (1971) were of questionable reliability because of major methodological flaws (Bandura, 1973). Replication of the research without the methodological defects yielded findings that were not to the industry's liking (Wells, 1971). The study was never published. With financial sponsorship and co-production by CBS, Milgram and Shotland (1973) conducted studies showing that exposure to modeled thievery does not lead viewers to steal money from a charity box called Project Hope, a medical charity that treats poor children worldwide. The charity box, with a dollar bill hanging from it, was mounted on a poster showing a physician treating a little girl and a picture of the hospital ship with the words "Where there is Hope there is life." This experimental setup was analogous to demonstrating that televised modeling of theft has no adverse effects by showing that viewers will not rip off a tiny charitable contribution to Mother Teresa. As the saying goes, there is honor even among thieves concerning a charitable humanitarian cause. The studies were published as a book and distributed free of charge by the network. This research did not survive conceptual and empirical scrutiny.

There were more chapters to the exercise of political leverage regarding research on media effects. The National Commission on the Causes and Prevention of Violence was about to release its report concluding, in the mass media volume, that the empirical evidence taken as a whole supported a positive relation between televised violence and aggressive behavior (Baker & Ball, 1969). In a surprise move, Senator John Pastore, a supporter of the broadcast industry (Butler, 1972) who chaired the Communications Subcommittee, instructed the surgeon general, with President Richard Nixon's endorsement, to assemble a committee of experts to evaluate the effects of televised violence and to allocate $1 million for new research on this topic. The first meeting of the evaluation committee took place at the Center for Advanced Study at Stanford. Ed Parker—who with Wilbur Schramm and Jack Lyle coauthored *Television in the Lives of Our Children* (1961)—and I were invited to sit in on the meeting. We were surprised to find that five of the members of the committee were tied to the broadcast industry—two network researchers, two network consultants, and a former research executive at CBS.

We enlisted the help of Senator Lee Metcalf to obtain information on the selection procedure. Health, Education, and Welfare Secretary Robert

Finch explained that each network was allowed to veto, without explanation, any of the nominees on the list submitted by professional associations and the broadcast networks. I was one of eight researchers, including Len Berkowitz, Percy Tannenbaum, the child psychiatrist Leon Eisenberg, and the sociologists Leo Bogart and Otto Larsen, who were vetoed. Finch provided two justifications for the veto procedure—precedent and objectivity. He explained that the tobacco industry was given veto power in the formation of the committee to evaluate the health effects of smoking. The media report would have greater impact, he claimed, if the committee members were entirely objective. Senator Metcalf was astonished to learn that the tobacco industry was also given sole veto power in the panel selected to evaluate the research on the health effects of smoking. He questioned the selective privilege of veto power given to the broadcast industry and how stacking the committee with folks tied to the television industry would ensure impartiality.

Writing the report created headaches for the broadcast-linked members because the empirical data were not friendly to the conclusion of cathartic or null effects. The report was written in opaque psychobabble that was better suited to confusing than to informing the public. Rose Goldsen (1972), a Cornell sociologist, dubbed the report "science in wonderland." Several social scientists reported on the perversion of the scientific review process. Mathilda Butler (1972) wrote a piece on the violence done to TV-violence research. In *TV Violence and the Child*, a book devoted to this controversial episode, Cater and Strickland (1975) traced the evolution and fate of the report. *Science* published a lead article documenting and condemning the misuse of the scientific advisory system for policy initiatives (Boffey & Walsh, 1970).

Before the report was released, a copy was leaked to Jack Gould (1972) of the *New York Times*, who published a column on the report under the misleading headline "TV Violence Held Unharmful to Youth." The researchers who conducted the studies for the committee were incensed at the misrepresentation of their findings in the report. They protested to Senator Pastore, who then scheduled an open Senate hearing on the committee's report. The National Film Board of Canada filmed the proceedings (Chatwin & Low, 1972). After years of obfuscation, negation, and disparagement of research programs by the broadcast industry, its own chief researcher, Joseph Klapper, acknowledged at the hearings, "There were indications of a causal relationship.... The catharsis theory had no empirical support" (Chatwin & Low, 1972).

President Lyndon Johnson once remarked that politics is like sausage making. You don't want to examine what goes into it. Social scientists seek to advance knowledge that can inform public policy. As revealed in the stealthy workings of the sociopolitical forces swirling around the issue of television violence, we also need to study how politics and power, which shape public policy, determine how knowledge is used. Policy research is difficult to conduct. We do little of it.

Attribution of Blame to Viewers

In disengaging moral self-sanctions from television fare by attribution of blame, media personnel fault the viewers and their social environment for any associated detrimental behavior. Joseph Klapper attributed positive relations between viewing violence and aggressive behavior to preexisting dispositions of viewers. This placed the cause entirely in the viewer. It is not that televised violence fosters aggression, he argued, but rather that viewers' dispositions drive them to violent programs. However, the nature of the disposition was left in foggy ambiguity: "[C]ertain personality traits lead to a taste for violent media material, and...this material serves some sort of ill-understood function" (Baker & Ball, 1969).

Parents also are blamed for any adverse effects of televised violence. Viewed from a producer's perspective, "Are kids from unstable environments triggered by television violence? They're [sic] not having parents is a more serious problem" (Baldwin & Lewis, 1972). Parental culpability is often linked with the familial antidote argument: By providing a warm, secure, and wholesome home environment, parents, it is claimed, can neutralize any potential negative impact of massive exposure to inhumane conduct. If they cannot create a counteracting environment they should control what their children watch on television. "Today's mothers don't acknowledge that kind of responsibility; instead, they expect television to be a babysitter for them" (Baldwin & Lewis, 1972). Parental monitoring requires advance information about the violence levels of given programs. Parents and child advocates lobbied for a violence-rating system. On the one hand, the television industry preaches to parents that they bear responsibility for what their children watch. On the other hand, as will be explained later, the industry adamantly opposes granting parents the information to do so.

A variant on the dispositional disclaimer of accountability is that only a few emotionally disturbed viewers may be adversely affected by televised violence. In testimony before the National Commission on the Causes and Prevention of Violence, Joseph Klapper expressed contradictory views on the effects of televised violence. On the one hand, he contended, "I don't know what effect the depictions of violence have." On the other hand, he was highly certain that they had no adverse effects except on a rare psychopath: "It is my personal opinion that in reference to fictional portrayals of violence—portrayals of violence in fiction—the likelihood that witnessing depictions of violence would lead anybody other than an occasional psychopath into acts of violence is very, very unlikely" (Baker & Ball, 1969). Rare events, of course, should not dictate what can be shown to the general public. As some of the producers put it, "You can't modify all programming to leave only shows like *Bewitched* on the possibility that a few disturbed people will be triggered.... To remove what might adversely affect a few would be like prohibiting medications because of a side effect which they may have on one person out of 7,000. Follow this line of reasoning and we'd stop giving prescriptions: we'd stop doing all kinds of hazardous things; we'd stop driving our automobiles" (Baker & Ball, 1969).

This causal attribution makes internal pathology, rather than televised fare, a contributor to the harmful behavior. The problem with this explanation is that media effects are common occurrences, not rare ones. In the case of vicarious learning, virtually all viewers learn most, if not all, of the aggressive style of behavior being modeled (Bandura, 1965). In tests of performance effects of modeled aggression, it is not merely a few viewers who become more aggressive (Anderson & Bushman, 2001). Similarly, habituation and desensitization to human cruelty through massive exposure to televised violence is a common emotion-blunting phenomenon, not a selectively rare one. Images of reality shaped by media influences are widely adopted (Bryant & Oliver, 2009).

Emotional arousal can enhance aggressive behavior (Berkowitz, 1990; Zillmann, 1988), but this does not mean that the aggression is a product of an internal pathology. There is a difference between impulsive aggression, in which emotional arousal figures prominently, and instrumental aggression, which is governed by its functional value and positive evaluation. One can get people, whatever their makeup, to adopt aggressive forms of behavior more readily by modeling, legitimizing, socially sanctioning, and rewarding such behavior than by instilling an "emotional disorder" in them. It should be noted in passing that media representatives never describe what they mean by "emotional disorder." All too often the pathology is inferred from the very behavior it supposedly causes, which is a circular explanation.

This discussion of parental control of children's viewing habits is concerned with broadcasters' use of causal attribution as a moral disengagement strategy for dealing with troublesome media effects, not with the feasibility or utility of a violence-rating system. Efforts to create a functional rating system get mired in bickering over what constitutes aggression and how to categorize it. It is more fruitful to focus efforts on increasing the availability of beneficial programs than on rating detrimental ones. We shall revisit this issue in an evaluation of alternative remedies for the commercialization of violence.

Interpersonal aggression is a social matter, not just a private family affair. Nonviewers can be secondarily affected by televised violence if they emulate the conduct of influenced viewers, or if they are victims of viewers' modeled aggression. For example, the thousands of airline passengers whose vacation or business plans were thrown into disarray by extortionists modeling the bomb threat from *The Doomsday Flight* suffered the consequences even though none of them might have watched this TV film. Children whose parents limit their exposure to modeled aggression may, nevertheless, be victims of aggressors whose parents do not care what their children watch.

Dehumanization of Viewers and Disparagement of Challengers

Some writers and producers divest viewers of human sensibilities or invest them with base qualities that justify serving them gory offerings: "Man's mind is connected to his stomach, his groin, and his fists. It doesn't float five feet above his body. Violence, therefore, cannot be eradicated" (Baldwin & Lewis, 1972). Viewers allegedly hanker for brutality: "If he doesn't beat the hell out of him, I want my money back." This presumption is based on the belief that people find violence inherently gratifying. This view is vividly conveyed in a memorandum from a script reader to a writer: "Not as much action as some, but sufficient to keep the average bloodthirsty viewer fairly happy" (Senate Hearings, 1962).

The widely shared belief among broadcasters is that violence is an expression of the meanness of human nature. Broadcasters claim that in a highly competitive entertainment market, viewers' craving for violence compels them to include violence in their plotlines. Television is simply responding to the desires of viewers. This jaundiced conception of human nature also justifies the necessity for violent conflict resolution: "There must ultimately be some kind of physical settlement. The audience doesn't see a jail sentence. It will feel emotionally cheated and complain, Christ, what a dead ending that was" (Baldwin & Lewis, 1972). Seeing the villains get killed supposedly gives viewers a feeling of fulfillment: "Make the villain bad and have the hero kill him to give the audience a sense of fulfillment." Failure to do so also violates the dictates of the "action and adventure" genre: "As an end to certain dramatic situations, if the good guy simply puts handcuffs on the bad guy and says, 'I'll see you in court,' the audience will feel dramatically cheated" (Baldwin & Lewis, 1972). Seeing the defeat of malevolent foes depicted as justified retribution heightens viewers' aggression in contentious situations (Berkowitz et al., 1972).

The myth that the prevalence of televised violence is determined by the base desires of viewers is widely accepted, despite empirical evidence to the contrary. Diener and DeFour (1978) correlated levels of program violence and viewership as measured by the Nielsen index of the number of households tuned in to given programs. The correlation that they found, $r = 0.05$, revealed no relation whatever between the amount of program violence and how many households watched it. Programs aired at the same time by competing networks can affect the viewership of a given program. In an experimental test of whether counterprogramming might affect the correlation, Diener and DeFour found that a program containing its original violence was no more attractive to viewers than the same program with most of the violence deleted. These findings provide no empirical support for the myth that violence sells. Nor does the annual viewership for the top-ranked series support this myth. Situation comedies populate the top 10 year after year. As one television producer said, There is one maxim that is always true. The network with the most comedy shows is the dominant network.

Contrary to the view that people are attracted to gore, networks have to sanitize the violence by deleting the gory parts to get people to watch it. A script reader instructs a producer to cut down on the gore: ...[b]e careful in shooting this beating of Allison. As described it is much overdone and overdescribed. Cut down on the lashes—the blood, the 'raw and bloody' face, the fall downstairs, etc. All this—plus the number of people killed in the closing scene—makes this a pretty horrible 10 minutes" (Senate Hearings, 1962).

Screenwriters and producers shield viewers from revulsion at vicious beatings and mangled bodies by having the characters beaten or killed off camera. This solution disembodies the physical violence. An overseer of scripts, checking for inappropriate material, instructs the scriptwriter to "kill Hazel off camera, ...kill pigeon [informer] off camera....[In s]cenes of the fight, keep blood to a minimum" (Senate Hearings, 1962). Killings that may be especially unsettling to viewers are likely to occur off camera. In a memo to the producer of the especially violent series *The Untouchables*, the executive producer, Quinn Martin, acknowledged that a group of Mexican girls imported for prostitution might have to be massacred off camera: "This scene is the roughest I have ever seen and I don't know if we can get away with it, but let's leave it in. Have a feeling you may have to kill the girls off camera" (Senate Hearings, 1962).

The networks' overseers of scripts appear more concerned with how to portray violence without turning off the viewers than with the gruesomeness of the violence itself and the morality of exploiting it. An issue worthy of study is whether producing violent programming desensitizes and habituates the producers to violence as it does the viewers.

Cinematic staging and editing techniques are widely used to make gory events tolerable to viewers. This is another structural means of mitigating moral reactions. For example, the camera focuses on a body part such as a hand in a death reaction rather than on the dying person. However, overseers of scripts instruct writers to avoid bizarre death reactions: "Don't show the knifing—or any grotesque death reaction....If seen at all, the woman's body should not be grotesquely sprawled" (Baldwin & Lewis, 1972). Writers are also told to avoid depicting injuries that may be revolting to viewers. For example, they won't show a physical beating but will show teeth falling into the spaghetti (Senate Hearings, 1962). Through these disembodying and sanitizing techniques, brutal beatings and killings are portrayed as relatively clean. There would be no need to launder violence in these ways if viewers craved it and found it inherently gratifying.

Not only is violence sanitized but its social repercussions are rarely, if ever, shown. There are no anguished widows or crying children whose lives are scarred forever by the murder of their father. Moreover, the violent characters are stripped of a mental life. They do not struggle with inner conflicts over their use of violence, nor do they have any afterthoughts or feelings about taking a human life. Heroes who achieve worthy ends by violent means have no need for remorse. Why admonish oneself for good deeds? Aggressing in a nonchalant way also conveys the social acceptability of such means.

Inner feelings and thoughts are manifested through self-reflective, revealing dialogue. The character-driven series *Wyatt Earp* was structured around Earp's remorse at having killed a man and how it shaped his approach to maintaining public peace and order (Senate Hearings, 1962). As we shall see shortly, the "action and adventure" genre, which avoids talk like the plague, has little room for an inner life that reflects the interplay of motivating forces governing the actions of the characters.

If violence does not sell, what accounts for its prevalence in televised fare? People's television preferences are constrained by what they are given to choose from. Research during the early phase of television showed a marked discrepancy between what people would have liked to see on television and what they were shown. The offerings that are broadcast are determined mainly by commercial considerations. Programs that capture large audiences are discontinued if the people they attract do not fit the age or income categories that advertisers wish to influence. Popular programs that deliver the wrong kinds of viewers from a commercial standpoint are retired due to unfavorable "demographics" despite their wide acceptance because they fetch low advertising rates (Brown, 1971).

Program production costs per thousand viewers strongly influences what is televised. Action formats are prevalent because they are relatively cheap to produce. The Western drama required only a few horses, a weathered saloon, a superhero-type lawman, transient evildoers, some dancing girls which the industry refers to as "candy for the eyes," and the open range with natural lighting. A producer could grind out endless episodes at a price that yielded higher profits than more popular programs that incur higher production costs. Westerns were supplanted by the "space wars" genre, in which a good share of a program is devoted to computer-generated spaceships in lengthy battles with weird-looking enemies from other planets. The crime genre has its share of drawn-out chase scenes and fights by stuntmen and stuntwomen doubling for the actors to reduce production costs. Long-running programs of better quality are typically canceled at the height of their viewership because of the ever-increasing salaries of the stars and annual raises for the writers and production crews. These soaring costs make popular programs less profitable.

Time constraints are another factor that makes violence the preferred vehicle of conflict and its resolution. Violence is an easy way to initiate conflict, advance the plotline, and achieve a quick, decisive end to it. There is no time, say the broadcasters, for reflective thought. It only slows things down. "To have a person wrestle with a problem before acting may be objected to by the network executive because it slows down the action" (Baldwin & Lewis, 1972). Nor is there time for adjudicating guilt and punishment: "Without some kind of violence, you couldn't resolve the show. Instead of being able to hold a protracted court trial, you need to end the show in a couple of minutes" (Baldwin & Lewis, 1972). In one writer's taxonomy of conflict, "man against man," which usually takes the form of physical violence, is the only viable option for television:

> Man against nature. "This is usually too expensive for TV."
> Man against God. "Too intellectual for TV."
> Man against himself. "Too psychological, and doesn't leave enough room for action."
> Man against man. "This is what you usually end up with." (Baldwin & Lewis, 1972)

High-decibel action is also a means of attentional control. Viewers are not all that attentive to what is being shown, with a host of distracters around them competing for their notice. While watching television they are talking, thumbing through reading material, snacking, walking around, dozing off, or doing any number of other things. Broadcasters try to capture and hold viewers' attention through fast-paced physical action with rapid scene changes on the screen. As shown earlier, talented writers can portray conflict in captivating ways without resorting to physical violence. However, formula shows hold little interest for them. Those who try their hand at them but resist pressures to inject violence into their plotlines either leave or are dismissed.

Finally, the widely shared misbelief throughout the broadcast industry that violence keeps programs on the air fosters its gratuitous use. Violence allegedly garners high ratings. Even though this idea is unfounded, if broadcasters believe it and their success rests precariously on ratings erroneously attributed to violence, they have a strong incentive to include beatings and killing in their programs. In sum, the answer to the abundance of televised violence lies more in production costs, program time constraints, a limited talent pool, and a mistaken belief about people's craving for violence than in viewers' supposedly base human nature.

Shifting blame for aggression to brutish human nature, negligent parents, and viewers' own psychopathology is self-exonerating. So is disparagement of critics and overseers of their work. Members of congressional committees that focus on the broadcast industry came in for heavy derogation (Senate Hearings, 1962). They were considered unqualified to pass judgment on the industry. They were blamed for hounding the television industry rather than addressing societal problems, which made them considerably more culpable for the adverse human condition: "[F]ailure to improve the slums, improve educational opportunities, and get out of Vietnam is a much greater failure to improve society than that of television" (Baldwin & Lewis, 1972). Broadcasters viewed

Congress as having no business infringing on the constitutional rights of the broadcast industry: "But the government has no right to decide what is right and what is wrong with society. It has no right to dictate to private industry. It has no right to legislate morality, certainly in the arts" (Baldwin & Lewis,1972). Critics from the broadcast industry enlisted exonerative comparison in portraying the dangers of governmental regulation: "If the government does control these matters, the result will be like that in Hitler's Germany"(Baldwin & Lewis, 1972). The most vituperative critiques were directed at Senator John Pastore, the chair of the Communications Committee: "Pastore is a publicity-oriented fool with a limited, dogmatic approach. To make TV a scapegoat for the ills of our society is preposterous." Pastore is also disparaged comparatively: "He is likened to an infamous demagogue. "He's got an issue—like Joe McCarthy. It's a nice way to get reelected" (Baldwin & Lewis, 1972).

Nor were the industry overseers of scripts for objectionable content spared disparagement. The more combative producers called them "assholes, idiots, cookie-cut network executives, page boys, shop girls, and small people." Their decisions were referred to as "illiterate," "simplistic," "asinine," "ludicrous," and "stupid" (Baldwin & Lewis, 1972). These are not the kinds of folks who make the producers' Christmas card lists. Producers were angry at being told by low-level overseers to degrade their creativity: "I resent their flyspecking against my creativity. I'm being told what the public wants and how a scene should go by someone who got an A in English composition back in Kalamazoo" (Baldwin & Lewis, 1972).

Having belittled the overseers of their scripts, producers fought to overrule their judgments: "We never let the network decide, if we can help it—not for conscience's sake, but for effective operating procedure. We fight them as hard as we can in regard to their absolutely asinine decisions. You can get away from the rules by going to the top." The irate critic adds a bit of sexism: "It's useless to argue with a shop girl, so you go to the store manager. I call the boss and say, 'Would you like to hear what your people are doing? Isn't that asinine?' And he's likely to agree" (Baldwin & Lewis, 1972). Some figured out how to outwit their overseers: "The easiest way to deal with a censor is to load [a script] with things you know they'll take out, leaving what you want" (Baldwin & Lewis, 1972). Moral considerations were shortchanged in this power struggle.

Producers voiced frustration at being unable to pin down who was responsible for directives to change their scripts: "When they tell you to change something and you ask, 'Who's pressing for this?' there's never any particular man. It's always 'they.'...That guy 'they' is a fantastic character in my life." "'They' won't allow it. And the 'they' keeps going up the ladder. Like in the military, the private puts the blame on the corporal, the corporal on the sergeant, etc." (Baldwin & Lewis, 1972).

Producers who dispute any ill effects of televised violence see their creativity marred by meddlesome overseers of limited talent, and resent being unfairly chastised by those they regard as opportunistic politicians using television for political gain and as a scapegoat for their legislative failures. Given this combative view, producers have no reason to feel any qualms about their work. Rather, they regard themselves as protectors of free speech.

ANTIDOTES AND REMEDIES FOR TELEVISED INHUMANITIES

A number of possible remedies have been proposed for the exploitation of gratuitous violence. In one approach, the public demands congressional remedies. The congressional route, however, has little effect for a variety of reasons. Constitutional protection for free speech restricts the government from regulating the content of television programming. (Recall the Supreme Court ruling on this matter.) Although the public wants Congress to make the broadcast industry clean up its act, they do not want official agencies prescribing what they can watch. The "public" is diverse, not monolithic. The prospect of many interest groups objecting to particular content evokes a slippery-slope scenario in which restricting one type of content will launch demands for restricting a slew of other types.

Although Congress can do little about the content of televised fare, it cannot ignore common public concerns and demands. So it schedules hearings. Congressional hearings come and go, but the level of televised violence remains high. Like drama series, Congressional investigations have protagonists playing stylized roles, with the common tale of little or no results. After the networks are commended for serving the public in many ways, their record of gratuitous violence is presented, along with testimony by researchers on the psychological effects of exposure to such influences. Broadcasters challenge the criteria for judging violence and dispute that they use it intentionally. Social scientists present empirical evidence of media effects. Industry researchers contest the empirical evidence. At the conclusion of such hearings, the chairperson issues threats to the effect that if the industry fails to improve its self-regulation, the government will have to intervene. Broadcasters, in turn, reaffirm that they have not been misbehaving; besides, the objectionable practices are a thing of the past, and they will continue to abide by the industry's code of good conduct.

Broadcasters use the congressional pseudo-threat to reframe the issue from viewers against broadcasters to broadcasters against big government, with denunciations of governmental censorship like that during notorious dictatorships. This scares the public into opposing a governmental remedy. The government can take action against grossly irresponsible practices through the licensing power of the Federal Communications Commission. There is little danger, however, that a television station would ever lose its license due to commercial overuse of violence. Not only would such rulings provoke endless semantic disputes over what violence is, but they also would be challenged on constitutional grounds. Being recipients of campaign contributions and subject to other corporate pressures, legislative bodies and regulatory agencies are heavily influenced by the very industries they are supposed to oversee. In reality, the industry fears adverse publicity more than the threat of censorship. Because televised fare draws little official attention after the hearings have concluded, broadcasters have few reasons to discontinue their customary practices. After a time, public pressure on Congress again mounts, prompting another congressional hearing. The lethality of media violence has increased over time but no longer results in public protests or congressional hearings. The parents of today were raised on a heavy diet of televised violence. Does the public quiescence of recent years reflect parental desensitization and habituation to human violence?

The commotion generated by governmental pseudo-threats blocks consideration of constructive changes that do not involve infringement on free expression. As a public service, some amount of broadcasting time could be set aside for children's programming without advertisements that manipulate youngsters into pressuring their parents to buy products that they don't want or don't need or can't afford. Freed from the constraints of sponsors, producers could devote their talents to creating entertaining, quality programs for children. However, this would be a partial remedy, at best, because children also watch adult shows that feature a lot of beatings and killings.

Promoting children's programming legislatively is, of course, easier said than done. A predictor of what people watch is the channel to which their television set is tuned. Because of the continuity problem of adults switching channels from children's shows, broadcasters shun children's programming. They offer animated cartoons on Saturday mornings in which heroes beat up evildoers under the sponsorship of cereal, snack, and toy companies. Congressional efforts to mandate even a few hours of genuine children's programs testify to the difficulty of achieving legislatively even minor changes. With heavy dependence on corporate funds, lawmakers want to be on the side of those who replenish their campaign coffers. Those who receive campaign contributions from broadcasters and advertisers have few incentives to press the issue.

After years of bickering, in 1990 Congress passed and the president signed the Children's Television Act, with FCC guidelines mandating broadcasters to provide three hours each week of educational and informational programming for children. This mandate revived a long-running debate in formulating the guidelines on what constitutes children's programs. In a plan that would subvert enforcement of the law, the Federal Communications Commission, under pressure from broadcasters, would free commercial stations of the obligation of providing some programs for children by allowing them to pay another station in the same market to do so. Peggy Charren, the founder of Action for Children's Television, had this to say about the outsourcing of this obligation as though being granted use of the public airways carries no public responsibility: "What kind of idea is this, trading away children's rights and having one station fulfill the obligation of others?... Allowing stations to simply pay another station to do programming does not fulfill stations' obligations to serve the needs of children" (Hall, 1995).

In commenting on the networks' reneging on their promise to reduce gratuitous violence at a Senate hearing given years earlier, Senator Thomas Dodd voiced his frustration and a sense of powerlessness to effect change: "I am out of patience, and I think we have waited long enough, 5 years with promises of improvement, and instead of improvement, we got deterioration. I don't know what we will do after this" (Senate Hearings, 1962).

A second approach to promoting social responsibility in television programming relies on the industry's system of self-regulation. However well intentioned many practitioners might be, when they are left to internal regulation, profits will dictate content. In the face of strong financial pressures and weak public sanctions, the operating guidelines are quite pliable. As previously documented, given the industry's rejection of adverse media effects and the subordinate status of script overseers, the implementers of broadcast standards are more concerned with protecting the industry from public criticisms than in rooting out gratuitous violence. The level of brutality that is permitted testifies to a rather low standard. The fact that producers can get the upper echelons to overrule the judgments of their subordinate overseers indicates that the standards are easily circumvented. Righteous standards are fine for public relations, but neither the performance record nor frank statements by industry personnel inspire confidence that the broadcasters' self-regulatory practices will curb objectionable excesses.

The third approach relies on public pressure linked to a violence-monitoring system. This solution is based on the belief that broadcasters will behave differently if the violence ratings of their programs are publicized than if no one examines what the networks are doing. However, social monitoring without performance consequences has little effect. To cite but one example, congressional public exposure of flagrant broadcast practices did not change them. When public sanctions are considered, they usually take the form of complaints to sponsors and threats to boycott their advertised products. Such threats do not carry much force. This is because very few people take action and those who do rarely stick with it for long. They are easily dismissed as oddballs or reactionaries bent on imposing their values on others.

For years parents lobbied Congress to mandate that television sets be equipped with a V-chip that can electronically block violent programs. Eventually it was mandated, only to be neutralized in a dispute over the coding of programs. The industry proposed an age-based rating system by which it judges what may be appropriate for given ages. The broadcasters' rating system provides a summary judgment about age appropriateness but otherwise leaves parents poorly informed about the content of programs. Children's advocates vigorously opposed the system. They wanted parents to make the judgment on the basis of the violence of programs. Jack Valenti, the spokesman for the television industry, warned that it would challenge legally any ratings system other than its own age-based one as an infringement on First Amendment rights. Some content-related rating systems were created, but they were presented in a form that many parents found indecipherable. Prohibitions can make the programs more enticing (Bushman & Cantor, 2003). Parents ended up with an essentially functionless program-monitoring system. So much for the public-pressure remedy.

All of the preceding remedies seek to alter media practices by coercive and restrictive means. Coercion is not a reliable way of achieving lasting changes in human behavior. The failed congressional efforts to mitigate the detrimental aspects of televised fare testify to the weakness of this approach.

It is a well-established psychological principle that it is easier to eliminate detrimental behavior by providing a more attractive alternative than by trying to prohibit the detrimental one. The fourth approach is founded on this principle. The power of attractive alternatives is nowhere better illustrated than in children's programming, which had aroused the greatest public criticism. For years parents complained about the heavy diet of violence on prime-time television and the weekend commercial fare served their children.

The creation of *Sesame Street* and its broadcast on public television changed all that. It entertained and educated generations of children both at home and abroad in partnership with foreign producers tailoring the program to their cultural interests. Close collaboration between producers and social scientists served the dual purpose of enhancing the quality of children's programming and furthering understanding of how television can promote positive child development. Research on other children's programs on public television, featuring the creative and prosocial aspects of children's lives, verifies their beneficial effects (Johnston & Ettema, 1986). A financially secure public broadcasting system, free of sponsor pressures, is perhaps the best vehicle for providing the quality children's programming that the commercial networks shun. This still leaves the issue of the exploitation of gratuitous violence in prime-time offerings. Although intended for adults, adult programs have a sizable child viewership.

THE CHANGING MEDIA SCENE

The rich body of information for the preceding microanalysis of the moral aspects of the television entertainment industry was provided by two sets of cultural events in the 1960s. The first was concerned parents' persistent pressure on Congress to do something about the pervasive brutality on television. This social pressure launched the 1962 Senate hearings, which examined virtually every aspect of the entertainment industry and the key players in it. The second event was the assassination of Senator Robert F. Kennedy. President Lyndon Johnson established the National Commission on the Cause and Prevention of Violence in America, whose research staff commissioned and published 13 volumes, one of which addressed the role of the media in violence. This volume also examined in considerable detail the practices of the television industry.

The entertainment media have undergone many transformations since the 1960s. The multibillion-dollar teenage market became big business for pop music producers, clothing manufacturers, fast-food franchises, and the beverage industry. Marketers commercialized a teen counterculture with new entertainment media that could serve their purposes well. A PBS documentary, *The Merchants of Cool*, provides a glimpse into how marketers crafted the media to shape the buying habits of teenagers (Dretzin & Goodman, 2001). Through "cool hunting," marketers looked for what was cool and the trendsetters and early adopters. The hunters must become cool themselves to avoid being seen as establishment outsiders.

Marketers were no longer developing advertising campaigns. Rather, they were fashioning a youth culture as the vehicle for their commercial purposes. The prototypic male model in this culture was a crude, angry "mook" who glorified violence. The female model was a libidinous "midriff" who flaunted her sexuality. In commenting on the merchandizing of this seamy, dumbed-down teenage counterculture, the consulting producer Douglas Rushkoff asked, "So is there anywhere the commercial machine won't go? Is it leaving any room for kids to create a culture of their own?" (Dretzin & Goodman, 2001).

The documentary graphically chronicled teenage exploitation by underhanded, unsavory means. However, marketing and conglomerate media executives were never asked to reflect on their practices. The one moral justification they voiced was that they were merely responding to the demands of the youth culture rather than creating that culture. The teens were to blame. We have countless studies on media effects on youth but essentially none on the media system that produces the influential programming. Despite access to the top marketing and media executives, the documentary lost an opportunity to examine how the media influencers managed the moral aspects of the means they used to shape youth buying habits.

In an ironic turn of events, broadcasters may be agents of their own reform through program replacement by financially more attractive alternatives, though the change is not in an enlightened direction. Reality shows that feed on suspenseful competition and the seamier side of human relationships have unexpectedly become the vehicle of change. The reality shows, which incur minimal production costs, are a gift from television heaven.

They have no expensive superstars and no writers, expensive staging, filming in pricey locations, or union representation to urge improvements in living and work conditions. These shows hold viewers' interest, in large part, through suspense about which contestant will triumph. Advance knowledge of the winner would kill interest in the program. Contestants are, therefore, threatened with severe penalties were they to leak the information. Reality shows not only have lower production costs but also draw younger audiences, which bring higher advertising revenue. Because rivalries can be staged for most any activity, this lucrative genre has proliferated.

The music-based version, featuring amateur singers, was also a lucrative format that dominated the airways for a long time. These alternative genres muscle out violent programs in the "action and adventure" genre. For example, *American Idol*, a contest for talented amateur singers, was the number one television show for eight years, drawing more than 30 million viewers an episode (Koblin, 2015). It launched careers of talented participants, boosted slumping record sales, and yielded millions in ticket sales from concerts featuring the contestants.

At an earlier time, the Ed Sullivan variety show, which featured the talents of all types of entertainers, was immensely popular for 23 years. Norman Lear was the most prolific and creative producer of situational comedies that addressed controversial and socially relevant issues in humorous but emotionally touching ways (Campbell, 2007). He aired multiple sitcoms at the same time achieving top viewership. Each week over a million viewers were tuned in to these masterful socially relevant programs. These different types of hugely popular programs provide testimony that creative nonviolence sells.

The revolutionary advances in communication technologies in the current digital media culture have vastly diversified the sources of aggressive modeling. Through the capacity for interactivity, they have increased the power to personalize the valuation and legitimization of aggressive conduct. As the former FCC commissioner Nicholas Johnson has observed, the social costs of dealing heavily in violence are not only the untoward effects. An even greater casualty, he explained, is the squandered opportunities to use this powerful vehicle for human understanding and betterment. Chapter 8 reviews media-based social applications worldwide in which television serves as a powerful force for good.

Chapter 4

■ ■ ■ ■ ■ ■ ■

THE GUN INDUSTRY

The role of guns in our society and how they are managed has fueled intense public disputes. In his book *The Politics of Gun Control*, Robert Spitzer (2014) traces the historic changes in the functions that guns have served over the years. The form these changes have taken has inflamed the controversy over guns even further. The veneration of guns is rooted in this nation's heritage, with citizen militias fighting for independence, the U.S. Cavalry protecting settlers from Native Americans, and legendary heroic citizens stamping out rampant lawlessness in the frontiers of the Western expansion. Through events both historic and mythical, guns developed deep social and cultural roots in society.

During the agrarian period, hunting was a source of food. As society began to urbanize, hunting declined, but its heritage morphed into sport shooting. Modern urbanized society does not grow many hunters and gun sportsmen. Nor do heads of households go out to shoot a deer or a turkey for the family dinner. Growing urbanization, with ready access to lethal weaponry, begot gun crimes and fear of criminal victimization. These changes put into conflict two major constituencies residing in different regions in which guns are used for different purposes. In more rural regions of the country, guns are used mainly for hunting and sport shooting. Residents see themselves as law-abiding citizens pursuing their long-established way of life. In urban areas, guns are widely used to kill people in interpersonal disputes, criminal activities, and suicides.

In the gun controversy, progun groups are outraged by what they see as efforts to deprive them of their constitutional right under the Second Amendment to use guns for hunting and recreational activities, and to arm themselves for self-defense. Gun-regulation proponents are outraged at having their lives threatened and constrained by a radical gun lobby that opposes any sensible gun regulations. The Supreme Court's affirmation of gun ownership as a constitutional, individual right amplified the conflict between individual rights and public safety. Progun groups press their right to carry concealed weapons in formerly prohibited public places, whereas gun-regulation advocates are alarmed by the erosion of public safety. In this fray, gun advocates assert their unrestricted right to carry concealed weapons. The gun-regulation proponents assert their right to public safety.

Originally founded to promote training in marksmanship, the National Rifle Association (NRA) was formed by a former Union army general, who was dismayed by the deficient shooting skills of urban Union soldiers, and a military magazine editor. Another aspect of the NRA's mission was to support wildlife conservation by creating open lands for hunting. The latter program was funded by a tax on hunting rifles and ammunition. In its long history, the NRA adopted a moderate position regarding guns. It helped draft a number of laws that placed limits on gun sales, gun prototypes, and their use. For example, during the 1930s, NRA President Karl Frederick testified in support of a bill requiring a permit to carry a concealed weapon: "I do not believe in the general promiscuous toting of guns. I think it should be sharply restricted and only under licenses" (Rosenfeld, 2013). In the aftermath of the assassination of President John F. Kennedy with a military rifle purchased by mail order, NRA Executive Vice President Franklin Orth supported a ban on such sales. "We do think that any sane American, who calls himself an American, can object to placing into this bill the instrument which killed the president of the United States" (Rosenfeld, 2013). Helping to place limits on guns did not sit well with a group of NRA activists who opposed any gun regulations.

During the 1970s, the NRA decided to relocate its headquarters, considering Colorado more suitable to its mission than Washington, with its political climate. However, at the 1977 annual convention, dubbed the "Cincinnati Revolution," activists defeated the incumbents, a victory that transformed the NRA from a moderate association into a radical one. Under its new leadership, the primary focus shifted from hunters, sportsmen, and target shooters to lobbying for gun rights. In its politicization, the NRA gained legislative influence through coalitions with conservative lawmakers. The fight for gun rights was elevated to a wider struggle for freedom from intrusive government. Even some libertarians joined their ranks. Wayne LaPierre, the executive vice president and CEO, became the spokesman for the NRA. The movie star of biblical epics, Charlton Heston became its celebrity standard-bearer.

INNOVATIONS IN FIREARMS LETHALITY

The firearms that are produced and marketed have increased in lethality over time. In his richly documented book *Making a Killing: The Business of Guns in America*, Tom Diaz, a senior policy analyst at the Violence Policy

Center, demonstrates that the innovation of firearm lethality was driven by sagging gun sales rather than by consumer demand (Diaz, 1999). Several factors contributed to the stagnating sales of firearms. The shrinkage of rural populations eroded the hunting tradition. Urban youths were not socialized into hunting and sport-shooting activities. Another major problem facing the gun industry is that guns do not wear out, so owners have little need for new purchases. The growth market became mainly city dwellers arming themselves for self-defense, and criminal elements using guns for criminal activities. Andrew Molchan, the editor of a firearms magazine, described the problem of deficient market growth: "Without new models that have major technical changes, you eventually exhaust your market. You get to the point where 90% of the people who might want one have one already" (Ordorica, 1997).

William Ruger, a dominant gun maker, had a solution to stagnating sales—replacement through innovation: "We have a little moneymaking machine here. All we have to do is keep introducing the correct new products. . . . We operate on a philosophy that you have new stuff, and you have to have it annually" (Millman, 1992).

The gun makers innovated by increasing the killing power of their products rather than by improving their safety. This lethality took several forms. The new pistols are semiautomatics with larger magazines that hold more bullets of larger caliber. The manufacturers also made the pistols smaller for easy concealment. They call this type of pistol a "pocket rocket." Gun makers fight for a larger cut of the market share by boosting the firepower of their guns. Hemenway (1998) describes the gun makers' competition for greater lethality in their weaponry:

> Ammunition and accessories with "Rambo" appeal—bipods, flash suppressors, grenade launchers, laser sights, and expand bullets—have also been increasingly offered. Ammunition has come on the market with names like "Eliminator-X," "Ultra-Mag," "Black Talon" (whose razorlike talons could tear protective medical gloves, exposing doctors to infectious diseases), and "Starfire," (whose advertisements called it "the deadliest handgun cartridge ever developed for home or personal defense," with "fast knockdown" due to the "massive wound channel" it can create).

Juveniles and criminals switched from revolvers to the deadly semiautomatic pistols. The light, concealable, snub-nosed handguns called "snubbies" are criminals' favorite weapon (Albright, 1981). When James Oberg, the president of Smith and Wesson, was asked why the company sells "snubbies," he explained that the public demands it, "I sell the guns the market is demanding," as do the stockholders: "We supply dollars to our stockholders. For us, a great deal of the motivation is to run a profitable company" (Albright, 1981). After the interview, Oberg revised his statement in which profitability was tempered and serving public needs elevated as motivators for marketing this type of weapon.

These business practices are the unvarnished side of the right to bear arms. The enhanced lethality of weapons on the street sparked a "gun war." As police found themselves outgunned by more powerfully armed transgressors, they too switched to deadlier semiautomatic guns, in another financial boon for the gun industry. As a result, shootouts now are much deadlier.

The introduction of semiautomatic pistols boosted gun sales in an otherwise sagging market. Society has an inherently lethal commodity on its hands that is easily accessible and essentially unregulated in its form, distribution, marketing, and sales. Diaz (1999) brings a broader perspective on how society should look on guns and manage them. Because guns are a commodity that carries some public risk, he maintains that they should be regulated like other consumer products. However, as I consider later, with the Supreme Court providing constitutional protection for gun ownership and Congress granting the gun industry virtually blanket immunity from legal liability, the political climate favors deregulation rather than regulatory protections.

COSTS AND BENEFITS OF GUNS IN SOCIETY

Gun-friendly constituencies emphasize the benefits of guns. These include hunting and recreation as well as the sense of personal safety offered by firearms for self-defense. These constituencies also contend that an armed citizenry deters crime. However, it is difficult to get a reliable estimate of defensive gun use, let alone whether it is a crime deterrent (Cook, Ludwig, & Hemenway, 1997). There would be little public controversy if these were the only purposes for which guns were used. The societal problem stems from the laissez-faire commercialization of firearms of escalating deadliness coupled with lax regulations. Guns fall easily into the hands of juveniles and criminals who use them for criminal activities that incur heavy social and economic costs for society.

Progun constituencies typically consider only the social costs to criminal violence. The remedy they prescribe is tougher law enforcement, with stiffer prison terms for gun crimes. We will revisit this solution in a more detailed discussion of the broader social effects of guns. Guns come with a high cost to society that extends beyond criminal victimization. Most homicides occur in heated disputes among family members, acquaintances, and relatives rather than in criminal encounters. There are more deaths by gun suicide than by gun homicide (Brent, Perper, Moritz, Wartella, & Zelenak, 1991). This finding takes on added importance because it includes a rise in youth suicides. The presence of a gun in the home is a significant risk factor for adolescent suicides in part because young people tend to act impulsively. A despairing youth and a readily available gun make a dangerous mix (Brent et al., 1991). Children also figure prominently in accidental deaths by guns, often at home. Nonfatal injuries by semiautomatic firearms, which outnumber deaths, usually leave survivors with massive wounds that necessitate costly treatment and, in some cases, result in permanent disabilities. In their comprehensive analysis, Cook and Ludwig (2000) estimate that gun homicides, suicides, and accidental shootings cost society billions of dollars. *Mother Jones* enlisted economist Ted Miller, who quantifies societal costs of injurious activities, to assess the actual costs (Follman, Lee, Lurie, & West, 2015). He found that gun violence costs America $229 billion a year. They include huge prison costs, permanent physical disability and massive medical costs, lost productivity and quality of life, and a host of other long-lasting secondary costs.

The most pervasive effect of gun violence is its generalized impairment of the quality of life in a society. There are three properties of criminal victimization that enable a few violent incidents to instill widespread public fear. First, there is unpredictability, with no forewarning of when or where violence might occur. Random crimes are especially frightening because they make everyone feel vulnerable (Heath, 1984). The second property is the gravity of the consequences. Individuals are unwilling to risk being maimed or killed or having their child abducted, killed, or critically injured, say, in a school shooting, even if the probability is extremely low. Finally, there is the sense of uncontrollability, a perceived helplessness should one be the victim of an armed crime. The prevalence of gun violence in broadcast media and the heavy focus on murders on local network news reinforce the fear that one can become the victim of an armed crime.

The gun industry and the NRA, which is essentially the lobbyist of the industry, oppose virtually every gun regulation in the belief that even a sensible restriction to protect police, such as banning bullets that pierce bulletproof vests, disguises sinister intent on the slippery slope toward eliminating guns from society. Chris Cox, the executive director of NRA-ILA, the NRA's own lobbying arm, concisely expresses this slippery-slope mind-set: "Our opponents' long-term goal . . . is to ensure that no American can legally own or use any firearm for any purpose." In explaining the NRA's opposition to limiting gun purchases to one a month, Charlton Heston (1999) voiced the same argument, albeit via the metaphoric camel, and added a list of the most ruthless tyrants to underscore the perils of depriving people of guns: "It's the camel's nose in the tent. Look at Stalin, Mussolini, Hitler, Mao Zedong, Pol Pot, Idi Amin—every one of these monsters, on seizing power, their first act was to confiscate all firearms in private hands." Fear of a step-by-step march toward a complete ban on guns is a major obstacle to striking a balance between gun rights and public safety.

The gun industry faces a formidable moral challenge in justifying the production and marketing of large-caliber, semiautomatic rifles. They are unsuitable for recreation or hunting purposes. One man who went deer hunting with a semiautomatic rifle ended up killing five hunters and wounding three others (Butterfield, 2004)! In the competition for market share, new models have ever-increasing killing power. The gun manufacturers' moral evasion of the toll their products take in human life and the fear they engender in society at large requires skillful disengagement of moral self-sanctions. The sections that follow address the moral issue.

THE DISENGAGEMENT OF MORALITY

Moral and Social Justification

The social justifications clothe guns in the symbolism of patriotism, freedom, and individualism. The most embellished justification for the right of people to arm themselves was resoundingly presented by Charlton Heston when he was the president of the NRA. He framed his justification in terms of the Second Amendment: "A well regulated Militia, being necessary to the security of a free State the right of the people to keep and bear Arms, shall not be infringed." In his keynote address to the NRA, Heston (1999) provided a scary list of evil social forces, both governmental tyranny and criminal elements, against which armed people must protect themselves:

> The majesty of the Second Amendment, that our Founders so divinely captured and crafted into your birthright, guarantees that no government despot, no renegade faction of armed forces, no roving gangs of criminals, no breakdown of law and order, no massive anarchy, no force of evil or crime or oppression from within or from without, can ever define your Americanism. . . . The founding fathers guaranteed this freedom because they knew no tyranny can ever rise among a people endowed with the right to keep and bear arms. That's why you and your descendants need never fear fascism, state-run faith, refugee camps, brainwashing, ethnic cleansing, or especially, submission to the wanton will of criminals.

In an invited address at Stanford University sponsored by the Stanford Speakers Bureau, Heston's successor as president of NRA, Sandra Froman (2007), reaffirmed the constitutional right of individuals to have firearms to defend themselves:

> The simple truth, born of experience, is that tyranny thrives best where the government need not fear the wrath of an armed people. . . . I'm proud to be an American gun owner, and grateful to live in a

country where the basic human right of self-defense is guaranteed by a constitutional provision, and where that constitutional provision, the Second Amendment right to keep and bear arms, is there to protect all of the other rights that we hold so dear.

In 2011, the U.S. House of Representatives approved a bill granting individuals with a permit to carry concealed loaded weapons in their own states and the right to do so in other states, regardless of their gun policies. In justifying this law, Congressman Chris Gibson equated guns with freedom: "This bill is about freedom" (Collins, 2011). It is ironic that promoting a bill in the name of freedom takes away the freedom of inhabitants in other states that have chosen to disallow carrying concealed firearms.

In Froman's (2007) view, permission to bear arms has been especially liberating to immigrants and those of lower socioeconomic status: "If you look at history, gun bans have been used, many times, to prevent people of lower economic classes or immigrants from protecting themselves." The notion that guns are a blessing for immigrants and disadvantaged populations stands in stark contrast to reality. In fact, these are the very populations that are disproportionately the victims of gun violence (Cole, 2013). Guns take the heaviest toll of life in ethnic-gang turf wars, in fights over territorial rights for lucrative drug dealerships, and when used by others living a life of crime. Drive-by shootings in disadvantaged neighborhoods also take a toll on innocent lives. Nannette Hegerty, the police chief of Milwaukee, described the scene on the streets of the inner city: "We're seeing a very angry population, and they don't go to fists anymore, they go right to guns" (Zernike, 2006). We shall see shortly that the marketing practices of the gun industry make it easy for powerful firearms to fall into the hands of minors and criminals. Heston also used the poor to justify opposition to banning the easily concealed "snubbies": "The black and Hispanic women who clean office buildings until 3 a.m. and then walk home—of course, they want a handgun in their purse" (Hornblower, 1998).

In proclaiming the liberating power that subjugated people experience when armed, Ron Schmeits, one of Froman's successors as president of the NRA, told cheering gun-rights advocates that had the German people been armed during the Holocaust, "we wouldn't have had the tragedy we had there" (Altherr, 2009). The notion that a small group of armed citizens could have overthrown the crushing Nazi regime far exceeds any bounds of credibility. In the genocidal bloodbaths resulting from political mayhem in Africa, armed factions are slaughtering each other in appalling numbers with deadly weaponry supplied by Western nations.

Richard Feldman, an executive of a trade group representing gun manufacturers, invoked better self-defense as another type of justification for enhancing the lethality of guns: "If the gun has more stopping power, it is a more effective weapon" (Butterfield, 1999). The escalation of firepower is of the industry's own making. Recall that police were forced to adopt deadlier firearms because they were being outgunned by criminals. Some fringe groups with conspiracy mindsets are fueling rage over their marginalization and troubles with the law. They are heavily armed to protect themselves against an expected assault by governmental forces. However, the general public is not arming itself against social forces threatening to deprive them of their freedom of speech. Should such threats occur, they are countered by congressional and judicial means, not by armed force.

Euphemistic Language

Metaphors do the heavy lifting in sanitizing the policies and practices of the gun industry. In the opening remarks of her talk at Stanford University, Sandra Froman (2007) equated guns with freedom of speech and continued the metaphoric theme throughout her talk: "Now I'm sure you expected the President of the NRA to talk about guns, and I'll get to that. But the fight over your right to keep and bear arms and the fight over your right to speak out and make a difference are all a part of the same fight to protect and preserve the freedom that we Americans have as our brithright." People came to hear Froman address gun issues being debated nationally. Instead, they heard a diversional lecture devoted mainly to safeguarding the First Amendment. The students provided a forum for the NRA president to speak freely on gun issues.

After the metaphoric mutation of guns into free speech, Froman presented a historical analysis of the social changes in punitiveness for speaking out on controversial matters. She proclaimed her resolute defense of free speech against "social censors or government gag rule":

> What could happen to you in America if you said the wrong thing at the wrong time? In 1775, if you said the wrong thing at the wrong time, you could be tried for treason and hanged. In 1875, if you said the wrong thing, you might be ostracized by your peers or lampooned by the press. In 1975, if you said the wrong thing, you might get punched in the nose—on the other hand, you might get elected. Today, if you say or do the wrong thing, you might look up from your desk to find that you are today's thought police victim. . . . I'm here to defend outspoken points of view. I'm here to defend a marketplace of ideas that's not policed by social censors or government gag rules (Froman, 2007).

The point at issue is not the marketplace of ideas but rather the marketplace of guns. I am sure that Wayne LaPierre does not like being called a "gun nut," nor do advocates of gun regulation like to be called "loony leftists." However, both sides are free to say whatever they want about each other and their gun policies. They are doing so unrestrained by any formal social sanctions or legal prohibitions.

Froman (2007) then deplored the misuses of the First Amendment to justify protection of "marginal speech": "The First Amendment is supposed to protect our right to speak out on subjects of public importance. Yet the First Amendment has been treated so cavalierly of late that its core purpose, the protection of political speech, has been dangerously diminished. At the same time, the First Amendment has been used to justify protection of marginal speech that would make our founding fathers blush and turn over in their graves." Quite the contrary. The founders can repose serenely because the opposing constituencies are assailing each other unmercifully on the airwaves, in political campaigns, and on the floor of Congress with impunity.

The First Amendment was designed to protect all kinds of speech—including "marginal," offensive, deranged, or vile speech. Indeed, the Supreme Court has allowed very few exceptions to the constitutional protection of free speech. Froman suggests that protection of "marginal speech" diminishes the fundamental purpose of the amendment. Defending "marginal speech" does not diminish the amendment. Rather, it testifies to its robustness.

Froman did not name the "thought police" who she claimed prohibit free speech. Nor did she describe the nature of the "marginal speech": "People started twisting words as weapons, to gag their critics, to attack their political foes, to plead victimhood, or claim the moral high ground." Froman (2007) went on to describe the costs to society of silencing those it does not want to hear, citing Pasteur and Einstein as examples:

> In an open marketplace of ideas, you're always going to have a few crazy ideas, but by opening the door wide enough to allow those in, you also open the door to brilliant, world-changing ideas, from people like Louis Pasteur and Albert Einstein, both of whom were ridiculed at first by their professional colleagues for their uncommon views. The fact is, by seeking to silence those it doesn't want to hear, society is also silencing those it needs to hear.

Here again Froman focused on the wrong issue in the wrong marketplace, and on the wrong constitutional amendment. This triple evasion required a lot of linguistic camouflage.

In sum, speech about guns is not socially prohibited. By a linguistic sleight of hand that equates guns with free speech, Froman converted the Second Amendment, which affirms the right to bear arms, to a free-speech issue covered by the First Amendment. Her diversionary talk illustrates the power of language to mask what one does not want to talk about.

Most of the public alarm and controversy over gun violence centers on high-powered, semiautomatic rifles because of their enormous killing power. This type of firearm was styled after the military's automatic M-16, which was designed for instant mass killing on the battlefield. The civilian versions, with their large-capacity magazines, especially the Bushmaster AR-15, were used in mass killings (Follman, Aronson, & Lee, 2013).

Gun bans require specification of firearm features. The original federal assault weapons ban of 1994 listed several accessories of military rifles, including a pistol grip, detachable magazine, grenade launcher, and flash suppressor. In this compromise bill, a rifle was legal if it included only one of those features, so it was easy to circumvent the law. Semiautomatic firearms are vigorously protected by the gun industry because they are the most profitable items. As a result, heated semantic battles are fought over what a militarized rifle in civilian life should be called (Goode, 2013). Those who try to tighten gun laws call them "assault weapons." Gun advocates call them "modern sporting rifles." It is ironic that the gun industry itself advertised these rifles as "assault weapons" before linguistically sanitizing them as "sporting rifles." At first, the NRA refused to sell Phil Peterson's *Gun Digest Buyer's Guide to Assault Weapons* on its web site, but readily did so when Peterson retitled it *Buyer's Guide to Tactical Rifles*. Peterson said that after the 1994 ban, the gun industry "moved to shame or ridicule" those who called the militarized guns assault weapons (Goode, 2013). In the final analysis, restricting certain features would make little or no difference, because the gun industry will find ways to circumvent the bans.

After the gun lobby renders a ban ineffective, the difficulty in showing that the ban has any effect has been cited as evidence that gun regulations are ineffective. This neutering process is illustrated by a California law designed to slow down reloading. The law required empty magazines to be detached with a tool rather than with a finger ("Bullet button" used, 2012). It did not take gun makers long to find a way around this requirement. They simply devised a button that releases the magazine with the tip of a bullet and defined the bullet as a "tool." The gun makers called the "bullet button" assault weapon "California Legal." As this failed effort shows, whatever gun features are banned or altered the gun industry finds a way around them, mechanically and linguistically.

Advantageous Comparison

Reducing moral self-sanctions by means of advantageous comparisons is typically achieved by contrasting one's harmful activity with more egregious inhumanities. John Risdall, president of the gun manufacturer Magnum Research, used this common mode of corporate exoneration: "But don't tell me I'm immoral for selling this product. Did the people at Honeywell who were making components for nuclear weapons feel they could be doing something immoral? I don't think so. It was a business" (Diaz, 1999).

Heston used the Nazi persecution of the Jews in comparative justification for people arming themselves. He likened gun-regulation advocates to the Gestapo in terms of their pervasive dictatorial power: "I remember when European Jews feared to admit their faith. The Nazis forced them to wear six-pointed yellow stars sewn on their chests as identity badges. It worked. . . . So what color star will they pin on our coats? How will the self-styled elite tag us? There may not be a Gestapo officer on every street corner yet, but the influence on our culture is just as pervasive" (Heston, 1997).

The gun industry favors morally uplifting comparative associations, however. By equating guns with freedom of speech, the gun industry creates a comparison that is morally elevating. In an example of how the industry achieves this by linking its wares to just causes fought for by revered social reformers, Sandra Froman (2007) cited both Susan B. Anthony and Rosa Parks for moral uplift:

> Look at Susan B. Anthony. She demanded her rightful inheritance when she spent the last half of the 19th century fighting to give women the right to vote. And soon women everywhere realized that this was a birthright that should never have been denied. . . . What if Rosa Parks didn't reclaim her share of freedom, by refusing to move to the back of the bus? Thanks to Rosa Parks, no one has to go to the back of the bus, whatever your color.

Such comments are a diversionary, exploitation of the woman suffrage and civil rights movements in the service of the gun industry. Neither Susan B. Anthony nor those she inspired won women's voting rights with guns. Rosa Parks sparked the civil rights movement by nonviolent resistance to institutionalized discrimination. Given her commitment to social change by nonviolent means, she would probably be appalled to see her name used in support of the gun industry. For its comparative ennoblement, the NRA also recruited George Mason and Patrick Henry, who fought for the Bill of Rights, and distinguished scientists such as Einstein and Pasteur. Froman (2007) added other political figures and social reformers for comparative moral uplift.

> So before I go, I'd like to leave you with the wisdom of others who have also faced the decision of whether to fight or forfeit their own freedoms. 'To not speak one's thought, this is slavery.' That's Euripides. I say to each of you who has the courage to speak your thoughts: don't be afraid, you're reclaiming your freedom. President John F. Kennedy said, 'Conformity is the jailer of freedom.' And I say, political correctness, or 'PC,' as it's known, is just another way of asking you to please conform. . . . [M]ake up your own mind and say what you believe, even if someone disagrees with you. . . . And finally, 'Our lives begin to end the day we become silent about things that matter.' Martin Luther King said that.

To use President Kennedy and Martin Luther King Jr.—whose reform efforts were silenced when they were shot to death—to vindicate the problematic policies and practices of the gun industry is not only the height of irony. It is shameless.

No one is restricting people's freedom to talk about guns or to argue about whether the Second Amendment refers to an individual right or a collective right tied to an organized militia. Rather than misleading people with uplifting comparative metaphors, free speech is better served by public debate about the types of guns that are being produced, how they are marketed and sold, the need for background checks and safety instruction for those who want to buy them, and how to carve out the boundaries of gun-free zones.

Diffusion and Displacement of Responsibility

The gun industry does little to shift responsibility for the production of firearms itself. The constitutional protection of individual gun rights further reduces gun makers' qualms about how the gun business is run. However, the Second Amendment does not remove the moral issues involved in producing guns that are used for killing people rather than for sport and hunting. Lethal semiautomatic pistols are not designed for target practice or hunting elk. This section addresses the gun industry's moral disengagement from the manufacture of increasingly deadly wares, marketing and sales practices, and the granting of protections from civil liability.

Gun manufacturers make guns and then sell them to wholesalers who, in turn, sell them to retail dealers. Tracing guns used in crimes reveals that criminals often get their guns directly or indirectly through recent retail purchases rather than by theft. However, not all the guns used in crimes are recovered. About half a million guns are stolen annually, and about a third of incarcerated felons report that they get their guns by stealing them (Cook et al., 1997). In a Chicago sting operation, undercover police posing conspicuously as street gang members had no difficulty buying guns from licensed dealers (Butterfield, 1998). Weekend gun shows, where licensed dealers, unlicensed private sellers, and private individuals sell their firearms, are an unregulated marketplace for illegal gun sales. Another undercover operation was conducted by New York City in Nevada, Ohio, and Tennessee (City of New York, 2009). Undercover gun buyers told gun sellers that they probably could not pass a background check, or the seller allowed a female companion to purchase a gun in her name. The gun was then handed to the prohibited partner in an obvious straw purchase, in which someone buys guns legally for those who are barred from purchasing them (Keefe, 2009). Among private sellers, 67% sold guns illegally. And 94% of the licensed dealers sold guns to an obvious straw purchaser. In a similar sting operation in the online gun market, in over 60% of the cases, sellers were willing to sell guns to undercover buyers after they said they probably could not pass a background check or were too young to buy a gun (Goldstein, 2011). The high rate of illegal sales suggests that gun laws with inadequate regulatory oversight are of little value.

Gun lobbies oppose any effort to close the gun-show loophole. They compare gun shows with shows of benign products and characterize unregulated firearms sales as an expression of citizens' passion for freedom. Such portrayals are justifications for opposing background checks at gun shows. In the view of the NRA, such checks would criminalize law-abiding citizens:

> They [gun shows] are no different than book fairs, car shows or country cross-stitch shows—all of which share free speech, the right to assemble and the right to peaceable commerce between individuals. All of these assemblies represent the same thing: a gathering of Americans with a common passion—for freedom. . . . Anti-gunners call private individuals who sell a few guns from their personal collections—their personal property—the so-called 'gun show loophole' . . . [u]nderstand the 'closing' of the so-called 'gun show loophole' for what it means. It would make it a criminal act for peaceable, law-abiding citizens to buy or sell guns freely as they do today. (Keefe, 2009)

There are, of course, many local gun-control ordinances, some state laws, and a few federal ones. However, all too often they are of limited functional value because some of them are cosmetic, and most are unmonitored, unenforced, and easily circumvented. The gun lobby pressured Congress to defeat legislative efforts to close the gun-show loophole by requiring background checks at those sales. Having legislators justify their opposition to even minimal gun regulation makes it easy for gun sellers to justify their sales practices. Under a poorly monitored distribution system, manufacturers and wholesale distributors can shield themselves from knowledge of what happens to their guns in sales to the public. Unknowingness by design not only assuages moral concern, but permits deniability, nonresponsibility, and protection against legal liability. An executive representing gun manufacturers, Richard Feldman, succinctly described the nonaccountability for what happens to the guns that the industry produces: "We design weapons, not for the bad guys, but for the good guys. If criminals happen to get their hands on it, is not the manufacturer's fault. The problem is, you can't design a product and insure who is going to get it" (Butterfield, 1999). Ed Schultz, a Smith & Wesson executive, extended this view to children. The gun industry, he maintained, is faultless. Shooters are solely to blame: "The problem is not the guns. These people that they call children, in my mind, are little criminals and . . . ought to be held accountable" (Donn, 1995).

Built-in nonresponsibility in the gun-distribution system, exemption of gun dealers from reporting and accounting for missing guns in their inventory, unregulated sales at gun shows, and the absence of a national gun-tracking system allow everyone in the gun business to disown any responsibility for the guns used in crimes. Detrimental practices shielded from consequences do not change. The gun industry dumped in Southern states with lax gun laws firearms that ended up in the hands of young people and criminals in cities with tough gun laws. Ninety percent of the guns used in crimes in New York City were bought in other states. The city won a lawsuit against the gun dealer for negligent marketing and distribution practices (Kunkle, 2008).

A number of cities and counties in California filed a similar lawsuit. In an affidavit filed in support of the lawsuit, Robert Ricker, a former gun lobbyist and director of the main gun-trade organization who turned critic, reported that gun manufacturers knew that some corrupt dealers were selling guns to criminals through straw purchases. Gun makers agreed, under pressure from larger gun manufacturers, to maintain collective silence to protect against legal liability (Butterfield, 2003).

Ricker further contended that the gun industry resists weeding out corrupt dealers because doing so would acknowledge the problem. This could create potential liability. They even canceled formal meetings to discuss illegal sales, according to Ricker, for fear that it would be construed as admission of a problem and expose them to charges of negligence for their inaction. Not knowing what happened to their guns permitted deniability of responsibility. Noting the distinction in tort law between misfeasance and nonfeasance, Professor Richard L. Abel at the University of California at Los Angeles explains that it is much easier to adjudicate doing harm than doing nothing to prevent harm. Those within the industry willing to stop the illegal gun trade were pressured to remain silent. Ricker described it as a "see-no-evil, hear-no-evil" practice of evading firearms laws and regulations (Butterfield, 2003).

The California lawsuit was dismissed on the grounds that gun manufacturers cannot be held responsible because they are too far removed from the point of sale (Dolan, 2001). Wholesalers also argue that they, too, bear no responsibility because they are not selling guns to the public. Both the manufacturers and wholesalers use the additional exoneration that they are selling guns only to dealers with federal firearms licenses. They contend that it is not the industry's responsibility to monitor the dealers for what happens to the guns they sell them. They argue that this is the job of the federal Bureau of Alcohol, Tobacco, Firearms and Explosives, which licenses gun dealers. However, there are too few federal inspectors to oversee adequately what the dealers are doing. The agency lacks the resources to provide proper on-site inspections of how guns are sold. Given the high profits of illegal gun sales in the criminal market, corrupt dealers will figure out ways of getting around corrective measures if the responsibility is displaced entirely to understaffed and underfunded external regulators. The societal problem of inadequate gun regulation is exacerbated by the escalating lethality of the types of guns being manufactured. In short, the gun industry has created a distribution system with scant oversight that institutionalizes a culture of nonresponsibility for an extremely lethal product.

Sandra Froman portrayed the NRA as a tiny underfunded organization run by a skeleton staff. She explained that they achieve so much legislation with such meager resources because of their high credibility with lawmakers, who have great respect for NRA lobbyists:

> What I continue to find amazing is that we do so much with so little. People don't realize we really don't have a lot of people: we really have a very sparse staff. . . . And we're really able to accomplish a lot. Mostly because we have a lot of credibility on [Capitol] Hill, we always back up what we say with empirical data and our lobbyists are really well respected. . . . The NRA is still playing catch up. We still need to be better of making sure we have a secure financial foundation to continue to protect this fundamental right. (Froman, 2007)

Froman's characterizations of the NRA could not be further from the truth. The NRA is a powerful player in gun politics, not only by virtue of its ability to mobilize a passionate membership dedicated to gun rights as a superseding issue. With an apathetic electorate, a dedicated group organized around a narrow issue can exercise electoral power well beyond its numbers. Moreover, as we will see later, the American legislative system grants disproportionate power to small states with a sizable share of rural residents. The NRA wields powerful influence over legislators through both carrots (campaign contributions) and sticks (the threat of electoral opposition) (Spitzer, 2014). Although over half the state legislatures have granted the gun industry immunity from legal liability, the successful New York City liability lawsuit struck fear in the industry. It made enactment of a federal immunity law, which would preempt state laws, an uppermost priority and exercised its power to achieve it.

In 2003, Senator Larry Craig of Idaho and House members Don Young of Alaska and Barbara Cubin of Wyoming, states with small populations but significant progun constituencies, sponsored a bill in both houses of Congress to grant the gun industry special exemptions from legal liability. The bill received the White House's blessing. Senator Craig, who was sometimes referred to as the "senator from the NRA," was on the board of the NRA, as were Young and Cubin.

A group of law professors wrote to the Senate, opposing the bill because it had only a few immunity exceptions. In their view, the bill "would largely immunize those in the firearms industry from liability for negligence. . . . No other industry enjoys or has ever enjoyed such a blanket freedom from responsibility for the foreseeable and preventable consequences of negligent conduct" (Clark, 2003). The bill passed the House with a sizable majority, and 56 senators added their names to it. However, progun supporters had several problems with the bill that required bringing further pressure to bear on legislators. More senators had to be lined up to make it filibuster-proof. Opponents to the bill had added two amendments that the NRA strenuously opposed. These would extend the federal ban on assault weapons and the requirement of background checks on those seeking to buy guns, both of which were due to expire in 2004. The bill could have passed easily, but it was pulled from the Senate floor and reintroduced in 2005, after the expiration of the assault weapon ban and the required background checks.

The Brady Campaign to Prevent Gun Violence submitted a request to the House and Senate ethics committees to examine the conflict of interest of Craig, Cubin, and Young's co-sponsoring the liability exemption bill while serving on the NRA board. Their request fell on deaf ears. When the bill was reintroduced in the Senate, it passed handily, granting gun makers and dealers sweeping liability exemption for misuse of firearms. An amendment to narrow the bill to permit cases to go forward against gun dealers who engaged in "grossly negligent" or reckless sales practices was defeated. Another amendment to narrow the bill by barring suits by municipalities claiming group damage but preserving the right of individuals to sue was also summarily defeated.

In a statement following the vote, Senate Majority Leader Bill Frist, who had pulled the original bill from the Senate floor the previous year, defended the gun industry as being unjustly targeted: "America's crime problems will be solved not by unjustly targeting the gun industry for the criminal actions of others" (Murray, 2005b). Supporters for blanket immunity justified it on the grounds that frivolous lawsuits would bankrupt the domestic gun industry, leaving the nation dependent on foreign gun makers for weaponry. Frist voiced this justification: "The Department of Defense faces the very real prospect of outsourcing side arms for our soldiers to foreign manufacturers" (Murray, 2005a). The Brady Campaign planned to challenge the constitutionality of the law.

Senator Edward Kennedy of Massachusetts expressed moral outrage at the blanket exemption of gun dealers from responsibility for negligent conduct: "The unholy alliance and control of the legislative process against the safety of our citizens is immoral, and it's a disgrace" (Murray, 2005a). Senator Jack Reed of Rhode Island expressed concern about barring individuals who have been seriously harmed from suing irresponsible dealers: "This legislation would bar the door to courthouses for real people" (Murray, 2005b).

Behaving in ways that displease the gun industry is not only politically risky, especially in southern and midwestern states, but it can be financially costly as well. Smith & Wesson agreed to set restrictions on how dealers sold its handguns. The NRA denounced the firm as capitulators. The nation's largest gun wholesalers refused to distribute Smith & Wesson guns. Some shooting-match organizers told the firm to stay away from their events.

The company was vilified in Internet chat rooms, ostracized within the gun industry, and promptly terminated as a client by a law firm representing other gun manufacturers (Butterfield & Hernandez, 2000). These concerted punitive actions had the semblance of antitrust activity. A spokesman for the company had this to say about the pummeling: "We've been getting beat up pretty bad, and the whole idea seems to be a boycott of Smith & Wesson products." The chastisement brought the wayward company back in line. It submitted a clarification that watered down the agreement to meet the dealership instructions.

Minimization of Adverse Effects

Disputes about the effects of guns depends, in large part, on the different functions they serve in rural and urban settings. In rural life, guns mainly are used for hunting and recreation. In urban life, guns are mainly instruments of interpersonal violence and criminal activity. Rural residents fear that gun regulation will lose them their way of life. Urban residents fear that inadequate gun regulation can lose them their lives. In progun states and rural regions within states, politicians are gun shy about even sensible safety regulations.

As noted earlier, the production and marketing of deadly semiautomatic firearms compared to the earlier firearms lack social and moral justifiability. Semiautomatic firearms are a quantum leap in lethality. Sandra Froman (2007) camouflaged this issue with her oft-used misleading comparative metaphors and minimization of the escalation of lethality:

> The analogy between old-style firearms and modern firearms isn't too different from the analogy from hand-written manuscripts and the old printing presses that we had to the internet today. The technology has changed, but the need for the protection has not. . . . It's true for the First Amendment as well as the Second Amendment.

These lethal firearms, in Froman's view, are no more than a technologically advanced way of protecting free speech. Lawrence Keane, a spokesman for the gun industry's trade association, tried to cloak the lethality of the semiautomatic assault rifle in benign recreational terms as a "modern sporting rifle" (Shear & Davis, 2015). These rifles are military-style assault weapons, not sport-hunting rifles. An executive of a trade group representing gun manufacturers trivialized the deadly escalation of firepower as a standard competitive business practice: "Just like the fashion industry, the firearms industry likes to encourage new products to get people to buy its products" (Butterfield, 1999). The problem with this comparative exoneration of the gun industry is that guns can impair the quality of life in communities by heightening people's fear of becoming the victims of criminals wielding lethal firearms. Changes in fashions have no injurious public consequences.

Sandra Froman (2007) argued, by minimization through advantageous comparison, against states' requiring gun purchasers to receive instructions on how to operate guns safely, except in some shortened form that can be easily turned into a token gesture: "And why should we have training at all? We don't have a literacy test for people to vote. That's a right that you have, just like the Second Amendment is a right." She compared the requirement for instruction in gun safety with Jim Crow–era literacy tests intended to disqualify mainly African American voters. This is a strange comparison, indeed, of framing the requirement of safety instruction as violating a civil right.

In a speech he delivered at the National Press Club, Charlton Heston trivialized public concern over armor-piercing bullets and easy access to small concealable pistols that are the preferred weapon in criminal activities. He characterized regulatory initiatives regarding these menacing products thus: "I want to save the Second Amendment from all these nitpicking little wars of attrition, fights over alleged 'Saturday night specials,' plastic guns, cop-killer bullets and so many other made-for-prime-time non-issues invented by some press agent over at gun-control headquarters that you guys buy time and again" (Seelye, 1997). Efforts to regulate guns were, in his view, "merely tyranny with manners."

The Bureau of Alcohol, Tobacco, Firearms and Explosives is the main federal agency responsible for overseeing the enforcement of gun regulations. However, under the pressure of the gun lobbyists, Congress has succeeded in keeping the bureau leaderless, understaffed, and underfunded. These obstructions have prevented the bureau from doing its job of safeguarding the public from gun violence. In the past, the president had the authority to appoint a director without the approval of Congress. However, doing the gun lobby's bidding, lawmakers changed the law, requiring Senate confirmation of a nominee (Schmidt, 2013). Because of the Senate's delay in voting on nominees, this bureau has had six acting directors in the past eight years.

Attribution of Blame

The gun industry attributes the blame for the escalating lethality of its firearms to public demand. Recall Olberg's explanation of why Smith & Wesson was selling small lethal pistols that are easy to conceal: "I sell the guns that the market is demanding" (Albright, Alexander, Arvidson, & Eason, 1981). As we have seen, innovative lethality was driven by sagging gun sales and the battle among gun makers for the small-gun market, not by consumer demand.

Another form of moral evasion by selective attribution of blame is to disembody the gun from the shooter in a false dichotomy that places the blame entirely on the shooter. This is apparent in the NRA's exonerative causal slogan "Guns don't kill people. People kill people." Removal of the gun from the mix of causal factors absolves guns—and by extension their manufacturers—of any role in gun violence. This causal detachment is analogous to claiming that it is people, not carcinogenic cigarettes, that are a major determinant of lung cancer. Human agency is executed through means. The gun toter is the agent. The gun industry provides lethal means to achieve desired ends.

Guns vary in killing power. In a mass shooting with a semiautomatic rifle, the size of the magazine and the ease of reloading determine the scope of the slaughter. For example, in the massacre in Fort Hood in 2009, Nidal Hasan was able to exact a heavy toll by extending the 10-round magazine to 30 rounds with easy reloading: "He was dropping his magazines and reloading in a matter of seconds" (Fernandez, 2013). Because of the semiautomatic feature, mass shootings last less than five minutes (Schmidt, 2014). The make of the gun and the size of the magazine in the hands of the shooter determine how many people die and are maimed. For someone intent on killing a lot of people, a semiautomatic weapon with a large-capacity magazine is the means of choice. Its killing power is tragically displayed in the rash of mass shootings. In accord with modeling theory, the recent years have witnessed a sharp rise in the number of mass shootings and the number of people killed in each tragic assault (Schmidt, 2014).

A gun is inanimate, but through its intended firepower it also influences a person's sense of agency (Selinger, 2012). The agentic transformative power of a gun is captured in an ad from an earlier era for the Colt .45 gun. It was often called the great equalizer that made the little man as big as the largest man in the West. The amount of carnage in a shooting spree is determined by the complex interplay of the psychological makeup of the shooter, the social conditions that drove the shooter to commit mass murder, the nature of the setting, and the lethality of the gun. From a moral standpoint, in addition to the shooter, the gun industry bears some responsibility for developing and marketing guns of ever-greater lethality in the competition for market share. The gun lobby is also a contributor to the causal mix by blocking any gun reforms regarding the lethality of the firearms and bullets being marketed and by staunchly defending easy access to them. Lawmakers beholden to the gun lobby are facilitators as well. In short, mass killing is determined by a complex array of facilitators, rather than solely by the psychological makeup of the assailant.

The causal cliché is widely used for deflecting accountability. William Ruger, a gun manufacturer, argued, "Guns are a matter of individual responsibility. You keep coming back to the fact that people kill people, not guns" (Ayres, 1994). Professed helplessness to do anything about mass killings is another form of moral evasion for opposing any constraints on the gun industry. One lobbyist used this type of evasion in opposing a community's effort to ban bullets that can penetrate police body armor. In his argument, in which he euphemistically refers to armor-piercing bullets as "objects," he claimed that you can't moderate behavior by controlling objects. Quite the contrary. Fewer police are likely to be slain with armor-piercing bullets if they are banned with strict enforcement than if the bullets are freely available.

Claimed Futility of Gun Regulations

Construing gun regulation as futile is a novel form of moral disengagement in gun violence operating at the effects locus of moral control. In a mass shooting at a movie theater in Aurora, Colorado, one of the weapons was a military-style semiautomatic rifle. As we have seen, this type of assault weapon had been banned for civilian use. However, lawmakers allowed the ban to expire in 2004. Immediately after the mass killing, the governor of Colorado argued against stricter regulation of the gun industry: "If there were no assault weapons available and no this or no that, this guy is going to find something, right? He's going to know how to create a bomb" (Crummy, 2012).

Recall that the killing power of firearms is heightened by enlarged ammunition clips and semiautomatic firing. The Aurora gunman used a semiautomatic rifle equipped with a 100-bullet magazine. Countless lives were spared because his gun jammed partway through his planned massacre. The governor used the alleged inevitability of mass killings by other means as a justification for exempting firearms from regulatory consideration.

Little attention is paid to the government's obligation to protect the public's right to safety. A gunman in a suburban Wisconsin town killed three women and wounded four others in a spa where his estranged wife worked. The mayor of the town repeated the futility justifications that fend off public demands for gun reforms: "Try as we might, these can't be avoided" (Yaccino & Davey, 2012).

Gun-rights advocates point to the fact that killers obtain guns legally as evidence that regulations won't stop massacres. They argue that mentally unstable people, not guns, are the problem. A gunman intent on killing as many people as possible obviously can massacre more of them with magazines that hold 30 rounds than with ones that hold 10 bullets. In arguing against a proposed law in Colorado to limit the capacity of ammunition clips, one lawmaker claimed that "it makes no difference to public safety if there are 10 rounds in a magazine, whether there are 15 rounds in a magazine or whether there are 30 rounds" (Frosch, 2013).

Gun advocates who oppose the regulation of firearms on the grounds that they cannot be regulated run the risk of hoisting themselves in their own petard. If a society faces the threat of repeated massacres of innocent people by killers using military-style weapons that no amount of regulation can prevent, society has a moral obligation to protect its citizens by banning such weapons. It cannot be a helpless victim of a gun industry. What the claim of the futility of gun regulations ignores is a fundamental question: What are military-style semiautomatic weapons with unlimited ammunition clips doing as merchandisable lethal products in a civil society?

In keeping with the selective allocation of blame, the solution proposed by the gun industry is to increase the severity of punishment for crimes committed with a gun. This translates into lengthier prison terms, "Harsh sentences for gun criminals," as Froman (2007) puts it. The massive growth of the prison population is imposing increasing social and economic burdens on society. We turn to the high societal cost of the remedy proposed by the gun industry next.

Types of Public Victimization by Crime

Crimes victimize people in three major ways. The crime itself victimizes them. It also impairs the quality of life in the community at large. A few random shootings can strike fear in an entire community. Fear for their own safety permeates people's lives. Many people are arming themselves. They live behind bolted doors, avoid most downtown areas, and desert their streets at night. A district attorney describes in concrete terms the life-constricting effects of feared violence: "Gun violence is what makes people afraid to go to the corner store at night" (Ludwig & Cook, 2003). Crime rates have been declining but, paradoxically, fear of criminal victimization is rising. A campaign to arm the populous requires high arousal of public fear. Carrying concealed guns in public places has been legalized by state and local legislatures. The fact that people are walking around with concealed weapons renders more of the public environment threatening. One senator introduced a bill on the Senate floor that would allow individuals from states permitting concealed gun carrying to arm themselves while visiting other states (Collins, 2009). The senator argued, for example, that this interstate gun-carrying license would make Central Park "a much safer place." The ill-chosen example, which probably contributed to the narrow defeat of his bill, backfired. Introducing guns into Central Park could not make it safer because there had not been a gun homicide in the park for years. Converting Central Park into a gun-carrying zone could only make it a scary place.

The second societal cost of gun violence, which bears on the gun industry's prescription of longer jail terms, is the heavy drain of prison costs on tax revenues. Lengthier and mandatory prison terms cram the prisons. In California it costs about $47,000 per year to incarcerate an inmate (Legislative Analyst's Office, 2014). Lengthier prison sentences have a significant impact on how governmental resources are spent. Higher education and prisons compete for money from the same general fund. The public demands that criminals be put away for long stretches, but is unwilling to pay the heavy costs. Indeed, legislators get voted out of office if they raise taxes. As a consequence, prisons are draining funds for higher education. After adjustment for inflation, since 1980 spending has decreased by 13% for higher education but has swelled by 436% for prisons. California now spends more on prisons than on higher education (Sankin, 2012). As university budgets and financial aid shrinks, tuition increases are used to cover the shortfalls. The diversion of scarce resources from education to prisons drives out the neediest students from higher education. The irony of this budgetary diversion is that education provides the best escape from crime and poverty.

In the third public victimization by crime, the huge cost of operating the prison system detracts from educational and developmental programs during children's early formative phase of life. The enabling guidance equips them with personal resources for a prosocial life path. School failure, accompanied by association with antisocial peers, forecloses many prosocial options in later life (Patterson, 1986). Dropping out of school increases the likelihood of incarceration and joblessness, which incur high social and economic costs (Sum, Khatiwada, McLaughlin, & Palma, 2009). Once youths get into trouble with the law, they cycle through the prison system, with most coming out worse than when they went in. Investment in developmental programs that cultivate children's interests, aspirations, competencies, and resilient beliefs in their efficacy to realize their hopes pays large future dividends.

Hawkins and his collaborators demonstrate how early efforts to promote academic and social development yield huge long-term benefits (Hawkins, Catalano, Kosterman, Abbott, & Hill, 1999). In this school-based program offered in the elementary grades, teachers were taught how to manage classroom behavior and promote academic development. Parents were taught parenting skills and how to support their children's academic work. And the students were taught how to manage interpersonal problems and resist peer pressure to engage in transgressive activities.

The effects of this early multifaceted effort were assessed in a six-year follow-up when the students were 17 years old and in high school. Compared with children in matched control schools that did not offer the program, those who had the benefit of this early developmental aid were more likely to remain in school, were less likely to repeat grades, had higher academic achievement, and were less likely to commit violent crimes, take up heavy drinking, father a baby, or give birth to one. The children from poor, crime-ridden areas benefitted the most. Society can provide prosocial guidance for children living in disadvantaged conditions or pay dearly later. Youth violence is better reduced by investment in education than investment in incarceration.

Derogation of Opponents

A poorly regulated lethal product that is shielded from civil liability and incurs high economic and social costs predictably draws heavy critical fire. Challenges to the morality and civic responsibility of the gun industry's troubling practices are met with infuriated reactions by progun advocates. They see themselves as patriotic defenders of freedom, unjustly attacked by an arrogant, elitist minority bent on banning guns from society. During his presidency of the NRA, Charlton Heston launched the most blistering counterattack. He directed his heaviest fire at the press, especially their coverage of publicly alarming shootings (Heston, 1999). In his portrayal, "[t]his harvest of hatred is . . . sold as news, as entertainment, as governmental policy" as "reporters perch like vultures" and "news anchors race to drench their microphones in the tears of victims" (Heston, 1999). The reason for the "screeching hyperbole leveled at the gun owners" is that "their story needs a villain. . . . And we're often cast as the villain." Concerning media requests for interviews after a tragic shooting, Heston said, "The countless requests we've received for media appearances are in fact summons [*sic*] to public floggings, where those who hate firearms will predictably don the white hat and hand us the black." Heston turned his wrath on political advocates of gun regulation as well. Members of the Clinton administration, whom he called "Clinton's cultural shock troops," were his archenemies (Heston, 1997).

With his election to the presidency, Obama drew the heavy fire. Wayne LaPierre likened him to a "South American dictator" bent on eradicating the Second Amendment. In his conspiratorial analysis, LaPierre warned NRA members that Obama was trying to "lull gun owners to sleep to win re-election." "Lip service to gun owners," LaPierre warned, is just "part of a massive Obama conspiracy" to deceive voters and hide his true intentions to destroy the Second Amendment during his second term (Markon, 2012). In his rallying cry at an NRA convention, LaPierre (2012b) beseeched his followers to "save America and our freedom."

Other members of the NRA also characterize gun policies in terms of repressive police control. For example, gun regulation is called "political terrorism." Development of a gun-tracking system is "police control," and federal agents are "jack-booted government thugs." Proponents of gun regulation are "loony leftists." It works both ways, however. One former top lobbyist for the gun industry had some uncharitable things to say about the NRA: "You have a situation where you have a bunch of right-wing wackos at the NRA who are controlling everything" (Butterfield, 2003). And the NRA resents being called a "merchant of death."

The fierce factional dispute is not about guns per se, Heston explained. Rather, it is just one aspect of the larger cultural war construed by progun advocates as between arrogant elitists and rank-and-file Americans who love their country and are courageous guardians of America's cherished values and freedoms (Heston, 1997). The reframing of the nature of this war is larded with widely used oppressive imagery of "thought police," "lock-step conformity," "cultural warlords," "self-appointed social engineers," "Clinton's cultural warriors," and "apologist for criminals." Within this wrathful declamation, Heston (1999) incongruously presents himself as a judicious conciliator seeking to restore harmony between the warring factors. "I am asking all of us, on both sides, to take one step back from the edge of that cliff. Then another step and another, however many it takes to get back to that place where we're all Americans again."

The mission of the NRA, in Heston's clarion call to his constituents, is to defend hard-fought freedoms from zealous gun haters. In the emotive discourse, guns are linked to a list of other types of freedoms:

> Our mission is to remain a steady beacon of strength and support for the Second Amendment, even if it has no other friend on the planet. We cannot let tragedy lay waste to [sic] the most rare and hard-won human right in history. A nation cannot gain safety by giving up freedom. This truth is older than our country. "Those who would give up essential liberty, to purchase a little temporary safety, deserve neither liberty not safety." Ben Franklin said that. If you like your freedoms of speech and of religion, freedom from search and seizure, freedom of the press and of privacy, to assemble and to redress grievances, then you'd better give them that eternal bodyguard called the Second Amendment. The individual right to bear arms is freedom's insurance policy, not just for your children but for infinite generations to come. That is its singular, sacred beauty, and why we preserve it so fiercely." (Heston, 1999)

Guns are sanctified not only by association with other cherished freedoms but also by linkage to broader sociopolitical matters that resonate strongly with most NRA constituents. This is achieved by establishing one's moral credentials through past conduct. Having behaved charitably or righteously establishes one as a good person with license to behave prejudicially in the future. This process of self-entitlement to prejudicial conduct is well documented by Monin and his collaborators across diverse areas of functioning (Effron, Cameron, & Monin, 2009; Monin & Miller, 2001). Heston used his march with Martin Luther King Jr. for civil rights as his moral voucher to courageously champion "white pride" in the nation's founders, who created the constitutional gun right. This moral self-license spilled over into indiscriminate condemnation of entire categories of people who, in Heston's view, undermine the social and moral order, including feminists, homosexuals, African Americans, and new age religionists:

The Constitution was handed down to guide us by a bunch of those wise old dead white guys who invented this country. Now some flinch when I say that. Why? It's true . . . they were white guys. So were most of the guys who died in Lincoln's name opposing slavery in the 1860s. So why should I be ashamed of white guys? . . . Now, Chuck Heston can get away with saying I'm proud of those wise old dead white guys because Jesse Jackson and Louie Farrakhan know I fought in their cultural war. I was one of the first white soldiers in the civil rights movement in 1961, long before it was fashionable in Hollywood, believe me, or in Washington for that matter. . . . Mainstream America is depending on you, counting on you to draw your sword and fight for them. These people have precious little time or resources to battle misguided Cinderella attitudes, the fringe propaganda of the homosexual coalition, the feminists who preach that it's a divine duty for women to hate men, blacks who raise a militant fist with one hand while they seek preference with the other, and all the New-Age apologists for juvenile crime, who see roving gangs as a means of youthful expression. . . . Freedom is our fortune and honor is our saving grace. (Heston, 1997)

This call to arms also illustrates the moral engagement subfunction in the mechanism of social and moral justification. Fighting gun regulation becomes a source of patriotic honor, moral courage, and self-pride. Each year the National Council of Teachers of English presents its Doublespeak Award to public figures or organizations employing deceptive, euphemistic, or self-contradictory ways. In 1999, the award went to the National Rifle Association, with special recognition of Charlton Heston for his "artful twisting of language to blur issues," and the "invocation of patriotism, reverence, love of freedom, and the opposing use of dread words to color the opposition" (National Council of Teachers of English, 1999).

Former mayor of New York Michael Bloomberg, who cofounded a coalition of mayors and supports grassroots activism for gun reform, has been especially targeted by gun enthusiasts. They have branded him a "nanny statist fascist" and an "anti-gun bigot" (Barbaro & Goldstein, 2013). Their intense hatred went beyond words. One man sent letters to him and the director of his advocacy organization that were laced with the poison ricin. The letters asserted that the right to bear arms is a "God-given right" that the sender would protect to his death.

The NRA's uncompromising opposition to any restriction on firearms gives gun-regulation advocates a lot to be incensed about. Here are some of the restrictions opposed by the NRA on the basis of the slippery-slope scenario: banning semiautomatic assault weapons, armor-piercing bullets, and easily concealable street crime guns; requiring safety trigger locks; limiting purchases to one gun a month; background checks for purchases at gun shows; requiring gun dealers to examine their inventories for lost or stolen guns; implementing a national system for tracing guns used in crimes; imposing civil liability for egregious sales practices; and banning gun carrying in public parks and recreational areas.

ESCALATION OF THE GUN WAR

The Second Amendment had always been interpreted to mean that individuals can own guns to answer the call as a civilian militia to defend their country. In a controversial split decision across ideological lines, the Supreme Court granted gun rights to individuals independent of militia service (*District of Columbia v. Heller*, 2008). Professor Michael Waldman (2014) of the New York University School of Law has traced the political machinations, spearheaded by the NRA, that turned the Second Amendment permitting citizens to bear arms for the militia defense of a free state into a private right of self-defense. Now that the Supreme Court has ruled that gun ownership is constitutionally protected, court battles are being fought to determine the limits of the right to bear arms. The Second Amendment is ambiguously crafted and mentions only militias. In its narrow ruling, the Supreme Court affirmed a constitutional individual right to keep handguns in one's home for self-defense and hunting. This ruling, involving federal jurisdiction in the District of Columbia, left many issues unresolved. It ruled on only half of the amendment, the gun ownership part, but not on the ambiguous "bear arms" portion. The Supreme Court's ruling on the right to gun ownership did not extend to state gun laws or what people can do with their guns outside their homes. In a subsequent ruling, the Supreme Court reaffirmed that individual gun rights are protected against state and local gun laws (*McDonald v. Chicago*, 2010). It will take further litigation to spell out what "bearing arms" means in this day and age. As in other amendments, a gun right is not an absolute one. Vigorous court battles will be fought over which restrictions are constitutional and which are not.

The legislative battles have now begun over regulations of who can own guns, their commercial sale, and how and when they can be carried. An attachment to a credit card reform bill has granted individuals the right to carry loaded firearms in national parks. A political conflict brewing in Tennessee is a harbinger of battles to come over sensible gun regulations. Not to be outdone by the federal government, Tennessee legislators extended the right to carry concealed guns to playgrounds, campgrounds, underdeveloped recreational areas, and nature trails (Good sense in Tennessee, 2009). More people packing guns in public places can make them more dangerous through criminal gun use or accidental shootings. However, the law granted major cities and suburban counties the right to ban guns from these public places. Some cities imposed a ban. The law permitting concealed weapons in public recreational places is tearing apart the social fabric of communities. In a community that lifted the gun-carrying ban, the president of a group of nature park patrons called this action putting "guns over children." Many families plan to avoid public recreational areas, fearing for their safety. A school will not schedule athletic contests and events in parks where concealed firearms are allowed. In response an NRA spokesperson said the law can be improved by having parks post gun-free times when school events are being held.

The gun lobby is bringing pressure to bear on legislators to deny localities the right to enact ordinances that place any restrictions on guns (Good sense in Tennessee, 2009). Revoking local jurisdiction by preemptive legislation shifts local control to state legislators, who are more easily influenced by lobbyists. Safety concerns have roused the public in the otherwise gun-friendly state of Tennessee to confront their politicians on whether they will side with the gun lobby or with their constituents. As one mother put it at a local hearing, "Are you going to hear the voices of the unarmed?" (Good sense in Tennessee, 2009). This example foreshadows the types of challenges the gun lobby is likely to mount against efforts to institute some regulatory limits to protect the public from being victimized by guns given their ready availability.

The U.S. Senate chamber is another powerful locus of control over gun legislation. Its disproportionate rural representation tends to favor progun initiatives. With a population of 37 million, California is represented by 2 senators. The 20 smallest states—in many of which a significant portion of the population is rural—are represented by 40 senators, even though their combined population is less than that of California (MacGillis, 2009). The founders created the Senate to safeguard the rights of the smaller states. Ironically, they now wield considerable legislative power over the big, heavily urbanized ones. Progun constituents regard the Senate as an ally in the drive to remove gun restrictions and curtail civil liability.

The conflict over firearms spilled over to funding research designed to inform public policy (Luo, 2011). The Centers for Disease Control and Prevention funded research on gun-related injuries and deaths as a public health issue. Ken Cox, the chief lobbyist for the NRA, pressed for the elimination of the injury center on the grounds that "they were promoting the idea that gun ownership was a disease that needed to be eradicated." Efforts by progun legislators to eliminate the center failed, but they stripped the budget for it. The congressman who spearheaded the budgetary amendment reflected on the reason for the prohibition: "We have the right to bear arms because of the threat of government taking over the freedoms that we have." Funding for firearms research has been cut not only at the CDC, but at the Justice Department as well.

Thousands of gun dealers along the Mexican border are running a brisk business in military-style weapons, some of which end up in the hands of violent drug cartels. These weapons take a heavy toll on human life and strike fear in the society at large. In an effort to stem gun trafficking, the Bureau of Alcohol, Tobacco, Firearms and Explosives requested an emergency rule requiring gun dealers in this border region to report bulk sales of assault rifles. Wayne LaPierre of the NRA objected to reporting gun sales on the grounds that it would penalize U.S. hunters and those arming themselves for self-defense without solving Mexico's violence problems (McKinley, 2009). He did not explain why thousands of gun dealers set up shop along the Mexican border to sell military-style weapons. In response to a *New York Times* editorial, a National Shooting Sports Foundation blogger challenged the alleged amount of gun trafficking (Brassard, 2009). The writer also objected to the requirement to report such sales as an infringement on Second Amendment gun rights because the sales take place in a foreign country. He reiterated the view that gun regulation is a step toward gun ban: "Registration is a necessary precursor to confiscation, which is precisely what many politicians ultimately would do with many classes of firearms" (Brassard, 2009). The request for the emergency rule was shelved. The NRA filed a lawsuit against the firearms bureau requiring gun dealers along the Mexican border to report bulk sales of semiautomatic rifles (Savage, 2011).

During a killing spree in Tucson that left Congresswoman Gabrielle Giffords gravely injured and many others dead or wounded, the assailant was subdued while trying to reload his pistol with another large-volume magazine clip to continue the massacre (Lacey & Herszenhorn, 2011). He would have killed more people, but he dropped the magazine while trying to reload, and a woman kicked it away. In a tragic irony, a nine-year-old girl who was among the dead had appeared in the book *Faces of Hope*, featuring children born on the day of the terrorist attacks on the World Trade Center and the Pentagon. The Tucson killings prompted yet another showdown between gun rights and public safety. Gun rights handily carried the day. Proposed legislation to ban large-volume magazines and improve background checks at gun sales never materialized. Lawmakers who controlled the agenda refused to consider any gun legislation. A short time after this killing spree, the Crossroads of the West Gun Show convened, with business as usual, a few miles from the scene of the shooting. An undercover investigator was sold a gun at the show after he told the private seller that he probably couldn't pass a background check (Lacey, 2011).

At the national trade show in Las Vegas at about the same time, Lawrence Keane, vice president of the National Shooting Sports Foundation, proclaimed that "gun control is a failed social experiment, and it is time to move on" (Nagourney, 2011). In attribution of blame, Keane explained that guns were not the problem. It was the failure of the mental health systems and the kin of the assailant who were at fault in the Tucson massacre. The maker of the high-capacity magazines that the assailant used enlisted the familiar advantageous comparison in opposing any restrictions on the sale of enlarged magazines: "To point any fingers at the gun industry is ignorant. That's like pointing a finger at Ford and blaming them for car deaths." The comparison was not a smart choice. Hundreds of Ford Pinto drivers, in fact, perished in flames because of faulty car design. The magazine manufacturer added another exonerative advantageous comparison that trivialized public calls for safety legislation, "It's the same kind of panicked reaction you get after a hurricane. It's over, and everyone wants to get shutters." Gun dealers were confident that public shock would not spur any legislative initiatives. The president of the National Shooting Sports Foundation voiced the view that Congress is fully on the side of gun rights.

The Tucson shootings produced no congressional action, even though a congresswoman was targeted and suffered severe head wounds. Concerned over negative media attacks in reelection races, congressional proponents of gun safety decided not to oppose gun rights initiatives in the gun fight (Democrats and gun control, 2011). In an effort to depoliticize the gun controversy and salvage some modicum of gun reform from the Tucson tragedy, President Obama proposed bringing together people with different views on the issue—gun-rights and gun-safety proponents, law enforcement officers, retailers, and manufacturers—to come up with some legislative or administrative remedies (Calmes, 2011). However, a White House advisor explained that this search for common ground should focus on the people, not the guns, that is, on how to keep lethal weapons out of the hands of the unfit.

Despite the concessionary agenda, in a blatant show of power, Wayne LaPierre turned the president down with the constitutional justification: "Why should I or the NRA go sit down with a group of people that have spent a lifetime trying to destroy the Second Amendment in the United States?" He placed the blame for shootings on harmful people: "It shouldn't be a dialogue about guns; it really should be a dialogue about dangerous people." LaPierre not only rebuffed the president's efforts to protect the public against mass shootings, but urged his followers "to vote against Mr. Obama so that he couldn't try to deprive them of gun rights through Supreme Court appointments in a second term" (Whitney, 2012).

Buoyed by the Supreme Court's ruling on guns in public places, the gun lobby redoubled efforts to push for extensions of gun rights that alarmed citizens who have no interest in arming themselves. With the growing ascendancy of the NRA, advocates of gun reform shifted their efforts from regulating guns to regulating the public places where people can carry concealed firearms. Even this limited regulation, however, met with little success, especially in gun-friendly states. This hurried campaign, especially in state legislatures, is essentially designed to make the Second Amendment an absolute right to carry concealed guns anywhere at any time. In a growing assertion of states' rights, the governors of Wyoming and North Dakota signed bills proclaiming that federal regulation of firearms is invalid if the guns are produced and used in their states (Johnson, 2010). A Montana sports shooting association filed a lawsuit challenging federal interstate commerce authority to regulate guns. In a rush to expand gun rights, Virginia approved bills that permit individuals to carry concealed weapons in bars and repealed the ban restricting gun purchases to one gun per month (Urbina, 2010).

The politicization of guns has moved onto college campuses, one of the safest societal settings, where gun violence is rare. In the polarizing divide, Students for Concealed Carry campaign for the right of students to be armed and Students for Gun Free Schools want guns off campus (Pérez-Peña & Saulny, 2013). Colorado passed a law granting college students the right to carry concealed firearms on campus. The armed students are being housed in a separate dormitory (Frosch, 2012). Some faculty members fear that having armed students in classes creates an intimidating climate that can stifle free and open discussion of controversial issues. Some faculty refuse to see armed students in their offices, a prohibition that will undoubtedly be challenged legally. Exploiting notorious cases of campus sexual assaults, gun-rights advocates and the gun lobby pressured states to pass laws permitting faculty members and students to be armed on college campuses (Schwarz, 2015). The legislative response has split mainly along political party lines, with Republican-controlled states legalizing concealed guns on campuses. This gun controversy illustrates how a campus that was free of any gun violence was drawn into a socially polarizing conflict by the assertion of gun rights.

An enacted federal law now permits people to carry guns in their luggage on Amtrak trains. The NRA filed a lawsuit challenging the constitutionality of a federal law prohibiting people aged 18 to 20 from buying handguns and carrying them concealed in public places. Progun advocates assert that 18- to 20-year-olds who can defend their country should have the right to defend themselves. Critics characterized the move to arm teenagers as "breathtakingly irresponsible" (Handguns for 18-year-olds?, 2010). The 2012 Republican national platform opposed any gun legislation that would restrict the capacity of ammunition clips for semiautomatic guns (Cooper, 2012). A loosely organized "open carry" movement lobbied for the unrestricted right to carry visible firearms that would make it an ordinary practice as individuals go about their everyday activities.

Gun-rights advocates use self-defense as the main justification for laws granting individuals the right to carry concealed handguns in public. However, this justification does not fare well when compared with how concealed handguns are actually used. An extensive analysis of concealed-carry shootings found that only 3% were lawful self-defense (Violence Policy Center, 2015). Rather, most of the guns were used for criminal homicides, murder-suicides, and suicides. These findings indicate that carrying concealed weapons risks lethal violence rather than preventing it.

Under the initiative and pressure of the NRA, the state of Florida passed a law called "Stand Your Ground." It permits individuals to use deadly force in public places with protection from criminal prosecution if they believe they face harm. Unlike under existing self-defense laws, under the new statute, individuals do not have the duty to retreat first. They can legally resort to deadly force if they believe they are in imminent peril. The NRA's chief lobbyist lauded the law as a "critical turning point in what has become our proactive approach to gun-rights activism" (Brown, 2012). In a preemptive defense of the law, viewed as advancing "firearm freedom," she forewarned that the "anti-gun media" will misrepresent the law as a return to the days of the Wild West of "shoot first and ask questions later" (Brown, 2012). NRA lobbyist Marion Hammer, who had a heavy hand in promoting the legislation, justified it as needed because "activist judges and prosecutors" favor criminals. She reassured tourists that they had nothing to fear as long as they were law abiding. LaPierre issued a warning to lawmakers. "Politicians are putting their career [*sic*] in jeopardy if they oppose this type of bill" (Brown, 2012).

Florida's expanded self-defense law became a model for other states that quickly adopted it under pressure from the NRA, despite opposition by police, judges, prosecutors, defense lawyers, and bar associations. Mark Glaze, the director of Mayors against Illegal Guns, said of the NRA drive to expand the public places where concealed weapons can be carried: "Both directly and with cutouts like ALEC [the American Legislative Exchange Council], the N.R.A. is slowly and surely and methodically working at the state level to expand the number and kind and category of places where people can carry concealed, loaded weapons and use them with deadly force" (Goode, 2012).

George Zimmerman, a self-appointed community watch volunteer, acting on suspicion suggestive of racial profiling, pursued and killed an unarmed black teenager, Trayvon Martin. Martin was returning home from a local store with candy and iced tea. Zimmerman left his car and continued to pursue Martin on foot even though the police dispatcher told him not to do so. In the ensuing altercation, Zimmerman shot and killed Martin. Zimmerman was set free without being charged with the shooting or any judicial review of it, because he claimed he was acting in self-defense. Zimmerman displaced the responsibility for killing to divine agency, expressing no regret over it because he was following "God's plan." "We must worship a different God," replied the father of the slain teenager, "because there is no way my God would have wanted George Zimmerman to kill my son" (Robles, 2012). The teenager became a victim by being in the wrong place at the wrong time and because of the existence of a hazardous self-defense law. Critics argued that the passage of a law that gives people the right to shoot someone if they feel threatened makes public places more dangerous, not safer.

Martin's tragic death sparked massive public outrage, demonstrations, and demands that the assailant be arrested and brought to trial. New York Mayor Michael Bloomberg launched a national grassroots campaign to get state legislators to amend or repeal the law that gives individuals a "license to murder" in public places if they feel threatened (Anderson, 2012). He argued that the law undermines the integrity of the justice system, threatens public safety, and makes it difficult to prosecute suspected shooters. Speaking for the NRA, LaPierre used diversionary offense as the mode of defense. He impugned the media for singling out the Florida killing: "You manufacture controversy for ratings," he charged. "You don't care about the truth, and the truth is the national news media in the country is a national disgrace" (Yaccino, 2012).

In the face of national outrage, Zimmerman was charged with second-degree murder. The trial turned the unarmed victim into a criminal assailant. The jury acquitted Zimmerman on all counts. This outcome raised again the issue of race and justice in society. Public protest regarding the broader issue of public safety fell on deaf ears. In a show of power wielded by the NRA, in less than two weeks after the shooting, two U.S. senators introduced legislation requiring states to permit visitors to carry concealed weapons licensed in another state. In response to the Florida shooting LaPierre again used the strategy of offense as the best defense (Yaccino, 2012). He blamed the media for sensationalizing the Zimmerman case and accused them of ignoring the crimes of everyday life because they do not attract ratings and sponsors.

The verdict inferring that one is legally justified in shooting and killing an unarmed person on the basis of perceived threat struck fear in families nationwide. It belied the NRA slogan that an armed American is a safer America. Because the unarmed Martin, walking home, posed no actual threat, the shooting made any youth from a negatively stereotyped group vulnerable. Clothing associated with racial profiling and supposedly indicating dangerousness—a "hoodie" in Martin's case—raised the risk. Parents considered changing their children's clothing and advised their children to behave deferentially and cautiously outside the home so as not to provoke an attack. The lax self-defense law apparently made the social environment scarier for families.

The NRA's stated aim is to make carrying a gun a common, normative practice. A fearful populace, primed for self-defense with guns, is a huge boon for the gun industry, and more so if women are arming themselves. Spin-off businesses treat lethal weapons as innocuous accessories. For example, the fashion industry is marketing stylish clothing with special pockets for concealing a weapon. This enables armed women to look stylish while carrying a gun. The industry also markets fashionable handbags with a special compartment for a weapon. Catchy names for clothing include Elite Discreet and Gun Tote'n Mamas for handbags. Stylish male gun accessories also are being marketed. Turning a lethal device into normative gear is a significant change in cultural values and morality.

Exercise of Political Power to Block Gun Reforms

As described earlier, under a change of leadership the NRA shifted its focus to political advocacy and vigorous opposition to gun-regulation laws. The NRA portrays itself as a defender of the interests of hunters, sportsmen, and those who want to protect their households and families. Lily Raff McCaulou (2012), a hunter and sportswoman, takes issue with being lumped with the gun-rights lobby. She argues that the NRA shows little interest in hunting. Rather, its major focus is on opposition to the control of militarized rifles, large-capacity ammunition clips, and buyer background checks. This agenda mainly serves the interests of gun makers. The hunting tradition, McCaulou explains, is threatened not by bans on rifles and ammunition magazines but by the devastation of habitats. To serve the interests of hunters, she contends, the NRA should be a strong defender of the environment, as it was originally.

The NRA mounts well-financed campaigns, both directly and through its affiliates, to increase its political clout in statehouses and Congress, not only in general elections but also in primary contests, in which candidates are selected. When in power, each of the two major political parties carves out districts with large majorities for its side to ensure victory. Incumbents either have no opponents or face only token challengers from the opposing political party. However, the battle for political control is fought even in safe districts in primary contests. Because of low voter turnout in primaries, a well-organized faction with an extremist agenda can defeat established incumbents. The NRA unseats even progun incumbents in primary contests, if these lawmakers do not fully hew to the NRA line. Debra Maggart, the leader of the Republican lawmakers in the Tennessee statehouse, was a staunch supporter of gun rights, including the right to carry guns in bars (Confessore, Cooper, & Luo, 2012). Then she balked on a bill, euphemistically called the "Safe Commute Act," that would allow people to have guns in their cars in parking lots. The NRA collaborated in a harsh campaign to defeat her, using mass media ads, billboards, and mailings. She described the multipronged assault that ran her out of office: "They said I was shredding the Constitution, I was putting your family in danger, I was for gun control, I like Barack Obama" (Confessore et al., 2012). At the national level, Senator Richard Lugar of Indiana was defeated in the primary by a challenger whose beleaguered national campaign was mired in the issue of whether God wants rape victims to become pregnant. Such defeats in primary elections added a new verb to the political lexicon: being Lugared.

In genuinely competitive general elections, the NRA's political clout is considerably weaker than the political power attributed to it (Johnson, 2012). In many of these races the NRA-backed candidates win the primaries but lose in general elections despite heavy financial backing from the NRA. Nevertheless, enough well-established incumbents have been defeated in primary elections to make the NRA politically intimidating. Extreme tactics by well-organized minorities in primary contests fuels the politically polarized divide.

The advent of digital production technology has ushered in a transformation in manufacturing. It enables freelancers to alter banned gun components and customize guns to their liking from digitalized models and print them on home 3D printers. Cody Wilson, the founder of Defense Distributed, commented on the futility of banning gun components in the era of digitalized production: "This isn't 1994." He declared, "The Internet happened since the last assault weapons ban" (Greenberg, 2013). He was already preparing a preemptive strike against the gun ban that Senator Diane Feinstein, the NRA's prime nemesis, was planning to introduce in the Senate: "We want to preempt Feinstein, to eat their lunch" (Greenberg, 2013). Wilson uploaded his blueprint for a 3D-printable gun magazine, which several thousand individuals downloaded. Wilson, who calls himself a "crypto-anarchist," cast the controversy over guns as a fight between individual freedom and state control. His followers found his combative approach much to their liking. "The liberty crowd loves it," he declared (Greenberg, 2013).

Congress renewed the ban on plastic guns, which don't show up on metal detectors and scanners. This has become a serious problem with the advent of 3-D printing. However, the lawmakers left a huge loophole. The bill requires a metal part, but it can be snapped on and off, which essentially defeats the purpose of the law (Condon, 2013). Senator Charles Schumer could not imagine why anyone would undermine public safety over a non-removable piece of metal on a plastic gun: "Who in God's name wants to let plastic guns pass through metal detectors at airports or stadiums?" (Fram, 2013b). He underestimated the tight control the NRA exercises over a group of lawmakers. The NRA announced that it would oppose any law requiring a permanent metal part on the grounds that a nonremovable metal piece "would infringe on our Second Amendment rights." Schumer's proposal for a permanently attached metal piece was defeated. Because it is a 10-year renewal of the detachable version, this law will not be revisited for a long time. This type of regulation is further testimony that lawmakers apparently still are unable to pass a law regulating guns, whatever form they take and whatever threat they pose.

The new manufacturing technology elevates the challenges to the management of guns in a society to a new level. As the preceding examples illustrate, without moderation in the nation's gun culture war or moral restraint in the manufacture, marketing, and sale of guns of mass killing power, not only the gun industry can easily circumvent any new regulations. Private individuals using digital manufacturing technology can now do so. In a deeply divided society that cannot find common ground even on modest gun reforms, anyone with customized guns will elevate the threat to public safety.

The NRA has a wide reach well beyond the legislative arena. A number of cities have arranged voluntary gun buyback programs, in which people turn in their guns for privately funded gift certificates. On the second anniversary of the serious wounding of Congresswoman Gabrielle Giffords and the killing of others in a mass shooting in Tucson, the city scheduled a voluntary gun buyback program funded by private donations and Safeway gift cards. Todd Rathner, a Tucson, Arizona NRA national board member, threatened to sue the city for illegally destroying guns. The city attorney countered that the law applies to guns seized by police, not to guns turned in voluntarily by their owners. If the city did not comply, Rathner warned, he would get state lawmakers to pass a law to prohibit the practice. In a show of power, he asserted, "[W]e'll pursue it either through litigation or legislation" (DaRonco, 2012). Gun promoters would not welcome images of long lines of people turning in their guns. This effort to suppress a voluntary benign activity that is privately funded appeared to be more concerned with image management than with gun preservation.

TEST OF SOCIETY'S ABILITY TO ADOPT SENSIBLE GUN LAWS

Mass shootings come and go, but their impact on public attitudes regarding gun laws is much the same. Immediately after a gun massacre, there is a small increase in public support for tightening gun laws. However, such massacres rapidly fade from public consciousness and legislative concern until the next rampage arouses brief concern anew. This pattern of attitudinal change repeats itself regardless of whether the massacres occur in elementary schools, high schools, colleges, theaters, shopping centers, churches, military bases, or workplaces. No public place provides people with safety from semiautomatic guns and their spray of multiple rounds of bullets. Nor is any particular group safe from random killing sprees in the public places they frequent. Gun violence is a form of threat where a few incidents can change the quality of life in society at large because of the unpredictability of the threat and the gravity of its consequences (Bandura, 1986).

Vanquished Hope for Gun Reform

Shortly before Christmas in 2012, Adam Lanza assembled a huge arsenal of guns and ammunition. He shot his mother to death, then drove to the Sandy Hook Elementary School in Newtown, Connecticut. Before committing suicide, he killed 20 first-grade children and six adult staff members with 154 bullets fired in under 5 minutes. The death toll would have been much higher were it not for teachers who sacrificed their own lives to protect the children. One of the teachers crammed a group of children in a closet and cupboards, enabled others to run away, and was shot shielding the ones remaining in her classroom. The nation was shocked and enraged by the massacre of little children. The polarized collision between gun rights and public safety rights, reactivated by this dreadful event, shed light on how moral disengagement at the individual and social-systems levels influenced the ongoing gun dispute.

Despite the horrific nature of this tragedy, reactions by the NRA in the aftermath followed the same scenario that is reenacted after each new mass killing. The NRA offers condolences but lies low, knowing that massacres are quickly supplanted in public consciousness by other newsworthy events. The issue quickly fades from congressional debate as well. Another strategy, designed to stifle any talk of gun reforms, condemns any talk about the role of guns in the massacre as political opportunism that exploits people's grief in a time of mourning. Wayne LaPierre set the tone: "While some have tried to exploit tragedy for political gain, we have remained respectfully silent" (Goldstein, 2012). In an even more outlandish charge of opportunism against President Clinton after the Columbine shooting, LaPierre contended that Clinton was "willing to accept a certain level of killing to further his political agenda and his vice president, too" (Pear, 2000).

After the Newtown shooting, several progun lawmakers accused their critics of exploitation. The aide to Congressman Jim Jordan proclaimed that it was "time to mourn, not to debate policy" (Shear, 2012). Iowa Congressman Steve King joined in the denunciation, "political opportunists didn't wait 24 hours before they decided they were going to go after some kind of a gun ban" (Shear, 2012). His aide, Brittany Lesser, echoed the talk taboo "amidst the funerals of these brave young children and adults" (Shear, 2012). King also trivialized the effect of real guns by comparing them to childhood cap guns: "We all had our cap pistols when I was growing up, and that didn't seem to cause mass murders in the street." In his prepared statement as the top Republican on the Judiciary Committee hearing on the causes of gun violence, Iowa senator Chuck Grassley extended the prohibition beyond gun talk to suspending any congressional action: "Although Newtown and Tucson are terrible tragedies, the deaths in Newton should not be used to put forward every gun control measure that has been floating around for years" (Grassley, 2013).

It was widely assumed, especially among those favoring tougher gun laws, that the Newtown shooting would be the galvanizing event that finally forced polarized factions to find common ground for reasonable gun laws. The president of the Brady Campaign to Prevent Gun Violence, Dan Gross, found reason to be optimistic: "It's different because no decent human being can look at a tragedy like this and not be outraged by the fact that it can happen in our nation." The collective outrage, he reasoned, would force change, "because this time, we're really poised to harness that outrage and create a focused and sustained outcry for change" (Cooper, 2012). The governor of New York, Andrew Cuomo, also considered the tragedy a "wake-up call for aggressive action" (Cooper, 2012). Senator Richard Blumenthal of Connecticut explained why this was different: "The atrocity was so staggering and brutal that I think it struck a chord and captured attention in a way that is unique" (Salant, 2013). Even the ultraconservative media mogul Rupert Murdoch announced that the time had come for a change in gun policies: "When will politicians find courage to ban assault weapons?" he asked (LoGiurato, 2012).

Others found plenty of reasons for pessimism. Pointing to the long record of failed attempts to regulate guns, they saw poor prospects for significant changes in gun laws. One mass killing after another elicited condolences and outrage but no gun reforms. Under the more forceful pressure in the aftermath of the Newtown massacre, lawmakers may make some token changes with relief that another gun crisis has been weathered. What came as a surprise was the swift, collective moral disengagement by progun proponents while the young victims were still being buried. Wayne LaPierre announced that the NRA would fight any legislative efforts to tighten gun laws (Stolberg & Kantor, 2013).

With an enraged public and President Obama vowing gun reform, the usual silent strategy by the NRA no longer worked. After a week without making a statement, the NRA took to the airwaves. Wayne LaPierre called a press conference but disallowed any questions (Lichtblau & Rich, 2012). In a defiant statement, he exempted the gun industry from any role in school shootings, instead blaming Hollywood, video games, a violent pop culture, and gun-free school zones. They "demonized" gun owners and insinuate "that guns are evil and have no place in society," he complained (LaPierre, 2012). He depicted lawmakers who oppose arming school personnel as enablers of school violence: "They tell every insane killer in America that schools are the safest place to inflict maximum mayhem" (Collins, 2012c). The root cause of gun violence, he claimed, resides in mental illness. Senator Schumer of New York likened LaPierre's displaced causal attribution to analyzing the causes of lung cancer without talking about cigarettes. In the TV appearance, LaPierre characterized the news media as "an anti–Second Amendment industry in [Washington, D.C.]" (Hersh, 2012). LaPierre's proposed remedy for school shootings was to place armed security guards and armed volunteers in every school in the nation. Teachers could be armed as well.

The NRA's press conference and La Pierre's appearances on national talk shows did not go well. The tragedy was too horrific to be neutralized by oft-used moral justifications for lax gun regulations. Congressman Tim Murphy, who represents the Newtown district, described the transcript of LaPierre's news conference, which he received while leaving the funeral of one of the children, as "the most revolting tone deaf statement I've ever seen" (Briand, 2012). People were taken aback by the compassionless gun extremism defiantly expressed as the murdered children were being buried.

The NRA's call to arm schools drew opposing reactions. Progun states welcomed the proposal. The NRA publicized workshops instructing teachers on how to handle guns. Proregulation states were appalled by the proposal. Families that did not want guns in their schools denounced the NRA directive. New York tabloids dubbed LaPierre a "Gun Nut" and the "Craziest Man on earth." Arming schools to defend themselves drew harsh criticism from other quarters as well. The governor of New Jersey, Chris Christie, objected on the grounds that it would turn schools into "an armed camp for kids" without making them safer (Cosker, 2012). LaPierre opted for comparative self-defense of his proposal: "Why is the idea of a gun good when it's used to protect the president of our country or our police, but bad when it's used to protect our children in our schools?" (Castillo, 2012).

New York State promptly passed the strictest gun regulations in the nation. Governor Andrew Cuomo stated his position bluntly, "No one hunts with an assault rifle. No one needs 10 bullets to kill a deer" (Halbfinger & Kaplan, 2013). Governor Dannel Malloy of Connecticut voiced his objection to arming schools as a violation of his state's values: "That is not who we are in Connecticut, and it is not who we will allow ourselves to become" (Applebome, 2013).

President Obama appointed Vice President Joe Biden to convene a task force to formulate a set of proposals on how to reduce gun violence. The response of the NRA to the announcement of the task force made it clear that there would be no search for common ground. After attending a meeting of the Biden task force, NRA officials defiantly stated that the organization will fight any legislative attempt to tighten the nation's gun laws (Jennings, 2013). The NRA officials declared that they were defending law-abiding gun owners and the Second Amendment, and singled out "criminals," "madmen," and the "collapse of the federal prosecution of violent criminals" as those who should be blamed for gun violence. They threatened to block any proposed gun regulations: "We will not allow law-abiding gun owners to be blamed for the acts of criminals and madmen." They further announced that they would enlist lawmakers in this effort: "[W]e will now take our commitment and meaningful contributions to members of congress [sic] of both parties who are interested in having an honest conversation about what works—and what does not" (O'Keefe, 2013).

Even before the Biden task force met, David Keene, the president of the NRA, dismissed Vice President Biden as an antigun ideologue: "This is somebody who's bombastic and really does think that anybody who disagrees with him is not only wrong but crazy" (Baker, 2012). After President Obama's reelection, Keene announced, "We have to be prepared to fight him on each front, rally friendly elected officials, persuade those in the middle and let all of them know that gun owners will not stand idly by as our constitutional rights are stripped from us" (Cooper, 2012).

In their efforts to ward off any legislative initiatives to strengthen gun laws, gun advocates faced the task of defending lax regulations that provide the means for mass gun violence. This required reducing moral qualms about the types of guns being manufactured and how they are being sold and used. The constitutional protection of gun rights was a major justification. Some of the more ardent progun activists construed the Supreme Court ruling as granting law-abiding citizens the absolute right as citizens to buy whatever type of gun they want and to carry it wherever they go. In response to the Newtown massacre, Governor John Kasich of Ohio declared that "we don't want to erode the Second Amendment rights of law-abiding citizens" (Nagourney, 2012). Charlton Heston, then the president of the NRA, faced a similar situation in 1999 when thousands protested the NRA Convention in Denver shortly after the mass killing at Columbine High School in Colorado. Heston proclaimed "we cannot, we must not let tragedy lay waste to [*sic*] the most rare, hard-won right in history," he said, referring to the Second Amendment right to bear arms (Hendren, 1999).

A hearing of the Connecticut state legislature added a human face to the conflict between gun rights and public-safety rights. At the hearing a grieving father whose son was slain in Newtown testified in favor of a ban on military-style weapons. He questioned the justification for these types of firearms: "I still can't see why any civilian, anybody in this room, in fact, needs weapons of that sort. You're not going to use them for hunting, even for home protection," he said. Gun devotees shouted "Second Amendment," as he spoke (Muskal, 2013). A staunch gun advocate paraphrased Heston's rallying cry—"You can have my guns when you take them from my cold, dead hands"—and spoke with equal passion against any gun regulations: "I will tell you here today, you will take my ability to protect my Victoria from my cold, dead hands" (Codrea, 2013). The attendees applauded their advocates' arguments as if it were a debate.

Causal Displacement to Mental Illness

Affirming a constitutional gun right cannot entirely eliminate moral qualms about the bodies of little children ripped apart by bullets. The mode of moral disengagement that does heavy duty—attribution of blame—shifts the focus from unjustifiable lethal firearms to the mental health of the gunman and the inadequacy of mental health services of the nation. Causal analysis, which severs agents from their means of action, has a long history in the justification of gun violence. It goes back to the causal cliché that people, not guns, kill people. This disjointed view of causation continues to be recited. "I think it's more of a mental health problem than a gun problem," said one congressman (Shear, 2012). Another House member also claimed that the mass killing of children is not a gun problem: "It's a people problem. It's a culture problem" (Collins, 2012c).

There have been proposals to create a national database of the mentally ill to prevent them from buying guns (Brennan, 2012). Wayne LaPierre explained the necessity for a national mental illness registry: "We have a mental health system in this country that has completely and totally collapsed. We have no national database of these lunatics" (Gertz, 2012). Given his organization's staunch opposition to a national gun registry on privacy grounds, the proposal to invade the privacy of people with mental illness is the height of hypocrisy. An overwhelming majority of the mentally ill are nonviolent; many of them do not own guns and have no intention of buying any. Moreover, a good number of them may be proponents of banning guns altogether. There is a marked difference between requiring individuals who want to buy guns to undergo background checks and listing individuals on a national registry as mentally ill who are not seeking to buy guns. This Orwellian scheme violates people's privacy rights for the sake of shifting attention away from guns of mass destruction to mental illness.

Human violence is a product of a complex interplay of personal characteristics, environmental influences, precipitating events, and sometimes fortuitous occurrences. Hence, prediction of violence from personal characteristics alone is disappointing because it is founded on a truncated causal model that ignores the other interacting determinants of behavior. A causal model that omits interacting social determinants of violence is inherently limited in its predictiveness. Mental illness is only a minor factor in predicting gun violence (Swanson, 2011). Only about 4% of violence in its varied forms is attributable to mental illness (Monahan, 2014). If all mental illness could be cured, Monahan argues, it would leave 96% of violence that is due to other causes. Everyday gun violence has more to do with fights for proprietary rights over lucrative illegal drug markets, gang warfare, organized crime, and other subcultural norms that legitimize gun use and ready access to lethal firearms.

The public greatly overpredicts violence by the mentally ill. When individuals are asked to judge the violent proclivity of a person in a vignette, 61% rate the individual as likely violent if the person is dubbed a schizophrenic, but only 17% do so if the person is dubbed a troubled person (Pescosolido, Monahan, Link, Stueve, & Kikuzawa, 1999). The mainstream media coverage of the mass shootings reinforce the stereotype that, as a group, the mentally ill are dangerous people. Wayne LaPierre (2012a) elevated the demonization to the utmost, characterizing the mentally ill as "genuine monsters . . . that are so deranged, so evil, so possessed by voices and driven by demons that no sane person can even possibly comprehend them." In point of fact, over 90% of those with serious mental illness are not violent. The violence rate is even lower if they do not abuse alcohol or drugs or have no history of aggressive behavior. For the small number who do aggress, their actions most often involve hitting a family member rather than assaulting a stranger (Monahan, 2014). The seriously mentally ill use guns mainly to kill themselves rather than to kill strangers.

Predicting mass shootings is even more daunting because of their rarity. Rare events are the result of a unique constellation of factors interacting with each other such that, were one or a couple of the factors absent, the shooting would not occur. Unique constellations of causes provide few predictive commonalities. Moreover, factors contributing to a unique combination of influences lose some of their predictiveness when they are considered separately from each other, because some of their causative influence may derive from their mutual influence. For example, neither bizarre beliefs alone nor substance abuse alone may be conducive to aggression, but in combination, they may increase the likelihood of aggressive behavior.

Researchers try to create a profile of mass killers from case studies of them. Because many of them die by their own hand or by police bullets, researchers have to rely on psychological postmortems to judge a killer's psychic life and motivation from whatever public information is available. Of special interest are early signs of odd behavior that foreshadow later violence. One of the commonly mentioned attributes of mass killers is that they tend to be loners, isolated from family and friends and alienated from mainstream society. If they lead reclusive lives, as many of them do, they shield bizarre beliefs from corrective social feedback. They plan their assault methodically and carry an arsenal of firearms and ammunition to take as many lives as possible. Apparently, most of these assailants expect to die either by suicide or by forcing the police to kill them.

The problem with such profiles is that they yield high false-positive predictions, with nonviolent individuals being judged as prone to violence. Countless loners with bizarre beliefs do harbor resentments, but fortunately the vast majority conduct their lives as best they can without acting on those beliefs. However, some who lead bleak, despondent lives with festering grievances, conspiratorial attributions for their personal failures, and radical ideological beliefs can be provoked by precipitating events to act violently on their grievances. Whether or not disturbed individuals act violently will depend, in large part, on their self-regulatory ability to keep their psychological troubles in check. Alcohol and drug abuse, which impair self-control, and instances of rash behavior are often indicants of deficient self-regulatory capabilities.

In an opening statement on *Meet the Press*, Charlton Heston (1997) elaborated the causal cliché that it is bad people, not guns, that do the harm: "There are no good guns. There are no bad guns. Any gun in the hands of a bad man is a bad thing. Any gun in the hands of a decent person is no threat to anybody—except bad people . . ." However, guns differ in their inherent lethality. Consequently, a "bad" person will kill many more people with a gun of mass killing capacity than with a gun of limited killing capacity. Treating guns as inherently identical, neutral tools and ascribing the problem solely to the mental health of the gunman, for which no one bears responsibility, makes it easy to achieve collective moral exoneration for recurrent killing rampages.

Robert Levy, the chairman of the Cato Institute, used causal displacement to mental illness and the futility justification to argue against gun regulation. He argued that with millions of guns in circulation, any restrictions on new guns would have little effect. Instead, "early detection and treatment of mental illness" can reduce the risk of mass killings (Baker & Landler, 2012). Governor Hickenlooper of Colorado noted, "The common element of so many of these mass homicides seems to be a level of mental illness" (Nagourney, 2012). What is conspicuously missing in this truncated causal analysis is the fact that semiautomatic firearms are *always* present in the recent spate of mass shootings.

Faced with massacred young children, Governor Hickenlooper reversed his position on the need to tighten gun laws. The state legislature overrode the unrelenting pressure by gun advocates to fight any gun legislation. Colorado enacted laws requiring universal background checks and limited ammunition magazines (Bartels & Lee, 2013). Dudley Brown, the director of Rocky Mountain Gun Owners, threatened political retaliation: "The Democrats have just handed me a sledgehammer, and I get to walk through their china shop in the 2014 election."

With NRA backing, Colorado gun advocates collected sufficient signatures to vote two vulnerable Democratic state senators out of office in a special recall election. The two senators were unseated amid charges of voter suppression (Healy, 2013a). Mail ballots are permitted in regular Colorado elections, but a court ruling required in-person voting in this case, which reduced the number of votes cast. The results of the recall election changed the state senate composition slightly but made no difference to the strict gun law. One of those ousted, John Morse, had been the president of the senate. Before the recall election, he explained his stance that the massacre of children demanded gun reform, whatever the political costs: "There may be a cost for me to pay, but I am more than happy to pay it" (Healy, 2013a). The recall election was viewed as a test of NRA political clout. However, the clout was short lived. In the regular midterm election, the recently elected progun senators were ousted. Despite intense NRA effort to unseat him, Governor Hickenlooper was reelected.

Some liberally oriented states have tightened gun regulations on their own. In 2014, voters in Washington State approved an initiative mandating background checks on gun sales, including at gun shows and online sales (Siddiqui, 2014). The NRA promoted an opposing initiative barring background checks unless required by federal law, which is replete with loopholes. Arguing by pernicious comparison, the NRA lobbyist Brian Judy likened expansion of background checks to Nazi Germany (NRA representative, 2014). Voters defeated the NRA initiative and closed the loopholes. These victories were heralded as the beginning of a gun-regulation movement that would bypass Congress and state legislatures by going directly to voters via state ballot initiatives (Steinhauer, 2015). The movement is billed as promoting public health and gun safety rather than gun control. When allowed to do so, voters have passed gun regulations that Congress refuses to consider or defeats if it is brought to a vote.

Using odd logic, Wayne LaPierre extended the futility argument against universal background checks for gun buyers. "My problem with background checks is you're never going to get criminals to go through universal background checks" (Hunt, 2013). In a companion futility argument, he pointed out that many mass killers obtained their guns in compliance with existing gun regulations. Gun regulations do not prevent mass killings, he argued. There are several notable problems with this line of reasoning. Semiautomatic, militarized rifles with large ammunition clips are the weapons of choice for quick massacres. Congress refused to renew the ban on these firearms and opposes any restrictions on the capacity of bullet magazines. To evaluate the effectiveness of gun regulations when the main tool of death is exempted is but a token gesture. It is a logical fallacy to argue from evidence that some individuals were undeterred by existing gun regulations that those regulations had no deterrent effect on others.

Shifting the blame for mass killings solely to mental illness reframed the debate as a mental-health problem rather than a gun problem. The focus on mental illness also diverted attention away from everyday gun violence. The causal shift apparently resonated with the general public. When asked in a Gallup poll after the Newtown massacre what should be done to prevent future school shootings, the public favored increasing school security and mental health programs over doing something about guns of mass killing power (Newport, 2012). However, the average values mask a huge political divide. Democrats heavily favored banning assault weapons (61%), whereas Republicans' support for banning such weapons (26%) was much lower. Democrats were also less supportive of having an armed school official in every school (27%) than were Republicans (49%). Rather, Democrats strongly favored increased spending on mental health screening and treatment (67%), whereas Republicans were much less supportive of this approach (35%), despite attribution of mass shootings to mental illness. The priority in mental health measures is not surprising. Communities welcome programs that add federal funds to their coffers. However, those priorities would rapidly change if communities had to tax themselves to pay for them.

In a Pew poll also conducted shortly after the Newtown massacre (Pew Research Center, 2012), Democrats (72%) were considerably more supportive of gun regulation than were Republicans (27%). Republicans (63%) believed more strongly than Democrats (33%) that guns protect people from crime. In contrast to liberals, (12%) more Republicans (42%) believed that ownership of assault weapons makes the country safer. The marked political polarization indicated that shock and outrage at the massacre of young children would produce no gun reforms at the federal level.

A society should foster the mental health of its youth for its own sake. However, this is a byzantine and highly costly way of preventing mass killings. In a pluralistic society, people differ over what constitutes mental health, how to promote it, and how to treat psychosocial disorders. A national program aimed at mental health is likely to rekindle the culture war over faith-based approaches versus secular ones. Mike Huckabee, a former governor of Arkansas and the former host of a Fox News talk show, provides a glimpse of the form the debate might take. The day after the Newtown massacre, he blamed it on the removal of prayer from public schools: "[S]hould we be so surprised that schools would become a place of carnage?" he asked (Collins, 2012b).

NRA Campaign Against Preventive Measures

Drawing on the work of the Biden task force, President Obama offered a package of nine proposals to reduce gun violence. They included bans on assault weapons, on magazines with more than 10 rounds, and on armor-piercing bullets; background checks for all gun sales and increased penalties for buying guns for others; and increased funding for street police, training in handling shootings, school emergency-response planning, and mental health programs for youth.

As soon as President Obama presented these proposals, the NRA aired a controversial ad denouncing him as an "elitist hypocrite." Advantageous comparison was the means of attack. The narrator in the ad referred to Obama sending his own daughters to a private school under Secret Service protection, then questioned whether putting guns in schools will provide school safety: "Why is he skeptical about putting armed security in our schools when his kids are protected by armed guards at their schools?" (Glueck, 2013). The narrator concluded by raising the issue of elitism: "Are the president's kids more important than yours?"

The ad elicited intense public criticism, not least for referring to the president's children. The White House condemned it as "repugnant and cowardly." Even some conservatives were appalled by it. Joe Scarborough, a former Republican congressman and talk show host, noted that the NRA had changed into a "fringe organization. . . . What the NRA once was, it no longer is. This extremism is so frightening and so over the line" (Moore, 2013).

However, ardent gun advocates defended it with exonerative justifications. Some invoked the First Amendment. Larry Pratt, the director of Gun Owners of America, justified the ad as an expression of free speech: "This is a democracy. This is a country where we are all equal before the law" (Glueck, 2013). When criticized for using the president's children in the ad, David Keene blamed Obama for bringing the problem on himself through public exposure of his daughters and including other children at official events, which Keene claimed were used to advance political agendas (Dwyer, 2013).

As the time for Congress to address the administration's gun-law proposals drew near, partisan conflict intensified. Several progun states passed laws preemptively opposing any new gun regulations (Healy, 2013b). A law in Montana designated any restrictive federal law "unenforceable," even though federal laws preempt state laws. Wyoming went further in its defiance with a law that said any federal agent who attempted to enforce new gun regulations would be charged with a felony. A number of sheriffs announced that they would not enforce federal laws on constitutional grounds. "I don't plan on helping or assisting with any of the federal gun laws because I have the U.S. Supreme Court and the U.S. Constitution on my side" (Frosch, 2013). The defiance in statehouses was backed up by congressional representatives. Tim Huelskamp of Kansas proclaimed, "The Second Amendment is nonnegotiable" (Baker & Shear, 2013). Dan Benishek of Michigan declared a similar defensive stand: "I will fight any efforts to take our guns. Not on my watch" (Baker & Shear, 2013).

Haunted by the children's massacre, some of the gun-safety states began to tighten their gun laws. For example, New York State banned assault weapons, limited the capacity of ammunition clips, and instituted stringent universal background checks. Gun advocates reacted in shocked disbelief that lawmakers passed such sweeping gun laws with bipartisan support. They denounced the new laws, threatened civil disobedience against having to register their assault weapons, and vowed to overturn the laws on constitutional grounds (Kaplan, 2013).

In the midst of the political maneuvering, one voice addressed the troubling societal cost of the inability to find common ground on managing guns. It was congresswoman Carolyn McCarthy, whose husband was killed and her son severely wounded in 1993 in a mass shooting on a Long Island Railroad train. When asked to comment on the massacre of children in Newtown, she replied, "I just don't know what this country's coming to, I don't know who we are any more" (Collins, 2012b). Gabrielle Giffords, severely impaired by a shot in the head, pleaded at the Senate Judiciary Committee hearing on gun control for gun reforms (O'Keefe & Fahrenthold, 2013). "Speaking is difficult but I need to say something important. Violence is a big problem. . . . We must do something. It will be hard, but the time is now," she said haltingly. "Be courageous. Americans are counting on you."

Congressional Rout of Gun Reform

In the Senate Judiciary Committee hearings and extensive media campaigns, the Newtown massacre became just another incident in the partisan gun fight rather than the expected turning point for bipartisan efforts to enact some sensible changes in the nation's gun laws. Despite impassioned pleas for gun reform, this entire legislative effort became just another intractable gridlock among lawmakers, who were deeply split along party lines. The Democratic members of the committee unanimously approved a proposed set of laws for action by the entire Senate, whereas, except for one dissenter on curbing gun trafficking, the Republican members unanimously rejected every proposal. So much for common ground. Senator Patrick Leahy, the chair of the committee, submitted the watered-down gun proposals to the Senate floor with a note of urgency that "lives are at risk when responsible people fail to stand up for laws that will keep guns out of the hands of those who will use them to commit murder, especially mass murder" (Naylor, 2013). Proponents of gun-law reforms resigned themselves to the speedy death of major proposals designed to reduce the killing power of guns and shifted their efforts to salvaging at least some of the lesser ones.

Appeals to conscience and concern over public safety fell largely on deaf ears. When the gun-regulation proposals were presented for a vote on the floor of the Senate, the Republicans adamantly opposed them. The Republican Senate leader, Mitch McConnell of Kentucky, argued that tightening gun laws would infringe on the Second Amendment (Wing, 2013). Drawing on advantageous comparison, Senator Ted Cruz of Texas likened a ban on military-style assault rifles to an infringement on freedom of speech by banning some types of books. He was reminded that there are limits to constitutional rights. Child pornography, for example, is banned under the First Amendment. Senator John Cornyn of Texas mocked the effort to ban assault weapons: "We're going to give the American citizens a pea-shooter to defend themselves with" (Fram, 2013a). In an odd line of reasoning, Senator Charles Grassley of Iowa opposed universal background checks because such a law would lead criminals to steal guns or get them by straw purchases. Senator Charles Schumer of New York acknowledged that this might still be possible, but noted that such a line of reasoning has never been applied to any other law: "We shouldn't have laws because the bad people will get around them anyway" (Steinhauer, 2013b).

In a vote split along political lines, Democrats approved the gun reforms, whereas Republicans, along with a few Democrats from conservative states, rejected them. Lawmakers defeated the ban on military-style assault rifles, the restriction of the capacity of ammunition magazines, and universal background checks on gun sales, but approved stiffer penalties for individuals who buy guns for someone who cannot pass a background check. Not only were the gun-safety measures roundly defeated, but progun lawmakers also turned the effort for gun safety into a further expansion of gun rights. They approved an amendment allowing residents with a permit to carry concealed guns in their home state to do so in other states as well, regardless of their gun laws. However, no gun laws were enacted because a group of Republicans and the few Democrats from the conservative states blocked votes on the proposals with a threatened filibuster. The lawmakers ended up legislating nothing.

The Senate suspended any further consideration of gun legislation. This was a staggering defeat for gun reform. Hopes and expectations that the massacre of young children would make a difference made no difference. In a dramatic ending to this legislative rout, Patricia Maisch, who saved lives in the Tucson mass shooting by kicking away the bullet magazine the gunman dropped while reloading, stood up in the Senate gallery and shouted, "Shame on you."

Ironically, heightened social concern over gun violence became an impetus for Congress to further hamstring the ability of the Bureau of Alcohol, Tobacco, Firearms and Explosives to reduce gun violence. Members of the House and Senate appropriations committees added riders on appropriations bills to prohibit the agency from requiring gun dealers to conduct inventories for lost or stolen weapons or creating a federal registry for tracking illegal guns. The committees also required the agency to add a disclaimer that data about guns "cannot be used to draw broad conclusions about firearms-related crimes" (Steinhauer, 2013a). Because the appropriations bills concerned budgets that keep the government running, gun-reform advocates were forced to compromise by accepting the attached gun riders.

With the congressional ban on even interpreting gun-related data, the gun lobby has a complete stranglehold on Congress on any issue concerning guns. Lawmakers of all stripes shun gun-law proposals. Progun advocates oppose them. Those favoring gun regulations know that, even if the majority of legislators support tightening gun laws, they cannot muster the votes needed to override a filibuster. So they have become resigned to the reality that they cannot enact gun reforms at the federal level. In the past, when partisanship was less extreme, some gun laws were enacted, including a ban on semiautomatic military-style rifles. However, those laws were generally watered down, limiting their effectiveness. Gun makers found it easy to circumvent any prohibitions.

Occasionally an especially horrific massacre, such as the one at Newtown, forces Congress to address gun reform. It did so only reluctantly, with predictable results. The legislative effort merely rekindled the congressional partisan battle. With the individualization of the Second Amendment, even gun regulations supported by a majority of senators were defeated by the threat of a filibuster, on the grounds that any proposed gun regulations violate individual gun rights bestowed by the Second Amendment. Legislative defeat in the Senate spares the House representatives from having to address the gun issue at all.

The political divide on gun rights and public safety continued unabated in state laws enacted in the aftermath of the Newtown massacre (Siddiqui, 2014). States in which the legislatures and governorships were under Republican control further weakened gun regulations. State legislatures and governorships under Democratic control tightened gun regulations.

When legislators occasionally pass some weak gun laws, they hobble regulators from conducting effective oversight of them. Gun lobbyists and progun lawmakers adopt a hypocritical stance when it comes to monitoring guns. On the one hand, they obstruct regulators from doing their job. On the other hand, they criticize regulatory agencies for doing a faulty job of overseeing existing laws while trying to create new ones. They exhibit the same duplicity regarding gun sales. On the one hand, they demand that guns be kept out of hands of criminals and the mentally ill. On the other hand, they adamantly oppose universal background checks on the grounds that they impose needless burdens on law-abiding gun owners and will lead to a national gun registry. As a result, there are no background checks on about 40% of all gun buyers, who get their guns at gun shows and on the Internet regardless of their criminal background or mental health status (Luo, McIntire, & Palmer, 2013). In addition to the issue of public safety, the large gap in background checks makes it difficult to trace guns used in crimes.

Sound gun policies require reliable data based on genuine gun reforms that are fully implemented, closely monitored, and adequately assessed. Vigorous political battles are fought over questionable data based on weak, easily circumventable gun regulations that are poorly enforced. By intimidating federal agencies for funding gun research and barring them from interpreting gun-related data, Congress keeps the public uninformed about the social effects of guns in society.

Given the inhospitable congressional environment for gun reform, achievement of any significant change in gun policies requires massively expressed public pressure. However, in a nation deeply divided over guns, calls for goal-oriented grassroots activism only energizes the opposing factions to work harder for the gun policies they favor. One faction pushes with strengthened resolve to tighten gun laws, whereas the opposing faction jostles to protect existing lax laws and to fend off the enactment of new ones. The net result is congressional gridlock, with partisanship superseding the common good.

With gridlock at the federal level, the states have gone their opposite ways. Liberal-leaning states are regulating guns for public safety, whereas conservative-leaning rural and southern states are enacting more laissez-faire gun laws favoring gun rights. The human tragedies and moral voices get drowned out by unyielding factionalism. The escalating lethality of gun technology has outpaced moral consideration of the type of society we want to be and the role of guns within it.

No society can either prevent or predict mass killings with certainty. However, it is within a society's power to limit the extent of the human toll a killing spree exacts. This is tellingly revealed in cases where the death toll was cut because the gunman's semiautomatic weapon jammed (Johnson & Kovaleski, 2012). Society can exercise some measure of control over the scope of massacres by limiting two features of gun design: banning semiautomatic, military-style rifles and restricting the bullet capacity of magazines. One does not need enormous killing power for self-defense, hunting, or sport shooting. Limiting magazine capacity alone could reduce the number of people killed in a shooting rampage. However, unless gun regulations are negotiated in good faith, they are easily circumventable. Recall how gun makers altered the design for virtually instant reloading to circumvent the California law. A simple design change turned an intended safety measure into a more lethal one.

Deterring Pursuit of Sensible Gun Policies

Because of high demand and lax gun laws, the United States is the largest importing market worldwide for civilian guns (Kramer, 2012). It has the most heavily armed citizenry and the highest rates of gun homicides, gun suicides, and accidental shootings of children in households. The states with the weakest gun laws have the highest rates of gun violence (Beauchamp, 2013). Guns are even deeply ingrained in metaphors of everyday speech: Candidates "target" their opponents, lawmakers "stick to their guns," advocacy groups "take aim" at legislation they don't approve, and reporters write about a White House "under fire" (Baker, 2013). Presidents will not negotiate "with a gun at the head of the American people."

Despite recurring gun massacres, American society remains deeply divided on the matter of firearms, unable to adopt sensible policies. There are two principal ways of addressing the gun crisis. In the politically safer and customary approach, lawmakers ascribe the gun problem mainly to mental illness, pass some minor gun-regulation measures, enact a few watered-down laws that gun makers easily evade, and hamstring regulators from doing their oversight work. In the reformative approach, polarized factions work together for gun reforms that strike a balance between gun rights and public safety rights. In addition, Congress provides regulators with the resources needed to ensure that the laws are adequately implemented.

Individuals in the gun subculture feel vulnerable to criminal victimization, are vigilant against potential threats to their safety, and are equipped to use lethal force in self-defense. They also distrust the government, which they perceive as scheming to take their guns away from them. With the Supreme Court decision in *District of Columbia v. Heller* granting individual gun rights, gun advocates have little basis for fearing that the government will confiscate all guns. In national surveys, about 70% of current and former NRA members favor many reasonable gun regulations. If this sizable majority truly supports moderate gun polices, it is puzzling why the membership does not moderate the extreme gun policies of their organization from within.

In some influential progun circles, a moderate view regarding gun rights is a punishable offense. A case in point is the uncompromising exercise of influence by the gun industry over gun journalism (Somaiya, 2014). In one of his columns in *Guns & Ammo* magazine, the distinguished gun journalist Dick Metcalf wrote that constitutional rights have limits: "[A]ll constitutional rights are regulated, always have been, and need to be" (Somaiya, 2014). Punishment came swiftly. Gun manufacturers threatened to withdraw financial backing for the magazine and for Metcalf's TV program if he was not dismissed. He was promptly fired, but the magazine linked his firing to sponsors' possible concern that customers would boycott their products. Richard Venola, a former editor of the magazine, explained the necessity for the absolutist position on gun rights: "We are locked in a struggle with powerful forces in this country who will do anything to destroy the Second Amendment" (Somaiya, 2014). In his view, there is no place for a moderate voice in the fight for gun rights: "The time for ceding some rational points is gone."

A moderate but dormant social force that appears leaderless and voiceless within the NRA carries no influence in shaping the gun policies that affect the quality of life in a society. Were moderate gun owners to form an alternative organization, it would create the political conditions conducive to legislation of sensible gun policies and their effective implementation. A moderate progun voice would defuse the polarized gun battle and remove the electoral intimidation that blocks legislative reforms. However, instead of moderates exerting their influence, an even more militant group called Gun Owners of America spun off the NRA (Steinhauer, 2013c). This group criticizes the NRA for compromising too much on gun legislation and for being too lax in rating the voting behavior of lawmakers. Although fewer in number than the NRA, they are vociferous in pressuring lawmakers. They rate lawmakers not only on every vote taken on gun initiatives but also on various conservatively oriented legislative initiatives. Without activism by moderates and with many gun-shy politicians doing the bidding the NRA, legislative initiatives supporting a laissez-faire gun culture will likely continue to trump public safety and welfare.

Any efforts to change gun policies must contend with the elephant in the room—the gun manufacturers who are at the heart of the firearms culture war. They operate in concert with the NRA and the industry trade organization. The introduction to this chapter traced the evolution of escalating gun lethality, driven mainly by commercial pressures. As explained earlier, the gun business is a peculiar one. Gun manufacturers face a major challenge to economic growth because they sell a product that does not wear out. They have two ways to promote economic growth within the United States. The first strategy is to increase the number of gun buyers, usually by heightening fear of criminal victimization. For example, the women's market is a new major source of sales growth. The secondary criminal market brings additional revenue from unregulated sales, legislated deficient regulatory oversight, and heavy gun trafficking across state lines from states with lax gun laws to those with stringent laws. Also, the Bureau of Alcohol, Tobacco, Firearms and Explosives is prohibited from creating a central database of gun sales. These practices make it easy for criminals to buy guns and to evade detection.

In the second source of economic growth, gun manufacturers compete for market share by producing guns of escalating lethality. They achieve a competitive edge by adding accessories from military-style automatic assault weapons with large capacity magazines. Manufacturers strenuously oppose efforts to ban militarized rifles because they are the most profitable big-ticket items. Spokespersons for the industry trade association, as well as wholesalers and retailers, promote increasingly lethal guns in the language of gun rights and self-defense. They also do damage control in the aftermath of tragic mass killings. The NRA, in turn, applies its political power to keep lawmakers in line.

Socializing a New Generation to Guns

Mass urbanization has created a major economic problem for the gun industry. Present-day city dwellers do not go hunting for food, nor are many of them sport-shooting enthusiasts. It is the cyberworld that commands the attention of today's youth. The gun industry has mounted a broad campaign to socialize a new youth generation to guns. Mike McIntire (2013) describes the scope of socialization: "The industry's strategies include giving firearms, ammunition and cash to youth groups; weakening state restrictions on hunting by young children; marketing an affordable military-style rifle for 'junior shooters'; sponsoring semiautomatic-handgun competitions for youths; and developing a target-shooting video game that promotes brand-name weapons, with links to the Web sites of their makers." This large-scale campaign to cultivate a future generation of gun lovers relies heavily not only on direct indoctrination of children. The Hunting Heritage Trust and National Shooting Sports Foundation commissioned studies on how to enlist peer influence in the recruitment campaign (National Shooting Sports Foundation, 2012). Articles in *Junior Shooters*, cited by McIntire, urge youngsters to become "peer ambassadors" by introducing their friends to target shooting. The public opinion researcher group that was commissioned to do the study recommended that the ambassador peer models use social media as important modes of influence. It also recommended that peer recruitment be likened to other sport and youth-group activities. "Participation in the shooting sports should not be all about the activities themselves," it advised, "but also about socializing, meeting new friends and having a fun time" (National Shooting Sports Foundation, 2012).

Children were also urged to prod their parents to support their participation in the gun program. "Who knows?" an article in *Junior Shooters* remarked merrily. "Maybe you'll find a Bushmaster AR-15 under your tree some frosty Christmas morning!" (McIntire, 2013). The Bushmaster is the assault weapon of choice in mass shootings. Advisors counseled that children's recruitment of parental support be cast in euphemisms of fun-filled family outings, "like sharing the experiences." The advisors provided explicit instruction on the form of the parental persuasion, "Such a program could be called 'Take Me Hunting' or 'Take Me Shooting'" (McIntire 2013).

The lack of early institutional access to child populations poses a major problem in the generational conversion to a widespread embrace of guns. A target-shooting program in middle schools would serve this purpose. In selling the program to school systems, advisors recommended that it be presented as serving prosocial purposes: "When approaching school systems, it is important to frame the shooting sports only as a mechanism to teach other life skills, rather than an end to itself" (McIntire, 2013). State laws limiting hunting by children are another obstacle to engaging them with guns early in their development. Changing these legal barriers centers on lowering or eliminating age limits or providing children a provisional hunting license under adult supervision.

Wielding guns that can injure or kill if mishandled is intimidating to novices. Graduated mastery experiences eliminate apprehension (Bandura, 1997). The architects of the gun-socialization program specify a graduated strategy to enable children to shoot high-powered semiautomatic firearms: "The point should be to get newcomers started shooting something, with the natural next step being a move toward actual firearms" (McIntire, 2013). In desensitizing children to gun use, advisors suggest removing humanity from the inaugural phase by not having newcomers practice shooting at human silhouettes.

To alleviate any moral qualms about putting high-powered, semiautomatic firearms in children's hands, the promoters rely on exonerative comparison. A reader of *Junior Shooters* challenged the justification of military-style semiautomatic firearms: "Why do you need a semiautomatic gun for hunting?" The editor of the magazine, Andy Fisk, reacted to the objection with the worn comparative justification, "They're a tool, not any different than a car or a baseball bat." He went on to focus on the similarity in the mechanics of different types of rifles while completely disregarding their differential lethal properties: "It's no different than a junior shooting a .22 or a shotgun. The difference is in the perception of the viewer" (McIntire, 2013). The human toll in mass shootings is not a perception problem.

In another form of comparative exoneration, proponents of the generational program argued that cheerleading and playing softball are more harmful than gun use. Gun violence is a social action inflicted on another person with grave consequences, not a personal injury in an activity of one's own choosing. Those training children to shoot lethal firearms do not know how the youngsters will use guns later in life. Adam Lanza, who massacred the children in Newtown, was well trained in semiautomatic firearms and often accompanied his mother for sport shooting. He ended up using that gun training in a killing rampage.

THE CONSTITUTIONAL PHASE
OF THE GUN BATTLE

This next phase of the gun battle is marked by stiff resistance to achieving a political accommodation that would strike a balance between public safety through sensible regulation of firearms and the right of law-abiding citizens to use guns for hunting and recreation. Gun-regulation advocates are reframing the political debate away from the polarizing gun-rights versus gun-control battle to gun rights with public responsibility for safe gun use that does not jeopardize public safety rights. However, with considerable imbalance in congressional power favoring gun-rights proponents, there is little incentive to compromise for common good.

In many states in the past, permission to carry a concealed gun in public required a permit issued by the police department after a thorough background check. The Supreme Court's narrow ruling in *McDonald v. Chicago* permitting a gun in the home for self-defense is widely misread as granting absolute gun rights. States rapidly stripped away these public safeguards after a politically driven national gun-rights campaign. These changes created a largely laissez-faire policy toward guns.

The Supreme Court ruling does not forbid regulating the types of guns that are manufactured, how they are sold, or the public places where they may be carried. The Court has yet to rule on these qualifying conditions. Legal challenges will determine which public safety measures can be reinstated constitutionally. Gun laws are now being challenged in lower courts. An Illinois law that had virtually no chance of surviving the Supreme Court banned carrying loaded guns in public (Liptak, 2012). This blanket prohibition was declared unconstitutional by the Seventh Circuit Court of Appeals. In a qualified prohibition, the District of Columbia challenged the right to possess semiautomatic assault weapons and handguns with magazines containing multiple rounds. The appeals court ruled that the District has the right to ban such firearms. It argued that military-style rifles belong on the battlefield and banned gun magazines with more than 10 rounds of ammunition. This ruling, if upheld by the Supreme Court, places some limits on gun rights regarding the lethality of firearms.

New York State has a law requiring individuals to demonstrate a special need for self-protection for a permit to carry guns in public (Liptak, 2013). The NRA filed a lawsuit challenging it, but the Supreme Court refused to hear the case. A federal judge upheld the law except for the arbitrary magazine limit of 7 rounds. The judge viewed the constitutional challenge as more of a political issue than a judicial one. However, as mentioned earlier, the U.S. Court of Appeals ruled unconstitutional Illinois's blanket ban on carrying concealed guns in public and Chicago's ordinance requiring gun owners to register their firearms (Yaccino, 2013). The latter prohibition makes it difficult for law officials to track guns and the flow of guns from other states. These types of lawsuits in defense of unlimited gun rights will eventually be settled by the Supreme Court.

The lethality of guns and limits on the public places where concealed guns may be carried have yet to be determined. These aspects of gun rights are beginning to be litigated. A federal appeals court ruled that a visitor from a state that allows people to carry concealed guns cannot do so in Colorado without a permit. A preliminary decision by the Supreme Court suggests that it would support some limits on the Second Amendment. A New Jersey law requires individuals to demonstrate a "justifiable need" to carry a gun in public for self-defense. The Supreme Court rejected a challenge to that law (Liptak, 2014). Eventually, many of these lower court decisions will reach the Supreme Court for formal review. The Court has its own ideological divisions. Its future rulings on the constitutionality of particular gun restrictions will determine how the balance between gun rights and public safety is played out in the factional gun battle.

Chapter 5

■ ■ ■ ■ ■ ■ ■

THE CORPORATE WORLD

This chapter addresses moral disengagement in the corporate world in terms of two major classes of activities. The first concerns transgressive practices in the finance industry, mainly large-scale financial activities in the form of home mortgages, commercial loans, and stock trading. They include not only private trading but also speculative investments of institutional and retirement funds, thereby affecting people's livelihoods and the economic life of society. Some of these financial operations are global in scale, so they affect vast populations, and in the recent economic crisis, the integrity of financial recovery measures.

The second class of activities concerns the development and marketing of commercial products that impair human health, and the use of workplace production methods that are seriously injurious to the health of workers. Some corporations, such as those in the tobacco industry, make products that are harmful to consumers. Others, such as the mining industry, expose workers to harm during the production process. Some do both. To do either requires moral disengagement at the corporate level.

Triadic Deterrents of Transgressive Activities

As explained in chapter 1, transgressive behavior can be deterred by three types of sanctions—legal, social, and self-evaluative ones that are rooted in personal moral standards (Bandura, 1986). A comprehensive theory of deterrence based on negative sanctions must explain how these modes of influence operate in concert in regulating transgressive behavior. Their deterrent strength may vary for different types of unlawful activities. For example, self-sanctions may be less influential in property crimes than in interpersonal crimes. Individuals may condemn themselves for injuring another person, but not for cheating on their income taxes. Moreover, the relative contribution of these sanctions to deterrence can change over time as cultural values change.

According to the legal deterrence doctrine, the threat of punishment is intended to work in two ways. In direct deterrence, transgressors are punished to dissuade them from repeating their crimes. In vicarious deterrence, transgressors are punished to discourage others from committing similar crimes. The prospect of certain, swift and severe punishment is assumed to keep people law-abiding. This form of deterrence is plausible in theory but works poorly in practice (Bandura, 1986).

If legal sanctions are to deter, they must be credible. Zimring and Hawkins (1973) document that the perpetrators of most criminal activities run only a small risk of being caught and punished. About half of crimes committed are never even reported. The culprits of many reported crimes cannot be found. Of those arrested, many are released because of insufficient evidence or settle on lesser charges. Of the cases brought to trial, some are dismissed. Only a limited number of those convicted serve prison time. The threat is least credible when crimes are commonplace but arrests and convictions are infrequent. The explanatory challenge is not the occurrence of crime, but rather why it is not more frequent, given such low rates of apprehension and punishment.

Deterrence depends on perceived risk rather than actual risk. Those who abide by the law overestimate the risk of getting caught, whereas those who engage in unlawful activities, most of whom get away with it, perceive the risk of punishment as low. The views of the lawbreakers are more in line with the actual probabilities (Claster, 1967). Longitudinal studies confirm that perceived risk decreases with criminal engagement. People who are planning to commit crimes do not act on wholly rational calculation, weighing costs and benefits as do utility maximizers (Cook, 1980). They are swayed more by anticipated payoffs of crimes than by the likelihood of legal penalties. For example, in the financial sector, insider trading is acknowledged to be pervasive, but few culprits are caught and punished. In his thoughtful book *The Limits of Criminal Sanction*, Herbert Packer (1968) concludes that legal sanctions are a cumbersome and very costly way to regulate human behavior. With the low risk of penalty, a society cannot depend on legal sanctions alone to deter criminal behavior.

The second source of deterrence stems from social sanctions. For individuals who have a stake in the social system, being charged with and convicted of a crime can have devastating consequences on reputation, career, and livelihood. This line of theorizing focuses mainly on marginalized individuals who have little or nothing to lose socially for unlawful activities. Indeed, they may be admired and applauded by their peers for their proficiency in antisocial pursuits. For example, a trader applauds a fellow trader for his adroitness in criminal price-fixing of foreign currency, "mate yur getting bloody good at this libor game…think of me when yur on yur yacht in Monaco wont yu" (Chappell, 2015).

In recent years, the social stigma of criminal conviction has eroded. Crimes are being committed by individuals of status and power who have high stakes in the system. They act in the belief that they can outsmart the system and that their privileged status puts them above the law. Power holders wield their influence to build their privileges and immunity into laws (Gardner, 1972). Corporate practices that cause widespread harm are sanitized as "white-collar crimes," typically punished impersonally as faceless organizations that pay fines. When wrongdoers are named, most rebound quickly from their downfall to resume their former status. Some even become media celebrities. For these reasons, social sanctions are not always reliable deterrents to unlawful activities.

The most powerful deterrent to criminal conduct operates through self-sanctions. People constantly preside over their own behavior and have to live with their self-evaluation. In this mode of self-regulation, individuals do not transgress because it results in self-condemnation. Indeed, many adhere to the law not because they fear legal penalties but because they subscribe to the values embodied in the law. Hence, they would be law abiding on the basis of self-sanctions alone even if there were no legal penalties. Evaluating the incremental deterrent force of these various sanctions requires assessment of all three forms—legal, social, and self-evaluative. Tittle (1977) studied various sanctions that deter young adults from a wide array of illegal activities. Lawful behavior was best predicted by moral self-sanctions and fear of social censure. Fear of legal consequences was the weakest contributor in the triadic mix. Although moral self-sanctions are the most reliable deterrents to transgressive behavior, they are often neutralized by selective disengagement from detrimental conduct. This chapter analyzes how disengagement is practiced in the corporate world.

THE FINANCE INDUSTRY

The lure of wealth, social status, and power has spawned one scandal after another in the corporate world. Varieties of corporate deceit and fraud change over time, but the crises recur in one form or another. After many of these scandals, the public ends up picking up the tab in bailouts. Some transgressive practices undermine whole industries in the broader economy and have widespread social consequences. The sections that follow analyze the forms that corporate transgressions take and how moral restraints are put on hold in various businesses and industries.

The Electrical Price–Fixing Scandal

During the 1950s, the electrical manufacturing industry faced falling prices in competitive bids for large contracts with government agencies and private industry because competitors were undercutting each other. In a massive conspiracy to control the price and bidding war, fourteen electrical manufacturers divided the market for lucrative contracts, rigged the prices of the bids, and took turns being the lowest bidder. They divided the profits according to an agreed-on formula. With competition eliminated, prices were fixed at high levels. These artificially inflated prices raised the cost of electricity for consumers, with national ramifications. General Electric (GE), headed by Robert Paxton, and Westinghouse, led by Mark W. Cresap Jr., were the main players in this conspiracy, which continued for about six years. Unless cited otherwise, the material for this analysis of moral disengagement in these practices in the electrical industry was drawn from *The Great Price Conspiracy*, by John Herling (1962).

The loss of corporate profits through competitive undercutting was the main justification for devising the scheme to fix prices and rig bids. Because this remedy relied on illegal methods, it had to be implemented surreptitiously to avoid legal detection. Those taking part in the scheme also had the vexing psychological problem of how to retain their self-respect while engaging in criminal conduct. This required sanitizing the illegal behavior and diminishing personal responsibility for it.

The participants in the conspiracy spoke in euphemisms that masked and sanitized their unlawful activities. "Meeting with" and "speaking to" competitors meant price-fixing and bid rigging. To "stabilize prices" meant to rig them. The "problem" was the violation of antitrust law. Conspiratorial meetings became "social meetings." GE gained a reputation for speaking in "vague and elliptical" ways. The company adopted a covert code of communication: the "code of the wink," which was a surreptitious, nonverbal way for officials to authorize illegal antitrust activities. Subordinates also used it to inform top officials that they had fixed prices or rigged bids. The head of the company first learned its meaning when it was used to explain to him that he lost a bid to a competitor because it was rigged. He was angry at being "made a damn fool of" (Herling, 1962). The wink became a fixture in his firm's surreptitious nonverbal communication.

The corporate executives at GE circulated an antitrust directive that prohibited price discussions with competitors. However, this directive was designed mainly to provide legal cover for executives because they made little effort to monitor and enforce it with consequences for violations. Executives cautioned their managerial officials against engaging antitrust activities while tacitly urging them to do so.

Displacement and diffusion of responsibility were the main mechanisms of moral disengagement for those distancing themselves from the fraud. The conspiracy was the product of group decision making. This collective effort allowed individual participants to minimize their roles in the operation.

Smaller firms viewed themselves as too unimportant to the industry giants to have had any influence on the illegal scheme: "[I]n an industry like this, we couldn't have been the initiators of anything like this" (Herling, 1962). They also viewed their participation as more or less compulsory if they were to survive the fierce competition: "You are a little fellow in a big industry, and you have to go along" (Herling, 1962). One need not feel guilty for behavior performed under conditions of perceived powerlessness and coercion.

Managerial officials believed they had tacit approval from above to participate in the antitrust activities. This absolved them of a sense of personal responsibility for their actions. Some felt constrained by their position in the chain of command to report that their supervisors were clandestinely supporting antitrust activities: "I had no power to go higher. I do not report to anyone except my superiors" (Herling, 1962). Still others knew about the price-fixing and bid rigging but remained silent because higher authorities might be covertly approving these very illegal activities. They feared that reporting the activities upward could cost them their jobs or advancement in their careers. Many employees simply worked hard at keeping themselves uninformed about what was going on.

The head of GE acknowledged that he had an inkling that something was going on, but in classic intentional self-deception, he took no action to find out what it was: "[I]t was something that was going on outside of my orbit and I wasn't curious about it" (Herling, 1962). Nor did he ask any of his division managers whether they had been meeting with competitors. He explained to the Senate's Antitrust and Monopoly subcommittee that he did not pursue the issue because he found such "tale-bearing" "distasteful" and "womanish." Through willful inattention the readily knowable remained unknown to him. By this self-exoneration, he shielded himself from charges that he had prior knowledge of the antitrust scheme.

Unlike GE, which vigorously denied corporate fraud, Westinghouse admitted to the price-fixing. Although Mark Cresap, the chairman of Westinghouse, admitted that some of his managers had violated the antitrust law. In testimony before the Senate Subcommittee on Antitrust and Monopoly he repeatedly denied that he had any prior knowledge of the illegal activities going on about him. A frustrated, skeptical senator on the subcommittee remarked, "If you couldn't see it, you ought to be able to smell it" (Herling, 1962). The architects of this conspiracy not only disavowed responsibility for their actions but even dissociated an agentic role in the selection of bid winners. They created a system in which the phase of the moon determined which firm won the bid in a particular competition on a given day. With a proxy lunar agency, no one could be held personally responsible for picking bid winners.

With newspapers exposing the conspiracy, corporate blatant disregard of antitrust policies, and the Justice Department closing in, GE executives took self-protective actions. They selected the manager of the transformer division as the fall guy. They informed him and his subordinates that they would be demoted and eased out of the company. Smith was angry at this selective punishment, given that the company disregarded its antitrust directive and that operational managers were participating in price-fixing meetings with their competitive counterparts. With decentralization into divisions and divisional profits key to advancement, tacit directives to use unlawful means of increasing profits carried weight. The head of the transformer division complied faithfully with the company's covert policy, only to find that his own company considered him expendable. In addressing the assembled managers, the chairman of the GE board of directors absolved corporate executives of any responsibility. He proclaimed, with righteous indignation, that any violators of federal antitrust law were on their own in defending themselves against criminal indictments. Herling (1962) described this self-exonerating meeting as one in which "[the chairman] sanctimoniously consigned the miserable sinners—whose sin was none of his knowledge—to the secular arm of government" (Herling, 1962).

The corporations assumed that their antitrust violations would be handled in the customary, lenient way as "a gentleman's misdemeanor—and a gentleman was never sent to jail for violating the antitrust law" (Herling, 1962). They further assumed that they would settle on a plea of no contest (*nolo contendere*), neither admitting nor disputing the charges against them, and pay a token fine. However, much to their chagrin, they had to deal with Robert A. Bicks, acting U.S. assistant attorney general in charge of the litigation. He had a reputation as a highly knowledgeable, aggressive prosecutor who was reluctant to use the *nolo* plea on the grounds that it disrespected the law and the public's desire for justice. He persuaded the attorney general to reject *nolo* pleas because they are not an admissions of guilt.

The sins of willful omission by chief executives resulted in neither personal fines nor long jail sentences. The electrical corporations paid medium-size fines, as did a number of their managerial officials. Those more deeply involved in the conspiracy received light prison sentences as well, although virtually all of the sentences were suspended. In corporate cultures where unlawful behavior is profitable and top executives are shielded from the consequences of their wrongdoing, the moral disengagement drama is repeated. We shall revisit it in analysis of systemic financial transgressions of global proportions.

The Savings and Loan Crisis

Federal housing programs are created to enable citizens of lesser means to realize their dream of homeownership and to fuel economic growth. These loans are insured by the federal government. Financiers and other moneyed self-interest groups use their considerable political clout to remove regulations not to their liking and to weaken regulatory oversight, which they characterize as burdensome and implemented by obstructive governmental bureaucracies. Weak regulatory oversight creates fertile ground for faulty management, exploitive practices, and outright fraud.

The 1980s saw the savings and loan crisis following its deregulation during the Reagan administration. Among the changes in the savings and loan, or thrift industry, deposits toward the purchase of a home could now be used for risky loans, resulting in unsafe commercial investments, fraudulent insider transactions, and corruption. Over half of the thrifts failed. Taxpayers ended up footing a bill of $3.5 billion dollars. The slowdown in the financial and real-estate markets contributed to the economic recession of the early 1990s. This was the origin of mortgage securities that, in a more complex form, spawned the global economic crisis and recession a decade later.

Charles Keating Jr., chairman of the Lincoln Savings and Loan firm, became the face of corruption in the thrift industry. He persuaded customers to switch their federally insured deposits to uninsured high-risk ones, which eventually defaulted as worthless bonds. L. William Seidman, the former head of the Federal Deposit Insurance Corporation, characterized the deceitful switch of savings as "one of the most heartless and cruel frauds in modern history" (Dougherty, 2014).

Keating viewed himself as a victim of "incompetent, wrongheaded" regulators (Carlson & Keating, 1990). He directed his most intense blame at the chairman of the Federal Home Loan Bank Board, whom he regarded as "ignorant," and on a "power and ego trip." "[He] wrecks it and then says the greatest financial debacle in the history of the world is Keating's fault." Using the "bad apples" exoneration, Keating attributed the savings and loans collapse to a few "miscreants" in the industry who were mismanaged by the regulators. He alleged that the "miscreants" had singled him out as a scapegoat to intimidate others in the industry: "The government is doing a fantastic job in making an example of me for everybody else to shut up." When asked whether he had the temperament to be in a regulated industry, he shifted his personal failings to his nemesis, the regulators: "If there is a problem, there is something wrong with the regulators." It was ironic that Keating blamed regulations for the demise of the thrift industry—which was brought on by deregulation! Disavowal of responsibility for the extensive harm he caused extended even to disassociating himself from his own actions. When asked about his exorbitant salary he replied: "It was braggadocio and grandstanding. That isn't me."

What was conspicuously absent in Keating's self-reactions was concern for those he harmed—many of them elderly who lost their life savings—or guilt over his injurious actions. The lack of empathy and remorse comes as no surprise, considering the low regard he had for his unwitting clients. In a memo he advised bond salesmen, "And always remember the weak, meek, and ignorant are always good targets" (McFadden, 2014). Maltreating those who are devalued does not rouse much guilt.

Keating enlisted the help of five prominent senators, known as the "Keating Five," who benefited from his perks and substantial campaign contributions. They included Alan Cranston of California, John McCain and

Dennis DeConcini of Arizona, John Glenn of Ohio, and Donald Riegle of Michigan. Keating located his savings and loan firm in California, lived in Arizona, and owned property in Ohio and Michigan. The senators all claimed him as a constituent. Keating recruited them to intervene on his behalf when he was having trouble with federal agencies. The senators collectively complained to federal officials that they were overregulating Keating's thrift operation and should back off. Keating also used a report prepared by Alan Greenspan, whom he had hired earlier in his career as a consultant. Greenspan argued that Lincoln Savings should be exempted from some regulations because it posed no foreseeable "risk," and was in the hands of "seasoned and expert management" (McFadden, 2014).

All of the senators vigorously denied that they had done anything wrong in defending Keating. They claimed that they were merely acting on behalf of a constituent's request, which senators do all the time. In exonerating himself by trivial comparison, Senator McCain minimized his intervention as a constituent service by likening it to "helping the little lady who didn't get her Social Security check" (Bethell, 1989). There is a major difference between an unfamiliar constituent making a small request and interventions by five senators, recipients of large campaign funds from their "constituent," collectively pressuring a regulatory agency to lay off a debt-ridden, rogue real-estate firm that was about to be shut down. Keating was not reticent about buying political favors. When asked whether his campaign contributions brought results he remarked, "I want to say in the most forceful way I can: I certainly hope so" (McFadden, 2014).

Senator Cranston was reprimanded by the Senate Ethics Committee, but no charges were filed against the other senators. Cranston claimed that the chairman of the Federal Home Loan Bank Board, whom he called a "political hack," targeted him because the mortgage crisis happened on the chairman's watch. This construal made the chairman's self-protectiveness rather than Cranston's self-interest the problem. In his self-defense Cranston vigorously denied the charges, implying that others in the Senate do what he did. Alan Dershowitz, his attorney, added, "We can prove that other senators engaged in similar linkage but simply did a better job of covering up their tracks" (Fritz, 1991). Cranston's Senate colleagues angrily condemned his insinuation as "arrogant, unrepentant and a smear on this institution" (Fritz, 1991).

Keating was fined $250,000 for bankruptcy fraud, but served a relatively short prison sentence because his convictions were overturned on the grounds that the jury was given faulty instructions. The senators vigorously denied that they intervened improperly. The Senate Select Committee on Ethics reprimanded Cranston for "impermissible conduct" and criticized the other senators for poor judgment and acting improperly. The lenient reprimand was roundly criticized as a "whitewash," a "cop-out," "wrist tap," and "shameless." Others were cynical about lawmakers investigating themselves. In public opinion polls people called for campaign finance reform.

Keating was a notable example of the selective exercise of moral agency. As an ardent antipornography crusader, he served on the President's Commission on Obscenity and Pornography, testified at congressional hearings, filed lawsuits against pornographers and spearheaded a national campaign against pornography. Dubbed "Mr. Clean," Keating founded Citizens for Decency through Law, an additional vehicle in this effort that enlisted a large national following. In ironic moral detachment from the suffering he caused countless people, Keating voiced concern over the growing societal erosion of morality: "The moral fiber of our nation seems to be rapidly unraveling." He excluded himself as an exemplar of this ethical decline, but this was not a case of superficial hypocrisy. Keating deeply invested morality in the pornography sphere but disengaged it from the financial suffering he inflicted on his clients.

No lesson was learned by the finance industry or Congress from this costly debacle. As we will see later, the practices of the subprime home mortgage industry, which spawned the 2008 global financial meltdown, essentially replicated this scenario. However, more ingenious methods were devised that wreaked massive financial havoc internationally. Bad subprime home mortgages were bundled in perplexing derivatives. Technological advances that enable financers to monitor and move instantaneously huge amounts of wealth globally accelerated the transactions. These developments vastly expanded the scope and depth of the harm inflicted on societies.

The Insider Trading Crisis

The 1980s also saw insider trading violations that threatened the integrity of the stock market. Corporate insiders leaked information about confidential corporate developments to select investors prior to public announcement. The investors traded on that advance information. The corporate insiders and the tipped-off investors shared the profits. Before his downfall for insider trading in merges and hostile takeovers, Ivan Boesky delivered the commencement address at the University of California, Berkeley, announcing, "Greed is all right....I think greed is healthy. You can be greedy and still feel good about yourself" (Stewart, 1991). The students greeted this conversion of greediness to a virtue with laughter and applause. Healthy greediness eventually got Boesky a stint in jail and a $100 million fine for insider trading.

How can a person preserve positive self-regard while committing gross illegalities that jeopardize the integrity of the stock market and adversely affect the lives of countless people? Boesky seems to have achieved it by transforming the moral issue of inflicting harm into a lesser ethical violation of trader rules: "I think 'immoral' is probably the wrong word to use....I prefer the word 'unethical'" (Stewart, 1991).

Ayn Rand (1966), who attained a sizable following in libertarian, neo-conservative, and corporate circles, championed the secular morality of self-interest in her version of laissez-faire capitalism. In her view, happiness through productive achievement is the basis of a moral life. (Productive achievement is not inherently moral. In fact, it can be detrimental, as in the tobacco industry.) An unfettered free market, she argued, is the only inherently moral social system. She justified the morality of self-interest and rejected "ethical altruism" as based, in large part, on making achievers feel guilty about the fruits of their labors.

In response to the Boesky case, some young traders shifted the blame to isolated "bad apples." "It's like knowing someone with cancer. You feel it for awhile. But say to yourself, 'Hey, it's not me,' and you go on" (Martz, Powell, McCormick, Thomas, & Starr, 1986). Given the excesses on Wall Street, some of the elders in the business viewed the blurring of the line between right and wrong as pervasive. As one of the elders put it, "The 'bad apples' speeches are crap."

Illegal insider trading is an easy crime to commit. It is simply a matter of passing on secret information to a fellow trader who cashes in on the advance information and shares the profits or provides a generous payment. It therefore comes as no surprise that Preet Bharara, the U.S. attorney for the Southern District of New York, reports that insider trading is not only rampant many years later, but may even be on the rise. He calls this common practice a "financial steroid" (DeCambre, 2010). A case we will explore later reveals that the manipulation of the stock market through insider trading occurs even at the uppermost ranks of the finance industry.

The human capacity for cognitive reconstrual of transgressive conduct as minor or even worthy knows no bounds. Research on résumé fraudsters sheds some light on the type of cognitive construal processes by which anyone can turn a moral issue into a lesser infraction. To demonstrate the pervasiveness of résumé fraud, the Port Authority of New York and New Jersey ran a phony ad for electricians with expertise in the Sontag connector (McGarvey, 1993). The Port Authority received résumés from 170 applicants who claimed familiarity with this apparatus. Over half of them claimed they were licensed Sontag experts with over 10 years of experience. Some even listed projects in which they used the Sontag connector. However, this seemingly masterly set of applicants outwitted themselves: There is no Sontag connector. This is a surprisingly high level of fraud with applicants claiming proficiency on a contrivance that does not exist!

Wexler's (2006) ethnographic study of résumé fraudsters in high managerial positions sheds some light on how lying can be transformed into an indicant of admirable occupational attributes. These executives were dismissed after their résumé deceptions were discovered. This deceit apparently carried no moral stigma, because they found even higher-paying jobs within a few months. The fraudsters recruited the entire set of moral disengagement mechanisms in the service of self-exoneration. They trivialized lying about their qualification as a harmless minor matter: "It's silly to hold me in a negative light when no one is complaining" (Wexler, 2006). They sanitized their actions as "résumé enhancement," not lying. In their view, their deceit paled in comparison to the dishonesty, licentiousness, and hypocrisy of those who dismissed them. As further comparative self-exoneration, they invoked the corruptness of the corporate system itself: "I feel like a just man in an unjust system. Others are stealing, padding expenses and raising Cain, but are not losing their jobs" (Wexler, 2006). Life in the fiercely competitive corporate world was likened to a game in which everyone is driven to do shady things to win.

The fraudsters even viewed themselves in valiant terms: "I am precisely what the firm wants, needed, and advertised for—a bold, risk-taking innovator who pushes the boundaries" (Wexler, 2006). Their résumé embellishment, they explained, was strong testimony to their motivation and commitment to becoming valued members of the company. They maintained their positive self-regard as good, decent people who should be judged by the results they produce: "Good people get results and create more benefits than costs. I am using this definition of a good person" (Wexler, 2006).

If fraudsters turned out to be productive contributors in the workforce, organizations would likely forgive indiscretion on job applications. An apology with remorse would bring forgiveness. What sparked reexamination of the executives' résumés, whether their fraudulent behavior generalized to their work lives, and whether they lived up to their inflated self-presentations remain unknown. They all found well-paying jobs in a short time but in different industries where their past transgressions would not haunt them. In applying for a new job, only one of the managers gave the reason for the job change; all continued to doctor their résumés. Apparently justified and sanitized deception removes a need for ethical self-reform.

The Enron Accounting Debacle

The fraudulent behavior of the Enron Corporation toward the end of the 1990s primarily involved faking its account books. Enron began as an energy company but quickly expanded into an assemblage of other types of businesses, many of which proved unprofitable. To keep the losses off its financial statements, the company devised outside partnerships and moved its debts and losses to those entities. By hiding its losses, Enron created the illusion of vast profits even as it continued to lose money. The company's share price soared. For six years in a row, *Fortune* magazine cited Enron as the most innovative U.S. corporation (McLean & Elkind, 2006). Little did the raters know that Enron's real innovation was fraudulent accounting. Enron executives sold their shares in the company while telling their investors to buy more shares because the stock would rise in value. The company's massive debts could be hidden for only so long. The deception began to unravel. Eventually, the Enron Corporation collapsed in bankruptcy, leaving in its wake thousands of laid-off employees, billions of dollars in shareholder losses, and the demise of its corporate auditor, Arthur Andersen, a renowned global auditing firm.

Both Enron's CEO Kenneth Lay and Jeffrey Skilling, the company's chief executive officer, claimed they were unaware of what was going on. Sherron Watkins, vice president of economic development sent Lay a memo warning him that Enron might "implode in a wave of accounting scandals" (Associated Press, 2006). A law firm with a conflict of interest that was appointed to look into the matter concluded that a broad investigation was unwarranted and would risk "adverse publicity and litigation" (Yardley & Schwartz, 2002). Skilling also claimed he did not understand the complexities of the accounting practices. At a congressional hearing, he displaced responsibility for the erroneous financial statements onto the auditors. "I am not an accountant, I relied on our accountants. Andersen had taken a hard look at this structure. They believed it was appropriate. The board approved it after accountants signed off on it" (Collapse of the Enron Corporation, 2002). According to the court testimony of Andrew Fastow, Enron's chief financial officer, Skilling was neither blind to the fraudulent machinations nor naive about them. Fastow reported that Skilling pressured him to get "as much of that juice as you can" in hiding the debts in the partnerships the company created (Levine, 2006). In his instructions to the jury, the presiding judge explained that if the defendants intentionally shielded themselves from discovering what was going on, they could not claim ignorance (Barrionuevo, 2006).

Skilling viewed himself as unjustly victimized in a sensationalized witch hunt: "We are labeled hucksters and criminals with complete disregard for the facts." He went on to complain that in his view, Enron's downfall was caused by the "classic run on the bank," set off by declining market confidence. "People don't stop long enough to look at the facts. People are angry, people lost money, they lost jobs. The easiest thing to do is look for the witches" (Pasha, 2006). Enron founder Kenneth Lay died of a heart attack shortly after his conviction. Chief executive Jeffrey Skilling is serving a 14-year prison term, and chief financial officer Andre Fastow is serving a 6-year prison term.

Another notable casualty of Enron's downfall was the venerable Arthur Andersen accounting firm. The founder adhered to high accounting standards and to the ethos that their accountants are responsible to investors, not to corporate governance. The firm went awry through conflicting interest between their auditing responsibilities and consulting fees for advising Enron on, among other matters, how to capitalize on loopholes. Joseph Berardino, Andersen's managing partner and chief executive officer, shifted the blame for not warning the public about Enron's financial condition to the constraints of the audit rules. A firm can only "pass" or "fail" the financial reports (Spiegel, 2002). The only option he had, he explained, was to "give it a pass or give it the death penalty." A failing grade could destroy the company. At a congressional hearing, Berardino angered lawmakers with his deniability replies that he had no direct knowledge of the accounting fraud. While technically true, in that he was not a member of the audit team, his denial of responsibility undermined his credibility. In describing the dilemma his firm faced on how to rate the suspect financial reports, he had to have been fully informed about the auditing misdoings (Enron warned, auditor insists, 2001).

Arthur Andersen was convicted of obstructing justice for shredding Enron audit documents. They trivialized their actions by portraying the shredding as "routine housekeeping." David Duncan, who had led the Enron audit team, shifted responsibility for the shredding to institutional pressure. He signed an agreement to present a united front that nothing wrong was done (Andersen guilty in Enron case, 2002). After "soul searching," Duncan became a witness for the prosecution. However, the conviction was overturned by the Supreme Court because the jurors were instructed improperly on the law. A venerable company founded on high ethical standards ended up shielding a client's illegalities, obstructing justice, and self-destructing.

The Madoff Ponzi Scheme

Bernard Madoff, a wealth manager, used a familiar fraud, running the largest pyramid, or Ponzi, investment scam in U.S. history. He deposited some of his clients' money in a bank account rather than investing it. He paid high returns based not on profit from investments but from the clients' own money or money from subsequent investors. The Ponzi scheme eventually collapsed, with losses of over $60 billion when Madoff could not meet redemptions. Academic institutions and charities lost their endowments, thousands of people lost their life savings, and offshore hedge funds and other investors suffered heavy financial losses.

Madoff ran his operation for a long time without a large cadre of smart money manipulators wielding intricate financial instruments. This was a readily detectable fraud. However, Madoff's brother, who oversaw the compliance program, circumvented regulators by filing phony documents and fraudulent tax returns (Lattman & Protess, 2012). The banks and prospective investors who flocked to Bernard Madoff seemed more interested in his high returns than in how he achieved them. In an interview with Steve Fishman (2011), Madoff described the regulatory failures and complicities between banks and investors that enabled him to continue the Ponzi scheme. The Securities and Exchange Commission, he said, "looks terrible in this thing." Chairmen of major banks were paying him visits, seeking to invest with him. "All of a sudden, these banks which wouldn't give you the time of day, they are willing to give you a billion dollars." He described the heady experience of these financial courting visitations. "It is a head trip....It feeds your ego." When they asked for facts about his financial operations, he told them, "You don't like it, take your money out. Which of course they never did."

Madoff acknowledged his wrongdoings but found relief in moral self-exonerations. He explained that he benefited others by making money for the earlier investors; only the latecomers bore costs. He tried to return funds to some individual clients when he realized that he could not extricate himself from his elaborate fraud. In advantageous comparison, he viewed himself as a small fish in a pervasive climate of greed and unlawful complicity in the financial industry: "Everyone was greedy and I just went along." Regarding the banks and hedge funds, "the attitude was sort of, 'if you're doing something wrong we don't want to know" (Henriques, 2011). The financial and investment "market is a whole rigged job," he claimed. Nor did he spare the lawmakers and the regulatory agencies, whom he regards as enablers of financial excesses and abuses: "The whole new regulatory reform is a joke. The whole government is a Ponzi scheme."

He felt no sorrow for clients who profited from his legitimate investments with net gain, despite later losses, but act as though "they're living out of Dumpsters." He blamed his clients for pressuring him to invest their money while ignoring the face that his underhanded high returns were attracting them to him. In his view, he was the object of social pressure rather than the agent of fraud: "People just kept throwing money at me....I allowed [myself] to be talked into something, and that's my fault." In minimizing the harm he caused he found further solace in the belief that "these people probably would've lost all that money in the market." These various self-exonerations left him with the self-view that "I am a good person" (Ghosh, 2011).

Madoff's reflections on his life provide some clues as to why he ceded virtually everything to financial celebrity (Ghosh, 2011). "How could I have done this? I was making a lot of money. I didn't need the money." However, he felt marginalized and excluded from the inner circle of Wall Street power holders. It was not money per se that drove him. Money mainly was a means for him to purchase the symbols of lofty status so that he could display the trappings of privileged rank. "I woke up one morning and said, 'Well listen, I need to be able to buy a boat and a plane, and this is what I'm going to do'" (Fishman, 2011). "I lived very extravagantly. In the end, I bought a plane with another person. I had a boat [and four homes]. You're talking about someone who had a billion dollars" (Ghosh, 2011). However, his lavish lifestyle came at great financial and human costs.

Bernard Madoff will spend the rest of his life in a prison cell, estranged from his family and friends, resented by those he defrauded, and haunted by the suicide of a son he admired.

Rajaratnam: Big-Time Insider Trading

In 2011, amid global financial losses tied to devalued mortgage-based securities, Raj Rajaratnam, the head of the Galleon Group and a hedge-fund billionaire superstar, was convicted under racketeering law for engaging in the largest insider trading conspiracy in U.S. history. The legal term for this type of criminality is "trading on material, nonpublic information." Rajaratnam cultivated a large network of insider tipsters such as former classmates from business school, corporate executives, consultants, and industry experts. They fed him confidential information about developments in publicly traded companies. Trading on the basis of these tips brought windfall profits for his hedge fund and large payments or a share of the profits to the tipsters—motivating them to pass along even more inside information.

Being a foremost hedge fund titan bestows considerable financial and social power. Rajaratnam wielded that power unsparingly in recruiting a cadre of tipsters. On the financial side, the payments were huge. This created a strong sense of obligation to produce illegal tips. Anil Kumar, a senior executive at a global consulting firm with access to corporate secrets, described his sense of obligation to provide inner corporate secrets when pressed for details, "I felt that I owed him something, given how much money he was paying me" (Lattman & Ahmed, 2011). Generous acclaim for profitable tips served as another influential incentive. When a tip about a secret forthcoming merger produced a large trading profit, Kumar was praised profusely: "That was fantastic. 'We're all cheering you at the office right now. You're a star. You're a hero.'"(Lattman & Ahmed, 2011).

Anil Kumar initially turned down the offer to become a tipster in exchange for payment through a hidden Swiss bank account or for a share of the profits from illegal trading, both of which he regarded as criminal. However, he agreed to the offer when he and Rajaratnam found a way to bundle the corrupt money with payments for lawful consulting services, thus adding a semblance of legitimacy to his activities. Masking the unlawful payment weakened restraint over transgressive conduct but did not diminish the self-devaluative costs. Kumar ended up viewing himself as a "reluctant felon" (Lattman & Ahmed, 2011).

Others traded morality for substantial payments coupled with friendship. This was the case for Rajaratnam's business-school classmate Rajiv Goel, who passed on corporate secrets at Intel. He described the influence of friendship on his illicit activities: "He was a good man to me. I was a good pal, a good person to him, so I gave him the information" (Lattman & Ahmed, 2011). Their social bond and Goel's longing for approval overrode consideration of the moral and legal consequences of his unlawful behavior. What he feared was that some of his tips might prove wrong, jeopardizing their friendship.

Some of the tipsters got caught up in the intensely competitive culture of investment trading. Using a military metaphor, Adam Smith, an executive in the Galleon Group, compared having the competitive edge of research-based findings and illicit tips with having two torpedoes: "If one of them misses, the other is likely to hit" (Lattman & Ahmed, 2011). He found the fierce competition of the financial markets "exhilarating" but seemed to find little time for self-reflection on the broader purpose and morality of his work life. For Danielle Chiesi, a former beauty queen, sexual conquest was the driving force. She extracted confidential information through affairs with corporate insiders. She boasted to Rajaratnam about one of her conquests: "I just got a call from my guy. I played him like a finely tuned piano" (Lattman & Ahmed, 2011). She evidently got more from her conquests than just company secrets: "It is mentally fabulous for me."

What drove Rajaratnam, an eminent financier known for his pride, to self-destruction and the ruin of so many other business executives? Several years earlier, in an interview for the book *The New Investment Superstars*, Rajaratnam described himself as a relentless competitor (Peltz, 2009). In commenting on his financial success, he explained that he tied his sense of pride to unmatched victories, especially in risky undertakings. "It is pride and I want to win. After a while, money is not the motivation. I want to win every time. Taking calculated risks gets my adrenaline pumping" (Peltz, 2009). However, winning illegally got him an 11-year prison term. This is another case in which morality apparently yielded to overbearing competitive ambition.

Rajat Gupta was another wealthy corporate executive driven to self-destruction in the pursuit of exorbitant wealth as a marker of elite status (Lattman & Ahmed, 2012). In a telephone conversation, Rajaratnam and Anil Kumar discussed Gupta's drive for more money to make it into the "billionaire circle." Some members of the corporate establishment coined a new psychological malady, "billionaire envy" (Lattman & Ahmed, 2012).

Rankings invest competitive activities with import and excitement. For example, if football and soccer teams had no rankings, it would rob them of spectators and fans. *Forbes* magazine's list of the world's richest people fuels the competitive money drive. In a talk at Columbia University, Gupta affirmed his drive to amass money, "When I look at myself, yeah, I am driven by money" (Raghavan, 2013). This relentless drive brought him considerable wealth, he explained, but also chagrin over the materialistic person he had become. He forewarned his audience that "money is very seductive" and enormously difficult to resist. "However much you say that you will not fall into the trap of it, you do fall into the trap of it" (Raghavan, 2013). His downfall later testified to its powerful allure.

Gupta was convicted and sentenced to a two-year prison term for feeding secret information to Rajaratnam when he was a Goldman Sachs board member. In handing down the sentence, the presiding judge noted, "He is a good man. But the history of this country and the history of the world is full of examples of good men who did bad things" (Lattman, 2012). This apt observation is very much in keeping with the organizing theme of this book: that good people can do harmful things by disengaging moral self-sanctions from their transgressive conduct. The judge reduced the sentence because of Gupta's philanthropic work, which included advising the Gates and Clinton foundations. Gupta's lawyer argued to keep Gupta out of prison because "the loss of his reputation was a punishment far worse than incarceration" (Lattman, 2012).

James Fleishman at Primary Global Research elevated insider trading to a regularized financial service. Preet Bharara, the U.S. prosecutor, described Fleishman's activities as "verging on a corrupt business model." Fleishman served as a matchmaker, connecting money managers to corporate executives and consultants who leaked illegal stock tips (Lattman, 2011). He was convicted and sentenced to 30 months in prison (Pavlo, 2011). The number of money managers who have been convicted or pled guilty of insider trading is growing. It was over 80 at the last count (Goldstein & Protess, 2015).

An extravagant lifestyle, which comes with a huge price tag, has become a marker for arrival in the circle of elite financiers. Insider trading has become rampant because it is easy to do and is highly profitable for both the tipster and the recipient of confidential information. For traders lured by superrich status with its resplendent trappings, illegal means provide a quick shortcut to get there. Joseph Skowron, an orthopedic surgeon, quit his practice to become a hedge fund manager, trading stocks in the health field. He got caught bribing a physician for advance information on a failed clinical drug trial on which the physician was a consultant. Skowron also lied while trying to cover up the criminal activities that got him a 5-year prison term. He blamed the lure of "relativism" for his downfall (Bray, 2011): "I allowed myself to slip into the world of relativism where the ends justify the means." In reflecting on the course his life took, he voiced puzzlement as to how he had changed: "Quite frankly, it is very hard to imagine how I became that kind of person."

Criminal transformations usually begin with small offenses. As time goes on, larger infractions are justified by successive moral compromises. Eventually one becomes a different person, whose life is characterized by major moral failings. Some of these disastrous life courses are akin to a Shakespearean tragedy in which a character flaw drives one to self-destruction.

To complicate matters in adjudicating insider trading, a federal appeals court overturned a few insider-trading convictions. The court ruled that insider trading is illegal only if the tipster benefits tangibly in exchange for private information. Law professor Michael Perino was perplexed and highly critical of this narrow decision, because "allowing executives to give away information to whomever they choose so long as they get nothing in return simply makes no sense" (Henning, 2014). An appeals court denied the U.S. prosecutor's request to reconsider the ruling (Goldstein & Protess, 2015).

This partial legitimization is likely to spawn creative insider trading, through intermediaries with hidden benefits to tipsters, that will be difficult to prosecute successfully. Indeed, Andrew Stoltmann, a securities lawyer who handles fraud cases, expects the new rule to dissuade prosecutions of insider trading. "It will likely lead to less [*sic*] cases being filed and fewer convictions and that is unfortunate given what many perceive to be rampant insider trading" (Prial, 2014). If this turns out to be the case, it would further deepen public distrust of the financial market.

The Global Economic Meltdown

The federal government encourages financial institutions to offer affordable loans to people with limited financial resources and property assets by insuring those loans. However, lobbying by the finance industry resulted in decreased down-payment requirements, weakened underwriting standards for affordability documentation, and emasculated regulatory oversight. Government-backed guarantees of debts with scant oversight provided fertile ground for reckless risk taking. In the subprime lending crisis, exploitative and predatory lenders sold, with trivial credit documentation, homes that borrowers could not afford (Duca, 2013). The sales pitch transformed unaffordable dwellings into seemingly affordable ones. With scanty down payments and initially low interest, these mortgages seemed to be within the means of unqualified borrowers. These deceptively cheap mortgages quickly changed into increasingly costly variable-rate ones. The unwitting borrowers were led to believe that they would be able to raise money to cover their increased mortgage payments from the growing value of their homes.

Not all moneylenders engaged in predatory practices. However, selling unaffordable homes to people of limited means required misleading them or persuading them that the value of their homes would increase indefinitely. To sell home loans initially on the cheap with subsequent escalating variable-rate loans served as a lure. Instead, the housing bubble burst, leaving lenders with accumulating repossessed homes and few, if any buyers. When the housing bubble burst home values plummeted and continued to fall with a glut of unsold foreclosed homes. New homeowners lost their homes, and established homeowners, many of whom borrowed against their home values, abandoned theirs when the debt on their homes exceeded their value.

The lenders also assumed that home values would continue to increase, which would ensure that they could resell the dwellings in the event of defaults. Instead, many people lost their homes when they could not keep up their mortgage payments. Some simply abandoned their homes when the debt on them exceeded their value and the houses were said to be "underwater." The glut of unsold, foreclosed homes caused housing prices to plummet. Financial institutions found themselves saddled with mounting defaults, "toxic" loans, and devalued homes. Investment brokers bundled the bad home loans with safer ones and sold the bundles, called derivatives, as mortgage securities to pension funds, mutual funds, insurance companies, and other investors worldwide. The value of the packaged jumble of loans and the risks they posed were difficult to estimate. They were sold under weak regulations that were unenforced and easily circumvented. In his book *The Return of Depression Economics and the Crisis of 2008*, the economics Nobelist Paul Krugman (2009) characterized the lack of regulatory oversight as "malign neglect." Warren Buffet (2003) called the derivatives "financial weapons of mass destruction."

These irresponsible mortgage practices occurred in the context of large-scale bank deregulation. The Glass-Steagall Act, enacted in 1933, had prohibited commercial banks from engaging in the securities and investment sectors. In 1999, the banks succeeded in having Glass-Steagall repealed with the help of Alan Greenspan, the chairman the Federal Reserve Board. Greenspan argued that Glass-Steagall's regulations handicapped American banks in competing with their foreign counterparts, thereby stifling their economic growth (Prins, 2014). The combination of faulty, or subprime, home mortgages embedded in complex securities that were traded under deficient federal oversight created the conditions for the global financial crisis. Paul Volcker, Greenspan's predecessor as chairman of the Federal Reserve, expressed regret for failing to speak out strongly against Congress's wholesale deregulation of the financial industry (Uchitelle, 2010).

As defaults and foreclosures mounted, the banks found that the now-toxic loans were hard to unload. In a cynical innovation, Goldman Sachs secretly bet on the failure of the subprime mortgage bonds they were selling to their unwitting clients. In a linguistic sanitization, Goldman Sachs claimed they did not mislead investors but merely gave them "incomplete information" (Prins, 2014). Jamie Dimon, the head of J.P. Morgan Chase, used a comparative metaphor to express his displeasure with how federal officials interpreted financial losses during the economic crisis: "So we made a stupid error. I mean, if an airplane crashes, should we stop flying all airplanes?" (Prins, 2014). Goldman Sachs and J.P. Morgan were fined for negligence, but no one was charged with misleading investors. The executives profited from their companies' misleading financial practices but distanced themselves from any responsibility, claiming that they knew nothing about those practices. Fabrice Tourre of Goldman Sachs was the lone trader whom the Securities and Exchange Commission (SEC) sued for selling bad mortgage securities (Story & Morgenson, 2011b). Tourre was convicted of civil fraud.

Shifting blame to subordinates occurs not only within corporations but also in federal agencies prosecuting corporate crimes. The Goldman Sachs fraud case was settled with a hefty fine. However, a federal jury found Tourre liable on six counts of civil securities fraud. Jurors wondered why Tourre was the only one on trial, rather than the top Goldman Sachs executives (Craig, Protess, & Stevenson, 2013). They sympathized with Tourre as the fall guy but found him liable as a contributing functionary: "We don't think he deserved to take the blame for everything but he did play along" (Craig et al., 2013).

There are several reasons that prosecutors may be reluctant to go after the corporate upper echelon. The assemblage of corporate legal power is highly intimidating. If deniability for profitable transgressive practices is built into the corporate governance structure of a company, top executives can easily absolve themselves of responsibility. Federal officials justify their reluctance to prosecute the top management of prominent banks by pointing out that it could set in motion events that cripple the economy. The "too big to fail" problem, solved by public bailouts, also shields corporate executives from the consequences of their misbehavior. Charges of wrongdoing are usually settled by fines that companies pay without any individuals being indicted and "while neither admitting nor denying any wrongdoing" (Wyatt, 2012). A faceless corporation becomes the agent of wrongdoing. A settlement in which there is no acknowledgement of wrongdoing and there are no identified wrongdoers shields corporations and their top executives from the full consequences of their transgressive behavior. They resist any admission of wrongdoing because it makes them vulnerable to lawsuits by shareholders.

The "London Whale," the chief investment officer at J. P. Morgan's office in London, specialized in large and complex investment packages. His deals lost the company over $6 billion. Two other traders were accused of falsifying records to hide the losses from those trades (Hurtado, 2015). A loss that immense is hard to sweep under the rug, however powerful the control Wall Street wields over federal regulators. In a rare move, under a new chairperson, the SEC filed civil charges against the firm. J.P. Morgan settled the charges by agreeing to pay an unprecedentedly large $200 million fine, admitting the SEC's charges, and acknowledging publicly that it broke federal laws on securities. The SEC filed no charges against the upper echelon. However, it did charge the two London traders with criminal fraud for concealing the losses and, as of May 2015, they haven't been convicted. Both are citizens of other countries who will not extradite them. Both claim innocence of any wrongdoing (U.S. Securities and Exchange Commission, 2013).

The problem of sheltered executive unaccountability for unlawful corporate practices is deeply rooted in the norms of how corporate offenses are prosecuted. This helps explain why a midlevel trader gets convicted of civil fraud, whereas the executives managing the fraudulent behavior get off scot-free.

Faulty financial products were highly profitable for the traders but ruinous to people's lives worldwide. Sales of derivatives containing subprime mortgages brought high fees and commissions. However, these socially detrimental financial practices were disconnected from corrective consequences. This disconnect undermined the rational market system. Because banks borrowed heavily, with insufficient capital requirements to cover the losses of their risky loans, they fell deeply in debt. Because they were so intricately embedded in the economic lives of entire countries, banks also got those countries heavily in debt. Whereas financiers raked in huge personal profits, taxpayers bore the costs of bailing out banks that were considered "too big to fail."

The worldwide financial market spun out of control. The massive public bank bailouts swelled national debts. The financiers left in their wake nations teetering on the brink of bankruptcy, spawned widespread failures of financial systems, and the financial systems shut down as credit markets tightened. The economic crisis left vast populations deeply in debt and chronically unemployed by the ensuing global recession, faced with retrenched social services and looming tax hikes to repay budgetary deficits. Family homes were foreclosed when breadwinners lost their jobs. Those of lesser means suffered the most. The grim economic austerity generated by the recession will persist for some time. The use of public funds to bail out financial institutions fueled divisive political battles. Severe austerity measures instituted to pay off debts caused by the mistakes of bankers and financiers set off social discord.

Not much in the way of moral self-correction seemed evident. As one trader reported, "I leave my ethics at the door." Some executives expressed their cynicism openly (Gouet, 2012), proclaiming, "Ethics is a liability in business." In an e-mail to his girlfriend, Fabrice Tourre expressed no regret for selling toxic mortgage bonds that were destined to fail: "Anyway, not feeling too guilty about this, the real purpose of my job is to make capital markets more efficient and ultimately provide the U.S. consumer with more efficient ways to leverage and finance himself, so there is a humble, noble and ethical reason for my job ;) amazing how good I am at convincing myself!!!" (Eder & Wutkowski, 2010). In another letter to his girlfriend, Tourre boasted that he sold risky bonds to "widows and orphans"—Wall Street euphemisms for unsuspecting investors. Tourre was convicted of defrauding investors in mortgage investments and fined just under $1 million (Raymond & Stempel, 2014). Prosecutors characterized him as lacking "contrition or appreciation of his misconduct." His defense lawyers, who argued for a smaller fine, portrayed him as a "scapegoat" who was treated unjustly.

In an act considered traitorous in the industry, Gregory Smith (2012), an executive at Goldman Sachs, went public in criticizing the firm's ethos of exploiting its clients to increase corporate profits. In addition to documenting these exploitive practices, he described traders disparaging their clients as "muppets" (British slang for a stupid person who is easily manipulated) and talking about "ripping eyeballs out," and analysts of derivatives asking, "How much money did we make off the client?" Smith resigned from the firm when he could "no longer in good conscience" compromise his values.

Financiers rely heavily on economic justifications of their business practices. They argue that when it is free from obstructive regulations, the finance industry promotes economic growth by supporting innovations and providing capital for productive industries. Economic growth raises the standard of living and contributes in other ways to the common good. At the height of the global economic meltdown of the financiers own making, Lloyd Blankfein, chief of Goldman Sachs, extolled how the financial industry serves the greater good: "We help companies to grow by helping them to raise capital. Companies that grow create wealth. This, in turn, allows people to have jobs that create more growth and more wealth. It's a virtuous cycle. We have a social purpose." He described himself as "doing God's work" (Carney, 2009). Viewing oneself as promoting the common good through holy work obviates the need for self-censure. The missionary claim might be dismissed as spoken in jest. However, given the financial meltdown, one must believe in the goodness of one's work to preserve a sense of self-respect.

While financiers extolled their vital contribution to the economic well-being of society, their critics denounced them as "vulture capitalists" and "economic vandals." Matt Taibbi (2010) of *Rolling Stone* magazine penned a memorable metaphor when he referred to Goldman Sachs as "a great vampire squid wrapped around the face of humanity, relentlessly jamming its blood funnel into anything that smells like money."

Rising Income Inequality

Escalating income disparity raises the broader social issue of the values of the corporate culture. In a massive income shift, a tiny segment of society continues to amass ever more wealth. In stark contrast, the middle class is eroding, with many of its members under- or unemployed. Low-wage workers receive an hourly salary that is insufficient for the basic necessities of life. A growing number of struggling families are seeking federal assistance through the food stamp Supplementary Nutrition Assistance Program. Much of the dispute over compensation centers on the morality of relative income inequality. The morality of paying workers so little that they have difficulty providing the necessities of life for their families receives little attention. The minimum wage set by the federal government has stagnated for decades. In a recent year, generous Wall Street bonuses far exceeded the combined paychecks of over 1 million workers paid the federal minimum wage of $7.25 per hour (Anderson, 2015). A number of lawmakers, mainly those of a conservative bent, oppose raising the minimum wage a few dollars on the grounds that it will drive businesses abroad and result in worker layoffs. This justification conveys the uncharitable implication that it is in the self-interest of low-wage workers to remain underpaid for their labor if they want to keep their jobs.

Shifting blame was used for exonerative purposes in the collapse of the housing market. Homeowners who had fallen behind on their mortgage payments were blamed for buying homes they should have known they could not afford. In the controversy over who is to blame for the global crisis, the columnist Charles Krauthammer (2008), representing the conservative view, argued that the government's affordable housing policies, not the banks, had caused the crisis: "What could be a more worthy cause? But it led to tremendous pressure on Fannie Mae and Freddie Mac—who in turn pressured banks and other lenders—to extend mortgages to people who were borrowing over their heads. That's called subprime lending. It lies at the root of our current calamity." David Min (2011), a financial analyst at the Center for American Progress, empirically refuted this displacement of responsibility. High-risk home mortgages precipitated the financial problem, but evidence pointed to unregulated banks as major contributors to the global economic crisis. They bundled the bad loans into obscure derivatives and sold them worldwide. A large cast of players had a hand in the economic disaster, including Wall Street bankers, lawmakers beholden to them, mortgage finance companies, subprime lenders, and federal regulators. Krauthammer exonerates the finance industry by invoking the isolated "bad apples" argument, as though only a few predatory lenders and traders brought down financial systems worldwide. Paul Krugman (2011) demonstrates the global financial crisis was the product of top-down financial recklessness, not bottom-up pressure from unqualified home buyers.

The Dodd–Frank Wall Street Reform and Consumer Protection Act

The magnitude of the economic crisis shattered faith in the heralded self-corrective power of the free market. But it did not diminish the efforts of Wall Street to water down legislative regulatory initiatives designed to rein in the financial industry. Despite the disastrous human consequences and the urgent need for reforms, efforts to enact financial regulations met with stiff opposition. Corporate executives and legions of lobbyists for the financial industry fought vigorously to defeat regulation of their financial practices. A united partisan group of lawmakers, some of whom received disproportionately large contributions to their reelection campaigns shortly before the vote on the Dodd-Frank financial reform bill, joined the financial lobbyists in opposing the bill (Lipton & Lichtblau, 2010). They justified their votes on the grounds that regulations would cripple the economy; stifle job growth, expand the government's costly, obstructive bureaucracies; undermine international competitiveness; and distort the self-correcting power of the free-market system (Dennis, 2010).

Legislative initiatives designed to remedy problems are often subverted or neutralized by opposing interest groups using the 4D strategy: defeat, defang, deregulate, and dismantle. In the initial defeat phase, congressional leaders oppose efforts to introduce legislative initiatives disliked by campaign contributors, or they try to defeat a proposal in congressional committee to save legislators from having to record a public vote that their constituents may not like.

If a bill is passed by Congress and signed into law by the president, opposing special-interest groups shift the battle to the defanging phase in an effort to weaken and circumvent the law. The defanging strategy takes a variety of forms. Laws are mainly general statements of intent. The task of converting enacted laws to operational rules is delegated to regulatory agencies, which spell out the legal specifics. Lobbyists can use their influence to water down a proposed law until its intent is subverted. If that happens, the legislative initiative can end up toothless. Targeted industries also enlist their resources and talent to find loopholes in a law to turn intended regulations into unintended profits.

A common strategy in the defense phase is to devise creative ways to outwit a law. An even more creative scheme is to find ways to exploit the law to one's benefit. Even positive economic incentive systems can be corrupted for a new source of lucrative profits (Rosenthal & Lehren, 2012a). In an effort to reduce global warming, the UN rated gases according to their power to warm the atmosphere. The UN wanted to phase out a certain coolant used in air-conditioning and refrigeration that has a huge warming effect and depletes the ozone layer. Manufacturers, mainly in China and India, figured out that they can make huge profits by increasing production of this coolant and destroying the waste gases released in its manufacturing for generous carbon credits that they can sell in the international market. This well-intended incentive system got corrupted into a subsidy for increased production of the coolant!

If countercontrol fails in the defanging phase, the battle shifts to weakening the implementation of the regulatory rules by deregulating the regulators, watering down their oversight rules or cutting their budgets so they lack the personnel and resources to enforce the law adequately. This strategy is known as "starve the beast." Effective oversight also requires transparency of the organizational activities being monitored. Regulators can be foiled by obfuscation and concealment, so battles are fought over transparency rules.

Implementation is also thwarted by the "revolving-door" practice. Many lawmakers, regulators, and top staff members become high-paid lobbyists shortly after leaving government. A sizable number of lawmakers who preside over legislative policies affecting particular industries, as well as regulators who implement the laws, have an eye on a lucrative career change as lobbyists for the very industries they are overseeing. Under this conflict of interest they act on behalf of the industry instead of regulating it. Special interests are eager to recruit them because they know how Congress works and how to use their congressional connections to influence the polices being legislated. Eisinger (2014) describes government work for those seeking life in the lobbying world as "an internship program for law firms and large corporations." With the lure of campaign contributions and the prospect of a lucrative lobbying career, lawmakers are not especially keen to reform these revolving-door practices.

It is difficult to repeal a law in its entirety. However, under lobbying pressure, it can be obliterated by piecemeal dismantling of its essential regulatory features. Incremental dismantling cripples the already starved beast. Most regulatory agencies are ill equipped to oversee adequately laws that are already on the books. Given the complexities of innovative financial products, overseers are likely to be even less equipped to do their job without increased operational resources.

The financial reform bill survived the first phase of the 4D strategy but was scaled back in the defanging phase. When major banks merge their deposit and trading functions, risky, speculative trading can incur huge debts, threatening the collapse of the financial system. Structural financial reforms separate safe deposit services from risky trading operations (as did the Glass-Steagall Act), or devise ways of limiting negative effects of the speculative trading sector on the deposit sector. The Dodd-Frank reform bill did not institute structural changes in the financial industry. It left things pretty much as they were, but with more oversight and regulation of industry practices. It also provided some new consumer protections. Paul Krugman (2009) considered these remedies insufficient against the magnitude of the financial crisis.

Paul Volcker, the former chairman of the Federal Reserve Board, favors restricting federally insured banks from risky trading that is not on behalf of their clients. Volcker gave the watered-down bill an "ordinary B, not even a B plus" (Uchitelle, 2010). He preferred a simpler rule that was readily enforceable: "I'd love to see a four-page bill that bans proprietary trading and makes the board and chief executive responsible for compliance" (Stewart, 2011). Volcker's second requirement is a key feature of an effective regulatory system: personal accountability for unlawful corporate practices. It shifts the major responsibility for adherence to the law from regulators to the officials managing the firms. Volcker also wanted vigilant regulators: "And I'd have strong regulators. If the banks didn't comply with the spirit of the bill, they'd go after them." The former senator Ted Kaufman, now a professor at Duke University School of Law, describes how adding exemptions to the rule opened a Pandora's box of rules covering 300 pages: "Here's the key word in rules: 'exemption.' ... [A]s soon as you see that, it's pronounced 'loophole'" (Stewart, 2011). Kaufman comments on the cleverness of "Wall Street guys" in exploiting exemptions: "They're smart as hell. You give them the smallest little hole, and they'll run through it" (Stewart, 2011). All those exemptions can result in a law that is essentially unenforceable.

The lobbying also shifted to the defang phase to where the operative rules are drafted. The effectiveness of lobbies is typically gauged in terms of their power to sway lawmakers. Appelbaum (2010) highlights the power of information management as another key aspect of the power of the lobbies. Bills can easily run into thousands of pages, making them difficult to fathom. They involve many uncertainties regarding the extent of the benefits, possible costs, and unintended adverse effects. Well-funded corporations mobilize lobbyists and law-firm personnel, many of whom are former lawmakers or agency officials, to scour the bills for unfavorable provisions and regulations. They provide legislators with the economic and social justifications to water down proposed legislation further.

The former senator Christopher Dodd, who shepherded his namesake financial-reform bill through the Senate, reminded the public that no one can legislate the competencies, commitments, and allegiances of regulators. Although some regulators become cozy with those they are supposed to oversee, the fate of bills that become law rests, in large part, in the hands of lawmakers, not regulators. Lawmakers can water down reform initiatives and cut funds for enforcement of the laws they pass. Dodd began to express concern over Congress's lack of success in reforming the finance system: "Here we are 17 months after someone broke into our house and robbed us...and we still haven't even changed the locks" (Foley, 2010).

The Revised Volcker Rule

After three years of arduous deliberation, federal regulators produced a revised Volcker Rule designed to rein in risky trading that can result in disastrous bank losses (Eavis, 2013). The new rule prohibits banks from trading depositors' money with taxpayer backing for the banks' own profit. However, it is difficult to distinguish allowable trading that benefits depositors from proprietary trading for banks' own profit. Compromises in drafting the Volcker Rule created exemptions that left many potential loopholes for circumventing the regulations.

The revised Volcker Rule also tried to change the trading-incentive system. Traders will not be paid bonuses up front as a percentage of profits from trades, regardless of the merits of those trades. If corporations object to regulations, they try to find a way to circumvent them. Banks fought the bonus skirmish semantically by disguising them as "allowances" and "reviewable salary" (Anderson & Eavis, 2014).

In the view of Sheila Bair, the former chairperson of the Federal Deposit Insurance Corporation, it would have been easier to reinstate the Glass-Steagall law of the 1930s, which separated commercial and investment banking. Senator Elizabeth Warren of Massachusetts, a nemesis of Wall Street and its supporting lawmakers, was also highly skeptical of the effectiveness of this effort to prevent future bank failures requiring costly taxpayer bailouts: "[W]e should not accept a regulatory system that is so besieged by lobbyists for big banks that it takes years to deliver rules, and the rules that are delivered are often watered down and ineffective" (Mattingly & Hopkins, 2013). Even the creator of Citigroup, Sanford Weill, acknowledged the need for a more comprehensive regulatory system along Glass-Steagall lines. "What we should probably do is go split up investment banking from banking" (Mattingly & Hopkins, 2013). Financial wrongdoings, however, go beyond risky proprietary trading. The toxic securities that banks traded before the 2008 crisis drew heavily on faulty, unregulated mortgage lending.

Exemptions to the expanded Volcker Rule give regulators leeway on how to interpret and enforce the rule. Sometimes regulators are lax in their oversight; sometimes they protect the interests of the very corporations they are supposed to regulate. The financial crisis testified to the languid enforcement of existing laws. Morgenson (2013) cites a number of financial authorities who express strong skepticism that regulators are up to the task of vigorously enforcing the modified Volcker Rule. They describe exceptions as large enough to drive a "large truck through." They call for the establishment of a system to hold regulators accountable, with consequences for deficient regulatory behavior. If lawmakers, some of whom side with financial institutions, provide insufficient staff and funding for regulators to do the job right, they also are responsible for stripping the rule of its regulatory intent.

A striking feature of the catastrophe is that the finance industry, through its reckless practices, caused a global financial disaster without anyone being held responsible for it. Amid the financial crisis, sanitizing language and animistic forces were called into service for self-exonerative purposes. Bear Stearns, an investment bank that collapsed, portrayed itself as a victim of a "once-in-a-lifetime tsunami" that was unforeseeable and uncontrollable (Cohan, 2009). In fact, Bear Stearns collapsed because of a risky policy of maximizing profits with speculative investments, using borrowed money with limited capital as backup. When the company could not cover its losses and was denied bailout funds, it went out of business. In short, it was a participating agent in the economic meltdown, not the helpless victim of an inscrutable, animistic force.

A comprehensive Senate report on the business practices that spawned the financial crisis implicated a wide array of contributing factors (Final Report, 2011). They include misleading and predatory mortgage lenders; investment banks that engaged in deceptive practices, including a lack of transparency and disclosure of the scope of risks being undertaken; credit rating agencies with conflicts of interest; and neglectful regulators who sided with the institutions they were overseeing or sought to join them as lobbyists. Lawmakers with close ties to the financial industry were also highly significant players among this diverse cast of enablers.

Individual and institutional change requires accountability, with consequences for harmful practices. Without personal consequences, people do not learn from their faulty judgments and practices. Alan Greenspan, the chairman of the Federal Reserve and an Ayn Rand disciple and strong advocate of free competitive markets, was "nibbling away at regulation" (Heffernan, 2011). Congress removed many of the likely social and legal consequences for questionable financial practices. In deference to corporate lobbying, lawmakers not only deregulated the financial industry but also cut the budget required for investigating financial wrongdoing. Few rules and little chance of getting caught violating those that existed resulted in a sense of invulnerability.

Story and Morgenson (2011a) provide a detailed account of how widespread machinations caused the economic debacle without anyone's feeling accountable for it. They cite William Black, a law professor who directed litigation during the savings and loan crisis of the 1980s. He called the existing atmosphere a "criminogenic environment." He contrasted the vigorous litigation of the savings and loan transgressions with the lethargic federal response to the global economic catastrophe: "There were no criminal referrals from the regulators. No fraud working groups. No national task force. There has been no effective punishment of the elites here."

None of the major players in the global financial crisis were charged or prosecuted for financial fraud. Henry Pontell, a professor of criminology at the University of California, Irvine, described the difficulty of doing so when bank regulators make no criminal referrals: "When regulators don't believe in regulation and don't get what is going on at the companies they oversee, there can be no major white collar crime prosecutions" (Morgenson & Story, 2011). Not only had referrals dwindled to a trickle but, according to Pontell, regulators did not understand the nature and scope of the transgressive activities. "If they don't understand what we call collective embezzlement, where people are literally looting their own firms, then it's impossible to bring cases" (Morgenson & Story, 2011). Mortgage executives were raking in millions in pay while their companies were collapsing.

The anti-oversight mind-set spilled over into intra-agency conflict. When the Washington Mutual Bank failed to correct hundreds of poor lending practices, Sheila Bair, chairperson of the Federal Deposit Insurance Corporation, downgraded the bank's soundness rating. John Reich, the director of the Office of Thrift Supervision, the agency with oversight responsibility for Washington Mutual, responded angrily to her action: "I cannot believe the continuing audacity of this woman" (Story & Morgenson, 2011a).

Various governmental forces also acted to protect possible wrongdoers. There were reports that some lawmakers used their influence to abort committee hearings related to corporate fraud, and memos from the Justice Department telling the FBI not to shift agents to mortgage fraud cases. These reports were met with the usual denials and collective memory losses of those involved. Eventually Congress allocated funds so that the FBI could investigate mortgage fraud, but the amount was insufficient to do the job.

Partisan lawmakers who side with Wall Street tried to curb the independence of the Consumer Finance Protection Bureau and to water down the regulatory rules for the Dodd-Frank financial reform bill. They blocked confirmation of nominees for leadership and regulatory positions in key agencies, leaving them in limbo (Wyatt & Protess, 2011). What began as a legislative effort to rein in the detrimental practices of Wall Street turned into a concerted effort to rein in the regulators.

Another part of Dodd-Frank requires large investment banks to hold sufficient capital to cover their losses. This forces banks rather than taxpayers to pay for their mistakes. Having the wrongdoer pay restores consequential responsibility for fraudulent financial practices. Investment bankers oppose higher capital requirements on the grounds that it will diminish their competitiveness. This justification received a sympathetic hearing from congressional supporters of the financiers.

A uniquely striking feature of the catastrophe is that the finance industry, through its reckless practices, caused a global financial disaster without anyone being held responsible for it. It was widely assumed that the massive financial collapse would force a wave of reform. Instead, it left a catastrophe with no guilty parties. Wrongdoers do not change when they are sheltered from the consequences of their harmful conduct. As a result, the basic structure of the industry remains essentially unchanged. Wall Street did not foreswear extravagant salaries, stock options, or bonuses. Banks that were shored up with public bailout funds continued to offer lofty salaries and unmerited bonuses to themselves while people struggle to rescue their livelihood under bleak employment conditions. Financiers justify multimillion-dollar salaries as necessary to ward off competitors' raids on their talent and to prevent brain drain from Wall Street to countries with financial systems unfettered by regulations. The irony in this justification is that this is the talent that caused the enormous economic mess. Vigorous lobbying efforts to emasculate even the modest financial reform bill indicate little change in the priorities and ethical climate in the financial sector.

The long-standing "gentleman's agreement" of fining offending corporations without admission of wrongdoing and shielding upper-echelon executives from accountability is highly resistant to change. However, public pressure for indictments of those responsible for the economic crises mounted because of the magnitude of the corporate harm and the spectacle of senior executives continuing to enjoy extravagant salaries and traders receiving generous bonuses while many in the general public are struggling to save their livelihoods. The Justice Department began to pursue more aggressively some of the offending banks. J.P. Morgan, for example, paid a $13 billion settlement for its faulty mortgage practices and failure to inform investors of risks in their bundled securities, which included the toxic residential mortgages (Protess & Silver-Greenberg, 2013a). The bank reluctantly admitted wrongdoing but shielded upper-level wrongdoers. Bart Naylor of Public Citizen criticized the

Justice Department for pursuing civil penalties instead of criminal charges: "Unless you hold the executives accountable, it really is just the cost of doing business" (Protess & Silver-Greenberg, 2013a).

J.P. Morgan profited from many of the fraudulent transactions that Bernard Madoff conducted through the bank. The bank was charged with failing to report Madoff's suspicious financial activities to federal authorities, which is a criminal offense (Protess & Silver-Greenberg, 2014b). The Justice Department had to decide whether to pursue a criminal indictment or adjudicate the case in a more lenient way. The officials opted for the prosecutorial settlement known as deferred prosecution, commonly applied in settlements of corporate criminal activities. In this legal procedure, prosecutors dismiss criminal charges in exchange for a fine, various concessions, and a pledge to adopt prescribed corporate reforms. These settlements also grant waivers to offending firms that exempt them from some laws that carry penalties. Concessions are granted because companies refuse settlements without the waivers they demand. This practice further weakens consequences for criminal conduct. Prosecutors are averse to acknowledging exempting companies from certain laws and penalties, so waivers are rarely mentioned in media announcements of settlements.

The term *deferred prosecution* puts a linguistic mask on the nature of the practice. It suggests that the criminal trial has been put off to a later date. In practice, it essentially says "We will let you off this time with a fine and a promise to reform, but change your ways and don't do it again." The Michigan law professor David Uhlmann (2013) argues that this type of settlement should be limited to first-time wrongdoers whose violations are not too severe. In cases of serious violations, he contends, "They should be prosecuted, not be allowed to buy their way out of criminal liability" (Uhlmann, 2013).

The bank settled for a deferred prosecution agreement with a $2 billion dollar fine but without having to plead guilty to a criminal charge (Protess & Silver-Greenberg, 2013b). Critics of the settlement objected to the fact that no bank employee was charged with wrongdoing. Commenting on the habitual practice of detaching corporate wrongdoers from their financial wrongdoing, Dennis Kelleher, head of the advocacy group Better Markets, reconnected the detached human agency. "Banks do not commit crimes; bankers do" (Protess & Silver-Greenberg, 2014b).

Not only is corporate wrongdoing agentless, but even the depersonalized consequences are watered down. Multibillion-dollar settlements are not as punitive as they appear (Cohen, 2015). Corporations are allowed to write off billion-dollar fines as tax-deductible business expenses. For example, a sizable share of J.P. Morgan's $13 billion dollar fine was tax deductible. Similarly, BP also was able to write off much of the billions that it was fined after the Gulf of Mexico oil disaster. As Phineas Baxandall, an analyst at the Public Interest Research Group observed, allowing tax deductions for fines amounts to "subsidizing bad behavior" (Cohen, 2015). Taxpayers bear the dual costs of corporate wrongdoings. They pay the losses from reckless corporate practices and lose tax revenues because the fines are deductible. Under the sway of corporate influence Congress rejects efforts to close this tax windfall.

Adjudication of criminal charges has produced a new form of displaced responsibility—banks are too bureaucratically complex to convict. In this form of exoneration, a bank's complexity is at fault, not the bankers. There were warning signs within J.P. Morgan that Madoff was running a fraudulent scheme (Protess & Silver-Greenberg, 2014b). One employee noted that Madoff's returns were "possibly too good to be true." He cautioned against a deal because there were "too many red flags" (Protess & Silver-Greenberg, 2014b). A bank risk manager explained that a bank executive told him that "there is a well-known cloud over the head of Madoff and that his returns are speculated to be part of a Ponzi scheme" (Protess & Silver-Greenberg, 2014b). The multiple explicit warnings prompted a request for a meeting with Madoff, who refused (King, 2007).

Despite growing suspicion that Madoff was running an enormous Ponzi scheme, the bank allowed him to "still move billions of dollars in and out of his Chase accounts, no questions asked" (Henriques, 2011). Madoff claimed, "They were deliberately ignoring the red flags" (Henriques, 2011). When the "Oz-like signals" became "too difficult to ignore" (Silver-Greenberg & Protess, 2013), J.P. Morgan quit doing business with Madoff. His arrest came as no surprise to bank officials. However, the responsibility for ignoring the warning signs remains in foggy ambiguity within the bureaucratic maze. Speaking on the bank's behalf, Joseph Evangelisti defended the bankers' innocence: "We do not believe that any J.P. Morgan Chase employee knowingly assisted Madoff's Ponzi scheme" (Tseng, 2014). Smart officials do not engage in profitable suspect activities knowingly. They do so tacitly with an organizationally structured system of deniability for the upper echelon.

The J.P. Morgan settlement was widely criticized for its leniency. U.S. Attorney General Eric Holder cautioned prosecutors against bringing criminal charges against firms and their executives for fear that it could damage domestic and world economies—but quickly backtracked from that statement (Breslow, 2013). The former Wall Street executive Nomi Prins (2014) argues that it is not that banks are too big to jail but that banks are too powerful to restrain. The case of Credit Suisse, one of the world's biggest banks, is a notable example. Credit Suisse was charged with criminal offenses for helping wealthy Americans evade taxes. Bank officials pleaded with U.S. prosecutors and regulators not to file criminal charges against their parent company (Protess & Silver-Greenberg, 2014c). Instead, they proposed settling the government's case against them with "modest guilty pleas from their subsidiaries." To escape criminal charges and penalties bank, officials predictably turn to fear control. Guilty pleas, they argue, will wreak widespread havoc in financial markets. The threat of catastrophic financial consequences intimidates prosecutors into settling for lesser charges and penalties.

Credit Suisse agreed to a guilty plea and was fined $2.6 billion, a modest cost for a huge bank. As part of the deal, the bank was not required to release the names of its American clients on the grounds that doing so would violate Swiss law. Moreover, the bank was granted a waiver, allowing it to continue doing business in the United States despite the criminal conviction. In the view of Protess and Silver-Greenberg (2014c), "other than fines and the reputational stain of being a felon, the implications are likely to be limited."

This turned out to be the case. The business catastrophe predicted by the bank's officials never materialized. Rather, the bank enjoyed an abrupt rise in its stock price! Professor Rebel Cole of DePaul University noted, "If there are no consequences from a criminal conviction, they are just dumbing down a criminal conviction" (Eavis, 2014).

The French bank BNP Paribas was criminally charged with illicit financial transactions with blacklisted countries, such as Iran and Sudan, in its U.S. operation. The bank went to great lengths to cover up those transactions and allegedly suggested extending the deception to the settlement itself. Individuals briefed on the proceedings reported that BNP proposed creating a new subsidiary and retroactively assigning the guilt to it (Protess & Silver-Greenberg, 2014a). BNP pleaded guilty to the criminal charges and was fined $8.9 billion. A unit of the bank was temporarily suspended from doing business, but its U.S. license was not revoked. The assistant district attorney reported that "[t]his conspiracy was known and condoned at the highest levels of BNP" (Protess & Silver-Greenberg, 2014a). However, neither the condoning executives nor their offending subordinates were criminally charged.

These bank settlements reflect a shift in policy from civil settlements and deferred prosecutions to requiring corporations at least to admit to criminal practices. The Justice Department is apparently no longer scared by the "Chicken Little routine," as the U.S. attorney Preet Bharara calls it, that admission of corporate criminal wrongdoing will do serious damage to world economies. This new phase of adjudication includes admission of corporate guilt, but corporate crimes continue to be treated as personless crimes. Top executives still remain above the law.

If banks are too big to fail, indict, convict, and jail, they require structural changes, not modest fines with promissory pacts of future good behavior. Otherwise, the same bank structure with weak or industry-friendly oversight provides a fertile breeding ground for civil and criminal wrongdoings that will bring on the next financial crisis. The most protective structural reform, which was provided by the repealed Glass-Steagall Act of the 1930s, separates commercial from investing banking. Under this structure, if banks get heavily into debt through poor investment practices, they pay with their own money rather than shifting the burden to taxpayers to bail them out.

With a new Congress that is more sympathetic to Wall Street, the Dodd-Frank Reform and Consumer Protection Act is entering the dismantling phase. The lawmakers' proposed changes, as reported by Gretchen Morgenson (2015a), would weaken or eliminate key sections of the law. The changes, designed to benefit mainly Wall Street firms, were linguistically minimized as "technical corrections" in a bill with the misleading title Promoting Job Creation and Reducing Small Business Burdens Act (Morgenson, 2015a). Marcus Stanley, the policy director of the nonprofit Americans for Financial Reform, regarded the Dodd-Frank legislation as weak to begin with: "Any further compromise and it tends to collapse into nothingness," he warned (Morgenson, 2015a). If financial firms dismantle regulations to the precrisis level, the public is likely to end up bailing out Wall Street again.

In his defense of the banking industry general counsel at Bank of America Gary Lynch criticized the regulatory efforts in the aftermath of the financial crisis (Norris, 2013). He dismissed the Volcker rule as meaningless and as forcing banks to second-guess regulators in trying to run their business. He cites the caustic criticism by the head of the Deutsche Bank of Wolfgang Schäuble, German finance minister, for suggesting the need for additional bank regulations, "banks still show great creativity in evading regulations," (Ibid). Finding ways of circumventing regulations is a common corporate practice not an outlandish claim. However, the top banker discredited Schäuble as an "irresponsible" official resorting to "populist" rhetoric. As for bankers not going to jail, Lynch minimized the trading violations, "it is not a crime to make stupid mistakes" (Ibid). These "mistakes", wreaked havoc with financial systems worldwide and devastated people's lives. It does not serve the public interest to grant top executives immunity from the consequences of corporate wrongdoing.

General counsels for Wall Street firms complained about increased regulations and escalating fines levied on banks (Norris, 2013). Gary Lynch, a general council at Bank of America, expressed frustration over the continuing distrust of banks: "At which point does this stop," he asked. General Council at J.P. Morgan was troubled by the heightening fines, "We should all be concerned that there doesn't seem to be a natural end point to how high fines could go." The head of the Deutsche Bank berated Wolfgang Schäuble, German finance minister, for suggesting the need for additional bank regulations: "Banks still show great creativity in evading regulations," he said (Norris, 2013). Finding ways of circumventing regulations is a common corporate practice not an outlandish claim. However, the top banker discredited Schäuble as an "irresponsible" official resorting to "populist" rhetoric.

At an industry conference, Gary Lynch noted the increase in "regulatory fervor" and enforcement of regulations, which he expected to continue for several years (Campbell & Geiger, 2013). At the same conference, Stephen Cutler commented on the number of government agencies investigating the banks: "In some cases there have been interviews of our people taking place in auditoriums because there are so many different agencies involved"

(Patel, 2013). Self-commiseration and perceived injustice of penalities for wrongdoing are not conducive to corrective change.

Big banks placed the responsibility for the 2008 financial crisis on faulty mortgages and maintained that, in selling them, they never violated any laws. Eventually 18 of them, including Goldman Sachs and Bank of America, were charged with criminal conduct for deceptively selling packaged defective mortgages worldwide (Eavis, 2015). Because of banking interconnections these duplicitous practices contributed to the widespread collapse of the mortgage market. Under a "nonprosecution agreement," the banks settled out of court except for two foreign ones that went to trial and were found guilty. The presiding judge bluntly described the extensive underhanded sales: "The magnitude of falsity, conservatively measured, is enormous" (Eavis, 2015).

In criminal conduct in the foreign exchange business four international banks—Citigroup, J.P. Morgan Chase, Barclays, and Royal Bank of Scotland— were fined over $4 billion in penalties for criminal antitrust violations in rigging interest rates and foreign currency prices (Corkery & Protess, 2015). Like the illegal price fixing in the electric industry of yesteryear (Herling, 1962), bankers colluded in manipulating the average interest rate banks charge each other for shorter term loans (Libor). However, taking advantage of the Internet, traders did it pretentiously in chat rooms. They referred to their illegal operation as "the cartel" and "the mafia." They used coded language in their chat rooms with venturesome group names like The Three Musketeers (Mufson & Marte, 2015). The profitability of price fixing was dazzling, "It's just amazing how Libor fixing can make you that much money" (Taibbe, 2013). One of the traders described succinctly the prevailing illicit culture, "If you ain't cheating you ain't trying" (Corkery & Protess, 2015). With federal authorities exempting some activities in the foreign exchange market from regulatory oversight, and providing no government agency to monitor bank practices, manipulation of the price of foreign currency was difficult to detect.

Michael Corbat, chief executive of Citigroup, minimized the seriousness of the criminal conduct, characterizing it as "an embarrassment to our firm." Chief executive Jamie Dimon of J.P. Morgan Chase shifted the blame to a few renegade traders: "The lesson here is that the conduct of a small group of employees, or of even a single employee, can reflect badly on all of us" (Mufson & Marte, 2015). Executives are acutely aware of the profitability of their traders but exhibit collective blindness to the means they use.

In "deferred prosecution" and "nonprosecution" settlements corporations are treated as the agents of wrongdoing and fined for criminal behavior. High-echelon officials are granted immunity buttressed by diffused responsibility and deniability built into the corporate structure itself. With little chance of convicting high officials under these self-protective conditions, prosecutors opt for civil settlements of criminal conduct. Professor Michael Greenberger at the University of Maryland warned of the societal harm caused by shielding chief executives from personal consequences for corporate crimes: "But when the attorney general says, 'I don't want to indict people,' it's the Wild West. There's no law" (Taibbi, 2013).

An agentless, corporate model has evolved in the banking industry. Transgressing corporations shield their upper-echelon executives from accountability for their harmful practices and pay fines without having to admit wrongdoing. They receive taxpayer bailouts for financial losses and turn financial penalties into tax benefits by writing off fines as business expenses. They do so with the tacit consent of lawmakers who depend heavily on corporate funding of their political campaigns. This set of exonerations makes it easy to strip morality from harmful practices. With faulty corporate practices disconnected from adverse consequences for wrongdoers, the free-market system loses its corrective influence. Because the general public is unfamiliar with the specifics of judicial settlements, there is little public pressure on lawmakers for essential oversight. With the public incensed that no one has been held responsible for the global financial crisis, "gentleman's agreements" were hard to defend. The Securities and Exchange Commission now requires major offenders to at least admit wrongdoing, but culpability still remains agentless (Morgenson, 2015b).

The recurrent financial crises are systemic moral failings, not just systemic financial failings. Morality cannot be mandated or legislated, but when it is supplanted by reckless ambition, new financial products designed to circumvent existing regulations will bring about future financial crises. You can plug the hole in a leaking water barrel but with disengaged morality enterprising individuals will drill another one. In wisdom born of a wealth of knowledge, Paul Volcker explains that "There is a certain circularity in all this business. You have a crisis, followed by some kind of reform, for better or worse, and things go well for a while, and then you have another crisis" (Uchitelle, 2010). Much creativity in the financial industry will, in all likelihood, be devoted to figuring out how to circumvent the new financial reforms with new schemes. Without a change in the moral climate, legislative reforms will continue to play catch-up with new financial transgressive creativity.

INJURIOUS PRODUCTS AND PRODUCTION PROCESSES

The preceding analysis centered on moral issues related to egregious practices and products of the finance industry that had ruinous economic and social repercussions. In some industries, morality concerns are related to commercial products that cause harm to others, and to production practices that take a heavy toll on human health. This section analyzes the moral disengagement by the tobacco, lead, vinyl chloride, and silicon-producing industries. Cigarette smoking causes almost half a million deaths annually in the United States alone. Lead poisoning can cause neurological disorders, convulsions in adults, and mental retardation, attention disorders, poor impulse control, and other neurological and behavioral deficits in children. Most exposure to lead was through its use in household paint and as a gasoline additive, until it was banned from both products in the 1970s and 1980s. Vinyl chloride (VC) is used in a host of construction and consumer products. Its health effects include degenerative bone disease and liver cancer. Silicosis is a respiratory disease common among workers in the mining, foundry, sandblasting, and other "dusty trades." It is caused by the inhalation of silica dust and increases the chance of contracting tuberculosis. The disease can continue to progress even after workers have left these industries.

Disputes over the adverse health effects of the products marketed by these industries have a long history. Through litigation, a vast array of internal corporate documents have become available for analysis. The tobacco documents have been archived by, and are accessible through, the University of California, San Francisco's Legacy Tobacco Documents Library (https://industrydocuments.library.ucsf.edu). Documents from the other three industries were also obtained though litigation and reported by David Rosner of Columbia University and Gerald Markowitz of the City University of New York Graduate Center (Markowitz & Rosner, 2002; Rosner & Markowitz, 1991). These documents include copies of corporate research reports, conference proceedings, letters, internal memos, internal planning documents, correspondence, public statements, and newspaper articles. The authors also have included documents authored by corporate scientists, executives, lawyers, public relations and marketing personnel, and scientific consultants working with these industries.

Major battles continue to be fought over evidence of harmful health effects of products and production processes. If they can be shown to cause no harm, there is no moral predicament or any reason for moral qualms about one's work life. Disputes about empirical evidence of harmful effects take a variety of forms. They include engaging in straightforward denial, distortion, or minimization of adverse health effects; creating questionable exposure thresholds below which the exposure is claimed to be harmless; fabricating controversies to confuse the general public about the overall evidence; denying access to industry data showing harm; and exaggerating the adverse consequences of regulating or eliminating the product.

Numerous studies have documented how industries influence research activities to negate the evidence of harmful effects and to weaken or block regulatory policies (Bekelman, Li, & Gross, 2003; Bero, Oostvogel, Bacchetti, & Lee, 2007; Cho & Bero, 1996; Levine, Gussow, Hastings, & Eccher, 2003; Lexchin, Bero, Djulbegovic, & Clark, 2003; Nestle, 2002). In a study using this extensive data set, White, Bandura, and Bero (2009) shed some light on moral disengagement practices in the manipulation of research and how findings are used. This section draws on the findings of this study, and broadens the analysis to include a wider range of corporate practices.

The Tobacco Industry

Cigarettes, which are essentially a vehicle for nicotine, are one of the deadliest products that is marketed worldwide. Cigarettes are the only legalized drug-delivery device that can sicken and kill you if used as intended. Smoking is the leading cause of premature deaths; (McGinnis & Foege, 1993). In countries with high smoking rates, such as China and France, about a third of men will die prematurely of chronic lung disease or lung cancer (Lam, Ho, Hedley, Mak, & Peto, 2001). John Seffrin, the former head of the American Cancer Society, characterized smoking as "the only weapon of mass destruction used against people all over the world." Smoking is the leading cause of premature deaths; (Smoking biggest killer, 2004).

To remain profitable, the industry must recruit new people to take up smoking. If youngsters do not start smoking in their teens, they are unlikely to start later in life (Lynch & Bonnie, 1994). Evidence that the industry was tracking teenage smoking was dismissed as "anomalies" (Dedman, 1998). Subpoenaed memos from R. J. Reynolds describe the need to target young age groups. As one of the memos puts it, "To ensure increased longer term growth for Camel filter, the brand must increase its share penetration among the 14–24 age groups, which have a new set of more liberal values and which represent tomorrow's cigarette business" (Meier, 1998b). This was not an isolated case, however. Other memos called for more active recruitment of young smokers: "We must get our share of the youth market. We are presently and I think unfairly constrained from directly promoting cigarettes to the youth market" (Memos highlight importance, 1998).

Tobacco advertising glamorized smoking and depicted it as a rite of passage from childhood to adulthood (Proctor, 2011). Marketing campaigns targeted young women smokers as liberated and offer promotional gifts of hip clothing in exchange for coupons from cigarette packs. Sponsorship of sporting, entertainment, and other cultural events further burnish the positive image of tobacco products (Proctor, 2012). Exposure to tobacco ads and promotions fosters tobacco use (Lynch & Bonnie, 1994).

Each day, over 3,000 American youngsters take up smoking. A third of them will die of smoking-related diseases. Lung cancer has now replaced breast cancer as the leading cause of cancer deaths in women. There are other health costs as well. Cohen, Tyrell, Russell, Jarvis, and Smith (1993) have shown experimentally that smoking increases vulnerability to infections following exposure to viruses. Moreover, the toxic chemicals in secondhand smoke take a toll on the health of nonsmokers. Children exposed to secondhand smoke are especially vulnerable to respiratory illnesses and suffer stunted lung growth.

Following the 50th anniversary of the U.S. surgeon general's landmark report on the harmful health effects of smoking, new scientific evidence shows that smoking is even deadlier than previously reported (Office of the Surgeon General, 2014). Smoking contributes to a much wider range of diseases as well as impairing immune function. Evidence indicates that the cigarette design makes them more addictive by requiring smokers to inhale more deeply, thereby drawing more nicotine into the lungs. Cigarette smoking contributes to over 480,000 deaths annually in the United States alone. An additional 60,000 smoking-related deaths from disease not previously included brings the smoking death toll to over half a million per year. As the leading cause of premature deaths, the total death toll in the past 50 years from smoking is near is 21 million (Office of the Surgeon General, 2014).

A comprehensive study of nearly a million people who were followed over 10 years revealed that smoking is even more harmful than previously was known (Carter et al., 2015). The study found more diseases linked to smoking. Several aspects of the new findings verify these linkages. The heavier the smoking, the higher the death rate. Among former smokers, the longer the period since quitting, the lower their death rate.

The tobacco industry has pursued a multipronged justification of the value of tobacco products for personal well-being and for society at large. One form of justification is cast in terms of constitutional protection and individual rights. In an article in the *Legal Backgrounder*, Jonathan W. Emord (1992), an ally of the tobacco industry, affirmed the constitutional protection of tobacco products by equating them with free speech. Recall that the gun industry used the same linguistic sleight of hand, equating use of a product with free speech. This argument shifts the debate to whether one is for or against free speech. No one is prohibited, either socially or legally, from talking about smoking. This is how Emord frames the displaced justification: "Muzzling the speech rights of the tobacco companies and establishing a speech orthodoxy on the issue of tobacco consumption violates the basic tenets of the First Amendment. Singling out one industry for discriminatory treatment violates the basic tenants of the Fifth and Fourteenth Amendments" (Emord, 1992).

In a strategy to counteract Ralph Nader's petition to ban smoking in airliners, Ross Millhiser (1970) an executive at Philip Morris, recommended focusing on individual rights:

> Let's support Mr. Nader but ask that smoking seats and/or areas wherein smoking is permitted be provided in planes, buses, etc. We are simply thereby endorsing and upholding the right of each individual citizen to be protected from infringement upon his privacy, or whatever the right word is, by other individuals. We do not want an individual's rights to be infringed upon even by products of our manufacture.

Millhiser commented on how advertising could turn Nader's initiative to ban smoking in airplanes into a prosmoking individual right exercised aloft: "Rather than react negatively to Mr. Nader's proposal, inherent in this memo is the suggestion that we seize the initiative at the outset in supporting what the public sees as being in their interest" (Millhiser, 1970).

To neutralize antismoking campaigns, the industry created an instructional memo on how to prepare a kit for distribution to smokers for the Great

American Smokeout held annually on the third Thursday of November (Sabatino, 1986). It stressed the importance of "emphasizing the rights of smokers to use a legal product." A video showed a celebrated actor smoking a cigar while extolling the importance of "freedom of choice." Bennett and Di Lorenzo (1997) likened tobacco regulation to fascism and communism masquerading as the public interest: "And there certainly is nothing new about governments seeking more control over people's lives. Recall, however, that the two major ideological political movements of our century, Fascism and Communism, sought just this while claiming the best interests of the governed peoples—with tragic consequences" (Bennett & Di Lorenzo, 1997).

The tobacco industry also enlists economic justifications. Vast numbers of people—including farmers, manufacturers, advertisers, retailers, and many others—depend on the tobacco industry for their livelihood. It also generates tax revenues. The industry argues that it is vital to the national economy: "Tobacco, and its use for smoking[,] is a vital and dynamic part of the American heritage dating back to the nation's founding. Its use in all forms is legal and it is a major contributor to the U.S. economy and to its tax revenues" (Carlson, 1976). The industry also linked the self-interest of labor unions to their side. A memo explains how the Tobacco Institute placed a tobacco workers ad in left-leaning magazines: "Text reminds traditional friends of labor that when they attack tobacco, they're attacking organized labor" (Chilcote, 1984). Job threats pay off. The union representing hotel and restaurant employees, a tobacco industry ally, issued a press release criticizing efforts by the U.S. Occupational Safety and Health Administration (OSHA) to regulate secondhand smoke in workplaces and arguing, "A government ban would have a devastating impact on our members because it would lead to a marked decline in the number of international visitors, most of whom smoke.... American workers should not lose their jobs to regulations based on faulty scientific data" (Hotel Employees and Restaurant Employees International Union, 1995).

Despite smoking's heavy toll, the tobacco industry touted the health benefits of smoking as an additional justification, characterizing the cigarette as a "portable mild bio-stressor" that enhances performance on routinized tasks requiring sustained attention, and that is a tranquilizer for the stresses of modern life. It is also portrayed as a safer drug:

> Nicotine is not only a very fine drug, but the techniques of administration by smoking has psychological advantages and a built-in control against excessive absorption. It is almost impossible to take an overdose of nicotine the way it is only too easy to do with sleeping pills. (Ellis, 1962)

In addition to these health benefits, smoking brings feelings of satisfaction and pleasure: "people gain considerable satisfaction from smoking, satisfaction that in their eyes exceeds the expected costs" (Bennett & Di Lorenzo,

1997). The tobacco industry not only stressed the benefits of smoking but also warned of the dangers to mental health of quitting smoking:

> It is a reasonable inference that the mental health of the smokers would be even worse if they were deprived of smoking. Professor I. Mills (University of Cambridge) has pointed out that underlying depression can be masked by the increasing level of arousal and many subjects resort to this mechanism to cope with depression. Smoking would appear to be one method of sustaining high levels of arousal. If...the masking mechanism is withdrawn for any reason a catastrophic change in behavior usually occurs, varying from the so called nervous breakdown to suicide. (Thornton, 1977)

In the actual calculus, the inventory of psychological benefits comes at heavy costs to health and society.

The tobacco industry advertised and marketed cigarettes with deceptive descriptions such as "low tar," and "light" suggesting that they were less hazardous to health. In handing down a ruling against the tobacco companies for deceptive practices, Judge Gladys Kessler charged them with having "marketed and sold their lethal product with zeal, with deception, with a single-minded focus on their financial success and without regard for the human tragedy or social costs that success exacted" (Shenon, 2006). The industry was unrepentant. Mark Smith, an R. J. Reynolds spokesperson, reported that executives were "gratified that the court did not award unjustified and extraordinarily expensive monetary penalties." Judge Kessler's decision was upheld on appeal, and the tobacco companies had to disclose their deceptive practices to the public.

In exoneration by advantageous comparison, tobacco is likened to other common consumer products. "The product is a 'common consumer product intended for personal consumption, such as sugar, castor oil, alcohol, tobacco and butter" (British American Tobacco, 1987). Bennett and Di Lorenzo (1997) regard a host of substances people consume and activities they perform persistently as addictions. "Many substances, including caffeine and alcohol, can produce physical or psychological dependence. 'Chocoholics' are 'addicted' to chocolate, and compulsive eaters are 'addicted' to food. Addiction can also arise from participating in physical activities....But government does not attempt to regulate or ban most of these 'addictive' substances or activities" (Bennett & Di Lorenzo, 1997). The industry complained of being unfairly targeted because these other "addictive" products go unregulated. However, these activities do not contribute to about half a million early deaths annually with high costs to societies.

Continuing with the exonerative comparative strategy implemented by proxy agents, in a strategy planning document Philip Morris urged enlistment of health advocacy groups to attack governmental funding of smoking cessation programs. "At both the state and Federal levels a number of Health Advocacy groups could also attack Sullivan for failing to address major health care issues—AIDS, prenatal care, teen-pregnancy, affordable health care, child immunization—instead of wasting more Federal dollars on anti-smoking programs" (Slavitt, 1992). Bennett and Di Lorenzo, (1997) also argue comparatively that targeting young people with cigarette ads glamorizing smoking is nothing unusual: "Every product is produced with some 'target group' in mind." They cite as an example: "Dental adhesive is aimed at people who wear false teeth" (Bennett & Di Lorenzo, 1997).

Advantageous comparison was also used to play down the health risk of secondhand smoke. In a strategy document, executives at Philip Morris recommended that the company "[i]dentify a strategy in risk assessment methodology that allows comparison of ETS [environmental tobacco smoke] to other indoor air (volatile organic chemicals), foods (pesticides), and water (lead, fluorine). Design a communications package that illustrates the significant risks associated with everyday life that includes ETS as a 'negligible risk'" (Philip Morris USA, 1989).

The harmful effects of smoking were masked by sanitizing language. In internal communications, industry scientists converted the carcinogenicity of their products to "specific biological activity" or simply "specific activity" (Brown & Williamson Co., 1984; Evelyn & Esterle, 1977). Secondhand smoke became "indoor air pollution," or "ambient smoke," that give rise to "passive smoking." There is nothing passive about having to breathe the exhaled smoke of others in the workplace, in restaurants, and other public places. This is forced smoking, not passive smoking.

Language can also be used to circumvent regulations. For example, pipe tobacco and cigars are taxed at a much lower rate than cigarettes. In circumventive ingenuity, to avoid the higher tax some tobacco companies relabeled tobacco used to roll one's own cigarettes as pipe tobacco (Rabin, 2012). By altering the size of a cigarette product and relabeling it, the industry was able to get around additional taxes and regulations. Cigarettes in the form of small cigars are also taxed at a lower rate. Additionally, the U.S. Food and Drug Administration had banned fruit flavors in cigarettes, which had been added to lure youngsters to smoking, but the ban does not cover pipe tobacco or cigars. Linguistic and design maneuvers enabled companies to evade both cigarette taxes and flavor bans. Regulators usually find themselves playing catch-up because, for every solution they come up with, those being regulated will find a loophole.

Industries that produce products that have adverse effects dispute that they cause harm. If the products are not harmful, there is no blame to shift elsewhere. However, displacement of responsibility involves using proxies (front organizations, recruited scientists and consultants, etc.) to negate scientific evidence, argue against regulations, and discredit researchers. Philip Morris recruited two Japanese scientists to refute Hirayama's influential paper demonstrating that secondhand smoke was associated with lung cancer (Hirayama, 1981; Hong & Bero, 2002). Philip Morris's director of science and technology discussed with the company's top lawyer how to hide their involvement in the research:

> This is NOT [sic] a project that should be funded by CIAR [Center for Indoor Air Research, an industry research group], although there

> MAY [*sic*] be... a reason to say it was sponsored by CIAR so as to "hide" industry involvement.... Proctor [a scientist working with Philip Morris]... may be necessary to help get this done... but this should be a Japanese study: Proctor should not be a coauthor on any publication that comes out of it. (Pages, 1991)

For years, the tobacco industry denied the addictive properties of nicotine (Glantz et al., 1996). The strategies took several forms, initially straightforward denial or minimization of adverse health effects. With mounting scientific evidence to the contrary, the strategy turned to sowing doubt and controversy about research findings. This was succinctly expressed by a Brown & Williamson executive in a company speech he gave on smoking and health. "Doubt is our product since it is the best means of competing with the 'body of fact' that exists in the mind of the general public. It is also the means of establishing a controversy" (Anonymous, 1969).

The tobacco industry spends billions of dollars annually glamorizing smoking in advertisements targeting youth, but argued contradictorily that advertisements have no effect. "Some young people use licit products which are advertised, and some use illicit substances which are not. Marijuana, for example, another substance which I know is of concern to you, is widely used despite the fact that it has never been advertised" (Kloepfer, 1985).

In a battle of symbols, Philip Morris launched a joint controversial project with the National Archives in a heavily advertised national tour to commemorate the 200th anniversary of the Bill of Rights (Pool, 1991). The tour opened with a patriotic parade, armored vehicles, and an honor guard of retired marines protecting an original copy of the Bill of Rights. Antismoking advocates were outraged that Philip Morris was associating the tobacco industry with patriotism and the "freedom" to smoke.

A creative group of public health advocates launched a countertour with a "Statue of Nicotina" (Wallack, Dorfman, Jernigan, & Themba, 1993). A cigarette replaced the torch in her upheld hand. Her eyes were closed in shame that she was made a symbol of tobacco. A chained pack of cigarettes represented their addictive properties. The inscription at her feet read: "Give me your poor, your tired, your women, your children yearning to breathe free." The cigarettes bought by youngsters formed the base on which she stood. Every 70 seconds a clock reported the toll of people who died of smoking-related diseases since the beginning of the Philip Morris tour. Nicotina, a captivating symbolic image, preempted the Philip Morris tour by arriving the day before and receiving extensive media coverage of smoking's toll on health and life. The countertour derailed Philip Morris's anticipated triumphant association of smoking with freedom.

The tobacco industry's own research was producing disconcerting findings regarding the addictive properties of nicotine and its adverse health effects. As the surgeon general's groundbreaking report was being prepared in 1964, Brown & Williamson's general counsel advised withholding from the surgeon general the troublesome results of commissioned research regarding cardiovascular disease: "Finch agrees submission Battelle or Griffith developments to surgeon general undesirable and we agree continuance of Battelle work useful but disturbed at its implications re cardiovascular disorders" (Yeaman, 1963). Manufacturers set the nicotine in cigarettes at a level that would ensure addiction. Independent researchers had found that smokers compensate for low nicotine delivery in so-called light cigarettes by inhaling more deeply or smoking more cigarettes. The smokers were blamed for the number of cigarettes they smoked. Brown & Williamson announced that "the choice of number of cigarettes smoked rests with the consumer and we don [sic] directly influence this decision in either direction" (Brown & Williamson Co., 1984).

Tobacco smoke contains hundreds of chemical compounds, many of which are carcinogenic. The smoke from the end of a lighted cigarette is even more harmful than that exhaled by smokers. The biggest challenge for the tobacco industry was growing evidence of the toxicity of secondhand smoke. Evidence that exposure to secondhand smoke is injurious to the health of nonsmokers was especially troublesome. Smoking was no longer a private matter that could be justified by freedom of choice. It became a public health problem affecting nonsmokers whose rights were being violated. Tobacco smoke, the industry contended, was erroneously blamed for respiratory problems because it is so visible. Industry officials attempted to rebut arguments about its adverse effects: "Conduct research to anticipate and refute claims about the health effects of passive smoking" (Irwin, 1983). In addition, industry officials challenged the reliability of the research findings: "The alleged harm done by smoking to innocent bystanders by 'environmental tobacco smoke' (ETS)...has been used with great success by the anti-tobacco activists to bolster the arguments for government intervention....However, the data continue to be inconclusive" (Bennett & Di Lorenzo, 1997).

What follows is the type of action plan developed for Philip Morris by the public relations firm Leo Burnett on how to respond to the Environmental Protection Agency's report which classified secondhand smoke as a group A carcinogen (U.S. Environmental Protection Agency, 1993). The first step was to create a "sense of doubt" about the EPA report, primarily by attacking the science as flawed (Leo Burnett, 1993). The agency also recommended shifting the focus away from secondhand smoke to general air-quality issues. Philip Morris executives devised a strategy document declaring that if they failed to discredit secondhand smoke as a health risk, they could minimize it by comparison with risks associated with everyday activities:

> Whether or not we succeed in discrediting the notion that ETS is a health risk, we can place the risk in context and thereby minimize it. Thus, non-smokers may still believe ETS is a health risk, but on par with driving a car, shoveling snow, etc. Low risk makes ETS an annoyance issue which can be handled by courtesy and tolerance (Philip Morris USA, 1989).

It is unclear whether or not Philip Morris adopted the proposed strategy.

In a press conference on the release of an updated report on the dangers of secondhand smoke, Surgeon General Richard Carmona announced, "[T]he debate is over: The science is clear" (O'Neil, 2006). There is no safe level of toxicity. Neither separate sections for nonsmokers nor ventilation systems are effective. Nevertheless, R. J. Reynolds continued to challenge the empirical evidence: "It seems unlikely that secondhand smoke presents any significant harm to otherwise healthy nonsmoking adults" (O'Neil, 2006).

The health hazards of smoking are being extended to thirdhand smoke. The harm is caused by the accumulated residue of secondhand smoke that clings for a long time to clothes, carpeting, sofas, bedding, and furniture, and at heavy levels in cars whose drivers smoke. It is evident in the telltale smell of rooms where people have been smoking. The toxic mix includes "hydrogen cyanide, used in chemical weapons; butane, which is used in lighter fluid; toluene, found in paint thinners; arsenic; lead; carbon monoxide; and even polonium-210, [a] highly radioactive carcinogen" (Rabin, 2009). Nearly all the other compounds also are carcinogenic. Infants and young children are especially vulnerable, because they are in the early stages of brain development, so their brains are sensitive to toxins. Also they spend a great deal of time crawling and playing on carpeted floors. Because the health hazards of thirdhand smoke have come to light only recently, future research will need to determine its effects. Hang et al. (2013) have reported preliminary evidence that thirdhand smoke damages DNA in human cells.

Tobacco companies also negate adverse health effects by treating tobacco smoke as a source of "social discomfort" rather than a carcinogen. Linguistically cleansing tobacco smoke of its chemical properties made the problem psychosocial rather than one of physical health:

> This report describes studies supporting the hypothesis that it is the smoker, rather than the chemical status of cigarette smoke itself which plays the key role in determining the non-smoker's psycho-physiological response to the passive smoking situation. (Hang et al., 2013)

Among the recommended studies was examination of the extent to which social discomfort is determined by the "degree to which the non-smoker has perceived control over the passive smoking situation" (Hang et al., 2013). In the industry's view, the problem with tobacco smoke is best dealt with by social accommodation: "Voluntary accommodation is a much more 'efficient' solution to the problem of indoor air pollution, for no one is forced to give up his or her rights and the rights of others are also respected (Bennett & Di Lorenzo, 1997).

With the shift of causation to nontobacco sources, the industry proposed environmental accommodation as well. These remedies included improved ventilation systems and design of separate public sections for smokers and nonsmokers. These were the remedies proposed in Proposition 188,

(Scott, 1994), a deceptive California smoking initiative that was misleadingly titled "Californians for Statewide Smoking Restrictions" and heavily funded by Philip Morris. The initiative was intended to repeal all local tobacco ordinances (Scott, 1994). The lobbyists argued that the patchwork of local ordinances should be replaced by a single statewide law, which would be easier for the tobacco industry to control. The proposed ballot measure increased fines for "knowingly" selling cigarettes to minors; regulated the placement of vending machines and billboards; banned undercover youth sting operations except by police; permitted smoking in restaurants, recreational settings and workplaces; designated separate smoking and nonsmoking sections; and mandated annual certification of ventilation systems.

Lee Stitzenberger, director of this prosmoking campaign, explained that they will not resort to "slick 30-second ads," but rather will inform the public and "ask people not to listen to the antis, the prohibitionists on cigarette smoking"(Hoover, 1994). The cynical brochure was distributed statewide, depicting smiling adolescents of diverse ethnicities and emblazoned with the words "the best way to keep young people away from cigarettes." The public saw through this underhanded cynical campaign and roundly defeated the ballot measure.

The tobacco industry disparaged research that demonstrated the harmful effects of tobacco. Robert Proctor (2011) compiled a two-page list of the massive ridicule. Here is but a small sample: "half truths in the hands of fanatics . . . Orwellian Official Science . . . Scientific malpractice . . . statistical jiggery pokery . . . claptrap . . . colossal blunder."

The industry attributed pathological conditions to people seeking regulation of tobacco products: "It should be recognized that smoking can be an emotional issue which can lead to obsessive behavior, reminiscent of the fanaticism spawned by the prohibition movement in the first third of this century" (Carlson, 1976). Bennett and Di Lorenzo, (1997) dubbed government officials "nannies" and countries that regulate cigarette advertising "nanny states."

In our study of moral disengagement in the corporate world (White et al., 2009), we recorded instances in which individuals adhered to their moral convictions under strong pressure to violate them. Instances of this kind of moral courage were disappointingly rare. Such employees probably get weeded out or seek employment elsewhere. However, occasionally individuals expressed reservations or concerns about the manipulation of research or the adverse effects of a product or production process, concerns unlikely to serve the financial or strategic interests of their employer. For example, the executives at Brown & Williamson became concerned because Franz Adlkofer, the scientific director of their research arm in Germany, objected to corporate criticisms of the landmark Hirayama study on the health effects of secondhand smoke (Hirayama, 1981):

> Dr. Adlkofer...believe[s] Hirayama is a good scientist and that his nonsmoking wives publication was correct....At a meeting of the board of the research arm, Adlkofer was asked how he could continue to support the projects if Hirayama's work was dead. He replied with a strong statement that Hirayama was correct, that the TI [Tobacco Institute] knew it and that TI published its statement about Hirayama knowing that the work was correct (Wells, 1981).

The production, protection, and merchandising of tobacco requires a vast supporting cast of talented and otherwise considerate people who perform subfunctions without moral qualms about the larger enterprise. The following sections briefly discuss these diverse functionaries.

The following incident illustrates how subsystems work in concert. As we have seen, for years, tobacco executives disputed evidence that nicotine is addictive and that smoking is a major contributor to lung cancer. Testifying in a state lawsuit, Geoffrey Bible, the chairman and chief executive of Philip Morris, stated that he would neither examine the company's past research nor order any studies of the effects of smoking. He exonerated himself by shielding himself from evidence of the harmful effects of his product: "I could spend the rest of my life looking backwards. I'm going to disengage for that debate" (Dedman, 1998). Tobacco executives enlist lawyers and paid consultants to challenge evidence of the harmful effects of smoking (White et al., 2009). When research in one of Philip Morris's laboratories verified that nicotine is addictive, lawyers in a tobacco-law firm warned the company that such findings are "undesirable and dangerous" because they provide fodder for lawsuits: "This kind of research is a major tool of our adversaries on the addiction issue. The irony is that the industry-sponsored research is honing that tool" (Meier, 1998c). To avoid learning about the health effects of their product, the company closed the laboratory.

Company scientists found that ammonia speeds the body's absorption of nicotine. This provided a means of increasing the nicotine "kick" without manipulating nicotine levels. Ammonia began to appear in cigarette products (Meier, 1998a).

It is illegal to manipulate nicotine levels, but permissible levels are sufficient to maintain smokers' addiction. A biotech company was indicted for conspiring with Brown & Williamson to genetically engineer a tobacco seed that doubles the nicotine content (Proctor, 2012). Leaked documents disclosed that the tobacco seeds were exported to Brazil under the deceptive label "special material" bound for "winter trials abroad" (Hall, 1998). Large amounts of nicotine-enriched tobacco were then imported illegally and used in several brands of cigarettes (Meier, 1998d).

Creative advertisers target young age groups with promotional and advertising schemes depicting smoking as a sign of youthful hipness, modernity, freedom, and women's liberation (Lynch & Bonnie, 1994; Proctor, 2012). American tobacco companies mount vigorous advertising campaigns abroad depicting smoking with this positive imagery. Through the power of social modeling, popular movie actors further influenced youngsters to take up smoking by agreeing to smoke in their movies in exchange for money and expensive gifts, a practice that began in the 1920s (Proctor, 2012). Pop celebraties are enlisted as endorsers of e-cigarettes (Elliot, 2013).

Congress defeats legislative efforts to regulate tobacco products and their advertising. The more tobacco money legislators receive, the more dutifully they block regulatory legislation (Moore, Lindes, Wolfe, & Douglas, 1993). To protect the tobacco industry further, Congress exempted nicotine from drug legislation, even though it is one of the most addictive substances known (Lynch & Bonnie, 1994). Moreover, states passed preemption laws that block communities from passing stronger local tobacco control laws. The Department of Agriculture essentially banned low-nicotine tobacco. Farmers are ineligible for government price supports if they grow low-nicotine varieties (Ryan, 2002).

Countries that run the tobacco business have a financial stake in promoting smoking (Efron, 1987). In the balance of priorities, short-term revenues usually override long-term societal health costs. In the United States this conflict erupted in the defeat of a Senate bill to fund health insurance for poor children with revenues from an increase in tobacco taxes. One of the arguments against the bill was that the tax would decrease smoking and thus reduce excise tax revenue to states. This argument led Senator Orrin Hatch to ask, "Does that mean that 419,000 Americans must die every year in order to preserve the state tobacco revenues?" (Clymer, 1997).

Growing awareness of the serious health effects of tobacco use stripped smoking of its glamour and turned much of the public against the tobacco industry. Nonsmoker rights against exposure to the toxic chemicals in secondhand smoke gained growing public support. A tobacco company official warned of the difficulties of containment strategies: "The antismoking movement is now so intertwined and interrelated that chopping off one arm, or the head, should not be viewed as a quick fix to containment" (Meier, 2000). In the face of this unfriendly normative change, the tobacco industry targeted developing countries with weak or nonexistent tobacco regulations as new growth markets. For a time, U.S. trade representatives threatened sanctions against countries that barred the importation of U.S. cigarettes.

With industry lobbyists and beholden legislators erecting protective barriers against the regulation of tobacco products, social battles over the adverse effects of tobacco use shifted increasingly to grassroots initiatives at local levels. People won smoke-free workplaces, restaurants, public buildings, and airliners through their own collective action, not through the governmental agencies responsible for protecting national health. To counter this movement, the tobacco industry mounted campaigns to revoke local regulatory ordinances and to ward off new ones. Pseudograssroots organizations (dubbed "astroturfers") and business coalitions were often used as vehicles for opposing local legislation (Samuels & Glantz, 1991). Another strategy focused on getting state legislators, who are persuadable by generous campaign contributions, to enact preemptive state laws to abolish local ordinances (Mowery, Babb, Hobart, Tworek, & McNeil, 2012).

The promotion and merchandising of tobacco use, along with vigorous efforts to block its regulation, has an international aspect as well. In order to evade excise taxes, ingenious employees in a subsidiary of R. J. Reynolds engaged in an elaborate operation that smuggled cigarettes into Canada through an Indian reservation in New York State (Drew, 1998). Philip Morris worked actively behind the scenes to defeat efforts in Switzerland, where many tobacco companies have their European headquarters, to restrict smoking in workplaces, restaurants, and airliners (Olson, 2001b). Earlier, the companies had run a campaign using a front organization and surrogates to undermine the efforts of the World Health Organization to regulate tobacco product advertising (Meier, 2000). They argued that WHO should stick to vaccines and communicable diseases. Philip Morris, along with British American Tobacco and Japan Tobacco, blocked WHO's initiative for a global ban on advertising and promotion of cigarettes (Olson, 2001a). Tobacco companies ship loads of cigarettes to the tiny Caribbean island of Aruba, which is the distribution point for drug lords who launder their narcotics money through the control of cigarette sales in some parts of Latin America. In 1999 a company official absolved the tobacco companies of responsibility: "We sell to distributors. It's not our business what they do with it" (Ronderos, 2001).

As more developing countries joined the WHO Framework Convention on Tobacco Control to limit the advertising and promotion of cigarettes, the tobacco industry launched a legal counteroffensive (Tavernise, 2013b). Despite the magnitude of the global epidemic of smoking-related diseases, tobacco firms threaten costly lawsuits against countries that impose limits on cigarette advertising. They justify the lawsuits on the grounds that limits on advertising violate trade and investment treaties. The U.S. Chamber of Commerce (despite its name, not a government agency) added its opposition to advertising limits, invoking the slippery-slope justification: cigarettes today, soft drinks tomorrow (Tavernise, 2013b). The WHO framework convention was not intended to allow international corporations to launch legal campaigns to eliminate the public health policies of their host countries.

Threatened with costly lawsuits, developing countries, which lack the legal resources to fight the lawsuits, have backed down on limiting advertising. Some developed countries have done so as well. Philip Morris International has many foreign subsidiaries, which, according to the law professor Robert Stumberg of Georgetown University, enables the company "to play the treaty game [much] more adroitly" (Tavernise, 2013b). Some companies even pay countries to be complainants in their lawsuits. For example, Ukraine was paid to file a complaint with the World Trade Organization against Australia for its requirements regarding cigarette packaging.

The peculiarity of this exercise of proxy control is that there is virtually no trading between these two countries. In commenting on the lawsuits, Dr. Margaret Chan, the director general of WHO, described the legal counteroffensive metaphorically: "The wolf is no longer in sheep's clothing, and its teeth are bared" (Chan, 2012).

The Bill & Melinda Gates Foundation and Bloomberg Philanthropies came to the aid of poorer countries by establishing a global legal fund that enables them to defend their smoking regulations against costly legal suits by tobacco companies (Tavernise, 2015a). The philanthropists are also creating a network of lawyers who are experts in trade litigation to assist the targeted countries. Dr. Chan underscored the growing legal threats used by the tobacco industry: "In an ominous trend, in some countries the battle between tobacco and health has moved into the courts. We will push back hard" (Tavernise, 2015a). Given the huge annual death tolls from smoking-related diseases, the exploitation of people in poorer countries shows a stunning lack of moral responsibility.

As documented earlier, the large-scale marketing of harm is not the work of a few unprincipled offenders and functionaries. Rather, it involves a host of good folks in all walks of worklife, all doing their part as best they can in the larger scheme of things. This analysis has identified major contributors in the tobacco industry and the roles they play in this collective operation. Evidence from other industries lends support to the generality of the psychological processes governing moral disengagement at the collective level.

Electronic Cigarettes

The advent of electronic cigarettes introduced a new nicotine delivery device. E-cigarettes are battery-operated vaporizers through which users inhale nicotine vapor. They are called e-cigarettes because, besides aerosol additives, nicotine, extracted from tobacco, is the main ingredient. The use of this device, which began as a fledgling activity free of regulation, is gaining popularity. Sales are rising sharply, especially among adolescents (Tavernise, 2015b).

E-cigarettes have become popular amid ambiguity about whether regulations governing traditional cigarettes apply to e-cigarettes as well. In a series of articles, Richtel reviewed at length the lively debates on what e-cigarettes should be called and whether they should be regulated and taxed. Advocates argue that e-cigarettes should be construed as "vapor products," not "tobacco products." To avoid any likeness, they call cigarettes "vape pens" and "hookahs," referring to a waterpipe that vaporizes flavored tobacco. Surprisingly, several states have ruled that e-cigarettes are not a tobacco product. In camouflaging prose, many other states have ruled that e-cigarettes do not belong in the "tobacco category" (Richtel, 2014d). This is a peculiar exemption given that nicotine, which is extracted almost entirely from tobacco, is almost the sole ingredient in e-cigarettes. These rulings say more about the power of the tobacco industry than about the contents of e-cigarettes. Linguistic denicotinization frees e-cigarettes from the excise taxes and regulations imposed on traditional cigarettes.

Proponents of e-cigarettes claim that their products are not only different from traditional cigarettes but also safer, because e-cigarettes do not burn tobacco, which produces carcinogens and a host of other toxins. They also allege that e-cigarettes save lives by helping conventional smokers to quit and by reducing harm in those who continue to smoke by providing them a safer alternative. The e-cigarette business was originally run by small independent operators. To expand their market, they focused on the harm caused by their big tobacco competitors. Sean Gore, the chairman of Oklahoma Vapor Advocacy League, described cigarette makers as "profiteers who don't care about people's health" (Richtel, 2014d). He called traditional cigarettes "cancer sticks." Craig Weiss, the cofounder and chairman of the NJOY e-cigarette company, berated the tobacco giants for selling products that "kill half their customers" (Richtel, 2013). Smokers can be liberated from addiction, advocates declare, by gradually reducing the concentration of nicotine in e-cigarettes. Saving lives and reducing harm are powerful moral justifications for this industry. However, e-cigarette makers are conflicted about how to characterize an addictive substance in socially desirable terms and how to avoid regulations. If e-cigarettes are promoted as a treatment device, they fall under medical regulations requiring proof of effectiveness and evidence that benefits outweigh risks. E-cigarette makers vigorously oppose medical regulation, so they are caught in a linguistic tangle when they claim therapeutic benefits while insisting that they make no such claims.

Gore also justifies opposition to regulations on humane grounds, in the belief that if e-cigarettes save lives, restricting their sale has deadly consequences. As he puts it, regulations take "a product that has the potential to save thousands of lives and give it back to the industry that is killing people" (Richtel, 2014d). Appropriateness regulation is based on similarity in nicotine content, not on appearance, but others use advantageous comparison in arguing against taxing or banning e-cigarettes. One advocate compares e-cigarettes with health food: "You wouldn't put a tax on Weight Watchers health food" (Richtel, 2014d). Another uses water as a justifying comparator: "We don't ban water because it looks like vodka" (Hartocollis, 2013).

E-cigarette makers also enlist proxy agents in their defense. As reported earlier, traditional tobacco companies often fund research institutes, scientists, and consultants who try to sway regulatory policies to the companies' liking. At the height of the European debate regarding the e-cigarette industry, lawmakers received a letter allegedly signed by ex-smokers who quit the habit with the aid of e-cigarettes. They pleaded with the European Parliament to vote against regulating e-cigarettes (Higgins, 2013). This heartfelt letter was actually written by an undercover astroturfer, a London lobbyist hired by an e-cigarette firm. The European Union eventually adopted much tighter regulatory standards for the e-cigarette industry by applying all the regulations for traditional cigarettes to e-cigarettes (Jolly, 2014).

In this unsettled atmosphere, the U.S. Food and Drug Administration (FDA) exercised its oversight authority regarding e-cigarettes. Officials issued an initial set of modest rules that banned sales of e-cigarettes to minors and prohibited sales in vending machines and offers of free samples. The FDA also required manufacturers to register their products, with full disclosure of the ingredients. However, at this early stage, the rules did not regulate the concentration of nicotine or e-cigarette advertising. Nor did they address the controversial practice of using tasty flavorings.

Regulations issued by the FDA require support by scientific evidence, which is woefully lacking for e-cigarettes. Long-term health effects need to be clarified. Nicotine has immediate cardiovascular effects, such as elevated blood pressure and heart rate as well as vasoconstriction, which reduces blood flow and oxygen to the heart (Benowitz & Gourlay, 1997). Whether or not e-cigarette smoking increases the risk of cardiovascular disease in the long term remains to be determined. Anecdotal evidence that e-cigarettes help to wean smokers from traditional cigarettes requires verification with controlled clinical trials. In a randomized controlled study, Bullen and colleagues (2013) compared the success of different methods of helping smokers quit the habit. In a six-month evaluation, the quit rates were 7.3% for e-cigarettes, 5.89% for nicotine patches, and 4.1% for placebo e-cigarettes whose vapors contained no nicotine. These miniscule quit rates do not differ significantly from each other. Although the smokers wanted to quit, almost all of those in the e-cigarette condition apparently adopted a dual smoking pattern in which they smoked traditional cigarettes where they are permitted and e-cigarettes in places where the traditional ones are banned. A comprehensive evaluation of e-cigarette effects should also examine whether secondhand nicotine vapor affects nonsmokers, especially young children.

Nicotine is a highly addictive substance. Continuing to smoke builds up cellular tolerance, so stronger doses and more frequent smoking are required to satisfy the craving for nicotine and reduce aversive withdrawal symptoms. What begins as a stimulant and relaxant imbedded in daily routines can develop into an addiction that needs to be fed throughout the waking hours. Ex-smokers continue to be haunted by nicotine cravings. Does this drive some e-cigarette smokers to traditional cigarettes because they are better in satisfying the craving for nicotine? This type of smoking may well become normalized and socially entrenched in everyday routines long before reliable evidence of its effects is available.

A further complicating factor in evaluating the effects of e-cigarettes is the speed of changes in smoking technology and style of smoking. These are described by Richtel (2014c) in his article on the "new smoke." Vapored nicotine provides a weaker nicotine rush than do traditional cigarettes. The changes are designed to intensify the nicotine rush. In one innovation, rather than filling the e-cigarette with liquid nicotine, creative smokers are trickling drops of nicotine on the battery-operated heating element. This mode of smoking is known as "dripping." An attachable mechanical dripping device is probably not far off. Another method calls for raising the temperature of the heating element so that the emitted vapor contains more nicotine. Increasing the heat releases more toxins into the vapor, some of which are carcinogenic. In a further technological change that may add toxicity to e-cigarette smoking, Philip Morris developed an alternative nicotine-delivery device. It heats tobacco at intense degrees, rather than burning it, to create a tobacco-flavored nicotine vapor that may be more appealing to smokers. Dr. Alan Shihadeh, a project director of the Center for the Study of Tobacco Products at the University of Virginia, remarked on the perplexing rapid changes in the tobacco industry: "Technology is way ahead of the science. We are creating this stuff, and we don't understand the implications" (Richtel, 2014c). The drive for a more potent nicotine-delivery device may ultimately reduce the difference in health hazards between e-cigarettes and traditional cigarettes.

Liquid nicotine is a deadly neurotoxin that currently is being sold without regulation in shops and online in varying concentrations, even by the barrel (Richtel, 2014b). Chip Paul, operator of a national franchise, described the e-nicotine industry as "the wild, wild west right now" (Richtel, 2014b). Children can be drawn to drink liquid nicotine because of the bottles' luminous, colored labels and aromatic flavorings. Lee Cantrell, a professor of pharmacy at the University of California, San Francisco, explains, "It's not a matter of if a child will be seriously poisoned or killed. It's a matter of when" (Richtel, 2014b). Reports of accidental poisonings among children, some as young as age two, are rising. Adults can poison themselves through carelessness in refilling their smoking devices. Additionally, the production and handling of liquid nicotine joins the ranks of dangerous workplace hazards.

With the growing popularity and soaring sales of e-cigarettes among young people, the major tobacco firms are entering the e-cigarette business with their own brands or acquiring small independent ones. The companies are well armed with proven marketing methods. These include targeting youngsters by sponsoring youth-oriented music and sports events where free e-cigarette samples are offered and advertising campaigns that feature celebrities (Elliot, 2013; Tavernise, 2013a). In addition, the firms run radio and television ads that glamorize e-cigarettes on youth-oriented programs. They also appear in social media ads and as product placements in media productions. To expand the women's market, women celebrities are shown endorsing e-cigarettes. Just as Philip Morris associated its traditional cigarettes with the Bill of Rights and freedom, Lorillard sponsored the Freedom Project, a national tour of bands with e-cigarette linkage. Young people are again being recruited as lifelong smokers in the name of freedom. Associating drug addiction with freedom is an oxymoronic linkage.

Matthew Myers, president of the Campaign for Tobacco-Free Kids, expressed alarm at the soaring amount of money spent on targeting young people to take up e-cigarettes. He fears that "with this marketing, cigarette makers will undo 40 years of efforts to deglamorize smoking" (Elliot, 2013). In contrast, Joana Martins, vice president for marketing at Fin Branding, views marketing that glamorizes e-cigarettes as a blessing for smokers who "are tired of being ostracized" (Elliot, 2013). Fin's "Rewrite the Rules" campaign promoted the view that "it's okay to smoke again." The chief marketing officer for NJOY, Geoff Vuleta, forecast metaphorically that the "renormalizing" of smoking will bring indoors the smokers banished to the frosty sidewalks (Richtel, 2013).

Delicious fruit and candy flavors serve as another lure. The "vape pens" are said to provide "kissable breath," satisfaction of nicotine craving, and "a medley of flavors, like Belgian waffle, vanilla cupcake, and peppermint blast" (Richtel, 2014a). These descriptors suggest an ice cream parlor serving a variety of flavors rather than a drug-dispensing device. As is usually the case, tobacco firms deny that their marketing and promotional activities are directed at youth.

The tobacco industry has a transformative mission for e-cigarettes. Murray Kessler, the chairman, president, and chief executive of Lorillard, describes the effort to remove the "social stigma" of nicotine addiction by making the e-cigarette look offbeat and "cool." In doing so it can become "a complete replacement" of traditional cigarettes. The goal of this ambitious mission "isn't to try to keep people in cigarettes, but to normalize smoking e-cigarettes and vaping as [sic] the next generation" (Richtel, 2013).

With traditional cigarette smoking declining, the tobacco industry acknowledged that e-cigarettes, although less profitable, are the nicotine-delivery method of the future. In takeover of the business, major tobacco companies are acquiring existing e-cigarette brands and creating their own (Esterl, 2013). With e-cigarettes still largely unregulated, tobacco firms have the resources and marketing apparatus to promote e-cigarette smoking on a large scale. They can also develop faster and higher-volume nicotine-delivery devices to match the levels delivered by traditional cigarettes. Time will tell whether the tobacco industry succeeded in "normalizing" the e-smoking habit and developing a sizable youth clientele of potential lifelong smokers.

If e-cigarettes are found to help smokers to quit the habit and are promoted as a replacement treatment, they should be regulated as a medical method. However, the tobacco industry is not in the business of creating nicotine-dispensing devices that can put them out of business. Their stated, ambitious mission is to remove the stigma associated with smoking and have it treated as a socially accepted, normal activity. In the heated debates about health risks and benefits, regulations and freedom, there is virtually no discussion about the morality of "renormalizing" smoking.

A survey of middle and high school students conducted by the U.S. Centers for Disease Control and Prevention (CDC) found that traditional smoking had declined, but e-cigarette smoking had tripled within a year (Tavernise, 2015b). One student described the attitudinal change regarding these two modes of smoking. He never took up cigarette smoking, he explained, because "Girls think they're gross." In contrast, e-cigarette vaporing was daring: "It is something for us to do that was edgy and exciting." Kessler and Myers (2015) expressed alarm that, with aggressive marketing reglamorizing smoking, the tobacco industry will addict a new youth generation to nicotine.

The Lead Industry

Lead was widely used over the years in metal products, industrial finishes, pesticides, and many consumer products such as household paints and gasoline. It was also spewed into the air with industrial emissions, especially from smelters. It accumulates in the body through food, dust, and drinking water. Lead damages the brain and nervous system, impairs kidney function, reduces male fertility through sperm damage, impairs development of the fetus during pregnancy, and causes mental retardation and behavioral problems in children.

The industry relied mainly on economic justifications for the widespread use of lead. In addressing the Public Health Service regarding the public health hazards of lead, Dr. Gilman Thompson, a medical director representing Standard Oil, General Motors, and DuPont, extolled the vital role that lead played during the industrial era: "Is this a public health hazard? Unfortunately, our problem is not that simple. We cannot quite act on a remote probability. We are engaged in the General Motors Corporation in the manufacture of automobiles, and in the Standard Oil Co. in the manufacture and refining of oil. On these things our present industrial civilization is supposed to depend" (U.S. Public Health Service, 1925).

Thompson framed the issue of individual risk versus national benefit in utilitarian terms: "We should look at the problem in the large, rather than be swayed by prejudice. It is often much easier to see the concrete immediate dangers than to evaluate the perhaps more important industrial advantages. We do not like to match the life of a man against the life of a Nation" (U.S. Public Health Service, 1925). Thompson cited other benefits as well. Lead preserved "a precious natural resource, petroleum, by making gasoline go much further than it would without these additives." Thompson questioned whether decisions vital to the industrial viability of a nation should be made on the basis of empirical evidence, which he trivialized: "Because some animals die and some do not die in some experiments, shall we give this thing up entirely?"

The Ethyl Gasoline Corporation decided to use the sanitizing term *ethyl* instead of *lead* for their gasoline additive, following a number of deadly accidents in lead-manufacturing plants: "Midgely told me his Company had decided to adopt the trade name 'ethyl gas.' Of course, their object in doing so are fairly clear, and among other things they are not particularly desirous of having the name 'lead' appear in this case" (Lind, 1923). The more innocuous label was used in internal correspondence as well: "I purposely avoided the use of 'lead' in the inter-bureau correspondence on this subject because of the fact that even in confidential investigations the Washington Office sometimes slips out information to the newspapers" (Lind, 1923). The term *ethyl* caught on and was used in marketing and research publications for decades.

A public outcry arose over the health hazards of lead after several lead-factory workers were injured or killed. The lead industry responded with ad hominem attacks. Dr. H. C. Parmelee, the editor of *Chemical and Metallurgical Engineering*, was quoted in the *New York Times*:

> It is a little short of a calamity, therefore, that the train of events of the past two months has developed a public controversy over this product that has been characterized by incompetent and hysterical testimony. One can imagine how chemical progress in the past might have been hampered by a similar crusade by self-appointed guardians of the public health. City gas and motor exhaust still claim their victims almost daily, but escape the tender ministrations of the crusader....The chemical industry...does want a reasonable degree of assurance that it is not to be tried and convicted by incompetent critics or forced to abandon its legitimate pursuits by misguided zealots. (Demands fair play for ethyl gasoline, 1925)

At a conference convened by the U.S. Public Health Service shortly after the series of deadly accidents in lead-manufacturing plants, Dr. Henry Vaughan, president of the American Health Association, used the following exonerative comparisons in arguing against regulation of lead manufacturing:

> I am sorry to say that we have on average one death each day from automobile accidents, approximately 300 to 350 each year, and yet there has been no legislation so far to do away with the automobiles. Furthermore, we annually have a few people who close themselves up in the winter months in their garages, and...insist upon choking themselves to death with carbon monoxide, and still we have not legislated against the construction of garages; nor have we said that such people cannot drive automobiles. It seems to be almost impossible to safeguard against all foolhardy accidents. (U.S. Public Health Service, 1925)

In the minimization of health effects, Robert Kehoe, head of the industry-funded Kettering Laboratory, was "a virtual commissar of lead toxicology" until the 1960s (Markowitz & Rosner, 2002). Throughout his lengthy career, Kehoe never publicly acknowledged that lead posed any public health risk.

He considered it "normal" for all human beings to have some lead in their bodies. The civil rights movement and the War on Poverty of the 1960s began to focus public attention on lead poisoning among the poor. Scientists began to challenge Kehoe's positions and his research, which never took into account the smaller body mass and developing neurological systems of lead poisoning's primary victims, children. Late in his career, Kehoe responded to criticism of his research by the Hazard Evaluation System and Information Service of the California Department of Health, claiming that his life's work was conducted with integrity.

In efforts to create a threshold, industry officials presented quantitative arguments that the amount of exposure to lead was insufficient to cause harm, even if their product was harmful in large doses. Although there was no evidence to suggest that lead content was safe below a certain threshold, they discussed establishing specific thresholds below which their products would not be considered toxic to humans. A physician consultant to the industry described an "experiment upon men to determine the amount of lead retention from an exhaust containing lead from 'ethylized gasoline' and found that, on the average, 85 percent of the lead inhaled was again exhaled.... [T]he amount inhaled and absorbed in the hazard under discussion is evidently far below the 'threshold' of toxicity" (Hayhurst, 1925).

More recent research, however, has demonstrated that even minute levels of lead poisoning affect neurological functioning, particularly in children, because of their small size and developing bodies. During the 1970s, Herbert Needleman and others demonstrated that even at blood-lead levels lower than 60 microg/dL, lead could decrease IQ and affect behavior. These levels that are not sufficient to produce the clinically obvious symptoms (renal failure, anemia, convulsions, etc.) that had been the focus of discussion in earlier years (Needleman et al., 1979). More recent research "suggests that there is no safe threshold for the toxicity of lead in the central nervous system" (Landrigan, 2000).

By 1945, the lead industry realized that it had a credibility problem in making its case for the safety of lead. Lead producers concealed their efforts to negate evidence of harmful effects by having proxies do it for them. The head of the Lead Industries Association (LIA) wrote to its executive committee:

> I feel that the word of the Lead Industries Association might carry even more weight if some other agency, used as a screen, were utilized in order to do the job for us.... This point may only be academic, however, as the plan to be submitted calls for the help of nearly all agencies in a position to do so. It is obviously not possible to procure the services of any education institution for what would be, in part, publicity or public relations purposes. (Wormser, 1945b)

In its 1956 annual report, the Lead Industries Association claimed that it had partially suppressed evidence of adverse effects through editing: "Getting wind of a forthcoming report on sustainability of plastic pipe for potable water supplies in preparation at the University of Michigan, we arranged to see the galley proof of the report and, through contacts with members of the advisory committee on the report, were able to secure elimination of a number of statements adverse to the use of lead stabilizers" (Bowditch, 1956).

As Herbert Needleman and Philip Landrigan demonstrated during the 1970s, children are especially vulnerable to the neurotoxic effects of exposure to lead. Their exposure risk is high because they often put things in their mouths, including toys and furniture painted with lead pigments and leaded paint chips from peeling paint. They also inhale lead dust from the friction of lead-painted surfaces such as window frames and window sills. Their developing bodies absorb lead more readily. A spokesperson for the Lead Industries Association placed the blame for childhood lead poisoning on the children themselves: "Dr. Aub told me that children who have sub-normal appetites, or the disease known as 'pica' which caused them to chew on inedible articles, were sub-normal to start with!" (Wormser, 1945a). Twelve years later, the LIA's director of health and safety blamed and disparaged "ignorant parents": "Of some, but secondary importance is lead paint mistakenly applied by ignorant parents to cribs, play pens and other juvenile furniture and subsequently chewed off and ingested.... Childhood lead poisoning is essentially a problem of slum dwellings and relatively ignorant parents" (Bowditch, 1957).

Because they made it possible to pin the blame for lead poisoning on parents, psychosocial remedies were proposed as the solution, rather than removing lead from house paint, children's toys, and furniture: "Elimination or minimization of exposure to lead can be successfully achieved through alterations in personal habits, increased public education and improvements in living conditions, particularly among population groups known to have higher likelihood of exposure" (Bowditch, 1957). However, the industry was pessimistic about eliminating the problem in poor families short of eliminating slums: "That until we can find means to (a) get rid of our slums, and (b) educate the relatively uneducable parent, the problem will continue to plague us" (Bowditch, 1957).

Lead was eventually banned from house paint and gasoline during the 1970s, but the health hazard for children lingered because of the lead paint that remained in millions of homes. In addition, Mattel, the world's largest toy maker, has had to recall millions of toys produced in Chinese factories because they contained lead-contaminated paint (Sellers, 2010). It is surprising that the Consumer Product Safety Commission has not listed lead among the top toy hazards. In 2007, Julie Vallese, then the spokesperson for the commission, minimized the omission by exonerative comparison: "It's not your child's dollhouse, when it comes to lead that's going to actually cause injury, it's your own house. And that's where parents should be focused if they want to really tackle the issue of lead" (CBSNews, 2007). The problem of deteriorating lead paint in old houses and other sources of lead dust does not justify excluding lead as a toy hazard, especially in this era of outsourced production to countries with weak safety standards and deficient enforcement of those they have.

The Chemical Industry: Vinyl Chloride

Vinyl chloride is a chemical widely used to make polyvinyl chloride (PVC) plastic products. In the past, it was used in aerosol sprays before it was banned for this purpose. Vinyl chloride is also released by factories producing vinyl products and is found in places where chemical wastes are stored. People are exposed to it through contaminated air and water supplies. Exposure to this chemical damages the liver, lungs, kidneys, and immune function. Workers in the plastics industry experience long-term exposure and are at risk for liver cancer, leukemia, and brain cancer.

When questions were raised about vinyl chloride's potential dangers, members of this chemical industry sought to shift the focus from concern over the carcinogenity of vinyl chloride to its vast human benefits. At an industry meeting discussing a proposed speech on "Industrial Problems in Environmental Health," Dr. A. Fleming advocated reframing the issue in the public debate: "[T]he speech should cite the benefits to mankind through chemicals. Hazardous chemicals *can* be used safely....Feeding the world will depend on the use of chemicals. We should work in some propaganda along this line. Chemicals are important for both protection and production of food" (Manufacturing Chemists' Association, 1960).

Years later Joseph Fath, the vice president of Tenneco Chemicals, was more expansive on the scope of benefits as justification for the use of PVC:

> I believe we can easily demonstrate how PVC has benefited all of us in the supply of economical consumer goods, has aided our defense industries in preserving our political system, our communications industry in enabling us to conduct the business of our modern society and has played a key role in assuring us through the plastics industry in particular and the chemical industry in general, of a continued increase in our standard of living. (Fath, 1974)

However, the accent on benefits was accompanied by efforts to obfuscate and negate polyvinyl chloride's harmful effects by other modes of moral disengagement. For example, in commenting on an epidemiological study of polyvinyl chloride workers, Robert Wheeler, a Union Carbide scientist, discredited the field of epidemiology, the main research method used to identify harmful substances in human populations. He applied comparative odds: "The epidemiology as presently practiced is too gross a tool to pinpoint a vinyl chloride problem with any certainty....The odds that a death caused by a neoplasm is untraceable are as poor as being compared to being run over by an automobile in Washington" (Wheeler, 1977a). Industry personnel also used the adverse effects of smoking on workers' health to exonerate vinyl chloride. They claimed that smoking, rather than vinyl chloride, caused workers' health problems. In a memo to a subcommittee of the Manufacturing Chemists' Association, Richard Henderson suggested "the terminology for vinyl chloride as 'hazardous chemical agent,' rather than its designation as a 'cancer suspect agent,' or 'carcinogen'" (Johnson, 1974).

By 1973, the MCA's own epidemiological and animal studies confirmed that exposure to vinyl chloride could cause liver cancer (Markowitz & Rosner, 2002). Nonetheless, in 1975 a physician at Pittsburgh Plate Glass wrote, "It is my feeling that the vast majority of abnormal liver function tests are caused by regular and rather heavy drinking of alcohol and I expect that the people who have abnormal liver tests as a result of this may be inclined to resume their previous habits as soon as they think they are okay" (Lovejoy, 1975).

In addition to being exposed through contaminated air and water supplies, consumers also come into contact with this chemical through a variety of plastic and vinyl products. These include housewares, packaging materials, wire coatings, and automobile upholstery. The MCA agreed to fund an epidemiological study in an effort to show that any adverse health effects are confined to workers handling the chemicals. The study would "hopefully be expected to...confirm that the condition is purely an occupational disease and in no way affects the general public using PVC products" (Nessell, 1967).

In discussing a response to a request for information from the National Institute of Occupational Safety and Health (NIOSH), MCA considered ways to withhold information about the potential health hazards of vinyl chloride: "All references to use of vinyl chloride in aerosol propellants were removed, since it is a minor part of the industry and is not a worker-exposure problem except for beauticians and can-fillers" (Wheeler, 1977b).

The occurrence of malignancies in factory workers was attributed to genetic aberrations. In commenting on an epidemiological study done for MCA that showed increased incidence of cancers among PVC workers, W. D. Harris, an industrial taxologist at Uniroyal, questioned the evidence because the cancer incidence did not seem to be dose-related. He opted for genetic predisposition: "There just is a suggestion that people who for some reason are susceptible to cancer will be affected and die within this period of time. If they don't die within this period, they won't" (Markowitz & Rosner, 2008). Regarding acroosteolysis (AOL), a degenerative bone condition associated with vinyl chloride exposure, a Monsanto scientist commented, "[U]ltimately we may find that AOL is related to a chromosomal aberration which if confirmed, may be used to select PVC and VCM workers" (Ingle, 1969). A similar suggestion was made by Exxon's Robert Eckardt at an OSHA hearing: "If employees with low susceptibility would be selected, it would greatly enhance the value of engineering controls" (Markowitz & Rosner, 2008). Causal attribution to genetic aberration inspired Eckardt to entertain a rather macabre personnel-selection policy: "One idea would be to only hire workers over 50 years of age to work with carcinogens." In this depersonalized view, workers are merely tools for hazardous operations.

Amid these exonerative machinations, there were some acts of principled objection. Zeb G. Bell of PPG Industries argued that employees should be fully informed about the carcinogenic properties of the materials they were handling and warned about the inadequacy of the odor threshold:

> I feel that transmittal of information to employees of the potential carcinogenic properties of vinylidene chloride should not be done on a low-key basis if we expect them to respect and avoid breathing vapors as specified in your memo....It should be emphasized that the odor threshold for VCDM is grossly inadequate in warning employees of the presence of VDCM. (Bell, 1974)

He also vetoed erroneous claims in a vinyl chloride video script: "I think you are stretching the credibility that food wrap (meaning saran [sic] wrap) has done as much for public health as penicillin. This statement has to be deleted" (Bell, 1976). In a memo to managers at MCA, George Best (1973) objected on moral grounds to the withholding of relevant information from the government: "There is also the aspect of moral obligation not to withhold from the Government significant information having occupational and environmental relevance, and the desirability of industry taking the initiative rather than at some later time having to defend another course." But the MCA did so anyway. W. D. Harris, who was partial to genetic vulnerability as a causative factor in workers' malignancies, nevertheless advocated dosage studies and an epidemiological study to confirm findings of cancer in animals: "[T]o make no attempt to develop better information would be inexcusable" (Harris, 1971).

Silicosis–Producing Industries

Silicosis is an occupational lung disease caused by inhaling silica dust. It gets embedded in the lungs, causing fibrosis and impairing breathing. The effects of long-term exposure include chronic, dysfunctional coughing, and severe breathing difficulties, all of which greatly impede everyday life. Silicosis also increases the risk of developing tuberculosis. In the terminal phase, people die of suffocation. The sources of silica exposure include mechanical mining and tunneling, stonework, sand blasting, glassmaking, cement manufacturing, and building and road construction, among other occupations.

As the secretary of the Tri-State Zinc and Lead Ore Producers Association, Evan Just was a leading spokesman for the mining industry in Kansas, Missouri, and Oklahoma. He minimized the risk of silicosis, arguing that lungs have too much excess capacity for inhaling silica particles to result in disability: "[T]he body is normally equipped with considerably more lung capacity than it needs" (Just, 1939). He also minimized functional impairment even in advanced stages of the disease: "Only in very advanced cases is any impairment of functions noticeable and this exists in shortness of breath in exercising" (Just, 1939). In the advanced stages of silicosis, individuals are suffocating rather than experiencing some windedness while exercising. Just attributed the cause of workers' health problems to poor living conditions rather than to unhealthy working conditions. Many of the miners lived in shabby shacks amid piles of dust. Just criticized them for making bad lifestyle choices: "[T]he wages paid in our industry are certainly adequate to support decent living. That many people who can afford better homes, prefer to live in small, unpainted two or three room shacks and spend their surplus funds on automobiles and radios cannot be charged against the mining industry" (Just, 1940).

Silica dust does not lend itself to justification in terms of personal and large-scale societal benefits. However, it is subject to the usual sanitizing language and mitigating comparisons; for example, silica dust becomes "nuisance dust." At a national conference, other industrial hazards were used to downplay the seriousness of silicosis: "From a statistical point of view, therefore, the problem of silicosis is not as serious or general as some other industrial problems, such as lead poisoning or industrial accidents" (U.S. Department of Labor, 1937). Scientists at the industry-funded Industrial Hygiene Foundation used other comparisons to deny the adverse health effects of silicosis.

Silicosis takes many years to develop. Symptoms may not appear until after a worker has retired. Corporations ignored the progressive nature of the disease and required workers to demonstrate an inability to work before they could be compensated. Using this criterion of disability, the industry absolved itself of responsibility for the health of workers who had retired, many of them due to the progressing silicosis itself: "The committee points out that since silicosis may be present without any demonstrable symptoms, silicosis per se should not carry with it a liability for compensation, but rather liability should attach only when the disease results in wage loss" (U.S. Department of Labor, 1937).

The seriousness of silicosis was trivialized: "Too few [physicians] have realized the prognosis with the so-called benign pneumoconiosis due to inert dust deposits is no more unfavorable than is the mild anthracosis of every city resident....Not infrequently we find nuisance dust exposures to be more injurious to the mechanical equipment than to workmen" (Sander, 1946). The industry also trivialized it by using a short time frame for the appearance of debilitating symptoms: "To the 105,000 workers who have silicosis, but no disability and no tuberculosis, the problem is not particularly serious. It is generally agreed that, if the dust is properly controlled at all times, such workers would be as well off in continuing at their present jobs as if they were discharged or transferred to other employment" (U.S. Department of Labor, 1937).

The silica industry also used the threshold of harm as another way of minimizing the health hazard of silica dust. Measurement instruments available during the 1930s were crude, resulting in dust concentration readings that varied by a factor of 4 or more (Rosner & Markowitz, 1991). Nevertheless, industry-funded scientists at a national silicosis conference identified a specific concentration as the threshold of harm: "For prolonged exposure a concentration of more than 5 million particles per cubic foot of a highly siliceous dust is dangerous" (U.S. Department of Labor, 1938). This level was arrived at because it was what could be achieved with current engineering methods. They thus ignored the long latency period for silicosis, which often extended well into retirement (Rosner & Markowitz, 1991).

Silicosis is associated with and sometimes misdiagnosed as tuberculosis. Industry officials preferred to attribute a worker's illness to tuberculosis rather than to silicosis. Two consultants to the industry claimed at a National Silicosis Conference, "In all the reports, and writings on silicosis the one thing that stands out is the extraordinary incidence of tuberculosis among silicotics. It is tuberculosis which disables and kills the silicotic" (U.S. Department of Labor, 1937).

A common way to forestall policy initiatives, even in the face of corroborative converging evidence from diverse methodologies, is to argue that the available information is insufficient and more research is needed. A decade after silicosis reached epidemic proportions among American mine workers, a scientist from a research center funded by the mining industry minimized the state of knowledge regarding silicosis in an article in the *Journal of the American Medical Association*: "The scarcity of factual information and lack of knowledge of already established facts are responsible for the major part of the medical expert's shortcomings. Additional study is certainly needed" (Wright, 1949).

After World War II, the silica industry claimed that silicosis was not only a minor problem but no longer existed. In 1946, scientists at the Industrial Hygiene Foundation (IHF) announced that "silicosis, once a great hazard to the health of industrial workers, is no longer a threat....The dangerous trades of our fathers have all but disappeared" (Industrial Hygiene Foundation, 1946). In fact, silicosis has remained a major problem for workers in contemporary workplaces and is often misdiagnosed and ignored in retirees (Rosner & Markowitz, 1991).

The head of the Mellon Institute for Industrial Research, a corporate-funded research group, suggested to industry leaders that they locate research on silicosis at the institute, using it as a proxy. That would enable individual corporations to sponsor research surreptitiously, thereby avoiding accusations of conflict of interest:

> If this work were to be centralized in Mellon Institute, it...could be carried out in a most confidential manner as to who was supporting the research and no one would know what industries or individuals were contributing to the fund. This would enable the organization to get soundly established, so that if later on it was desired to come out in the open this could be arranged. (Weidlein, 1935)

The use of respiratory masks as the first line of defense against silicosis has long been a contentious issue in the dusty trades. Traditional engineering controls included exhaust and ventilation systems, physical separation of dust-producing processes such as sand blasting, and administrative improvements, such as rotating workers in the dusty areas of a factory. However, these controls did not keep pace with the advances in high-speed sand blasting, which created ever more dust throughout factories. Smaller shops often could not afford the engineering improvements needed. The masks themselves are difficult to wear during an entire sweltering workday. Army Corps of Engineers regulations state, "Only when all engineering or administrative controls have been implemented, and the level of respirable silica still exceeds permissible exposure limits, may an employer rely on a respirator program" (U.S. Army Corps of Engineers, 1996). Rather than setting standards for effective exhaust and ventilation systems, however, the industry shifted the focus from needed structural improvements to workers' use of masks:

> With some men respirators are a continual complaint....But these men should be keenly aware of the gravity of the disease which may be suffered if they unnecessarily expose themselves to excessive concentrations. They should in no way resist the reasonable efforts of management to protect their own health. (U.S. Department of Labor, 1938)

In their efforts to ward off pressure from lawmakers and labor unions to address the silicosis problem, spokespersons for silica industries disparaged those who helped the victims, as well as the scientists and victims themselves. Lawyers working with injured workers were "shyster[s]," "racketeering lawyers," "ambulance-chasers" and "parasites." Doctors who diagnosed silicosis were "quacks" or "uninformed" (Hirth, 1936). A scientist at the Industrial Hygiene Foundation wrote of workers' "hysterical manifestations which undoubtedly exaggerated the symptoms" (Sander, 1946).

While acknowledging "bona fide cases of silicosis in which plaintiffs have been represented by lawyers of ability and integrity," the industry regarded most of the cases as without merit. They would have preferred to "exterminate" their "mutual malady—the system lawyer and quack doctor." They also would have liked to eliminate lay juries from liability cases: "We are not here dealing with the type of injury which the layman can visualize and understand, such as a broken arm or a broken leg, but with a very complex lung condition which is not understood even by the medical profession generally" (Hirth, 1936). In the industry's view, lay jurors were ill equipped to weigh conflicting testimony between the plaintiff's experts and those of the defendant, or testimony "couched in such language as to be wholly unintelligible to the jury and often to the Court" (Hirth, 1936). If the medical profession was bewildered by this lung disease, and testimony was unintelligible even to the court, then disputes over possible injury from chronic exposure to silica dust could not be litigated fairly. In this portrayal of the legal process, the industry often viewed itself as the victim of opportunistic plaintiffs who were manipulated by crooked lawyers and quack doctors and as judged by confused lay jurists. It was the system, they contended, not the industry that was at fault.

The Coal Industry

Coal mining not only involves health risks from coal dust but also poses grave danger to miners' very lives. The Center for Public Integrity revealed that the federal Mine Safety and Health Administration (MSHA) and the U.S. Department of Labor report an alarming resurgence in black-lung disease, which results from inhaling coal dust (Berkes, 2012). With regulations poorly enforced and mining companies providing false mine-dust samples, miners continue to contract this suffocating lung disease in hazardous working conditions. Despite substantial evidence of violations of safety standards there have been few prosecutions or convictions for illegal practices. Professor R. Larry Grayson of Penn State University, an authority on the health risks of mining, prescribed a consequential corrective: "We have to get these people with consequence so high they won't do it" (Berkes, 2012). However, with disengaged moral restraint and scant oversight, legal sanctions are readily circumventable.

It is more profitable to remove mountaintops for surface mining of coal reserves rather than digging the coal out from underground. Surface mining causes massive environmental degradation. Other cost-saving practices produced widespread water pollution, which takes a heavy toll on public health.

In April 2010, an explosion in the Upper Big Branch Mine in West Virginia, fueled by combustive coal dust and methane buildups, killed 29 miners (Tavernise, 2011). The mining operation was characterized as reckless, with poor ventilation in the coal tunnels, malfunctioning controls on safety equipment, and clogged machines that were supposed to dilute coal dust. Safety equipment was diverted to construction projects, safety inspections were thwarted, and only minor changes needed to pass inspections were made. Regulators were treated as "enemies." Fearing powerful corporate influence over their electability, politicians were reluctant to take action.

A roof bolter who escaped death because he called in sick the day of the explosion described the stifling heat in the tunnels: "It was literally like you were melting." A miner who closed a tunnel for lack of air was threatened with firing if he did not reopen it. On the day before he perished, one miner described the inhumane working conditions: "Man, they got us up there mining, and we ain't got no air. I'm just scared to death to go to work because I'm just scared to death something bad is going to happen" (Tavernise, 2011). It did.

Shortly after the disaster, Massey Energy, the owner of the mine, was bought by Alpha Natural Resources. Alpha agreed to a $210 million settlement that protects the company from further criminal liability, but leaves open the possibility of criminal prosecutions of individual employees for the miners' deaths (Mauriello, 2011). Cecil Roberts, the president of the United Mine Workers of America, expressed disappointment at the nonprosecution clause in the settlement, saying, "We remain hopeful that responsibility will be placed where it belongs: on upper-level management at Massey who created the safety-last culture at that company" (Mauriello, 2011).

David Hughart, a former official at subsidiary companies that controlled other Massey coal mines, was sentenced to jail for 42 months for conspiring to violate safety laws, hiding violations, and giving miners advance warning of surprise safety inspections. The federal prosecutor called Hughart "the highest-ranking mine official ever convicted of conspiracy to impede MSHA [the Mine Safety and Health Administration] or conspiracy to violate mine health and safety standards" (Berkes, 2013).

Don Blankenship was the CEO of Massey Energy at the time of the disaster. He was dubbed the "dark Lord of Coal Country," who exercised powerful control over the political and judicial systems in West Virginia, whose economy was heavily dependent on the coal industry (Goodell, 2010). Blankenship referred to federal lawmakers who called for tighter regulation of the mining industry as "crazies" and "greeniacs" (Cooper, 2009). He proclaimed global warming a "hoax" (Goodell, 2010) and set profits above miners' safety and environmental costs. With natural gas replacing coal in power plants, Blankenship's commanding control over the political system declined. Federal prosecutors indicted Blankenship for conspiracy to violate mine safety standards and conspiracy to impede federal mine safety officials (Segal, 2015). He pleaded not guilty, claiming that the mine disaster was an act of God and blamed the federal administration as a contributor to the explosion by changing ventilation systems (Goodell, 2010). Blankenship was given a three-month reprieve to prepare for the criminal trial, though it was later postponed.

AGGREGATE ANALYSIS

Comparative analysis, based on the data from the studies reviewed, revealed similar patterns of moral disengagement across the four diverse industries discussed above (White et al., 2009). The replication of similar modes of moral disengagement adds to the generalizability of the theory. Minimization and denial of harmful effects was the most frequently used mode of moral disengagement. Social, moral, and economic justifications were also widely used. Industry personnel attributed harmful effects, which could not be dismissed, to personal deficiencies of the victims or to other causative factors operating in the environment. Bad genes, personal vulnerabilities, and unhealthful lifestyles were invoked as the causes of health problems. The complexity of variables contributing to health status provides fertile ground for attributing harmful effects to a host of factors, while excluding the corporate products and production practices even as partial contributors to health impairment.

In most social systems, diffusion and displacement of responsibility figure prominently in self-exoneration for harm that is caused collectively. People do not feel personally responsible if they view their harmful actions as prescribed by authorities. The authorities themselves create mazy chains of authorization, sanction detrimental conduct surreptitiously, keep themselves intentionally uninformed, and devise insulating social arrangements that permit deniability of wrongdoing (Bandura, 1999).

There were no instances of displacement of responsibility to company officials authorizing detrimental practices except in the mining operations. This was because all of the industries steadfastly denied that their products and practices are harmful. Hence, there was no blame to displace or diffuse. A different form of nonresponsibility was widely practiced, however. It involved concealing efforts to shape scientific evidence by shifting responsibility to proxy agents to do the exonerating research and to influence regulatory policies. The industries enlisted scientists and consultants, funded research programs likely to vindicate the industries, and created front organizations to conduct research on their behalf under a cloak of independence and credibility. Outsourcing the research activities shifted the moral predicament to the proxy agents.

Chapter **6**

■ ■ ■ ■ ■ ■ ■

CAPITAL PUNISHMENT

All societies face troubling social and moral issues regarding what to do with murderers in their midst. Homicidal behavior has such dire social consequences that all societies make efforts to curb it. Not only do murderous offenders inflict personal suffering on their victims and their victims' loved ones, but on a broader scale they also threaten public safety and the social order. Through the fears they arouse, they change the quality of life in society and impose costly protective measures on society at large that involve law enforcement and judicial and prison systems.

Heinous crimes such as murder fuel public wrath and provoke societal demands to eliminate the offenders. The taking of human life is the ultimate penalty a state can impose. However, the institutionalized killing of a human being raises deep moral issues. To mitigate this moral problem, the state provides religious, philosophical, and utilitarian justifications that make executions individually and socially acceptable.

Murders occur in various forms and are committed under varying circumstances. Any judicial system must decide whether a murderer should be committed to lifetime imprisonment, receive a shorter sentence, or be put to death. When death is the sentence, society must decide on the means of execution. The methods, which vary across cultures and which may change within a culture over time, include decapitation, stoning, hanging, shooting, gassing, electrocution, and lethal injection. Executioners have the formidable task of putting a person to death.

Throughout history, virtually every society has punished wrongdoers with death for a variety of crimes. Over time, the number and types of crimes punishable by death have changed. With growing globalization, socioeconomic development, and democratization, countries worldwide have abolished the death penalty. The UN General Assembly has adopted a nonbinding resolution calling for a worldwide moratorium on the death penalty with the goal of abolishing it. Rupert Colville, a spokesman for the

UN Office of the High Commissioner for Human Rights (OHCHR), explained the need for such a moratorium: Many of the countries conducting executions violate international standards of due process, lack fair trial rules, force confessions from suspects, and execute people for crimes that fall below the "threshold of most serious crimes" (Minegar, 2013). About 150 countries have agreed to observe the moratorium. The European Union has abolished the death penalty altogether.

Retentionists and abolitionists differ markedly in the reasons for the positions they take toward the death penalty. Retentionists want murderers put to death as repayment in kind, because they deserve it, and to save taxpayers money (although, as we will see, this has been called into question). Abolitionists oppose the death penalty because it is wrong for the state to take a human life, because innocent individuals are sometimes wrongly executed, and because the death penalty violates their religious beliefs.

An anomaly among developed democratic nations, the United States finds itself a bedfellow with oppressive regimes that impose the death penalty (Spielman, 2012). However, within the United States, support for the death penalty is far from universal. Opinions can depend on how survey items are framed in public opinion polls. If people have only one choice of penalty for capital crimes, about 63% support the death penalty. However, when given alternatives, 45% favor lifetime imprisonment, and support for executions drops to 50%. In the historical trend support for executions is gradually declining, and preference for lifetime imprisonment is sharply rising (Jones, 2014).

The pattern of support for the death penalty varies regionally; it is carried out mainly in the Midwest and South. Within these regions only a few states—principally Texas, Oklahoma, and Missouri—carry out the majority of executions. Executions can be localized even further. Only states can actually carry out executions, but county district attorneys can decide to request the death penalty. Fifteen counties in the Midwest and Southwest—fewer than 1% of the U.S. total—account for almost one third of all executions since 1976 (Top 15 counties by execution, 2013). However, these findings need to be further analyzed, with controls for county population size. It also would be of interest to evaluate the extent to which district attorneys and prosecutors favor the death penalty or lifetime imprisonment in the trials they conduct in their counties.

It should be noted in passing that over the years, virtually all of the states have imposed the death penalty at various times. However, this seeming consensus is misleading. In fact, the nation is deeply divided on the issue of capital punishment. As documented earlier, the southern states are the most consistent practitioners of punishment by death, with about 80% of the executions carried out there, with most of them in Texas (Top 15 counties by execution, 2013). However, if corrected for population size, the Texas rate of executions may not differ from those of its southern brethren. Liberally oriented states also adopted the death penalty, mainly for electoral expediency, but practice a de facto moratorium on executions.

The most striking difference in views on capital punishment is in the partisan political divide on this issue. Republicans favor it highly (81%), whereas Democrats are much less supportive (47%). Over the years about 75% of Republicans regarded the death penalty as morally acceptable, whereas 43% of Democrats did so in a pattern of declining moral acceptability (Jones, 2013). The split in support of the death penalty is much the same across conservative and liberal orientations as it is across political party affiliation. The sociodemographic pattern of support also varies. Men (67%) favor capital punishment more than women (59%), as do older (65%) individuals compared with younger ones (52%). Considerably more Whites (68%) are in favor of executing offenders than are non-Whites (41%) (Saad, 2013).

Regional variations in support of the death penalty reflect public attitudes on this matter, as measured by Gallup polls (Saad, 2013). Residents in the Midwest (66%) and South (68%) favor the death penalty at higher rates than those in the East (54%). Religious background does not make a difference, but more gun owners (80%) favor the death penalty than do non–gun owners (55%) (Saad, 2013). This relationship, along with the political correlates, suggests that advocacy of capital punishment may be part of a more general threat-oriented mind-set that tolerates lethal means of curbing perceived dangers. In sum, strong advocates for the death penalty are conservative, older, gun-owning White males living in the Midwest and South.

Attitudes toward the death penalty itself are also interesting. The public is highly skeptical that executions save lives. Only about a third of the public (34%) believe that executions reduce murder rates. A major share of the public (59%) believes that innocent individuals have been wrongfully executed, and a significant percentage (35%) is of the view that the death penalty is unfairly applied. However, in the aggregate, skepticism about deterrence, legal unfairness, and wrongful executions do not seem to diminish support of executions (Jones, 2006). The support is driven mainly by the desire for restitution and revenge.

Support for the death penalty in the United States has varied widely, consistent with changes in the political climate. During the mid-1960s, the public was opposed to the death penalty, albeit by a small majority. Thereafter, public support for it rose to a peak of 80% during the Reagan and George H. W. Bush Republican administrations. Reagan voiced strong support for the penalty while he was the governor of California. His linguistic justification was that according to Hebrew scholars, the commandment "Thou shall not kill" should have been translated as "Thou shalt not murder." The Old Testament, he noted, also requires "an eye for an eye" (Reagan, 1967). In response to Christian ministers who tolled bells as the time for execution neared, Reagan replied, "If you toll your bells every time somebody is murdered, I won't mind if you do it every time the state executes a killer" (Ashcroft, 1998).

During his presidency, Reagan remained a stalwart advocate of the death penalty. He portrayed crime victims as maltreated by the criminal justice system and extended the death penalty to drug dealers who killed drug-enforcement officers. Troubled by social unrest and the perceived erosion of "family values," working-class Democrats defected to the Republican Party. These "Reagan Democrats," as they were called, were progun, pro–capital punishment, and antiabortion. They raised their voices in support of the death penalty.

In his 1988 bid for the presidency, the Republican candidate, George H. W. Bush, portrayed his Democratic opponent, Governor Michael Dukakis of Massachusetts, as soft on crime and national defense. During a prison furlough a convicted murderer, Willie Horton, fled from Massachusetts to Maryland, where he broke into a home, raped a woman, and beat and stabbed her fiancé. The infamous Willie Horton television ad, laced with racist overtones, was aired repeatedly as graphic evidence that Dukakis was soft on crime. During a presidential debate, the moderator asked Dukakis whether he would favor the death penalty if his wife was raped and murdered. He calmly explained his opposition to the death penalty. His didactic response to this horrid scenario not only reinforced the view that he was soft on crime but also suggested that he was cold and unresponsive to the fate of victims as well. This set of events contributed to Dukakis's defeat in the presidential election.

During the Reagan and George H. W. Bush presidencies, the death penalty enjoyed overwhelming public support. After peaking at 80% in 1994, support for it declined sharply (Saad, 2013). This drop was occasioned largely by reports of DNA evidence showing that innocent prisoners on death row were awaiting wrongful execution. Amnesty International USA has documented the faulty legal practices by which innocent people end up on death row. These include grossly incompetent defendant lawyering, misconduct by police and prosecutors, perjured testimony, racial prejudice, erroneous eyewitness testimony, and suppression of mitigating evidence (Amnesty International USA, n.d.). Death-row inmates in some of these cases were pardoned, others were acquitted on retrial, and still others saw the charges against them simply dropped. Review of evidence also has exonerated a number of innocent prisoners after they had been put to death. During the period when application of the death penalty was blatantly discriminatory, innocent people were probably executed at a higher rate. These executions raise fundamental questions about the morality of the death penalty. Unlike other penalties, the taking of human life is irrevocable. For some people, this irrevocability alone is enough reason for abolishing the death penalty.

Faced with evidence that innocent people have been wrongfully executed, the American public has conflicting views regarding state executions (Gross & Ellsworth, 2003). Although at a lower but still majority level, the public supports the death penalty but simultaneously doubts its deterrent value and acknowledges that the judicial system is often administered unfairly and cannot fully protect innocent defendants from being put to death.

Lawmakers play an influential role in whether capital punishment is retained or abolished in a society. In several high-profile cases, governors have lost elections in which their opposition to the death penalty was the Achilles' heel of their political campaigns. These outcomes reinforced the political view that staunch support for capital punishment wins elections, and opposition to it jeopardizes electability. Politicians therefore exploit capital crimes to further their political careers. Borrowing from the "Willie Horton" debacle, they portray their opponents as soft on crime, with mug shots of notorious criminals in their campaign materials and television ads.

Conflicts involving deeply rooted value commitments, such as that over the death penalty, rarely are definitively resolved. Although Canada and Great Britain abolished the death penalty years ago, retentionists continue to introduce legislative initiatives to reinstate the death penalty that legislators promptly defeat.

A rarity among politicians, New York State governor Mario Cuomo forcefully opposed the death penalty. In an op-ed piece in the New York *Daily News*, Cuomo (2011) explained that he understood the anger over egregious murders and the desire for revenge because he experienced the same emotions himself. However, retaliatory killing, he said, "is a surrender to the worst that is in us." He viewed capital punishment as an "abomination," a "stain on our conscience" that corrodes society. He challenged not only the morality of the death penalty but its utility as a deterrent as well. The taking of innocent human life, he declared, is "irreversible injustice."

When Cuomo was asked why he pushed an issue that jeopardized his reelectability, he explained that the problem is more fundamental than the death penalty, "It raises important questions about how, as a society, we view human beings." He further explained that "we should be better than what we are in our weakest moments" (Cuomo, 2011). A spokesman for the governor described the "politics of death" (Kolbert, 1989) in which legislators passed a law to reinstate the death penalty, whereupon the governor vetoed it. This scenario was repeated seven times. Legislators, in turn, rejected the governor's proposal to enact a law for mandatory life imprisonment without possibility of parole. Advocates of the death penalty saw it as a ruse to abolish the death penalty. An opposing legislator warned that he would not allow Cuomo to do so: "He'd like to have a vote on life without parole, so that he would in that way defeat the death penalty. But I am not going to give him that opportunity" (Kolbert, 1989).

In 1994, Cuomo was defeated by his Republican opponent, George Pataki. The following year, Governor Pataki fulfilled a campaign promise, signing legislation that reinstated the death penalty. On the first anniversary of the restored death penalty, Governor Pataki issued a press release describing the many benefits of the law he sponsored. He concluded, "I have every confidence that it will continue to deter murders, will continue to enhance public safety and will be enforced fairly and justly" (Pataki, 1996). However, the "politics of death" was replayed with a generational change in the governorship. Governor Andrew Cuomo, the son of Mario Cuomo, suspended the death penalty that his father could not abolish.

A few other high-profile political contests further strengthened lawmakers' risk-adverse mind-set regarding capital punishment. In his reelection bid for the California governorship, Pete Wilson was challenged by the state treasurer, Kathleen Brown (Stall, 1994). This election was held in the context of the abduction, rape, and murder of Polly Klaas, a young girl who was kidnapped at knifepoint from a slumber party at her home. The randomness of the crime, which was committed in a middle-class neighborhood, frightened the public with the realization that anyone can be a victim.

In response to this tragedy, legislators drafted a "one-strike law" whereby rapists would be sentenced to life imprisonment without the possibility of parole. Brown argued that it would be difficult to get convictions in rape cases under such an extreme law. She also opposed the death penalty on the moral grounds that it conflicted with her religious values but said that as governor she would enforce it. In addition to illegal immigration, Wilson made Brown's apparent "softness on crime" the mainstay of his reelection campaign. Television ads portrayed him as a tough crime fighter, questioned Brown's commitment to the one-strike law, and used her opposition to the death penalty as evidence that she lacked the courage to be tough on crime. The ads reminded the public that her father, Edmund, and her brother, Jerry—both California governors—opposed the death penalty as well. Brown objected to Wilson's misrepresentations of her position on crime and criticized him for "exploiting the pain of rape victims to cover up his failed record" (Stall, 1994). Brown's initially large lead rapidly eroded, and she was defeated in the election. Both this case and that of Michael Dukakis illustrate how a socially threatening, fortuitous event can help determine the outcomes of gubernatorial and presidential elections.

MECHANISMS OF MORAL DISENGAGEMENT

No amount of debate about capital punishment can dispel the reality that it involves killing a human being. Putting a person to death requires stripping morality from every phase of the execution process. When capital punishment is carried out, moral disengagement operates with increasing personal involvement at the societal, judicial, and execution levels.

The societal level centers on moral considerations in public support for the death penalty. Those who favor the death penalty are far removed from its implementation in the execution chamber. Moral disengagement can ease the public's qualms about state executions, especially when they are viewed in the abstract under the sanitized label of "capital punishment." People are less supportive of the death penalty if they have to serve as jurors on death-penalty cases (Ellsworth & Ross, 1983).

The moral predicament is graver at the judicial level, where jurors have to decide whether or not to sentence a person to death. Capital trials are structured to mitigate the moral weightiness of deciding who should live and who should die. Jurors decide the death penalty but are spared the task of having to put the convicted inmate to death. The weakening of moral self-sanctions achieved by the jurors' distal role in the execution process was captured by Sara Rimer (2000) in the remarks of a retiring warden: "If jurors had to draw straws to see who was going to pull the switch or start the lethal injection, there wouldn't be as many executions."

The gravest moral predicament is faced by the executioners, who must willfully kill a human being by their own hand. To do so they have to suspend moral self-censure. The following sections of this chapter address the ways in which moral disengagement at each of these levels enable societies to execute a human being.

Moral and Social Justifications for Capital Punishment

A variety of moral and social justifications are used to make the death penalty morally right. This enables a society to execute wrongdoers without serious moral qualms. A major share of the justifications are provided by two major theories of morality—the utilitarian and the retributive. Utilitarians justify the death penalty by citing the social benefits it produces. It prevents the murderer from killing again, deters would-be murderers, restores public safety, and provides solace for society. The utilitarian view is essentially the consequentialist theory of morality, whereby the rightness of an act is judged by its utility for the greatest number of people.

Opponents of this view question whether capital punishment delivers what it promises. Justification of executions on utilitarian grounds requires evidence that the death penalty has unique deterrent power over and above that of lifetime imprisonment. The latter penalty may be equally effective as a deterrent and also results in the incapacitation of murderers. The execution of innocent people who were wrongfully convicted is irreversible. The irreversibility of capital punishment applies, of course, to all theories of morality being used to justify executions.

Retributivists contend that wrongdoers deserve to be punished in the name of justice. The proportionate principle dictates that the severity of the punishment should fit the gravity of the crime. This principle is captured in the adage "an eye for an eye." Immanuel Kant was the foremost proponent of retributive justice. He argued that society has a duty to execute those guilty of the most serious offenses. Kant rejected utilitarianism, whereby wrong-doers are executed as a means of deterrence. The retributive view rests on the core assumption of autonomous agency. The execution of wrongdoers is construed as respecting their humanity. Viewed from this perspective, individuals have free will, rationality, and responsibility for the consequences of their actions. Rationality endows them with moral personhood. Hence, executing wrongdoers as a consequence of the choices they made freely is an affirmation of their moral personhood. Through their rational agency, they brought punishment on themselves; thus, they should get what they deserve.

The application of retribution is problematic in a number of ways. There are wide variations over time and across cultures in the types of offenses that are punishable by death. At one time the death penalty was imposed for kid-napping, adultery, robbery, theft, blasphemy, Sabbath violations, hijacking, counterfeiting, drug trafficking, prostitution, arson, and rape. In patriarchal cultures, females are killed for conduct believed to bring shame on the family. Such offenses usually involve violations of social norms and traditions. These so-called honor killings are socially condoned as justifiable or are punished with minor sentences. As evident from the diverse offenses, the proportionality principle has been seriously violated. For example, at one time individuals were hung for horse theft.

There is no established principle for judging what constitutes a proportionate punishment. Moreover, in some cases the proportionality principle cannot be applied (Schauer & Sinnott-Armstrong, 1996; Tollefsen, 2011). For example, rapists are not punished by being raped, nor are arsonists punished by being set on fire. Nathanson (2012) raises a more serious problem that applies even to murder. The reprehensibility of behavior cannot be judged solely from the behavior. Murder committed in self-defense is judged differently from premeditated murder. Mitigating circumstances alter its reprehensibility. In short, "an eye for an eye" has become a slogan rather than a principle for fitting punishments for crimes.

Conceptual differences between utilitarian and retributive morality at the abstract level fade in actual practice. Staunch retributivists argue for the death penalty on the grounds that it is a better deterrent. They also believe executions cost less than lifetime imprisonment. These are utilitarian justifications. In reality, people have to justify to themselves the morality of executing a human being. They use some combination of justice, deterrents, and a dose of vengeance. If they believe that executing human beings shows respect for their humanity, that makes executions even easier to carry out.

American Catholic scholars who analyze the morality of the death penalty are divided on its application. The more traditionally minded oppose the death penalty as a violation of the sanctity of life. Mandatory lifetime imprisonment, they argue, provides a nonlethal means of protecting the public from heinous criminals (McGuire, 2013). Pope John Paul II (2000) and more recently Pope Francis (2015) called for the unconditional abolishment of the death penalty worldwide. Those who view capital punishment from this moral perspective believe that the intentional taking of human life should not be used as deterrence or vengeance.

Social conservatives who generally are pro-lifers are proponents of the death penalty (Zmirak, 2013). They base their moral justification on retributive justice in the name of their faith. In theological support of their view, they cite incidents from the Bible when capital punishment was imposed. Some advocates draw heavily on Immanuel Kant's ideas on restitutive morality. As we saw earlier, Kant argued that society has a duty to execute those found guilty of the most serious crimes. In justifying the morality of capital punishment, advocates contend that if one accepts that punishment is legitimate and that the severity of punishment is proportionate to the gravity of the crime, then the death penalty is morally justified. Supreme Court Justice Antonin Scalia put it succinctly: "You kill. You die. That's fair" (Pew Research Center, 2012).

In reality, however, neither murder nor punishment is that definitive. Killing is viewed differently in different circumstances. Was it premeditated, committed in self-defense as a last resort, socially coerced, or the result of deranged thinking? Moreover, in practice the way murder is treated legally depends, in part, on the status of the defendant and the quality of the lawyering. Individuals of high social status defended by clever lawyers can, in many cases, literally get away with murder. By invoking mitigating circumstances, wrongdoers can get off with brief jail time for manslaughter or with a slightly longer stretch for second-degree murder. In the legal expansion of gun rights, lax self-defense laws make it easier to kill with impunity (Alvarez & Buckley, 2013).

Death-penalty statutes are being struck down as unconstitutional because they are administered unfairly and arbitrarily. This was why Supreme Court Justice Harry A. Blackmun gave up on the quest for fairness in executions (Greenhouse, 1994). However, the procedural fairness issue does not address the moral issue of putting a person to death when a nonlethal alternative is available. Pope John Paul II repudiated the authority of a state to deprive a human of life on behalf of the state: "A sign of hope is the increasing recognition that the dignity of human life must never be taken away, even in the case of someone who has done great evil" (Pope John Paul's II statements, 2000). The pope argued that society is obligated to punish wrongdoers to preserve public safety but is not morally required to kill them as punishment. This view conflicts with that of Saint Thomas Aquinas, who equated the murderer metaphorically with a diseased limb threatening the body, which represented the common good, and the death penalty with amputation of the limb to save the body (Kaczor, 2010). Pro-life advocates of capital punishment dismiss the pope's pronouncement as personal opinion that is not binding (Zmirak, 2013). Pope John Paul II's rejoinder in this metaphoric skirmish is that one should not amputate a diseased limb if it is treatable with medication. Tollefsen (2011) exposed the flaws in Aquinas's disease metaphor.

Philosophical battles have been fought over whether the dignity of personhood is divinely given or socially bestowed (Feser, 2011). In the latter case, dignity is developed by goodness and achievement and lost through wrongdoing. Intentional killings are easier to justify if human dignity is construed to have a social origin. Individuals who commit heinous crimes are judged to be unworthy of dignity and deserve to be stripped of it. Attributing subhuman and bestial qualities to evildoers implies that they can even be excluded from the category of common humanity. On the other hand, if the sanctity and dignity of life have a divine origin, abolitionists could charge the state with playing God by taking human life intentionally.

Vengeance is another justification for executing murderers. People often confuse restitutive punishment with vengeful punishment. Restitution is aimed at restoring justice, but with restitution, excessively harsh punishment is disavowed. In contrast, vengeful punishment—the harsher the better—is aimed at inflicting suffering on offenders.

Seeking solace and a sense of closure for family members of the victim and the public at large is another justification for executing murderers. However, executions evoke powerful, mixed emotions in family members— anger, hatred, anguish at reliving the brutal death of a loved one, vengeful feelings, and deep grief. Some family members report that the speed and ease of execution left them unsatisfied (Brownlee & McGraw, 1997). "You stand there and you watch a man take two gasps and it's over. We make it too easy," said a mother who watched the execution of the murderer of her two children (Haney, 2005). Some survivors reported that they want offenders to suffer painful deaths. The public regards harsh punishment of criminals as showing caring for victims. Others are angry at the lengthy appeals process, which extends offenders' lives: "He didn't deserve to live during those six years" (Haney, 2005).

Of the various justifications, the public favors retribution and vengeance, followed by economic savings and deterrence (Newport, 2011). Recent years, however, have witnessed a substantial decline in the view that the death penalty is morally acceptable, from a peak of 71% in 2007 to a low of 58% in 2012. Abolitionists regard state executions of human beings as a barbaric practice that should be abolished.

Ernest Van Den Haag (1968), a staunch supporter of capital punishment, argues that there is no such thing as a right to life. Hence, legally depriving a murderer of life is a deserved punishment. Citing Immanuel Kant, Van Den Haag contends that executing an egregious offender confirms his humanity by affirming his rationality and responsibility for his actions. Construing the death penalty as reverence for life and believing that abolishing the death penalty cheapens life further remove qualms about executing condemned prisoners. Staunch retributionists still have to deal with the nonlethal alternative of lifetime imprisonment. Their solution is to denigrate it as a suitable option.

Aaron Taylor (2013) challenges the notion that imprisoned offenders can do no harm. Future governors, legislators and judges, he argues, might renege on lifetime sentences and release dangerous prisoners. Even in prison, convicts can kill; this also is possible if they escape. Parole boards, which preside over the conditional release of prisoners, change members periodically and may release prisoners whose parole previously was denied. Cases of prisoners who commit murder while on parole are cited as evidence that life imprisonment does not guarantee public safety. Few if any governors are willing to risk the high political cost of releasing condemned prisoners who might go on to commit more crimes. Finally, executions are justified on controversial economic grounds. It is widely believed that executing offenders is cheaper than imprisoning them for life. This economic justification is disputed (Chammah, 2014).

Echoing Kant's duty-bound morality, Taylor questions whether respect for the sanctity of life is the ultimate moral value. Protecting the social order, he argues, is a higher common good than simply allowing offenders to continue living in prison without a further purpose. Granting states the right to execute wrongdoers based on judgments of their worthy purpose is a dangerous social policy. To further denigrate lifetime imprisonment as a nonlethal alternative to execution, Taylor cites Archbishop Fulton J. Sheen, who stated that "the refusal to impose just punishment is not mercy but cowardice" (Taylor, 2013). Some death-penalty advocates go further in condemning opposition to executing condemned prisoners by claiming that it is not merely cowardice. In accord with Immanuel Kant, they contend that it is immoral *not* to do so. Arguing along a similar line, John Zmirak (2013) characterizes lifetime imprisonment as a "mockery of justice" that shows "profound disrespect to...victims." In his pro-life view, "true justice and genuine mercy demand the hangman." In the promotion of punishment by death, retribution appears to be morphing into vengeance.

In sum, there are several elements in the retributionist justification for executing offenders. The first is proportionate punishment; the second is protecting public safety by executing convicted murderers so they cannot kill again; the third strips the lives of offenders of any value or purpose; the fourth construes execution as affirming the offender's humanity. This combination of justifications, or a subset of them, can remove any moral pangs about executing a human being, especially when someone else has to do it. How someone can coherently be pro-life and pro-death simultaneously remains to be explained (McGuire, 2013).

Euphemistic Language and Advantageous Comparison

A correctional record at an old Massachusetts state prison referred to the death penalty as "judicial homicide" (Moseley, 2014). That designation has been considerably sanitized since then. Killing a human being is a gruesome act. Hence, euphemisms and legal jargon are used to sanitize executions, making them more personally and socially palatable. Consider the term *capital punishment*. "Capital" suggests something serious. "Punishment" sounds like a reprimand and "penalty" like a fine, rather than an execution. Sometimes the death penalty is called "deprivation of life." A strong opponent of capital punishment, the French philosopher Albert Camus described it starkly as the "most premeditated of murders," which "[w]e smother under padded terms" (Camus, 1960). As we have seen, Supreme Court Justice Scalia calls capital punishment "fair." Archbishop Desmond Tutu does not: "To take a life when a life has been lost is revenge, not justice" (Lieblich, 2003).

There is no humane way to execute people. "Humane execution" is an oxymoron. However, the term *humane* is widely used in comparing execution methods, with each method being "more humane" than others. For example, electrocution replaced hanging on the grounds that it was allegedly "more humane." Richard Dieter, the former executive director of the Death Penalty Information Center, dubbed the merciful language as a "veil of humaneness" for a gruesome task (Berman, 2014b). Compare the euphemistic label with the grisly reality of executions as described by Supreme Court Justice William Brennan: "[T]he prisoner's eyeballs sometimes pop out and rest on [his] cheeks. The prisoner often defecates, urinates and vomits blood and drool. The body turns bright red as its temperature rises, and the prisoner's flesh swells and his skin stretches to the point of breaking. Sometimes the prisoner catches fire" (Ecenbarger, 1994). It is easy to understand why prison officials banned public witnesses and the media from observing executions.

What the execution of condemned inmates is called has social consequences. Polling for public support of executions is often based on these euphemisms. Were people shown the methods of death, the number of supporters would probably decline sharply. Analysis of sanitizing, euphemistic language should be extended to its impact on political debate and how it influences public policy on whether the death penalty should be adopted, maintained, reinstated, or abolished.

Electrocution was later replaced by lethal injection as a "more humane" method of execution. Lethal injection, which requires three different drugs, has the trappings of an antiseptic medical approach. However, its use has run into problems. Pharmaceutical companies in Europe and the United States refuse to supply the necessary drugs, and states find their supplies running low or depleted. Unable to conduct executions, officials searched for alternatives or ways to circumvent regulations. However, as will be described later, this effort ran into trouble as well. The use of untested drugs, which turned out to prolong the time it takes for a condemned inmate to die, heightened the dispute over legal injection (Lyman, 2013). Kent Scheidegger, the legal director of the Criminal Justice Legal Foundation and a major spokesman for the death penalty, dismissed the seriousness of the problem: "We've gotten namby-pamby to the point that we give murderers sedatives before we kill them" (Lyman, 2014). Botched executions, which involve prolonged torment, revived arguments against the lethal injection method on constitutional grounds as cruel and unusual punishment (Ford, 2015).

Responding to these executions and to legal controversy over state secrecy laws about the drugs used, U.S. Ninth Circuit Court chief judge Alex Kozinski argued that states should cease trying to sanitize executions, which he called "brutal, savage events" and instead restore the firing squad, which is "messy but effective" (Dolan, 2014). However, this mode of execution makes the task more difficult for executioners because they become direct agents of death, whereas lethal injection provides an elaborately diffused system of intentionally killing a human being. No one is the executioner.

The medical profession bans doctors, nurses, and anesthesiologists from participating in executions because it violates the code of professional ethics. Therefore, technicians of varying skill have to do it. The necessary drugs are becoming almost impossible to obtain in the United States, and in some cases the imported drugs were too weak to sedate inmates, who were conscious while being paralyzed. They were gasping for air and convulsing (Lyman, 2014). In other instances, members of the intravenous teams misjudged the inmate's level of unconsciousness, inserted the needle into muscles rather than in the vein, couldn't find the vein, or had to deal with blocked needles (Associated Press, 2014).

Proponents of the death penalty blame the reduction in executions on obstructive tactics by abolitionists. Kent Scheidegger, an avid advocate of the death penalty, claimed that the drug problem is an artificial one and casts the objection to the lethal injection method in broader conspiratorial terms: "There is no difficulty in using a sedative such as pentobarbital. It's done every day in animal shelters throughout the country. But what we have is a conspiracy to choke off capital punishment by limiting the availability of drugs" (Lyman, 2013). Professor Robert Blecker at the New York Law School likewise attributes the objections to an abolitionist strategy for rescinding the death penalty: "It's an abolitionist tactic to gum up the works. I know why they're doing it. From their perspective, every death delayed is a day in favor of abolition. It's just another tactic" (Lyman, 2013).

Scheidegger (2002) is linguistically unrestrained in his antipathy toward abolitionists. Armed with a DNA testing mandate, they are "saboteurs" hiding in the belly of a "Trojan Horse." The mission of their "holy crusade" is to "grind the system of capital punishment to a halt." He minimizes the number of innocent people on death row who have been exonerated by DNA tests to "a handful of cases" and disputes the extent of inadequate lawyering by public defenders: "In any large barrel one can always find some bad apples."

Echoing Supreme Court Justice Blackmun's decision to quit "tinkering" with the "machinery of death" (Greenhouse, 1994), critics declared that it is time to stop trying to find a way of killing a human being "humanely." David Fathi (2009), the director of the U.S. program at Human Rights Watch, commented on the cruel irony implicit in comparing human death by lethal injection with animal euthanasia: "It's shocking that California plans to put human beings to death using a method that's considered too cruel to use on animals." In 2014, a federal judge declared California's death-penalty system unconstitutional. In response to the constitutional challenge concerning the cruelty of death by lethal injections, federal and state judges temporarily suspended the use of the three-drug method (Eckholm, 2015; Richinick, 2015).

With thiopental unavailable states substituted a controversial anesthetic midazolam in executions by lethal injections. The U.S. Supreme Court upheld the use of midazolam, a controversial sedative that was used in prolonged executions in Arizona, Ohio, and Oklahoma. By a 5–4 vote, the Court ruled that the plaintiffs—three prisoners on Oklahoma's death row—failed to establish the merits of their claim that the use of midazolam violates the Eight Amendment's ban on cruel and unusual punishment. In a decision split along ideological lines, the Supreme Court upheld the use of the drug (Liptak, 2015). Writing for the majority, Justice Samuel Alito invoked a new rule requiring prisoners to prove that the existing method of execution is more cruel and unusual than any available alternative one.

Writing for the dissenters, Justice Sonia Sotomayor argued that his line of reasoning would allow torturous modes of execution as long as no more humane method was available. In a separate dissent, Justice Stephen G. Breyer, joined by Justice Ruth Bader Ginsburg, raised a more fundamental issue. Given evidence of executions of innocent people, false convictions of death-row prisoners, arbitrary death sentencing, a capital justice system tainted by discrimination and politics, and lack of evidence that executions are more deterring than lifetime imprisonment, Breyer argued that the constitutionality of the death penalty itself should be reexamined. Justice Scalia called Beyer's judicial analysis "gobbledygook" (Liptak, 2015).

Before becoming Pope Benedict XVI, Cardinal Joseph Ratzinger used military self-defense as justification by social comparison for the use of the death penalty. He explained that it is "permissible to take up arms to repel an aggressor or to have recourse to capital punishment" (Ratzinger, 2004). This justification is similar to one of the just-war principles except that it permits violent force only after nonviolent means have been exhausted.

Advantageous comparison in defense of the death penalty also comes into play when in unfortunate cases, innocent people are executed. The first part of the defense begins with minimizing the scope of the problem. Scheidegger (2005) contends that wrongful executions are rare: "Only a handful of capital cases involve genuine questions of innocence." However, DNA acquittals reveal wrongful death sentences to be more numerous than commonly claimed (Dwyer, Neufeld, & Scheck, 2000). The number of innocent individuals who have been put to death is undoubtedly an underestimate (Lopatto, 2014). DNA samples are unavailable for most inmates on death row. Some innocent people have been exonerated after their executions (Executed but possibly innocent, n.d.). Wrongful executions were probably more prevalent under the old capital-punishment statutes, which were administered in a discriminatory fashion. Minimizing wrongful executions as a systemically inevitable but minor problem cheapens the lives of innocent people who were put to death.

The second part of the comparative defense contrasts the size of the risk of wrongful execution with fatality rates for other activities. Death penalty proponent Wesley Lowe (The death penalty in the United States, 2011) complains that people find the "slim risk" of wrongful executions "unbearable" but "accept the average 45,000 person a year death toll in this nation due to car wrecks." Continuing with the comparative justification, there is "much paranoia on the slimmest and unlikely of risks," he stated, but tolerance of "mass murders and genocides." Lowe even cites Joseph Stalin for his "insight on human nature," in risk assessment when he said, "One death is a tragedy, but a million deaths are statistics." This statistical defense of the death penalty masks the utilitarian morality that it is acceptable to sacrifice a few innocent people for the benefit of many.

Efforts to add more procedural safeguards to prevent wrongful executions are often dismissed by retentionists as valuing the lives of the guilty above the lives of the innocent public. Calls for suspending the death penalty until legal flaws are remedied are also rejected on the grounds that more innocent people will be murdered. This view assumes that the death penalty is a better deterrent than lifetime imprisonment, which is very much in dispute empirically.

Displacement and Diffusion of Responsibility

Across the centuries, various popes have formulated different justifications for capital punishment. As we have seen, examples include the metaphor of amputating diseased limbs and the equation of executions with self-defense in a just war. However, Saint Augustine simply displaced responsibility to divine authority (St. Augustine, 2011). He explained that God temporarily suspends the commandment "Thou shall not kill" and permits civil authorities to carry out particular executions for a just reason. Construing the execution as performing God's bidding absolves the executioners of any sense of personal responsibility. Temporary suspension of the prohibitive commandment circumvents the conundrum that the Bible both prohibits and sanctions killing.

Although divine sanctioning helps to eliminate personal responsibly, intentionally killing a human being requires a great deal of displacement and diffusion of responsibility. Various methods have included hanging, gassing, firing squad, and electrocution. Death by firing squad is less disturbing for the executioners because it involves diffused responsibility. One member of the squad is randomly issued a gun containing a blank cartridge, whereas the others are issued guns with live ammunition. The blank cartridge, called a "conscience round," is intended to allay guilt because no one in the squad will know who fired the fatal shot (Firing squad, n.d.).

Electrocution replaced hanging as supposedly more humane, although the sight of the condemned's popped eyeballs, bloody vomit, and burning flesh is anything but humane. In electrocution, members of the execution team diffuse responsibility by each strapping different parts of the body to the electric chair. Lethal injection, in turn, replaced electrocution because it was perceived to be less gruesome. The execution process diffuses responsibility even more broadly with the addition of an intravenous team. The institutional arrangement diffuses the agentic subfunctions across a variety of individuals, each performing only a small task in the division of labor. The strap-down team escorts the condemned inmate to the death chamber. Each member straps a particular part of the body: left leg, right leg, left arm and torso, right arm and torso, and head, all under close supervision of the team leader. They approach their task with a strong sense of technical responsibility. As one team member put it, "We each have a small role on the team. We carry out a job for the state. The press and victims are watching. We have a certain duty and do it as efficiently as we can" (Osofsky, Bandura, & Zimbardo, 2005).

The medical technicians get the lethal drugs from the pharmacy, insert the intravenous lines for the syringes into the inmate's veins, and attach electrocardiogram electrodes to monitor the inmate's heart rate. The actual execution involves three different drugs in lethal doses: sodium thiopental, an anesthetic that suppresses death spasms; pancuronium bromide, which stops respiration; and potassium chloride, which stops the heartbeat. The executioner pushes the plungers on the syringes one by one so that each drug enters the bloodstream. If this is done correctly, death comes fast. The disinhibitory power of diffusion of responsibility through task fractionalization is reflected in the remarks of a guard in San Quentin who strapped down the offenders' legs to the electric chair in 126 executions (Marine, 1990). "I never pulled the trigger," he said. "I wasn't the executioner."

This discussion illustrates how the minute division of labor absolves the executioners of any agentic responsibility in the execution process. By placing capital punishment in a broader societal context they further absolve themselves as agents of their actions through displacement of responsibility. As one of the guards put it, they are merely following the orders of the state: "We have a job to do. . . . It is simply to carry out the order of the state." Some responsibility is displaced to the judges and juries: "It's not up to me to say yea or nay. That's for the judges and juries. I'm not a part of the deal-making process. I'm here to do the job. I'm assigned to do it and have the job to do" (Osofsky et al., 2005). Displacement of agency relieves emotional distress: "It don't bother me at all. The law says this, and I follow it, and that's it." The dictate of law gains added disinhibitory force when it is grounded in religious imperative, as shown by a prison chaplain who found justifications for the death penalty in religious decree: "I believe that when the laws of men correspond with the laws of God, the laws of men become the laws of God. That enables me to support the death penalty" (Osofsky et al., 2005).

Deterrence Effects

Some of the fiercest disputes about capital punishment center on the utilitarian justification that executions deter others from committing capital crimes. The issue concerning deterrence is not whether the threat of punishment by death deters homicides and other serious crimes but whether it does so more effectively than life imprisonment. It is the alleged unique deterrent influence of the death penalty that is disputed. Advocates of the death penalty contend that executions save lives by deterring homicides. Oppositionists argue that there is no credible evidence that it does so. Resolving this dispute empirically is not as straightforward as it may appear. Society is not at liberty to conduct randomized experiments in which half of the condemned prisoners in one region are executed and the other half are assigned to life imprisonment in a matched region. Researchers must therefore try to tease out the unique influence of the death penalty from among many naturally co-occurring influences that can affect homicide rates. A variety of methods has been used in an effort to resolve this dispute empirically.

Homicide rates were compared in neighboring states with and without capital punishment, such as Illinois, which at one point imposed the death penalty, and Michigan, which does not. The validity of this method depends on how well matched executing and nonexecuting states are for factors that affect murder rates. A second approach relies on time-series analyses. Societies impose, abolish, and reinstate the death penalty for capital crimes. Time-series data are analyzed to ascertain whether adoption of the death penalty reduces murder rates and whether its abolition is accompanied by a rise in murders. However, the interpretation of changes in murder rates over time is complicated by the fact that a host of social factors that can affect homicide rates change concurrently. This makes it difficult to disentangle the independent effects of a society's death-penalty policy. Moreover, it is necessary to compare changes in homicide rates under the adoption or abolition of the death penalty with the trajectory of change in crimes not punishable by death. This comparison controls for societal changes that alter the trajectory of crime rates as a whole.

Another approach examines whether publicized executions deter murders, at least in the short term. However, executions are not publicized in ways that provide vivid reminders that would be cognitive restrainers of violent conduct. Contemporary society wants to instill the imagery of death as a restraining influence while keeping executions hidden from public view. In the past, executions were publicized in the press. Opponents of capital punishment held vigils at execution sites. Nowadays, most executions go unnoticed except in certain cases. A credible threat, such as a mass murderer, must be salient and widely known. Without awareness of occasional executions in distant states and poorly publicized rare ones within their own jurisdiction, many people may not even know whether their state has the death penalty or how strictly it is enforced.

Verifying causal relations in human behavior is complicated by the multiplicity of possible causal factors. To complicate matters further, many factors correlate with each other to some degree, requiring statistical methods to estimate how much each of the various factors contributes to behavior on its own. A reliable casual theory is required, to provide guidance on which of many factors should be selected for the causal analysis. The strength of this analytic model lies in its ability to gauge the deterrent influence of the death penalty after the influence of other possible causes of murder rates are taken into account. However, controversy has arisen over its application. Some critiques are directed at the explanatory value of the causal model. This is a key issue because it determines which factors among the many possible causal ones are selected. Other concerns center on the quality and completeness of the data and whether they are measured at the individual or aggregated group level. Often, data for key factors are unavailable so researchers have to rely on secondary or proxy measures for them. For example, the unemployment rate might be used as a proxy for incentives to engage in criminal activities. Still other issues involve disagreements about the statistical methods used. Are the findings based on cross-sectional or time-series data? Are data on social conditions that are conducive to criminal behavior aggregated at the national level or for local jurisdictions? How do law enforcement and judicial practices affect the risks and consequences of crime?

Prior to the 1970s, research on the deterrent effect of the death penalty was conducted mainly by behavioral scientists and criminologists. More recently, empirical arguments regarding the death penalty have centered mainly on the econometric model of deterrent effects. In the inaugural application of this method, the economist Isaac Ehrlich (1975) studied murder rates as a function of the probability of being caught, convicted, and executed; income and employment; and expenditures in law enforcement.

He concluded from his economic analysis that each execution spares several lives. However, his research came under heavy fire on conceptual and methodological grounds (Fox & Radelet, 1989).

A variety of subsequent studies has yielded contradictory findings. Small changes in assumptions in causal models and choice of control factors produce different results (Lamperti, 1996). Despite improved analytic methods, the key issue of whether executions deter homicides more effectively than lifetime imprisonment without parole remains unsettled. Given the insufficient and equivocal quality of the data, claims that each execution saves a specified number of lives are highly questionable. The law professors John J. Donohue and Justin Wolfers described the difficulty of isolating a deterrent effect caused by a few executions within a mix of many other factors that influence murder rates. The penalty "is applied so rarely that the number of homicides it can plausibly have caused or deterred cannot reliably be disentangled from the large year-to-year changes in the homicide rate caused by other factors" (Liptak, 2007). Professor John Lamperti (1996) put it more succinctly: "The signal, if any, is hopelessly buried in the noise." Liptak (2007) describes a deep disciplinary divide in this field. Econometricians, acting on the tenet that if you raise costs of an activity its use will decline, often claim deterrent effects. By contrast criminologists, who question the appropriateness of economic theory as a research method on violent crimes, find no credible evidence that murders are deterred by the threat of the death penalty.

Retentionists dismiss negative empirical findings. Some argue that prolonged appeals processes obscure the link between crime and punishment. They also dismiss the evidence on the grounds that, although some states impose the death penalty, many of them rarely execute anyone. Retentionists focus on the methodological problem of shortage of executions without addressing the contradictory societal practices that surround the death penalty. On the one hand, states are filling up their death rows. On the other hand, except in a handful of states, officials cannot bring themselves to execute their condemned prisoners. I shall return to this conundrum later to analyze how society manages to sustain the death penalty with the help with the Supreme Court.

In sum, there is no consistent evidence that the death penalty deters would-be murderers (Fagan, 2006). In a comprehensive review of research on the effect of the death penalty, a committee of the National Research Council concluded that much of the research is flawed and provides no informative evidence of a deterrent effect (Nagin & Pepper, 2012). The report cautions against using unreliable findings as a basis for policies regarding capital punishment. The elusiveness of the relationship between the death penalty and deterrence indicates that threat of the death penalty has little effect on the individual dynamics of homicidal behavior. These personal factors reduce the restraint of self-sanctions over homicidal behavior

(Bandura, Caprara, Barbaranelli, Gerbino, & Pastorelli, 2001, 2003). Mismanaged conflicts often escalate to higher levels of aggression that ultimately culminates in physical violence (Toch, 1992). Emotion overwhelms any forethought of the consequences of what one is doing at the moment. The combination of low self-efficacy in managing stormy clashes and a gun can be lethal. In these charged encounters, armed assailants react impulsively, rather than thinking about the death chambers. A good number of homicides occur in the context of arguments between individuals in close relationships, for example, in domestic violence, in jealousies and disputes in other stormy relationships, and in conflicts with associates and acquaintances. When we consider the circumstances under which many homicides occur, it is not surprising that the prospect of the death penalty does not arise.

The incidence of aggravated assaults predicts murder rates, whereas the rate of executions does not (Clermont, 2012). Murders also occur in the course of bungled armed robberies. Here, too, the incidence of armed robberies predicts homicide rates, whereas the death penalty does not, nor do socioeconomic conditions, such as rate of unemployment. Assault-based murders are usually dubbed "crimes of passion" and are considered undeterrable by the death penalty or other legal sanctions. However, they are deterrable on a personal level if one cultivates skill in exercising control over one's anger arousal (Novaco, 2013).

It is interesting that opponents of gun regulation also tend to be proponents of the death penalty. Guns are the method of choice for committing murders because they do so swiftly, distantly, and safely for assailants, as opposed to killing the victim manually. The influence of the National Rifle Association in a state correlates positively with murder rates (Dezhbakhsh, Rubin, & Shepherd, 2003). Correlation, of course, does not mean causation. Vigorous debates over the direction of causation will undoubtedly continue. There are four possibilities: NRA political pressure for lax gun laws contributes to gun murder rates; high murder rates increase NRA pressure for easy access to guns; the influences work both ways; or NRA pressure and high murder rates are both influenced by other factors.

People do not have to be emotionally distressed to resort to violent means (Bandura, 1973). Many instances of human violence are motivated by the expected benefits of such behavior. For example, many homicides result from disputes over locality rights to lucrative drug dealerships. Self-efficacy in plying criminal trades supports the use of premeditated murder to maintain and expand control over profitable activities. Those who plan to commit murder devote their time to devising strategies to avoid getting caught rather than weighing possible legal consequences of their actions. In intentional murders, the various methods of moral disengagement come strongly into play. Murderers have to strip the moral self-sanctions from taking a person's life. When they kill in the name of religion and ideology, they persuade themselves of the morality of their homicidal actions. Viewing their victims as blameworthy and heinous also makes it easier to kill them. The death penalty is unlikely to deter killings of this type. For example, at his court-martial for the mass shooting at Fort Hood, Texas, the military psychiatrist turned Islamic extremist Nidal Hassan insisted on conducting his own defense. He also tried to plead guilty before the trial began, but military rules did not allow it. He was accused of trying to get the death penalty as an act of martyrdom that would be rewarded in the afterlife (Kenber, 2013).

We noted earlier that empathy for the plight of others and a sense of common humanity are powerful restrainers of harmful conduct. Low empathy and lack of prosocialness are a third class of personal determinants that can be conducive to homicidal behavior.

In the final analysis, empirical findings do not change people's minds regarding the death penalty. Many advocates say that they would still support the death penalty even if it was demonstrated conclusively to have no deterrent effect (Vidmar & Ellsworth, 1974). As shown in the poll cited earlier (Newport, 2011), they seek retribution and vengeance. Deterrence is low on their list. Conversely, abolitionists say they would oppose capital punishment even if it was demonstrated conclusively to deter homicides. They oppose state executions on moral grounds.

MORAL DISENGAGEMENT AT DIFFERENT LEVELS OF THE EXECUTION SYSTEM

The preceding discussion examined how the various mechanisms of moral disengagement enable otherwise considerate people to participate in the execution of a human being without suffering an agonizing loss of self-regard. This section analyzes how the various disengagement mechanisms operate in concert at the public policy, jury, and execution levels. The analysis is based on quantitative and qualitative research conducted among the general public and in judicial and penitentiary systems.

Public Policy

Earlier analyses identified a variety of sociodemographic factors that predict support for the death penalty. These findings are informative as a first stage of research. The appropriate analytic next stage in this area was to verify the psychosocial processes underlying the obtained correlations. The focus of this line of research tested the notion that moral disengagement is one of the mechanisms through which sociodemographic factors affect support for the death penalty (Bandura & McAlister, 2015). In this research, randomly selected participants from telephone exchanges were drawn from different regions of Texas. They rated their views on items representing moral disengagement.

The morality of state executions was measured in terms of two of the mechanisms that are especially relevant to the endorsement of the death penalty. The first mechanism centered on moral, deterrent, and economic justifications for executing convicted defendants. The second mechanism assessed dehumanization of condemned inmates. Support for the death penalty was measured in terms of three different forms of this legal sanction—death penalty, life imprisonment without parole as an alternative to execution, and barring execution of defendants judged to be of "exceptionally low intelligence."

Fifty-nine percent of the respondents favored the death penalty, 49% supported the option of life imprisonment without parole in capital crimes, and 75% supported the law barring execution of defendants of low intelligence. However, support for the death penalty varied depending on the sociodemographic characteristics of the respondents. Figure 6.1 summarizes the variations in moral disengagement as a function of sociodemographic characteristics. Those of lower education exhibited higher moral justification for capital punishment than the higher educated. Compared to females, males were higher moral disengagers for the death penalty, and more inclined to dehumanize condemned inmates. Age groups did not differ in their moral justification of executions or in dehumanization of inmates. However, participants differed in their moral justification of the death penalty as a function of race. African Americans were considerably less likely to justify the morality of executions and to dehumanize inmates than were

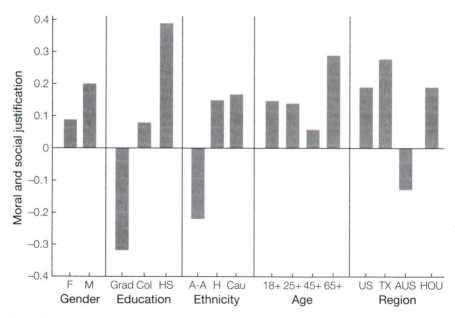

Figure 6.1 Level of moral disengagement associated with different sociodemographic characteristics. From Bandura and McAllister (2015).

Caucasians and Hispanics, who did not differ from each other. Sociodemo-graphic factors were also shown to work through moral disengagement in support of military force following the terrorist attacks on the World Trade Center and the Pentagon (McAlister, Bandura, & Owen, 2006).

Many culturally oriented analyses use regions as proxies for the inhab-itants' psychological orientation (Bandura, 2002). For example, American southerners are said to be especially prone to justifying aggression because their "code of honor" obliges them to challenge an offender (Cohen & Nisbett, 1994). However, territorial ascriptions can mask notable diversity in moral disengagement within regional groupings. This is borne out by regional dif-ferences obtained in the same study. Residents in the more liberally oriented region of Austin, Texas, were much less likely than their counterparts resid-ing in more conservative southern regions to cite a moral justification for the death penalty.

After controlling for the influence of sociodemographic factors, moral justifications for the death penalty contributed significantly to every aspect of capital punishment. High moral justifiers favor the death penalty, oppose life imprisonment without parole, and are against exempting defendants of low intelligence from execution. Dehumanization did not contribute to support of the death penalty or to the stand taken on life imprisonment as an alternative to execution. However, those who dehumanized condemned inmates were more strongly opposed to exempting those of low intelligence from execution. As reported above, the higher the moral disengagement for a given sociodemographic factor the stronger the support for the death pen-alty (Bandura & McAlister, 2015).

The Jury System

Jurors in capital trials face a grave moral predicament. In states that have the death penalty or in certain federal cases, the jury's verdict determines whether the defendant will live or die. Jury duty in a murder case is an unusual morally laden situation. Ordinary citizens are recruited by civic requirement, rather than by choice, to make a weighty moral decision with the most serious consequences—without being schooled in the intricacies of the law. As jurors they observe and listen while prosecutors and defense lawyers argue over testimony and raise nuanced legal issues. They also must balance conflicting testimony from expert witnesses. If they reach a guilty verdict, they have to decide the defendant's fate.

In states with the death penalty, capital trials are divided into two phases—the guilt phase, in which jurors determine the verdict, and the sentencing or penalty phase, in which they determine the severity of punishment. Jurors in such trials face two vexing moral problems. The first is rendering a ver-dict of guilty or not guilty. The second problem—in the penalty phase of the trial, following a verdict of guilty—is deciding whether the sentence will be life in prison or the death penalty. If the jurors call for the death penalty, they will have to live with the knowledge that they will be parties to the intentional killing of a human being. They also have to distance themselves from the consequences of a death sentence. To allow jurors to make this decision, capital trials are structured so that the jurors do not see themselves as responsible for sentencing a human being to death. They achieve self-exoneration through social justification, diffusion of responsibility, and minimization of consequences.

In his influential research on capital punishment, Craig Haney (1997, 2005) provides a richly nuanced analysis of how enlisting the various mechanisms of moral disengagement enables jurors to sentence a person to death. Individuals who unalterably oppose the death penalty on religious or moral grounds are eliminated from the pool of prospective jurors. Those who survive the peremptory challenges are already prone to regard the death penalty as morally acceptable or as essential for preservation of the social and legal order. Some subscribe to the utilitarian justification that executions save human lives. Prospective jurors who favor the death penalty are not only prone to convict but also believe that it is worse to let a guilty defendant go free than to convict an innocent one wrongly (Young, 2004).

Jurors' judgment can be strongly influenced by empathy for defendants or their victims. Hence, during the jury-selection process, both prosecutors and defense lawyers look for jurors who will sympathize with their cause. They typically invoke commonality in life experiences—reflected in ethnicity, race, gender, and socioeconomic status—as indicants of potential jury empathy. Perceived similarity heightens empathic reactions to the plight of similar others (Bandura, 1992; McHugo, Smith, & Lanzetta, 1982).

People who favor the death penalty in the abstract hesitate to impose it when given information that personalizes the murderer (Ellsworth, 1978). In explaining this variation, Ellsworth suggests that when people have minimal information about a convicted inmate, they conjure up a prototype of a most heinous murderer. During the trial, therefore, prosecutors and defense lawyers battle over the dehumanization of criminal defendants. Prosecutors often portray defendants who are accused of terrible crimes as frightening fiends. The grisly nature of the crime facilitates dehumanization. This eases jurors' moral qualms about executing the convicted defendant. Defense attorneys, in turn, try to personalize and humanize defendants in order to dissuade jurors from imposing the death penalty after a guilty verdict.

The structure of trial proceedings also affects the depersonalization and dehumanization of defendants. Capital trials are divided into two phases—the guilt phase that produces the verdict and the sentencing phase that determines the severity of punishment. During the guilt phase of a capital trial, prosecutors discourage humanizing aspects. Depersonalization in this phase can color how jurors view the convicted inmate during the sentencing phase, when jurors consider aggravating factors that enhance the gravity of the crime and mitigating factors that lessen its seriousness. Jurors can personalize convicted prisoners to some degree if they show remorse and if the jurors find that extenuating circumstances figured significantly in the crime, such as provocation, duress, impaired cognitive self-regulatory capacity, and little in the way of prior violence. Leniency based on sympathy can sway jurors to favor life imprisonment over execution. Aggravating factors are another matter, however. Premeditated, vicious, torturous murders committed by defendants with a history of felony convictions arouse revulsion and fear of future dangerousness. Prosecutors prompt jurors to visualize such a murder—and the depravity of the defendant—by highlighting the most gruesome details of the crime and the weapons used. These graphic presentations underscore the derangement and dangerousness of defendants. A vicious crime implies a beastly disposition.

Jurors distance themselves in a variety of ways from the decision to condemn a person to death. They displace responsibility by construing their decision as compelled by the sentencing instructions. Jurors are provided with decision rules and a set of mitigating and aggravating factors that they must take into account in deciding the severity of the penalty. In tests of comprehensibility, jurors have only a poor understanding of sentencing instructions (Eisenberg & Wells, 1993; Haney, 2005). Jurors are unclear about what constitutes mitigating and aggravating conditions. They are also unaware of how to weigh these factors in the rules for deciding between a sentence of death or lifetime imprisonment. When one jury asked the judge to clarify the two conditional factors, he referred them to the guidelines, which they did not understand:

> The first thing we asked for after the instruction was, could the judge define mitigating and aggravating circumstances. Because the different verdicts that we could come up with depended on if mitigating outweighed aggravating, or if aggravating outweighed mitigating, I said, "I don't know that I exactly understand what it means." And then everybody else said, "No, neither do I," or "I can't give you a definition." So we decided we should ask the judge. Well, the judge wrote back and said, "You have to glean it from the instructions." (Haney, Sontag, & Costanzo, 1994)

The jurors also complained about the opaque legal language of the sentencing instructions: "To twelve people...off the street, to use the word 'willful' versus 'deliberate' versus 'intentional'—all that becomes foggy" (Haney et al., 1994).

Eisenberg and Wells's (1993) characterization of jury instructions as causing "deadly confusion" is amply supported by jurors' accounts of their bewilderment over prescribed rules for determining who should live and who should die. However, rewriting sentencing instructions in more understandable language produced little improvement in level of comprehension (Haney, 2005). These findings indicate that the comprehension problem involves more than wording. As Haney points out, death sentencing involves a profound moral decision concerning the life and death of a human being. In order to perform their service jurors have to absolve themselves of responsibility for a decision involving grave consequences. Here is a juror from the Zimmerman trial analyzed earlier expressing regret for acquitting the defendant, despite believing that he was guilty. She felt that she could not have done otherwise because of the constraints of the sentencing rules, "They give you a booklet that basically tells you the truth, and the truth is that there is nothing that we could do about it" (Cadet, 2013).

Some jurors in the study by Haney and colleagues explicitly distanced themselves from the responsibility for their decisions: "My justification of the whole thing is, it's not really my decisions, it's the laws decision" (Haney et al., 1994). The instructions to one jury depicted the guidelines as doing the deciding: "I think having those questions sort of takes that burden off of you because if you can answer 'yes' to the questions, well then he— that makes him eligible for the death penalty" (Costanzo & Costanzo, 1994). Here is a juror's expression of relief that the sentencing rule decided the outcome: "We are not sentencing him to death—we are just answering this question. We talked about it. We are just answering these questions—to get a clear mind so as not to feel guilty I sentenced him to die. That's how the law has it—just answer these questions" (Haney et al., 1994).

The factors included in the conditional list can influence the penalty that the jury is likely to impose. For example, the scope of the mitigating factors tend to be more limited and, because the jurors already have found the defendant guilty, they have more difficulty weighing mitigating circumstances, which would decrease the gravity of the crime. The sequencing of the two decisional phases also favors a death verdict. Given that jurors have already judged the defendant guilty in the guilt phase of the trial, they tend to focus on aggravating factors in the penalty phase as further justification for their decision to impose the death penalty. Haney (2005) coined the phrase "structural aggravation" to identify this built-in focus on aggravating factors, which arises out of the jurors' desire to punish the person whom they have already found guilty.

The discussion thus far has centered on jurors' self-exoneration from responsibility for imposing the death penalty. Further analyses examine how jurors deal with moral aspects of the execution itself. The three disengagement mechanisms that figure prominently in this aspect of the death penalty include social justification, diffusion of responsibility, and minimization of outcomes. Jurors who qualify for capital trials generally invoke social justification, believing that executions save lives. They also hold the mistaken belief that convicted inmates are released after serving only a short time in prison. They call for the death penalty to ensure that dangerous criminals remain imprisoned. As one juror put it, "The only way I can guarantee [that he will stay in prison] is to vote the death penalty" (Haney et al., 1994). Fear of future dangerousness and the belief that convicted criminals eventually will return to society provide justification for executing them to protect the public. A record of felony convictions provides further justification for a death sentence.

Those who are sentenced to death can go through various stages of appeals regarding issues concerning conviction and sentencing. These appeal processes can go on for decades. As a result, the connection between the death sentence and execution may span many years; in many cases, execution never occurs. The greatest moral self-exoneration is the belief that executions do not really happen. Except in a few southern states, jurors can point to the fact that inmates sentenced to death are rarely if ever executed. In a study of capital-case jurors (Haney et al., 1994), one participant describes how some jurors cited the low execution rate in their deliberations to persuade other, more reluctant jurors to vote for the death penalty: "We talked about the fact that if you have a hard time voting for the death penalty, are you really not just voting for life imprisonment? Because there hasn't been an execution in over 20 years in California. And so, you know, is it really more a statement than it is an actuality." However, jurors in southern death-penalty states also deny that their verdicts are consequential. Jurors do not see themselves as deciding whether defendants live or die. They view their decisions as merely provisional, because at some point in the appeals process, an appellate judge ultimately will decide the question. Even if a death sentence is upheld, jurors point to evidence that convicted inmates are rarely executed. As one juror said, "Ninety-nine percent of the time they don't put you to death. You sit on death row and get old" (Sarat, 1995).

Sarat (1995) notes that the greater the protective legal reviews and appeals to prevent the execution of innocent people, the greater the diffusion of responsibility across legal jurisdictions. Diffused responsibility makes it easier for jurors to vote for the death penalty. Retentionists want fewer protections and speedier action on appeals and executions of those sentenced to death. Sarat argues convincingly that if protections are reduced and executions are increased, jurors will be more reluctant to sentence a defendant to death because they would be faced with evidence that their decisions are, in fact, consequential. In many respects, the policy of capital punishment and its implementation is an elaborate, painful, and costly undertaking in which society fills death rows but is reluctant to execute in large numbers those it sentences to die for their crimes.

The decisiveness of jury verdicts has been further weakened in the state of Alabama, where judges are granted authority to override them. Alabama judges are elected by the public rather than being appointed by the governor. This arrangement makes judges highly vulnerable to political pressures. Their record of judicial activism seems to bear this out (Editoral, 2013).

In over 90% of their decisions, judges override jury verdicts of life imprison-ment in favor of death sentences. In an earlier dissent, then Supreme Court Justice John Paul Stevens argued that this type of judicial practice detaches "the death penalty from its only legitimate mooring" (Editorial, 2013)—that is, from community values. When elected judges are concerned that their rulings will affect their reelectability, they are heavily invested in the partisan political climate of their communities—a situation that does not necessar-ily ensure justice. Indeed, when a ruling majority in a society disregards the rights and liberty of minority members, the result is injustice. It remains to be determined whether the diffusion of jurors' responsibility for the conse-quences of their verdicts by judges who overrule their sentences of lifetime imprisonment increases jurors' likelihood of choosing the death penalty.

Jurors' decisions are made under diffused responsibility. The guilt phase in a capital trial has an unusual structural aspect. A group of strangers with diverse backgrounds, attitudes, values, and political views must deliberate over a vast body of legally complex and often conflicting testimony and arrive at a verdict beyond a reasonable doubt. They have to make a life-or-death decision with almost no help on how to do it. For a diverse group to reach a unanimous verdict requires a great deal of social persuasion and, in the case of hold-outs, even social coercion. Besides the social influences operating within the jury, judges pressure jurors to continue their deliberations when they report being hopelessly deadlocked. Under increasing pressure from the judge or their fellow jurors, many holdouts eventually subjugate their views to that of the majority and reluctantly give in. Under this type of pressure, jurors can discount their personal responsibility for the group verdict. For example, in the acquittal of George Zimmerman of killing an unarmed African American teenager under the stand your ground law, the lone holdout eventually gave in, but disassociated herself from that verdict after the trial (Cadet, 2013).

The Executioners

The gravest moral predicament is faced by executioners, whose job requires them to kill a human being up close and by their own hands. Unless they suspend moral self-sanctions against the intentional taking of a human life, they will have difficulty doing their job and will be burdened with a trouble-some mental and social life.

   The depersonalization of executions through pride in operational profi-ciency is illustrated by the last British hangman. (Great Britain permanently abolished the death penalty in 1969.) Hooding the offenders helped neutralize the execution process by stripping them of any personhood. "He was a crafts-man, like a carpenter," the hangman's widow explained to reporters. "He took pride in his job but he wasn't a callous man" (Associated Press, 1994).

His self-esteem was linked to the speed he brought to his task: "Nobody suffered, he was very quick," his widow explained. Indeed, he took special pride in achieving the fastest execution time, seven seconds. However, his penchant for gallows humor ended his career as a hangman when he offended his superior.

The role of moral disengagement in the execution process was explored intensively by Osofsky, Bandura, and Zimbardo (2005) in penitentiaries in three southern states. In each of the three prison systems, three groups of prison personnel were studied, each with a different type and degree of involvement in the execution process. Members of the first group, the *execution team*, perform key roles in the execution itself. They are under the most pressure to justify the morality of their actions to themselves.

The second group included members of the *support team*, who carry out the more humane services during the execution. They provide solace and emotional support to the families of the victim as they await the execution, alleviate the trauma of the homicide, and provide support for the families and relatives of the condemned inmate as they meet with him for the last time. The final partings are the most difficult for the support team: "I'm a mother. It's hardest on the mothers and that's what touches you. It's the last day her child will live. Watching the mothers say goodbye—that's the hardest thing" (Osofsky et al., 2005).

Spiritual advisors offer prayers of support immediately before the inmate is escorted to the death chamber. As one spiritual advisor explained, "I prayed with him at the end.... He tried to hug me through the bars. Fifteen minutes later he was dead." One of the members aptly described their supportive role: "You have to be compassionate or else you can't perform your work" (Osofsky et al., 2005).

Members of the support team also provide counseling and spiritual guidance to inmates while they are on death row. Their greatest supportive involvement with the inmates is on the day of the execution, "I spent time with him the day of the execution. As soon as I left my work, I went to him and stayed with him during the day. The only time I left was to eat lunch (Osofsky et al., 2005)." Some expressed frustration over how little they had to offer: "I'm in a helping profession, but there isn't a damn thing I can do for these guys". Although they are part of the execution team, they approach their work from an entirely different perspective, as one of the members explained: "I didn't feel like I was a part of taking life. I was there for life, not death" (Osofsky et al., 2005). The more the members of the support team humanize their services, the more helpful they can be.

The *control* included randomly selected prison guards who had no involvement in the execution process. They provided a control for the effects of being a prison guard working in a penitentiary where executions are carried out. Their noninvolvement with the executions minimized their need to disengage moral self-restraints.

The various forms of moral disengagement regarding executions were measured with a multifaceted scale completed anonymously by every participant. The items assessed the eight mechanisms through which moral self-sanctions are disengaged in support of the death penalty. All of the participants in the support and execution subgroups, but not the subgroup of guards who had no involvement in the execution, were also interviewed in an open-ended format for their views and experiences regarding the execution policy and process. Quotations from the interview cited in the Execution section are from the following study: (Osofsky, Bandura, & Zimbardo, 2005).

In an extraordinary level of cooperation encouraged by the wardens, every member of each of the three groups in each of the three penitentiaries participated in the study. Total participation removed any possible bias that could result from some refusals to take part in the study.

In their interviews, members of the execution team saw themselves as doing society's work as in other jobs in an institutional service facility. I'm here to do the job." Their focus is not so much on the morality of their activity, but on performing their role proficiently: "Our job was to execute this man and we were going to do it in a professional manner". As these comments reveal, after lethal activities become routinized into separate subfunctions, participants shift their attention from the morality of their activity to the operational details and efficiency of their specific jobs. Some of the medical technicians even swab the inmate's arm with alcohol to prevent possible infection—ironic in a person they are about to execute! In his insightful analysis of diffusion of responsibility, Kelman (1973) documents a similar shift in focus from morality to operational proficiency in other deathly activities.

Active institutional efforts are generally made to create a sense of dignity in the execution of an individual:

> A warden of one of the penitentiaries described this dignifying effort, however ironic it may appear to outsiders and to those who revere the dignity of life: "There's an awful lot of dignity in carrying out executions in our prison. The act may seem barbaric, but it isn't carried out by barbaric people. We try to carry out the act with as much dignity and respect for all people involved." The custom is reinforced by members of the support team, "My responsibility is to follow the law. I can't change the law, but I can be compassionate and caring. I can provide dignity to the man and all those involved in the process."

Efforts to dignify execution creates a moral paradox in which offenders are being treated in a dignified way during the act of killing them. In the executioners' comments about the process of putting a human being to death, "dignity"—which traditionally means being worthy of honor or esteem—is construed as operational proficiency performed dutifully without vengeance: "He did a deed and it is our job to kill him. We did a professional job".

A constellation of factors is necessary to enable a state to execute a convicted inmate. Scriptural and societal justifications provide moral support. Fractionating the killing into small parts means that no one person is the sole executioner. Viewing inmates as dehumanized public threats weakens qualms about putting them to death. Tight compartmentalization of the job keeps it from intruding on the home and social lives of prison personnel.

Executioners varied in their reactions to participating in executions. Some took pride in their emotional toughness: "I take pride that I can do it without falling apart mentally". Many others expressed concerns that taking human life would turn them into insensitive, uncaring persons. "My biggest concern is that I'll be there and won't feel anything. I have a real concern that it wouldn't concern me any longer to put someone to death". Evidence that an executioner had already begun to change in the feared direction was especially distressing: "The hardest thing for me is that the first one really affected me and the next two to three didn't. It affected me that it didn't affect me". "When I came back to work the next day it was as if nothing had happened. That was the worst feeling". A few members of strap-down teams had apparently become what their cohorts feared in their own course of change: "After an execution, I just come into work and it is business as usual," "Give me some clean rags, wipe the gurney up, and let's do it again". In the view of one of the interviewees, being an executioner is inevitably psychologically damaging, unless one is completely devoid of any moral standards: "Those executions, if you have a conscience, you can't deal with that and be psychologically stable." This view assumes that conscience is an invariable regulator of moral conduct. In accord with the integrating principle of this book, conscience can be selectively disengaged from lethal conduct or engaged in the service of a worthy cause without loss of self-regard.

Executioners grounded their role in the death penalty in moral justifications: "We are taking a perfectly healthy human being and executing him. I had to make sure it was all right between me and God". Virtually all of the members believe that executions save lives: "I believe in the death penalty. There needs to be a death penalty to deter people from committing murder". However, members of the execution team also justify it on economic and security grounds: "I am for the death penalty. It is all in a day's work. I'm not callous or hardened. Death Row inmates are here too long, it is wrong for the taxpayers, families, and us".

Putting an inmate to death requires a large cast of participants, each performing a tiny aspect of the execution process. Widely diffused collective responsibility is individually self-exonerating. Recall the San Quentin guard who participated in 126 executions but did not regard himself as an executioner because he only strapped a condemned inmate's leg. The displacement and diffusion of agentic responsibility was prevalent among prison personnel regardless of whether they provided emotional supportive services or carried out the executions.

Depersonalization is another method prison systems use to reduce moral self-restraints against taking a human life. Members of the execution team are discouraged from getting emotionally close to inmates on death row. The executioners also try to distance themselves on their own from condemned inmates: "I don't try to get to know them. You can't be too friendly. I keep my distance". One of the members explains the benefits of depersonalization: "It makes it really stressful getting to know the inmates. By not knowing them, you can do your job. Getting to know them makes it tough". A negative view of the inmates also helps: "When you think about Death Row, you can't think about the inmates. They are in 'high street' and have pen pals and are milking the system. You really need to think about the victims. You have to think about what your client did to others". If they are troublemakers on death row their executioners will not be remorseful: "I really didn't feel too much remorse around his execution because he was always a problem—banging and beating on his bars for no reason."

The analysis thus far has centered on how moral disengagement enables executioners to take a human life. Participating in executions can have ramifications for everyday social and emotional life beyond prison walls. The in-depth interviews shed some light on how executioners manage the social and emotional aspects of their lives. To begin with, they strictly compartmentalize their prison lives and home lives. They never talk at home about what they do in prison: "My life is like a switch. I turn it on when I get here and turn it off when I leave. I won't let myself take my job home". The compartmentalization of their worklife extends to their other social relationships as well: "We don't speak about it and we don't talk about what we do back there. We do our job proudly, but we don't want to talk about it with anyone". Social silence is motivated by the fear that being identified as an executioner is likely to change their social identities in terms of the worst prototype of an executioner. Public dispute over the morality of the death penalty is stressful for executioners because it threatens their justifications for it: "Having the whole country concerned about the death penalty creates more stress for us than the actual execution".

Compartmentalization eases the social problem. However, there is the additional problem of managing one's intrapsychic life. For many of the executioners thoughts of the execution intrude on their everyday lives: "After it is over, you get to thinking about him. You try to block it out, but you can't—his death is there" (Moseley, 2014). Some members of the strap-down team reported unwanted intrusive thoughts as a lingering problem: "After it was over, I was satisfied with the way it had turned out and that we had done such a good job with no glitches. I was really pleased, but at the same time, the execution kept bringing up a lot of emotions". Personalization of death-row inmates, whereby they come to be known "as people, not killers," heightens the emotional problem. Executioners try to block the perturbing thoughts by suppressing them. This strategy only exacerbates the thought-control problem, because the very negation of the thought contains the thought (Wegner, 1989).

In managing stressors, individuals can focus on changing the perturbing realities that cause them or on alleviating the emotional distress they cause (Bandura, 1997; Lazarus & Folkman, 1984). Executions leave little leeway for task-oriented coping strategies because the individual jobs cannot be restructured: nor do they allow alternative solutions. Therefore, executioners have to rely heavily on stress-reducing cognitive strategies so they can put a person to death without paying a heavy emotional toll. Positive reconstrual of the execution is one such strategy for mitigating its emotional aversiveness (Bandura, 1997; Gross, 1998). Construing executions as serving high moral and societal purposes changes the meaning of putting a person to death in ways that makes it less emotionally disturbing. For some, religious belief sanctifies executions: "I'd stop if I felt it were against my morals and the bible [sic]." For others, the law legitimizes them: "It don't bother me at all. The law says this and I follow it".

Multiple executions did not produce further increases in moral disengagement in executioners above their initial level. However, performing the executions reduced the level of distress. The executioners described the desensitization through routinization: "No matter what it is, it gets easier over time. The job just gets easier." The routinization is fostered by a sense of duty and professionalism in carrying out the executions: "The process has become very routine and the next day is easy. It should be that way. The job is something that must be taken care of. It is a duty of my job that has to be done".

The reports by members of the execution team on how they managed their roles in the execution process put a human face on the implementation of the death penalty. Their accounts are very much in keeping with results from the quantitative analysis. In empirical testing of the differential disengagement of morality, it was predicted that members of the execution team would exhibit the highest level of moral disengagement. The prison guards, who had no involvement in executions, would have little need to disengage moral self-restraints. To be helpful in their role, members of the emotional support team had to humanize their ameliorative services. Additionally, their professional training as psychological and spiritual counselors supported a humane orientation in their work. It was therefore predicted that they would disavow stripping morality from the execution process.

Figure 6.2 summarizes the level of moral disengagement for the three groups of prison personnel. The patterns of moral disengagement were much the same for the three penitentiaries. Members of the execution team, who face the most formidable moral problem, made the heaviest use of all of the mechanisms for disengaging moral self-sanctions. They adopted moral, economic, and societal security justifications for the death penalty. They ascribed subhuman qualities to the condemned inmates and disavowed a sense of agentic responsibility in the executions. In their view, society had

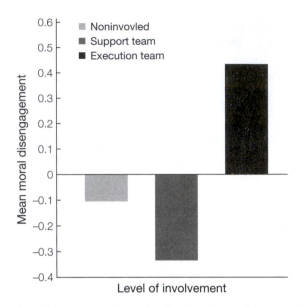

Figure 6.2 Extent of moral disengagement as a function of the type and degree of involvement in the execution process. From Osofsky, Bandura & Zimbardo, 2005. © 2005 American Psychological Association. Reprinted with permission.

assigned them a job that saves lives and protects the social order, and they performed that job professionally. In contrast, members of the support team were wary of the common justifications for executing condemned inmates and disavowed attributing subhuman and bestial natures to them. Noninvolved guards displayed a similar pattern of moral involvement but to a much lesser degree.

Figure 6.3 presents the changes in moral disengagement by members of the execution and social-support teams as a function of the number of executions in which they participated. The executioners were moral disengagers at the outset and remained so across multiple executions. However, members of the support team began as moral engagers but gradually became moral disengagers with more frequent participation in executions. By the 15th execution they become moral disengagers and no longer differed in this regard from their counterparts on the execution team.

With repeated exposure to, and engagement in, injurious behavior, people eventually become desensitized and habituated to it (Bandura, 1973). As a result, they are no longer emotionally aroused by it. However, the personal transformation from moral engagement to moral disengagement suggests a more complex process. In the course of providing ameliorative services, support personnel hear the families of the victim recount the brutal ways in which their loved ones were murdered. Repeated exposure to graphic accounts of heinous crimes can gradually instill revulsion toward the inmates. One of the support members described the struggle to counteract

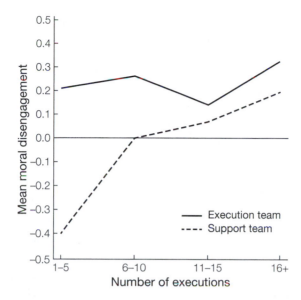

Figure 6.3 Changes in moral disengagement by the members of the support and execution teams as a function of the number of executions in which they had participated. From Osofsky, Bandura & Zimbardo, 2005. © 2005 American Psychological Association. Reprinted with permission.

developing into a callous person: "I close my mind to what the inmates have done. It is easier to work with it in that way. I prefer to be in denial than to let everything come to the surface". Support personnel who learn the details of many murderous tragedies seem to have lost the compassion battle. However, the present findings are based on cross-sectional evidence. It remains for future research to verify the transformative personal change longitudinally.

The extension of research on moral self-regulation and its selective disengagement to other aspects of the enforcement and judicial systems would further our understanding of the ways in which moral self-sanctions influence how these systems operate in practice. There is a notable difference between the formal law and the law that is applied on the streets. Police officers have considerable discretionary power over those they investigate and arrest. In his informative field study, Albert Reiss (1971) found that police tend to apply the law selectively, according to their personal standards. The role of moral disengagement in police enforcement practices remains to be explored. Similarly, state prosecutors have discretionary power over which cases become capital ones. It would be of interest to examine whether those prosecutors who frequently call for the death penalty differ in levels of moral disengagement from those who are reluctant to try murders as capital cases and prefer a maximum penalty of life imprisonment.

THE FUTURE OF THE DEATH PENALTY

The exercise of the death penalty and the justification for it are in social, political, and legal confusion and flux. We legislate, constitutionalize, and try to implement what, as a society, we cannot make ourselves do. Public fear of crime sways many lawmakers to be strong advocates of the death penalty. Indeed, virtually every lawmaker of note and every recent president has, at various times in their careers, professed support for the death penalty. If they do not, they are branded "soft on crime" and as wanting to "coddle criminals." Many politicians believe that proclaiming support for the death penalty helps them win elections. Opposing the death penalty, they claim, jeopardizes their electability. They cite as evidence the defeats of high-profile opponents of the death penalty. Establishing their credentials as tough on crime by declaration enables them to evade informing the public about their policies for reducing and preventing crime in society.

Condemned criminals are continually being added to death rows where, after appellate reviews, they await execution. Society is evidently loath to carry out this grim task. For example, California has 746 prisoners on death row (Death row inmates, 2015). However, in the past 38 years only 13 have been executed. New York State has adopted, abolished, and reinstated the death penalty, which ultimately was declared unconstitutional, as we have seen. New York had not executed a single convicted inmate since 1963 (Latest news and developments, 2015). Except for some southern states, the others that enforce the death penalty have executed none or only a few inmates over several decades. David Von Brehle, a commentator on the death penalty, characterized this disconnect between committing prisoners to death and not executing them as Alice in Wonderland (Totenberg, 2015). Because of the huge backlog of over 3,000 prisoners awaiting execution, society would have the ghastly task to execute them daily over a long period to deplete their numbers or do it faster by staging mass daily executions.

The U.S. Supreme Court spares society the ghastly job of having to kill a great many people by voiding, on constitutional grounds, the sentences under which the prisoners were convicted. Rather than being retried, prisoners typically see their death sentences commuted to life imprisonment (Shulman, 2011). In its landmark *Furman* decision, the Supreme Court struck down Georgia's death penalty statute, because imposing and carrying out the death penalty would constitute cruel and unusual punishment in violation of the Eighth and Fourteenth Amendments. Jurors often applied it unfairly, arbitrarily, and in racially discriminatory ways (*Furman v. Georgia*, 1972). This ruling cleared the nation's death rows. In response to the narrower opinion of the justices, some states adopted new statutes that mandated the death penalty in a more consistent, less arbitrary manner. The Supreme Court upheld some of these statutes but struck down others, arguing that jurors should consider aggravating features such as premeditation and torture, which increase the reprehensibility of a crime, and mitigating circumstances, which reduce culpability. The nation's death rows were repopulated with prisoners convicted under the new statutes.

As we saw earlier, in a dissenting minority opinion in a 1994 Texas case, Supreme Court Justice Harry Blackmun, who had supported the death penalty in past decisions, announced that he would no longer support it (Greenhouse, 1994). Because Justices William Brennan and Thurgood Marshall, both of whom considered the death penalty unconstitutional, had retired, Justice Blackmun's was the lone dissenting voice.

Blackmun's strong personal opinions were essentially statements of conscience. In his dissenting opinion on a pending execution, he wrote that the case was "perilously close to simple murder" (Greenhouse, 1994). In his dissent in the 1972 *Furman* decision—in which he had upheld the death penalty—he described the personal moral toll of presiding over a system he regarded as unfair: "Cases such as these provide for me an excruciating agony of the spirit" (Greenhouse, 1994). In his concurring majority opinion in the 1994 Texas appeal, Supreme Court justice Antonin Scalia argued that personal conviction was no excuse for banning the death penalty, which had been ruled constitutional and was not cruel and unusual punishment. He argued comparatively that the crime is worse than death by lethal injection, "The death-by-injection which Justice Blackmun describes looks pretty desirable next to that" (Greenhouse, 1994). In arguing that capital punishment is constitutional not immoral, Scalia reminded Blackmun that he has the duty to apply the law, not to rewrite it.

In his dispute with Justice Blackmun on the justness of capital punishment, Justice Scalia cited a murder committed 30 years earlier: "For example, the case of the 11-year-old girl raped by four men and then killed by stuffing her panties down her throat. How enviable a quiet death by lethal injection compared to that!" (Mazza, 2014). Two brothers of low intelligence were sentenced to death for this crime on the basis of a coerced, fake confession that they later retracted, rather than on physical evidence linking them to the crime. Justice Scalia used this case as an example of the justness and comparative benignness of the death penalty. In an ironic twist, the same case later became an example of judicial injustice. After 30 years of imprisonment, the brothers were exonerated by DNA evidence from the crime scene that linked the murder to a sex offender imprisoned later for another rape (Mazza, 2014). Periodic DNA exonerations indicate that there are other innocents on death row.

In a further effort to devise a constitutionally fair death-penalty statute, some states have enacted a law that is inherently contradictory. It limits the factors jurors can consider in deciding between death or nonlethal punishment while granting them some discretion in considering mitigating and aggravating circumstances. The law is both mandatory and discretionary. The Supreme Court acknowledged the contradictory nature of the statute in that it mandates execution of convicted murderers but allows discretion in sentencing them. Nevertheless, they ruled the statute to be constitutionally acceptable. Given deeply ingrained human biases, there is every reason to expect that unfairness and discrimination will creep into the discretionary aspect of jurors' decisions. Jurors have leeway in the weight they give to aggravating and mitigating factors. If they have a strong bias for conviction, they can even turn mitigating factors into aggravating ones (Haney, 2005). It is highly likely that the statute will also eventually be declared unconstitutional. If this turns out to be its fate, judges will have succeeded in again clearing the nation's death rows of condemned prisoners sentenced under this version of the statute. On the other hand, if it continues to pass the constitutional test, states will have to start executing the offenders they are placing on death row.

After a botched execution in Oklahoma, four death row inmates who were scheduled for execution petitioned the court to bar executions using the drug that resulted in the torturous execution. Writing the majority opinion, Justice Samuel A. Alito argued that the inmates failed to identify a preferable alternative method of execution (Liptak, 2015). He blamed the problem on opponents of the death penalty for pressuring pharmaceutical companies to refuse to supply drugs for executions. Justice Sonia Sotomayor criticized the ruling as allowing highly painful methods if available alternatives are even more barbarous.

In his dissent Justice Steven G. Beyer, joined by Ruth Bader Ginsburg, argued that the Supreme Court should address the more basic question of whether the death penalty violates the Eighth Amendment of cruel and unusual punishment. He documented the tragic failings of the death penalty: Execution of innocent people; exoneration of death row inmates because of false convictions; arbitrary imposition of death sentences; and corruption of the capital justice system by racial discrimination and politics. Justice Antonin Scalia derisively called Justice Breyer's proposal "gobbledygook." (Liptak, 2015)

Postconviction national legal reviews reveal an extremely high rate of serious flaws (68%) in capital convictions (Liebman, Fagan, & West, 2012). These include highly incompetent defense lawyers as well as prosecutors who suppressed evidence favorable to defendants. Aggregation of evidence of prejudicial judgments and prosecutorial misconduct in individual cases reveals group socioeconomic and racial biases. Liebman and his collaborators (2000) describe the typical scenario in death sentences fraught with errors:

> The capital conviction or sentence will probably be overturned due to serious errors. It'll take about nine years to find out, given how many other capital cases being reviewed for likely error are lined up ahead of this one. If the judgment is overturned, a lesser conviction or sentence will probably be imposed.

This process costs millions of dollars per case. The authors ask why American society tolerates a social system with such incredibly high error rates, heavy costs, and potentially deadly consequences.

Ernest Van Den Haag (1986) accepted some inequality as "unavoidable as a practical matter in any system." He disputed reported evidence that execution is costlier than life imprisonment. In putting a more benign face on execution, he contended that life imprisonment degrades an individual's humanity more than execution does. In his view, an individual convicted of murder is unworthy of living. Any degradation, he argues, is self-inflicted. Van Den Haag acknowledged that there is no consistent evidence that execution is a better deterrent than lifetime imprisonment, but argued contradictorily that execution is more feared than imprisonment, so it deters some prospective murderers. The fear of lifetime imprisonment probably deters some likely murderers as well. The issue in dispute is not whether fear of execution or of lifetime imprisonment may deter some murderers. The dispute concerns *marginal* deterrence gain. Is the threat of execution a better deterrent of homicides than lifetime imprisonment?

The way in which executions are conducted is another reflection of American society's conflict over the death penalty. Executions are usually carried out at midnight, hidden from public view. The media are banned from filming them. For utilitarians, who claim that executions prevent homicides, executing the condemned in semisecrecy defeats its assumed deterrent purpose. Stealth executions will not strike fear in violence-prone individuals. Because executions are rare and secluded, some individuals may not even know whether their state employs capital punishment.

The death penalty is being abolished around the world. The United States is virtually alone among developed democratic nations in applying this lethal penalty. Even as the legal and empirical disputes continue, support for the death penalty is waning. Public opinion on the morality of the death penalty is sharply declining. Many states have abolished or suspended it. Most of those that retain it rarely execute the condemned inmates on their death rows, so they are practicing de facto abolition. In a surprising move, some governors in death-penalty states are refusing to implement the death penalty. For example, then governor John Kitzhaber of Oregon, a physician, announced that he would not allow any prisoners to be executed during his tenure in office on moral grounds and because of the arbitrary and unfair application of the death penalty (Yardley, 2011). Joining the governor of Colorado, the governor of Washington likewise suspended executions, arguing that the capital punishment system is too flawed for states to carry out the death penalty (Lovett, 2014). Richard Dieter, the former executive director of the Death Penalty Information Center, commented on the changing times regarding political opposition to the death penalty: "The fact that governors can now stand up and say these things, when they

used to get pilloried, is a sign of the changing views on the death penalty"
(Lovett, 2014).

States that retain the death penalty are finding that executions are more
difficult to carry out (Eckholm & Zezima, 2011a). Domestic drug manufacturers refuse to supply drugs for executions (Lyman, 2013). The American Pharmacists Association voted to ban its members from taking part in executions
by lethal injection (Goldschmidt, 2015). The European Union has banned
the export of drugs used in executions (Ford, 2014). States are resorting to
covert means of questionable legality to find the needed drugs and suppliers. Federally unapproved drugs imported from unlicensed foreign suppliers
are confiscated (Eckholm, 2014). As states turn increasingly to unregulated
compounding pharmacies for drugs, battles are being fought over the legality
of these practices. Some states are flirting with the idea of granting suppliers
anonymity by listing them as part of the execution team, whose identity is
not revealed. To overcome drug makers' refusal to supply drugs for executions, some states have enacted secrecy laws that conceal their suppliers and
the drugs being used. These laws are being challenged on the constitutional
grounds that secrecy prohibits evaluation of whether the method of execution is cruel and unusual punishment (Eckholm, 2014). The U.S. Supreme
Court has yet to rule on the legality of state secrecy laws. It is ironic to see
states skirting the edge of illegality in conducting executions with trial-and-
error drug combinations from secret sources.

The death penalty faces a new constitutional challenge. As previously documented, states that retain the death penalty continue to add
condemned inmates to their death rows but execute only a few, if any, of
them. As a result, the backlog keeps growing. The inordinate delays in the
few executions that do occur are due mainly to states' aversion to carrying
out death sentences rather than to inmate appeals. A federal appeals court
judge recently ruled California's death penalty system unconstitutional
because it was "arbitrary" and "completely dysfunctional" and therefore
inflicted cruel and unusual punishment (Berman, 2014a). California has
746 inmates on its death row, Florida has 401, Texas has 271, and so on
(NAACP, 2015). If the U.S. Supreme Court upholds this ruling, states will
face the ghastly task of mass executions—if the states can find executioners
to carry them out.

Prosecutors' sentencing preferences also have changed (Eckholm, 2013).
They increasingly favor lifetime imprisonment without parole over execution. Richard Dieter viewed the sharp decline in seeking the death penalty
as part of a broad "societal shift" away from the death penalty. In response
to a bungled execution in Oklahoma, Richard Barnett, a former Supreme
Court law clerk, raised the fundamental issue of the morality of the death
penalty: "The Constitution allows capital punishment in some cases, and so
the decision whether to use it or abandon it, and the moral responsibility for
its use and misuse, are in our hands" (Levs, Payne, & Botelho, 2014). As a

nation with the death penalty, the United States forfeits its moral authority to condemn autocratic regimes for their executions.

Previous U.S. Supreme Court rulings on the constitutionality of death-penalty statutes; suspension or abolition of the death penalty in some states; wrongful executions of innocent inmates; DNA exonerations of prisoners on death row; arbitrary, and unfair disparities in trials and executions for capital crimes; and repeated failures to devise a constitutionally fair death penalty statute have shaken the public's confidence in the death penalty. If public support for the death penalty continues to wane, society may well end up with a constitutionally permissible lethal punishment that no one wants to carry out any longer.

Chapter 7

■ ■ ■ ■ ■ ■ ■

TERRORISM AND COUNTERTERRORISM

The scourge of terrorism has become deadlier and more pervasive. This form of violence involves some unique aspects in the suspension of moral control. This chapter presents a two-part analysis of the role of moral disengagement in terrorism. The first part focuses on the nature of terrorism and how terrorists manage the morality of using terrorizing violence as a means of social change. The second part addresses the moral predicaments that military counterterrorism raises, the forms it takes, the legitimacy of the justifications for it, and the morality reflected in its execution.

TERRORISM

Terrorism is a strategy of violence designed to force desired sociopolitical changes by instilling fear in the public at large. Public intimidation is a key element that distinguishes terrorism from other forms of violence. In conventional violence, victims are personally targeted. Terrorism relies on third-party violence in which the identity of the victims is incidental to the terrorists' purposes. Terroristic violence is directed at civilians and essential infrastructure to pressure the government to change its policies and practices. It is neither the ends nor the severity of the operational means but the third party that characterizes terrorism.

The term *terrorism* is often misapplied to violent acts that dissident groups direct at government officials or agencies. So defined, terrorism becomes indistinguishable from straightforward political violence. Personalized threats are certainly intimidating to the authorities who are targeted for assassination and can create apprehension about the social aftermath of such acts. However, these threats do not necessarily terrify the general public as long as ordinary civilians are not the targets. As we will see, terrorists use public intimidation as an offensive weapon for a variety of purposes.

Erlich (2010) cites as a case of terrorism the Zionist Stern Gang's assassination of the UN mediator Count Folke Bernadotte for advocating that the UN administer Jerusalem as an international city. However, this was not a terrorist act that deliberately targeted civilians. In contrast, the violence that the Irish Republican Army (IRA) directed at their opponents was terroristic in nature. The bombs that they planted in London and other cities in England took a heavy toll in civilian lives. The IRA believed that the devastation would frighten the British public into pressuring the government to withdraw its troops from Northern Ireland.

In his effort to specify conditions under which terrorism is morally acceptable, Andrew Valls (2010) deletes from the definition of terrorism its two distinguishing features, indiscriminate targeting of innocent individuals and frightening the populace into forcing changes in the current regime and its practices. Valls incorrectly regards these characteristics as "nonessential." This stripped-down version of terrorism becomes indistinguishable from common political violence.

The United States has also had a hand, mainly through the Central Intelligence Agency (CIA), in supporting terrorist activities by insurgents serving as proxy terrorists. This was especially the case in Latin America, where the CIA orchestrated covert operations designed to curb the spread of leftist regimes in the wake of Castro's successful 1959 revolution in Cuba. In what became known as the Iran-Contra affair, officials in the Reagan administration secretly and illegally sold arms to Iran with the long-term goal of freeing American hostages who had been captured by Iranian terrorists in Lebanon. They then diverted funds from the weapons sales to support a guerilla war against the leftist Sandinista regime in Nicaragua. The CIA trained and armed the right-wing rebels, known as contras, who conducted terrorist activities designed to undermine public support for the leftist Sandinista regime. The contras targeted schools, health clinics, agricultural cooperatives, and other public services. The contra leader Horacio Arce described the strategy: "We attack a lot of schools, health centers, and those sorts of things. We have tried to make it so that the Nicaraguan government cannot provide social services for the peasants, cannot develop its project. . . . [T]hat's the idea" (Erlich, 2010).

Terrorist acts include several features that allow a few incidents to incite widespread public fear even though the likelihood of being a victim of a terrorist attack is exceedingly low. The first feature is the unpredictability of who will be targeted and when or where terrorists will strike. Terrorists could attack busy markets, crowded streets, public events, public transportation, or airliners, making anyone a potential victim. The second feature is the gravity of terrorist acts. With the increasing lethality of conventional and improvised weapons, terrorists can wreak destruction on a massive scale.

The third feature is the sense of uncontrollability that they instill. People feel that there is little they can do personally to protect themselves from becoming victims of a terrorist attack.

The fourth feature that contributes to a heightened sense of personal and societal vulnerability is the highly centralized nature of essential service systems in modern life. When populations were more widely dispersed, the consequences of any given aggressive act were confined mainly to the persons against whom the behavior was directed. However, with increasing urbanization, the welfare of millions of people depends on the smooth functioning of intricate, interdependent service systems. A single destructive act can instantly harm vast numbers of people and frighten many more by disrupting communications, transportation, and electricity or contaminating water and food supplies. The combination of unpredictability, grave consequences, perceived inability to protect oneself, and vulnerable interdependence is especially intimidating and socially constraining (Bandura, 1997).

Terrorist acts incur high economic costs and impair the quality of life in societies in ways other than through generalized intimidation. The use of airliners as instruments of terror, for example, forced the worldwide adoption of costly electronic surveillance systems for screening passengers. To board an aircraft, passengers have to spend countless hours in serpentine lines and shed coats, belts, and shoes in security routines that proliferate with each new type of threat. Terrorist tactics can quickly outstrip the countermeasures. As the saying goes, for every 10-foot wall you build, terrorists will build an 11-foot ladder. Advanced security systems can provide the impetus for terrorists to devise ever more sophisticated destructive devices, requiring additional intrusive electronic surveillance. Some of these surveillance systems infringe on civil liberties, human rights, and privacy.

In coping with terrorism, societies are faced with a dual task. The first is how to reduce the number of terrorist acts. The second is how to combat the fear of terrorism. The likelihood of becoming a victim of a terrorist attack is infinitesimal, but fearfulness is high. Events that are relatively unlikely but that have grave consequences heighten the perception of personal vulnerability and fear. A number of factors can amplify fear arousal. As we noted earlier, people have a low sense of efficacy that they can personally reduce their risk. News broadcasts repeatedly portray the carnage of terrorist strikes worldwide. Debates about national security underscore the vulnerability of the nation's infrastructure and vital utilities, and a lack of faith in the government's ability to protect its citizens against terrorist attacks. The Department of Homeland Security's frequent color-coded alerts of imminent terrorist threats added salience to the threats. Frightened, angry citizens can be easily talked into supporting extreme and misdirected countermeasures, because they do not spend much time agonizing over the morality of lethal modes of self-defense. Later, we will see how politicians have manipulated Americans' fear to gain support for the war on terrorism.

Terrorists face an especially troublesome moral paradox: Because they take innocent lives indiscriminately as a means toward a sociopolitical end, their actions belie the very liberation values they espouse. From a psychological standpoint, seemingly random third-party violence is much more morally perturbing than violence directed against specific officials who are blamed for contributing, in one way or another, to people's aversive life conditions. It is easier to persuade individuals who harbor strong grievances to kill officials they loath or to abduct advisors and consular personnel of foreign nations that support oppressive regimes. However, to slaughter ordinary men, women, and children going about their lives requires more powerful psychosocial machinations to neutralize moral conflict in ways that enable terrorists to live in peace with themselves. Intensive psychological training in moral disengagement is necessary to create the capacity to kill indiscriminately without self-condemnation. Recall the intensive psychosocial program that transformed ordinary Greek soldiers into cruel torturers who took pride in their brutality (Haritos-Fatouros, 2003; see chapter 2).

The Making of a Terrorist: A Process Analysis

There has been much debate on where to look for the causes of terroristic violence. Dispositional theorists place causes in the individual. They search for defining attributes of terrorists. Studies that include only terrorists, as is often the case, can be misleading because the attributes that are singled out may not be unique to terrorists. Previously, it was widely believed that terrorists generally are impoverished, poorly educated, mentally unstable, and driven to violence by a sense of powerlessness and hopelessness. This characterization did not survive empirical scrutiny (Bandura, 1973). The search for a distinctive "terrorist personality" is misdirected.

A low sense of efficacy to effect change by one's actions and belief in the futility of effort breeds apathy, not violence (Bandura, 1997). In civic strife, college students, who are nurtured in self-efficacy in their formative years, usually spearhead militant activism, not those who have lost hope (Lipset, 1966). The most vociferous protesters against the Vietnam War, for example, came from elite universities, not from junior colleges or from underprivileged groups (Bandura, 1973). The leaders of al Qaeda, who came from wealthy upper-class families, were well educated. Osama bin Laden was a civil engineer; Ayman al-Zawahiri was a physician. The September 11 hijackers also came from advantaged families rather than from the ranks of the downtrodden. Comparative studies were hard pressed to show that terrorists are more emotionally unstable than nonterrorists (Abrahms, 2008). This finding comes as no surprise. Terrorist groups weed out emotionally unstable recruits because they are too unreliable and could jeopardize the safety of the group. For example, examination of Indonesian Islamic terrorists found them to be imbued with al Qaeda's ideology and trained to fight for it, but they "were not ignorant, destitute, or disenfranchised outcasts" (Bonner, 2003).

Situational theorists place the causes of terrorism in the environment. According to this view, people are driven to violence by aversive life conditions characterized by poverty, social inequities, humiliation, and oppression. Theories that try to predict terrorism from the environment alone tend to overpredict terrorist proclivity because, except for a small number, people living under conditions of unrelenting misery do not resort to terroristic violence. It is not that personal and environmental factors do not contribute to the adoption of violent means. They do. But they operate through an intricate mix of determinants. As we noted in chapter 1, human behavior is a product of the complex interplay of personal attributes, behavioral proclivities, and environmental influences.

The likelihood that a particular person will become a terrorist is exceedingly rare. This is why personal and environmental risk factors that are considered in isolation yield high rates of false-positive predictions. These predictions are based largely on categorical indices such as ethnicity, race, religion, and nationality rather than on personal attributes. Such indices treat individuals within these groups as though they all think and behave alike. Thus characterized, many harmless people are stereotyped as dangerous suspects.

Rare events are the product of an idiosyncratic constellation of influences, some of which may occur fortuitously. Once initiated on a path to terrorism, individuals undergo intensive socialization into the role of terrorist. They are indoctrinated in ideology; persuaded of the morality of the cause; taught guerilla hit-and-run tactics; and trained to use firearms, build bombs, and carry out suicide bombings (Meadows, 2010; Powers, 1971). The IRA's training manual spelled out the training regimen in full detail. It also prepared recruits for the harsh interrogation they would face should they be captured and how to withstand it (Green Book, n.d.).

This transformative socialization is usually carried out in a closed environment that becomes the recruits' pervasive new reality, with new kinships, strongly held group beliefs and values, all-encompassing codes of conduct, few vestiges of individuality, and substantial rewarding and coercive power—all with the purpose of completely transforming recruits' personal lives (Bandura, 1982). Those in charge further enhance the power of communal influence by curtailing recruits' personal contacts and exposure to countervailing influences outside the group. Immersion in heavily prescribed activities that leave the recruits with little time to think or to explore other milieus has similar encapsulating effects. Regardless of the particular constellation of influences that shape the path to terrorism, every terrorist faces the moral problem of having to kill innocent people. Skill in disengagement of morality also requires intensive training to be able to inflict pain and suffering with equanimity (Haritos-Fatouros, 2003).

As we saw in chapter 1, the case of Diana Oughton illustrates concretely key elements in the process model of terrorist development (Franks & Powers, 1970). These include her start on the path to terrorism through a chance meeting; her socialization into the life of a terrorist; her further intensive radicalization in an overbearing, insular environment; and her suspension of any sense of the morality that she had absorbed during her formative years. This case is especially informative because it involves a radical transformation from a humanitarian life to a ruthless, terroristic one. This case also illustrates that, given the right circumstances, almost anyone can become a terrorist.

Diana Oughton was a gentle, lighthearted young woman whose background and personal attributes were the antithesis of the common correlates of political activism. She came from a privileged conservative family and a congenial, conventional upbringing. However, even early in life she voiced concern over the family's affluence. At age 6 she asked her nanny, "Ruthie, why do we have to be rich?" She continued to exhibit discordance between her conservatism and altruism. On the one hand, having adopted her parent's conservative values, she rejected socially beneficial programs as examples of the evils of big government. On the other hand, for her extracurricular activity at Bryn Mawr College, she tutored children living in the ghetto.

After she graduated from Bryn Mawr, Diana's humanitarian concerns led her to service as a volunteer with the Quaker organization VISA (Voluntary International Service Assignments). Working with the Indians of a remote village in Guatemala, she became deeply sensitized to human suffering caused by social inequities. In a chance encounter during a visit to Guatemala City, she met Alan Howard, a Fulbright Scholar who had grown cynical about the prospects for peaceful social change. He belittled her tireless efforts as superficial and argued that only violent revolution would bring the needed sweeping reforms. This encounter, along with her frustration at the poverty she found in the village, and exposure to American intervention in Guatemalan politics and military and critiques of the United States during her year of study abroad, launched her on a path of militant action.

On her return to the United States she became increasingly involved in Students for a Democratic Society (SDS), which at the time was splintering into opposing ideological camps. She was drawn into the violent Weathermen faction, not by studied design but through affectional attachment to Bill Ayers, a leader of this faction, whom she met as a fellow teacher at a makeshift community school in Chicago. After the failure of their call for violent street protests to effect social change during the four "Days of Rage," the group changed its name to the Weather Underground and literally went underground, where they adapted a radical remedy for the moral problem (Powers, 1971). They imposed on themselves an unmercifully brutal regimen to eradicate their "bourgeois morality," violating sexual mores to "smash monogamy," desecrating cemeteries by tumbling gravestones, engaging in revolting activities such as eating tomcats, and disparaging what they had been taught to value and revere. They likened themselves to the "barbarians" of old who destroyed decadent societies. Freed from moral restraints and sound judgment, they set out to bring the Vietnam War home to what they considered the mother country of imperialism. To do so they were ready to take on the police, whom they bestialized: "Sure there's going to be pigs hitting people like before, but this time there's going to be people hitting pigs" (Sprinzak, 1990).

When their destructive forays and street battles with the Chicago police failed to produce the heralded revolution, the Weather Underground resorted to bomb attacks. Diana's brief career as a revolutionary ended abruptly in a Greenwich Village townhouse. A bomb she was assembling, intended to destroy the society she had come to hate, exploded and took her life instead.

MODES OF MORAL DISENGAGEMENT

Moral and Social Justifications

A variety of justifications are moral disengagers for involvement in terroristic activities. In sacred justifications, terrorists view themselves as doing God's bidding, willing to kill others and martyr themselves for rewards in the afterlife. Secular justifications rely heavily on consequentialism. Secularly oriented terrorists aim to dislodge oppressive social practices and topple tyrannical regimes, thereby improving peoples' lives. Terrorists who espouse utilitarian justifications believe that the harm their terroristic acts cause is minor compared with the widespread social benefits they will usher in for the aggrieved. With idiosyncratic justifications as a basis for terrorism, personal grievances are the moral disinhibitors for vengeful, costly actions.

Some terrorists are freelance paramilitary groups with all the trappings of a military force. They perpetrate atrocities in weak states and ungoverned regions in parts of Africa and the Middle East. For example, Boko Haram, an Islamist militant group in Nigeria, has embarked on a mission to eradicate anything Western in their drive to create a pure Islamic state. They regard the education of girls as forbidden. They abducted over 270 schoolgirls and offered them in exchange for release of their jailed comrades (Mark, 2014). Otherwise, they threatened to sell them off. The government refused the exchange on the grounds that it would only encourage further abductions. The fate of most of the girls remains unknown.

As previously noted, terrorism is not a homogeneous phenomenon. It takes diverse forms that serve diverse purposes. Hence, analysis of its determinants functions, and strategies for curbing it, must be tailored to its particular form. Critics dispute moral justifications for terrorism. Michael Walzer (2010) rejects the claim that terrorists exhaust all legitimate options before turning to terroristic means, as well as the related claim that under extreme power imbalance, terrorism is the only option available. A good share of terrorism involves indiscriminate retaliation rather than acts carried out in the name of liberation.

The claim that terrorism works is also disputed. Mass nonviolent protest is a morally grounded strategy that is more likely to achieve sociopolitical change than the indiscriminate killing of innocent people. The power of mass nonviolent resistance that is aided by social modeling of strategies is graphically illustrated in the rapid toppling of oppressive regimes. For the first time in history, people worldwide watched on television as mass civil resistance brought the ouster of the repressive regime in East Germany. The power of overwhelming numbers could not be suppressed. People from East and West Berlin joined in demolishing the Berlin Wall. This dramatic success became a model of political change. Mass nonviolence resistance was quickly adopted by people in other Eastern European countries. They dislodged Soviet-backed rulers in Czechoslovakia, Romania, Hungary, and other nations (Braithwaite, 1994).

By overthrowing its despotic ruler through mass nonviolent resistance, Tunisia triggered a wave of political change in the Arab world called the "Arab Spring." However, except for reforms in Jordan and a few other countries, most attempts at nonviolent or even violent revolutions in the Middle East have failed. In some countries, the rise of radical militant groups has only made the situation worse (Botelho, 2015). Mass nonviolent resistance is an effective vehicle for large-scale sociopolitical change. Building a representative government in the aftermath is another matter. Dislodging despotic rulers liberates oppressed factions who vie for power in the governance vacuum. Initial euphoria usually gives rise to disillusionment over controversial changes and the slow pace of change. What is lacking are prosocial models on how to meld diverse self-interest into common cause for humane representative governance.

Euphemism and Advantageous Comparison

Most perpetrators use euphemistic, convoluted jargon to cloak their inhumane activities in innocuous, opaque terms. In the case of terrorism, however, perpetrators strive to publicize their activities rather than camouflaging or neutralizing them. Their linguistic sanitizing centers mainly on how they construe their mission and view themselves in carrying it out. They regard themselves as "freedom fighters" in a war of liberation from oppressive rule, corruption, and humiliation.

The extensive manipulation of language occurs in counterterrorism as well when a nation embraces methods that breach its venerated values and laws. A good example is the "war on terror," which has involved a great deal of linguistic camouflage. To begin with, the term itself is a misnomer.

Terror is a state of intense fear. One cannot wage war against an emotion. U.S. forces used "enhanced interrogation" methods that inflict severe pain and distress—methods that are especially controversial, because they border on torture, which is internationally banned. Outsourcing such interrogations to other countries was called "extraordinary rendition." Secret prisons run by the CIA in foreign countries, outside U.S. legal jurisdiction, were dubbed "black sites." These are but a few examples of euphemistic practices that will be analyzed in greater detail later in this chapter.

Advantageous comparison is an especially important mode of self-exoneration from the harm terrorists cause because they acknowledge responsibility for it. From the terrorists' perspective, the harm their attacks cause pales when compared with the widespread suffering inflicted on downtrodden people by oppressive power holders who are often backed by foreign patrons. Advantageous comparison also is a handy self-exonerative device for the lethal methods that are used. The renegade CIA agent and international weapons merchant Frank Terpil justified his sale of torture equipment: "by comparison with Dow Chemical selling napalm"—which the United States used as a weapon against the Vietnamese people (Thomas, 1982).

Displacement and Diffusion of Responsibility

Construal of responsibility in terrorism differs in several important ways from that in conventional forms of wrongdoing. Those who commit conventional misdeeds minimize, deny, or dispute the harmful effects in an effort to prove that they have done no harm. They intentionally obscure the link between themselves and the detrimental effects of their acts, making it difficult to know who is responsible. In contrast, those who carry out terrorist destruction for religious or humanistic social causes claim responsibility for the mayhem they cause and rejoice in its success. Some are even willing to take their own lives as an act of martyrdom to fulfill what they regard as a divine mandate.

Consider the outspoken Dutch film director and journalist Theo van Gogh, who was gruesomely murdered for his criticism of intolerance in the name of Islam. At his trial, the accused killer, Mohammed Bouyeri, a Dutch Moroccan national, declared, "I take complete responsibility for my actions. I acted purely in the name of my religion" (Friedman, 2005). Suicide bombers are heralded as martyrs; some families even take pride in offspring who sacrifice their lives in defense of Islam. Claiming responsibility for death and destruction also serves another important function. Well-organized terrorist operations use destructive exploits as a show of power over their enemies. These successes strengthen the motivation to forge ahead with their cause and to attract recruits (Kydd & Walter, 2006).

Notable exceptions were the September 11 airplane attacks in New York City and Washington, D.C. The suicidal hijackers were affiliated with and trained by al Qaeda, but its leader, Osama bin Laden, at first denied any involvement in the mission, despite every indication that he was involved in planning and financing it. He later claimed responsibility for it. His initial denial reflects the difficulty of living with compromise when one claims the moral high road. On the one hand, bin Laden distanced himself from the September 11 attacks on the grounds that Islam forbids harming innocents. On the other hand, he defended indiscriminate attacks that harm women and children: "We do not differentiate between those dressed in military uniforms and civilians; they are all targets in this fatwa" (Ludlow, 2001). This rationale assumes that democracies are politically monolithic. In fact, they contain partisan factions, some of which oppose, sometimes vehemently, governmental policies with which they take issue. Children, who are among the victims in some terrorist attacks, do not exercise control over governmental policies. It should be noted that claims of responsibility are made in the name of the terrorist group as a faceless collective.

The enormity of the twin towers pulverization, in which thousands of workers and hundreds of first responders and airline passengers perished, defy vindication by Islamic values and law. Husayn al-Musawi, a leader of Hezbollah, faced the same moral contradiction. When he was reminded that holding innocent people as hostages is forbidden by Islamic law, he justified it with a contextual, exonerative metaphor: "It is the same as with alcohol. Alcohol is forbidden under Islam, but when it is a medicine you are allowed to take as much as you need for your recovery" (Kramer, 1990). Democracies confront the same moral self-contradiction when they preach freedom, justice, and inalienable rights while supporting, for reasons of self-interest, dictatorial regimes that abuse their own people.

In an incongruous moral justification, the terrorist group that contaminated Israeli oranges exported to Europe in 1978 claimed responsibility for the act but disclaimed intent to kill people, declaring that their goal was "not to indiscriminately kill . . . [the] population, but to sabotage the Israeli economy" (Sprinzak & Karmon, 2007). The fact that the mercury injected into the oranges sickened but did not kill innocent consumers does not negate the morally reprehensibility of the act.

Terrorist attacks that take a heavy toll of civilians in consecrated and memorial settings create special pressures to lay the blame elsewhere because it can alienate even a group's supporters. IRA guerrillas planted a large bomb that killed and maimed many adults and children attending a war memorial service in a town square in Enniskillen, Northern Ireland (Bomb kills 11, 1987). The British prime minister, Margaret Thatcher, condemned the attack as desecrating the war dead. The IRA promptly ascribed blame for the civilian massacre to the British army, which they accused of detonating the bomb prematurely with an electronic scanning device. The guerrillas claimed that the bomb was meant to strike a procession of British army forces and the Royal Ulster Constabulary. The British government denounced "this pathetic excuse," because no scanning equipment was in use at the time (Raines, 1987).

Displacement of responsibility also operates when hostages are taken in violation of terrorists' religious canons. When Sayyid Abbas al-Musawi of Hezbollah was asked whether the "oppressed" were responsible for taking hostages, he shifted the blame to international foes: "Only the United States, France, and Israel are responsible, since they provoke such actions by their hateful policy toward the Muslim people and their barbaric practices, the consequences of which they must accept" (Kramer, 1990). The same attribution of blame occurs concerning the safety of hostages during their captivity. Terrorists warn officials of targeted nations that if they take retaliatory action, they will be held accountable for the lives of the hostages. At different phases in negotiations for the release of hostages, terrorists continue to displace responsibility for their safety to the reactions of the nations they are fighting. If the captivity drags on, terrorists blame the suffering and injuries they inflict on the hostages on the officials who fail to make what they regard as warranted concessions to remedy social wrongs.

Nation-states sponsor terrorist operations through disguised, roundabout routes that make it difficult assign blame. Moreover, the intended purpose of state-sanctioned destruction is usually linguistically disguised so that neither sponsors nor perpetrators regard the activity as censurable. When culpable practices are exposed, officials deny that their country had anything to do with the attacks.

Minimizing, Distorting, or Disputing Harmful Effects

The perpetrators of most inhumanities go to extraordinary lengths to deny that they cause harm and suffering. There is no need for self-censure or to change one's ways if one is doing no harm. Harm management takes an entirely different form in terrorism. As we have seen, terrorists usually magnify the harm they cause. The purpose of terrorist violence is to cause wide-scale destruction to compel access to an international forum to air the groups' grievances, justify the desperateness of the extreme means, and stress the need to redress the inhumane and humiliating maltreatment of those victimized by oppressive social systems.

Attribution of Blame

Faced with legitimate charges of maltreatment of those they harm, terrorists readily vindicate themselves by blaming their adversaries for bringing their suffering on themselves. The terrorists' own grievances take varied forms and can be more or less grave. They may include racial, ethnic, religious, economic, and social persecution. Governments may wield coercive and punitive institutional power to maintain entrenched social inequities, obstruct legitimate efforts at change, silence critics, and override institutional checks and balances. Widespread governmental corruption also fuels social wrath. Terrorists do not confine their disputes to internal foes, however. Often, they direct much of their enmity and rage at foreign nations that prop up dictators who control strategic locations and essential resources. Attribution of blame works both ways, with terrorists considering themselves victims driven to lashing out against oppression. The net result is an escalating cycle of violence and retaliation with mutual condemnation wrapped in righteousness.

Terrorists contend that fundamental changes can be achieved only if they take up arms against blameworthy oppressive, corrupt regimes. They frame the battle for social change in a war metaphor, seeing themselves as "freedom fighters" and "revolutionaries" selflessly battling despotic enemy forces on behalf of the marginalized and maltreated (Cordes, 1987). In her analysis, Cordes notes that terrorist groups are not monolithic but have internal disputes over the justification of violence, the forms it should take, and whether to target the foe discriminately or indiscriminately. Sometimes they split over the disagreement, as in the case of the Weathermen, with one faction taking the more violent route (Sprinzak, 1990).

Dehumanization

Rival extremist groups on both sides of conflicts resort to inflammatory metaphors cast mainly in terms of bestiality and disease. This practice has a long history. In launching the Crusades, Pope Urban II portrayed his Muslim foes as "barbarians" who are "despicable, degenerate and enslaved by demons." In contemporary times, some of the most prominent leaders of the extreme Christian Right have encouraged hatred of Muslims as a whole (Johnson, 2011). The Reverend Jerry Falwell branded the Prophet Muhammad a "terrorist" (McKay, 2002). The evangelist Pat Robertson called the Prophet "an absolute wild-eyed fanatic" (Kristof, 2003). The Reverend Franklin Graham, the heir to his father's evangelical dominion, characterized Islam as a "very evil and wicked religion" (Kristof, 2003). And the Reverend Jerry Vines, a former president of the Southern Baptist Convention, angered Muslims by proclaiming at an annual meeting that Islam was inferior to Christianity (Muslims angered, 2002). He poured additional fuel on the polemical fire with other inflammatory remarks such as "Islam was founded by Muhammad, a demon-possessed pedophile" (Kristof, 2003). In reciprocal dehumanization, Osama bin Laden dubbed his American enemy "debauched infidels" who perpetrate heinous acts "that the most ravenous of animals would not descend to" (Ludlow, 2001). He labeled allied nations "slaves" to the United States.

The Nazi regime carried dehumanization to the ultimate extreme (Wistrich, 2010). This campaign, applied with a vengeance, laid the foundation for the national genocidal mission. Jewish people were derogated as a genetically inferior race that had to be eradicated from society. They were segregated in ghettos where they were denied any rights or dignity. The Nazis converted the Star of David to a symbol of shame and portrayed Jews in demeaning caricatures as money-grubbing, scheming, and filthy. Movie posters depicted Jewish people as rats. In the death camps they were stripped of their personal identity and assigned numbers, which were tattooed on their skin. By depriving Jews of any human qualities and investing them with revolting ones, Germans eliminated moral qualms about exterminating an entire class of people.

Anti-Semitism has been deeply entrenched in many societies for centuries. Shakespeare wrote his play *The Merchant of Venice*, which addressed anti-Semitism through the character of Shylock, the Jewish moneylender, in 1596. The intractable Israeli-Palestinian conflict has generated a flood of dehumanizing speech about Jews in the Arab mainstream press, on television, and on radical websites. Jews are depicted in the most malignant and demonic terms and vilified as "Nazi occupiers" (Wistrich, 2010). Radical clerics have promoted dehumanization further. In a sermon at the Grand Mosque in Mecca, a prominent imam declared that Jews are "the scum of the earth whom Allah cursed and turned into apes and pigs" (Stalinsky, 2004). Dehumanizing speech is also practiced by a good part of the Mideast body politic. In his anti-Semitic address to the International Conference on National and Islamic Solidarity for the Future of Palestine, President Mahmoud Ahmadinejad of Iran declared, in a metaphor combining disease and bestial qualities, that the "[w]orld powers have created a black and dirty microbe named the Zionist regime and have unleashed it like a savage animal on the nations of the region" (Goldberg, 2009).

Hateful language poses particular problems for Western societies that have constitutional protections for speech. Hate speech, especially defamation of religion, rouses social pressures to place legal restrictions on it. Opponents object to criminalizing hateful expressions because it would infringe on free speech. Given the controversy over what constitutes hateful speech, they argue that such restrictions can be used to stifle any dissenting voices. In the absence of legal sanctions, some aggrieved groups have attacked press offices and, in some cases, assassinated the perceived defamers. Islamic extremists firebombed the Paris offices of *Charlie Hebdo*, a satirical magazine that lampoons virtually all authority (Jolly, 2011). Its editor, Stéphane Charbonnier, asserted his right to free speech: "If we can poke fun at everything in France, if we can talk about anything in France apart from Islam or the consequences of Islamism, that is annoying" (French satirical paper, 2011). He expressed his resolve to continue criticism of radical Islam. "There is no question of giving in to Islamists (if [they are] behind the bombing)" (Samuel, 2011).

Abdoulaye Wade, the president of Senegal, had a different view on the matter: "I don't think freedom of expression should mean freedom from blasphemy. There can be no freedom without limits" (Callimachi, 2008). As this case illustrates, the battle over what constitutes hate speech and where to draw the line does not lend itself to easy resolution.

An Egyptian American Coptic Christian wrote and directed a crude anti-Muslim film depicting the Prophet Muhammad as a philanderer and a violently oriented religious phony who condoned child sexual abuse. When clips from the short film were dubbed into Arabic and uploaded to the Internet, enraged Muslims staged violent protests worldwide. Ultraconservative factions attacked the U.S. embassy in Cairo. Armed militants overran the U.S. consulate in Benghazi, Libya, killing an American diplomat, among others (Associated Press, 2012).

At the height of this tumult, *Charlie Hebdo* published disparaging cartoons of Muhammad (Sayare & Clark, 2012). Using a comparative argument of equitable treatment, an Egyptian spokesman urged the French judiciary to condemn the newspaper, citing the precedent that Holocaust denial is legally prohibited in France. The government announced that it would block protests against the offensive cartoons. Charbonnier challenged the decision on the grounds that it infringed on freedom of speech. "We have the right to express ourselves, they have a right to express themselves, too" (Sayare & Clark, 2012). Critics argued that pouring fuel on a raging fire was an inflammatory way of affirming freedom of speech and was likely to incite acts of violence.

In retaliation against *Charlie Hebdo* for insulting the Prophet Muhammad, two militants sponsored by al Qaeda (Schoichet & Levs, 2015) stormed the journal's offices and shot Charbonnier and most of the staff, shouting, "God is great!" during the attack (Bilefsky & de la Baume, 2015b). The killings aroused worldwide condemnation and massive public support in defense of free speech; many protesters carried signs saying, "I am Charlie." The massacre roused worldwide condemnation and massive public support in defense of free speech. However, the fervent defense of free speech did not last long. In the face of terrorist threats France is broadening laws permitting mass domestic surveillance of communications on the Internet with weak judicial oversight (Rubin, 2015).

Muslim leaders denounced the perpetration of atrocities in Allah's name. In contrast, supporters rejoiced on social media, praising the avenging "soldiers of Allah" (Black, 2015; MEMRI, 2015). The editor of the weekly was bestialized as "that dog Charb[onnier]." Twitter followers were told that through the vindictive slaying "the honor of [Allah's] prophet has been cleansed." One graphic showed the Eiffel Tower with the black flag of the self-proclaimed Islamic State and the caption "We are everywhere" (MEMRI, 2015). One Twitter user warned, "This is the first reaction. You'll not live in safety again" (Black, 2015).

The few surviving members of the newspaper staff published the next issue with a cover showing Muhammad shedding a tear while holding up a sign saying, "I am Charlie," under the headline, "All is forgiven" (Bilefsky, 2015b). Islamic radical leaders warned that the cartoon would further inflame the cultural conflict between "the secular West and observant Muslims" (Bilefsky, 2015b). They also complained about the apparent double standard for free speech, accusing Western countries of banning hate speech against some groups but allowing it against Muslims.

Dehumanization is not confined to speech but can also be expressed in actions. Dehumanization that motivates terrorist actions should be distinguished from actions designed to dehumanize. The Nazis dehumanized their victims by stripping them of any personal identity and subjecting them to a subhuman level of existence. In the animalization that occurred in Abu Graib prison, guards forced detainees to wear dog leashes and rode on their backs as if they were beasts of burden. Islamic terrorists carried physical dehumanization to the ultimate extreme by beheadings and other atrocities. Genocidal terrorists debase women by using rape as a weapon of war.

Terrorists rarely achieve their goal of bringing down the social order. However, they succeed in other ways. They instill fear in the general population. Authorities must subject the public to costly surveillance and safety procedures. Terrorist threats result in laws that implement scrutiny of people's private lives. These outcomes detract from the quality of life.

Moral Compromises in the Merchandising of Weapons

Terrorists need deadly wares to inflict their destruction. The merchandising of weapons is fractionated and spread across a variety of enterprises, both legitimate and otherwise. Weapons dealers who supply tyrannical regimes with the lethal means to terrorize their own people make heavy use of the same modes of moral disengagement that serve terrorism. The sales they make arm terrorist groups either directly or through circuitous routes.

Frank Terpil, who became a weapons entrepreneur after he fell from grace at the CIA, provided detailed and remorseless testimony on the arming of evildoers through a large network of legitimate suppliers (Thomas, 1982). The details of Terpil's deadly operation are especially informative because they reveal, in stark detail, that those who trade in human destruction do not do so alone. They depend heavily on the collective moral disengagement of a vast network of reputable citizens who manage respectable businesses. Terpil masked his destructive operations in euphemisms suggesting a legitimate business fulfilling "consumer needs" under the sanitized name Intercontinental Technology. To spare himself any self-censure for contributing to atrocities, he actively avoided knowing the purposes to which his weapons would be put. "I don't ever want to know that," he said (Thomas, 1982). When asked whether he was ever haunted by thoughts about the suffering his wares might cause, he explained that a weapons dealer cannot afford to think about consequences. Banishing thoughts of the injurious results of one's actions frees one from restraints of conscience: "If I really thought about the consequences all the time, I certainly wouldn't have been in this business. You have to blank it off [*sic*]" (Thomas, 1982).

Probes for any signs of self-reproach only brought self-exonerative comparisons. When asked if he felt any qualms about supplying torture equipment to Idi Amin, the ruthless dictator of Uganda, Terpil justified his actions by advantageous comparison with the workers who manufactured napalm at Dow Chemical. As he put it, "I'm sure that the people from Dow Chemical didn't think of the consequences of selling napalm. If they did, they wouldn't be working at the factory. I doubt very much if they'd feel any more responsible for the ultimate use than I did for my equipment." When pressed about the atrocities committed at Amin's torture chambers under the sanitized designation State Research Bureau, Terpil repeated his depersonalized view: "I do not get wrapped up emotionally with the country. I regard myself basically as neutral, and commercial" (Thomas, 1982). To give legitimacy to his "private practice," he claimed that he aided British and American covert operations abroad as well. What began as a psychological analysis of a commercial operator of a death industry ended unexpectedly in an international network of supporting legitimate businesses run by upstanding business operators.

One might imagine that only a small group of unsavory individuals is involved in merchandising the weapons used in terrorism, but this is far from the case. A worldwide network of reputable, high-level members of society contribute to this deadly enterprise by fractioning the operations, farming them out to different firms, displacing and diffusing responsibility, and distancing themselves from the uses to which the weaponry is put. One group might manufacture the tools of destruction. Others might amass arsenals for legitimate sale at trade shows. Still others operate storage centers for them. Others procure export and import licenses to move the weaponry among different countries. Others obtain spurious end-user certificates that get the weapons to embargoed nations through circuitous routes. And still others ship them. Major banks process the financial transactions.

Arms trafficking is a highly lucrative business. The cogs in this worldwide network include weapons manufacturers; former government officials with political ties; former diplomatic, military, and intelligence officers who provide valuable skills and contacts; weapons dealers and shippers who operate legitimate businesses; and bankers who launder and move money through legitimate financial systems. Even producers of the CBS television program *60 Minutes* contributed to Terpil's coffers (Thornton, 1983).

Terpil skipped bail and fled to a foreign sanctuary after he was caught trying to sell assassination equipment to undercover agents. He was tried and convicted in absentia. The district attorney confronted Mike Wallace, the reporter who interviewed Terpil, about a payment of $12,000 to an intermediary who had arranged the interview. Wallace and CBS admitted paying an intermediary but self-exonerated by denying knowledge that the intermediary had passed the money on to Terpil.

VARIETIES OF TERRORISM

In his analysis of terrorism, David Rapoport (1990) distinguishes secular terrorism from sacred terrorism on the grounds that they differ in means and in ends. In sacred terrorism, violence serves religious purposes, so it is justified morally in terms of obedience to God's will. Secular terrorists are not tightly bound by a particular dogma. For them, violence can serve different purposes, and they justify it in different ways, depending on what rationale is likely to gain the most public support. Nor are secular terrorists restricted to particular means but select them for their utility in promoting desired outcomes. The success of the means to advance one's cause becomes its own moral justification.

Secular Terrorism

Secular terrorism takes a variety of forms (Cordes, 1987; Reich, 1990). Whether it is the "anarchic" type embracing revolutionary rhetoric, or the "nationalistic" type seeking redress of long-standing grievances and an independent state; whether it is left wing or right wing; and whatever the sociopolitical context might be, secular terrorists face the same moral predicaments. They have to justify the morality of their violent means to win public support for their cause. But even more important, they have to justify it to themselves so that they can remove the restraint of moral self-sanction to inflict death and suffering without being haunted by guilt.

Terrorist groups are driven underground, where they operate secretly. As a result, we have little detailed information on how they orchestrate each of the mechanisms of moral disengagement in the service of their cause. As we have seen, terrorists typically frame their violent activities in a war metaphor, envisioning themselves as liberators and freedom fighters, not terrorists, courageously battling inhumane systems on behalf of the oppressed. In its training manual, the leadership of the IRA proclaimed that the Irish people were morally justified in fighting a war of liberation against British occupational forces. Among many grievances, the IRA cited the injustice of political impotence, impoverished living conditions, exploitation of labor and natural resources, and the destruction of the Celtic culture by repressive British rule. Their enmity, transmitted through many generations, has a long history. Sean O'Callaghan, a former IRA militant, recalled the advice his grandmother gave him when he was 9 years old: "When you shoot a British policeman, dig him up and shoot him again because you can never trust them" (Bennhold, 2013).

The IRA leadership was insightful about the power of moral justification to disengage self-sanctions from lethal action. They explained in the training manual that pervasive injustice provided the moral grounds for IRA volunteers to be able to "kill someone without hesitation and without regret" (Green Book, n.d.). Absolved of moral constraint, they were told to "kill as many enemy personnel as possible." Their moral justification was based primarily on the commonly used necessitarian argument that they had no other option (McIntyre, 2001).

The power of ideology to dispel moral restraint is illustrated in cold-blooded assassinations. Sean O'Callaghan, the young IRA militant, entered a pub and shot at close range a Catholic police inspector erroneously rumored to be abusing IRA prisoners in detention centers (O'Callaghan, 1998). In reflecting on the killing he disclaimed any wrongdoing: "I had done no wrong. I had not committed a crime, a sin. I had no reason to feel guilty." The worthy purpose was his moral exoneration: "I was fighting for a righteous cause" (O'Callaghan, 1998). Although remorseless about the assassination, he experienced a residual live-with-yourself problem. He was haunted by an intrusive thought—"You're going to have to pay for this someday"—which he tried to suppress: "I pushed that troublesome thought away. 'Get your act together, you halfwit,' I told myself."

Intense hatred of foes obliterates any sense of shared humanity that would arouse some empathy and compassion. When Kevin McKenna, an adjutant general of the IRA, was told that the militants had killed a policewoman he remarked, "Maybe she was pregnant and we got two for the price of one" (O'Callaghan, 1998). At a meeting to decide what to do with an informant whom O'Callaghan tried to protect, McKenna asked whether he had any children. When told he had eight children, McKenna grimaced and ordered, "Kill him." Afterward, as the assassins were leaving the scene of the killing, one of them urinated on the spattered blood. These types of events, including the 1979 assassination of the British statesman and naval officer Lord Mountbatten, made O'Callaghan increasingly concerned about the terrorist activities he had become involved in. In a highly dangerous act of courage, O'Callaghan became an informer for the Irish police while subverting terrorist plots from within as a high-ranking member. Eventually he surrendered to the authorities. After pleading guilty to many crimes, he was sentenced to prison but was pardoned after serving eight years of his 539-year term (Bennhold, 2013). In the end he transformed himself from a callous revolutionary to a spokesperson for peace and human rights.

The IRA was able to maintain social support for its violent campaign over three decades. Sarma (2007) provides an insightful analysis of how members exploited the methods of moral disengagement in a media campaign to persuade people to suspend moral reactions to behavior they would ordinarily regard as morally reprehensible. Sarma's work is a novel extension of research on the role of moral disengagement in terrorism because it focuses on disengaging the morality of members of the general public. Through this mechanism terrorists can gain support for violent means and silence their opponents.

Suicide bombing is one of the most frightening modes of terrorism. A suicide bomber wears a specially designed body vest packed with explosives and shrapnel that produce widespread carnage when the bomb is detonated in a crowded area. The Tamil Tigers, a Sri Lankan separatist group, exploited this technique. Known for their ruthless tactics in their drive to carve out a Tamil homeland, for decades Tamil insurgent militants controlled substantial territory in northern and eastern Sri Lanka until they were routed by the Sri Lankan army. Their suicide bombers assassinated Rajiv Gandhi, the former Indian prime minister, and the Sri Lankan president. They justified the moral legitimacy of their guerilla warfare as the only means of freeing themselves from the oppressive rule of the Sinhalese majority.

The Tamil Tigers institutionalized suicide bombing, teaching its use formally in training camps (Weitz & Neal, 2007). The Tigers celebrated suicide bombers as heroic figures. They immortalized their first suicide bomber, memorialized on Tamil Tigers Day all those who had sacrificed their lives, and even named orphanages after suicide bombers. Recruiters glorified death in combat, telling potential recruits, "If you die fighting, you get a hero's death. But if you die naturally, you die a coward" (Meadows, 2010). They often used women as suicide bombers and recruited child soldiers as well. Fighters wore pendants containing cyanide pills so that they could kill themselves if captured. In the brutal final phase of fighting, the government's military offensive effectively destroyed the Tamil Tigers as a fighting force. Countless civilians perished when they were used as human shields. Each side blamed the other for the heavy death toll.

Insurgents in Iraq and Afghanistan carefully studied the Tamil Tigers' suicide-bombing techniques and adopted them as part of their offensive tactics. Their vision of a blessed afterlife through martyrdom overrode the drive for self-preservation. This mode of terrorism is especially frightening because people can do little to protect themselves from individuals who are not deterred by the fear of death and are willing to sacrifice themselves for a higher cause.

Sacred Terrorism

Perpetrators of sacred terror believe that they are on a divine mission to do God's bidding. Examples of how they sanctify violent means for religious ends were presented in chapter 2. Pope Urban II declared that Christ commanded all Christians to launch the Crusades. He called on Europeans to fight "under the guidance of the Lord" against "a race [that was] despicable, degenerate, and enslaved by demons" (Geary, 2010). Osama bin Laden ennobled his global jihad by calling it a holy imperative against decadent infidels who seek to enslave the Muslim world, "We will continue this course because it is part of our religion and because Allah, praise and glory be to him, ordered us to carry out jihad so that the word of Allah may remain exalted to the heights" (Banerjee, 2007). Yigal Amir, who assassinated Prime Minister Yitzhak Rabin, claimed a divine mandate. Amir invoked the rabbinical pursuer's decree because Rabin had ceded some West Bank territory from which Amir believed Palestinian radicals would threaten Israel. Paul Hill, a former Presbyterian minister, believed he was divinely chosen to follow God's will in killing a doctor and his assistant at an abortion clinic: "God has used people who are willing to die for their cause to save human life, and I'm certainly willing to do that" (Kuntz, 1995).

In an interfaith meeting for peace hosted by Pope Benedict XVI, religious leaders from around the world—Christians, Jews, Muslims, Hindus, Taoists, Shintoists, and Buddhists—condemned violence and terrorism committed in God's name (Pullella, 2011). The pope acknowledged "with great shame" that over the ages Christianity had justified violence as divinely mandated. The religious leaders pledged to promote interfaith understanding and to work against the use of violence.

Violent means present a special moral dilemma for religious terrorists because killing innocent people to advance a cause is sacrilege. However, the notion that religious terrorism differs from secular terrorism in its methods is mistaken. Throughout the long history of sacred terror, religious terrorists have sanctified violence. The Lebanese Hezbollah is a good example of the cognitive machinations by which violence is justified. Hezbollah, which is led mainly by Shiite clerics, presents itself as a political party: Its very name means "party of God." The sacred mission of its armed unit is to turn Lebanon into an Islamic state and to destroy Israel. To do so Hezbollah must defeat foreign forces, which it considers a threat to Islamic values and an Islamic way of life.

Clerics of any denomination face a moral paradox when the militant strategies they favor, either directly or indirectly, belie the sacred values they espouse. Kramer (1990) describes the great lengths to which Shiite clerics go to create moral justifications for violent acts that breach Islamic law, such as suicide bombings and taking innocent people as hostages. The clerics must persuade themselves of the morality of their actions not only to preserve their positive self-regard but also to uphold their integrity in the eyes of rival clerics and in the international arena. In reality, Islam permits neither suicide by any means nor the terrorizing of innocent people. The clerics justify such acts by invoking situational imperatives and utilitarian reasons. They frame the issue in terms of their foes' overwhelming tyrannical power, which drives oppressed people to resort to unconventional methods of self-protection.

Until his death, Ayatollah Muhammad Hussein Fadlallah, a senior Shiite cleric affiliated with Hezbollah, was one of Lebanon's leading authorities on Islamic values and laws. He argued that overpowering oppressive regimes requires unconventional means of self-defense: "The oppressed nations do not have the technology and destructive weapons America and Europe has. They must thus fight with special means of their own. . . . We view this as religiously lawful warfare against the world's imperialist and domineering powers" (Kramer, 1990). This is the necessitarian moral justification mentioned earlier. To vindicate the morality of the suicidal means, Fadlallah argued that the unconventional means of dying in a suicide bombing for a moral cause is no different from dying at the hands of any enemy soldier. "There is no difference between dying with a gun in your hand or exploding yourself" (Kramer, 1990). Kramer notes the contradiction in the moral logic. On the one hand, Fadlallah said that suicide bombing is a necessitated unconventional means, but on the other hand, he said it is just a commonplace type of death in battle. Suicide bombing cannot be both unusual and usual.

Hijackings and the abduction of innocent foreign nationals as hostages were other practices that violated Islamic law and hence required moral justification. Hezbollah often used hostages as leverage to release its detained fighters and to publicize its cause worldwide. Fadlallah could find no Islamic moral or legal exoneration of hostage taking (Kramer, 1990). Nevertheless, clerics who were not schooled in Islamic law offered a variety of justifications. Militants accused their hostages of being spies, which warranted treating them as foes. This linguistic solution, however, defied credibility when it came to hijacking airplanes. It was highly implausible that whole planeloads of passengers, most of whom were tourists, could be spies. Overwhelming power imbalance then became the justification. Faced with tyrannical might, the terrorists claimed they had "no other choice than to adopt this means" (Kramer, 1990). They used the same justification that Fadlallah devised for suicide bombing. Hostage taking became indiscriminate. Professors were abducted for corrupting students with decadent Western values and foreign journalists for spying.

Fadlallah argued that according to Islamic law it is "forbidden to kidnap or kill an innocent person because one has a score to settle with a head of state" (Kramer, 1990). It is interesting that he sanctified suicide bombing even though Islam morally and legally forbids suicide. The contradiction probably has more to do with the relative effectiveness of different pernicious means than with inherent theological nuance. Being a moral authority is not an easy job, especially when one must justify violent means that prove effective in advancing one's cause. Moral compromises create logical paradoxes. Hezbollah militants eventually stopped taking hostages because they came to regard it as harmful to their cause, tarnishing the image of Islam with few benefits to show for it.

Because of the shaky moral logic and questionable reinterpretations, clerics sanction terrorism indirectly and vindicate successful ventures retrospectively but do not endorse terrorist operations beforehand. The radical group Islamic Jihad claimed responsibility for the deadly Beirut suicide bombing, in which terrorists detonated explosives loaded in trucks, killing and injuring hundreds of American marines and sailors and many French soldiers as well. They were part of an international peacekeeping force installed following the withdrawal of guerrillas from the Palestine Liberation Organization from Beirut, where Israeli forces had besieged them. The peacekeepers, whom the terrorists accused of favoring the Christian side in the conflict, soon withdrew from Lebanon. The terrorists were emboldened by their victory. Although denying any involvement in the terrorist attack, Husayn al-Mussawi, the leader of Islamic Amal, praised Islamic Jihad for carrying it out: "I supported their glorious attacks against the U.S. and French forces in Lebanon. I have said repeatedly that I have no connection with them, but we respect them and we support them fully and we bow our heads to the greatness of their work" (Kramer, 1990).

Domestic Terrorism

The rise of homegrown terrorism presents a new challenge to those charged with protecting American lives and territory. A number of factors make it especially difficult to detect threats and prevent attacks. As U.S. citizens, domestic terrorists blend in with the general public, pursuing ordinary daily routines. Because many of them are not affiliated with militant terrorist groups, there is no "chatter" in phone and online conversations among group members to provide clues about planned actions. If they operate as loners, there are no groups for informers or undercover agents to infiltrate. Moreover, if the terrorists have no records of previous arrests, they do not attract the attention of law enforcement. However, some do belong to groups but are instructed to dissociate themselves from the group before they take action, so that neither the group nor the group's leader is compromised (German, 2005).

There is no one pathway to domestic radicalization. Some who resort to violence view the federal government as a tyrannical force that is dismissive of "traditional" American values and that threatens their safety, freedom, and way of life. Antigovernment talk radio outlets and blogs abound with stories of diabolical conspiracies, fueling their wrath. Some white supremacists take up arms against the government. In the deadliest act of domestic terrorism, in 2001, Timothy McVeigh detonated a truckload of explosives that destroyed much of a federal office building in Oklahoma City, killing 168 people and injuring over 500 (Michel & Herbeck, 2001). He claimed that the bombing was revenge for a controversial, deadly confrontation in 1993 between the Federal Bureau of Investigation (FBI) and members of a religious sect suspected of gun violations. After a long siege, many members of the sect perished in the flames of their Waco, Texas compound.

Another route to domestic radicalization is through Islamic extremism. Among first-generation Muslim immigrants, those who struggle in their efforts to adapt to their adopted country are vulnerable to jihadist recruitment. As their alienated lives unravel, they gravitate to Islamic terrorist web sites that provide them with justification for their resentments and a sense of identity and purpose for their lives. Some act on their radicalization. Faisal Shahzad set out to bomb Times Square, but his effort failed because his car bomb malfunctioned (Moynihan & Cohen, 2010; Shifrel & McShane, 2010). At the Boston Marathon, the Tsarnaev brothers' homemade bombs took the lives of three people and seriously injured over 260 (Levitz, 2015; Schmitt, Mazzetti, Schmidt, & Shane, 2013). The older brother, Tamerlan, was the more alienated and troubled one. Most troubled individuals with extremist views do not resort to violence. Other factors obviously come into play. The suspension of moral self-sanctions for the taking of innocent lives clearly plays a critical role.

Like foreign terrorists, domestic terrorists target innocent civilians, carry out their attacks surreptitiously while aiming for maximum publicity, and—unless they are suicide bombers—try to get away safely. They all massacre innocent people, including children, out of devotion to their ideology. McVeigh, who was deeply involved in the white-supremacist militia gun culture, viewed himself not as a terrorist but as a principled warrior, defending freedom against governmental abuse of power. He felt no remorse over the massacre. Shahzad saw himself as only defending his religion: "We are only Muslims trying to defend our religion, people, honor, and land," he announced at his sentencing (Shifrel & McShane, 2010). He took pride in doing so: "If you call us terrorists for doing that, then we are proud terrorists, and we will keep on terrorizing until you leave our land and people at peace" (Shifrel & McShane, 2010). In the note he wrote while hiding in a boat, the surviving Tsarnaev brother, Dzhokhar, called the Boston Marathon bombing retribution for the Muslims killed in the wars in Afghanistan and Iraq (Boston Marathon bombings, 2013). In the often-used military euphemism, he called the Boston victims "collateral damage" and referred to his brother, who died in a gun battle with the police, as a martyr.

These cases illustrate the dual function of moral justification. Radical ideology engages morality in the service of the terroristic mission but disengages morality in its lethal execution. By selectively excluding classes of vilified people from their definition of humanity, perpetrators can feel proud to maim and kill numerous victims. Domestic terrorists can be Islamists, white supremacists, anarchists, or some other ideological variety.

Unconventional Terrorism

Unconventional modes of terrorism are also used to alarm the populace. Poisoning threats are one such example. In 1978, a group purporting to be the

Arab Revolutionary Army sent letters to European and Middle Eastern health ministries, warning that its agents had injected poison into Israeli citrus products (Sprinzak & Karmon, 2007). The letter claimed that the "oppressed Palestinian workers in the occupied territories have been poisoning the oranges in a widespread campaign." Foreign governments were alarmed by the threat. However, only a few Europeans were sickened by eating oranges that were found to be laced with mercury. The "Arab Revolutionary Army" turned out to be a phony organization. The perpetrators were suspected to be radical Germans sympathetic to the Palestinian cause. Although the threat was greatly overblown, it damaged Israeli export of agricultural products. In predictable modeling, other groups launched poisoning scares, requiring Western countries to beef up surveillance and safety measures.

Even a lone terrorist can impose permanent societal costs by a simple but deadly act. In 1982, a person or persons unknown laced Extra-Strength Tylenol capsules with cyanide, causing seven deaths (Fletcher, 2009). This case of product tampering, along with a rash of copycat incidents, terrorized the public and forced the permanent, costly adoption of tamperproof packaging of over-the-counter products. Some of the tamperproof packaging is so unyielding that it can turn otherwise serene individuals into raving ones.

Moral Justifications and the Mass Media

Terrorists try to exert influence over targeted officials and nations through intimidation of the public and arousal of sympathy for their social and political causes. Without widespread publicity, terrorist acts can achieve neither of these outcomes. The mass media, especially television and the Internet, provide the best access to the international community because of their strong drawing power. Terrorists exploit the Internet as a major vehicle of social and moral justification for their causes and the violent means they employ to further them. They gain sympathy and support for their cause by presenting themselves as risking their lives for the welfare of a victimized constituency whose legitimate grievances they disregard.

Unless terrorist groups gain appreciable social support and build on it, they cannot survive for long. Potential supporters may sympathize with their cause but reject violent means of promoting it. Terrorists face the difficult task of calibrating the level of their violence so as not to alienate their sympathizers. This is not easy to do when terrorist activities raise moral qualms in partisans and can make their lives more miserable. The natural tendency in the face of failed attempts is to escalate the level of violence, which only makes it more socially alienating. However, a clever campaign in moral disengagement can get supporters to accept extreme terrorist acts as morally justified (Sarma, 2010).

More and more, terrorists use electronic media to legitimize and gain support for their causes and to discredit those of their foes. For example,

Al Jazeera, a satellite television channel based in Qatar, broadcast the video-tapes and audiotapes that bin Laden prepared in which he justified the moral-ity of his global jihad. The televised tapes, usually dropped off anonymously at Al Jazeera's offices, also were a recruitment device, a tool for communicating with widely dispersed terrorist cells, and a source of inspirational support for his followers. The media, in turn, come under heavy fire from targeted offi-cials who regard granting terrorists a worldwide forum as aiding their causes. Nor do security forces appreciate it when media personnel record their con-duct and broadcast tactical information that terrorists can put to good use.

During the Sri Lankan civil war, the Tamil Tigers exploited mass media in their decades-long control of substantial territory in northern and eastern Sri Lanka until they were routed by the Sri Lankan army. The government realized that it was losing the public-image war in the international media to the Tigers: "They were better at this than we were. They were trying to tell the world that we were killers and racists and barbarians and that we will not allow their women to come out of their houses without killing and raping them" (Meadows, 2010). So the government mounted its own media campaign to promote a favorable image in the world community: "They have six websites to talk about their cause. And we have ours."

Broadcasting claims of responsibility for death and destruction serves another important function. Well-organized terrorist organizations use destructive exploits as a show of power over their enemies. Terrorist successes—or the image terrorists project of having the power and will to inflict heavy losses on their opponents—can attract recruits and help broaden a group's support base (Kydd & Walter, 2006).

In their cross-border war, the Israeli and Hezbollah paramilitary forces were shelling and bombing each other until the United Nations put a stop to it. Hezbollah claimed victory when their suicide bombers drove the Amer-ican and French peacekeeping forces out of Lebanon. With limited flight training and box cutters a few al Qaeda hijackers struck a devastating blow against the United States, the militarily most powerful nation in the world, and got it embroiled in a costly war in the Middle East.

In this electronic era, terrorist groups seek and radicalize recruits largely through the Internet, via social media platforms such as Facebook and Twitter. They post boastful videos of their exploits (and atrocities) on You-Tube. Many websites promoting extremist ideologies also provide practi-cal instructions on building weapons. In some instances, society has been spared terrorist massacres because homemade bombs malfunctioned or because execution of the plan was inept. As large-scale, cross-border terrorist attacks become more difficult to carry out because of improved security measures, foreign terrorists try to recruit domestic proxies to act for them (Shane, 2013b). Before his death in an American drone strike, Samir Khan, an American citizen who became an ardent al Qaeda propagandist in Yemen, was a prime recruiter through his website. "I strongly recommend all of the brothers and sisters coming from the West to consider attacking America in its own backyard," was a typical exhortation. He went on to explain the advantage of undetectability: "[T]hese types of individual decision-making attacks are nearly impossible for them to contain."

The Internet, which enables any tech-savvy individual to publicize his or her views worldwide, has transformed the role of communications in terrorism. The Internet's influence goes beyond the expression of viewpoints, however. Terrorist websites provide detailed instruction on how to assemble bombs from easily available materials, build detonators, plant explosives strategically, make bomb vests, and use surface-to-air missiles to down aircraft, as well as on how to dress to avoid suspicion and which secret roads to take to safe houses to elude capture (Curiel, 2005). Terrorists look for ardent followers of their web sites, Facebook pages, and Twitter feeds and try to recruit them. One such recruit, a Sudanese student, announced, "I'm off to Iraq to be martyred. Wish me luck" (Curiel, 2005). His death by suicide bombing was called a "martyrdom operation." Videos of hostage beheadings and even more horrific murders are also available on the Internet. At the most basic level, the websites and other Internet platforms provide instruction on how to use the Internet in the service of terrorism. Such media outlets are essentially uncontrollable. If they are disabled, they come back under new names.

MORAL DISENGAGEMENT IN MILITARY COUNTERTERRORISM

The preceding discussion centered on how terrorists invoke moral standards to justify their brutal deeds but selectively disengage those standards when they actually carry out such activities. In contrast, fighting terrorism with military force involves two-sided moral disengagement. The use of physical force in self-defense is easy to justify morally. Counterterrorists bring moral disengagement into play in devising and executing their campaigns. However, such means pose more troublesome moral problems for democratic societies than for totalitarian ones. Totalitarian regimes have fewer constraints against using institutional power to crush internal dissent and to sacrifice individuals for the good of the state. They have few qualms about using unrestrained lethal force to combat terrorist threats. Terrorists can therefore wield greater power against nations that place a high value on human life and personal liberties. A commitment to humanitarian values limits the types of means that are morally acceptable and how they are used in self-defense.

The just war moral framework specifies the morally permissible rules of combat in military self-defense against aggressors (Walzer, 2010). These rules include necessity, justness of the cause, rightness of intention, proportionality, discrimination, and humanity. Some of these rules address moral justification for the use of military force. Others address moral justification for how that force is applied. According to the necessity rule, military force is used only after peaceful alternatives have been exhausted. These may include economic, diplomatic, and other nonmilitary means. In such circumstances, nations resort to military force for a just cause and the right intention to eliminate a threat rather than for vengeance or material gain or as a pretext for gaining control of resources or geopolitical advantage. According to the proportionality rule, a military campaign should be limited to the level of force needed to eradicate the threat rather than to inflict excessive death and destruction. Wanton force does more harm than good. The discrimination rule refers to the moral limits of military actions, which should be directed at enemy combatants, not at innocents. This is difficult to do when combatants hide among civilians and civilians are active supporters of the combatants. The humanity rule dictates that warfare be conducted in ways that minimize civilian casualties. The following analyses address the ways in which nations use moral disengagement to circumvent just war principles in military counterterrorism.

A comprehensive analysis of terrorism must address how targeted nations grapple with terrorist violence. Extreme retaliatory attacks that cause widespread death and destruction may advance the terrorists' political cause by arousing a backlash of sympathy for innocent victims and moral condemnation of brutal attacks. Fighting terrorism with morally undisciplined force can also generate a ready supply of recruits prepared to die for their cause, even by suicidal actions. In addition, brutal means also provide new justifications for violence that escalate terrorism rather than diminish it. Indeed, some terrorist activities are strategically designed to win worldwide support and to provoke governments by breeding public disaffection with the system. In these various ways, extreme countermeasures can play into the hands of terrorists.

Adding to the problem of countercontrol, efforts to reduce societal vulnerabilities with better counterterrorist technologies can beget better terrorist tactics and devices. Recall the security officer who characterized such escalating adaptations metaphorically, "For every 10 foot wall you erect, terrorists will build an 11-foot ladder." Technological advances are producing highly sophisticated devices that, when terrorists adopt them, increase social vulnerability to attack. Some nations promptly answer attacks with massive, deadly retaliation, whatever the costs might be, on the grounds that this is the price they must pay to check terrorism. Opponents of such policies argue that excessive countermeasures only make matters worse by creating more terrorists and increasing public sympathy for the causes that drive them to violence. Vigorous debates rage over whether massive retaliation curbs terrorism or exacerbates it.

At the geopolitical level, nations increase their vulnerability to terrorism by making foreign marriages of convenience to prop up oppressive regimes, as in the United States' backing of the authoritarian theocratic monarchy of Saudi Arabia, which severely restricts the human rights of its citizens. Countries with these types of life conditions—which spawn resistance, anger, and political instability—can become breeding grounds for terrorism. The short-term solution is to crush terrorists and make them bear the consequences of their destructive acts. Here the issue of concern is whether military force is applied in accordance with just war principles or for vengeance, violating society's moral standards and undermining its moral authority. Long-term solutions require instituting social reforms that better the people's living conditions. A focus on fighting violence with violence while neglecting needed social reforms is likely to produce an escalating cycle of terror and retaliation.

Morally calibrated countermeasures that involve restrained and discriminate use of military force help gain and maintain domestic and international support. Cooperation among nation-states is essential, because the uprooting of terrorist threats must be an international enterprise. The aid of allies is even more critical for the tough and lengthy occupation and reconstruction program required in the aftermath of a military campaign. Because many modern terrorist groups are nonstate actors, affiliated with no single country but dispersed worldwide, success requires a unified effort by many countries to eliminate not only the terrorists in their midst but also the ills within their societies that embitter and alienate their people. States must ameliorate poor living conditions largely through change from within. In the eyes of the Muslim world, foreign unilateral interventions can readily convert an antiterrorism campaign into a holy intercultural war.

The Impact of the September 11 Terrorist Attacks

The devastating terrorist attacks by the al Qaeda network on American soil, as well as attacks on U.S. consulates and military installations abroad, presented a grave national threat with reverberating domestic and international consequences. They shattered Americans' sense of national invulnerability, heightened cultural clashes between secular modernists and religious fundamentalists within Muslim nations and against Western nations, reordered geopolitical debates and international alliances, and provoked widespread retaliatory military campaigns abroad to root out terrorist sanctuaries. The attacks were a different order of terrorism, conducted by a well-financed, elusive enemy operating through a worldwide network whose aim was fomenting a holy war between the Western world and the Muslim world. The September 11 attacks resulted in calls for national protective countermeasures to deter further terrorist strikes.

Fighting terrorists with military force presents moral dilemmas on how to conduct the fight. Alfred McAlister and his collaborators conducted a nationwide study on selective disengagement of moral agency in support of lethal military force (McAlister, Bandura, & Owen, 2006). The nationwide sample was randomly selected from telephone registries. Midway through the study, the nation witnessed the demolition of the World Trade Center and part of the Pentagon by agents of the al Qaeda network. The participants studied prior to the terrorist attack were comparable in sociodemographic characteristics to those studied three days after the strike. They were tested for moral disengagement regarding the use of military force. The study measured support for two international military campaigns—the aerial bombardment of Iraq and attacks on suspected terrorist sanctuaries.

Moral disengagement was measured shortly after the attacks, when support for the preemptive bombardment of Iraq increased from 70% to 81%. Both the searing nature of the al Qaeda attacks and assessment of their effects just after they happened lend credence to the interpretation that the changes were due to the attacks, which thoroughly dominated public consciousness. Whatever other events may have occurred at the time paled in comparison with the enormity of suicidal terrorism.

As shown in Figure 7.1, the September 11 attacks raised the level of moral disengagement. The greatest increases were in moral justification ("MJ" in the figure) for the use of military force and the dehumanization

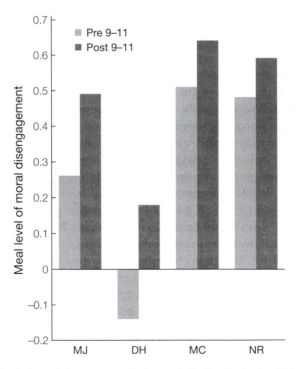

Figure 7.1 Mean level of moral disengagement before and after the September 11 terrorist strike. MJ = moral justification; DH = dehumanization; MC = minimization of consequences; NR = nonresponsibility. From McAlister, Bandura, and Owen (2006), with permission from Guilford Press.

("DH") of the enemy. The latter was the most striking change, from disavowing dehumanization to viewing the enemy in the most dehumanized form. This finding is all the more striking because dehumanization was measured in terms of a beastly nature. The less extreme forms of dehumanization tend to characterize terrorists and enemy leaders as inherently evil and devoid of any moral sense rather than as beastly creatures. A likely explanation for this moral reversal was the enormity of the intentional massacre of a huge number of innocent people and the heightened sense of personal vulnerability participants felt after the attack on their homeland.

In tests of the paths of influence, which are summarized in Figure 7.2, the effects of the terrorist attack on support of bombardment of Iraq were entirely mediated through moral disengagement. Participants backed the use of lethal military force only to the extent that they justified it to themselves, minimized civilian causalities, and bestialized the enemy.

Participants in the McAlister et al. study were considerably more supportive of a military campaign against Iraq (81%) than of counterstrikes against suspected terrorist sanctuaries (48%). Although the level of support for the use of military force against al Qaeda and against Iraq differed, the role of the various forms of moral disengagement participants used when considering attacking terrorist sanctuaries and attacking Iraq was virtually identical. The only difference was that bestialization was a stronger contributor to endorsement of counterstrikes against the terrorists. This difference comes as no surprise, given the role of al Qaeda in the September 11 attacks.

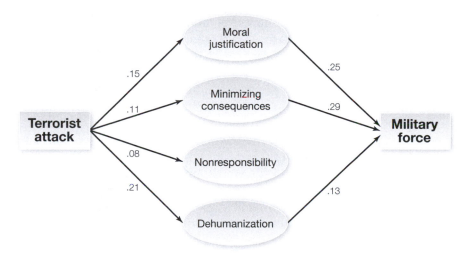

Figure 7.2 The paths of influence through which the terrorist attack on September 11 affected support of the use of military force. From McAlister, Bandura, and Owen (2006), with permission from Guilford Press.

The surprising disparity in choice of target may be explained in several ways. The Bush administration portrayed Saddam as being linked to al Qaeda terrorists and as a potential supplier of lethal weapons for their attacks. The administration was preparing the country for a war with Iraq. The findings of a *New York Times*/CBS News poll lend support to this explanation (Clymer & Elder, 2002). When the source of the potential terrorist threat was called "another country," 47% of those polled opposed a preemptive strike and 40% favored it. In contrast, when the country was called Iraq, 61% of those polled favored the preemptive attack and only 26% opposed it. Some of the respondents' comments mirrored the administration's erroneous justification for the preemptive military attack: for example, "Every day we wait to attack, Saddam is building more chemical weapons, and some sources say he already has nuclear weapons" (Clymer & Elder, 2002). As a fluid group with no national borders, al Qaeda was an elusive target. Its adherents quickly fled to Pakistan, where they established sanctuaries and received the unspoken approval of Pakistani intelligence. Bombarding the new sanctuaries would have required targeting Pakistan.

Of course, displacement and diffusion of responsibility are an important moral neutralizing device for the people who have to devise military campaigns and fight the battles (Bandura, 1999; Kelman & Hamilton, 1989). Because the general public is not doing the fighting, this means of moral disengagement may be less relevant to its advocacy of warfare. However, in the hierarchically organized systems of military forces with their strict chains of command, displacement and diffusion of responsibility are built into the policy and operational structure. In the public's view it is the policy makers and the commanders who should bear responsibility, not the soldiers who have to carry out their orders. Absolving soldiers of responsibility for undisciplined actions is unrelated to support of military campaigns.

Every nation has the right of self-defense to protect its people from outside attacks. The September 11 attacks called for national countermeasures against further terrorist strikes. However, military means can vary in their form, scope, and intensity. Not all forms of military self-defense may be morally permissible (Boyle, 2003). The use of military force also brings into play international constraints and supports that pose further moral dilemmas.

Military counterterrorism involves two-sided moral disengagement with terrorists on one side and counterterrorists on the other side. We already have addressed the ways in which terrorists enlist the mechanisms of moral disengagement. However, targeted nations also must morally justify lethal means and disengage moral self-sanctions so that they can gain public support for intervention with force and mount military campaigns that will necessarily inflict death and destruction.

For reasons given earlier, even when military interventions meet the moral standards for a justifiable war, a nation has to invest its military campaign with moral purpose to mobilize public support. It must convince its citizens that intervention will prevent more harm than it causes. Knowing that its soldiers will experience firsthand the gory horrors of war, it must persuade them of the morality of their mission, relieve them of responsibility for the effects of military operations over which they have no control, dehumanize their foes, and fault them for the suffering and deaths of innocent civilians. The sections that follow analyze how the United States managed these various moral issues in the war on terror and the Iraq war.

Mounting a counterterrorist military campaign requires a moral persuasion campaign through the mass media on the nature of and justification for the military intervention. M. Brewster Smith (2002) provides a thoughtful analysis of the Bush administration's metaphoric labeling of its retaliatory countermeasures as the "War on Terrorism." War metaphors create a mind-set for war that helps to mobilize patriotic public support for military actions. Actual wars involve battles between nation-states, usually with one of them getting the better of it in the end. In contrast, al Qaeda is decentralized, a loosely interconnected network operating surreptitiously worldwide without a clear structure and extending its reach by coordinating the activities of its dispersed affiliates. It is a new type of global enemy that is mobile, has no fixed geographic boundaries. It cannot be eradicated by eliminating its leader. Suicidal terrorism, which it exalted as an act of martyrdom, has become one of its most uncontrollable weapons.

Al Qaeda's geographical dispersion and mobility preclude a conventional end to a military strike, because dismantling a terrorist operation in a particular locale does not eliminate the threat elsewhere. For example, with porous borders and proxy ground forces of suspect allegiance, the massive military campaign in Afghanistan relocated, rather than eradicating, the core al Qaeda leadership. Although weakened with the killing of bin Laden and some of the top officials, al Qaeda has continued to operate as an insurgent force, spreading terrorism worldwide against an expanding range of Western foes. In addition to selecting targets of high symbolic and economic value, al Qaeda has broadened its aim, arousing international fear as its agents hit easily accessible targets that were neither predictable nor protectable. With globally dispersed semiautonomous terrorist cells and ample replacement recruits for captured or slain operatives, this was not a readily defeatable foe. Recurrent terrorist attacks heightened sociopolitical pressures to deploy electronic tracking systems for large-scale domestic and international surveillance.

Moral and Social Justification

The justification for going to war with Iraq took varied forms. The initial justification was that Saddam Hussein had stockpiled biological and chemical weapons of mass destruction (WMD) and was building a nuclear bomb.

Condoleezza Rice, then president George W. Bush's national security advisor, sounded the alarm: "The problem here is that there will always be some uncertainty about how quickly he can acquire nuclear weapons. But we don't want the smoking gun to be a mushroom cloud" (Blitzer, 2002).

The chief weapons inspectors in Iraq, Hans Blix and Mohamed ElBaradei of the International Atomic Energy Agency, could find no "smoking guns," either chemical or nuclear. Some strong advocates of a military invasion continued to cling to the belief that President Saddam Hussein of Iraq possessed lethal weapons but had hidden them, so it might take a long time to find them. A companion justification was that the September 11 attacks were supposedly linked to Saddam, whom President Bush called "the guy that wanted to kill my dad" (Kinzer, 2006). The administration pressured its national security staff to search for evidence that would implicate Saddam. No credible evidence that he had a hand in the terrorist attack could be found. In reflecting on the rightness of going to war with Iraq, Richard Clarke, the administration's chief counterterrorism specialist, remarked to Secretary of State Colin Powell, "Having been attacked by Al Qaeda, for us now to go bombing Iraq in response would be like our invading Mexico after the Japanese attack at Pearl Harbor" (Kinzer, 2006).

The erroneous claim that Saddam was allied with al Qaeda and suggestions that he had a hand in the September 11 terrorist attacks added urgency to calls for immediate military intervention to destroy his lethal weapons and dismantle his nuclear capabilities. In a forceful speech to the UN Security Council, Secretary of State Colin Powell presented richly documented proof, including aerial photographs and even a vial that could have been used for anthrax, that Saddam possessed lethal weapons and was building a nuclear bomb. Much to Powell's later chagrin, his entire case was founded on faulty intelligence (Jehl & Sanger, 2004). The British prime minister, Tony Blair, who was bent on ousting Saddam for "regime change," later asserted that the evidence then available that Saddam possessed weapons of mass destruction was "beyond doubt" (Smith, 2005). His certainty was based on a "sexed-up" dossier rife with disputable and faulty information (MacAskill & Norton-Taylor, 2003). On the U.S. side, CIA director George Tenet confidently reported, in an athletic metaphor that became his legacy, that the case against Saddam was a "slam-dunk" (Leibovich, 2004).

Deputy defense secretary Paul Wolfowitz was one of the hawkish architects of the Iraq war. In an uncharacteristically frank interview with *Vanity Fair*, he explained that weapons of mass destruction were selected as the major justification for going to war with Iraq for bureaucratic reasons: "The truth is that for reasons that have a lot to do with the US government bureaucracy, we settled on the one issue that everyone could agree on, which was weapons of mass destruction as the core reason." (After the publication of the article in *Vanity Fair*, the Pentagon stated that the quote was taken out of context and posted the complete transcript of the interview online; Wolfowitz, 2003; Deputy Secretary Wolfowitz interview, 2003.) With regime change per se a hard sell—and a violation of international law—the alleged imminent grave threat of lethal weapons in Saddam's hands became the reason for preemptive military action. The Bush administration having made the decision to oust Saddam, the intelligence and the facts were shaped to justify it.

When this initial rationale for the Iraq war was discredited, the administration presented another justification. This involved protecting human rights and promoting regional democratization. Administration policy makers, including President Bush, and many influential media pundits now championed military action as a humanitarian mission that would free the long-suffering Iraqis from Saddam's brutal, tyrannical rule. In this scenario, military intervention would establish a model of secular democracy that would spread to other Middle Eastern countries ruled by authoritarian regimes and pacify the region (Murphy, 2011). Some prominent liberal intellectuals, dubbed "humanitarian hawks," also became advocates of military intervention, citing the 1999 invasion of Bosnia as evidence that military power could be used for humanitarian ends (Packer, 2002).

Secretary of Defense Donald Rumsfeld firmly believed that with the use of advanced surveillance systems, remote-controlled armed drones, and other military technologies, Saddam's military could be defeated with relatively few ground forces. Paul Wolfowitz painted a rosy scenario for the proposed humanitarian military campaign (Packer, 2002). Just weeks before the invasion began, Vice President Dick Cheney, appearing on NBC's *Meet the Press*, claimed that American forces would be "greeted as liberators" (Interview with Vice-President, 2003). Rumsfeld and Wolfowitz claimed that Iraqi oil would pay for rebuilding the war-torn country (Murphy, 2011). Limited combat forces would be sufficient to bring down Saddam's regime. Rumsfeld and Wolfowitz dismissed the estimate by Army Chief of Staff General Eric K. Shinseki that several hundred thousand troops would be needed for the postwar occupation (Schmitt, 2003). Using what one writer referred to as the "Pottery Barn" rule (which the real Pottery Barn disavowed), Secretary of State Colin Powell also warned that "once you break it, you are going to own it" (Ideas and Consequences, 2007). Shinseki's unwelcome scenario became reality (Shanker, 2007).

All too often, foreign-policy disasters are the product of groupthink (Janis, 1972). In this group decision-making process, conformity pressures prevent the airing and critical evaluation of alternative courses of action. The voices of dissent are either weeded out or silenced by self-censorship of doubt by social pressure for consensus. Groupthink also taints decisions by biasing the sources that are selected, the type of information that is gathered and how it is interpreted. Both the Bush and Blair administrations politicized the intelligence agencies and pressed for information that would justify the invasion of Iraq (Risen, 2003; Tyler, 2004).

Groupthink theory focuses heavily on the psychological processes that bias decision making in insular groups. However, the makeup of the advisors in the inner circle also is a factor in causing bias. Government advisors usually have had previous successful careers in academia or the corporate world, sometimes with stints in various governmental bureaucracies. But they rarely have any battlefield experience and often inadequately understand the culture in which they are intervening. Great achievements build a strong sense of personal efficacy. However, in a new context, inadequate assessment of the challenges and risks of interventions can foster overconfident judgments regarding how easily desired sociopolitical changes can be achieved (Bandura, 1997). White's (1998) revision of groupthink theory underscores the role of advisors' faulty collective efficacy in foreign military fiascoes. In his book *The Best and Brightest,* David Halberstam (1972) recounts a conversation between Vice President Lyndon Johnson and House Speaker Sam Rayburn. Johnson described the brilliance of President John F. Kennedy's advisors, who later presided over the disastrous escalation of the Vietnam War. "You may be right, and they may be every bit as intelligent as you say," Rayburn replied, "but I'd feel a whole lot better about them if just one of them had run for sheriff once." Halberstam cites Rayburn's concern about the advisors' lack of appropriate experience as the difference between intelligence and wisdom gained through hard-won experience.

Given the death and destruction wrought by war, policy makers and their advisors have to find moral justification for a war for their own wellbeing, to enlist public support for it, and to enable soldiers to do the fighting. Military actions, whether successful or not, usually are launched with a tenacious belief in the rightness of the cause. In the case of Iraq, opponents of the Bush administration's policies argued that the underlying reason for overthrowing Saddam was to gain some measure of control over the country's huge oil industry. The resulting increased leverage could be used to obtain highly profitable oil leases for Western companies, influence oil prices, and help stabilize global oil supplies needed to power the West's high-energy-dependent economies and lifestyles. Anthony Cordesman, a senior analyst at the Center for Strategic and International Studies, characterized oil as the covert agenda: "Regardless of whether we say so publicly, we will go to war, because Saddam sits at the center of a region with more than 60% of all the world's oil reserves" (Scott, 2007). Allied countries were subtly informed that failure to support regime change would shut out their oil companies from gaining access to Iraq's oil reserves (Scott, 2007). Alan Greenspan, the former head of the Federal Reserve Bank, also spoke the unspeakable: "I am saddened that it is politically inconvenient to acknowledge what everyone knows: the Iraq war is largely about oil" (Greenspan, 2007). For someone known for his "oracular obscurity," this was an uncharacteristically clear, unequivocally bold statement. Were it not for oil, this region would have little that is vital to U.S. interests.

This major reason for invading Iraq is strongly supported in some quarters (Jones, 2012).

Osama bin Laden's terrorism against the United States also had an oil connection. Bin Laden was an ardent follower of the austere Wahhabi sect of Sunni Islam. He deeply resented the presence of U.S. military forces protecting oil reserves in Saudi Arabia—the location of Islam's two holiest places, Mecca and Medina—and the Saudi monarchy, whose legitimacy he challenged. He relocated to Sudan, where he set up training camps. Because of his activism, the Saudi regime stripped bin Laden of his citizenship and froze his assets in the kingdom. During a U.S. mission to bring famine-relief supplies to Somalia, bin Laden sent his followers to train the warlords whom the U.S. forces were trying to disarm. In this conflictual context, he declared a holy war against the United States: "It wants to occupy our countries, steal our resources, impose on us agents to rule us" (Zernike & Kaufman, 2011).

After the U.S. incursion in Afghanistan, the hunt for the elusive bin Laden and other leaders of al Qaeda became secondary to the preemptive military campaign in Iraq. The Bush administration's metaphoric war on terrorism was evolving into an actual counterinsurgency war. As we have seen, encouraged by conservative clergy, many Americans reflexively associated Islam with terrorism (Kristof, 2003). Some evangelicals believed that the only solution was to convert Muslims to Christianity (Goodstein, 2003). Leaders of the Christian Right believed that the invasion of Iraq qualified as a just war, because Saddam Hussein was threatening to use biological or even nuclear weapons (Goodstein, 2002).

Also as we have seen, some nations viewed the war on terrorism as a pretext for taking control of Iraq's vast petroleum reserves and ending the dominance of the Organization of the Petroleum Exporting Countries and its monopoly on oil prices (Banerjee, 2002). Critics viewed the diplomatic haggling with France and Russia over the UN resolution on inspection of Saddam's weapons arsenal and the threshold for waging war as partly driven by their established stake in the development of Iraq's lucrative oil (Henley, Younge, & Walsh, 2003). The Polish government also supported the invasion; shortly afterward, Poland's foreign minister expressed hope that Polish oil companies would gain access to oil reserves with the overthrow of the Saddam regime (Poland seeks, 2003). Osama bin Laden, who had been presumed dead, resurfaced on Al Jazeera to praise recent terrorist attacks, trumpet the evil intentions of the infidels poised to invade, and call "true Muslims" worldwide to action against the enemy (Whitaker, 2003).

Advantageous Comparison

The rightness of going to war with Iraq was further boosted with various advantageous comparisons. Gilovich (1981) demonstrated the importance of how military operations are framed when enlisting support for military interventions. For instance, in judging how the United States should respond to totalitarian threats against a small nation, people supported a more militaristic course of action when the international crisis was likened to another Munich, representing political appeasement of Nazi Germany, than when it was likened to another Vietnam, representing a military quagmire. President Bush designated three nations—Iran, Iraq, and North Korea—and "their terrorist allies" as the "axis of evil," deliberately invoking the term that described America's enemies of World War II to gain public support for the invasion of Iraq (Sanger, 2002). To bring the threat by comparative framing closer to home, Donald Rumsfeld likened the preemptive disarmament of Iraq to the Cuban missile crisis (Garamone, 2002). Condoleezza Rice also used the Hitler appeasement comparison to silence disputes between the United States and its allies on the UN Security Council about authorizing the use of military force against Iraq. She argued that it was "playing into the hands" of Saddam and compared it with the "appeasement" of Hitler (Bernstein & Weisman, 2003). As the Iraq war dragged on, in an address to a military audience on Independence Day, President Bush likened the war to the Patriots who fought for American independence from British rule: "Like those early patriots, you're fighting a new and unprecedented war—pledging your lives and honor to defend our freedom and way of life" (Rutenberg, 2007).

The comparative use of the war metaphor also supported restrictions on privacy rights and civil liberties in combating terrorists. Justification by advantageous historical comparison vindicated the restrictions. The public was reminded that Abraham Lincoln did this during the Civil War, and Franklin D. Roosevelt did so during World War II. When people feel threatened, concern for personal safety outweighs protection of privacy rights and civil liberties. Indeed, the public generally supported antiterrorism laws granting the government broad domestic surveillance powers to access, scan, and profile information on personal activities without public oversight and accountability (Langer, 2005).

In an atmosphere of heightened public fear, Congress quickly enacted and the president signed the Patriot Act, which was designed to intercept and disrupt terrorism. Its later reauthorization expanded the government's investigative power. In a later overreach of executive power, the federal government launched a massive surveillance program of foreigners abroad and of American citizens, to detect networks of suspicious terrorist activities (Schmitt, Sanger, & Savage, 2013). This electronic eavesdropping focused on patterns of associations in telephone calls and in online conversations, but not on the content of the interactions. The chief of staff to the former director of the CIA justified the massive scope of the surveillance program metaphorically: "If you're looking for a needle in a haystack, you need a haystack" (Schmitt et al., 2013). Edward Snowden, a staffer at a National Security Agency contractor, expressed shock at the immense surveillance and released secret documents about the program to the press (Greenwald, MacAskill, & Poitras, 2013).

Law-abiding citizens were taken aback to find themselves in the secret dragnet. They were especially upset to learn that federal intelligence agencies were requesting information about user accounts from the very communications companies through which they carried out their everyday transactions. Lawmakers who had speeded passage of the Patriot Act and its renewals were surprised by the scope of the surveillance and anxious about its political fallout. In defense, the Obama administration used the comparative justification that all other nations are doing it, and some are even sharing their information (Greenwald, Poitras, & MacAskill, 2013; Roberts & Ackerman, 2013). Foreign countries condemned electronic surveillance of conversations among their residents (Germany, Brazil to propose, 2013).

Within the United States, there were calls to limit the surveillance program to suspected terrorists, debates about how much the public should know about government programs designed to abort terrorist attacks, challenges to the constitutionality of secret unchecked judicial supervision, and recognition of the need to strengthen governmental and judicial oversight.

Facing a charge of violating the Espionage Act and theft of government property, Snowden fled the country seeking asylum elsewhere. In tests of its lawfulness, a federal appeals court ruled as illegal extension of the Patriot Act to bulk collection of domestic phone and e-mail records (Savage & Weisman, 2015). Opponents demanded evidence that the mass surveillance made the nation safer (Schwartz, 2015). The United States continues to be a target of terrorist attacks but largely has been spared tragic consequences by the incompetence of most of the terrorists carrying out the plots. As we have seen, these attacks involved two would-be suicide bombers on planes headed for Detroit and Florida and a botched attempt on New York's Times Square. All these attempts failed because the terrorists were unable to detonate the explosives. The tragic completed attack at the Boston Marathon killed three and maimed dozens more. The massive surveillance program did not detect these plots.

Forms and sources of terrorism continue to evolve. Through his popular blog Anwar al-Awlaki, a firebrand radicalizer who was assassinated by a drone strike, urged American extremists to mount terrorist strikes from within, as were the Boston and Times Square attacks. A rise in home-grown terrorism would heighten pressure for increased domestic surveillance to counter the threat. The dragnet approach needs to be seriously evaluated for evidence that it has detected and aborted terrorist attacks and analyzed for why even the unsuccessful plots were missed. The NSA claimed that it had foiled over 50 such plots (Nakashima, 2013). The mass surveillance approach will be reined in legislatively and legally. Whatever form the new version takes, it should strike the right balance between civil liberties and national security.

One must distinguish between justification of self-defense by military means and justification of the military means used in that self-defense.

Routing al Qaeda from its sanctuaries in Afghanistan and overthrowing its host, the oppressive Taliban regime, were justifiable in terms of some of the just war standards. U.S. armed forces achieved it with remarkable swiftness with unrelenting aerial bombardment and a proxy army of Afghan warlords—although Osama bin Laden himself escaped to Pakistan (Lister, 2011). Many of the international reactions, especially in Muslim societies, centered on the massive military means, the civilian toll, and the rightness of intention in the expansion of the war on terror to Iraq. As we have seen, the way in which force was wielded and used for geopolitical purposes violated a number of just war principles.

Drawing on historical contrast, Donald Rumsfeld acknowledged the inevitability of civilian casualties but added, "We can take comfort in the knowledge that this war has seen fewer tragic losses of civilian life than perhaps any war in modern history" (Shanker, 2002). General Tommy Franks, the commander of the U.S. Central Command, downplayed reports of civilian casualties in Afghanistan on the grounds that they were impossible to estimate reliably: "And so all of us have opted not to do that" (Lehrer, 2002). When questioned about the number of Iraqi soldiers killed, he replied, "We don't do body counts" (Broder, 2003). In the public view, precision-guided weapons spared the innocent. Rumsfeld also minimized the physical abuse and humiliation in Abu Ghraib prison by contrasting the abuses with beheadings: "Does it rank up there with chopping off someone's head off on television? It doesn't. It doesn't. Was it done as a matter of policy? No" (Lumpkin, 2004).

The administration also enlisted exonerative comparison to fend off criticism of its failure to follow up on specific warnings that al Qaeda was planning a major terrorist attack on U.S. soil. In addition, instructors at some flying schools warned the FBI that suspect Arabs enrolled in flying schools—later identified as the September 11 suicide pilots—were pressing for instruction on flying jumbo airliners. When asked whether the terrorist attack could have been averted, Rumsfeld replied with exonerative comparison that the United States could not predict the Japanese attack on Pearl Harbor (Beschloss, 2011).

Televised scenes of Afghans celebrating their liberation from the brutally tyrannical Taliban regime documented the humanitarian aspect of the military campaign. U.S. and allied forces suffered few casualties, providing mainly aerial surveillance and tactical bombardment while native proxy ground forces did the fighting, with seemingly minimal "collateral damage." The swift, successful outcome persuaded even vocal critics that military force could serve as a humanitarian intervention.

In 1995, NATO's tactical aerial bombardment had worked surprisingly well in Bosnia. Here was a model of warfare that the general public could support without moral qualms. Bosnia became the operative military model for the times (Packer, 2002). Overthrowing the autocratic regime in Bosnia with a finite military operation did not incite a worldwide Serbian network to terrorize the United States and its allies. In contrast, routing al Qaeda from Afghanistan only relocated the terrorist network, resulting in an open-ended battle with Islamic extremists operating worldwide in what they regard as a holy war. Bosnian military forces were unified and well equipped for fighting an effective ground war against NATO ground forces and air cover. In contrast, Iraq was split into contentious Sunni, Shiite, and Kurdish factions, all vying for control. Arming the factions to fight against a common foe risked turning them into sectarian militias fighting each other.

In the end, the Bosnian military model, which depended on unified ground forces, was unsuited to the sectarian dissension in Iraq. Overthrowing Saddam's regime unleashed ethnic conflicts held in check by his autocratic rule. The allied forces, caught in the middle of a civil conflict among Sunnis, Shiites, and Kurds, ended up fighting insurgents during years of occupation, rebuilding battered service facilities, and pressuring the contentious factions to form a functional government. With the departure of allied forces, fighting among various sectarian groups renewed (Ghazi & Arango, 2014).

The sorrowful American experience in Vietnam resulted in low tolerance for a protracted war with ever-increasing casualties and ever-eroding public support. As a consequence, military doctrine favored "overwhelming force" to get the job done fast. The military doctrine of rapid dominance, dubbed "shock and awe," was designed not only to inflict massive physical destruction but to annihilate the enemy's will to fight. In Iraq, shock and awe took the form of a "decapitation strategy" of unrelenting midnight aerial bombardment against Saddam and his top military leaders. Depending on how this doctrine is executed, it may be hard to square with the discriminative targeting, proportionality, and casualty standards of morally justifiable war.

The utilitarian standard provided justification for armed intervention in Iraq as an eventual necessity, even if the United States acted alone. Proponents of this justification argued that a preemptive strike would prevent a projected massive future threat to humanity. The public was reminded that Saddam was a monstrous despot who terrorized and gassed his own people and who had invaded a neighbor state (Kuwait). The United States was in a weak position to assert moral authority because it had been a strong supporter of Saddam during the Iran-Iraq war of the 1980s, providing him military intelligence and arms even though he was abusing his own people. Although he had been militarily contained and had no ties to al Qaeda, the U.S. administration portrayed him as a grave threat. Advocates of military intervention argued that, in defiance of UN restrictions, he not only had obstructed arms inspections but also was producing chemical and biological weapons that he might pass on to organized or freelancing terrorists. Moreover, his efforts to create nuclear weapons posed an even graver international threat. The utilitarian justification presented stark alternatives:

inflict limited preemptive harm now or witness massive human destruction later by a despot with nuclear weapons. The projected human threat was personalized, immense, and pervasive because a "dirty" bomb (combining conventional explosives with radioactive dispersants) could be smuggled into any city and detonated. No one was safe any longer from a nuclear strike. The clear choice in this humanitarian crisis: responsible preventive military offensive or international timidity. In the bleak contrast of dichotomous options frightened people are willing to forfeit privacy for safety. They also give low priority to moral considerations and potential international repercussions.

Some observers vigorously contested the utilitarian benefits of a military campaign against Iraq (Kaysen, Miller, Malin, Nordhaus, & Steinbruner, 2002). The U.S. administration depicted the outcomes in predominantly positive terms—removal of a horrific regional threat of mass destruction, democratization of a despotic regime, and liberation of its terrorized people. Detractors argued that the administration mischaracterized the planned intervention as a "preemptive" war to disarm and supplant a regime whose power to wage war actually was constrained by inadequate military forces and by severe economic sanctions. After the first Gulf war of 1991, Saddam was boxed in by no-fly zones in the northern Kurdish region and the southern Shiite region, with continuous aerial surveillance by American, British, and French war planes and bombardment of any defense and communication facilities that fired on those planes. Some nations questioned the U.S. administration's justification of the priority of the threat and the timing of a preemptive strike against Iraq, which did not seem to pose much of a threat under such stringent containment. They lobbied for inspecting and dismantling weapons of mass destruction and their production facilities under the UN charter and auspices rather than armed invasion with a troublesome aftermath of uncertain scope, magnitude, and duration. Extending the no-fly zone over the rest of Iraq and imposing a strict embargo on imports would place severe constraints on what Saddam's military could do. War, in their view, was not the option of last resort.

Critics enumerated a host of potentially disastrous consequences of military intervention (Kaysen et al., 2002). It would inflame the wrath of the Muslim world; derail global efforts to eradicate terrorism spawned by the al Qaeda network and other Islamic terrorist groups; expand the ranks of ultra-conservative Islamists and undermine the efforts of modernists and reformers working toward Islamic pluralism; unleash ethnic warfare on the Middle East; damage relationships and partnerships with allies in the region; subvert international laws that protect the rights of nations and ensure the equitable application of laws; undermine the United States' moral position as a force for good by violating its own values; and burden the United States with staggering long-term costs of warfare, occupation, peacekeeping and national reconstruction. The U.S. administration countered these sobering predictions with a more optimistic consequential scenario: (1) Saddam rules through fear, not loyalty; (2) an invasion will bring a quick end to his terrifying reign; and (3) rapid military success will turn detractors and private approvers into appreciative public supporters of the democratization of the region.

The Iraqi regime, depicted as posing an imminent grave biochemical threat to international security, conspiring with terrorists, and poised to unleash weapons of mass destruction if attacked, was speedily routed, proving to be an enemy of disorganized and rogue combatants rather than a mighty military machine. Geopolitical disputes arose over who should preside over and reap lucrative contracts for the nation's reconstruction. With Saddam's removal, the power vacuum in this deeply fissured, multireligious nation was quickly filled by exiles with political ambitions, ethnic separatists, and clerics jockeying for power to turn a pluralistic, secular country into an Islamic theocracy. The sociopolitical war presented more daunting challenges than did the military one.

Sanitizing the Gore of War Euphemistically

The initial foray into sanitizing the Iraq war turned out to be a linguistic fiasco. The U.S. administration labeled the war on terrorism as a "crusade" fought under the code name Infinite Justice. Because of the incendiary historical connotation, labeling the invasion a crusade was the worst possible choice. Translated into Arabic, "infinite justice" suggested the trumping of Allah. This ill-judged metaphor inflamed Islamic fundamentalists. The military invasion was renamed Operation Iraqi Freedom.

The Iraq war spawned a whole new vocabulary of camouflage. Here is a brief sampling from one website featuring euphemisms the U.S. administration used to characterize military actions in Iraq (What is a euphemism? n.d.). Understandably, most of them are intended to neutralize killing. For example, "extreme prejudice" meant killing without any qualms. "Dead checking" meant killing all wounded men in a house suspected of harboring insurgents. "Friendly fire," the former term for accidentally killing one's fellow soldiers, was renamed in Iraq as "blue on blue." "Clean bombing" meant bombing with absolute accuracy.

Another set of sanitizers had to do with military operations. An "operational pause" occurred when a military mission bogged down. With irony, war was called "assertive disarmament." Weapons were "assets." Pinpoint bombing was "discriminative deterrence." A "hunter-killer team" or "special mission unit" was a military assassination squad. Individuals contracted out by private companies as security guards and armed escorts were called "mercenaries" by the soldiers but "civilian contractors" or "private military contractors" by the military establishment (McKenna & Johnson, 2012). Their employment was called "greenbacking" (What is a euphemism? n.d.).

Euphemisms were widely used to sanitize the horror of torture. The CIA relied heavily on outsourced torturers who used some of the most brutal methods under the sanitized label "enhanced interrogation." These inhumane practices included shackling prisoners, naked and diapered, to the ceiling for hours on end; repeated simulated drownings by waterboarding; prolonged sleep deprivation; locking prisoners in coffin-sized boxes; shackling prisoners in stress positions for days; rectal feeding of pureed foods; and rectal rehydration for refusing food and water (Laughland, 2014). Imprisonment without charges was "protective custody." Suspected terrorists held as unregistered prisoners outsourced abroad to secret detention centers were "ghost detainees." Suspected detainees held at Guantánamo were "unlawful combatants."

These brutal practices were justified using the ticking time bomb metaphor. In this scenario an individual knows the location of a ticking time bomb that will kill countless people when it explodes. The utilitarian justification condones torturing the person to get the location, because it saves the lives of many. In a correlated justification, the CIA claimed that torture worked, allegedly enabling the CIA to abort terrorist plots and to capture of al Qaeda officials (Rose, 2008).

As another casualty on the war on terrorism, the American Psychological Association (APA) got itself embroiled in legitimizing psychologists' participation in abusive military interrogations euphemistically called "harsh interrogation." Its code of ethics prohibits psychologists from participating directly or indirectly in any forms of cruel, degrading, and inhuman practices. However, some APA officers and leaders violated the association's humanistic core values and ethical mandate (Risen, 2015a). In the aftermath of the 9/11 terrorist attack, detainees were forcefully interrogated for actionable information to avoid future attacks. As previously noted, the Bush administration legally legitimized use of abusive forms of interrogation as not constituting torture by their narrow definition of torture. If it could be shown that the practices were also safe because they were monitored by health professionals, it would further legitimize their use and provide cover for authorizers of abusive methods and interrogators who implement them (Hoffman et al., 2015). It was also necessary to construe the methods as safe and not torture to evade international laws banning torture. The American Medical and Psychiatric Associations refused to participate in the interrogation program because it violated their ethical standards. The APA ended up providing the certification of safety.

The APA convened a special task force, led by Stephen Behnke, director of the ethics office, to examine whether psychologists could ethically play the interrogatory role (Risen, 2015a). However, the task force was heavily stacked with Department of Defense (DoD) personnel interested in crafting an ethics code that placed no additional constraints on the DoD interrogation practices. In a weekend meeting, one of the few nonmilitary psychologists in the task force felt as though she was in a charade with a prearranged outcome (Hajjar, 2015). Based on this brief meeting, the group issued a report declaring that psychologists play a valuable and ethical role in training and advising interrogators. The APA altered its code of ethics, stating that psychologists have a dual ethical obligation—to refrain from inflicting harm on others and to protect the security of the nation. The latter addition to the code of ethics provided honorable justification in the name of national security for psychologists to participate in military interrogations. The APA board of directors declared an emergency meeting where they approved the report as official policy and then expedited its publication. The purpose for the hasty publication was to use it as an antitorture public relations statement in anticipation of a *New Yorker* article about to be published on the interrogation program.

Some psychologists on the CIA advisory committee added their voice in support of an interrogation role for psychologists (Hoffman et al., 2015). Adopting a situationist view of ethics, Melvin Gravitz explained to the CIA that a code of ethics must be used flexibly depending on circumstances. He invoked the national obligation justification for involving psychologists in military interrogations. A former APA president reassured the CIA that prolonged sleep deprivation is not torture.

Two former military psychologists, James E. Mitchell and Joseph Jessen, who were not members of the APA, had served in an air force simulated program that trained military personnel how to resist and endure torture if captured. They also served as consultants to the CIA advisory committee. Although they lacked experience in interrogating detainees, the CIA outsourced to them, with a multimillion-dollar contract, the task of designing and implementing the interrogation program at Guantánamo and overseas facilities. They also served as liaisons between the CIA and foreign intelligence agencies. Mitchell and Jessen also personally conducted interrogations using abusive methods on "high value" detainees (Dilanian, 2014). Mitchell minimized the brutality of the practices by advantageous comparisons. "It's a lot more humane, even if you are going to subject them to harsh techniques, to question them while they are still alive," he argued, "than it is to kill them and their children and their neighbors with a drone" (Dilanian, 2014).

Some members of the APA protested the association's support of psychologists' involvement in abusive military interrogation. They were disparaged as "bullies" and "antimilitary dissidents." Their allegations were dismissed by the APA as baseless, false, and inflammatory (Boyd, 2015; Hoffman et al., 2015). The Senate Intelligence Committee released a scathing report saying that the abuses in CIA detention and interrogation programs were much worse than presented to policy makers, were ineffective in eliciting accurate actionable information, and damaged the U.S. standing in the world. Mitchell and Jessen were named as contractors for the interrogation program (Senate Select Committee on Intelligence, 2014). The international outrage to the graphic images of prisoner abuse at Abu Ghraib served as the backdrop for the disturbing revelations of abuse.

After years of denial, in response to the Senate report that Mitchell and Jessen were architects of the interrogation program, the APA board of directors commissioned a former federal prosecutor David Hoffman to investigate the allegations. If the board expected the investigation to show the allegations were baseless, they were in for a jarring report documenting disturbing organizational practices. Hoffman issued a highly critical report of collusion and compromise of ethical standards to fit the needs of the DoD and the CIA. As he summarized it, "APA chose its ethics policy based on its goals of helping DoD managing its PR [public relations], and maximizing the growth of profession" (Hoffman et al., 2015). The report described a variety of incentives for currying favor with the DoD. It is one of the largest employers of psychologists. It funds research grants and contracts and underwrites conferences. It also supported a demonstration project testing the feasibility of granting psychologists prescription privileges.

Speaking on behalf of the APA, President Nadine Kaslow attributed the collusion in changing the code of ethics mainly to organizational failings in oversight. "Our internal checks and balances failed to detect the collusion, or properly acknowledge a significant conflict of interest, nor did they provide meaningful field guidance for psychologists" (American Psychological Association, 2015). The misleading mea culpa conveys the impression that a few rogue lower-ranking officials operating under faulty radar autonomously changed the APA code of ethics. The undetected "bad apples" exoneration was implausible because senior staff members and leaders presided over the ethics revision and its expedited adoption as official policy. Collective willful blindness weakens or eliminates moral restraints over detrimental practices. APA officials displayed an exceptional lack of curiosity about what psychologists were doing in detention centers. They took no steps to find out. As described in the Hoffman Report, they "intentionally avoided seeking more information in the face of substantial indications of psychologist involvement in abuses at Guantanamo" (Hoffman et al., 2015).

Regarding another part of the linguistically nebulous statement, it is not that the APA failed to "provide meaningful field guidance." The policy change explicitly permitted psychologists to participate in military interrogations. The original APA code of ethics would have prohibited psychologists from being in the military interrogation field to begin with. The policy change involved more than simply an oversight lapse in APA governance. The board of directors, that included a president and vice-president, played an active role in selecting the task force stacked with DoD personnel. Some APA officers also sat in on the deliberations. The phony claim of collective organizational blindness has no basis in fact. The biased task force was created designedly not unintentionally and unknowingly. Freed from having to speak for the APA, Nadine Kaslow led the fight for a stringent code of ethics (Risen, 2015b).

APA took swift action to restore its credibility and commitment to the humanistic core values of the psychology profession. The chief executive officer retired, several top officials resigned, and Ethics Director Stephen Behnke, who played a key role in the behind the scenes collusion with the DoD, was fired. APA overwhelming approved a stringent code of ethics that banned psychologists from participating not only in harsh interrogations but in noncoversive interrogations as well (Risen, 2015b).

The massive report by the Senate Select Committee on Intelligence (2014) documented that in no case did torture yield unique information as the CIA claimed. Rather, other agencies obtained actionable knowledge through nonabusive methods before the CIA tortured detainees. The Senate committee also dismissed the CIA claim that it found bin Laden through torture as "inaccurate and incongruent with CIA records" (Savage & Risen, 2014). Although admitting mistakes, James Clapper, the director of national intelligence, defended the implementers of the brutal CIA program (Ackerman, Rushe, & Borger, 2014). He described them as doing their duty: "The officers who participated in the program believed with certainty that they were engaged in a program devised by our government on behalf of the president that was necessary to protect the nation, that had appropriate legal authorization, and that was sanctioned by at least some in the Congress" (Ackerman et al., 2014). The morality of the inhumane practices was lost in the defense of their legality.

In a rare news conference, the new director of the CIA, John O. Brennan, acknowledged that some CIA officers used unauthorized methods, but otherwise, the interrogators were "patriots" (Mazzetti & Apuzzo, 2014). During the news conference, Brennan referred to "E.I.Ts," shorthand for the euphemistic term *enhanced interrogation techniques*. He never used the word *torture* in response to questions. Brennan argued that, contrary to the Senate report, the harsh methods were useful, but their effects were "unknowable" (Mazzetti & Apuzzo, 2014).

Neither the concoctors of the brutal methods nor the higher-level officials who authorized their use were held accountable for the program, which they carried out in the name of national security. In a height of irony, George Tenet, who had presided over the CIA and had asserted that Iraq had weapons of mass destruction, was awarded the Presidential Medal of Freedom by President George W. Bush.

Displacement and Diffusion of Responsibility

The exercise of moral responsibility requires clearly designated rules of behavior, unambiguousness about the authorizers, and sanctions for violating rules. An evident system of accountability provides a basis for judging how well individuals are discharging their duties and whether they are breaking any rules. In the aftermath of the September 11 attacks, conflicts arose among some counterterrorist practices, moral principles, and international laws. The U.S. administration believed that painful interrogation procedures would force detainees to divulge valuable information about al Qaeda operations. The war on terror generated a strong incentive to justify such practices as legally defensible and vital to safeguarding national security against an ominous threat.

The challenge was to make the infliction of severe pain morally acceptable so that interrogators could do it, socially acceptable to provide institutional and popular support for it, and internationally defensible to protect authorizers against legal suits by the World Court. Lawyers in the Departments of Justice and Defense as well as at the Pentagon prepared documents that essentially legalized torturous practices. They further declared that the president, as commander in chief, was not bound by federal or international laws in the effort to protect the nation. In his memo, widely regarded as outrageous, Jay S. Bybee of the Office of Legal Counsel in the Justice Department defined torture in the narrowest terms as "inflicting intense pain or suffering of that kind that is equivalent to the pain that would be associated with serious injury so severe that death, organ failure, or permanent damage resulting in a loss of significant bodily functions will likely result" (Novkov, 2013). This definition of torture only as extreme injury placed virtually no limits on the use of severe physical and psychological methods of interrogation short of organ failure or death, essentially legitimizing torturous practices. This made interrogators immune from punishment for using such practices on the grounds that they were following orders from officials higher up in the chain of command.

Another problem remained: how to circumvent the Geneva Conventions, which ban torture and maltreatment of prisoners. Professor John Yoo (2004), a former deputy assistant attorney general in the Justice Department's Office of Legal Counsel, declared that al Qaeda and the Taliban were a new type of enemy in disguise that, unlike conventional armies, intentionally attacked civilians. An especially consequential decision was the labeling of detainees as "unlawful combatants" rather than prisoners of war. Yoo (2003) argued that the Geneva Conventions did not protect them. As we saw in chapter 2, White House counsel Alberto Gonzales (2005) the Conventions "quaint" and "rendered obsolete" by the war on terror. As further immunity for interrogators, administration lawyers decided that they could not be tried for crimes on the basis of the federal War Crimes Act because they were seeking information, not acting on intent to cause lasting harm. Nor were they subject to federal war crimes charges because the Guantánamo facility was not part of the United States. These memos, laying the legal foundation for torture in intricate legalese, were accepted by Attorney General John Ashcroft, who later rescinded them (Associated Press, 2008). In testimony at a congressional hearing, Ashcroft refused to answer questions about interrogation policies and practices on the grounds of executive privilege and protecting information vital to national security (Shapiro, 2008). The torture policy was eventually revoked, but the torturous practices continued.

As we saw in chapter 2, Donald Rumsfeld issued changing lists of harsh interrogation methods, with instructions U.S. agents to "take the gloves off" while interrogating John Walker Lindh, the "American Taliban" (Serrano, 2004). In a handwritten note on a memo regarding interrogation methods at Guantánamo, Rumsfeld, who worked at a standing desk, called for increasing the intensity of the already harsh practices: "I stand for 8–10 hours a day. Why is standing limited to 4 hours?" (Jehl, 2004). Lieutenant General Ricardo Sanchez, in charge of the allied forces in Iraq, sent mixed messages on the types of interrogation methods that were permissible (Smith & White, 2004). Abuses arose after Major General Geoffrey Miller, commander of the Guantánamo detention camp, visited Abu Ghraib and recommended that military intelligence officers be in charge of the prison (Iraq abuse, 2004).

In addition, responsibility for torturous interrogation practices was displaced by outsourcing them to proxy agents. Abducted foreign suspects were shipped for interrogation to overseas countries that torture detainees. As one intelligence official put it: "We don't kick the shit out of them. We send them to other countries so they can kick the shit out of them" (Cosgrove-Mather, 2004). This brutal policy, carried out by proxy torturers, was cloaked in an innocuous name, "extraordinary rendition."

Diffused and disarrayed authorizations of abusive practices fostered a sense of nonresponsibility. Higher echelons pressured prison guards to "soften up" the detainees for the interrogators with rougher treatment. The interrogators from military intelligence (MI), the CIA, and the FBI became collective sanitizers and approved the abuse at Abu Ghraib prison under a shroud of anonymity. As we saw in chapter 2, Lynndie England, one of the prison guards, described the tacit and explicit sanctioning conditions: "But when you show the people from the CIA, the FBI and the MI the pictures and they say, "Hey, this is a great job. Keep it up," you think you must be right. They were all there and they didn't say a word. They didn't wear uniforms, and if they did they had their nametags covered" (Streck & Wiechmann, 2008).

The abuses occurred in a prison with all types of authorizers but no clear line of authority. These conditions created a climate of legitimization of torturous practices that incriminated no one. The graphic photos of abuse and humiliation at Abu Ghraib commanded worldwide attention, but the singular focus on Abu Ghraib made it easy to dismiss the abusive practices as isolated aberrations perpetrated by a few rogue guards who violated military rules. As the investigative report by the army's inspector general succinctly put it, "these abuses should be viewed as what they are—unauthorized actions taken by a few individuals" (White & Higham, 2004).

In his review of Mark Danner's book *Torture and Truth* and *The Abu Ghraib Investigations*, edited by Steven Strasser, Andrew Sullivan (2005) summarized the widespread use of the abusive practices: "They were everywhere: from Guantánamo Bay to Afghanistan, Baghdad, Basra, Ramadi and Tikrit and, for all we know, in any number of hidden jails affecting 'ghost detainees' kept from the purview of the Red Cross. They were committed by the Marines, the Army, and Military Police, Navy SEALs, reservists, Special Forces and on and on. The use of hooding was ubiquitous; the same goes for forced nudity, sexual humiliation and brutal beatings."

These systemwide abuses were carried out under confusing chains of command, justified in carefully crafted legalese and authorized with metaphors. Officials denied awareness of what was going on, absolving the upper echelon of any responsibility. Because administration officials blamed the problem on a few "bad apples," only guards did prison time. Many of the very officials who were the architects and enablers of the costly Iraq war and the resulting abusive practices received high national honors and career advancement.

Minimizing and Distorting Detrimental Effects

War takes a heavy toll on civilians, sanitized as "collateral damage." The trauma that war inflicts on children is especially heartbreaking because of their innocence and helplessness. In the Iraq war, sectarian violence also erupted with ceaseless bomb attacks.

Satellite broadcast technology heightened the war of words and imagery regarding "collateral damage." While the Western media were highlighting the humanitarian benefits of military force, the Qatar-based Al Jazeera Media Network was showing vivid images of the heavy civilian human toll of the military campaign in Afghanistan and Iraq, along with frequent images of carnage from the Israeli-Palestinian conflict. Al Jazeera expanded the scope of collateral damage to the disastrous aftermath of the military campaign, with huge displaced populations in squalid refugee camps left to fend for themselves for the basic necessities of life. Many of those with more means fled the country.

In applying the Bosnian military model in Afghanistan, the United States and its allies provided aerial surveillance and bombardment and committed a limited number of advisors and ground forces but otherwise relied on the Afghan warlords to do most of the ground fighting. The warlords also supplied some of the on-the-ground intelligence, some of it of questionable reliability. As tribal factions sought advantages in local power struggles, bombing runs wreaked havoc on villages and political rivals falsely depicted as Taliban adherents

The conflict in Afghanistan, which was the actual training and command center for al Qaeda, was downgraded by the diversionary war with Iraq.

The Afghan feuding warlords regained control over their fiefdoms. Some resumed the lucrative international heroin trade, and others even restored the medieval tyranny, especially toward women, that was the Taliban so brutally practiced. Generous payments to the warlords, allies of convenience, to fight the war and to hunt al Qaeda and its Taliban patrons nourished a state of anarchy.

Dehumanization

Most of the analysis of dehumanization in military contexts focuses on each side's need to portray its enemies as subhuman and bestial creatures to make it easier to kill them. Exterminating vermin arouses little guilt. Dehumanization also can foster degrading treatment of prisoners of war, as we have seen in the cases of Abu Ghraib and Guantánamo.

Dehumanization also operates at a broader social level. Among the reasons that Iraq veterans gave for opposing the war in Iraq was that it changed soldiers to the point where they began dehumanizing the Iraqi people (Hedges & Al-Arian, 2007). They did so by degrading and humiliating people at checkpoints, during raids on their homes, and in other aspects of their daily lives.

Dehumanization by the news media has even broader influence in shaping public policies and how foreigners are viewed. Steuter and Wills (2009) analyzed headlines in Canadian newspapers in their coverage of the Afghanistan and Iraq wars. For the most part, the media framed the war on terror as a battle between the barbaric East and the civilized West. The authors noted the stark contrast between the ideological dichotomy and the Canadian identity as respecting diversity, multiculturalism, and inclusiveness.

The newspaper portrayal of the Muslim enemy relied heavily on dehumanization in three metaphoric forms (Steuter & Wills, 2009). The first dehumanizing metaphor characterized the enemy in animalistic terms. The rat metaphor was the favorite one, perhaps because of the revulsive association it evokes. "Canadian soldiers mop up Taliban rat's nest in Afghanistan." "Captured: Saddam caught in hole 'just like a rat.'" "Terrorists, like rats and cockroaches, skulk in the dark." The second type of dehumanizing metaphor characterizes the enemy as a pernicious disease: "Only Muslim leaders can remove spreading cancer of Islamic terrorism." "Al Qaeda mutating like a virus." In the third dehumanizing metaphor, military actions designed to capture enemies are framed in animal-linked hunting metaphors. The enemy as "prey" is hunted, tracked down, snared, caged, and "kept on a short leash."

Dehumanization works both ways. As we have seen, Osama bin Laden used bestial dehumanization when he characterized Americans as "lowly people" committing acts that "the most ravenous of animals would not descend to." He launched his jihad to fight the "debauched" infidels who seek to enslave the Muslim world (Ludlow, 2001).

Although the present discussion concerns dehumanization, it should be noted that people have the capacity for humanization, even under trying military conditions that put morality on hold. One of the interviews with veterans of the war who turned against it shows the transformative power of humanization amid a spree of gunfire: "I'll tell you the point where I really turned. I go out to the scene and [there was] this little, you know, pudgy little 2-year-old child with the cute little pudgy legs, and I look and she has a bullet through her leg. . . . An IED [improvised explosive device] went off, the gun-happy soldiers started shooting everywhere and the baby got hit. And this baby looked at me, wasn't crying, wasn't anything. It just looked at me like—I know she couldn't speak. It might sound crazy, but she was asking me why. You know, why do I have a bullet in my leg? . . . This is—this is it. This is ridiculous" (Hedges & Al-Arian, 2007).

THE AFTERMATH

The United States responded to the terrorist attack on its soil with a massive military operation that continued for over a decade. It was ill suited for insurgency warfare against an elusive enemy moving across porous national borders. This prolonged military campaign took a huge toll on human lives, devastated communities and infrastructures that provide basic human services, and created a humanitarian crisis with millions of civilians fleeing to overwhelmed refugee camps. The nation was burdened with staggering debts, borrowing trillions of dollars to pay for the war in addition to operating national surveillance systems to detect terrorist plots. According to a report on the cost of the Iraq war by the Watson Institute for International Studies, "the United States gained little from the war while Iraq was traumatized by it. The war reinvigorated radical Islamist militants in the region. . . . [T]he $212 billion reconstruction effort was largely a failure with most of that money spent on security or lost to waste and fraud" (Trotta, 2013).

The prolonged war on terrorism did not make the nation feel any safer from terrorist attacks (Ekins, 2014). In the aftermath of the Iraq war only a small percent (14%) of the U.S. public believed that the war reduced the threat of terrorism. An overwhelming majority (83%) believed that it did not make the country any safer. Over a third (38%) believed that it increased the terrorist threat. Despite the killing of Osama bin Laden, the war on terrorism continues, with al Qaeda offshoots in Iraq, Syria, Pakistan, Yemen, and Somalia. The leader of the Syrian terrorist cell called the Khorasan group, who had been in bin Laden's inner circle, was plotting to blow up airlines with explosives in laptops and toothpaste undetectable by existing security systems (Baker, 2014). After his death in an airstrike, another terrorist cell in Syria called the al-Nusra Front declared a terrorist campaign against the United States.

These diverse endless threats have forced the U.S. government to maintain a high level of surveillance that conflicts with the American value of an open society. Prying into people's private lives also breeds societal distrust. Recurrent terrorist threats not only perpetuate mass surveillance but also have spawned a huge private security industry to which the government outsources security operations costing billions, with lax oversight and insufficient accountability (Risen, 2014). As the war on terrorism became deeply politicized and commercialized the term *terrorism* is is being used indiscriminately for all types of acts of violence.

After the attacks of September 11, Congress granted presidents the authority to take military action against al Qaeda sanctuaries, wherever they were. This legal authorization led to an expanding covert campaign using remote-controlled drones (Currier, 2013). Targeted killings of al Qaeda militants have been conducted from within the United States and from secret bases abroad in at least five countries. Legal justifications for the drone airstrikes argue that international law grants nations the right to self-defense and that al Qaeda militants pose an imminent threat to the nation. Opponents have criticized the use of drones because it is a covert operation with no oversight of the assessment of threat and the process by which individuals are judged to be plotting against the United States. The moral problem of civilian killings in drone strikes also has arisen.

Iraq Revisited

The departure of U.S. and allied forces left Iraq deeply divided along sectarian lines while struggling to create a representative government. After prolonged controversy Nouri al-Maliki, a highly divisive Shiite, was chosen to govern the nation. His discriminatory policies mistreated and essentially disenfranchised the Sunni minority. He further alienated them by arresting Sunni political leaders for terrorist activities. In retaliation, Sunni militants escalated their violence and suicide bombings against Shiite targets. Amnesty International charged the Shiite militia with abducting and killing Sunni civilians, which the militia justified on the grounds that they were terrorists. The Bush administration's vision that the overthrow of Saddam's repressive regime would result in a model of nation building that would democratize the Middle East collapsed in a large-scale humanitarian tragedy.

In an interview with Thomas Friedman (2014) President Obama succinctly summarized the strife in the aftermath. In Iraq a residual U.S. troop presence would never have been needed had the Shiite majority there not "squandered an opportunity" to share power with Sunnis and Kurds. "Had the Shia majority seized the opportunity to reach out to the Sunnis and the Kurds in a more effective way, [and not] passed legislation like de-Baath-ification," no outside troops would have been necessary. In the midst of this growing social unrest, a radical group of Sunni extremists, portraying themselves as Islamic jihadists and proclaiming the Islamic State in Iraq and Syria (ISIS), launched an offensive to establish a caliphate. With minimal resistance they quickly seized large regions straddling Iraq and Syria (Laub & Masters, 2014). They pursued their military campaign with barbaric zeal in God's name. After the defeat of the Ottoman empire in World War I, the French and British partitioned the Middle East into newly created coun-tries. The militants claimed that the region had been carved up to prevent the formation of an Islamic state. They portrayed their military campaign as directed at erasing the "Crusader partitions" and establishing a caliphate.

The self-styled ISIS rules by terror. They have forced conversions to their harsh version of Islam, massacred those who resisted them, beheaded captives and hostages, and used children, called "cubs of the caliphate," as fighters and suicide bombers. They have subjected women to brutal sexual violence, raping them, selling them as sex slaves with price tags to recruits, and forcing them into temporary serial marriages with fighters. Systematic rape of women is embedded in their perverted view of Islamic theology. A young escapee describes the religious ritual (Callimachi, 2015). After praying, "[h]e told me that according to Islam he is allowed to rape an unbe-liever." And by raping her "he is drawing closer to God." Sexual assaults become spiritual acts. ISIS uses religiously sanctioned sexual assault also as a recruitment tool. Christians and other religious minorities such as the Yazidis, who are persecuted as nonbelievers, their daughters forced into sex-ual slavery, have fled in huge numbers to escape the ethnic cleansing.

ISIS has expunged any moral self-sanctions against the most barbaric actions with supposed Quranic justifications for their atrocities. They con-strue attacks by their opponents as war against God. To crush any resistance to their ruthless rule, they staged public crucifixions (Spyer & al-Tamimi, 2014), citing passages from the Quran stating that crucifixion is an appro-priate punishment for those who "wage war on God and his messenger" (Spyer & al-Tamimi, 2014). Those "striving to cause corruption on earth" also deserve to be crucified. They have cited passages in which "Moham-med [sic], when faced with treachery, ordered that the perpetrators have their hands and feet cut off, their eyes gouged out with hot irons, and be left to die" (Goodenough, 2014). These gruesome acts presumably vindicated beheadings. In one of their most barbaric acts, they burned alive a captured fighter pilot locked inside a cage.

Drawing on the Crusader justification, ISIS portray their military mis-sion as the rightful displacement of the "Crusader partitions" with a unified caliphate in the Arabian Peninsula. Muslim scholars have vigorously dis-puted the group's claim that sexual enslavement of infidel women is justified by Islamic law. ISIS leaders blame President Obama for the beheadings they have performed, calling him a "crusader" and "apostate" for waging war on them with airstrikes (Goodenough, 2014). They debase their opponents as "infidels" and "devil worshipers." With this diverse set of moral justifications, there is no limit to the cruelty that they may inflict in God's name.

The fact that a good share of ISIS fighters are foreigners also may have contributed to their barbarity. Social distancing reduces moral self-restraints. The fighters terrorize, rape, and execute strangers. However, the leaders of this ruthless militia also have used a variety of incentives in socializing recruits in brutality. A Turkish militia fighter reported that participating in an execution was the badge of honor (Yeginsu, 2014). He was heralded as a full ISIS fighter for burying a man alive. If the recruits volunteer in the belief that they are doing God's work, they have sacred sanctions to carry out their brutal deeds in the name of Allah. Divine sanction was repeatedly declared during deadly violence. "Everyone shouts, 'God is the greatest,' which gives you divine strength to kill the enemy without being fazed by blood or splattered guts" (Yeginsu, 2014). Cold-blooded killings and barbaric executions require dehumanization of victims to eradicate any restraining moral qualms. It may be even easier to do it if victims are bestialized, with victims often degraded to "dogs." "Surely, the holiday [Ramadan] won't be complete without a picture with one of the dogs' corpses," a callous Egyptian recruit remarked in a Twitter post. A photo showed him kneeling beside a decapitated corpse (El-Naggar, 2015).

A UN report documented how ISIS lured and abducted children and socialized them in brutality as soldiers and suicide bombers (Arango, 2014). Shiite enemies were portrayed as "infidels" who massacre men and rape women so they have to be killed. In training camps children were taught military skills and indoctrinated in the ISIS ideology as the future Islamists of the caliphate. At a graduation ceremony the children were celebrated as a "generation of lions, protectors of religion, dignity and land" (Hilburn, 2014).

To model gruesome killings and desensitize revulsion to them, children were shown videos and witnessed beheadings and stonings. For one training session, after viewing beheading videos, the youth practiced beheadings on three captured Syrian soldiers. As described by a child attendee who defected, "[a]fterward, the teachers ordered the students to pass around the severed heads" (Belz, 2015). Gruesome behavior was likened to an ordinary culinary practice: "It was like learning to chop an onion. You grab him by the forehead and then slowly slice across the neck" (Belz, 2015). Another execution video showed a child shooting two suspected spies in the back of the head, spraying their writhing bodies with bullets and smiling proudly while applauded as a "lion cub." In a video of thorough dehumanization, children were shown playing with severed heads and poking fun at the decapitated bodies. There was no limit to the atrocities for which morality was suspended. Glorification of the child-committed atrocities was exploited on social media as a recruitment device and to frighten people from resisting the ISIS mission.

The Iraqi army did not seem to have any allegiance to the Shiite-dominated regime, fleeing and leaving military equipment behind when faced with advancing ISIS forces. Once again the United States became entangled in an Iraqi civil war between Sunnis and Shiites that grew in scope and brutality. The interminable bloodshed in Iraq came with sanitized labels—names such as Operation Desert Storm, Operation Desert Shield, and Operation Iraqi Freedom. The new war was called Operation Inherent Resolve. In his address to the nation, President Obama essentially declared war against ISIS via air strikes but reassured the public that this war would not include "boots on the ground." In addition, a cadre of military special forces would be dispatched to Iraq to advise the Iraqi military and coordinate air strikes from the ground.

In retaliation, ISIS staged videotaped beheadings of two American journalists. They warned that further American attacks would bring the war to the "far enemy" and "result in the bloodshed" of Americans (Shane & Hubbard, 2014). Seeing staged beheadings of one's fellow citizens activates a strong sense of moral obligation to put a stop to it. President Obama decided to intervene militarily in a more extensive way. What began as a very limited U.S. mission to halt the advance of ISIS forces instantly escalated into a war to eradicate ISIS. The beheadings and accompanying threats seemed designed to provoke the United States into another war that the militants could exploit as a war of the West against Islam. A display of ruthless invincibility also is used for enlistment of potential recruits.

In Afghanistan in 2001, the U.S. strategy essentially followed the Bosnian war model, in which the United States provided air cover and degraded enemy forces with air strikes while unified native ground forces did the fighting. However, this model of warfare is ill suited to the Middle East, where military forces are weak and divided across sectarian factions that have been fighting with each other for years. President Obama was correct in claiming that he was proposing a different type of war. In the previous Iraqi war, the United States and its allies were an outside occupational force that controlled how they fought the war with their own ground forces on their own terms. In the new war, Prime Minister Haider el-Abadi of Iraq announced that he welcomed the air strikes but would not allow any foreign ground forces. Even the air strikes would have to be approved by the Iraqi military.

There is only so much that aerial military campaigns can do. To mitigate the effects of the air strikes, the militants took cover amid civilians, split into small units, shifted locations rather than staying in established military compounds, and moved fighters and vehicles individually rather than in convoys. Not only was ISIS an elusive target, but the severe restrictions on the aerial campaign to spare civilians also did not leave much to bomb. Neither Iraq nor its neighbors provided air bases from which U.S. planes could attack ISIS forces in Syria. Aircraft missions therefore had to fly from aircraft carriers in the Gulf or bases thousands of miles away. In most of the missions, fighter planes returned without dropping their bombs because they could not find a permitted target (Schmitt, 2014). Because of these protective measures, the aerial campaign had a limited impact.

Urban warfare requires ground forces to defeat the enemy. Eradicating Islamic radicalism in the Arab world calls for a coalition of Arab ground forces to eliminate the entrenched scourge of violence in their midst. Friedman (2015) had this to say about strength of commitment to one's nation: "This has to be their fight for their future. If the fight against ISIS is not worth it to them, it surely can't be for us." The unending social strife cannot be resolved as long as sectarian factions continue their feud within their national government and their society at large. Regardless of whether Sunni or Shiite Muslims are being targeted, Western soldiers killing Muslims is more likely to exacerbate than alleviate the root sectarian problem.

Because ISIS has a stronghold in Syria, extending the war to Syria meant U.S. entanglement in dual messy civil wars involving still more feuding factions. In its efforts to crush an internal revolt, Bashar Al-Assad's regime has been killing its own people, attacking with poison gas and obliterating their cities. A mixed Syrian rebel force is fighting both Assad's forces and ISIS. ISIS is fighting the Shiite-dominated Iraqis and the Syrian rebels while seizing territory for their caliphate. The United States is bombing ISIS, and that unintentionally helps Assad and provides support to the Syrian rebels. The Sunnis in Iraq were caught amid the Shiite-dominated government that they distrusted and feared, Iran-backed Shiite militias that attack Sunnis with impunity, and ISIS militants who rule captured territory with their own brutal version of Islamic law.

A number of foreign policy and counterterrorist experts were highly critical of the rush to war without congressional debate about the plan for the military mission, the long-term strategy, and what it would accomplish in the end (Mazzetti, Schmitt, & Landler, 2014). Critics also questioned the justification for the war. The Obama administration justified going to war against ISIS on the grounds that it posed an immediate threat to the security of the nation, although security agencies reported that ISIS posed no immediate danger. Despite these assessments, House Speaker John Boehner sounded the alarm: "These are barbarians. They intend to kill us. And if we don't destroy them first, we're gonna pay the price" (Fuller, 2014). Heightened fear and wrath over the savage execution of the two journalists provided the driving force to strike back immediately and forcibly.

Given that only Congress has the power actually to declare war, critics questioned President Obama's authority to launch a new war (Rudalevige, 2010). The president argued that he has statutory authorization based on congressional approval for the Iraq war. He also argued that Congress granted presidents broad authority to take military action against al Qaeda militants worldwide, which he broadened to include ISIS on the grounds that many of its members are former al Qaeda terrorists. Representative Michael McCaul, a leader in the House on national security, used a bestial metaphor in justifying bombardment of ISIS on Syrian soil: "To defeat ISIS", he proclaimed, "we must cut off the head of the snake which exists in Syria" (Parkinson, Zeleny, & Dwyer, 2014).

The expansion of the aerial campaign to Syria created additional problems of justification. Legal analysts argued that military action against another nation without authorization by the UN Security Council is a violation of international law (Sengupta, 2014b). The legality of the justification became even more problematic when the United States decided to train and arm the Syrian rebels. A foreign country arming insurgents to overthrow their governmental system, however welcome it may be in despotic regimes, is also going against international law. The United States argued that it was protecting Iraq from the brutal Sunni jihadists. Because the Syrian regime was unable or unwilling to eradicate these militants from their sanctuary on Syrian soil, the United States had the right to do it. Besides, the United States argued, it was arming the Syrian rebels to fight ISIS, not the Assad regime. However, the rebels acknowledged that routing the Assad regime was a higher priority for them than fighting ISIS.

In a lack of moral and congressional responsibility, Congress evaded taking a vote on whether or not the nation should go to war. House Speaker John Boehner shifted the responsibility to the president, claiming that he already had the authority to do so. The House would not address the issue, he explained, unless the president requested it (Baker & Knowlton, 2014). Representative Justin Amash harshly criticized Congress for shirking its moral responsibility, declaring in a Twitter feed, "It's irresponsible & immoral that instead of debating & voting on war, congressional leaders chose to recess Congress for nearly two months" (Walsh & Caldwell, 2014). After waging the air war for months, the administration asked Congress to authorize it formally. Because of the congressional political divide, the Senate was gridlocked on the requested authorization of the ongoing war against ISIS. Conservative senators favored heavier military engagement, whereas liberal ones feared embroilment in another endless Middle East war (Carney, 2015).

The American public supported the limited military campaign to avenge ISIS's appalling barbarity and to degrade its military capability. But weary of years of open-ended wars with unsettled outcomes, it, too, would not support getting bogged down in another prolonged civil war in the Middle East. With UN Security Council authorization appearing unlikely, the United States decided to expand the aerial bombardment of ISIS in Syria without UN approval. Some Western and Arab countries joined in the aerial campaign but opposed bombardment of Syrian targets and deployment of ground forces in Iraq. The war against ISIS has been severely handicapped by lack of experienced military forces to fight the enemy on the ground.

The United States has focused on its military campaign against ISIS but has neglected the online media campaign, which was underfunded, uncoordinated, and of little interest to military and security agencies (Schmitt, 2015). In contrast, ISIS has made heavy use of social media to glamorize its mission, recruit fighters, and expand its reach through affiliates in the Middle East and North Africa. It has portrayed itself as fighting against the West's war with Islam. To counter ISIS's growing influence, the Obama administration created the National Center for Counterterrorism. In a counternarrative, the president argued that the United States is at war with terrorists, not with Islam. Muslim scholars and Islamic leaders condemned ISIS for violating tenets of Islam and self-proclaiming a caliphate by force (Markoe, 2014).

In warfare, words make a big difference. A socially consequential semantic controversy has arisen over what to call ISIS. Portraying its members as "Islamic jihadists" implies an Islamic religious war. To avoid being semantically lured into a war with Islam, President Obama dubbed ISIS "violent extremists." His critics objected to what they regarded as "evasive" language that, in their view, minimized the threat of terrorists masking criminality in the name of Islamic theology (Shane, 2015).

ISIS has franchised its ruthless brand of Islamic activism around the world. However, its military might was not sustainable. Its initial triumphant blitzkrieg was slowed by airstrikes and stiff opposition by Kurdish military forces. In a symbolic battle to preserve its image of invincibility, ISIS was locked in fierce combat in the Syrian city of Kobane with equally fervent Kurdish militants joined by Western volunteers. The dedicated Kurdish army, supported by air strikes, drove ISIS out of the city in defeat. It was also losing territory it had seized in Iraq in battles with Kurdish and Shia militias. The United States found itself in a conflictual predicament in this fight. On the one hand, it was working to rein in Iranian influences in the Middle East. On the other hand, it was relying heavily on Shiite militia, some of them commanded by Iranian officers to carry the fight against ISIS. Shiite militants took revenge on Sunnis suspected of being ISIS sympathizers. Such punitive actions could further inflame the already intense animosity between Iraqi Sunnis and Shiites.

The Syrian rebels are not a monolithic militia. Joshua Landis, a Middle East scholar, describes them as a parochial, leaderless group feuding among themselves: "The rebels often fight among each other and most are extremely regional and clan or village based" (Schulberg, 2014). Commenting on the hundreds of clans involved, Landis likened efforts to organize them to trying to herd cats. They did not look like a group on which to pin one's military hopes. Nevertheless, Congress voted funds to train and arm them, despite some concern about their effectiveness and fears that the arms might eventually end up in the hands of ISIS. In the debate on whether to arm the Syrian rebels, the CIA questioned the wisdom of doing so. The agency cited a long record showing that arming rebel forces rarely produces victories (Mazzetti, 2014).

ISIS is partly of the United States' own making. Many of its leaders are former officers in Saddam Hussein's army and former members of his political party (Breslow, 2014). ISIS faced the Americans anew, not as insurgents fighting the occupier of yesteryear, but as an invited obstacle on the road toward creating its caliphate. Many cynical Sunnis remarked on the irony that the present military campaign was directed against "an organization that evolved from jihadist groups fighting American occupation" (Barnard & Kirkpatrick, 2014). A Sunni housewife wished the military campaign well, "despite the fact that America was one of the reasons why this radical organization originally existed" (Barnard & Kirkpatrick, 2014).

The counteroffensive against ISIS was based on misjudgments that overestimated the competence and resolve of the Iraqi army and greatly underestimated the strength of ISIS, who was pursuing territorial conquests not just acting out resentments against the Shiite-dominated regime. Intelligence officials blamed the Obama administration for downgrading the seriousness of the militants' offensive (Baker & Schmitt, 2014). They attributed the low priority to the demands of other crises and the administration's reluctance to get bogged down in another Iraqi war.

The Iraqi government allowed the U.S. military mission only a severely restricted aerial campaign. Also hampering the effort, the Iraqi army had inadequate troops to fight the ground war. Iraqi ground forces were inexperienced, poorly equipped, and plagued with low morale and desertions. They were quickly routed by ISIS forces (Semple, 2014). Arab partners of the United States were unwilling to commit any ground forces of their own, although the military campaign needed well-trained troops immediately. Instead, they had to be recruited and trained, which takes a long time. Further complicating the situation, Iraqi army training programs were subverted by pervasive corruption and provided arms ending up in the weapons black market, where ISIS can buy them (Kirkpatrick, 2014). Sunni tribal leaders were difficult to recruit as allies in the fight. Some were in regions already occupied by the militants; others feared brutal retaliation if they resisted. Many who were alienated and resentful of the Shiite-led central government sympathized with the Sunni militants. Because of mutual distrust, the central government was reluctant to arm trained Sunni security forces for fear that they would sell their weapons to ISIS or join it themselves (Hubbard, 2014).

Early defeats in the fight against ISIS escalated military missions. The United States added Apache helicopters, which can be used for close-range combat, to the military force. However, they are vulnerable to small-arms fire, making it dangerous to deploy them (Semple & al-Jawoshy, 2014). Although the U.S. military is not engaged in frontline combat, American soldiers are on the ground as advisors. There has been some "mission creep," with more advisers being deployed. Were any of them to be captured, helicopters would be used in rescue missions, with high risk of deepening the military engagement.

Governments often attribute military escalation to compelling circumstances. Situational attribution reduces personal responsibility for choosing an escalative course. House Speaker John Boehner was highly skeptical that air strikes would defeat the militants, "At the end of the day somebody's boots will have to be on the ground," he explained (Frizell, 2014). When asked whether it would be American boots if other countries refused to commit ground troops he replied, "We have no choice" (Frizell, 2014). Former architects of the Iraq war and their supporters clamored for U.S. deployment of ground troops to Iraq and Syria. However, the public was deeply divided along political lines on this issue, with 57% of Republicans favoring troop deployment but only 39% of conservative and moderate Democrats and 27% of liberal Democrats supporting it (Growing support for campaign, 2015). Time will tell whether the United States can resist becoming involved in another lengthy ground war in the Middle East.

ISIS is a zealous military force with recruits from around the world and good supply lines for weapons, financed by huge revenues from oil sales on the black market from the regions they occupy. The group's wealth, romanticized media self-portrayals as builders of a caliphate, and rapid seizure of large regions to show for it, have persuaded thousands of foreign recruits from about 80 countries to join their mission. Not only have they joined this radical militia, but they also appeared on social media to recruit other fighters and to urge those at home to carry out terrorist attacks locally (Bilefsky & de la Baume, 2015a). Apprehensive countries have enacted laws to prohibit their citizens from joining the ranks of ISIS for fear that they would return as radicalized jihadists, ready to engage in terrorist activities at home. Lured by money, weapons, and territorial conquests, Islamic militants in other countries have shifted their allegiance from al Qaeda and other radical groups to international affiliates of ISIS. To foster survival, the ISIS leader delegated authority to key figures in his inner circle so that, were he to be killed, transfer of leadership would be seamless (Schmitt & Hubbard, 2015). Their rule by terror and dispersal in foreign affiliates in weak and failed states further adds to the difficulty of eliminating ISIS.

The political alliances in the Mideast region that shape the course of events, however, are convoluted and volatile. For example, Turkey maintained a tolerant attitude toward ISIS, treating it as an antidote against Kurdish militants, who are Turkey's foe but allied forces' most effective ground forces against ISIS (Barnard, 2015). Although Turkey refused to participate in the allied military campaign, after ISIS's suicide bombings and other attacks inside Turkey for proposing an ISIS-free zone along the Syrian border, Turkey branded ISIS a barbaric terrorist organization and joined the allied forces in the battle against ISIS.

With this political realignment the allies could use nearby bases in Turkey to launch their aerial campaign. By closing major supply lines and the route for foreign recruits through Turkey, they hampered ISIS's operations. To complicate matters, however, Turkey took advantage of the alliance to escalate its offensive against the Kurdish militants, imperiling a Kurdish peace settlement and weakening the Kurdish militia needed to fight ISIS, much to their allies' concern. The political bedlam makes it difficult to predict where the Mideast combat is going, how long it will last, and whether it ends democratically, chaotically, autocratically, or in stagnated exhaustion, only be replaced by a new form of insurgency.

On Addressing Root Problems

Once ISIS is eventually routed as occupiers of vast regions, new insurgent groups will spring up, creating fresh mayhem if sectarian factions cannot moderate their mutual animosity. Sectarian proxy wars will also continue in the region. An enduring solution requires sociopolitical reforms in sharing power that enable different ethnic and religious factions to live together without fighting each other. It remains to be seen whether the Iraqi political system can structure an effective government and whether its lawmakers are motivated to make the social reforms needed to achieve an inclusive society.

The Iraqi president nominated Haider al-Abadi as the new prime minister under vigorous protest by Nouri al-Maliki (Morris, 2014). As a first step toward establishing an inclusive government, Abadi has to win the trust of Sunnis and assimilate them into the political system so that they will have a stake in the life of the nation. Were the new government to achieve this reform, it would erode Sunni support for the Sunni extremists and remove the sociopolitical conditions necessary for the evolution of future insurgencies. However, Maliki did not take kindly to being ousted. He and his supporters have continued to attack and humiliate Abadi for his conciliatory approach toward the Sunnis and Kurds. As one Shiite politician put it, Abadi's opponents "really want to give him a bloody nose" (Semple, 2014). Even as the Sunni extremists approached the outskirts of Baghdad, the feuding within the Iraqi government continued unabated. Another major complicating factor is that many of the regional wars are proxy battles fueled by the rivalry between the Shiites of Iran and the Sunnis of Saudi Arabia.

The Iraqi government achieved an accord with the autonomous Kurds in northern Iraq. Under the terms of the agreement, the Kurds will share oil wealth and receive a budget allocation from the central Iraqi government, which also will provide resources for their security forces (Arango, 2014). Now that the relation with the Kurds is more settled, the Iraqi government faces the formidable challenge of making peace between the Shiite and Sunni factions, which dislike and distrust each other.

If terrorism is to be defeated worldwide, societies must address the life conditions that drive people to take up deadly terroristic missions. This is a daunting challenge not amenable to quick fixes. More advantaged individuals who have been alienated and radicalized by embittering experiences in their efforts to promote the social changes they desire usually spearhead militant activism (Bandura, 1973; Sprinzak, 1990). In cultural milieus that hail suicide bombers as gaining blessed martyrdom, this mode of terrorism is institutionally embraced and socially applauded as divine retribution for the humiliation and suffering inflicted by the enemy (Lelyveld, 2001). Educational development with opportunities for a desired livelihood provide the best escape from poverty and cultivate national advancement in the social and economic challenges modern societies face. These personal and social resources enable individuals to find meaning and satisfaction in modern life. But this institutional resource is squandered when educational systems are used more for indoctrination in reactionary theologies and ideologies than for developing the talents needed to thrive in a modern global society.

All too often, American foreign policy forges marriages of convenient self-interest with autocratic rulers who preside over their people with oppressive force to ensure self-preservation. These life conditions arouse wrath in disaffected populations toward the United States and its allies for propping up authoritarian regimes with approval and weapons. Enmity is further inflamed by Islamic fundamentalists who politicize religion. They rally support for terrorist operations against secularism and the enemies of their medievalist strain of Islam. The scourge of terrorism presents a humanitarian challenge in how to demonstrate that it is in people's self-interest to live together agreeably in a pluralistic society embedded in modernity and global interdependence. If the war on terrorism is to be won, it requires extensive enabling support of the moderate voices and the hopes and aspirations of a younger generation within these societies who have a progressive vision of how to integrate the benefits of modernization with humanistic principles that uphold human rights, equality, and dignity.

Chapter 8

■ ■ ■ ■ ■ ■ ■

ENVIRONMENTAL SUSTAINABILITY

The most urgent issue facing humankind in this century is the preservation of a sustainable environmental future. Harm to the earth is largely a product of human activity. All societies, therefore, have a moral obligation to preserve the environment so that future generations have a habitable planet. We are witnessing hazardous global changes with spiraling ecological consequences. They include earth's rising temperature, deforestation, expanding desertification, ice-sheet and glacial melting, flooding of low-lying coastal regions, severe weather events, depletion of topsoil and aquifers in major food-producing regions, acidification of oceans, depletion of fish stocks, extensive loss of biodiversity, and degradation of other aspects of earth's life-support systems. These diverse forms of environmental degradation indicate that we have already exceeded the earth's carrying capacity. In short, humans are destroying ecological systems that have evolved over eons and that keep the planet cool and habitable. Before addressing the sources of environmental degradation and the role that moral disengagement plays in them, we review people's conceptions of nature. These conceptions are important because they shape and provide exonerative justifications for the environmental practices that societies adopt.

CONCEPTIONS OF NATURE

Business

As Lakoff (2002) succinctly describes it, in conservative environmentalism, human exceptionalism—human domination over nature—is the natural order. Nature is a resource that individuals and societies can own and use in pursuit of their self-interest. Markets place a value on nature. According to this environmental ethic, transactions concerning natural resources should be governed by free-market principles without governmental intrusion. In this worldview, regulators are meddlesome bureaucrats masquerading as protectors of the public against harmful products and practices. Conservatives accuse them of hassling innovative, hardworking people who have achieved their success through self-reliant dedication. In the words of Newt Gingrich (1995), a conservative spokesman, "[t]o get the best ecosystem for our buck, we should use decentralized and entrepreneurial strategies, rather than command-and-control bureaucratic effort." In the free market, the products of the unfettered pursuit of self-interest within legal bounds contribute to the welfare of others. The intrusion of social-responsibility considerations in the market process area is viewed as a form of taxation that hampers productivity and profitability. Proponents believe that free-market forces will correct faulty practices. Under market-driven incentives, technological ingenuity will provide solutions for environmental problems (Pearce, 2013). It is ironic that human ingenuity is a source of many of the ecological problems we face.

This conception of nature is deeply rooted in economic libertarianism. Milton Friedman, the foremost proponent of a corporate-centered ethic, contends that the sole social responsibility of corporate officials is to make money for shareholders (Friedman, 1970). However, the effects of business activities extend beyond mutual benefits for firms and their shareholders. Some moneymaking activities adversely affect the lives of people who are not involved in those activities but nevertheless bear the penalty of collateral harmful life conditions. Business jargon linguistically sanitizes these human and environmental costs as "negative externalities." Life in the societies of today is increasingly shaped by transnational interdependencies and the power of international financial capital (Keohane & Nye, 1977). Many corporate shareholders do not live in the regions contributing to their wealth. This remoteness leaves harmful effects largely out of sight and out of mind. Costly collateral effects call for a broader ethical framework for corporate behavior than one based solely on shareholders' self-interest.

Religion

Religious beliefs also shape conceptions of nature that are environmentally consequential. For example, some radical Christians embrace the conception of nature as a bountiful resource placed on earth by God for the taking. According to this doctrine of human exceptionalism, nature exists for humans to use as they see fit. They find biblical justification for opposing environmentalists in passages that are environmentally unfriendly. In Genesis 1:28, for example, the Lord commands prolific reproduction and unmerciful domination of nature and its varied species: "Be fruitful, and multiply, and replenish the earth, and subdue it: and have dominion over the fish of the sea, and over the fowl of the air, and over every living thing that moveth upon the earth."

However, elsewhere the Bible advocates responsible stewardship of all of God's creations. These contradictory verses provide grounds for radical followers to oppose, in God's name, initiatives designed to curb environmental degradation. Some not only view resources as there for the taking but believe that God preferentially placed valuable ones in their homeland. As one tea party supporter said, "Being a strong Christian, I cannot help but believe the Lord placed a lot of minerals in our country and it's [sic] not there to destroy us" (Broder, 2010). At a political gathering, another adherent cited the Bible in arguing that global warming "is a flat out lie." He continued, "I read my Bible. He made this earth for us to utilize" (Broder, 2010).

In voicing his opposition to environmental protection measures, the Republican presidential candidate Rick Santorum trumpeted the anthropocentric view of human exclusivity: "We were put on this Earth as creatures of God to have dominion over the Earth, to use it wisely and steward it wisely, but for our benefit not for the Earth's benefit" (Hooper, 2012). Mainstream Catholic leaders reject conservatives' antienvironmental stance but welcome their political clout. The Catholic hierarchy's stern rebukes of liberal Catholics who promote stewardship for a sustainable environment often have raised questions about the church's commitment to alleviating global environmental problems. In a significant departure, Pope Francis's encyclical *Laudato si'* (Praise be to you; in English, On Care for Our Common Home) calls climate change a worldwide problem. He condemns industrialized nations' heedless destruction of the environment purely for commercial gain and points out that the poor suffer the most from environmental degradation. The encyclical calls on developed nations to help less-developed nations face the challenges to the environment (Yardley & Goodstein, 2015). The response from conservative Republicans, including several presidential candidates, has been sharply critical (Brody, 2015). However, the church's long-standing opposition to contraception may, in fact, exacerbate problems caused by unplanned childbearing.

Patriarch Bartholomew I of Constantinople, who leads the world's Orthodox Christians, interprets scripture in a similar way. This Green Patriarch, as he has come to be known, has declared that environmental conservation is a religious imperative: "Tending to and caring for this creation is not a political whim or a social fashion. It is divine commandment; it is a religious obligation" (Bartholomew, n.d.). His devoted environmental activism is rooted in a deeply spiritual worldview that environmental and biological diversity are God's creations and as such must be protected.

The Environmental Debate

An alternative form of environmentalism is grounded in a contrasting eco-logical ethos to human exceptionalism. It views human well-being as inextricably linked to the health of ecological systems. Ecosystems do not operate in isolation. Because they are intricately interdependent, degradation of a particular aspect reverberates throughout the network. In this view, species are interdependent on each other. Hence, destruction of one species jeopardizes the ecological support of all life. The earth's resources are not inexhaustible. Natural resources must, therefore, be used in a sustainable way to preserve a plentiful and habitable planet for future generations.

These diverse conceptions of nature differ markedly in the importance they place on preserving biodiversity. In the latter environmental ethic, species diversity is essential for sustaining the ecological supports of life. Because of the intricate interdependence of the earth's ecosystems, humans need all other species. The conservative environmental ethic favors the more anthropocentric view that humans are an exceptional species on this planet and that many of the so-called lowly species are of little or no consequence in the larger scheme of things. They view laws protecting endangered species as a cover for governmental intrusion in the free-market system.

Modern-day environmentalists draw their inspiration from prominent naturalists of the past: Ralph Waldo Emerson, Henry David Thoreau, and John Muir. John Muir not only viewed nature with awe, but he also was an indefatigable advocate for preserving it. Through his writings, his founding of the advocacy organization the Sierra Club, and his political activism, he was instrumental in protecting some of the most majestic American landscapes. Through his influence, Yosemite and the Grand Canyon were established as national parks for future generations to enjoy.

With advances in scientific knowledge, most conservationists subscribe to the view that the intricately interdependent ecological systems evolved over eons. These systems' nature and functioning, they contend, are governed by natural laws, not supernatural ones. John Dewey and Ernest Nagel provided the more contemporary philosophical foundation for naturalism in which knowledge is gained by scientific means (Papineu, 2009). The conflict between creationism and naturalism continues to be fought stridently in the culture war over environmentalism. Some seek to reconcile the conflict with the view that nature was created supernaturally but science can reveal how the ecological systems work. The supernatural cause, however, remains scientifically untestable. Large numbers of environmentalists subscribe to faiths that invest nature itself with divinity. In their worldview, it is sacrilegious to despoil nature.

The notion of nature as an economic commodity is in no way confined to a conservative ethic, however. It comes in all types of ideological forms. The locus of influence, which is becoming increasingly megacorporate and transnational, widely views nature in terms of market value rather than for its inherent value in local milieus. Even some of the most basic necessities of life are now being treated as commodities priced in terms of supply and demand. For example, the growing scarcity of clean water is a looming crisis, especially in developing countries with teeming populations, limited water resources, and inadequate delivery systems. Sinking water tables, receding glaciers that feed rivers, and heavy pollution of rivers that render the water undrinkable and hazardous to health foreshadow dwindling water supplies. Faced with large populations and lacking the infrastructures to deliver fresh water, some developing countries are subcontracting this function to outsiders whose primary motive is to make a profit on their investment (Mann, 2007). The poor may be priced out of a vital "commodity" they cannot forgo.

In times past, people were highly dependent on their immediate habitat for their livelihoods. This tight contingency strongly linked behavioral practices to environmental consequences. It was, therefore, in people's self-interest to conserve their environment and learn to live in harmony with it. These efforts were often backed up with ethical prescripts and normative sanctions. In contemporary societies, most of the peoples of the world live under congested urbanized conditions where they must harmonize more with a constructed concrete environment than with the natural world. The constructed environment feeds and clothes them, and provides clean water supplies, countless labor-saving devices, and the energy needed to power a high-tech lifestyle.

The necessities of life are produced by faceless proxy workers in far-off places. As long as consumers' daily needs are met, they have little incentive to examine the humaneness of the working conditions, the level of pollution caused by production processes, or the costs exacted on the environment to produce, ship, and market the profusion of goods and the disposal of wastes. Under these modernized conditions, lifestyle practices are disconnected in time and place from the very ecological systems that provide the basis for them. Environmental conservation becomes an abstraction rather than an experienced necessity. Ecological destruction by high-consumption lifestyles makes this type of consumerism an ethical issue. There is much to be said for a less congested and polluted planet with an inclusive, sustainable way of living in adaptive union with the environment.

The pursuit of unfettered self-interest and high-consumption lifestyles was of less concern when there were fewer people consuming less luxuriantly. Only a limited number of countries enjoyed privileged control over bountiful resources in their own milieus through territorial expansion or exploitive extraction from weak colonies. Their low-level technologies could not do much ecological harm. Any detrimental environmental effects were, for the most part, locally situated. It is a different story in the current era, with teeming populations seeking a life beyond a mere subsistence level. A host of developing countries with increasing economic means to adopt high-consumption standards of living are now competing vigorously for declining natural resources. Some of them wield powerful technologies that have a global ecological impact, affecting everyone in one way or another.

Consider an example of environmental devastation of potentially major global consequence. The earth has two sizable "lungs" that absorb a goodly amount of carbon dioxide from the atmosphere: the Amazon rain forest of South America and the dipterocarp forests of Southeast Asia. Given the billions of tons of heat-trapping gases that humans discharge into the air, they can ill afford to destroy these vital restorative resources. Nevertheless, humans treat these forests as resources to be used in ways that are destroying them.

The Amazon rain forest is being clear-cut and burned at a fast pace to create farmland. This valuable ecological resource is being converted from a carbon absorber to a carbon emitter. International environmental groups have made efforts to save the rain forest by funding the creation of protected natural reserves. These conservation projects have aroused vigorous opposition by powerful business and political groups (Rohter, 2007). Business interests want to open up the rain forest to mining, logging, and agricultural projects supported by a network of highways, dams, and ports. Political extremists on both sides branded the conservation effort as a new form of colonialism organized by a "Green Mafia." In the fight for public opinion, they claimed that the environmental movement was a pretext for a plot by the "hegemonic powers" to take over the Amazon rain forest "to maintain and augment their domination" (Rohter, 2007). Convinced that the environmental initiative by outsiders was a threat to Brazilian sovereignty, a major share of the Brazilian general public sided with the opposition forces. In this inhospitable political climate, Brazilians regarded the market approach of payment for halting deforestation and reducing carbon emissions as suspect.

Brazilian lawmakers passed a law granting amnesty to landowners who deforested areas illegally and opened up huge new areas of Amazon forest for farming and ranching (Romero, 2012). During the controversy over this Amazon deforestation, one legislator—who also is the president of the agribusiness trade organization—denounced international environmental groups for trying to "paralyze the growth of Brazilian agribusiness" (Romero, 2012). However, with support of the scientific community, the press, entertainers, some corporate leaders, and environmentalists enlisting the popular culture via social media, President Dilma Rousseff vetoed certain portions of the bill deemed too favorable to farmers and ranchers. Despite protests from some environmentalists who thought the bill was still too lenient, it became law (Boadle, 2012).

China has signed a multibillion-dollar deal with the Indonesian government to clear-cut over 4 million acres of its forest for lumber and to replace it with plantations for palm oil, which is used in cooking, detergents, soaps, and lipstick (Perlez, 2006). A clan elder explained that his people love their trees, but the logging will bring jobs and modernize their lives. As he put it, "People have told me, 'Wood is gold, you're still too honest.'" Vast areas of mangrove forests in this region have already been converted to cropland.

These vital lungs of the earth are falling victim to the ethic of nature as property for human exploitation. The massive deforestation will further fuel earth's rising temperatures. Waiting until the effects of massive deforestation become locally aversive before taking action will most likely launch an out-of-control feedback cycle of progressive, irreversible ecological degradation.

THE IDEOLOGICAL CULTURE WAR OVER ENVIRONMENTALISM

Clive Hamilton, at the Centre for Applied Philosophy and Public Ethics at Charles Sturt University in Australia, casts the battles over environmental conservation as a more deep-rooted culture war between conservative and liberal worldviews (Hamilton, 2010a). He notes that many of the attacks on environmentalism and climate science are spearheaded by conservative think tanks heavily funded by the petroleum and other energy industries. Conservative advocates in think tanks and like-minded media, he argues, are united in a "hatred of environmentalism ... variously seen to be the enemy of individual freedom, an ideology of smug elites, an attack on capitalism and consumerism, and the vanguard of world government" (Hamilton, 2010b). They brand human-based climate changes as a left-wing ideology masquerading as environmental protection.

Some critics of environmental initiatives view them through a conspiratorial lens. The way this view plays out at the local level is illustrated in a controversy over an environmental initiative planned by Carroll County, Maryland. More than 20 years ago the United Nations developed Agenda 21, which includes a set of nonbinding principles and plans for promoting sustainable development at local, national, and global levels. Those who consider the UN to be bent on one-world rule regard these principles as a scheme for global control over people's lives (Strzelczyk & Rothschild, 2009). Activists who share that view are quick to brand and denounce local conservation programs, such as introducing bike lanes, expanding public transportation routes, and preserving open space, as applications of the UN's hidden agenda (Kaufman & Zernike, 2012). One of the attendees at a local planning meeting in Virginia expressed her fear over the usurpation of her rights: "They get you hooked, and then Agenda 21 takes over. Your rights are stripped one by one." It is not just a few extremists who hold this view. Ted Cruz, a Republican senator from Texas and a 2016 presidential candidate, pledged to fight the "dangerous United Nations plan," which he regards as bent on abolishing "golf courses, grazing pastures and paved roads" (Collins, 2012a). He pointed to the Democratic financier George Soros as the man behind the alleged scheme. There are legitimate concerns over development policies that affect property and other rights. However, support for local developments that improve the quality of community life can be undermined by fights against alleged conspiracies.

In the face of a global climate problem of immense and enduring consequence, efforts to address it have degenerated into a cantankerous culture war. According to Ross Garnaut at the Australian National University, the sorry dispute about climate change has become "less civilized, noisier and more ignorant" (Della-Ragione, 2011). One of the grave moral concerns that gets lost in this heated feud is the future state of the earth and humankind if the belief about global warming is a myth. Myron Ebell (2006), the director of the Center of Energy and the Environment at the Competitive Enterprise Institute, which is heavily funded by the petroleum industry, argues that global warming makes life more pleasant in northern regions with fewer and less severe winter storms. This northern scenario suggests that the cost to human well-being of a false positive (belief in global warming that does not exist) is greater than a false-negative belief (denial of global warming that exists).

The consequences of these two types of false beliefs are asymmetric but opposite to the ones that Ebell foretells. The initiatives supported by a false positive belief would put a cost on carbon, reduce wasteful practices and the mountains of trash they produce, foster development of green technologies, reduce reliance on fossil fuel energy with renewable sources, promote environmental conservation practices, create efficient mass-transit systems, develop recreational areas, and produce less environmental pollution. Under these conditions, people would live in harmony with their environment. In contrast, the false-negative belief fuels the high-energy diet that results in environmental degradation and the depletion of nonrenewable resources and produces massive amounts of pollution.

One of the most alarming aspects of global warming is that it thaws the Arctic permafrost; this thawing releases vast amounts of methane and carbon trapped under the permafrost over many millennia (Walter, Zimov, Chanton, Verbyla, & Chapin III, 2006). Once this process is unleashed, it feeds on itself, uncontrollably producing ever-higher atmospheric temperatures. As the earth continues to get hotter, life will become more miserable for the generations to come. The false negative will produce disastrous irreversible global consequences.

A variety of conditions, some of which are documented by Wenk (1979), foster a foreshortened perspective when it comes to environmental practices. The immediate, bountiful rewards of high-consumption lifestyles easily can override distant adverse effects, especially if those effects accumulate slowly. Many of those effects are unanticipated and, to make matters worse, some are irreversible. The incentive systems of many business organizations are strongly oriented toward practices that bring profits in the short term. Intense competition for natural resources and the prospect of a good share of the global market create further pressure on businesses to do whatever is needed to succeed. To ensure their political survival, politicians cater to

parochial interest and lobby for local projects that are not always environmentally friendly. The media tend to focus on crises of the day rather
than on policy initiatives designed to avert future trouble in the long term.
A foreshortened perspective in a disastrous ecological course calls to mind
the apocryphal story that Donald Collins (2007) tells about the person who
jumps off the Empire State Building. As he passes the 68th floor, he thinks
to himself, "So far, so good." Rachel Carson dedicated *Silent Spring* (1962)
to Albert Schweitzer and quoted the alarm he sounded over the grave consequences of an unremitting foreshortened perspective: "Man has lost the
capacity to foresee and to forestall. He will end by destroying the earth."
Given the growing deterioration of the ecological health of the planet,
Schweitzer's foreboding prognosis is not as far-fetched as it then appeared.

SOURCES OF ENVIRONMENTAL DEGRADATION

Human-caused environmental degradation stems from three major sources:
population size, per capita consumption of resources, and damage to the
ecosystem caused by the technologies that support a high-consumption lifestyle (Ehrlich, Ehrlich, & Daily, 1995). A comprehensive approach to environmental sustainability must address all three sources.

Population Size

There are limits to the number of people the earth can support sustainably.
The world's population was 3 billion in 1959 and doubled to 6 billion over the
next 40 years. Currently it is increasing by about 1 billion every 15 years,
soaring toward an estimated 9 billion by 2044 (U.S. Census Bureau, 2015a).
These additional billions of consumers will take a heavy toll on the earth's
finite resources and ecological systems. The development of clean, green
technologies and renewable sources of energy and the adoption of sustainable consumer lifestyles are essential. Even so, billions more consumers will
offset a good share of the benefits of any green remedies. Lifestyle changes
must, therefore, be coupled with stabilization of the human population at
a level the earth can sustain in the long term. On the consumption side, for
the most part, we are making token gestures rather than the needed fundamental lifestyle changes. On the population side, population growth has
been excluded from the equation for ecological degradation. For reasons to
be presented shortly, it is a taboo subject that no one dares touch. Stabilizing
the soaring global population is critical for an environmentally sustainable
future. To reduce continued destruction of the planet both problems of overpopulation and unsustainable consumption must be addressed.

In his book *The Population Bomb*, Paul Ehrlich (1968) forecast that, within several decades, soaring population growth would cause widespread famine and spark civil unrest. The book gained popular success in an era when the public was becoming more ecological minded. However, it also drew a host of critics. The predicted catastrophes did not come to pass in the designated short term. Critics challenged the inevitability of scarcity as a result of population growth, citing expanded food production made possible by high-yield agriculture, pesticides, and fertilizer. They argued that hunger in developing countries was caused by corrupt governments and faulty distribution systems, not by overpopulation.

In his defense, Ehrlich argued that his forecasts were scenarios of possible outcomes, not explicit predictions. However, critics easily refuted his forecasts, because the proposed time frame was too short for catastrophic effects to occur. In a wager that was billed as a battle between Malthusians and Cornucopians, Ehrlich bet his archcritic, the economist Julian Simon, that the price of five commodity metals would rise over a decade. Ehrlich lost the bet. Conservative critics proclaimed that the population bomb had been successfully defused. It was not that Ehrlich's concern over the adverse effects of soaring population growth were groundless. Rather, he projected his forecasts over too short a time. This is true even for the famed metals wager. The investor Jeremy Grantham showed that the prices of the selected metals actually had risen in real terms when calculated over a more extended period (Rotella, 2011). Ehrlich lost the bet in the short term, but won it in the long term.

Some of Ehrlich's harsh remedies for population control drew heavy fire from both the ideological Right and Left. They pitted overconsumption against overpopulation as though they were antagonistic factors in the calculus of ecological degradation. The population taboo remains in full force despite exponential population growth and its mounting consequences. At the time that Ehrlich sounded the humanitarian alarm, the population was 3.8 billion, and natural resources still were abundant. However, within just five decades, the population has nearly doubled to 7 billion, with pervasive detrimental ecological and social effects (Brown, 2009; Heinberg & Lerch, 2010). Food scarcity is becoming an issue of growing concern.

A view currently in vogue contends that population growth is no longer an ecological problem (Ellis, 2013). This erroneous belief stems from the failure to consider the differential pattern of population growth across regions of the planet and shifting populations. The population growth problem must be addressed at the global level, not dismissed as a myth by selective focus on some industrialized countries with declining birthrates. As shown in Figure 8.1, the developed countries have stabilized their populations, whereas population growth is soaring in developing countries, which have high rates of unplanned childbearing. Among the developing countries,

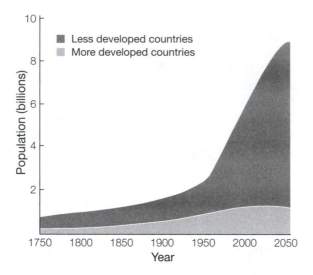

Figure 8.1 Population growth in developed and less-developed countries. With permission from Population Reference Bureau.

the poorest ones have the highest birth rates. Age demographics also differ markedly for developed and developing counties, as shown in Figure 8.2. In many developing countries, the major share of the population is under 20 years of age, a "youth bulge" that coincides with the most fertile period of the reproductive cycle. These populations will double in 20 to 30 years.

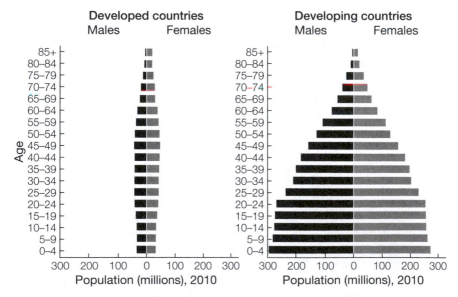

Figure 8.2 Age distribution in developed and less-developed countries. With permission from Population Reference Bureau.

Reports of falling fertility rates, at least in developed countries (see Figure 8.1), can instill a sense of complacency regarding the population problem. Because population grows exponentially, a paradox in population change arises that the general public may not understand. Falling fertility is accompanied by increased population for some time. Offspring may be less prolific, but there are more of them. As long as the falling fertility rate remains above a replacement level of 2.1 per woman, the population will continue to grow, albeit at a slower rate.

Damage to the Ecosystem

Studies of the effects of overpopulation focus heavily on ecological degradation. The Gallup World Poll (Clifton, 2012) sheds some light on how overpopulation degrades the quality of people's lives and creates barriers to bettering it. The poll found that what everyone worldwide wants is a good job. Gallup created a population-to-payroll index of economic security, defined as at least 30 hours of weekly employment on payroll. Using this index, Gallup reported that population growth far exceeds job growth, leaving huge numbers of people struggling for basic necessities, working makeshift jobs with earnings that are too low and unstable for a decent life. To compound the disparity, automation reduces the number of people needed to produce products and provide services. In societies burdened with inequities, those who are better off benefit from the economic growth from more workers and consumers, whereas the unemployed and underemployed are left to fend for themselves as best they can. In the poorest countries, population growth outstrips job growth, with most of the people struggling in an insecure, marginal existence. The youth population is currently the largest in history, with the highest percentage of young people in the poorest countries (Sengupta, 2014a). These countries will face tremendous social turmoil if they fail to prepare their young people for satisfying, meaningful lives.

Most of the recent violent conflicts are in countries with large youth populations that are uneducated, unemployed, and living in poverty under autocratic regimes that often are plagued with corruption (Leahy, 2007). The age structure, intense competition for limited resources, and widespread social discontent makes young men ripe for recruitment for civil wars and terrorist activities. Large youth populations living under repressive, poverty-ridden conditions will continue to be a growing threat to international security. Worsening this problem, water sources are shrinking as the demand by soaring human numbers outstrips the supply. The depletion of aquifers and of river flows from shrinking glaciers will spawn growing regional conflicts over the allocation of water from sources crossing national borders (Brown, 2007).

Compare the claim that the population bomb has fizzled with actual population-growth trends. The world's most populous nation, China, has 1.3 billion people and is adding about 7 million annually. India is adding about 17 million a year. It has passed the 1 billion mark and is on the way to surpassing China as the most populous country in the world (Ryerson, 2010). At its current fertility rate, India's population will double to 2 billion in less than 50 years. The population in the Middle East and North Africa is projected to double in about 50 years (Ryerson, 2015). Declining mortality rates add to the increase in numbers. As long as birth rates exceed death rates, the population will continue to grow. Although the rate of population growth globally has slowed somewhat, based on the rate of annual growth it is still on track to add about 1 billion people every 15 years. Global population growth cannot be disregarded indefinitely. Eventually, the mounting aversive consequences of environmental degradation will force the international community to address this problem.

Recent years also have seen mass migrations of people from heavily populated poor countries to more habitable or prosperous ones. Some are migrating from life under harsh economic conditions in search of a better life. Others are seeking a safe haven from internal civil or ethnic strife. And still others are environmental refugees forced to migrate because of the declining habitability of their region as fertile land turns into desert through prolonged drought and loss of water resources. Poor regions are especially vulnerable to rising temperatures, because if their crops fail or their water sources dry up, they have no reserves to draw on. The oft-repeated scene of hordes of emaciated people struggling to survive under squalid conditions in refugee camps is more likely to depersonalize and dehumanize them than to raise social compassion. These large-scale international migrations, which will swell with increasing environmental destruction, are transforming national populations, becoming the source of major regional upheavals that breed sectarian violence.

As Gwynne Dyer (2007) reminds us, the population bomb is rapidly ticking away despite being ignored as a major contributor to climate change and ecological destruction. Population growth is an escalating global problem, not a disappearing one. Through selective inattention to population demographics, soaring population growth disappears as a problem and population decline is elevated to an alarming one that "haunts our future" (Howe & Jackson, 2007). Even some of the leading environmental conservation organizations—which went from groups of active grassroots environmentalists to cautious bureaucracies accommodating political forces—disembodied ecological damage from population growth, a major contributor to the problem (Foreman, 2007; Kolankiewicz & Beck, 2001; Ryerson, 1998). The population of the United States was 150 million in 1950, grew to 300 million in 2006, and will reach 400 million in 2051 (U.S. Census Bureau, 2015b). Most of this increase stems from immigration (Wang, 2013). After a grueling internal fight over the role of immigration in population growth for fear of its racial implications, the Sierra Club, a leading environmental group, jettisoned domestic population growth from its environmental conservation agenda. Under new leadership, the Sierra Club more recently has become an advocate for immigration and has backed off from making comments about immigration's supposed impact on the environment. The new executive, Michael Brune, made this statement: "[T]he Sierra Club Board of Directors has voted to offer our organization's strong support for a pathway to citizenship for undocumented immigrants. Such a pathway should be free of unreasonable barriers and should facilitate keeping families together and uniting those that have been split apart whenever possible" (Brune, 2013).

Fear of alienating donors, criticism from the progressive left, and disparagement by conservative vested interests claiming that overpopulation is a "myth" were further incentives to reject the rising global population as a factor in environmental degradation. Population growth vanished from the agendas of other mainstream environmental organizations that previously had regarded escalating numbers as a major environmental threat (Nicholson, 2007). Years after Greenpeace announced that population "is not an issue for us," the organization currently favors family planning and contraception (Weyler, 2013). Friends of the Earth declared that "it is unhelpful to enter into a debate about numbers" but now also supports family-planning services (Childs, 2013). The common justification for the earlier stance was that consumption, not human numbers, created environmental problems, despite evidence that more people produce more ecological damage.

David Brower, a former director of the Sierra Club, would have viewed this retreat for political reasons as a tragic irony. He put it well when he said that there is no conservation policy if population is excluded. The rising global population is now a much more serious ecological threat. Noting that the current population exceeds the earth's carrying capacity, Chris Rapley, a former director of Britain's Science Museum, argued that stabilizing the population at an ecologically sustainable level is not much of a solution. In his view, we need fewer people to curb global warming (Clover, 2007). This requires slowing the rate of population growth, stabilizing it, and then reducing it to a level that is environmentally sustainable. High-consumption lifestyles that wreak havoc on the environment and harm other people's lives are a moral issue of commission. Evading the influential role of population growth in environmental degradation is a moral issue of omission.

THE POPULATION TABOO

The mention of population growth became politically incorrect for a variety of reasons. Almost three quarters of carbon dioxide (CO_2) emissions are produced by industrialized or industrializing nations: China, the United States, the European Union, India, the Russian Federation, Japan, and Canada. All other regions combined account for about 28% (U.S. Environmental Protection Agency, 2008). Targeting poor countries that suffer ecological harm from other countries' extravagant lifestyles is analogous to blaming the victim. It is ironic that ignoring poor people's need for help with planned childbearing and social support is mistreatment by neglect.

Immigration is a minefield in economic life. On the one hand, the manufacturing, agricultural, and service industries want a cheap labor supply. They rely heavily on migrant workers, regardless of their legal status, to perform the dirty and toilsome manual jobs that their own citizens will not do. Using economic justification, industries also argue that they need cheap labor to stay competitive in the global marketplace. They use their political clout to secure their labor needs. On the other hand, migrants are marginalized and denied adequate services and basic human rights. In some countries, they are even stripped of a national identity if their children born in the host country are denied citizenship. Better-off families are not about to groom their own offspring for toilsome menial jobs with paltry wages and lowly social status. So industrialized countries import or, by discriminatory practices, produce a disadvantaged ethnic underclass that remains largely unassimilated and is resented for its intrusion on the prevailing cultural norms, traditions, and practices.

To complicate matters further, in the political realm, immigration is an emotionally charged issue that evokes deeply ingrained prejudices against certain ethnicities and occupational strata, favoritism toward others, and indignation over illegal immigrants. These conflicting forces have spawned political correctness on both the Right and the Left. Some people exploit this contentious issue for political purposes, but most do not want to talk about immigration in terms of population growth for fear of being branded racist.

Religious opposition to contraception also diverts attention away from the ecological effects of growing overpopulation (Collins, 2007; Ryerson, 1998). The Catholic Church forbids contraception on the grounds that it dissociates sex from procreation. In a historical analysis, Phil Harvey (2012), the president of an international family-planning organization, documents that over the centuries, people and religious groups have been troubled by sex. In contrast to many, including the Catholic Church, he regards sexual pleasure as a fulfilling aspect of life. Contraception enables committed couples to enjoy, without the fear of an unwanted pregnancy, the pleasure of sex as a powerful experience that bonds them physically and emotionally. Various religious groups formed an alliance against planning the number and spacing of children with the aid of contraception.

The Vatican's efforts to control women's reproductive rights extend well beyond its own followers. A Catholic reform organization that supports women's rights regarding sexuality has argued that because of the church's unique, preferential status, which is granted to no other religion, the Vatican can vote on UN resolutions even though it does not meet the criteria for nationhood (Catholics for Choice, 2012). The UN requirement for consensus on resolutions grants individual members considerable say in the form that resolutions take. At UN conferences on environmental sustainability, the Vatican delegation argues against resolutions that acknowledge women's right to control their own fertility. The delegation agrees only to natural contraceptive methods, such as abstinence during the fertile phase of a woman's reproductive cycle. The Vatican considers morally unacceptable any family planning services that enable women to exercise control over their fertility with other contraception methods. The imposition of the Vatican's doctrine on women worldwide impedes confronting the environmental and social problems stemming from overpopulation.

Family planning also has become tainted with abortion politics. At the UN Rio + 20 Conference of 2012, the Vatican joined forces, mainly with countries with large Catholic populations, to delete any mention of women's reproductive rights from the final UN document (Herrmann, 2012). The Nicaraguan delegation branded "reproductive rights" a metaphor for abortion: "Every country knows [it] is a code at the UN for abortion" (Herrmann, 2012). The Chilean delegation claimed that the term *right to life* is "incompatible with the term reproductive rights" (Herrmann, 2012). The European Union remained silent because some of its members, such as Ireland, are strong pro-lifers. The delegations from African nations, which are undergoing exponential population growth, kept a low profile for fear of jeopardizing the limited financial support they receive from the UN for their overpopulation problems. The United States and other Western countries tried to finesse the resistance linguistically by linking the benign term *population dynamics* to "reproductive health," only to see it summarily deleted. Because of its consensus requirements, the UN is incapable of breaking the stranglehold of the population taboo. In an ironic twist, the Vatican wields stronger influence in blocking the UN from supporting voluntary family planning services for women worldwide than it does for its own followers. A large majority of sexually active Catholic women use artificial contraceptive methods, whereas only a small percentage use the church-prescribed natural approach.

Religious denominations differ regarding the morality of contraception. A group of leading theologians representing Christian, Jewish, Muslim, and other denominations issued an open letter through the Religious Institute affirming contraceptive access as a moral obligation. In their analysis of the issue, "contraception allows for a fulfilling sexual life while reducing maternal and infant mortality, unintended pregnancies, abortions, and sexually transmitted diseases" (Religious Institute, 2012). They regard denial of access to contraceptive methods as "coercive childbearing." Millions of women in developing countries want to exercise control over their fertility, but they cannot do so because they lack family planning and contraceptive services (Singh & Darroch, 2012). As a result, they have unplanned children whom they cannot care for adequately.

Heated disputes have erupted among Christian groups over whether global warming is a moral issue that should be part of their agenda (Goodstein, 2007). A coalition of prominent evangelical leaders, representing millions of followers, had declared that humans are stewards of God's creation and thus bear the moral responsibility to curb the earth's rising temperatures in order to save it from further degradation (Goodstein, 2005). This call to action drew heavy fire from leaders of conservative Christian groups, who argued that global warming has not been proved to be of human origin. They told the evangelicals to remove global warming from their agenda and restore their priority to sexual morality, which requires targeting abortion, homosexuality, and same-sex marriage, and teaching sexual abstinence to young people. They further warned the evangelical environmentalists against associating with "liberal crusaders," whom they regard as bent on limiting free enterprise as well as population growth. More recently, some evangelicals have begun to express concern about the disproportionate effects of environmental degradation on the world's poor (Gillis, 2015a).

In contrast, a number of Muslim countries are adopting a Pakistani program that trains health workers and medical school faculty to offer family planning services to their clients. The program also brought together religious scholars in a consensus that family planning does not violate Islamic principles as stated in the Quran (Mir & Shaikh, 2013).

Pope Benedict XVI issued a green message to young Catholics at a massive religious youth rally, urging them to save the planet from environmentally unsustainable development (Winfield, 2007). His proposed remedies included use of biodegradable packaging, recycling, installation of solar panels, and enrollment in carbon offsetting projects for reforestation. However, family planning to curb global population growth was conspicuously absent from his agenda for environmental salvation. Rather, his view on this issue exacerbated the environmental problem with forewarnings that low birthrates "cause enormous difficulties for social cohesion" (Stinson, 2007). Contrary to this claim, we saw earlier that throngs of people competing for basic necessities of life breed social discord not social cohesion. Growing more consumers means more pollutants that can overwhelm any gains from his prescribed mitigating practices. In his encyclical *Laudato si'*, along with his condemnation of environmental destruction, Pope Francis also criticized abortion and the idea that population control can solve the problems of the poor (Yardley & Goodstein, 2015).

Coercive birth-control schemes, such as those in China and India, have further tainted family planning. Libertarians, feminists, and human rights groups joined the ranks of religious and political opponents to forced participation. By the third population conference in 1994, the UN had shifted its focus from the population problem to the empowerment of women and to human rights issues (Foreman, 2007; Kolankiewicz & Beck, 2001). There was much talk about women's rights and empowerment but little to show for it. Slowing population growth and family planning became branded "coercive control," making both politically incorrect (Campbell, 2014). Funds for family planning from foreign agencies were slashed. Talk of human rights did not extend to women's right to control their pregnancies through ready access to contraceptives. Rather, women were being "forced to have pregnancies they did not want" (Campbell, 2014). Nor were women provided with increased educational opportunities to expand their prospects in life. The 2014 session of the UN Commission on Population and Development reviewed progress since the 1994 meeting and reaffirmed its commitment to the rights of women and girls, continuing efforts for the poor, strengthening youth participation, and to the inclusion of sexual and reproductive health as human rights (United Nations Population Fund, 2014).

The Nobelist Dr. Henry W. Kendall depicts the tragic human and ecological costs of the population taboo: "If we don't halt the population growth with justice and compassion, it will be done for us by nature, brutally and without pity—and will leave a ravaged world" (John, 2015).

To enable women to make informed choices about childbearing and methods of contraception, the British government and the Gates Foundation launched an international summit supporting women's reproductive rights aided by family planning and contraceptive services (Olson, 2012). The summit received pledges of billions of dollars along with social and political support to rejuvenate family planning services worldwide. Diverse faith-based organizations at the summit added their commitment to such services as well. Richard Cizik, the president of the New Evangelical Partnership for the Common Good, explained his group's basis of the support as follows: "Family planning is morally laudable in Christian terms because of its contribution to family well-being, women and children's health, and the prevention of abortion" (Olson, 2012). This large-scale global effort may help to break the stranglehold of the population taboo.

The scale of this bold effort, given the politicized nature of family planning, can go a long way toward remedying the unmet need of families to plan their future in terms of when and how many children to have. However, to ensure the benefit of this global initiative, it is necessary to address ethically the social and cultural impediments to women's development and control of their reproductive life. This broadened approach includes advancing human rights, promoting equitable education and enlightened future planning, and providing families access to the full range of contraceptive options.

THE CLARION CALL OF *SILENT SPRING*

Some of the technologies in the third major source of environmental degradation include toxic chemicals that adversely affect the ecological supports of life and impair human health. In 1962, Rachel Carson, a biologist and naturalist who held several positions at the U.S. Fish and Wildlife Service, published her ground-breaking book *Silent Spring*. This volume, written in a graceful, readable style, provided a rich synthesis of evidence on the environmental and health hazards of chemical pesticides. These harmful effects were powerfully captured in the title image of a spring without birdsong. Carson argued that toxic chemicals were being used indiscriminately without adequate tests of their effects, users were applying them in an uninformed way without safeguarding their health, and governmental regulations were poorly enforced. Her concerns were rooted in a sense of moral responsibility to foster the welfare of humans and nonhuman creatures alike.

The chemical industry and agribusiness went to great lengths to discredit Carson's credibility as a scientist. They criticized her as biased for not citing the benefits of chemical pesticides in eradicating insect-borne diseases. Robert White-Stevens, a former spokesman for the chemical industry, depicted Carson as a crusader who would lead the world backward: "If man were to follow the teachings of Miss Carson, we would return to the Dark Ages, and the insects and diseases and vermin would once again inherit the earth" (McLaughlin, n.d.). The National Pest Control Association waxed poetic in their disparagement (Cafaro, 2011): "Hunger, hunger, are you listening, To the words from Rachel's pen? Words which taken at face value, Place lives of birds 'bove those of men."

The journalist and author Edwin Diamond (1963) invested *Silent Spring* with nefarious evocative power. It "stirs the latent demons of paranoia," in which some "wicked 'they' were out to get 'us.'" Diamond disparaged not only Carson but also environmental advocates, linked stereotypically to the "anti-fluoridation leaguers, the organic-garden faddists and other beyond-the-fringe groups." He also criticized her, given the state of the evidence at the time, for linking chemical pesticides to cancer. Economic libertarians have continued to condemn *Silent Spring*, arguing that environmental regulations infringe on Americans' freedom to run their businesses as they see fit.

In her defense, Carson explained that she had never advocated a total ban of chemical pesticides, including their use to control insect-borne diseases: "I do not favor turning nature over to insects" (Rachel Carson, 1964). Rather, she objected to indiscriminate blanket spraying of pesticides and encouraged ecologically safer methods of insect control. She believed that with safer methods, human interests could be served without inflicting needless harm on the natural environment. Moreover, she had a more fundamental concern that should have made the chemical industry regard her as an ally rather than an opponent. With overuse or misuse of chemical agents, insects evolve resistance to them, rending those agents ineffective. Excessive use of the insecticide DDT is a good case in point. Carson (1962) expressed concern "that the insect enemy has been made actually stronger by our efforts. Even worse, we may have destroyed our very means of fighting."

The campaign against Carson backfired. People became concerned about the toxicity of pesticides and their effect on health and the environment. A commission convened by President John F. Kennedy to evaluate the state of the evidence upheld Carson's scientific credibility. *Silent Spring* became the inspiration for important initiatives in the environmental movement. Laws were enacted to regulate chemical pesticides. A variety of environmental advocacy groups were formed to work toward preserving a sustainable ecological future. The Environmental Protection Agency (EPA) was created to safeguard human health and the environment.

Over the years, vigorous assaults have been mounted to weaken or eliminate the EPA, which enforces environmental regulations. The former Texas governor Rick Perry called it a "cemetery for jobs" (Broder & Galbraith, 2011) and believers in global warming a "secular carbon cult" (Broder, 2011). The utility industry characterized the EPA's rules to curb pollution from coal-fired power plants a "regulatory train wreck" that will raise electricity bills, increase blackouts, and destroy jobs (Plumer, 2011). The war on the EPA continues unabated even 45 years after its creation. All the leading candidates vying for the 2012 U.S. Republican presidential nomination vowed to kill the EPA or strip it of a particular function, such as regulating the emission of greenhouse gases (Broder, 2011). In response to a stunning volume of bills introduced in Congress in 2011 that were designed to gut the EPA, John Walke of the National Resources Defense Council remarked, "It shows just a profound disgust and disdain for the regulatory state that is unhinged from any facts or concerns for the benefits from those rules" (McAuliff & Graves, 2011). With an eye toward the 2016 presidential election, three Republican contenders in the Senate supported a bill that would block the EPA's jurisdiction over bodies of water within the United States (Cama, 2015). In this legislative dispute, commercial considerations trump ecological and health effects.

Stymied by congressional opposition, President Obama exercised his executive authority to curb emissions through the EPA, which invoked its authority under the Clean Air Act to issue regulations aimed at reducing carbon dioxide emissions from coal-fired power plants in 28 states. In a constitutional challenge of the regulation, the Supreme Court upheld the authority of EPA to do so (Davenport, 2014c). However, this is not the end to what Peter Altman, the Natural Resource Defense Council's climate director, called "the Super Bowl of climate politics" (Eilperin & Mufson, 2014). Once the EPA finalizes the regulations, industry groups and some states intend to challenge them in federal appeals courts.

MORAL DISENGAGEMENT IN OPPOSING ENVIRONMENTAL INITIATIVES

The preceding section addressed many of the key issues concerning degradation of the ecological supports of life and the heated disputes about what, if anything, to do about it. Current generations are engaging in environmentally degrading practices that will make life worse for future generations.

Making the planet less habitable for those to come raises profound moral issues. This foreshortened, self-centered perspective is captured in a jesting banner hung from a freeway bridge: "What have future generations done for us?" (Gillis, 2014c). The crucial moral question concerns the changes we are willing to make to mitigate the harm inflicted on future people. Because our descendants seem like remote abstractions to us, it is difficult to arouse empathic concern and moral self-sanctions, both of which would curb environmentally harmful practices. The remainder of this chapter analyzes the role played by moral disengagement in this highly consequential drama.

Social and Moral Justification

Social and moral justifications in the environmental domain are designed to confer moral legitimacy on harmful practices by investing them with worthy purposes. These justifications take a variety of forms: gaining societal benefits or economic advantages in the competitive global marketplace, strengthening national security, protecting the free enterprise system, and curbing intrusive government. National, constitutional, and economic justifications also do heavy duty in promoting production processes that are hazardous to the environment and to human health (White, Bandura, & Bero, 2009). The benefits that industries depict usually are accompanied by dire warnings of the costs to society and human well-being were those practices subjected to governmental regulation or halted altogether.

The need to fund the pensions and health costs of America's aging population are used as economic justifications for increasing the size of the population. These justifications, and the media portrayals they spawn, are infused with pejorative stereotypes of the elderly as idle simpletons leading barren lives, draining precious societal resources but having little to contribute to the life of society (Signorielli, 1985). The people of today are aging more successfully than did those of earlier eras (Baltes & Baltes, 1990; Bandura, 1997; Rowe & Kahn, 1998). They are healthier, more knowledgeable, more intellectually agile, and able to work productively for longer. In the current realities of late adulthood, life is characterized more by a shift in pursuits and personal renewal than by withdrawal from an active life (Bandura, 1997; Carstensen, 2011). But societal structures and practices lag behind the capabilities of the elderly, so their skills and knowledge are largely untapped (Riley, Kahn, & Foner, 1994).

The elderly often are blamed for problems that actually result from societal structural impediments to the continuance of their productive lives. China, which is easing its family planning laws to produce more workers, is a good case in point. The problem is partly a product of China's mandatory early retirement policy, which retires blue-color workers at age 55 and professionals and government workers at age 60. Women are required to retire even earlier (French, 2007). Allowing capable people who are good at their work and who derive satisfaction and other benefits from working to keep their jobs longer would relieve the pressure on the pension system. The government is considering a schedule whereby it would raise the retirement age three months a year for several years, or perhaps raising women's retirement age first, starting in 2017 (Wong, 2015). However, this structural solution is politically unpalatable and already has sparked dissent in Chinese social media. Moreover, extending employment for older workers can increase unemployment among younger ones, which risks political unrest. Although the workforce problem arose partly from governmental retirement policies, the government attributed it to population decline, and the proposed remedy of population increase would only worsen China's social and environmental problems down the line. Kotlikoff and Sachs (1998) advocate policies that provide incentives for workers to save more toward their retirement as another way of easing the pension problem, rather than using population growth as a remedy.

In certain countries, some social and moral justifications are aimed at heightening concern over decline in fertility rates. Fearing that a declining population will stifle economic and consumption growth, some of these countries have launched campaigns granting generous incentives to women who have more babies. These incentives include cash payments for each childbirth, lengthy maternity leaves, good child care, compensation for lost wages, more flexible work arrangements, and even pension supplements. In some European countries, sex education courses subtly encourage students to have more babies when they grow up (Hakim, 2015). Countries conducting these fertility campaigns regard babies as a means toward future economic growth. Babies are the future workers and consumers. However, for financial, environmental, and lifestyle reasons—and because many countries are still recovering from the Great Recession of 2008—many young, educated couples are resisting governmental pressure to produce a baby boom. Opposition to such campaigns is arising in both developed and developing countries (Erdbrink, 2014).

A few European countries have witnessed a recent slight rise in their birthrates. The German minister of family affairs reported that the baby boomlet "filled me with delight" (Stinson, 2007). The basis for her joy is puzzling, to say the least. It takes many years, with substantial familial costs and hard work coupled with extensive societal resources, to grow babies into adult workers. Not all of them turn out well. As Mother Nature becomes harsher, many of them may end up as environmental activists! To achieve continual economic growth, industries need workers now, not 20 years hence, so they have to import them rather than waiting for the homegrown ones to mature. Production of goods can be outsourced to places that provide cheap labor. However, countries also seek the educated and skilled from abroad and use migrants from disadvantaged countries to do menial jobs cheaply that homegrown workers won't do. Families in developed countries who are paid to produce more babies do not envision their sons growing up to be garbage collectors and menial laborers or their daughters to be domestic workers and marginalized caregivers.

Writing from a feminist perspective, the essayist Katha Pollitt (2007) commented on the irony that some of the developed countries do the right thing in providing supportive aid to working mothers but for the wrong reason—that is, to produce more babies. Pollitt suggested that societies should develop the talents of the countless millions they already have but write off, rather than embarking on national fertility campaigns to increase their populations. Pollitt suggested that the quickest way for countries to enhance their social capital would be to ban gender inequality and educate girls and women. She declared that the same is true for ethnic minorities who are marginalized rather than provided with the developmental resources to nurture their talents. The moral issue here concerns the harm caused by social exclusion from the opportunity structures of a society.

In this electronic era, promoting educational development will contribute more to innovation and economic growth than will merely breeding more people. As previously noted, children are expensive to raise, require costly societal services, and if inadequately educated and then marginalized, they become social and economic burdens on society. Adding more people in struggling, overpopulated countries detracts from economic growth. Revenues should be used to provide for the basic necessities of life rather than for investment in national development. Ryerson (2010) summarized it well when he characterized population as a multiplier. It not only aggravates existing problems but also creates a host of new ones.

In some countries, the pressure on women to have more children includes punitive threats as well. To enlarge the working population in Japan, women are pressured to have more babies and chastised for not doing so. The former prime minister of Japan, Yoshiro Mori, suggested that women who bore no children should be barred from receiving pensions: "It is truly strange to say we have to use tax money to take care of women who don't even give birth once, who grow old living their lives selfishly and singing the praises of freedom" (McAvoy, 2003). One politician expressed the need for baby production in stark, dehumanizing terms when he characterized women who limit their childbearing as "recalcitrant baby-making machines" (Pollitt, 2007). Joseph A. Cannon (2007), the editor of the *Deseret Morning News*, reminds his readers that God commanded humankind to "multiply and replenish the Earth." In Cannon's view, it is not only "selfishness" but also "self-actualization" and "secularism" that are to blame for the impending "empty cradle."

Social, economic, political, and religious justifications are offered for the seemingly paradoxical practice of working to increase birthrates despite a global population that already exceeds the planet's carrying capacity. Proponents for greater fertility argue that an expanded young workforce is needed to support an aging population. This remedy may provide some short-term benefits but at the cost of worsening the economic and environmental problems in the long term. Enlarging a young cohort creates a new wave of population growth that, in turn, will require an even larger growth in population to support it in old age. This is a population Ponzi scheme. Population promoters do not explain how societies should fund the growing pension and health costs that progressively expanding populations will incur when they age. Adding more people will increase a workforce but is troublesome in the long term for a society that has to care for them through old age. Free-market fundamentalists compound this problem, probably because they want women to bear more babies, but fight against taxes to cover the costs of raising them and caring for them when they become elderly on the grounds that taxes are bad for business.

With an average birthrate of 5.2 children per woman, Africa is undergoing the fastest population growth in the world (Pflanz, 2013). Africa's population will more than double from 1.1 billion to over 2.4 billion by mid-century. Most of this population growth will be in the poorest sub-Saharan countries. Niger is an illustrative case of the negative multiplicative power of soaring population growth. This nation has a large, young population with an average fertility rate of 5.5 children. One half of Niger women are entering their peak childbearing years (Rosenthal, 2012). In rural areas the fertility rate is over seven children, with traditional-minded men wanting a dozen as the ideal. The nation's current population of 170 million is crammed into a small country and projected to soar to 400 million by mid-century. Peter Ogunjuyigbe, a Niger demographer, puts a human face on the multiplicative consequences: "Population is key," he explained. "If you don't take care of population, schools can't cope, hospitals can't cope, there's not enough housing—there's nothing you can do to have economic development" (Rosenthal, 2012).

Droughts accompanying climate change have fueled fights over scarce water and arable land in heavily populated sub-Saharan Africa. Under these pressures, the fragile environment is becoming increasingly uninhabitable for millions of people. Masses of displaced refugees in squalid camps fighting for basic necessities of life are but a small preview of things to come. Even with the present population, millions of people are living in hovels in megacities. They are struggling to survive with scarcities of food, fresh water, basic sanitation, medical services, and other necessities of life. According to the UN Development Goals Project, 14% of the world's people live in dire poverty, down from 47% in 1990, largely due to efforts by China (Sengupta, 2015). Nevertheless, the outlook for the world's poorest children remains grim (Gladstone, 2015). Swelling populations are creating a humanitarian crisis.

Reducing unplanned pregnancies is the fastest, most cost-effective way of curbing accelerating ecological destruction. Moreover, its benefits are immediate. Trying to change a people's customs is a tough undertaking. It is costly and vulnerable to the vagaries of competing influences, may have unintended adverse consequences, and usually involves long time lags before any benefits are realized.

Developed countries with declining birthrates also justify increasing their populations to forestall a troubled future of societies in decline. Howe and Jackson (2007) foresee dire consequences for countries with falling birthrates—economic stagnation, huge fiscal deficits, slashed budgets for national development, a demoralized populace, and loss of geopolitical power. The Cornucopians view the earth as providing bountiful natural resources that permit virtually limitless growth (Simon, 1998). According to the cornucopian view, increasing numbers of workers and consumers are needed to fuel continual economic growth. Moreover, growing populations require expanding industrial activity to provide employment for them. Failure to increase industrial facilities spells social trouble.

The ethics of extravagant and wasteful consumerism, rooted in a market-driven model, also warrants comment. This type of lifestyle degrades ecological systems, sometimes with extinction of plant and animal species. It is promoted by striving for perpetual economic growth with exemption from the environmental costs. The cost/benefit analyses omit the pollution, health, and environmental costs. Critics describe this calculus of benefits relieved of environmental costs as economics overruling ecology (Humphrey, 2010). Booming economic activities and hard-driving competitiveness raise value issues concerning the purposes to which human talent, advanced technologies, and resources are put. Much of the intense market activity devoted to consumerism promotes lavish consumption that neither uses finite resources wisely nor leads to a better quality of life. Many of these practices may be profitable in the short term, but as previously noted, they are unsustainable in the long term. This issue has grown in importance as powerful transnational market forces shape local economic activities that have significant impact on the ecological systems and natural resources on which those activities depend. Such practices are likely to take a heavier toll on the environment if the transnational forces adhere to an ethic of unbridled economic self-interest aimed at maximizing profits with little regard for the ecological costs they incur.

Advantageous Comparison

How lifestyle and industrial practices are viewed is colored by what they are compared against. Through exploitation of the contrast principle, proponents can make detrimental practices seem righteous. If used skillfully, framing the issue by advantageous comparison can make the lesser of two evils not only socially acceptable but even morally right. In the battle over pesticides, Edwin Diamond (1963) made extensive use of advantageous comparison to minimize any adverse effects of pesticides and to discredit public concerns following the publication of *Silent Spring*. He reported that more people die from misuse of aspirin and bee stings than from pesticides. "But no one," he went on to say, "has seriously proposed eliminating the use of aspirin or exterminating all bees." This erroneous comparison fails to recognize that, unlike aspirin and bee stings, misuse of pesticides kills a wide range of species on a large scale. He likened public concern over the ecological and health effects of pesticides to Joseph McCarthy's anticommunist witch hunt. Diamond also took issue with the environmental ethic that humans should live in balance with nature, arguing that human interests should not be subordinated to those of nonhuman species. He achieved this comparative exoneration by downgrading the value of lower species: "If DDT kills some cats but saves many humans, if weed killer destroys a pocket of wildlife shelter but increases highway safety, so much the better."

The most consequential use of advantageous comparison is in many nations' stiff resistance to making the lifestyle and economic changes needed to curb global warming. Mitigating concentrations of greenhouse gases in the atmosphere requires substantial reductions in emissions in the immediate future, that is, absolute reduction of emissions, not just slowing the growth rate. The disputes over the Kyoto Protocol, which was adopted in 1997 and went into effect in 2005, illustrate how, through exonerative comparison, both sides of the controversy feel righteous about their high output of greenhouse gases. This protocol required developed countries to cut their national emission of heat-trapping gases depending on their per capita output. But developing countries were exempted because they were minor contributors to the global climate problem. The United States and Australia rejected the protocol on the grounds that it would hamstring their economies and place their nations at a competitive disadvantage in the global marketplace. Opponents argued further that the protocol was unfair because large, developing countries, such as China and India, are surging ahead as competitive economic powers free of any emission limits. With their booming economies raising consumption levels in huge populations, they have become major producers of greenhouse gases.

Developing countries, in turn, rejected caps on their countries' greenhouse gas emissions on the grounds that global warming is a problem that the rich, industrialized countries created, so they should be the ones to cut their emissions. They asked why countries striving to modernize should stifle their economic and industrial growth for a problem that was not of their making. From their perspective, they argued, they have the same right to modernize their societies and raise their people's standard of living as did the rich, industrialized countries. They, too, want to live prosperously. This usually involves modeling the "good life" of Western consumerism. Through comparative exoneration, the contending parties freed themselves of restraint over their polluting practices and felt righteous about it.

At the 2011 UN Climate Change Conference in Durban, the delegates agreed to remove the major stumbling block to achieving a worldwide agreement—the exemption of developing countries that are high emitters, such as China and India. Withdrawing this exemption removed the handy economic and equity justifications that developing countries used for resisting any change. However, the conference did not produce a protocol that is legally binding for all countries. Rather, it produced a pledge to frame the future treaty by 2015 and implement it by 2020 (Black, 2011). Given the disconcerting history of negotiations, disputes will likely arise over mandatory emission limits, surveillance procedures, and enforcement mechanisms. Another challenge is persuading each country to ratify the treaty. With a host of impediments, achieving an enforceable worldwide treaty will require much greater political will and efficacious leadership. Considering that adverse climate change is the most urgent problem of the century, the remarkable thing about the global warming problem is the low sense of urgency to abate it. The current lethargic pace of incremental change will end up doing too little, too late.

A series of annual UN summits, with delegates from 194 countries protecting their own interests while arguing over resolutions on how to reduce heat-trapping emissions, is not a recipe for progress. At the beginning of the 18th climate conference in Doha in 2012, the U.S. special envoy for climate change, Todd D. Stern, announced that it was time to close the chapter on the Kyoto two-track division into industrial and developing countries and to begin a new chapter of "conceptual thinking" on the form of a comprehensive treaty of the future (Broder, 2012b). Instead, preserving the comparative justification for inaction, the conference simply extended the deficient Kyoto agreement for a few years while talking about behavioral changes that are expected to result in an action pact in 2020, to be implemented in 2025. The participants did note that in the meantime, global temperatures would continue to rise (Broder, 2012a).

Official reports on climate change typically begin with the bad news that adverse effects are becoming worse and are occurring faster than predicted. Moreover, serious environmental damage already has happened, rather than being likely to come in the distant future. Despite nearly two decades of annual UN-sponsored summits to enact a policy to curb global warming, emission of greenhouse gases continue to rise. A multipart 2014 report by the UN's Intergovernmental Panel on Climate Change (IPCC) documents in grim terms the damage that global warming is already causing and calls for large cuts in greenhouse gas emissions to avert future devastating global consequences (Gillis, 2014b). This report warns urgently that the window for doing so is rapidly closing.

Not all was bad news, however. In a section of the report released earlier in 2014, panel members pointed to recent advances in renewable energy technologies, indicating that they will play a much larger role than expected as sources of energy (Smith, 2014). Furthermore, renewables previously had been regarded as fringe players in energy generation. In a surprising development reviewed later in this chapter, rooftop solar is on the rise. Prices are plummeting to the point where solar energy is becoming competitive with fossil fuels. Scientific advances show promise of further transformative development of solar power (Evans-Pritchard, 2014). The IPCC panel also reported that placing a price on emissions can further limit the discharge of pollutants into the atmosphere without adverse economic effects. The potential for change gave the panel "modest hope" (Smith, 2014). A concerted effort to curtail emissions of greenhouse gases can still prevent the earth's climate from getting much worse and forestall disastrous, uncontrollable environmental consequences.

Natural gas is being heralded as friendly to the climate and as an abundant, cleaner, and cheaper source of energy for powering high-energy lifestyles. However, as a fossil fuel it is turning out to be not as clean as claimed. Hydrocarbon-based fuel sources such as coal, petroleum, and natural gas have accumulated over eons in reservoirs in the earth's substructure. When these fuels are extracted and burned for energy, the residue is released as heat-trapping greenhouse gases into the global atmosphere. According to the International Energy Agency, two-thirds of fossil fuel reserves should be left underground to limit global warming to 2 degrees Celsius, or 3.6 degrees Fahrenheit, above preindustrial levels to forestall irreversible, devastating environmental changes (McDonald, 2013). We cannot keep digging up underground hydrocarbons and depositing their byproducts into the global atmosphere, where they trap heat for centuries, warming the planet.

Renewable energy sources are criticized for their limited capacity, fluctuating output, and costs. Germany, which decided to phase out all nuclear power after the 2011 Fukushima earthquake and tsunami, has reported optimistic evidence that renewable sources can provide a good share of the energy needs of a country (Gillis, 2014a; Kirschbaum, 2012). In 2014, 26% of Germany's electric power came from renewable sources (Zha & Nicola, 2015). With careful preparation, Germany and other European countries were able to keep their solar power grids running during a total eclipse (Eckert, 2015). Recently, in Germany, solar power generation alone provided, in middays, a third of the electricity needs on workdays and nearly 50% on Saturdays when offices and many factories are closed (Kirschbaum, 2012). The latter measures address the energy supply side of the challenge. High-consumption lifestyles coupled with soaring population growth, both of which escalate demands for energy, magnify the impediments to keeping the global climate from getting much worse.

Euphemistic Language

Language shapes the appearance of things. Moral self-sanctions can be reduced by cloaking harmful activities in sanitized, convoluted, and innocuous language. Doublespeak renders them benign and socially acceptable (Lutz,

1996). For example, the acid rain that is killing lakes and forests is disguised as "transit particle deposition from an unidentifiable source" (EJ focus 2, 1988). The convoluted language of doublespeak disguises by piling on inflated words that do not add meaning (Lutz, 1987). In his book *Telling It Like It Isn't*, Dan Rothwell (1982) characterizes the sanitizing form of euphemisms as "linguistic Novocain" for the conscience that numbs us to unpleasant and harmful realities and the convoluted form as "semantic fog" that obscures and conceals detrimental practices.

The U.S. Environmental Protection Agency sanitized its lexicon to neutralize public perception of environmental hazards (Rogers & Kincaid, 1981). In this linguistic cleansing operation, a senior official at the agency banished the word *hazard* because it is "a trigger word that excites the American public needlessly" (Stiff, 1982). The justification for keeping people uninformed about carcinogens and other toxic chemicals in their environment was to spare them unnecessary uneasiness. The agency extended its linguistic detoxification to the titles of its offices. The Office of Hazardous Emergency Response was renamed the Office of Emergency and Remedial Action. Even the regulatory personnel were sanitized. The "enforcement personnel" were renamed "compliance assistance officers" as if they were helpmates rather than enforcers of environmental laws (Associated Press, 1981).

In the George W. Bush administration's linguistic ecological camouflaging (Salant, 2003), the distant vision of the hydrogen-powered "Freedom Car" powered by "Freedom Fuel" was intended to deflect the public's attention from the need to reduce carbon emissions by increasing fuel efficiency in the here and now. President Bush's proposed rewrite of the Clean Air Act, named "Clear Skies," was intended to spare the power industry from upgrading plants to reduce pollutant emissions. An initiative that favored the timber industry with liberal logging privileges in national forests was dubbed "Healthy Forests."

The National Council of Teachers of English bestowed its 1979 Doublespeak Award on the nuclear power industry for devising a unique lexicon for sanitizing nuclear mishaps. An explosion became an "energetic disassembly," a fire became "rapid oxidation," a reactor accident was a "normal aberration" or a "plant transferent," and plutonium contamination was dubbed "infiltration" or "plutonium has taken up residence" (National Council of Teachers of English, n.d.). What to do with radioactive waste from nuclear power plants is a daunting challenge. The Nuclear Regulatory Agency solved a good part of it linguistically by redefining radioactive waste material (Lutz, 1996). About a third of it was classified as BRC, "below regulatory concerns." This allowed the nuclear power industry to dispose of it any way they wished. A uranium processing plant was called the "Feed Materials Processing Center," suggestive of an animal feed processing plant. Its radioactive waste contaminated the ground water for almost four decades (Associated Press, 1988).

Officials at Tokyo Electric Power announced that "a big sound and white smoke" were recorded near a reactor (Tabuchi, Belson, & Onishi, 2011). One would not know from the sanitized description of the massive nuclear disaster that the "incident" was radioactive release from an explosion at the Fukushima Daiichi nuclear plant.

Linguistic camouflaging of the detrimental effects of social policies and practices is a flourishing morally neutralizing strategy (Bolinger, 1980; Lakoff, 2002; Lutz, 1987; Rothwell, 1982). Sanitizing language is not just a word game, however. It shapes people's perception of reality and increases their willingness to engage in detrimental activities (Bandura, 1999). For example, economic models are founded on the concept of continual growth. Economists use this concept as the core index of societal economic viability, which is highly prized and vigorously pursued. However, growth comes at the price of environmental degradation and depletion of resources for future generations. To mitigate the moral consequences of this degradation, proponents of continual growth cloak it in admirable terms. There is much loose talk, as Albert Bartlett (1994) documents, about "sustainable growth." He regards the term as an oxymoron because limitless economic growth cannot happen without increased consumption of nonrenewable resources. The belief that there will always be plentiful resources for future generations removes any moral concerns.

Eben Fodor (2012) calls "smart growth" a myth because it is based on the idea of unlimited growth with no consequences. Continuing destruction of the ecological supports of life and depletion of resources inevitably retrenches growth. Proponents append the terms *smart* and *sustainable* to *growth* as camouflage in promoting high levels of consumption. A loose coalition of logging, mining, petrochemical, and land development enterprises, along with some libertarian and fundamentalist religious groups, formed a movement to defeat environmentalist groups (Arnold, 1996). Under the benign title of the wise use movement (expropriated from the conservation movement), its proponents fight governmental regulations and champion laissez-faire commercial practices, many of which are environmentally unsustainable.

Advocates for environmental preservation sometimes manage to undermine their own mission with languid, misleading metaphors. Rather than portraying the harmful effects of human practices in vivid, concrete terms, they characterize those practices in metamorphic terms as leaving an "ecological footprint." We are beginning to witness footprint creep, with the "carbon footprint," the "decision footprint," and the "consumption footprint." Other types of footprints may be in the offing. However, a static footprint is a bad metaphor for agentic activities that degrade the quality of the environment. Deforestation, for example, does not leave a static footprint. Deforested land becomes an active carbon emitter. When carbon dioxide is deposited in the atmosphere, it remains there as a heat-trapping agent for thousands of years. The public is energized to collective action by aversive life conditions and warnings about worsening crises, not by visions of a metaphoric footprint.

What environmental changes are called makes a big difference in their social impact. When earth's rising surface temperature is called "global warming," people are more likely to view it as worrisome, a personal threat, catastrophic in its effects, already happening, requiring higher governmental priority, and evoking climate activism than if it is called "climate change" (Leiserowitz, Maibach, Roser-Renouf, Smith, & Dawson, 2013). People believe that glaciers are melting faster in the context of "global warming" than in the context of "climate change." The term *climate change*, which refers to diverse, long-term changes, is less emotionally engaging than images of high temperatures and extreme weather events evoked by the term *global warming*. I doubt that the metaphoric "footprint" rouses much of anything.

Displacement and Diffusion of Responsibility

Moral control comes into play when people acknowledge that they are contributing to harmful outcomes. When they shift the responsibility for the harm they cause to others or to external factors, they spare themselves self-reproach. It is easy to discern personal causation when one's actions produce highly noticeable, local effects in the short term. It is difficult to do so when the relationship between action and outcome is too slow to be noticeable and is obscured by intertwined chains of causation that take a long time to produce widespread observable effects. As a result, either individuals see no relationship between what they do and its effect on the earth's environment, or they view their contribution as too infinitesimal to make a difference in the global scheme of things. This sense of personal innocuousness is a form of self-exoneration for aggregate harm, but global effects are the cumulative products of just such local actions. The slogan "Think globally, act locally" is an effort to instill a sense of personal accountability for collective environmental harm. The belief that root causes can never be assigned because of the bewildering array of intertwined determinants is also self-exonerating.

Displacement of responsibility is often enlisted in industrial disasters where the blame is blatantly evident. Corporate vindication is achieved by shifting the blame. For example, the world's worst industrial disaster occurred in Bhopal, India, in 1984, when 40 tons of methyl isocyanate gas escaped from Union Carbide's pesticide production plant. Thousands of people were killed, others were seriously injured or partially disabled, and nearly 200,000 were severely affected in other ways (Weir, 1987). The U.S parent company displaced responsibility by blaming the Indian government for its failure to regulate the plant and for allowing people to live nearby (Bandura, Caprara, & Zsolnai, 2002). However, the company's attempt to blame the government for the residential zoning was not credible, because some of the worst affected communities were in existence before the factory was built in their midst, near the train station for convenient shipping. Union Carbide also blamed the explosion on sabotage, an assertion that environmental groups rejected.

Critics of conservationists blame global warming on natural cyclic changes in climate, claiming that we just happen to be in a warming phase. Making the planet itself the doer absolves high-consumption lifestyles and population growth of any responsibility for the earth's rising temperatures. Nor is there any need for moral self-evaluation if Mother Nature is the doer. As will be shown later, exoneration of the human connection is at odds with a mounting body of scientific evidence documenting it. Forests removed by clear-cutting, water supplies polluted by discharges of industrial and agricultural wastes and raw sewage, fish stocks depleted by overfishing with vast nets, and species made extinct by destruction of their habitats are but a few examples of environmental degradation that are plain to see, quantifiable, and unquestionably of human doing.

At the global level, the earth's temperature rise is linked to the number of people (Meyerson, 1998). However, in some quarters and media accounts that thrive on controversy, the emerging alarm over the rise in heat-trapping emissions is peculiarly disembodied from the growing multitude of consumers as a problem requiring attention. More people consuming more resources produce more environmental damage and generate more greenhouse gas emissions. This relationship underscores the influential role played by population growth in climate change.

Another common displacement strategy is disguising responsibility for subverting public policies designed to protect the environment. This is achieved through the creation of front organizations that masquerade under benevolent names and conceal their real purpose (Lutz, 1996). Industry-financed "scientific skeptics" add further credibility to the deceptive schemes (Gelbspan, 1998). Typical scenarios for the front organizations depict concerned citizens fighting big government, with its voracious appetite for laws and regulations that work against the public interest. If front organizations are cloaked in a seeming grassroots campaign, they gain an even greater sense of independence and credibility.

William Lutz (1996) provides a rich catalogue of ways that lobbying groups have creatively disguised their efforts to shape laws and regulations to weaken protection of the environment. Timber industries fight restrictions on cutting forests under the cloak of the Forest Protection Association. Corporations masqueraded under the name Citizens for Sensible Control of Acid Rain to defeat bills curbing acid rain. Utility companies and other organizations created the Endangered Species Reform Coalition to eviscerate the endangered species law. A host of polluters joined forces under the benevolently labeled Clean Air Working Group to gut the Clean Air Act. Real estate and gas and oil companies formed the National Wetlands Coalition, a seemingly environmentally friendly organization, to open up the nation's wetlands for commercial development. The fishing industry cloaked itself in the Sea Lion Defense Fund, not to save endangered sea lions but to remove limits on fishing the sea lion's favorite foods (Berlet, 1995).

Disregarding, Minimizing, and Disputing Detrimental Effects

When people pursue activities that serve their interests but produce detrimental effects, they avoid facing the harm they cause, or they minimize it. If minimization does not work, they can discredit scientific evidence of harm, generating doubt and controversy despite substantial evidence to the contrary. As long as one ignores, minimizes, or discredits the evidence of the harmful results of one's conduct, one has few reasons to activate self-censure or any need to change behavioral practices.

Because global effects are the products of multiple determinants, codetermination provides fertile ground for disputes about the true causes of detrimental outcomes. To further complicate assessment of effects, minor changes can set in motion cyclic processes that feed on each other in ways that eventuate in large-scale changes. For example, as previously noted, global warming thaws vast Arctic regions of permafrost, releasing methane and carbon dioxide that had been trapped in the frozen soil for thousands of years (Walter et al., 2006). Although methane is not so long lasting, it is better able than carbon dioxide to trap heat in the atmosphere. The trapped heat thaws more permafrost, which, in turn, further raises the earth's temperature in a vicious positive feedback cycle. The rate of methane release is much faster than expected, and the amount of carbon dioxide released vastly exceeded the amount emitted annually by burning fossil fuels (Bora, 2013). Implementing practices with little forethought for their consequences and disputing their human origin when they occur is a highly risky business.

Sound scientific theory provides knowledge on how human lifestyle practices affect interdependent ecological systems, suggests reliable proximal markers of long-range outcomes, and identifies factors for risk assessment. Using established knowledge to extrapolate the results of different courses of action enables people to take corrective measures to avert possible disastrous outcomes. A forward-looking focus is especially critical for environmental protection, because some of the detrimental changes that human practices unleash may turn out to be uncontrollable and irreversible.

Coby Beck (2007) has categorized the various stages of denial and rejection of global warming. The first stage is outright denial or treating global warming as nothing new. Naysayers argue that climate changes simply reflect the natural historical cycle of colder or warmer phases or that earth just happens to be in a hot phase. They claim that we must evaluate global climate change in terms of trends over a long time. Sometimes naysayers select a specific time or place that seems to provide contradictory evidence, challenging the conclusions of climate scientists. The general public often confuses weather, which fluctuates in the short term, with climate, which is an aggregated trend over long periods. As one skeptic, Donald Trump, put it, "[i]t's record cold all over the country and world—where the hell is global warming, we need some fast!" (Atkin, 2015).

The next stage of negation acknowledges that the earth may be warming, but we don't know why it is happening and, besides, predictions are unreliable. The conceptual models are alleged to be faulty, global systems are inherently chaotic so they are unpredictable, and scientific consensus is really collusion. Critics claim further that there is no proof that carbon dioxide causes global warming, which they attribute to a host of natural causes, such as volcanic eruptions, water vapor, cosmic rays, solar cycles, ozone, and the sun (Cook, 2015).

In the third stage, skeptics acknowledge that global warming is real and that humans contribute to it, but the effects are trivial or even beneficial. Warmer weather is said to make life more pleasant and productive in cooler northern regions. This may be personally comforting as long as one disregards the millions of people living near the equator whose lives are disrupted and dislocated by rising temperatures elsewhere. Arguments in the final stage claim that human actions cannot affect the earth's temperature and that regulatory policies to curb carbon emissions will be economically disastrous. The climate is not changing—or even if it is, the changes are not of human origin or remediable by human action—so there is no need to change lifestyle practices. Nor is there anything to get morally exercised about, and harmful behavior is freed from the restraint of moral self-sanctions.

Policy makers are fighting vigorously to shape our collective response to climate change. The stakes are high, everyone is a contributor to it, and it affects everyone in one way or another. Judging severity of the global threat for collective action requires prediction from scientific knowledge, which always contains some uncertainties. But despite those uncertainties, the need is urgent to take corrective measure before the scope of change becomes irreversible.

To address growing concerns over the global climate, the World Meteorological Organization and the United Nations Environmental Panel created the IPCC to assess research on changes in climate. Leading scientists worldwide evaluated the scientific and technical literature on climate change and concluded that the earth's temperature is rising and that the greenhouse gases emitted by human activities contribute significantly to global warming (Intergovernmental Panel, 2007).

The evidence available at the time of the 2007 IPCC report probably underestimated global warming, because that report did not include the release of greenhouse gases from the thawing permafrost. There is every reason to expect that the earth's temperature will rise faster than previously predicted, and some evidence already indicates that this is happening (Clark, 2009).

The physics professor Richard Muller, a leading scientific skeptic regarding global warming, assembled a distinguished group of scientists at the University of California, Berkeley, to reanalyze the large body of evidence along with climate changes much farther back in time (Muller, 2012). Their findings provided convincing evidence that, indeed, global warming is real and that human-caused emissions of greenhouse gases account for virtually all of it. These findings are stronger than those reported in the IPCC consensus statements, which had to be watered down to gain unanimity. The Berkeley reanalysis used more sophisticated analytic methods with more complete atmospheric data from as far back as 1753. Natural occurrences that skeptics invoked as the true cause of global warming, such as volcanic and solar activity and ocean currents, had small, short-lived effects or no effect at all. Adjustments for these various factors did not alter the relation between human greenhouse gas production and rising temperatures.

Muller suggested natural gas as the energy remedy for global warming, proposing that China should play a central role. China depends heavily on high-polluting coal for electricity to power its burgeoning industrial activities. It has now surpassed the United States as the leading emitter of greenhouse gases; as it rapidly builds more coal-fired plants, the emission rate will rise. The solution, in Muller's view, is for China to replace dirty coal with cleaner natural gas (Muller, 2012).

The IPCC's conclusions did not sit well with skeptics and denialists, who disagreed that the earth's climate was becoming warmer. They questioned the impartiality of the scientists, their forecasting models, and their analyses of the data. Amid the controversy, hackers downloaded files containing batches of e-mails and documents by climate scientists at the University of East Anglia's Climatic Research Unit. In an incident that became known as Climategate, climate skeptics claimed that the hacked documents showed that the scientists withheld and manipulated data. These allegations added further fuel to the already heated debate. Skeptics alleged that the scientists were not only biased but had committed outright fraud.

The British government commissioned eight independent investigations, some of which addressed the scientific conduct of particular climate scientists. An external Science Assessment Panel summarized the main findings (House of Commons, 2011). The investigations found no evidence of fraud or scientific misconduct. However, the external reviewers rebuked the scientists for sometimes being reluctant to share data and for a lack of transparency. The reviewers also noted the need for some changes in how the scientists reviewed the evidence. The investigations reaffirmed that the huge body of converging evidence from diverse scientific fields showed that human activity is driving up the earth's temperature (Gillis, 2010).

The science historian Spencer Weart, formerly at the American Institute of Physics, commented on the unprecedented assault on an entire group of scientists and the accusations that they had committed a massive scientific fraud: "We've never before seen a set of people accuse an entire community of scientists of deliberate deception and other professional malfeasance" (Freedman, 2009). Sherwood Boehlert, the former Republican chairman of the House Science Committee, regarded the attacks on climate scientists as diverting attention from a serious undertaking: "The attacks on scientists were a manufactured distraction" (Eilperin, 2010). He welcomed the end of the furor: "This exoneration should close the book on the absurd episode in which climate scientists were unjustly attacked." However, Myron Ebell, a spokesman in media appearances for skeptics of global warming and climate science, dismissed the investigations as a "whitewash" (Eilperin, 2010). There is no longer serious scientific dispute over the credibility of the evidence.

Senator James Inhofe of Oklahoma, who once brandished a snowball on the Senate floor as proof that climate change was a myth, has characterized global warming as the "greatest hoax ever perpetrated on the American people" (Sheppard, 2015). In his attacks on climate science, he sees himself as "doing the Lord's work" (Johnson, 2011). Ironically, Pope Benedict had a different view on God's will. The pope invoked a "global responsibility" to find the "moral will" to fight the "threatening catastrophe of climate change" (Johnson, 2011). When Pope Francis published his environmental encyclical *Laudate si'*, Inhofe—currently the chairman of the Senate Environment and Public Works Committee and still adamantly denying climate change—opined, "The pope ought to stay with his job, and we'll stay with ours" (Goldenberg, 2015). Emboldened by the climate scandal, Inhofe proclaimed that "[t]he credibility of the IPCC is eroding. The EPA's endangerment finding is collapsing. And belief that global warming is leading to catastrophe is evaporating" (Shiner, 2010). He described his alarmist nemesis, Al Gore, as "drowning in a sea of his own global warming illusions" and "running for cover" like an "ostrich." Inhofe joined forces with congressmen Sensenbrenner, an outspoken critic of climate science, in calling for investigation of climate scientists for possible criminal activities. Former Senator Rick Santorum, vying for the Republican presidential nomination, voiced his conspiracy theory of the true motivation behind the global warming claims. It is "an absolute travesty of scientific research that was motivated by those who, in my opinion, saw this as an opportunity to create a panic and crisis for the government to be able to step in and even more greatly control your life" (Johnson, 2012).

In August 2015, President Obama released his Clean Power Plan, intended to reduce emissions from power plants 32% nationwide by 2030 (Jackson, 2015). Before the White House even had made the plan public, Mitch McConnell, the Senate majority leader, wrote to all 50 state governors, calling on them not to comply with it (Malloy & Serfaty, 2015). Fifteen states filed petitions in federal court to block the EPA from implementing the plan (Reuters, 2015). The Democratic candidates in the 2016 presidential race generally had praise for it. Energy industry representatives and nearly all the Republican candidates criticized it as a costly federal overreach (Malloy & Serfaty, 2015). Climate change is on track to be a major issue in the 2016 presidential election.

Some observers promote natural gas as a cleaner fossil fuel that provides a new source of power while reducing carbon emissions. Hydraulic fracturing, or fracking, is the process of extracting natural gas and oil from shale rock deep in the earth by injecting water, sand, and toxic chemicals under high pressure. The industry claims that fracking does not release pollutants, but environmentalists have long claimed that fracking releases toxic chemicals, such as methane gas, into the water table, contaminating drinking water and even making it flammable (Marder, 2012). In addition, fracking releases methane gas into the atmosphere, which is considerably more damaging to the climate than carbon dioxide (Magill, 2015a). After extracting the natural gas, companies pump millions of tons of wastewater back into the earth, because there is at present no other way to dispose of it. The reservoirs of wastewater have been implicated in a rising number of earthquakes in states where fracking takes place, such as Oklahoma (Oskin, 2015).

One study posits that focusing on natural gas as an abundant, cheap source of energy is a distraction from investing resources to develop renewables (Magill, 2014). Hal Harvey, the CEO of Energy Innovation, voiced this concern: "Will it be a transition to a clean energy future, or does it defer a clean energy future?" (Friedman, 2012). With the fossil fuel industry wielding strong influence over lawmakers, deferral is the more likely option.

The energy supply-side remedy ignores the growing demand-side problem that fuels the need for high energy production. Given that global warming is largely the product of human activity, transformative changes must address its two intertwined, main sources—per capita consumption and population growth. People are the agents; their activities produce the emissions as by-products. There is much more to the environmental impact of human activity than climate change. Moreover, the multiplicative power of population size has increased markedly. In the earlier phases of the Industrial Revolution, smaller populations in developed countries pumped large amounts of greenhouse gases into the atmosphere. In contrast, despite larger populations, developing countries emitted fewer pollutants because of their much lower per capita consumptions of resources. For example, on average an American consumes more energy in a week than an inhabitant in India does in an entire year (Scheer & Moss, 2012).

Another environmental issue concerns opposition to models of change designed to mitigate global warming by placing a cost on carbon emissions. There are two ways of pricing carbon emissions: a carbon tax or a carbon market based on the cap-and-trade system. In this market incentive approach, manufacturers and utilities can purchase carbon emissions credits from more environmentally efficient industries that sell their unused emissions allowances. The level of allowed pollution is gradually lowered. Cap-and-trade's heralded market approach provides economic incentives to curtail polluting practices and to develop cleaner technologies.

President Obama's original cap-and-trade proposal fell victim to the culture war (Who pays, 2009). Former active supporters of this economic remedy turned against it by reconstruing it as a tax. Using this market approach for environmental protection, they claimed, was a subterfuge to impose taxes on families that could ill afford it: "An economy-wide tax under the cover of saving the environment is the best political moneymaker since the income tax" (Who pays, 2009). Critics further reconstrued the cap-and-trade program as an infringement on freedom in which the government manufactures a right to pollute that industries are then forced to buy. "Once the government creates a scarce new commodity—in this case the right to emit carbon—then mandates that businesses buy it, the costs would inevitably be passed on to all consumers in the form of higher prices" (Who pays, 2009). They also viewed it as a stealth scheme to redistribute income and wealth, taking money away from struggling businesses to give it to rich Silicon Valley and Wall Street "green tech" investors" (Who pays, 2009). The House of Representatives passed the bill, but it did not survive in the Senate (Power, 2010). The Nobel economist Paul Krugman (2014) comments on the irony that free-market proponents, who fervently believe that the "market can surmount all obstacles," rejected the use of financial incentives to reduce carbon emissions for political reasons.

Many analyses have compared the relative merits of an outright carbon tax and the cap-and-trade system. Even Thomas Crocker, who cocreated the cap-and-trade approach, acknowledges that it has some limitations. It is difficult to develop the permit exchanges; to link the system to myriad sources of pollution; to know how high to set the carbon permit prices; and to know how many carbon allowances to give the main industrial polluters. Further complicating matters, it is difficult to change the trading system once it is set up and to monitor and enforce it internationally without an agency empowered to oversee it (Hilsenrath, 2009). With lax oversight, the market system is easily corruptible. The cap-and-trade system is better suited, Crocker explains, for discrete, local pollution problems, as in the successful application that reduced acid rain in the northeastern United States.

In his keynote address at the international meeting on climate change in Copenhagen, Professor William Nordhaus of Yale University (2009) presented a strong case for an outright carbon tax. It is easily understandable as a tax per ton of emitted carbon; it is transparent; it can address carbon emissions from diverse sources such as energy, industry, and transportation; and it is highly flexible in implementation (Nordhaus, 2009). Whether an outright carbon tax can ever be enacted into law is another matter. The

European Union adopted the carbon market trading system but set the carbon permit prices too low, inadvertently changing an intended incentive market into a disincentive market with a glut of cheap carbon permits (Reed, 2014). Industrial polluters had few reasons to reduce their greenhouse gas emissions or to adopt green energy technologies.

President Obama's 2015 Clean Power Plan contains a cap-and-trade program whereby states that produce excess clean energy could sell that excess to less green states (Upton, 2015). Already some states and industries are challenging the plan (Reuters, 2015).

Carbon emissions have come under sharp scrutiny because, once spewed into the atmosphere, carbon remains there for centuries. Other heat-trapping pollutants dissipate rapidly but also increase global warming in the short term (Zaelke & Ramanathan, 2012). These include hydrofluorocarbon used in coolants; methane, a major ingredient of natural gas; lower-level ozone; and the carbon in soot. Curtailing emissions of these substances can help to reduce the earth's temperature but may distract from the primary goal of reducing carbon emissions.

People who minimize or deny adverse environmental changes or attribute them to natural causes are unlikely to alter their high-consumption lifestyles or support environmental conservation policies. In national surveys, 64% of Americans believe that global warming is real, but only about half believe that it is caused by human activity. Nor do they feel any need for more information about it. Only about one third see it as a threat to themselves and their local communities, and they do not believe that it is harming others at the present time (Leiserowitz, Maibach, Roser-Renouf, Feinberg, & Rosenthal, 2014). This is not a pattern of beliefs that is enduringly motivating for environmental conservation.

However, global warming has become a partisan issue. For the most part, individuals with a conservative worldview are more skeptical of human-caused global warming, whereas the liberal-oriented acknowledge it. Staunch supporters of initiatives to curb the earth's warming believe that it is real, human caused, harmful, and solvable (Ding, Maibach, Zhao, Roser-Renouf, & Leiserowitz, 2011).

The "Climategate" scandal over climate scientists' e-mails at the University of East Anglia further eroded the public's belief in global warming and fueled distrust of climate scientists (Leiserowitz et al., 2013). Although the scandal faded with time for most people, conservatives became even more convinced that the evidence for human causation of global warming is counterfeit. They used the erroneous claim that climate scientists are deeply divided in their views to undermine trust in the scientists and the reliability of their analyses. Over half of Americans are either unaware of the scientific consensus or believe that climate scientists disagree among themselves on this matter. When informed of the overwhelming scientific consensus (97%) among climate scientists that global warming is happening, people become more accepting that the climate is getting warmer and that humans contribute to it (Lewandowsky, Gignac, & Vaughan, 2013).

The scientific community and the mass media must do a better job of informing the uninformed and correcting the misinformed to build strong public support for social change (Maibach, Myers, & Leiserowitz, 2014). Whether or not people turn environmental concerns into sustainable practices depends in part on their shared belief that they can effect environmental changes through collective action. For example, in a national study in India, communities with a high sense of collective efficacy, aided by mass media campaigns, were better at ensuring an adequate supply of drinking water than were communities with a weak belief in their efficacy (Thaker, 2014). As we will see, findings on social change through media productions founded on social cognitive theory indicate that the mass media not only can inform communities but also can enable them to work toward an environmentally sustainable future.

The global financial crisis of 2008 diverted concern over environmental conservation and provided economic justifications for ecologically hazardous industrial practices that formerly had been restricted (Paulson, 2014). Restoration of economic growth trumped environmental consideration. Talk of regulating or taxing carbon emissions became politically perilous for electability. Abundant cheap natural gas stiffened resistance to subsidizing clean energy initiatives. Some observers thought that increased use of natural gas, especially in power plants, had caused a drop in carbon emissions, but it turned out that decreased consumption of energy during the Great Recession was the actual cause (Magill, 2015b).

Because climate change has become so contentious, it was never even mentioned in the 2012 American presidential campaign. Lack of global leadership and perennial stalemates at UN climate summits further lowered the status of climate change in the public agenda. Domestic political shunning of environmental issues and industrial and partisan public opposition to environmental reforms downgraded climate change further. In this inhospitable social climate, even the media deserted it as a newsworthy item. In the meantime, people worldwide are experiencing unprecedented environmental disasters wreaking death and destruction and obliterating livelihoods. Firsthand experience of aversive environmental consequences can restore public support for social policies that mitigate climate change. We will revisit how motivation can be enlisted for this purpose.

The increase in severe weather events, topped by Hurricane Sandy's massive devastation of the densely populated New York City area in 2012, forced the issue on the public agenda. People argue about whether extreme events, such as heat waves or superstorms, were caused by global warming (Gillis, 2012). This narrow focus addresses the issue in misleading terms. Any extreme event is the product of a unique constellation of factors such that, if one or more of them is absent, the event would not occur. Global warming operates in intricate interaction with other factors that influence the severity and pattern of extreme weather events. The increasing warming of the planet provides many of the ingredients for superstorms, raising sea levels through glacial melting, warming ocean temperatures that fuel the storms with high precipitation, and altering the trajectories of jet streams toward land areas or seaward. Rising sea levels and more powerful hurricanes heighten the vulnerability of low-lying coastal regions to devastating storm surges. There is scientific consensus that human-caused climate change is an important contributor to extreme weather events. Scientists and engineers warned officials in the New Orleans and New York regions a few years earlier that they would be battered by supersized storms (Glanz & Navarro, 2012). Their warnings and their calls for protective measures went unheeded.

A strong pressure ridge over Greenland turned Hurricane Sandy inland rather than out to sea. Having experienced three storms of historic proportions in a short time, New York State governor Andrew Cuomo characterized such extreme weather events as the "new normal" (Cuomo, 2012). Hurricane Sandy overwhelmed the region's aging infrastructures and relief efforts, causing massive flooding of low-lying areas and shutting down much of the area's transportation system. Millions of people were cut off from help amid demolished, burned, or submerged homes, without food, water, electricity, fuel, and medical services. At the height of this colossal tragedy, Art Horn (2012), a climate skeptic, took Governor Cuomo to task for declaring extreme weather the "new normal." Hurricanes happen all the time, including some big ones, Horn stated, but most steer seaward. In his view, it is just Mother Nature acting up again. He went on to explain that we should neither feel at fault nor try to control the weather. "The 'new normal' is the old normal, it just comes and goes in cycles."

In the aftermath of this disaster, there was much talk about erecting sea walls against future devastating storms, but none about preventing such disasters by reducing emissions of heat-trapping gases into the atmosphere. Such protective measures raise thorny ethical issues, because barriers divert surging water to neighboring regions, which then are flooded even more heavily. What if the inundated neighboring areas are heavily populated? Who decides, by what means and criteria, which areas will be protected and which will be more heavily flooded? With rising sea levels, lowland coastal regions—many of which are major densely populated cities—will be underwater, requiring mass relocations. Tidal surges fueled by fierce storms may flood even some higher elevations.

Dehumanization and Disparagement

Repudiation of the messengers of unwelcome ecological news takes a variety of forms. Antienvironmentalists portray them as mentally unstable, acting on suspect motives masquerading as environmental protection, doing "junk science" that yields faulty data, or cherry-picking evidence to their liking. Those who believe the environment is not deteriorating feel certain that they have nothing to be concerned about, including the morality of detrimental practices. Nor do they need to make major changes in their lifestyles.

One of the nastiest assaults on a bearer of unwelcome empirical evidence was directed at biologist Rachel Carson, on the publication of *Silent Spring* (Beyl, 1991). Recall the earlier analysis of the great lengths to which the chemical and agricultural industries went to discredit Carson's credibility as a scientist. She was portrayed as a "hysterical" woman who cared more about the deaths of cats than about the "10,000 people throughout the world who die from malnutrition and starvation *every day*" (Diamond, 1963). The conservative magazine *Human Events* bestowed on *Silent Spring* honorable mention in compiling its list of the "Ten Most Harmful Books" of the 19th and 20th centuries (Ten most harmful books, 2005). The scientific community and the general public thought otherwise. *Silent Spring* has appeared on dozens of lists of the best nonfiction books of the 20th century. The woman who was criticized as emotionally unfit to evaluate the effects of toxic chemicals received countless awards and honors, including, posthumously, the highest U.S. civilian award, the Presidential Medal of Freedom.

It is easy to remove other species from moral consideration and to destroy their habitats when they interfere with one's self-interest. Such species are regarded as lowly pests that stand in the way of economic development and destroy people's livelihoods. Opponents single out an endangered bird, rodent, or reptile to ridicule legislative protections and disparage those who promote them. Those who vilified Rachel Carson portrayed her as more protective of insects and vermin than of humans. Given the intricate interdependence of species, humans can ill afford to wipe out species on which they must depend. The recent alarm over the surprising decline of honeybees worldwide, due to a number of possible causes, underscores the grave risks of indifference to the health of other species (Schwartz, 2014). The disappearance of honeybees, which pollinate fruits, nuts, and vegetable crops, would set off a worldwide food crisis.

The changing oceans provide another example of how human activity threatens the intricate interdependencies of ecological systems. Humans have had a hand in the destruction of the maritime environment and are not merely passive blameless observers of its natural cycle. Carbon emissions are increasing the ocean's acidity, threatening destruction of organisms at the base of the marine food chain that supports stocks of food fish (Chu, 2015; Kleypas et al., 2006). Such developments make interdependent environmentalism a lived reality, not just an abstract ethos. Massive overfishing to feed growing populations has already obliterated some fish species and has decreased the numbers of others. Undoubtedly other crises are in the making through the extinction of other species lower in the food chain. People may see no inherent value in them, but utterly ignoring their functional value is perilous.

Depersonalizing classes of people or treating them as lesser human beings can disengage or blunt moral self-sanctions. Human suffering at the global level is, in large part, indirectly rather than directly inflicted. We saw earlier that the world's wealthiest countries produce most of the heat-trapping gas emissions that are raising global temperatures. The people who live in poor, developing countries in sub-Saharan Africa and Central Asia bear the brunt of the adverse climate shift. As the receding glaciers in mountain ranges are further melted by the earth's rising temperature, the rivers they feed provide less water for personal, agricultural, and industrial use. Water shortages, crop failures, and expanding desertification are forcing mass migrations of people who lack the resources and means to protect themselves against the degradation of their environment. The displacement of millions of people is creating a growing humanitarian crisis. Their meager livelihoods contribute little to the temperature rise, but they suffer from its adverse consequences.

Myron Ebell (2006), one of the most prominent critics of climate science, extols the benefits of global warming. He argues that it makes life more pleasant for people in northern regions. Moreover, he claims, cold spells kill more people than do heat waves. For him, therefore, a bit of global warming not only saves lives but also makes life more pleasant. As he explains it somewhat self-centeredly, "Given our obvious preference for living in warmer climates as long as we have air-conditioning, I doubt that we're going to go on the energy diet that the global warming doomsters urge us to undertake."

A sense of common humanity arouses empathy and compassion for the plight of the needy and most vulnerable. Such sentiments motivate efforts to improve their life conditions (Bandura, 2004). Ebell's trivialization of the effects of global warming raises moral issues and disregards the evidence that the energy-rich diet of wealthier countries is making life more miserable for those of lesser means in marginal regions: If they cannot adapt to less hospitable environmental conditions, so be it. To extol the benefits of a rich energy diet with apparent indifference to the environmental and human costs to vulnerable others raises moral issues.

Ebell extends a harsh Darwinism to lower species as well. "If the oceans are warming, or the acidity is changing, that will benefit some species more than others" (Shnayerson, 2007a). He goes on to explain that the extinction of sea life is of little concern: "Some will take over, others will die out or move on somewhere else" (Shnayerson, 2007a).

Some of the proposed technological remedies for global warming create new moral predicaments through unintended harm to needy people. Efforts to address the energy-supply problem, for example, focus on a fix rather than on reducing demand through conservation. Some Western governments have invested billions of dollars in ethanol and other biofuels as a partial solution to the heavy dependence on fossil fuels. However, the government-subsidized diversion of U.S. corn crops from food supplies to ethanol has raised the cost of corn worldwide (Gillis, 2015b). Increasing world hunger by placing staple foods in competition with biofuels is a matter of humanitarian concern. Especially in countries where corn is a staple, the poor find it harder to feed their families and are priced out of the basic necessities of life. Because livestock are fed corn, the diversion has raised the prices of milk and other dairy products, as well as prices of a wide variety of foods made with corn or corn by-products. Waste from other plants and from lumber processing also goes into manufacturing ethanol. As food prices soar, foreign food-aid money can feed fewer hungry people (Dugger, 2007). Also, doubts have begun to surface about whether biofuels actually do benefit the environment. For example, ethanol has corrosive properties (Clemente, 2015). Some analysts (GRAIN, 2007) report that the rush to agrofuels will cause huge environmental and social damage as forests and small-scale food farming are converted by agribusiness to large-scale cultivation of plants for biofuels. Recent research indicates that small-scale farming and other environmentally efficient practices may be the key to feeding the world's hungry (Bambrick, 2015).

Disparaging climate scientists and dismissing their scientific analyses as fraudulent neutralizes moral concerns that one's own lifestyle practices may be environmentally harmful. The messengers of adverse effects in both the scientific community and the general public are disparaged as "doomsayers," "scaremongers," "global whiners," "environmental wackos," "tree huggers," "Malthusian alarmists," or "technological Pollyannas." Bloggers who claim that environmental problems are partly of human doing are called "kooks" and "nutters." Critics christened the indefatigable environmentalist Al Gore "ozone man" and a "false prophet." The British press labeled Prince Charles, who called for a sustainable stewardship of the environment, a "loony eccentric: the prince who talked to plants" (Shnayerson, 2007b).

Passions run high on both sides of the global-warming debate. Individuals who acknowledge that global warming is real but minimize its impact are called "lukewarmers." A petition urged the media to call those who reject the vast body of evidence of climate science "deniers," not "skeptics" (Gillis, 2015c).

Scientists come in for especially harsh treatment because they bear disturbing news about what is happening to our battered planet (White et al., 2009). Critics ascribe nefarious motives to them and disparage them as "self-appointed guardians," "hysterical crusaders," or "misguided zealots." Their research is discredited as "junk science" and their findings dismissed as fraudulent. In his blockbuster techno-thriller *State of Fear* (2004), Michael Crichton debunks global warming by portraying environmentalists as eco-terrorists. In an appendix to the fictionalized message that environmentalism is a deceitful religion rather than fact-based science, Crichton adds his personal view, likening the zeal of environmentalists to that of the eugenicists of the Nazi regime.

PROMOTING HUMAN WELL-BEING AND ENVIRONMENTAL CONSERVATION BY PSYCHOSOCIAL MEANS

The widespread and mounting degradation of the environment is, in large part, of humans' own doing. Walt Kelly created a famous poster featuring his beloved comic-strip character, Pogo, that captured the harm being done to the environment. As Pogo surveys a deforested, trash-filled landscape, he remarks, "We have met the enemy and he is us." Altering this detrimental course requires altering the behaviors that contribute to it. Because of the magnitude of the environmental problems and the urgent need for solutions, large populations must have strong motives for making such changes.

People acquire new styles of behavior and change preexisting ones via two basic modes of influence. Through firsthand experience of trial and error, they learn from the positive and negative effects of their actions. Constraints of time, resources, and mobility can impose severe limits on the situations and activities that humans can explore in their own lived environments to acquire new knowledge, competencies, and worldviews. The second mode of influence, which operates through the power of social modeling, bypasses the trial-and-error method and vastly expands the available information for self-development and change (Bandura, 1986). Revolutionary advances in electronic communications and the development of entertainment-education allow large-scale social and lifestyle changes to be modeled and rapidly diffused worldwide, enabling people to transcend the confines of their physical locations (Bandura, 2006a; Braithwaite, 1994). Through electronic media, social programs, grounded in modeling theory, are alleviating some of the most pressing problems and improving the quality of people's lives around the world (Bandura, 2006a; Singhal, Cody, Rogers, & Sabido, 2004).

Serial Dramas: Vehicles of Change

Long-running serial dramas are the principal vehicle for promoting personal and social changes (Bandura, 2006a; Singhal et al., 2004). These dramatic productions are not just fanciful stories. The plotlines portray the realities of people's everyday struggles, fears, and aspirations, as well as the positive and negative effects of various social practices. The dramas help people to see a better life and provide the strategies and incentives to enable them to make personal and social changes so they can realize their hopes and dreams.

Hundreds of episodes spanning several years allow listeners and viewers to form strong emotional bonds with the cast-member models, whose thinking and behavior evolve at a believable pace, inspiring and enabling viewers to improve their own lives. The flexibility of this format allows generalizability, versatility, and power. Multiple, intersecting plots and sub-plots address different aspects of people's lives at both individual and social structural levels, rather than focusing on a single issue. For example, the story lines of a serial set in Sudan included the benefits of family planning, educational opportunities for girls, the injustice of forced marriage, the risks of early childbearing, prevention of HIV infection, and the harm of embroilment in drug-related activities. The myriad issues in a Rwandan program included reproductive health, the prevention of HIV-AIDS, the preservation of wildlife habitats and natural resources, land conservation, sustainable farming practices, and the promotion of civil harmony.

Some societies present unique problems that require story lines specifically tailored to their cultural practices. The World Health Organization (WHO, 2014) estimates that over 125 million girls and women in Africa, Asia, and the Middle East have been subjected to genital mutilation. In a Sudanese radio drama devoted to this problem, Muslim clerics explained that Islam does not sanction these practices. The story line portrayed the devastating physical harm and psychological consequences suffered by a young woman whom viewers had come to adore (Greiner, Singhal, & Hurlburt, 2007). After the broadcast, the social norm shifted from support for female genital mutilation to a commitment to abolish it.

Another story line tailored to unique cultural problems addressed the pervasive practice of child trafficking in the West African countries of Mali, Ivory Coast, and Burkina Faso. Child traffickers trick poor parents with large families into giving up some of their children under the pretense that they will receive good care and schooling and will send money home. Instead, the traffickers sell the children for slave labor under inhumane conditions. The traffickers also sell children whose parents have died of AIDS. Some children are sold to the sex trade. The radio serial drama exposed these cruel practices. Listeners became aware of child trafficking, discussed exploitative child labor, and took action against it, more so than did nonlisteners (Population Media Center, 2004).

A radio drama set in Rwanda promoted various changes, including family planning, prevention of HIV-AIDS, soil conservation, and biodiversity. In one of the story lines, a farmer cannot feed his large family with his small plot of land. He clear-cuts an adjacent hill. The erosion from it destroys his small plot. In desperation he turns to poaching gorillas, which lands him in even more serious trouble. Eventually, with the help of a neighbor, he is able to resolve his difficulties (Population Media Center, 2007).

The psychosocial approach to fostering societywide changes consists of three major components. The first component is a *theoretical model* based on social cognitive theory (Bandura, 1986). It specifies the determinants of psychosocial change and the mechanisms through which those determinants produce their effects. This knowledge provides the guiding principles. The second component is a *translational and implemental model*. It converts theoretical principles into an innovative operational model. It specifies the content, strategies of change, and their mode of implementation. Miguel Sabido (Institute for Communication Research, 1981), a creative playwright and producer at Televisa in Mexico, pioneered the entertainment-education model by translating social cognitive theory into a dramatic format.

We often do not profit from our theoretical successes because we lack effective means for disseminating proven psychosocial approaches. The third component is a *social diffusion model* for adopting psychosocial programs to diverse cultural milieus. Population Media Center (Ryerson, 1994) and Population Communications International (Poindexter, 2004) are the diffusion systems worldwide. These organizations raise funds from the UN, institutional, corporate, and private donors to cover their production costs.

The serial dramas are not social programs foisted on nations by outsiders pursuing their own interests. They are created only by invitation from countries seeking help with intractable problems. Population Media Center works in partnership with media personnel in the host countries to create serial dramas tailored to their cultures and addressing their particular needs. The host production team draws on a wide variety of sources, including public health systems, religious organizations, women's groups, and other constituencies to identify unique life conditions, social practices, and prevailing values. This information helps them to identify the types of changes the dramatizations should address and provides culturally relevant information for developing realistic characters and engrossing, functional story lines. Once a program is aired, producers monitor how listeners or viewers perceive the characters, which ones they identify with, how they view the obstacles and the dramatized options, and what types of futures they envision. Scripts are amended on the basis of this feedback.

The dramatizations are ethically and culturally sensitive. Value disputes in the story lines often arise from wrangling over stereotypes with emotive, surplus meanings. Hence the stories present value issues in concrete, real-life terms of the detriments and benefits of particular lifestyles. These tangible values embody respect for human dignity and equitable familial, social, health, and educational opportunities. The dramatizations thus support common human aspirations as codified in UN covenants and resolutions.

Principles Governing Enabling Dramatizations

Five basic principles guide the construction of the dramatic serials: social modeling, enhancement of personal and collective efficacy, vicarious motivation, emotional engagement, and enlistment of environmental supports (Bandura, 2002a).

Social Modeling

The first principle enlists the power of social modeling for personal and social change. Characters in the dramas include models exhibiting beneficial, dysfunctional, or transitional patterns of behavior. By dramatizing alternative behaviors and their effects on the characters' lives, the dramas help people make informed choices in their own lives. Viewers and listeners are especially likely to draw inspiration from, and identify with, transitional models who overcome adverse life circumstances like their own. Seeing people similar to themselves succeed through sustained effort increases observers' belief that they, too, can improve their lives. The greater the assumed similarity, the more persuasive the model's successes and failures (Bandura, 1986). Modeling influences do more than build people's belief in their own capabilities. Through their behavior and expressed ways of thinking, competent models transmit knowledge and teach observers effective skills and strategies for managing environmental demands. Acquisition of better means increases perceived self-efficacy.

Perceived Personal and Collective Efficacy

Human well-being and accomplishments require an optimistic, resilient sense of efficacy. The usual daily realities are full of conflicts, impediments, adversity, failures, setbacks, frustration, and inequities. If people are to succeed in difficult undertakings, they cannot afford to be derailed by troublesome experiences. Belief in personal efficacy is not a Pollyannaish mind-set such as "I believe, therefore, I achieve." The most functional belief system for undertaking difficult tasks combines realism about tough odds with optimism that one can beat those odds through self-development and perseverant effort. A resilient sense of efficacy provides the needed staying power.

Many challenges involve common problems that require people to work together to solve them. A shared belief in their combined power to realize the future they seek is a key factor in the exercise of collective agency (Bandura, 2000). The greater a group's perceived collective efficacy, the stronger its members' motivational investment in their undertakings, the more resilient their staying power in the face of impediments and setbacks, and the greater their accomplishments.

When people attempt social change, often they challenge power relations and entrenched societal practices supported by individuals who have a vested interest in preserving them, even though they no longer serve the common good. Social change does not come easily. Not only do people have to challenge adverse traditions and inequitable constraints, but they also must be prepared for other obstacles.

The dramatic serials offer several ways of building resilient self-efficacy through social modeling of prototypical problem situations and effective ways of overcoming them. They also teach people how to manage setbacks by modeling how to recover from failed attempts and how to enlist guidance and social support for personal and social change from self-help groups and other agencies in their localities.

Vicarious Motivators

Self-regulation of motivation and action is partly governed by whether people expect their actions to produce beneficial outcomes or adverse ones. Unless people see the modeled lifestyle as improving the serial drama characters' welfare, they have little incentive to adopt it themselves or to stick with it in the face of difficulties. Contrast modeling vividly portrays the personal and social benefits of the favorable practices and the costs of the detrimental ones. Seeing beneficial outcomes instills positive outcome expectations that become incentives for change, whereas observed detrimental outcomes result in negative outcome expectations that become disincentives. Observing modeled outcomes increases motivation when observers see similarities to themselves in the inspiring models' sociodemographic characteristics and judge the modeled behavior as having functional value (Bandura, 1986).

Attentional and Emotional Engagement

Story lines that dramatize viewers' everyday lives and functional solutions get them deeply involved. They form emotional ties to models who reflect their own hopes and aspirations. Unlike brief exposures to media presentations that typically leave most viewers untouched, ongoing engagement in the evolving lives of models provides numerous opportunities to learn from them and to be inspired by them.

Viewers care deeply about the characters because they are personally relevant. In *Taru*, a radio serial broadcast in India with a listenership of about 25 million, a mother challenges restrictive cultural norms to promote her daughter Taru's education. Taru's story inspired formerly illiterate teenagers who had no access to education to become avid readers and pursue an education. Here is an example of Taru's powerful impact on teenage listeners: "There are moments when I feel that Taru is directly talking to me, usually at night. She is telling me, 'Usha, you can follow your dreams.' I feel like she is my elder sister . . . and giving me encouragement." Modeling the educational practices of Taru's mother, one of the viewers created a school for illiterate women. Several teenage girls started a school for poor children, who attend classes around the village water well. The teenagers fight for social justice and gender equality and against class discrimination and forced teenage marriage. Their efforts alter community norms to fit the changing times (PCI Media Impact, 2002).

After the broadcast of another serial drama in India, 400,000 viewers sent letters supporting, advising, or criticizing the various models in the drama. After a serial in Tanzania, women spotted a negative model at a market and drove him out under a rain of tomatoes and mangoes. In Brazil, 10,000 people showed up for the filming of a virtual "marriage" of two of the characters in a serial drama.

Environmental Supports

Motivating people to change has limited value if they have no access to appropriate resources and environmental supports for realizing those changes. Enlisting or creating environmental supports expands and sustains the changes promoted by the serial dramas. The dramatic productions are designed to operate via two pathways, first by informing, enabling, motivating, and guiding viewers. However, people also are socially situated in interpersonal networks (Bandura, 2006a; Rogers & Kincaid, 1981). Therefore, the second, socially mediated pathway connects viewers to social networks and community settings. These places provide continued personalized guidance as well as natural incentives and social support for desired changes. Behavioral and value changes are promoted within these social milieus. Epilogues, delivered by culturally admired figures, provide contact information for relevant community services and support groups.

GLOBAL APPLICATIONS

Worldwide applications of entertainment-education are raising literacy levels, enhancing the status of women, reducing unplanned childbearing to break the cycle of poverty and stem soaring population growth, curtailing the spread of HIV-AIDS, promoting environmental conservation practices, and fostering beneficial changes in other life conditions unique to particular cultures. The sections that follow summarize some of these applications and provide formal evaluations of their effects. These applications have been extensively reviewed elsewhere in greater detail (Bandura, 2002a; Singhal et al., 2004).

Promoting National Literacy

Literacy is vital for personal and national development. To reduce widespread illiteracy, the Mexican government launched a national self-study program. People who were skilled at reading were urged to organize small self-study groups in which they would teach others how to read with primers developed for this purpose. It was a good idea but enlisted few takers. As this creative effort illustrates, simply providing resources and ready access to them does not mean that people will take advantage of them. Turning opportunities into desired futures requires perseverant effort and mastery of difficulties along the way. The process of personal and social change is greatly facilitated by eliminating the psychosocial impediments to change and building people's beliefs in their own efficacy. Failure to address the psychosocial determinants of human behavior is often the weakest link in social policy initiatives.

Given the ineffectiveness of this national effort, Miguel Sabido (Institute for Communication Research, 1981) created a yearlong television serial drama to reach, enable, and motivate people to enlist in the literacy program. A popular performer was cast in the role of the literate model. To enhance the impact of modeling through perceived similarity, she recruited a diverse set of characters to represent the different segments of the population with problems of illiteracy.

A prior survey had revealed three principal barriers that dissuaded people from enrolling in the literacy program: perceived inefficacy, the assumption that they were too old, and a sense of self-unworthiness. Many believed that they were incapable of mastering such a complex skill. Others believed that reading skills are learnable only when one is young, so they could not learn to read as adults. Still others felt that they were unworthy of having an educated person devote time to them. These self-dissuading erroneous beliefs were modeled by characters in the drama and corrected by the mentor, who persuaded them that they could succeed. The episodes included humor, conflicts, and engrossing discussions of the subjects being read. The characters were shown struggling in the initial phases of learning and then gaining progressive mastery with self-pride in their accomplishments.

To provide vicarious motivators for pursuing the literacy program, the dramatic series depicted the substantial personal benefits of literacy and its contribution to national efficacy and pride. One of the epilogues, by an admired movie star, informed the viewers of this national self-education program and encouraged them to take advantage of it. The next day, 25,000 people showed up at the distribution center to enroll in the self-study program. To facilitate transfer from vicarious engagement to reality, the series used real-life settings, showing the actors obtaining the instructional material from an actual distribution center and eventually graduating in a ceremony for actual enrollees in the adult literacy classes.

Millions of viewers watched this televised series faithfully. Compared with nonviewers, viewers were much more informed about the national literacy program and expressed more positive attitudes about helping one another to learn. As shown in Figure 8.3, enrollment in the literacy program was relatively low in the year before the televised series but rose abruptly during the year of the series (Institute for Communication Research, 1981).

As people develop a sense of efficacy and competencies that enable them to exercise better control over their lives, they can become models, motivators, and even tutors for others in the circles in which they travel. Such exponential second-order influences can amplify the direct impact of televised

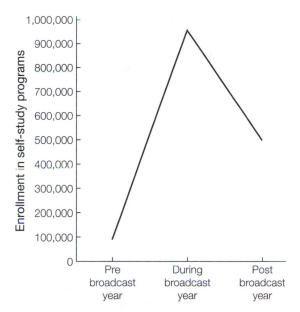

Figure 8.3 Enrollments in the national literacy program in the year prior to, during, and following the televised serial drama drawn from data in Sabido (Institute for Communication, 1981). With kind permission from Springer Science+Business Media.

modeling. In the year following the televised series, another 400,000 people enrolled in the self-study literacy program. Through the socially mediated path of influence, televised modeling can set in motion an ever-widening, reverberating process of social change.

Shaping Futures Through Family Planning

Some of the applications of social cognitive theory are aimed at slowing population growth, especially in developing countries struggling with widespread poverty. If they have high fertility rates, they could double their population in a short time. The psychosocial approach fosters personal and social change through enlightenment and enablement rather than by coercion (Bandura, 1997). Planned childbearing is addressed in terms of families' desired futures. Efforts to reduce the rate of population growth through family planning must address the broader issue of the role and status of women. Improving diverse aspects of people's lives, not merely targeting contraception, achieves the desired changes. Often the problem is not access to contraception but rather psychosocial impediments to its use. The challenges are greatest in societies in which women are marginalized, disallowed aspirations, denied access to education, forced into arranged marriages and early childbearing, granted little say in their reproductive lives, and denied liberty and dignity. Women's social and economic development requires eliminating cultural barriers to their education.

In patriarchal societies, male resistance to contraception and the idea that offspring are symbols of virility add to the family count. Another Mexican serial drama promoted family planning to help break the cycle of poverty, which is heightened by a high rate of unplanned childbearing. The story focused on the lives of married sisters. The benefits that one sister gained by having a small family were contrasted with the experiences of the other sister, who was burdened with a huge family that lived in poverty and despair. Another story line portrayed a married daughter and her family, who lived in her parents' desperately crowded, destitute environment. She already had two children and was pregnant with a third. She was in conflict with her husband and felt distress over her desire to have a voice in her family's life. She wanted to stop having more babies, which she realized would condemn her family to poverty without the means to care adequately for them. The young husband and wife were the transition models. The young woman sought help from an aunt who worked in a family-planning clinic. This relationship was the vehicle for modeling a great deal of information about how to manage marital discord and *machismo*-based behavior, how to deal with male resistance to contraception and family planning, how to communicate openly in the family, and how to escape the many problems caused by a family overburdened with children.

The drama depicted the young couple gaining control over their family life and enjoying accruing benefits with the help of the family-planning center. With support of the Archbishop, a priest occasionally appeared in the epilogues, emphasizing the need for responsible family planning by limiting the number of offspring to those the family can afford to raise adequately. At the end of some of the programs, viewers were informed about existing family-planning services to facilitate media-promoted changes.

Compared with nonviewers, heavy viewers of the dramatic serial were more likely to link lower childbearing to social, economic, and psychological benefits. They also developed a more positive attitude toward helping others plan their families (Institute for Communication Research, 1981). Records from family-planning centers revealed a 32% increase in the number of new contraceptive users over the number for the previous year, before the series was televised. As shown in Figure 8.4, national sales of contraceptives changed little in the preceding two baseline years but increased sharply by 23% in the year the program was broadcast. People reported that the televised serial was the impetus for consulting the centers.

Land ownership is highly valued in Kenya. The creative tailoring of a serial drama in Kenya illustrates this key cultural value. One of the major story lines linked the impoverishing effect of large families to the inheritance of land. The contrast modeling centered on two brothers. One brother had one wife, a son, and several daughters, whereas the other brother had multiple wives, nine sons, and a number of daughters. They squabbled over how to pass the family farm to the next generation. At the time the series was broadcast, only sons could inherit property. The monogamous brother

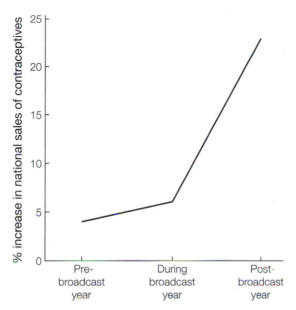

Figure 8.4 National sales of contraceptives in the two years preceding the serial drama promoting family planning and during the year it was broadcast. Drawn from data in Sabido (Institute for Communication, 1981). With kind permission from Springer Science+Business Media.

argued that his lone male heir was entitled to half the land. The polygamous brother insisted on dividing the farm into ten small plots that would provide, at best, a marginal subsistence for them all. In a concurrent plotline, a teacher pleaded with a young girl's parents to let her continue her education, which she desperately desired. The parents wanted her to quit school, be circumcised, and submit to an arranged marriage. The serial, which was broadcast via radio to reach rural areas, attracted 40% of the Kenyan population each week as the most popular program on the air. Contraception use increased by 58%, and desired family size declined 24%. A survey of women who came to health clinics found that the radio series helped to persuade their husbands to allow them to seek family planning.

The impact of media exposure on adoption and consistent use of new methods of contraception is shown in Figure 8.5. Listeners were higher adopters of contraception than were nonlisteners. Examination of the relation between level of exposure to the serial drama and adoption of contraception, with appropriate controls for self-selection of exposure, is another analytic means of assessing media influence (Westoff & Rodríguez, 1995). This quantitative analysis included multiple statistical controls for other possible influences on contraception use, such as life-cycle status, number of wives and children, and a host of socioeconomic factors such as ethnicity, religion, education, occupation, and urban or rural residency. Level of exposure remained a significant contributor to adoption of contraception after applying the multiple statistical

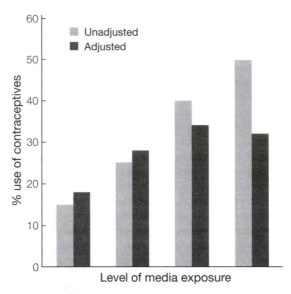

Figure 8.5 Percentage of women adopting contraceptive methods depending on the amount of exposure to family planning communications in the media. The dark bars report the level of contraceptive use after controlling for the women's demographic and socioeconomic characteristics and a host of other potential determinants. From Westoff and Rodriquez (1995).

controls. Surveys further revealed that media influence was a major factor in increasing motivation to adopt contraception.

Even stronger evidence for the effectiveness of serial dramas was obtained in a study in Tanzania, where regions with separate radio transmitters have little overlap of their signals. The separation provided a unique opportunity for an experimental comparison of adoption of contraception in broadcast and nonbroadcast regions, coupled with a delayed treatment design. At the time of the study, Tanzania's population was 36 million. The fertility rate was 5.6 children per woman and was projected to double in 25 years. No amount of economic development can cope with this rate of population growth.

Before the study, the serial drama was broadcast by radio in one major region of the country; the other region was the control. The program addressed both family planning and sexual practices that increase vulnerability to infection with the HIV-AIDS virus. People had access to contraceptive methods and family planning clinics but did not take advantage of them. The problem was neither a lack of information nor unavailability. Rather, it was primarily motivational. The dramatic series provided the impetus for change.

In contrast with response in the control region, in the broadcast region, the serial drama raised listeners' perceived efficacy to determine family size, decreased the desired number of children, increased the ideal age of marriage for women, increased approval of family-planning methods, stimulated spousal communication about family size, and increased use of family-planning services and adoption of contraceptive methods (Rogers et al., 1999).

Figure 8.6 shows the mean number of adopters of contraceptive methods per clinic over time in the broadcast and control regions. Both regions increased slightly at the same rate during the three-year prebroadcast period. The adoption rate increased only slightly in the control region but at an abrupt, pronounced rate in the broadcast region. These effects were replicated when the serial was later broadcast in the control region. The replicated effects provide further support for the effect of the media. The experimental design, shown in Figure 8.6, raises confidence that the serial drama brought about these beneficial changes.

Just as the Kenya project verified the dose-of-exposure effect, the more often people listened to the broadcasts, the more women talked to their spouses about family planning and the higher the rate of adoption of contraception methods (Figure 8.7). These diverse effects remained after multiple controls for other potential determinants, including exposure to other radio programs with family planning and HIV-AIDS content, prebroadcast levels of and changes in education, increased access to family planning clinics, radio ownership, and rural–urban differences. People's beliefs in their efficacy to manage their reproductive behavior predicted their adaption of contraception.

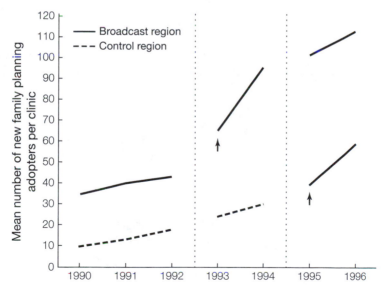

Figure 8.6 Mean number of new family planning adopters per clinic in the ministry of Health Clincs in the broadcast region and those in the control region. The values left of the dotted line are adoption levels prior to the broadcast: The values between the dotted lines are adoption levels when the serial was aired in the broadcast region but not in the control region; the values to the right of the dotted line are the adoption levels when the serial was aired in both the broadcast region and previous control region. Drawn from data in Rogers et al. (1999).

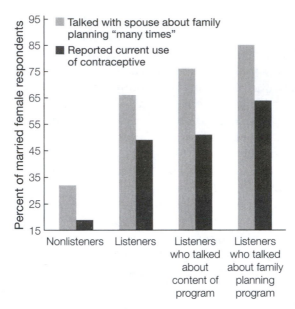

Figure 8.7 Impact of degree of involvement in the serial drama on spousal discussion of family planning and use of contraceptive methods. From Rogers et al. (1999).

Niger has one of the world's highest fertility rates, which thwarts any effort at social and economic development. Only about 15% of married women use contraceptive methods. Frequent childbearing is associated with high rates of maternal and infant mortality. In addition, many women suffer urinary incontinence from vesicovaginal tissue damage due to prolonged, obstructed labor without skilled assistance and too-close spacing of births. Childhood pregnancies greatly increase health risks.

A serial radio drama broadcast in Niger (Jah, Connolly, Barker, & Ryerson, 2014) modeled the benefits of planned childbearing and birth spacing and the adverse social and health effects of frequent unplanned childbearing. To enable listeners to turn their desired family futures into reality, the models taught them how to discuss intimate reproductive family matters when it was difficult to do so. Listeners were also taught how to prevent obstetric fistulas.

According to before-and-after assessments, listeners were twice as likely to discuss family planning and reproductive health after listening to the radio drama. They regarded smaller families as ideal, favored more space between births, and were less likely to believe that using contraceptives goes against the will of Allah or God. They increased adoption of contraceptive methods from 18% at baseline to 51% following the serial drama. In further testimony to the effectiveness of the serial drama, listeners reported significantly greater changes than did nonlisteners after the researchers took into account other possible influences.

Serial dramas promote a variety of environmental conservation practices that can improve the quality of life (Bandura, 2006a). For example, a serial in India motivated villagers to take collective action to improve sanitation, reduce potential health hazards, adopt fuel-conservation practices to reduce pollution, and launch a tree-planting campaign (Papa et al., 2000). Moreover, they persuaded other villages to adopt similar environmental practices.

However, sometimes the best humanitarian efforts meet with political resistance. Polluted drinking water is a major cause of illness and death worldwide. A Honduran radio serial drama enabled and inspired listeners to build safe drinking-water systems to protect their local water sources and conserve other natural resources. After a military coup, vested interests that opposed these conservation practices apparently forced the serial to be suspended indefinitely (PCI Media Impact, 2009).

In keeping with the rapid changes in modes of communication, weekly episodes of the Ecuadorian serial drama *Toque magico* were uploaded to Facebook and YouTube. TV Globo, based in Rio de Janeiro, broadcasts telenovelas dubbed into different languages, reaching hundreds of millions of viewers worldwide. Population Media Center helps create social themes that can be easily incorporated into these telenovelas, including gender relations, marital conflict, domestic violence, reproductive health, and contraception. Spanish-language telenovelas made in the United States also include public health themes (Kane, 2012).

Educating women and girls is often regarded as one of the best contraceptives. Indeed, education cuts teen pregnancies (Girma & Paton, 2015). Educated women generally adopt a small-family norm. They marry later and have fewer children with the use of contraception. Many join the labor force. These are major lifestyle changes. Through the acquisition of knowledge, competencies, and belief in their efficacy, schooling enables women to exercise greater control over their lives (Bandura, 1997). Self-development also provides the vehicle for socioeconomic advancement. Education is, therefore, regarded as one of the most important means of reducing fertility rates.

Although lauding educational initiatives for girls, Kavita Ramdas (2012), the former head of the Global Fund for Women, explains that these worthy efforts should be part of a comprehensive approach to gender equality. She calls attention to the fact that many environmentalists and women's rights activists shy away from talking about family planning because it is politically charged, even though women's control of their pregnancies is a fundamental right. Ramdas argues that advocates should not use the education of girls to evade the unmet need for family-planning services. A comprehensive approach includes both aspects. Impediments to voluntary contraception contribute to overpopulation.

It is easier to achieve educational development in egalitarian societies that have expanded human rights to include equal-gender educational rights.

The obstacles that women continue to face, even in developed countries, are less about access to education than about gender-role stereotyping, which undermines their perceived self-efficacy in activities traditionally performed by men despite comparable capabilities (Bandura, 1997; Hackett, 1995; Hackett & Betz, 1981). Entrenched institutional impediments also make it more difficult for women to realize their hopes and ambitions (Bussey & Bandura, 1999).

Many patriarchal societies devalue the education of girls and women, who are relegated to a subservient role in which they have little say about family matters and have few educational opportunities. These social constraints confine them to a life of early and frequent childbearing. In many countries with high fertility rates, after women have had several children, they do not want any more. Frequent unplanned childbearing compromises the kinds of lives that they can lead and the standard of living they can provide for their children.

Unless people see family planning as improving their well-being, they will have few incentives for adopting it. Indeed, adoption of contraceptive methods tends to be low even with full knowledge and ready access to them (Ryerson, 1995). Providing contraceptive services alone is not enough. Nor are brief media campaigns, exhortations, motivational slogans, or moral appeals for responsible parenthood. Stemming population growth requires not only providing family-planning services but also changing social norms and removing the psychological impediments to contraception in spousal relationships rather than placing the burden solely on women. It is within this broader familial context that entertainment-education programs model making informed decisions about the desired number and spacing of children and how to enlist family-planning services for this purpose. Planned childbearing is embedded in the larger issue of the type of future family members desire and the steps they can take to realize it.

Promoting psychosocial conditions conducive to planned childbearing supports women's reproductive rights rather than infringing on them. John Cleland, a leading population expert, builds a strong case for revitalizing family planning in the world's poor countries (Cleland et al., 2006). He regards promotion of family planning as especially important because of the unusually broad scope of its benefits. It interrupts the cycle of poverty, decreases maternal and child mortality, liberates women for personal development by relieving the burden of excessive childbearing, enables universal primary education, and aids environmental sustainability by stabilizing the world's population.

Reducing unplanned childbearing is the fastest and most cost-effective way of easing population pressures on the world's ecological and social systems. Moreover, its benefits are immediate. In contrast, trying to change entrenched consumption habits takes far longer, is costly and vulnerable to the vagaries of competing influences, and may have unintended adverse consequences.

The correlation between education and fertility does not mean that families with little or no education cannot be helped to make informed decisions about the number and spacing of children. Serial dramas enable such families to control family size through planned childbearing and bypass the institutional and cultural barriers to women's education.

Any period of transformative change results in a temporary mismatch or structural lag between dated normative practices and contemporary social reality. Even in developing countries, the historic transition to the information era has seen intellect supplant brawn in many aspects of modern work. Serial dramas show how educated daughters, not just sons, can be productive providers. The dramas try to foster a better normative match to the challenges and opportunities of this new era. Societies with burgeoning populations need not wait until they become economically sound to bring birthrates down—nor can they afford to. Indeed, no country can achieve much national progress until it can bring its rate of population growth under control.

Serial dramas set in India, which has almost 1.3 billion people, address the myriad ways in which women are marginalized and denied educational aspirations. A strong cultural gender bias exists in India. Radiologists offer cheap ultrasound tests in villages to identify female fetuses, some of which are aborted. This practice has produced a growing imbalance of females to males, a practice that already is having huge social consequences.

In the Indian serial drama *Hum Log* (*We People*), subthemes devoted particular attention to harmony amid differences among family members, elevation of the status of women in family social and economic life, educational opportunities and career options for women, the cultural preference for sons and gender bias in child rearing, the harm of the dowry requirement, choice in spouse selection, teenage marriage and parenthood, spousal abuse, family planning, youth delinquency, and community development. Some of the characters personified positive role models for gender equality; others were proponents of the traditional, subservient role for women. Still others were transitional models. A famous Indian film actor reinforced the modeled messages in epilogues.

Hum Log was immensely popular, enjoying top ratings on television and eliciting hundreds of thousands of letters from viewers offering advice and support to the characters. A random sample of viewers reported that they had learned from the serial that women should have equal opportunities and a say in decisions that affect their lives, that programs advancing the welfare of women should be encouraged, that cultural diversity should be respected, and that family size should be limited. In India and elsewhere, the more aware viewers were of the messages being modeled, the greater was their support of women's freedom of choice in matters that affect them and of planning for small families (Brown & Cody, 1991; Rogers et al., 1999).

Intensive interviews with village inhabitants revealed that the drama sparked serious public discussions about the broadcast's themes, such as child marriages, dowry requirements, the education of girls, the benefits of small families, and other social issues (Papa et al., 2000). These social transactions went beyond talk to collective community action aimed at changing inequitable normative practices and improving the inhabitants' futures. Indeed, one village sent to the broadcast center a large poster letter, signed by its residents, stating that they would work to eradicate dowries and child marriages and support the education of daughters. The enrollment of girls in elementary and junior high schools rose from 10% to 38% in one year of the broadcast.

Many impediments to sociocultural change remain, but their force weakens over time as new practices gain support and collective benefits outweigh the social costs of harmful traditional practices. In one village in India, young boys and girls created a self-help action group to promote the changes modeled in another serial drama (Law & Singhal, 1999). These system-level effects illustrate how dramatizations that address social problems in enabling ways can bring about the development of collective efficacy.

With 1.4 billion people, China is the most populous nation in the world. The government's one-child policy has heightened the traditional cultural preferences for sons. The television serial drama *Bai Xing* (*Ordinary People*) addressed gender bias in Chinese society and fostered psychosocial changes to supplant coercive institutional controls on fertility with voluntary adoption of contraceptive practices and the preference for small families. The drama graphically portrayed the tragedy and injustice of social practices that force women into arranged marriages and the cultural devaluation of baby girls. The central theme aimed to alter discriminatory gender norms and practices. Viewers were inspired and strengthened by the determination and courage of female characters who challenged the subordinate status of women and who strove to change detrimental cultural practices.

Applications of the psychosocial model worldwide have uniformly yielded positive results in diverse cultural milieus and across many spheres of functioning. The serial dramas have proven to be highly effective vehicles for reaching vast numbers of people over the prolonged periods needed to achieve major change. Viewers become deeply involved in the lives of the characters, who inspire them to take steps that can improve their lives. Radio versions of the serial dramas can reach vast rural populations. Airing of the televised serials is typically followed by improvement in the status of women, preference for smaller families, and adoption of contraceptive methods and self-protection against sexually transmitted diseases. The strength of the social impact increases as a function of level of exposure to the broadcasts. The more that people become engaged by a media program, the more they talk about the issues that are aired, the more supportive they are of gender equality, the higher their perceived efficacy to regulate their reproductive behavior, and the more likely they are to adopt contraceptive methods.

Addressing Overconsumption Early

People are generally unaware of how the products they buy and consume affect the environment. If they are to make decisions that support environmental conservation, they need to be informed of the ecological costs of their consumer habits and enabled and motivated to turn enlightened concern into beneficial courses of action. Many lifelong consumer habits are formed during childhood. It is easier to prevent wasteful practices than to try to change them after they have become deeply ingrained.

The Cost of Cool, a video made for distribution to schools, addresses the environmental problems created by overconsumption and focuses on the buying habits of teenagers (Griffith, Griffith, Molina, Holland, & Paul, 2001). It tracks the energy and ecological costs of the manufacture, distribution, marketing, sale, and waste disposal of everyday items such as T-shirts and sneakers. Providing teenagers with sound information helps them make informed buying choices. As one viewer put it, "I'll never look at a T-shirt in the same way."

Popular entertainment formats, such as music concerts, recordings, and videos, also reach mass youth populations (Singhal & Rogers, 1999). The themes address critical social issues, substance abuse, violence, teen sexuality, and gender equality. The impact of these complementary approaches requires systematic evaluation. The increasing magnitude of the environmental problem calls for multifaceted efforts to alter behavioral practices that degrade the ecological supports of life.

FROM TOKEN GESTURES TO FUNDAMENTAL LIFESTYLE CHANGES

We hear much talk about environmental sustainability, but few explanations of what it means and the changes required to realize it. The mounting toll on the environment indicates that the current population size and rate of consumption already have exceeded the earth's carrying capacity. Even adoption of zero growth in population and per capita consumption would, at best, only stabilize the present level of unsustainability.

Achievement of a sustainable environmental future faces three major challenges. The first concerns the sources of energy needed to power the contemporary lifestyles of millions of people living mainly in densely populated megacities. Fossil fuels have been the major source of energy. The energy marketplace is distorted by generous federal subsidies to the oil and coal industries, but society bears the costs of damage to the environment and impairment of human health. This cost displacement makes fossil fuels economically attractive and puts renewable sources of energy at a competitive disadvantage (Greenstone & Looney, 2012). An underpriced but polluting competitor impedes transition to a clean energy economy. If we monetize the collateral environmental costs, as well as the global damage from greenhouse emissions, fossil fuels would be even costlier.

With energy production grounded in nonrenewable fossil fuels, renewable sources of energy—solar, wind, hydro, geothermal, and tidal power—have been treated as minor supplements whose development is underfunded. Critics have decried their limited capacity, fluctuating output, and costs. However, as we have seen, recent advances are making renewable sources more feasible in cost and scale, particularly in Germany. Germans will soon get about 30% of their electric power from renewable sources (Gillis, 2014a). A major added benefit of the increased capacity is a reduction in greenhouse gas emissions. To meet energy demands in an environmentally sustainable way requires phasing out the extraction of fossil fuels, eliminating governmental subsidies to the fossil fuel industry, taxing carbon emissions, divesting from industries that pose serious threats to the climate, rewarding energy efficiency, and vigorously promoting the development of renewable sources of energy.

To take advantage of the vast potential of renewable energy requires development of energy storage technologies (Huggins, 2010). Home storage systems depend on rechargeable batteries to provide a backup electricity supply. They can do so for about 24 hours. The new generation of batteries will have greater storage capacity but battery energy storage has limitations.

The different sources of renewable energy vary with location. The most reliable renewable energy delivery is provided by integrated electrical grids. For example, through an internationally-connected system the primary renewable source in Southern Germany is from rooftop solar systems. In Northern Germany and Denmark, energy is obtained mostly from windmills and numerous hydroelectric systems in Norway serve as a supplementary source. In the US, electricity is delivered through local electrical grids operating independently. This new era of clean energy generation and delivery requires building an infrastructure in which renewable electrical power in different locations can be delivered where and when needed via integrated electrical grids.

Plummeting costs of solar modules and batteries are cutting into the market share of profits from energy generation by fossil fuels (Denning, 2013). The Nobelist and former energy secretary Steven Chu called for a new electric business model (McMahon, 2014). In an effective model utility companies would deliver most of the electricity from diverse renewable sources via an integrated grid supplemented by energy generated by fossil fuels when needed as backup. Wall Street has dubbed technological replacement of fossil fuels a "death spiral" (Denning, 2014). The ascendency of renewables in energy generation gives hope for a low-carbon future.

The second major challenge concerns growth in population and per capita consumption. The depletion of nonrenewable resources has been a cause for great concern. However, this problem applies to many renewable resources as well. Burgeoning populations consume even renewable resources—for example, fish stocks—faster than the earth can replenish them. With growing demand outstripping diminishing supplies, renewables eventually could be obliterated. Despite religious and cultural taboos and impediments to family planning and access to contraceptives, many countries with high birth rates are stabilizing their populations to near zero growth. However, as stated earlier, if population stabilizes at an unsustainable level, exceeding the earth's carrying capacity remains possible.

Per capita consumption will rise as Western lifestyles become more affordable for billions of people worldwide. A high but unsustainable baseline presents daunting challenges in persuading people to scale down their style of living. Conceptual models for economic growth abound, and billions of dollars are spent promoting its products and services, but we have few models for scaling down excessive consumption.

One example of high consumption involves unintentional adverse environmental effects. The coolants that had long been used in air conditioners were destroying the ozone layer, which blocks carcinogenic ultraviolet rays. A substitute coolant spared the ozone layer—but turned out to be an enormously more powerful agent of global warming than carbon dioxide (Rosenthal & Lehren, 2012b). The populations of India and China are understandably installing home air-conditioning at a rapid pace. Alarmed climate scientists estimate that over a quarter of projected global warming will be due to the coolant gases by midcentury. Despite the seriousness of the problem, nations remain in a stalemate over the costs of conversion to a safer coolant. In the meantime, greenhouse gas emissions keep soaring. This will be a common scenario as developing countries with huge populations increasingly adopt the unsustainable Western lifestyle.

The third formidable challenge includes adoption and implementation of climate treaties that curb detrimental practices. As previously explained, the annual UN climate summits are an unwieldy mechanism for effecting change. They morphed into a predictable scenario combining ambitious goals with vague, unbinding pledges that are usually hammered out in a marathon session on the final day of the meetings and that defer corrective action to the next summit (Broder, 2012). Twenty years of summitry have produced little to show for it.

Because of heavy lobbying by the petroleum and coal industries, the U.S. Senate has been unwilling to ratify any international climate treaties, depriving the United States of leadership and moral leverage in reducing greenhouse gas emissions. Until recently, through its obstructiveness at UN summits, it had aroused resentment and derision: "American officials have been booed and hissed during international climate talks, bestowed with mock 'Fossil of the Day' awards for resisting treaties, and widely condemned for demanding that other nations cut their fossil fuel emissions while refusing, year after year, to take action at home" (Davenport, 2014e).

The three top polluters—China, the United States, and India—are impediments in any path to environmental salvation. To avert further harm to the global climate system, these major polluters must take the lead in devising climate policies that result in substantial reductions in heat-trapping gases. If they do not curb their emissions, others will find justifications for not doing so.

In a landmark accord, the United States and China agreed to achieve significant reduction in carbon emissions (Landler, 2014).This agreement eliminated the comparative justification that each country had used previously to continue its polluting practices. By exercising his executive authority, President Obama committed the United States to reducing carbon emission by up to 28% in 2025. Republican lawmakers denounced the agreement but could do little about it, because it is an accord rather than a treaty, which would require Senate ratification. The signing of the accord transformed the international view of the United States from being part of the pollution problem to being part of the solution (Davenport, 2014e). Observers hoped that seeing two of the top polluters commit to curbing carbon emissions would break the impasse in devising a global climate accord.

China is still on the path to peak carbon emissions with pressing need for energy to power its vast economy, still served mainly by coal-fueled plants. The government plans to shorten the time to peak level while increasing reduction of carbon emissions with renewable energy sources. To accelerate reduction in emissions China will implement a national cap-and-trade program (Davis & Davenport, 2015). This redoubled effort is motivated in part by growing public pressure for relief from a heavily polluted environment that is making life less livable. One study showed that air pollution causes 1.6 million deaths a year (Levin, 2015). Political pressure on the government is growing as the public demands a healthier living environment.

Millions of people in India have no access to electricity. The country has embarked on a national development program requiring huge increases in energy production. The nation's environment minister, Prakash Javadekar, explained that India's top priority is to eradicate poverty and improve its economy (Davenport, 2014b). He estimates that this massive national development, which depends heavily on coal-fired energy, will double carbon emissions, moving them beyond those of the United States and China. The country will make efforts to reduce the rate of increase but, in his view, it will take decades before a decline in emissions can be achieved. He argues that developed countries spent a century polluting the atmosphere, so they now bear the responsibility of making large cuts in greenhouse gas emissions. "The moral principle of historic responsibility cannot be washed away," he said (Davenport, 2014b). Some Indian megacities are among the most highly polluted in the world. A massive coal-fueled economy foretells a severely polluted future in which people's standard of living is raised, but at the cost of a less livable environment and a heavy toll on public health.

If successful, China's declaration of "war on pollution" could become a model for other developing countries on how to promote national development while preserving a livable and healthful environment (Reuters, 2014). China has an economic advantage by being increasingly involved in the renewable technologies business (Harrabin, 2015).

With increasing grim warnings climate scientists give notice that failure to keep the planet's temperature from rising more than 3.6 degrees Fahrenheit, or 2 degrees Celsius, will have devastating irreversible consequences. It could "threaten society with food shortages, refugee crises, the flooding of major cities and entire island nations, mass extinction of plants and animals, and a climate so drastically altered it might become dangerous for people to work or play outside during the hottest times of the year" (Gillis, 2014b).

The purpose of the 2014 summit in Lima, Peru, was to develop a framework for formalizing a global climate agreement in Paris in 2015. The members abandoned the ambitious goal of adopting a legally binding global climate accord in favor of a more modest voluntary one. Every country would pledge cuts in carbon emissions at an economically and politically feasible level (Davenport, 2014d). There are no sanctions for not submitting a plan to cut emissions or for violating the submitted ones. Compliance is based on "international scorn" (Davenport, 2014a). This frail climate accord is the product of almost two decades of summitry, during which time emissions of greenhouse gases have soared. Except for India, which refuses to decrease emissions until their poor are lifted from poverty, countries have submitted their pledged cuts. In the view of climate analysts, however, the pledges are insufficient to avert an irreversible catastrophic rise in global warming (Gillis & Sengupta, 2015). As nonbinding promises subject to domestic pressure, they are likely to fall short of what was pledged. U.S. Secretary of State John Kerry commented on the deficiencies of the remedy: "We are still on a course leading to tragedy" (Davenport, 2014d). Weaning the top polluters from fossil fuels will not be easy. However, change comes more easily through replacement than through prohibition. We are now at the dawning of a transformative change in energy production (Gillis, 2014a). Renewable energy, as generated through wind and sun power, is on the rise and costs are dropping sharply. As we have seen, Germany has become the model for this nascent transformative change.

On Bringing the Future Into the Present

Programs designed to control global warming have a better chance of succeeding if they embrace the basic principles of change (Bandura, 1997). The main emitters and activities that spew greenhouse gases into the atmosphere have to be identified. This information will specify what needs to be changed. Levels of emissions must, of course, be measured throughout the process. People motivate themselves by the goals and challenges they adopt if they are properly structured with unwavering commitment to them (Bandura, 1991b; Locke & Latham, 1990). Long-range goals provide a vision of a desired future. However, having a vision is not enough. There are too many competing influences in the present for distant futures to regulate current behavior.

The long-term goal adopted at the UN summits to slow the rise in the earth's temperature to 3.6 degrees Fahrenheit by the end of the century is a good case in point. This goal is disconnected from the reality of current behavioral practices that are raising carbon emissions globally to record highs (Gillis & Broder, 2012). The distant goal is wishful thinking rather than an actionable, genuine commitment to the behavioral changes needed to realize that goal. Observers already acknowledge that this goal is unattainable with current lifestyle practices. At the 2012 summit in Doha, the delegates expressed "grave concern" over the growing disparity between goals and the reality of rising global warming emissions. However, this concern did not move them to action (Broder, 2012).

Wishful thinking alone does not beget behavior change. Turning a vision into reality requires adopting progressive, short-term goals that provide guides, strategies, and motivators in the here and now. Goals without reliable feedback on progress have little or no effect (Bandura, 1991a). During a hot New Jersey summer, families adopted a goal of reducing their energy use by 20% (Becker, 1978). Half the group received feedback every two days on the amount of energy they used; the other half received no feedback on their energy use. Families that received performance feedback significantly reduced their energy use. In contrast, families that did not receive performance feedback achieved no change. Timely feedback identifies the corrective adjustments required to ensure continuous progress. Failure to adopt explicit goals with feedback on progress usually is the weakest link in change programs. However, designers of behavior-change programs often ignore knowledge from the social sciences on how to enable people to change their behavior.

In large-scale change programs, the incentives are built into policy initiatives. The incentives for environmental sustainability are not just material ones, however. The most powerful are the self-evaluative ones, which are rooted in moral values regarding the extinction of other species, the degradation of ecologic systems, and the excessive consumption that make the earth less habitable for future generations. Value-based incentives add force to the social incentives that are codified in the normative structure of a society. To gain public support for environmental initiatives, a change program must address denials of human-caused global warming and the justifications and exonerations that strip morality from environmentally destructive practices.

In collaboration with local governments worldwide, ICLEI—Local Governments for Sustainability USA (ICLEI-USA) developed a standardized method of measuring the human demand on ecological systems and the regenerative and the waste-absorption capacity of the biosphere (Borucke et al., 2013; PRNewswire, 2012). ICLEI-USA tracks annual biocapacity changes worldwide and identifies places where demands exceed ecological resources. The biocapacity values provide early warning signs. The findings show that ecological resources are being depleted and that waste is accumulating. The overshoot is especially prominent in the case of carbon emissions, which exceed carbon uptake by ecological systems.

Other applications of this methodology bring the change process closer to home. Working in partnership with local communities, ICLEI has developed a new protocol to assess levels of greenhouse gas emissions and pinpoint the sources, such as power plants, passenger vehicles, livestock, waste treatment plants, and the like (ICLEI, 2014). The organization then assists communities in developing programs to reduce their particular sources of greenhouse gas emissions. Cities anywhere in the world can apply this highly flexible technology at the grassroots level to any source of pollution. These types of social science applications need to be promoted on a large scale. As mentioned earlier, worldwide applications of social cognitive theory in the form of entertainment-education have addressed the contribution of overpopulation to environmental degradation.

In preserving the environment, people are motivated more by local problems, such as air and water pollution, health impairment, extreme weather events, and toxic waste, than by generalities about global harm. The lived experience of environmental degradation becomes part of people's daily lives. Motivating people becomes more challenging when the environmental harm is cumulative, reaching crisis proportions only in some distant future. The future cannot be a cause of current behavior because it has no material existence. However, cognitive representation can bring visualized futures into the present as current guides and motivators of behavior. It is difficult to change behavior that is disjoined from its consequences in the here and now. It is a daunting challenge to do so when harmful consequence are slowly cumulative and go unnoticed over a long period. Aversive life conditions today are the consequences of behavioral practices by faceless generations long ago. It is easy to talk about a moral obligation to protect the quality of future life, but prevailing behavioral practices often undermine the realization of that very future.

Reliable prediction models provide the means of portraying what environmental futures will look like under different levels of climate change and should employ vivid terms rather than nebulous terms or technical jargon. The worldwide flooding problem that is getting progressively worse is a good case in point. Glacial and ice sheet melting caused by global warming is raising sea levels. By measuring land elevation one can pinpoint low-lying cities and coastlines that are at risk of being permanently inundated under different rates of sea level rises. Benjamin Strauss, a climate scientist at the nonprofit Climate Central, and colleagues have published in extraordinary detail an analysis of the entire American coastline for level of risk of permanent inundation and the size of the population that would have to be relocated to higher ground under different sea levels (Strauss, Ziemlinski, Weiss, & Overpeck, 2012). High tides and storm surges, which are growing more intense, further raise the threat of widespread flooding. Searching Climate Central's database by ZIP code to see how your own local community would look under different sea levels makes the threat real and personal (Strauss, 2015). Strauss illustrates how much of the continental United States coastal regions will be underwater as the sea level rises.

Similar threat analyses of low-lying coastlines worldwide could mobilize vast populations to work toward curbing emissions of heat-trapping gases. Personalizing future outcomes is more likely to spur efforts to mitigate global warming and to plan protective measures than abstract discussions about environmental ethics concerning consequences that span generations. Critics of global warming dismiss forecasting models as unreliable, but advances in technology have brought more accuracy to them. When existing models do err, it is usually on the conservative side. Summaries of findings typically state that things are getting worse much faster than expected.

People are doing myriad things in their own lives in the name of environmental conservation. They are recycling, lowering their thermostats, insulating their homes, switching to more efficient light bulbs, installing energy-saving appliances, and getting more miles per gallon by driving more fuel-efficient automobiles. These practices are well worth the effort. However, given the increasing scale of ecological destruction, substituting token gestures for genuine lifestyle changes accomplishes too little too slowly. Moreover, halfhearted measures can instill a sense of complacency that defers the adoption of more fundamental changes. Some practices have unintended harmful consequences. For example, people prefer their cars to public transportation but take comfort in powering their cars with biofuel additives—which, as we have seen, imposes hardships on millions of people who can ill afford rising corn prices. As we also have seen, the contribution of biofuels to reducing carbon emissions was greatly exaggerated because of the large amounts of energy needed to convert plants into biofuels.

Some efforts to ensure an environmentally sustainable and habitable future have been surprisingly successful, and others have achieved modest success. However, some problems remain intractable and may be worsening. It is essential to keep most of earth's remaining hydrocarbons stored underground rather than using them as energy sources that produce heat-trapping gases. As we have seen, in a remarkable transformative change, the costs of solar and wind power have plummeted. These and other renewable energy sources, which are becoming economically competitive with fossil fuels, are filling a sizable share of the social demand for energy. Even Al Gore, who was dubbed the "prophet of doom" by climate-change deniers, has become a green investor with an optimistic view of curbing the rise in global warming (Schwartz, 2015). The generous government subsidies given to the fossil fuel industry should be diverted to enhancing development of renewable energy sources.

As we have seen, global population has been growing at an exponential rate. Despite the adverse effects of overpopulation on environmental sustainability and quality of life, in the past population growth was a topic that no one dared talk about. A false dichotomy prevailed that pitted overconsumption against overpopulation, with reasons for ignoring the latter. Recall that these factors are intertwined rather than operating independently. Fortunately, the stranglehold of the population taboo is weakening. Voluntary global initiatives now enable families to make informed reproductive choices and provide them with ready access to the contraceptive means to do so.

Developed countries have stabilized their populations at near replacement levels. A number of developing countries with high fertility rates are also achieving a steady decline in population growth. These are encouraging attainments in efforts to stabilize the human population within the earth's carrying capacity. However, more help is needed for poorer countries that are so overwhelmed by burgeoning population that they are unable to provide basic services and security for their people. The money available is spent on basic survival rather than on personal and national development. In these cases, the issue is not an unmet need for contraception but rather normative impediments to its use. Comprehensive programs that enable families to address family planning within a vision of a desired future have increased the use of contraception to realize that vision (Bandura, 2006a; Singhal et al., 2004). These voluntary international programs enhance personal freedom through self-development of competencies and expand individual rights rather than infringing on them.

Overconsumption is the nemesis of efforts to achieve an environmentally sustainable future. The goal of such efforts is to persuade people to consume less, whereas corporations spend billions annually to convince them to consume more. In this economic model, even population growth is profitable, because it produces both more workers needed to manufacture the promoted products and more consumers to buy them.

Recall that as people in developing countries acquire the means of improving their standard of living, they want the same high-consumption lifestyle as people enjoy in developed countries. Consumption rates may double or triple depending on countries' baseline rates and levels of industrial production. An increase in world consumption of this magnitude would far exceed the resources the planet can provide and replenish. Preventing the collapse of the ecological supports of life requires scaling down consumption rates and reducing the number of consumers. It may be easier to reduce population growth than to persuade people to consume less.

The success of societies is being judged, in large part, by overall output of goods and services (GDP). This indicator is often misinterpreted as reflecting national well-being. However, there is widespread dissatisfaction with the emphasis on the GDP as a single summary measure of national progress (Gertner, 2010; Stiglitz, 2009). It disregards whether the products are good or bad and does not take into account the environmental costs that their production incurs. Bad products can harm the environment and worsen quality of life in a society. It also disregards sustainability. For example, GDP can be boosted in the short-term by rapid depletion of resources as in rampant deforestation and depletion of fish stocks via bottom trawling by fishing fleets. Countries strive for what is measured as success. This invests the GDP indicator with distorting influence favoring extensive production of goods for high consumption lifestyles. The net result is an acknowledged flawed market indicator driving excessive and wasteful consumption that further burdens efforts to preserve an environmentally sustainable future.

Going beyond the GDP, some scholars created an expanded set of quality-of-life indicators grounded not only in commercial values but in environmental and human values (Stiglitz, Sen, & Fitoussi, 2015). Some of these indicators include quality of national health, educational advancement, employment opportunities, and equity. With growing environmental degradation, quality of the lived environment gains importance. In some major cities, such as Delhi and Beijing, the air is so heavily polluted that the cities are near uninhabitable (Sedghi, 2015, Wainwright, 2014).

The public can shape markets by favoring environmentally friendly products and practices and raising the costs of environmentally harmful ones. Prominent international companies have formed a coalition to convert to renewable energy and to provide environmentally responsible products consumers demand (Gillis & Fleur, 2015). Additionally, the coalition intends to pressure governments to boost efforts to curb climate change. Divestment of large pension and intuitional investments funds from fossil fuel stocks is part of this movement toward preserving a habitable environment.

Making minor adjustments to environmentally and commercially unsustainable systems will not beget a green future. Achievement of a green future requires major lifestyle changes rooted in shared values linked to incentive systems that make environmentally responsible behavior not only normative but also morally right. Failure to make such changes will pass on to future generations a planet that is much hotter, more crowded, less habitable, poorer in resources and depleted of biodiversity.

Ecological systems are intricately interdependent. Global-level changes therefore affect everyone, regardless of the source of the degradation. Because of connectedness of consequences, when the cumulated effects of individual behavior affect the well-being of others worldwide, lifestyle practices are a matter of morality. As responsible stewards of our environment for future generations, we must restore moral self-sanctions for environmentally destructive practices.

EPILOGUE

In this book, I present a large body of knowledge on how moral disengagement weakens or strips moral self-sanctions from inhumane practices at both the individual and social-system levels. Each chapter addressed a major sphere of life within the conceptual framework of moral agency and the social consequences of its selective disengagement. Agentic theory, grounded in the self-regulatory power of moral self-sanctions, was the integrating principle. Analysis of moral disengagement in natural contexts provided richly nuanced knowledge of how people compromise their moral standards in the moral predicaments they face in everyday life and still retain a positive view of themselves. The prevalence and consistency of moral disengagement across diverse spheres of life lend support to the generalizability of the theory.

Social cognitive theory specifies not only eight forms that moral disengagement takes but also the four *loci* in the self-regulation process at which they undermine moral control. This conceptual specificity designates the types of psychosocial measures required at each locus to counteract the disengagement of moral self-sanctions from detrimental conduct.

At the behavior locus, harmful behavior is justified in varied ways depending, in part, on the sphere of activity. The justifications can be religious, ideological, social, constitutional, or protective of national security. It is ironic that many inhumanities are perpetrated in the name of freedom. Drawing on the utilitarian principle, some individuals also argue that it is necessary do some harm to achieve the greater common good. Justifications by forceful metaphor also are common. Gerald Grow, who wrote a satirical guide to writing misinformatively, would be astounded by the euphemistic creativity designed to conceal detrimental practices.

Monolithic sociopolitical systems that exercise tight control over institutions and communications can wield a greater power of moral disengagement than can pluralistic systems that represent diverse perspectives, interests, and concerns. Political diversity and the institutional protection of a free press and of dissent allow challenges to the misuse of morality for inhumane purposes. Limited public access to the media has been a major obstacle to the exercise of public influence on detrimental social policies and practices. The advent of the Internet and other revolutionary advances in communication technologies have enabled people to bypass, at least to some extent, media gatekeepers. Online influence, especially through social media, has become the principal vehicle for the exercise of social influence. Social media are instantaneous and wide reaching, transcending time, place, and national borders. Adherents morally legitimize and gain support for their causes and discredit those of their opponents largely through social media. However, as a political forum, the Internet is a double-edged tool. Unfiltered and unfettered, it is equally effective for mobilizing moral and social support for harmful purposes as for humane ones.

At the agency locus, individuals absolve themselves of responsibility in a variety of ways for the harm they cause. They shift the blame to others, create systems of personal deniability, keep themselves willfully uninformed about harmful activities perpetrated by those they oversee, and enlist proxies to distance themselves from transgressive practices. In collective activities, they downplay or dismiss any role in wrongdoings by their group. These types of self-exonerative strategies need to be exposed and widely known for what they are.

Responsibility is restored by consequences for culpable behavior. The market system malfunctioned because wrongdoers were shielded from the consequences of their detrimental actions. Instead, the public bore the costs of their faulty practices. Many such situations involve high-ranking officials, who command influence and power, which they use to shape protective self-policies and to craft settlements for harmful practices that guard them from legal penalties. For example, faceless companies are fined for corporate transgressions, but their chief executives are neither charged nor penalized nor even required to admit wrongdoing. It is difficult to reform transgressing organizations when they are considered agentless entities and allowed to treat fines as business tax write-offs. Although some progress has been made in getting transgressing corporations at least to admit wrongdoing, consequences need to be tied to individual executive wrongdoers, and corporations should not be allowed to treat financial penalties as tax benefits.

Assessing the harmfulness of given policies and practices is the major battleground at the effects locus of moral control. If given practices are judged to be harmless, there is no moral issue. Some deniers of detrimental effects subscribe to what have come to be called "zombie beliefs" that have been thoroughly debunked empirically. Other deniers disparage evidence of adverse effects as "junk science" and attribute discrediting nefarious motives to scientists.

With growing supporting evidence of the adverse effects of corporate practices and products, some industries have inaugurated misinformation campaigns designed to sow doubt in the public's mind concerning the soundness of the evidence against them. Often, members of industry-funded institutes are enlisted as proxy agents in this effort. Industries and companies mount pseudograssroots campaigns to sway the public against policies and regulations that they oppose. Scientists need to do a better job of informing the mass media, the general public, and policy makers of the effects of practices that have social consequences and should raise public concern. Transparency rules that identify funders of research projects and public campaigns help to inform debates and allow people to judge the credibility of supporting evidence on matters of consequence.

People get most of their information on important issues from traditional mass media and, increasingly, through social media, which have become the arenas for major battles over the effects of given policies and social practices. Individuals with smartphone cameras record events and evidence revealing harmful organizational and institutional practices, then upload the videos to the Internet for instant worldwide viewing. With ready public surveillance it is getting harder to conceal harmful activities as they are performed.

The final locus in the suspension of moral control centers on how opponents are viewed. Treating others as subhuman, demonic, or animalistic beings absolves perpetrators of moral self-sanctions through lack of any sense of shared humanity. To kill with moral impunity, soldiers in warfare strip their enemies of humanity and bestialize them. Societies that marginalize and maltreat certain classes and races of people diminish them as lesser beings. In conflicts of power, foes are characterized as wackos, zealots, and unsavory beings driven by degenerate motives.

A public that is well versed in the various modes of moral disengagement can see through self-exonerative practices, making it harder for wrongdoers to apply them successfully. As this book demonstrates, strategies designed to curb disengagement of morality from harmful practices must be tailored to the locus at which moral control is disengaged. This is a fruitful avenue of future research.

I devoted special attention to the influential role of moral disengagement in impeding environmental sustainability because of the increasingly urgent need to alter human practices that are rapidly and irreversibly degrading the habitability of the planet. Wasted decades of unproductive United Nations summitry have shortened the time available for adopting measures to forestall devastating, human-caused environmental changes. There is some progress in two of the three key remedies, slowing the rate of global population growth and shifting energy production from fossil fuels to renewable sources. The third remedy—curbing wasteful, excessive consumption—is not only failing but is worsening.

Consumption levels will continue to rise as Western lifestyles become more affordable for multitudes of people worldwide. This growth in consumption is driven by commercial models aimed at enhancing monetary gain through increases in the production and sale of goods. Although perpetual economic growth is unsustainable, it is difficult to modify excessive consumption even in the short term because it is vigorously promoted and profitable. Some industrial methods pollute and degrade the environment and annihilate species by destroying their habitats. Corporations are essentially exempted from these costs to the environment. There is little evidence that high-consumption lifestyles, in large part unfriendly to the environment, enhance people's satisfaction with their lives. Quality-of-life indicators may shift the focus from material values to environmental and human values that enhance people's sense of well-being.

One of the most striking findings of research on the suspension of morality is the extraordinary power of humanization to curb inhumane practices. Whether on the battlefield, in vengeful social relationships, or in the laboratory, people cannot persuade themselves to behave cruelly toward humanized others despite strong social pressure to do so. These findings shed some light on how to cultivate a humane society. Seeing common humanity in others arouses empathy and compassion toward them. It also instills a sense of shared responsibility for the quality of life in a society. The sense of common humanity is developed through shared relational experiences that link one's own well-being to the well-being of others. Commitment to humanitarian causes greater than oneself can further build commonalities. These interpersonal conditions are essential to the development of inclusive, socially just, and humane societies.

As this book extensively documents, the exercise of morality is not entirely an intrapsychic matter. Morality is socially grounded. Given the many psychosocial devices for disengaging moral self-sanctions, societies cannot rely solely on individuals, however righteous their moral standards. Regardless of the sphere of life, otherwise considerate people can behave cruelly yet retain positive self-regard. To function humanely, societies must establish social systems that uphold compassion and curb cruelty. Regardless of whether social practices are carried out individually, organizationally, or institutionally, it should be made difficult for people to delete humanity from their actions.

This book has focused on the moral dimension of life. Morality is governed socially rather than by inbred laws of nature, thus enabling people to shape the quality of life in their society. The choices they make will also profoundly affect the quality of life for future generations. Paul Sabin (2013) eloquently underscores the centrality of morality in the course humanity takes: "Neither biology nor economics can substitute for the deeper ethical question: what kind of world do we want to live in?"

REFERENCES

ABC News (2012, February 16). Underwear bomber Abdulmutallab: "Proud to kill in the name of God." Retrieved from http://abcnews.go.com

Abrahms, M. (2008). What terrorists really want: Terrorist motives and counterterrorism strategy. *International Security, 32*, 78–105.

Ackerman, S., Rushe, D., & Borger, J. (2014, December 9). Senate report on CIA torture claims spy agency lied about 'ineffective' program. *The Guardian*. Retrieved from http://www.theguardian.com

Admati, A. R., & Hellwig, M. (2013). *The bankers' new clothes: What's wrong with banking and what to do about it*. Princeton, NJ: Princeton University Press.

Adoni, H., & Mane, S. (1984). Media and social construction of reality: Toward an integration of theory and research. *Communication Research, 11*, 323–340.

Albright, J. (1981, September 2). Snubbies—instruments of crime. *Miami News*. Retrieved from https://news.google.com

Albright, J., Alexander, A., Arvidson, C., & Eason, H. (1981, November 22). Guns. *The Washington Post*, p. A2.

Alland, J. A. (1972). *The human imperative*. New York: Columbia University Press.

Alleyne, R. (2012, October 2). We were abused by Sir Jimmy Savile too: More damaging revelations about the Jim'll Fix It star. *The Telegraph*. Retrieved from http://www.telegraph.co.uk

Altherr, S. (2009, September 17). Hundreds of gun rights advocates attend conferences. *Newsday*. Retrieved from http://www.newsday.com

Alvarez, L., & Buckley, C. (2013, July 14). Zimmerman is acquitted in Trayvon Martin killing. *The New York Times*, p. A1.

American Psychological Association. (2015, July 10). Press release and recommended actions: Independent review cites collusion among APA individuals and defense department officials in policy on interrogation techniques. Retrieved from http://www.apa.org

Amnesty International USA. (2015). Death penalty and innocence. Retrieved from http://www.amnestyusa.org

Andersen guilty in Enron case. (2002, June 15). BBC News. Retrieved from http://www.bbc.co.uk/news

Anderson, C. A., Berkowitz, L., Donnerstein, E., Huesmann, L. R., Johnson, J. D., Linz, D., Malamuth, N. M., & Wartella, E. (2003). The influence of media violence on youth. *Psychological Science in the Public Interest, 4*, 81–110.

Anderson, C. A., & Bushman, B. J. (2001). Media violence and the American public: Scientific facts versus media misinformation. *American Psychologist, 56*, 477–489.

Anderson, J., & Eavis, P. (2014, February 14). Banks in London devise way around Europe's bonus rules. *The New York Times*, p. B1.

Anderson, S. (2012, April 11). Mayor Bloomberg launches campaign against stand your ground gun laws. The Huffington Post. Retrieved from http://www.huffingtonpost.com

Anderson, S. (2015, March 11). Off the deep end: The Wall Street bonus pool and low-wage workers. Institute for Policy Studies. http://www.ips-dc.org

Andrus, B. C. (1969). *The infamous of Nuremberg*. London: Fravin.

Anonymous (1969, August 21). [Memorandum]. Brown & Williamson Collection. University of California, San Francisco, Legacy Tobacco Documents Library. Retrieved from https://industrydocuments.library.ucsf.edu/tobacco/docs/#id=xqkd0134

Appelbaum, B. (2010, June 28). On finance bill, lobbying shifts to regulations. *The New York Times*, p. A1.

Applebome, B. (2013, January 10). Newtown shooting dominates opening of Connecticut legislative session. *The New York Times*, p. A19.

Arango, T. (2014, December 2). Iraqi government and Kurds reach deal to share oil revenues. *The New York Times*. Retrieved from http://www.nytimes.com

Armstrong, L., & Winfrey, O. (2012, May). Oprah talks to Lance Armstrong. *O, The Oprah Magazine*. Retrieved from http://www.oprah.com

Arnold, R. (1996). Overcoming ideology. In P. D. Brick & R. McGreggor (Eds.), *A wolf in the garden: The land rights movement and the new environmental debate* (pp. 15–25). Lanham, MD: Rowman & Littlefield.

Arras, J. (2010). Theory and bioethics. In E. N. Zalta (Ed.), The Stanford Encyclopedia of Philosophy (Summer 2013 ed.). Retrieved from http://plato.stanford.edu

Ashcroft, J. (1998). *Lessons from a father to his son* (pp. 138–139). Nashville, TN: Thomas Nelson.

Associated Press. (1981, November 21). Doublespeak '81: Haig, EPA, and Moral Majority take prizes. *The Telegraph*. Retrieved from https://news.google.com

Associated Press. (1988, October 15). 37-year leak at nuclear arms plant disclosed. *The Los Angeles Times*. Retrieved from http://articles.latimes.com

Associated Press. (1994, November 2). Britain's last surviving hangman dies at age 73. Retrieved from http://www.apnewsarchive.com

Associated Press (Trans.). (2001, October 7). Text: Bin Laden's statement. *The Guardian*. Retrieved from http://www.theguardian.com

Associated Press. (2006, March 15). Enron whistleblower tells of "crooked company." NBCNEWS.com. Retrieved from http://www.nbcnews.com

Associated Press. (2008, July 17). Ashcroft: "Not hard" to reject torture memos. NBCNews. Retrieved from http://www.nbcnews.com

Associated Press. (2012, September 12). Muhammad film: Director goes into hiding after protests. *The Guardian*. Retrieved from http://www.theguardian.com

Associated Press. (2014, July 24). Three executions gone wrong: details of lethal injections in Arizona, Oklahoma, Ohio. *San Jose Mercury News*. Retrieved from http://www.mercurynews.com

Atkin, E. (2015, January 8). Yes, it's cold. Global warming is still real. ThinkProgress. Retrieved from http://thinkprogress.org

Ayres, B. C. J. (1994, March 19). Gun maker on mayhem: That is not our doing. *The New York Times*, p. A8.

Baker, P. (2012, December 30). Biden is back for a 2nd run at gun limits. *The New York Times*, p. A1.

Baker, P. (2013, January 16). In gun debate, even language can be loaded. *The New York Times*, p. A14.

Baker, P. (2014, September 23). In airstrikes, U.S. targets militant cell said to plot an attack against the West. *The New York Times*. Retrieved from http://www.nytimes.com

Baker, P. & Schmitt, E. Many missteps in assessment of ISIS threat. *The New York Times*. Retrieved from http://www.nytimes.com

Baker, P., & Knowlton, B. (2014, September 28). Obama acknowledges U.S. erred in assessing ISIS. *The New York Times*. Retrieved from http://www.nytimes.com

Baker, P., & Landler, M. (2012, December 17). "These tragedies must end," Obama says. *The New York Times*, p. A1.

Baker, P., & Shear, M. D. (2013, January 17). Obama to "put everything I've got" into gun control. *The New York Times*, p. A1.

Baker, R. K., & Ball, S. (1969). *Violence and the media: A staff report to the National Commission on the Causes and Prevention of Violence*. Washington, DC: U.S. Government Printing Office.

Baldwin, T. F., & Lewis, C. (1972). Violence in television: The industry looks at itself. In E. A. Rubinstein & G. A. Comstock (Eds.), *Television and social behavior: Vol. 1. Media content and control* (pp. 290–373). Washington, DC: U.S. Government Printing Office.

Ball-Rokeach, S. J., & DeFleur, M. L. (1976). A dependency model of mass-media effects. *Communication Research, 3,* 3–21.

Baltes, P. B., & Baltes, M. M. (1990). *Successful aging: Perspectives from the behavioral sciences*. Cambridge: Cambridge University Press.

Bambrick, G. (2015, March 19). The best way to feed the billions. Tufts Now. Retrieved from http://now.tufts.edu

Bandura, A. (1965). Influence of models' reinforcement contingencies on the acquisition of imitative responses. *Journal of Personality and Social Psychology, 1,* 589–595.

Bandura, A. (1973). *Aggression: A social learning analysis*. Englewood Cliffs, NJ: Prentice-Hall.

Bandura, A. (1976). New perspectives on violence. In T. B. Brazelton & V. C. Vaughan III (Eds.), *The family* (pp. 41–55). Chicago: Year Book Medical Publishers.

Bandura, A. (1978, October). "Doomsday Flight" TV story leads to copies. *Stanford Observer*.

Bandura, A. (1982). The psychology of chance encounters and life paths. *American Psychologist, 37,* 747–755.

Bandura, A. (1986). *Social foundations of thought and action: A social cognitive theory*. Englewood Cliffs, NJ: Prentice Hall.

Bandura, A. (1991a). Self-regulation of motivation through anticipatory and self-reactive mechanisms. In R. A. Dienstbier (Ed.), *Perspectives on motivation: Nebraska Symposium on Motivation* (Vol. 38, pp. 69–164). Lincoln: University of Nebraska Press.

Bandura, A. (1991b). Social cognitive theory of moral thought and action. In W. M. Kurtines & J. L. Gewirtz (Eds.), *Handbook of moral behavior and development: Theory, research and applications* (Vol. 1, pp. 71–129). Hillsdale, NJ: Erlbaum.

Bandura, A. (1992). Social cognitive theory of social referencing. In S. Feinman (Ed.), *Social referencing and the social construction of reality in infancy* (pp. 175–208). New York: Plenum.

Bandura, A. (1997). *Self-efficacy: The exercise of control.* New York: Freeman.

Bandura, A. (1999). Moral disengagement in the perpetration of inhumanities. *Personality and Social Psychology Review, 3,* 193–209.

Bandura, A. (2000). Exercise of human agency through collective efficacy. *Current Directions in Psychological Science, 9,* 75–78.

Bandura, A. (2002a). Environmental sustainability by sociocognitive deceleration of population growth. In P. Schmuck & W. Schultz (Eds.), *The psychology of sustainable development* (pp. 209–238). Dordrecht: Kluwer.

Bandura, A. (2002b). Growing primacy of human agency in adaptation and change in the electronic era. *European Psychologist, 7,* 2–16.

Bandura, A. (2002c). Selective moral disengagement in the exercise of moral agency. *Journal of Moral Education, 31,* 101–119. Retrieved from http://web.stanford.edu

Bandura, A. (2002d). Social cognitive theory in cultural context. *Applied Psychology: An International Review, 51,* 269–290.

Bandura, A. (2004). Selective exercise of moral agency. In T. A. Thorkildsen & H. J. Walberg (Eds.), *Nurturing morality* (pp. 35–57). Boston: Kluwer Academic.

Bandura, A. (2006a). Going global with social cognitive theory: From prospect to paydirt. In S. I. Donaldson, D. E. Berger, & K. Pezdek (Eds.), *Applied psychology: New frontiers and rewarding careers* (pp. 53–79). Mahwah, NJ: Erlbaum.

Bandura, A. (2006b). On integrating social cognitive and social diffusion theories. In A. Singhal & J. Dearing (Eds.), *Communication of innovations: A journey with Ev Rogers* (pp. 111–135). Thousand Oaks, CA: Sage Publications.

Bandura, A. (2006c). Toward a psychology of human agency. *Perspectives on Psychological Science, 1,* 164–180.

Bandura, A. (2008). The reconstrual of free will from the agentic perspective of social cognitive theory. In J. Baer, J. C. Kaufman, & R. F. Baumeister (Eds.), *Are we free? Psychology and free will* (pp. 86–127). Oxford, UK: Oxford University Press.

Bandura, A. (2011). Self-deception: A paradox revisited. *Behavioral and Brain Sciences, 34,* 16–17.

Bandura, A. (2014). Bobo Doll studies. In M. S. Eastin (Ed.), *Encyclopedia of media violence* (pp. 54–56). Thousand Oaks, CA: Sage Publications.

Bandura, A., Barbaranelli, C., Caprara, G. V., & Pastorelli, C. (1996). Mechanisms of moral disengagement in the exercise of moral agency. *Journal of Personality and Social Psychology, 71,* 364–374.

Bandura, A., Caprara, G. V., Barbaranelli, C., Gerbino, M. G., & Pastorelli, C. (2003). Role of affective self-regulatory efficacy in diverse spheres of psychosocial functioning. *Child Development, 74,* 769–782.

Bandura, A., Caprara, G. V., Barbaranelli, C., Pastorelli, C., & Regalia, C. (2001). Sociocognitive self-regulatory mechanisms governing transgressive behavior. *Journal of Personality and Social Psychology, 80,* 125–135.

Bandura, A., Caprara, G. V., & Zsolnai, L. (2002). Corporate transgressions. In L. Zsolnai (Ed.), *Ethics in the economy: Handbook of business ethics* (pp. 151–164). Oxford, UK: Peter Lang.

Bandura, A., & McAlister, A. (2015). *Moral disengagement in support of the death penalty.* Manuscript in preparation.

Bandura, A., McAlister, A., & Owen, S. (2006). Mechanisms of moral disengagement in support of military force: The impact of September 11. *Journal of Social and Clinical Psychology, 25,* 141–166.

Bandura, A., Ross, D., & Ross, S. A. (1963). Imitation of film-mediated aggressive models. *Journal of Abnormal and Social Psychology, 66,* 3–11.

Bandura, A., Underwood, B., & Fromson, M. E. (1975). Disinhibition of aggression through diffusion of responsibility and dehumanization of victims. *Journal of Research in Personality, 9*, 253–269.

Bandura, A., & Walters, R. H. (1959). *Adolescent aggression*. New York: Ronald Press.

Banerjee, I. (Ed.) (2007). *The Internet and governance in Asia: A critical reader*. Singapore: Asian Media and Information and Communication Centre.

Banerjee, N. (2002, September 16). OPEC feels pressure to produce more oil. *The New York Times*. Retrieved from http://www.nytimes.com

Barbaro, M., & Goldstein, J. (2013, May 31). Mayor's fierce stand against guns creates lighting rod. *The New York Times*, p. A15.

Barchia, K., & Bussey, K. (2011). Individual and collective social cognitive influences on peer aggression: Exploring the contribution of aggression efficacy, moral disengagement, and collective efficacy. *Journal of Aggressive Behavior, 37*, 107–120.

Barnard, A. (2015, July 29). Turkey's focus on crushing Kurd extremists complicates ISIS efforts. *The New York Times*, p. A4.

Barnard, A., & Kirkpatrick, D. D. (2014). Arabs give tepid support to U.S. fight against ISIS. *The New York Times*, p. A1.

Barrett, P. (2012, December 17). Gun makers' silence won't deter a sales surge. Bloomberg Businessweek. Retrieved from http://www.businessweek.com

Barrionuevo, A. (2006, May 11). Judge in Enron case delivers a serious blow to the 2 defendants. *The New York Times*. Retrieved from http://www.nytimes.com

Bartels, L., & Lee, K. (2013, March 20). 3 new gun bills on the books in Colorado despite its Wild West image. *The Denver Post*. Retrieved from http://www.denverpost.com

Bartholomew [His All-Holiness the Ecumenical Patriarch of Constantinople]. [n.d.]. Quotes by His All-Holiness the Ecumenical Patriarchate [sic] of Constantinople on peace and the environment. Spiritual Ecology. Retrieved from http://spiritualecology.org

Bartlett, A. A. (1994). Reflections on sustainability, population growth, and the environment. *Population and Environment, 16*, 5–35.

Bateson, G. (1941). The frustration-aggression hypothesis and culture. *Psychological Review, 48*, 350–355.

Baylis, F., & Robert, J. (2004). The inevitability of genetic enhancement technologies. *Bioethics, 18*, 1–26.

Bazelon, E., & Levin, J. (2012, July 12). The most damning verdict. Slate. Retrieved from http://www.slate.com

Beauchamp, Z. (2013). Study: States with loose gun laws have higher rates of gun violence. Think Progress. Retrieved from http://thinkprogress.org

Beck, C. (2007). How to talk to a climate skeptic: Responses to the most common skeptical arguments on global warming. Grist. Retrieved from http://grist.org

Becker, L. J. (1978). Joint effect of feedback and goal setting on performance: A field study of residential energy conservation. *Journal of Applied Psychology, 63*, 428–433.

Bekelman, J. E., Li, Y., & Gross, C. P. (2003). Scope and impact of financial conflicts of interest in biomedical research: A systematic review. *Journal of the American Medical Association, 289*, 454–465.

Bell, Z. G. (1974, October 4). [Memo to J. A. Clapperton]. Federal Register, Vol. 39, No. 194, part 2, OSHA Exposure to Vinyl Chloride, Occupational Safety and Health Standards. 35890–35898.

Bell, Z. G. (1976, April 15). [Memo to F. C. Ludden]. Retrieved from http://www.deceitanddenial.org

Belson, K. (2012, June 12). Former coach testifies against Sandusky. *The New York Times*, p. B17.

Belz, M. (2015, Janurary 24). Suffer the children, ISIS Islamic terrorism is decimating a generation. WORLD. Retrieved from http://www.worldmag.com

Bennett, J. T., & Di Lorenzo, T. J. (1997). *CancerScam: Diversion of federal cancer funds to politics*. New Brunswick, NJ: Transaction Publishers.

Bennhold, K. (2013, October 12). Behind flurry of killing, potency of hate. *The New York Times*. Retrieved from http://www.nytimes.com

Benowitz, N. L., & Gourlay, S. G. (1997). Cardiovascular toxicity of nicotine: Implications for nicotine replacement therapy. *Journal of the American College of Cardiology, 29,* 1422–1431.

Berkes, H. (2012, July 13). Federal mine agency considering tougher response on black lung. NPR. Retrieved from http://www.npr.org

Berkes, H. (2013, September 10). Former Massey exec gets 42 months in mine disaster case. NPR. Retrieved from http://www.npr.org

Berkowitz, L. (1990). On the formation and regulation of anger and aggression: A cognitive-neoassociationistic analysis. *American Psychologist, 45,* 494–503.

Berkowitz, L., Leyens, J. P., Parke, R. D., Sebastian, R. J., & West, S. G. (1977). Some effects of violent and nonviolent movies on the behavior of juvenile delinquents. In L. Berkowitz (Ed.), *Advances in Experimental Social Psychology* (Vol. 10, pp. 135–172). New York: Academic Press.

Berkowitz, L., Parke, R., Leyens, J.-P., & West, S. (1974). The effects of justified and unjustified movie violence on aggression in juvenile delinquents. *Journal of Research in Crime and Deliquency, 11,* 16–24.

Berlet, C. (Ed.). (1995). *Eyes right! Challenging the right wing backlash*. Boston: South End Press.

Berman, M. (2014a, July 16). Federal judge says California's death penalty system is "unconstitutional." *The Washington Post*. Retrieved from http://www.washingtonpost.com

Berman, M. (2014b, April 29). Inmate dies following botched Oklahoma execution, second execution delayed. *The Washington Post*. Retrieved from http://www.washingtonpost.com

Bernard, V., Ottenberg, P., & Redl, F. (1965). Dehumanization: A composite psychological defense in relation to modern war. In M. Schwebel (Ed.), *Behavioral science and human survival* (pp. 64–82). Palo Alto: Science and Behavior Books.

Bernstein, R. (1984, March 12). Nicaragua in U.N. protest. *The New York Times*, p. A4.

Bernstein, R., & Weisman, S. R. (2003, February 17). NATO settles rift over aid to Turks in case of a war. *The New York Times*. Retrieved from http://www.nytimes.com

Bero, L. A., Oostvogel, F., Bacchetti, P., & Lee, K. (2007). Factors associated with findings of published trials of drug-drug comparisons: Why some statins appear more efficacious than others. *PLoS Medicine, 4,* e184.

Beschloss, M. (2011, February 12). Book discussion on *Known and unknown: A memoir*. C-SPAN. [Video]. Retrieved from http://www.booktv.org

Best, G. (1973, March 6). [Memo to John D. Bryan, Conoco Chemicals and Continental Oil]. Retrieved from http://www.deceitanddenial.org

Bethell, T. (1989, November 12). When "service" looks like "corruption": Lincoln S&L; Lawmaking has degenerated so far that the senators' intervention did not greatly differ from the routine. *Los Angeles Times*. Retrieved from http://articles.latimes.com

Beyl, C. A. (1992, April/June). Rachel Carson, *Silent Spring*, and the environmental movement. *HortTechnology*. Retrieved from http://www.hort.purdue.edu

Bickel, A. (1974). Watergate and the legal order. *Commentary, 59*, 19–25.

Bilefsky, D. (2015, January 13). Charlie Hebdo's defiant Muhammad cover fuels debate on free speech. *The New York Times*. Retrieved from http://www.nytimes.com

Bilefsky, D., & de la Baume, M. (2015a, January 29). French video tries to blunt Jihad's allure among youth. *The New York Times*. Retrieved from http://www.nytimes.com

Bilefsky, D., & de la Baume, M. (2015b, January 7). Terrorists strike Charlie Hebdo newspaper in Paris, leaving 12 dead. *The New York Times*. Retrieved from http://www.nytimes.com

[bin Laden interview]. (2001, November 10). 'Muslims have the right to attack America.' *The Guardian*. Retrieved from http://www.theguardian.com

Black, I. (2015, January 15). Charlie Hebdo killings condemned by Arab states— But hailed online by extremists. *The Guardian*. Retrieved from http://www.theguardian.com

Black, R. (2011, December 11). UN climate talks end with late deal. BBC. Retrieved from http://www.bbc.com

Blitzer, W. (2002). Interview with Condoleezza Rice. CNN.com transcripts. Retrieved from http://cnn.com

Blumenfeld, L. (2002). *Revenge: A story of hope*. New York: Simon & Schuster.

Blumenthal, M. D. (1972). *Justifying violence: Attitudes of American men*. Ann Arbor: Institute for Social Research, University of Michigan.

Boadle, A. (2012, October 18). Brazil's Rousseff enacts forest law in blow to farm lobby. Reuters. Retrieved from http://www.reuters.com

Boffey, P. M., & Walsh, J. (1970). Study of TV violence: Seven top researchers blackballed from panel. *Science, 168*, 949–952.

Bok, S. (1980). The self deceived. *Social Science Information, 19*, 923–936.

Bolinger, D. (1980). *Language: The loaded weapon; The use and abuse of language today*. London: Longman.

Bonner, R. (2003, January 16). Radical Islamists a threat to Southeast Asia even if al Qaeda is eliminated, Singapore says. *The New York Times*, p. A11.

Bora, K. (2013, November 26). Double the rate of methane release from Arctic seafloor creates fear of new "climate-change-driven factor." *International Business Times*. Retrieved from http://www.ibtimes.com

Borenstein, J. (2008). The ethics of autonomous military robots. *Studies in Ethics, Law, and Technology, 2*(1).

Borger, J. (2001, October 7). Rhetoric to arouse the Islamic world. *The Guardian*. Retrieved from http://www.guardian.co.uk

Borucke, M., Moore, D., Cranston, G., Gracey, K., Iha, K., Larson, J., Lazarus, E., Morales, J. C., Wackernagel, M., & Galli, A. (2013). Accounting for demand and supply of the biosphere's regenerative capacity: The National Footprint Accounts' underlying methodology and framework. *Ecological Indicators, 24*, 518–533.

Boston Marathon bombings: Suspect Dzhokhar Tsarnaev left mesage in boat calling victims "collateral damage." (2013, May 16). CBS News. Retrieved from http://www.cbsnews.com

Botelho, G. (2015, March 28). Arab Spring aftermath: Revolutions give way to violence, more unrest. CNN. Retrieved from http://www.cnn.com

Bowditch, M. (1956, April 24–25). *Report of Health and Safety Division*. 28th Annual Meeting of the Lead Industries Association, Lead Industry Association Papers.

Bowditch, M. (1957, December 26). [Letter to R. Kehoe, head of Kettering Laboratory]. Lead Industry Association Papers.

Boyd, J. W. (2015, July 18). How the largest association of U.S. psychologists colluded in torture. *Newsweek*. Retrieved from http://www.newsweek.com/how-largest-association-us-psychologists-colluded-torture-354870s

Boyle, J. (2003). Just war doctrine and the military response to terrorism. *Journal of Political Philosophy, 11*, 153–170.

Braithwaite, J. (1994). A sociology of modeling and the politics of empowerment. *British Journal of Sociology, 45*, 445–479.

Branigin, W. (2005, January 6). Gonzales pledges to preserve civil liberties. *The Washington Post*. Retrieved from http://www.washingtonpost.com

Brassard, B. (2009). The New York Times errs on guns and Mexico [Web log post]. Retrieved from http://www.nssfblog.com

Bratman, M. E. (1999). *Faces of intention: Selected essays on intention and agency*. New York: Cambridge University Press.

Bray, C. (2011, November 19). 5-year sentence for insider. *The Wall Street Journal*. Retrieved from http://online.wsj.com

Brennan, M. (2012, December 23). As NRA is criticized on shooting response, bullets sell. CBS News. Retrieved from http://www.cbsnews.com

Brent, D., Perper, J., Allman, C., Moritz, G., Wartella, M., & Zelenak, J. (1991). The presence and accessibility of firearms in the homes of adolescent suicides: A case control study. *Journal of the American Medical Association, 266*, 2989–2995.

Breslow, J. M. (2013, May 16). Eric Holder backtracks remarks on "too big to jail." *Frontline*. Retrieved from http://www.pbs.org

Breslow, J. M. (2014, October 28). How Saddam's former soldiers are fueling the rise of ISIS. *Frontline*. Retrieved from http://www.pbs.org

Briand, X. (2012, December 23). Gun lobby defends call for armed guards at schools. Reuters. Retrieved from http://www.reuters.com

British American Tobacco. (1987, October 5). The Legacy Tobacco Documents Library. Retrieved from https://industrydocuments.library.ucsf.edu/tobacco/docs/znjj0212

Brock, T. C., & Buss, A. H. (1964). Effects of justification for aggression and communication with the victim on postaggression dissonance. *Journal of Abnormal and Social Psychology, 68*, 403–412.

Broder, J. M. (2003, April 2). U.S. military has no count of Iraqi dead in fighting. *The New York Times*. Retrieved from http://www.nytimes.com

Broder, J. M. (2010, October 20). Climate change doubt is tea party article of faith. *The New York Times*. Retrieved from http://www.nytimes.com

Broder, J. M. (2011, August 18). Bashing EPA is new theme in GOP race. *The New York Times*, p. A1.

Broder, J. M. (2012a, December 9). Climate talks yield commitment to ambitious, but unclear, actions. *The New York Times*, p. A13.

Broder, J. M. (2012b, November 26). U.N. climate talks promise little drama. *The New York Times*. Retrieved from http://www.nytimes.com

Broder, J. M., & Galbraith, K. (2011). EPA is longtime favorite target for Perry. *The New York Times*, p. A13.

Brody, R. (2015, June 18). Views you can use: Cool to Francis' climate views. *U.S. News & World Report*. Retrieved from http://www.usnews.com

Brown, C. (2012, March 22). A look back at the NRA's effort to pass Florida's Stand Your Ground Law [Web log post]. Retrieved from http://www.mediamatters.org

Brown, L. (1971). *Television: The business behind the box*. New York: Harcourt Brace Jovanovich.

Brown, L. R. (2007, July 24). Water tables falling and rivers running dry. Earth Policy Institute. Retrieved from http://www.earth-policy.org

Brown, L. R. (2009). *Plan B 4.0: Mobilizing to save civilization*. New York: W. W. Norton.

Brown, W. J., & Cody, M. J. (1991). Effects of a prosocial television soap opera in promoting women's status. *Human Communication Research, 18*, 114–144.

Brown & Williamson Co. (1984, July 9–12). Proceedings of the smoking behaviour—marketing conference, session III. Bates no. 1226-1301. University of California, San Francisco, Legacy Tobacco Documents Library, Brown & Williamson Collection, Bates no. 1226.01, 223. Retrieved from https://industrydocuments.library.ucsf.edu

Brownlee, S., & McGraw, D. (1997, June 16). The place for vengeance. *U.S. News & World Report, 122*, p. 24.

Brune, M. (2013, April 25). A path to the future [Web log post]. Coming Clean: The Blog of Executive Director Michael Brune. Retrieved from http://sierraclub.typepad.com

Bryant, J., Carveth, R. A., & Brown, D. (1981). Television viewing and anxiety: An experimental examination. *Journal of Communication, 31*, 106–119.

Bryant, J., & Oliver, M. B. (2009). *Media effects: Advances in theory and research*. Mahwah, NJ: Erlbaum.

Buffett, W. E. (2003, February 21). Letter to shareholders. Berkshire Hathaway. Retrieved from http://www.berkshirehathaway.com

Bullen, C., Howe, C., Laugesen, M., McRobbie, H., Parag, V., Williman, J., & Walker, N. (2013). Electronic cigarettes for smoking cessation: A randomized controlled trial. *The Lancet, 382*, 1629–1637.

"Bullet button" used to get around California gun laws. (2012, May 1). CBS San Francisco. Retrieved from http://sanfrancisco.cbslocal.com

Bumiller, E. (2011, December 19). Air Force drone operators report high levels of stress. *The New York Times*, p. A8.

Bunge, M. (1977). Emergence and the mind. *Neuroscience, 2*, 501–509.

Burns, J. F., & Cowell, A. (2013, January 12). Report depicts horrific pattern of child sexual abuse by BBC celebrity. *The New York Times*, p. A8.

Burns, J. F., & Somaiya, R. (2012, November 2). A shield of celebrity let a BBC host escape legal scrutiny for decades. *The New York Times*, p. A8.

Burt, M. R. (1980). Cultural myths and support for rape. *Journal of Personality and Social Psychology, 38*, 217–230.

Bushman, B. J., & Cantor, J. (2003). Media ratings for violence and sex: Implications for policymakers and parents. *American Psychologist, 58*, 130–141.

Bussey, K., & Bandura, A. (1992). Self-regulatory mechanisms governing gender development. *Child Development, 63*, 1236–1250.

Bussey, K., & Bandura, A. (1999). Social cognitive theory of gender development and differentiation. *Psychological Review, 106*, 676–713.

Butler, M. (1972). *Social policy research and the realities of the system: Violence done to TV research*. Stanford, CA: Institute for Communication Research, Stanford University.

Butt, R., & Asthana, A. (2009, September 28). Sex abuse rife in other religions, says Vatican. *The Guardian*. Retrieved from http://www.guardian.co.uk

Butterfield, F. (1998, November 28). New data point blame at gun makers. *The New York Times*, p. A9.

Butterfield, F. (1999, February 14). To rejuvenate gun sales, critics say, industry started making more powerful pistols. *The New York Times*. Retrieved from http://www.nytimes.com

Butterfield, F. (2003, February 4). Gun industry ex-official describes bond of silence. *The New York Times*. Retrieved from http://www.nytimes.com

Butterfield, F. (2004, November 23). Rare weapon to hunt deer. *The New York Times*. Retrieved from http://www.nytimes.com

Butterfield, F., & Hernandez, R. (2000, March 30). Gun maker's accord on curbs brings pressure from industry. *The New York Times*, p. A1.

Cadet, D. (2013, July 26). Zimmerman trial juror says he "got away with murder." The Huffington Post. Retrieved from http://www.huffingtonpost.com

Cafaro, P. (2011). Rachel Carson's environmental ethics. In C. J. Cleveland (Ed.), *Encyclopedia of earth*. Washington, DC: Environmental Information Coalition. Retrieved from http://www.eoearth.org

Callimachi, R. (2008, March 14. Muslim nations: Defame Islam, get sued? *USA TODAY*. Retrieved from http://usatoday30.usatoday.com

Callimachi, R. (2015, August 14). Enslaving young girls, the Islamic State builds a vast system of rape. *The New York Times*, p. A1.

Calmes, J. (2011, March 12). Administration invites NRA to meeting on gun policies, but it declines. *The New York Times*, p. A22.

Cama, T. (2015, April 17). 2016 GOP hopefuls unite to block EPA water rule. *The Hill*. Retrieved from http://thehill.com

Campbell, D., & Geiger, K. (2013, November 23). N. Y. Fed counsel says punish banks to change culture. BloombergBusiness. Retrieved from http://www.bloomberg.com

Campbell, M. (2014). Ending the silence on population. In M. Hempel (Ed.), *Facing the population challenge: Wisdom from the elders*. Redlands, CA: Blue Planet United.

Campbell, S. (2007). *The sitcoms of Norman Lear*. Jefferson, NC: McFarland & Company, Inc., Publishers.

Camus, A. (1960). *Resistance, rebellion, and death: Essays*. New York: Modern Library.

Cannon, J. A. (2007, July 12). Is Earth's impending empty cradle due to selfishness? *Deseret Morning News*, p. G2.

Cantor, M. G. (1972). The role of the producer in choosing children's television content. In E. A. Rubinstein & G. A. Comstock (Eds.), *Television and Social Behavior: Vol. 1. Media content and control* (pp. 259–299). Washington, DC: U.S. Government Printing Office.

Caprara, G. V., Regalia, C., & Bandura, A. (2002). Longitudinal impact of perceived self- regulatory efficacy on violent conduct. *European Psychologist, 7*, 63–69.

Carey, B. (2011, November 1). Decoding the brain's cacophony. *The New York Times*, p. D1.

Carlson, C. J. (1976). Provision of designated "no-smoking" areas aboard aircraft operated by certificated air carriers. Civil Aeronautics Board.

Carlson, M., & Keating, C. (1990, April 9). Interview with Charles Keating: Money talks. *Time*. Retrieved from http://content.time.com

Carney, J. (2009, November 9). Lloyd Blankfein says he is doing "God's work." Business Insider. Retrieved from http://www.businessinsider.com

Carney, J. (2015, May 16). Senators struggle with ISIS war bill. *The Hill*. Retrieved from http://thehill.com

Carson, R. (1962). *Silent spring*. Boston: Houghton Mifflin.

Carstensen, L. L. (2011). *A long bright future*. New York: PublicAffairs.

Carter, B. D., Abnet, C. C., Feskanich, D., Freedman, N. D., Hartge, P., Lewis, C. E., Ockene, J. K., Prentice, R. L., Speizer, F. E., Thun, M. J., & Jacobs, E. J. (2015). Smoking and mortality—Beyond established causes. *New England Journal of Medicine, 372*(7), 631–640.

Castillo, M. (2012, December 21). NRA clear on gun debate stance: Arm schools. CNN.com. Retrieved from http://www.cnn.com

Cater, D., & Strickland, S. (1975). *TV violence and the child: The evolution and fate of the surgeon general's report*. New York: Russell Sage Foundation.

Catholics for Choice (20120). The Vatican at Rio +20—What's at stake? Catholics for Choice. Retrieved from http://www.catholicsforchoice.org

CBS (1964). A review and evaluation of recent studies on the impact of violence. Office of Social Research, CBS.

CBSNews. (2007, November 19). Calif. sues over lead-contaminated toys. Retrieved from http://www.cbsnews.com

Chagnon, N. (1968). *Yanomamö: The fierce people*. New York: Holt, Rinehart and Winston.

Chammah, M. (2014). Six reasons the death penalty is becoming more expensive. The Marshall Project. Retrieved from https://www.themarshallproject.org

Champlin, T. S. (1977). Self-deception: A reflexive dilemma. *Philosophy, 52,* 281–299.

Chan, M. (2012, March 20). The changed face of the tobacco industry. Keynote address at the 15th World Conference on Tobacco or Health, Singapore. Retrieved from http://www.who.int

Chappell, B. (2015, May 20). Big banks pay $5.6 billion, plead guilty to felonies over currency and rate-fixing. NPR. Retrieved from http://www.npr.org

Charlton Heston's speech to the NRA annual meeting in Colorado. (1999, May 1). Land of the Free. Retrieved from http://www.thelandofthefree.net

Chatwin, L., Low, C. (Producers), & Ferguson, G. (Director). (1972). *The question of television violence* [Motion picture]. Montréal: National Film Board of Canada.

Check, J., & Malamuth, N. (1986). Pornography and sexual aggression: A social learning theory analysis. In M. L. McLaughlin (Ed.), *Communication Yearbook* (Vol. 9, pp. 181–213). Beverly Hills, CA: Sage.

Chilcote, S. D. (1984, November 5). Memorandum to Tobacco Industry Labor Management Committee. Retrieved from dl.tufts.edu/file_assets/tufts: UA084.88115765

Childs, M. (2013, August). Briefing: Global population, consumption and rights. Friends of the Earth. Retrieved from http://www.foe.co.uk

Cho, M. K., & Bero, L. A. (1996). The quality of drug studies published in symposium proceedings. *Annals of Internal Medicine, 124485–124489*.

Christofferson, J. (2012, February 7). Retired Cardinal Egan criticized for abuse comments. Associated Press. Retrieved from http://www.guardian.co.uk

Chu, J. (2015, July 20). Ocean acidification may cause dramatic changes to phytoplankton. *MIT News*. Retrieved from http://news.mit.edu

Church, R. M. (1959). Emotional reactions of rats to the pain of others. *Journal of Comparative and Physiological Psychology, 52*, 132–134.

City of New York. (2009). Gun show undercover: Report on illegal sales at gun shows. Retrieved from http://www.nyc.gov

Clark, D. (2009, July 27). World will warm faster than predicted in next five years, study warns. *The Guardian*. Retrieved from http://www.theguardian.com

Clark, S. J. (2003). Protection of Lawful Commerce in Arms Act. *Congressional Record*. Retrieved from http://thomas.loc.gov

Claster, D. S. (1967). Comparison of risk perception between delinquents and non-delinquents. *Journal of Criminal Law Criminology and Police Science, 58*, 80–86.

Cleland J., Bernstein, S., Ezeh, A., Faundes, A., Glasier, A., & Innis, J. (2006). Family planning: The unfinished agenda. *The Lancet, 368*, 1810–1827.

Clemente, J. (2015, June 17). Why biofuels can't replace oil. *Forbes*. Retrieved from http://www.forbes.com

Clermont, W. R. (2012). An econometric analysis of the death penalty and other measures of punishment. Selected Works. Retrieved from http://works.bepress.com

Clifton, J. (2012, September 5). The right global employment metric: Payroll to population. Gallup. Retrieved from http://www.gallup.com

Cline, V. B., Croft, R. G., & Courrier, S. (1973). Desensitization of children to television violence. *Journal of Personality and Social Psychology, 27*, 360–365.

Clover, C. (2007, July 24). We need fewer people to halt global warming. *The Telegraph*. Retrieved from http://www.telegraph.co.uk

Clymer, A. (1997, May 20). Child insurance bill opposed as threat to cigarette revenue. *The New York Times*. Retrieved from http://www.nytimes.com

Clymer, A., & Elder, J. (2002, September 8). Poll finds unease on terror fight and concerns about war on Iraq. *The New York Times*. Retrieved from http://www.nytimes.com

Codrea, D. (2013, February 4). Newtown father defies legislators on "gun control." Examiner.com. Retrieved from http://www.examiner.com

Cohan, W. D. (2009, March 12). A tsunami of excuses. *The New York Times*, p. A23.

Cohen, D., & Nisbett, R. E. (1994). Self-protection and the culture of honor: Explaining southern violence. *Personality and Social Psychology Bulletin, 20*, 551–567.

Cohen, P. (2015, February 4). When company is fined, taxpayers often share bill. *The New York Times*, p. B1.

Cohen, S., Tyrell, D., Russell, M., Jarvis, M. J., & Smith, A. P. (1993). Smoking, alcohol consumption and susceptibility to the common cold. *American Journal of Public Health, 83*, 1277–1283.

Cole, D. (2013, January 2). Who pays for the right to bear arms? *The New York Times*, p. A19.

Collapse of the Enron Corporation: Hearing before the Committee on Commerce, Science and Transportation, United States Senate, 107th Cong. 2 (2002).

Collins, D. A. (2007). The great population debate: An opinion paper. *Journal of Social, Political, and Economic Studies, 32*, 75–87.

Collins, G. (2009, August 1). Have gun, will travel. *The New York Times*, p. A17.

Collins, G. (2011, November 17). Something to shoot for. *The New York Times*, p. A31.

Collins, G. (2012a, August 1). For God, Texas and golf. *The New York Times*. Retrieved from http://www.nytimes.com

Collins, G. (2012b, December 15). Looking for America. *The New York Times*, p. A23.

Collins, G. (2012c, December 22). Wish you a gun-free Christmas. *The New York Times*, p. A25.

Condon, S. (2013, December 10). Plastic guns ban extended. CBS News. Retrieved from http://www.ktva.com

Confessore, N., Cooper, M., & Luo, M. (2012, December 18). Silent since shootings, N.R.A. could face challenge to political power. *The New York Times*, p. A25.

Cook, J. (2015). Global warming & climate change myths. Skeptical Science. Retrieved from https://www.skepticalscience.com

Cook, P. J. (1980). Research in criminal deterrence: Laying the groundwork for the second decade. In N. Morris, & M. Tomy (Eds.), *Crime and justice: Annual review of research* (Vol. 2, pp. 211–268). Chicago: University of Chicago Press.

Cook, P. J., & Ludwig, J. (2000). *Gun violence*. Oxford, UK: Oxford University Press.

Cook, P. J., Ludwig, J., & Hemenway, D. (1997). The gun debate's new mythical number: How many defensive uses per year? *Journal of Policy Analysis and Management, 16,* 463–469.

Cooper, D. (2009, March 19). Coal CEO: I've been around West Virginia long enough to know that politicians don't stay bought. The Huffington Post. Retrieved from http://www.huffingtonpost.com

Cooper, M. (2012, December 16). Debate on gun control is revived, amid a trend toward fewer restrictions. *The New York Times,* p. A27.

Cordes, B. (1987). When terrorists do the talking: Reflections on terrorist literature. *Journal of Strategic Studies, 10,* 150–171.

Corkery, M., & Protess, B. (2015, May 21). Banks admit scheme to rig currency price. *The New York Times,* p. A1.

Cosgrove-Mather, B. (2004). Outsourcing torture. CBS News. Retrieved from http://www.cbsnews.com

Cosker, G. J. (2012, December 21). Gov. Chris Christie: Adding armed guards to schools is 'the easy way out.' Examiner.com. Retrieved from http://www.examiner.com

Costanzo, S., and Costanzo, M. (1994). Life or death decisions: An analysis of capital jury decision making under the special issues sentencing framework. *Law and Human Behavior, 18,* 151–170.

Cowell, A. (2012, October 27). Investigation of BBC host examines dropped cases. *The New York Times,* p. A9.

Craig, S., Protess, B., & Stevenson, A. (2013, August 3). In complex trading case, jurors focused on greed. *The New York Times,* p. B1.

Crichton, M. (2004). *State of fear.* New York: HarperCollins.

Crummy, K. E. (2012, July 22). Hickenlooper: Tougher gun laws would not have stopped shooter. *The Denver Post.* Retrieved from http://www.denverpost.com

Cullen, T. A. (1961, March 20). The Eichmann Story—No. 1 'I shall leap to my grave laughing.' *The Tuscaloosa News,* p. 3. Retrieved from http://news.google.com/newspapers

Cumming-Bruce, N. (2013, May 31). U.N. expert calls for halt on robots for military. *The New York Times,* p. A9.

Cumming-Bruce, N. (2014, May 7). Vatican tells of 848 priests ousted in decade. *The New York Times,* p. A8.

Cuomo, A. (2012, November 15). We will lead on climate change. *The Daily News.* Retrieved from http://www.nydailynews.com

Cuomo, M. M. (2011, October 2). Death penalty is dead wrong: It's time to outlaw capital punishment in America—completely. *The Daily News.* Retrieved from http://www.nydailynews.com

Curiel, J. (2005, July 12). Terror.com. *San Francisco Chronicle.* Retrieved from http://www.sfgate.com

Currier, C. (2013, February 5). Everything we know so far about drone strikes. ProPublica. Retrieved from http://www.propublica.org

Dahlburg, J.-T. (2003, September 2). Killer of abortion doctor faces death Wednesday. *San Francisco Chronicle,* p. A7.

Dalby, D., & Donadio, R. (2011, July 13). Irish report finds abuse persisting in Catholic Church. *The New York Times*. Retrieved from http://www.nytimes.com

Dao, J. (2004, March 7). From picture of pride to symbol of abuse. *The New York Times*, p. A1.

Darley, J. M., Klosson, E. C., & Zanna, M. P. (1978). Intentions and their contexts in the moral judgments of children and adults. *Child Development, 49*, 66–74.

DaRonco, D. (2012, December 29). NRA may fight gun buyback in Tucson. *The Arizona Daily Star*. Retrieved from http://tucson.com

Davenport, C. (2014a, December 14). A climate accord based on global peer pressure. *The New York Times*. Retrieved from http://www.nytimes.com

Davenport, C. (2014b, September 24). Emissions from India will increase, official says. *The New York Times*. Retrieved from http://www.nytimes.com

Davenport, C. (2014c, April 30). Justices back rule limiting coal pollution. *The New York Times*. Retrieved from http://www.nytimes.com

Davenport, C. (2014d, December 13). Nations plod forward on climate change accord. *The New York Times*. Retrieved from http://www.nytimes.com

Davenport, C. (2014e, December 11). Strange climate event: Warmth toward U.S. *The New York Times*. Retrieved from http://www.nytimes.com

Davis, J. H., & Davenport, C. (2015, September 25). U.S. says China will announce cap-and- trade emissions plan. *The New York Times*, p. A1.

Death Row inmates by state and size of death row by year. (2015, April 1). Death Penalty Information Center. Retrieved from http://www.deathpenaltyinfo.org

DeCambre, M. (2010, October 22). Taped crusader. *The New York Post*. Retrieved from http://nypost.com

Dedman, B. (1998, March 12). Executive says he's uncertain about tobacco harm. *The New York Times*, p. A16.

Delgado, J. M. R. (1967). Social rank and radio-stimulated aggressiveness in monkeys. *Journal of Nervous and Mental Disease, 144*, 383–390.

Della-Ragione, J. (2011, November 1). The voice of the climate change critics. Express. Retrieved from http://www.express.co.uk

Demands fair play for ethyl gasoline. (1925, May 7). *The New York Times*, p. 10.

Democrats and gun control [Editorial]. (2011, April 23). *The New York Times*, p. A18.

Denis, L. (2014). Kant and Hume on morality. In E. N. Zalta (Ed.), The Stanford Encyclopedia of Philosophy (Winter ed.). Retrieved from http://plato.stanford.edu

Denning, L. (2013, December 22). Lights flicker for utilities. *The Wall Street Journal*. Retrieved from http://www.wsj.com

Dennis, B. (2010, July 16). Congress passes financial reform bill. *The Washington Post*. Retrieved from http://www.washingtonpost.com

Deputy Secretary Wolfowitz Interview with Sam Tannenhaus, *Vanity Fair*. (2003, May 9). [Transcript]. Washington, DC: U.S. Department of Defense. Retrieved from http://www.defense.gov

Dezhbakhsh, H., Rubin, P. H., & Shepherd, J. M. (2003). Does capital punishment have a deterrent effect? New evidence from postmoratorium panel data. *American Law and Economics Review, 5*, 344–376.

Diamond, E. (1963, September 28). The myth of the pesticide menace. *The Saturday Evening Post*, pp. 16–18.

Diaz, T. (1999). *Making a killing: The business of guns in America*. New York: New Press.

Diener, E., & DeFour, D. (1978). Does television violence enhance program popularity? *Journal of Personality and Social Psychology, 36*, 333–341.

Diener, E., Dineen, J., Endresen, K., Beaman, A. L., & Fraser, S. C. (1975). Effects of altered responsibility, cognitive set, and modeling on physical aggression and deindividuation. *Journal of Personality and Social Psychology, 31,* 328–337.

Dilanian, K. (2014, December 10). Psychologist defends harsh CIA interrogations. *The Huffington Post.* Retrieved from http://www.huffingtonpost.com/2014/12/10/psychologist-james-mitchell-cia-torture_n_6302526.html

Ding, D., Maibach, E. W., Zhao, X., Roser-Renouf, C., & Leiserowitz, A. (2011). Support for climate policy and societal action are linked to perceptions about scientific agreement. *Nature Climate Change, 1,* 462–466.

District of Columbia v. Heller, 554 U.S. 570 (2008).

Dobzhansky, T. (1972). Genetics and the diversity of behavior. *American Psychologist, 27,* 523–530.

Dodge, K. A. (1991). The structure and function of reactive and proactive aggression. In D. J. Pepler & K. H. Rubin (Eds.), *The development and treatment of childhood aggression* (pp. 201–285). Hillsdale, NJ: Erlbaum.

Dolan, M. (2001, August 7). Gun makers not liable in crimes, state justices say. *Los Angeles Times.* Retrieved from http://articles.latimes.com

Dolan, M. (2014, July 23). Executions should be by firing squad, federal appeals court judge says. *Los Angeles Times.* Retrieved from http://www.latimes.com

Dominick, J. R. (1973). Crime and law enforcement on prime-time television. *Public Opinion Quarterly, 37,* 241–250.

Donadio, R. (2012, March 20). Vatican inquiry finds progress in Irish abuse scandal. *The New York Times,* p. A5.

Donn, J. (1995). Smith & Wesson attempts turnaround in new gun age. Associated Press. Retrieved from http://www.apnewsarchive.com

Donohue, B. (2012a). (January 9). Boston victims' summit bombs. Catholic League. Retrieved from http://www.catholicleague.org

Donohue, B. (2012b). (June 22). Philly jury says no to conspiracy. Catholic League. Retrieved from http://www.catholicleague.org

Donohue, B. (2012c). (August 30). Fr. Groeschel under fire. Catholic League. Retrieved from http://www.catholicleague.org

Donohue, B. (2012d) (September 7). Assessing Bishop Finn's guilt. Catholic League. Retrieved from http://www.catholicleague.org

Doomsday Flight: Serling regrets movie script. (1971). *Palo Alto Times,* p. 5.

Dougherty, D. (2014, April 3). Keating's techniques were replicated by those who helped trigger the 2008 financial collapse. *Phoenix New Times.* Retrieved from http://www.phoenixnewtimes.com

Drape, J. (2012, June 22). Sandusky convicted of sexual abuse of 10 young boys. *The New York Times.* Retrieved from http://www.nytimes.com

Dretzin, R. (Writer), & Goodman, B. (Director). (2001). The merchants of cool. [Television documentary]. In A. Collins (Director), *Frontline.* United States: PBS Home Video.

Drew, C. (1998, December 12). RJR subsidiary pleads guilty to smuggling. *The New York Times,* p. A1.

Duca, J. V. (2013, November 22). Subprime mortgage crisis. Federal Reserve History. Retrieved from http://www.federalreservehistory.org

Dugger, C. W. (2007, September 12). As prices soar, U.S. food aid is buying less. *The New York Times,* p. A1.

Duncker, K. (1938). Experimental modification of children's food preferences through social suggestion. *Journal of Abnormal Social Psychology, 33,* 489–507.

Dwyer, D. (2013, January 16). NRA President defends ad attacking Obama, vows "battle" ahead. ABC News. Retrieved from http://abcnews.go.com

Dwyer, J., Neufeld, P., & Scheck, B. (2000). *Actual innocence: When justic goes wrong and how to make it right*. New York: Doubleday.

Dyer, G. (2007, March 12). Population bomb still ticking away. *New Zealand Herald*. Retrieved from http://www.nzherald.co.nz

Eavis, P. (2013, December 11). "Long and arduous process" to ban a single Wall Street activity. *The New York Times*, p. B1.

Eavis, P. (2014, May 21). In Credit Suisse settlement, a question of justice. *The New York Times*. Retrieved from http://www.nytimes.com

Eavis, P. (2015, May 12). Judge's ruling against 2 banks finds misconduct in '08 crash. *The New York Times*, p. A1.

Ebell, M. (2006, December 26). Love global warming: What's wrong with mild winters anyway? *Forbes*. Retrieved from http://www.forbes.com

Ecenbarger, W. (1994, January 23). Perfecting death: When the state kills it must do so humanely. Is that possible? *The Philadelphia Inquirer Magazine*.

Eckert, V. (2015, March 20). European power grids keep lights on during solar eclipse. Reuters. Retrieved from http://www.reuters.com

Eckholm, E. (2013). In death penalty's steady decline, some experts see a societal shift. *The New York Times*, p. A30.

Eckholm, E. (2014, April 22). 2 executions in Oklahoma are stayed, ending tussle. *The New York Times*, p. A13.

Eckholm, E. (2015, April 30). Supreme Court justices hear Oklahoma inmates' lethal injection case. *The New York Times*. Retrieved from http://www.nytimes.com

Eckholm, E., & Hurdle, J. (2012, March 27). In a first, a trial tests whether a church supervisor is liable for abuse by priests. *The New York Times*, p. A11.

Eckholm, E., & Zezima, K. (2011a, January 22). Drug used in executions dropped by U.S. supplier. *The New York Times*. Retrieved from http://www.nytimes.com

Eckholm, E., & Zezima, K. (2011b, January 12). U.S. supplier drops a drug for executions. *The New York Times*, p. A1.

Eder, S. (2013, January 2). Governor sues over penalties to Penn State. *The New York Times*. Retrieved from http://www.nytimes.com/

Eder, S., & Wutkowski, K. (2010, April 25). Goldman's "Fabulous" Fab's conflicted love letters. Reuters. Retrieved from http://www.reuters.com

Editorial: Death meted out by politicians in robes. [Editorial]. (2013, November 19). *The New York Times*, p. 24.

Editorial: Father Greeley, defender of the faithful. [Editorial]. (2013, May 31). *The New York Times*. Retrieved from http://www.nytimes.com

Effron, D., Cameron, J. S., & Monin, B. (2009). Endorsing Obama licenses favoring whites. *Journal of Experimental Social Psychology, 45*, 590–593.

Efron, E. (1969a, November 26). A child is not a rat. *TV Guide*.

Efron, E. (1969b, November 15). The man in the eye of the hurricane. *TV Guide*, 34–37.

Efron, S. (1987, May 18). Japan slow to tell consumers tobacco is a health hazard. *San Francisco Examiner*, p. A14.

Ehrlich, I. (1975). The deterrent effect of capital punishment: A question of life and death. *American Economic Review, 65*, 397–417.

Ehrlich, P. R. (1968). *The population bomb*. New York: Ballantine Books.

Ehrlich, P. R., Ehrlich, A. H., & Daily, G. C. (1995). *The stork and the plow: The equity answer to the human dilemma*. New Haven, CT: Yale University Press.

Eilperin, J. (2010, July 1). Penn State clears Mann in Climate-gate probe. *The Washington Post*. Retrieved from http://views.washingtonpost.com

Eilperin, J., & Mufson, S. (2014, June 2). Everything you need to know about the EPA's proposed rule on coal plants. *The Washington Post*. Retrieved from http://www.washingtonpost.com

Eisenberg, T., & Wells, M. T. (1993). Deadly confusion: Juror instructions in capital cases. *Cornell Law Review, 79*, 1–17.

Eisinger, J. (2014, February 5). Maintaining ethics in the move from regulator to regulated. The Trade. Retrieved from http://www.propublica.org

EJ focus 2: The progress of public doublespeak. (1988, March). *English Journal*, 3.

Ekins, E. (2014, October 10). Poll: 66% favor airstrikes against ISIS, but 52% oppose US sending ground troops. Reason-Rupe Public Opinion Survey. Retrieved from http://reason.com/poll/2014/10/10/poll-66-favor-airstrikes-against-isis-bu

El-Naggar, M. (2015, February 19). From a private school in Cairo to ISIS killing fields in Syria. *The New York Times*, p. A1.

Elder, G. (1994). Time, human agency, and social change: Perspectives on the life course. *Social Psychology Quarterly, 57*, 4–15.

Elliot, S. (2013, August 30). E-cigarette makers' ads echo tobacco's heyday. *The New York Times*, p. B1.

Elliott, D. S., & Rhinehart, M. (1995). *Moral disengagement, delinquent peers and delinquent behavior*. Unpublished manuscript, Institute of Behavioral Science, University of Colorado.

Ellis, C. (1962, May 29). The smoking and health problem. University of California, San Francisco, Legacy Tobacco Documents Library. Retrieved from https://industrydocuments.library.ucsf.edu

Ellis, E. C. (2013, September 13). Overpopulation is not the problem. *The New York Times*. Retrieved from http://www.nytimes.com

Ellsworth, P. (1978). *Attitudes toward capital punishment: From application to theory*. Paper presented at the SESP Symposium on Psychology and Law, Stanford University.

Ellsworth, P., & Ross, L. (1983). Public opinion and capital punishment: A close examination of the views of abolitionists and retentionists. *Crime and Delinquency, 29*, 116–169.

Emord, J. W. (1992, July 10). Project "ASSIST": Federal funds for speech and behavior control. Washington, DC: *Legal Backgrounder, 7*(19). University of California, San Francisco, Legacy Tobacco Documents Library. Retrieved from https://industrydocuments.library.ucsf.edu

Englis, B. G., Vaughan, K. B., & Lanzetta, J. T. (1982). Conditioning of counter-empathic emotional response. *Journal of Experimental Social Psychology, 18*, 375–391.

Enron warned, auditor insists (2001, December 13). *Chicago Tribune*. Retrieved from http://articles.chicagotribune.com

Erdbrink, T. (2014). Urged to multiply, Iranian couples are dubious. *The New York Times*, p. A1.

Erlich, R. (2010). *Conversations with terrorists: Middle East leaders on politics, violence, and empire*. Sausalito, CA: PoliPointPress.

Esterl, M. (2013). Big tobacco begins its takeover of the e-cigarette market. *The Wall Street Journal*. Retrieved from http://blogs.wsj.com

Evans-Pritchard, A. (2014, April 9). Global solar dominance in sight as science trumps fossil fuels. *The Telegraph*. Retrieved from http://www.telegraph.co.uk

Evelyn, S. R., & Esterle, J. G. (1977, December 6). Biological research meeting: Minutes of the meeting held at Chelwood on 27th November 1977. University of California, San Francisco, Legacy Tobacco Documents Library, Brown & Williamson Collection. Retrieved from http://legacy.library.ucsf.edu/

Executed but possibly innocent. (n.d.) Death Penalty Information Center. Retrieved from http://www.deathpenaltyinfo.org

Fagan, J. (2006). Death and deterrence redux: Science, law and causal reasoning on capital punishment. *Ohio State Journal of Criminal Law, 4,* 255–320.

Fath, J. (1974, October 23). [Letter to John Lawrence, SPI]. Manufacturing Chemists' Association Papers.

Fathi, D. (2009, June 29). US: California execution procedure violates rights. Human Rights Watch. Retrieved from http://www.hrw.org

Fernandez, M. (2013, August 11). In testimony, witnesses relive horror of Fort Hood attack. *The New York Times,* p. A14.

Feser, E. (2011, October 13). Punishment, proportionality, and the death penalty: A reply to Chris Tollefsen. Public Discourse. Retrieved from http://www.thepublicdiscourse.com

Feshbach, S., & Singer, R. D. (1971). *Television and aggression: An experimental field study.* San Francisco: Jossey-Bass.

Final Report (2011, January). The Financial Crisis Inquiry Report. Submitted by the Financial Crisis Inquiry Commission. Washington, DC: U.S. Government Printing Office.

Fingarette, H. (1969). *Self-deception.* New York: Humanities Press.

Firing squad. (n.d.) Death Penalty Information Center. Retrieved from http://www.deathpenaltyinfo.org

Fishman, S. (2011, February 27). The Madoff tapes. *New York Magazine.* Retrieved from http://nymag.com

Flaccus, G. (2013, February 1). LA archbishop relieves retired cardinal of duties. Associated Press. Retrieved from http://news.yahoo.com

Flaccus, G. (2014, February 20). Los Angeles bishop Mahony kept altar boy list from police: Deposition. NBC Los Angeles. Retrieved from http://www.nbclosangeles.com

Fletcher, D. (2009, February 9). A brief history of the Tylenol poisonings. *Time.* Retrieved from http://content.time.com

Fodor, E. (2012, July 19). The myth of smart growth. Population Media Center. Retrieved from http://www.populationmedia.org

Foley, S. (2010, April 26). Detailed in emails, how Goldman lost a fortune and then made it back. *The Independent.* Retrieved from http://www.independent.co.uk

Follman, M., Aronson, G., & Lee, J. (2013, February 27). More than half of mass shooters used assault weapons and high-capacity magazines. *Mother Jones.* Retrieved from http://www.motherjones.com

Follman, M., Lee, J., Lurie, J., & West, J. (2015, April 15). What does gun violence really cost? *Mother Jones.* Retrieved from http://www.motherjones.com

Ford, M. (2014, February 18). Can Europe end the death penalty in America? *The Atlantic.* Retrieved from http://www.theatlantic.com

Ford, M. (2015, April 30). What makes a method of execution constitutional? *The Atlantic.* Retrieved from http://www.theatlantic.com

Foreman, D. (2007, June 6). Retreat on population stabilization. Rewilding Institute. Retrieved from http://www.rewilding.org

Fox, J. A., & Radelet, M. L. (1989). Persistent flaws in econometric studies of the deterrent effect of the death penalty. *Loyola of Los Angeles Law Review, 23*(1), 3.

Fram, A. (2013a, March 13). Assault weapons ban approved by Senate Judiciary Committee. The Huffington Post. Retrieved from http://www.huffingtonpost.com

Fram, A. (2013b). Congress renews undetectable gun ban for decade. AP News. Retrieved from http://bigstory.ap.org

Francioni, F., & Ronzitti, N. (2011). *War by contract: Human rights, humanitarian law, and private contractors.* Oxford, UK: Oxford University Press.

Francis (2015, March 20). Letter of His Holiness Pope Francis to the President of the International Commission against the Death Penalty. NEWS.VA. Retrieved from http://46.137.92.195/en/news/letter-of-the-holy-father-to-the-president-of-the

Franks, L., & Powers, T. (1970, September 14). Story of Diana—The making of a terrorist. United Press International. Retrieved from http://100years.upi.com

Freedman, A. (2009, November 23). Science historian reacts to hacked climate e-mails. *The Washington Post.* Retrieved from http://voices.washingtonpost.com

Freeman, J. B. (2001). *Affairs of honor: National politics in the new Republic.* New Haven: Yale University Press.

French satirical paper Charlie Hebdo attacked in Paris. (2011, November 2). BBC-News. Retrieved from http://www.bbc.com

French, H. W. (2007, March 22). China scrambles for stability as its workers age. *The New York Times,* p. A1.

Friedman, M. (1970, September 13). A Friedman doctrine—The social responsibility of business is to increase its profits. *The New York Times Magazine,* p. 32.

Friedman, T. L. (2005, July 12). A poverty of dignity and a wealth of rage. *The New York Times,* p. A21.

Friedman, T. L. (2012, August 5). Get it right on gas. *The New York Times,* p. SR13.

Friedman, T. L. (2014, August 8). Obama on the world. *The New York Times,* p. A19.

Friedman, T. L. (2015, May 27). Contain and amplify. *The New York Times,* p. A23.

Fritz, S. (1991, November 21). Cranston harshly rebuked, shows little remorse: Ethics: Panel calls "linkage" of contributions to aid for Lincoln Savings' Keating "improper and repugnant." But the senator says his colleagues do the same thing. *Los Angeles Times.* Retrieved from http://articles.latimes.com

Frizell, S. (2014, September 28). Boehner: U.S. may have "no choice" but to send troops to fight ISIS. *Time.* Retrieved from http://time.com

Froman, S. (2007, February 12). An evening with Sandy Froman. Civil Rights and Liberties: Stanford ItunesU. Retrieved from https://itunes.apple.com/us/itunes-u/assu-speakers-bureau/id384457889?mt=10

Frosch, D. (2012, September 23). University is uneasy as court ruling allows guns on campus. *The New York Times,* p. A22.

Frosch, D. (2013, February 1). Some sheriffs object to call for tougher gun laws. *The New York Times,* p. A19.

Fuller, J. (2014, September 28). John Boehner on combating the Islamic State: "Somebody's boots have to be there." *The Washington Post.* Retrieved from http://www.washingtonpost.com

Furman v. Georgia, 408 U.S. 238 (1972). Retrieved from http://www.oyez.org

Gambino, R. (1973). Watergate lingo: A language of non-responsibility. *Freedom at Issue, 22,* 7–9, 15–17.

Gandhi, M. K., Desai, M. H., & Nayyars, P. (1942). *Non-violence in peace and war.* Ahmedabad: Navajivan Publishing House.

Garamone, J. (2002, October 22). Rumsfeld draws lessons from Cuban missile crisis to today. DoD News. http://www.defense.gov

Gardner, J. W. (1972). *In common cause*. New York: W. W. Norton.

Gardner, R., & Heider, K. G. (1969). *Gardens of war: Life and death in the New Guinea Stone Age*. New York: Random House.

Gazzaniga, M. S. (2005). *The ethical brain*. New York: Dana Press.

Geary, P. J. (Ed.) (2010). *Readings in medieval history* (4th ed., p. 397). Toronto: University of Toronto Press.

Gelbspan, R. (1998). *The heat is on: The climate crisis, the cover-up, the prescription*. Reading, MA: Perseus Books.

Gerbner, G. (1972a). Communication and social environment. *Scientific American, 227*, 153–160.

Gerbner, G. (1972b). Violence in television drama: Trends and symbolic functions. In E. A. Rubinstein & G. A. Comstock (Eds.), *Television and Social Behavior: Vol. 1. Media content and control* (pp. 28–187). Washington, DC: U.S. Government Printing Office.

Gerbner, G., & Gross, L. (1976). Living with television: The violence profile. *Journal of Communication, 26*, 173–199.

Gerbner, G., Gross, L., Morgan, M., & Signorielli, N. (1980). The "mainstreaming" of America: Violence profile No. 11. *Journal of Communication, 30*, 10–29.

German, M. (2005, June 3). Behind the lone terrorist, a pack mentality. *The Washington Post*. Retrieved from http://www.washingtonpost.com

Germany, Brazil to propose anti-spying resolution at UN. (2013, October 25). Reuters: Retrieved from http://www.reuters.com

Germany, K. B. (2010). Lyndon B. Johnson and civil rights: Introduction to the digital edition. Retrieved from http://presidentialrecordings.rotunda.upress.virginia.edu

Gertner, J. (2010, May 13). The rise and fall of the G.D.P. *The New York Times Magazine*. Retrieved from http://www.nytimes.com

Gertz, M. (2012, December 23). *Meet the Press* interview exposes hole in NRA's mental health plan [Web blog post]. Retrieved from http://mediamatters.org

Ghazi, Y., & Arango, T. (2014, Janurary 5). Qaeda-linked militants in Iraq secure nearly full control of Falluja. *The New York Times*, p. 5.

Ghosh, P. (2011, February 28). Select quotes from Bernard Madoff in magazine interview. *International Business Times*. Retrieved from http://www.ibtimes.com

Gibson, J. T., & Haritos-Fatouros, M. (1986). The education of a torturer. *Psychology Today, 20*, 50–58.

Gillis, J. (2010, July 7). British panel clears scientists. *The New York Times*. Retrieved from http://www.nytimes.com

Gillis, J. (2012, August 7). Study finds more of earth is hotter and says global warming is at work. *The New York Times*, p. A13.

Gillis, J. (2014a, September 14). Sun and wind alter global landscape, leaving utilities behind. *The New York Times*, p. A1.

Gillis, J. (2014b, November 2). U.N. panel issues its starkest warning yet on global warming. *The New York Times*. Retrieved from http://www.nytimes.com

Gillis, J. (2014c, April 29). What does today owe tomorrow? *The New York Times*, p. D3.

Gillis, J. (2015a, June 20). For faithful, social justice goals demand action on environment. *The New York Times*. Retrieved from http://www.nytimes.com

Gillis, J. (2015b, January 29). New report urges Western governments to reconsider reliance on biofuels. *The New York Times*. Retrieved from http://www.nytimes.com

Gillis, J. (2015c, February 17). Verbal warming: Labels in the climate debate. *The New York Times*, p. D1.

Gillis, J., & Broder, J. M. (2012, December 2). With carbon dioxide emissions at record high, worries on how to slow warming. *The New York Times*. Retrieved from http://www.nytimes.com

Gillis, J., & Fleur, N. S. (2015, September 23). Global companies joining climate change efforts. *The New York Times*, p. B3.

Gillis, J., & Sengupta, S. (2015, September 28). Progress seen on warming, with a caveat. *The New York Times*, p, A1.

Gilovich, T. (1981). Seeing the past in the present: The effect of associations to familiar events on judgments and decisions. *Journal of Personality and Social Psychology, 40*, 797–808.

Gingrich, N. (1995). *To renew America*. New York: HarperCollins.

Gini, G., Albiero, P., Benelli, B., & Altoè, G. (2008). Determinants of adolescents' active defending and passive bystanding behavior in bullying. *Journal of Adolescence, 31*, 93–105.

Gini, G., Pozzoli, T., & Bussey, K. (2013). Collective moral disengagement: Initial validation of a scale for adolescents. *European Journal of Developmental Psychology, 11*, 386–395.

Gini, G., Pozzoli, T., & Hymel, S. (2014). Moral disengagement among children and youth: A meta-analytic review of links to aggressive behavior. *Aggressive Behavior, 40*, 56–68.

Girma, S., & Paton, D. (2015). Is education the best contraception? The case of teenage pregnancy in England. *Social Science and Medicine, 131*, 1–9.

Gladstone, R. (2015, June 22). Unicef report describes grim trends for the poorest children. *The New York Times*. Retrieved from http://www.nytimes.com

Glantz, S., Slade, J., Bero, L., Hanauer, P., Barnes, D., & Koop, E. (1996). *The cigarette papers*. Berkeley: University of California Press.

Glanz, J., & Navarro, M. (2012, November 5). Engineers' warnings in 2009 detailed storm surge threat to the region. *The New York Times*, p. A23.

Glueck, K. (2013, January 16). NRA ad attacked for including President Obama's daughters. Politico. Retrieved from http://www.politico.com

Goldberg, J. (2009, April 3). Questions about Ahmadinejad's famous quote. *The Atlantic*. Retrieved from http://www.theatlantic.com

Goldenberg, S. (2015, June 11). Republicans' leading climate denier tells the pope to butt out of climate debate. *The Guardian*. Retrieved from http://www.theguardian.com

Goldfrank, E. S. (1945). Historic change and social character: A study of the Teton Dakota. *American Anthropologist, 45*, 67–83.

Goldschmidt, D. (2015, April 3). Pharmacists discouraged from providing meds for lethal injection. CNN. Retrieved from http://www.cnn.com

Goldsen, R. (1972). *Science in wonderland*. Unpublished manuscript, Cornell University, Ithaca, NY.

Goldstein, B. (2012, December 22). The NRA's school safety plan: Round up the sick and arm the children. *The Washington Post*. Retrieved from http://www.washingtonpost.com

Goldstein, J. (2011, December 15). In its latest gun inquiry, city faults online sellers. *The New York Times*, p. A31.

Goldstein, M., & Protess, B. (2015, April 4). Court rejects Bharara's plea to reconsider insider trading ruling. *The New York Times*, p. B1.

Gomez, G. (2002). Problems in the timing of conscious experience. *Consciousness and Cognition, 11*, 191–197.

Gonzalez, J. (2005, January 6). Latino pride? Look again. *The Daily News*. Retrieved from http://www.nydailynews.com

Good sense in Tennessee [Editorial]. (2009, September 12). *The New York Times*, p. WK15.

Goode, E. (2012, April 12). N.R.A. push has resulted in broader laws on self-defense. *The New York Times*, p. A14.

Goode, E. (2013, January 17). Even defining "assault rifles" is complicated. *The New York Times*, p. A18.

Goodell, J. (2010, November 29). The dark lord of coal country. *Rolling Stone*. Retrieved from http://www.rollingstone.com

Goodenough, P. (2014, September 2). ISIS publication aims to lure recruits: Justifies atrocities by citing Mohammed. CNSNews.com. Retrieved from http://www.cnsnews.com

Goodstein, L. (2002, October 5). Evangelical figures oppose religious leaders' broad antiwar sentiment. *The New York Times*. Retrieved from http://www.nytimes.com

Goodstein, L. (2003, May 27). Seeing Islam as "evil" faith, evangelicals seek converts. The New York Times. Retrieved from http://www.nytimes.com

Goodstein, L. (2005, March 10). Evangelical leaders swing influence behind effort to combat global warming. *The New York Times*. Retrieved from http://www.nytimes.com

Goodstein, L. (2007, March 12). Evangelical's focus on climate draws fire of Christian right. *The New York Times*, p. A9.

Goodstein, L. (2011, May 12). 1960s culture cited as cause of priest abuse. *The New York Times*, p. A1.

Goodstein, L. (2012, March 13). Church using priests' cases to pressure victims' network. *The New York Times*, p. A1.

Goodstein, L. (2013a, July 13). Files show Dolan sought to protect Church assets. *The New York Times*, p. A10.

Goodstein, L. (2013b, January 23). New sexual abuse files cast shadow on legacy of Los Angeles Cardinal. *The New York Times*, p. A11.

Goodstein, L., Cumming-Bruce, N., & Yardley, J. (2014, February 5). U.N. panel criticizes the Vatican over sexual abuse. *The New York Times*. Retrieved from http://www.nytimes.com

Goodstein, L., & Eckholm, E. (2012, June 12). Church battles efforts to ease sex abuse suits. *The New York Times*, p. A1.

Goodstein, L., & Eligon, J. (2012, September 7). Bishop is guilty of bid to shield pedophile priest. *The New York Times*, p. A1.

Goodstein, L., & Medina, J. (2013, February 5). Los Angeles Archdiocese is accused of failing to release all abuse records. *The New York Times*, p. A15.

Goodwin, C. (1942). *The social organization of the Western Apache*. Chicago: University of Chicago Press.

Goodwin, D. K. (2005). *Team of rivals: The political genius of Abraham Lincoln*. New York: Simon & Schuster.

Goranson, R. E. (1970). Media violence and aggressive behavior: A review of experimental research. In L. Berkowitz (Ed.), *Advances in experimental social psychology* (Vol. 5, pp. 1–31). New York: Academic Press.

Gouet, H. (2012). Personal communication.

Gould, J. (1972, January 11). TV violence held unharmful to youth. *The New York Times*, p. 1.

Gould, S. J. (1987). *An urchin in the storm: Essays about books and ideas*. New York: W. W. Norton.

GRAIN. (2007, June). Stop the agrofuel craze! GRAIN. Retrieved from http://www.grain.org

Grassley, C. (2013, January 30). Grassley opening statement—Committee hearing on the causes of gun violence. Retrieved from http://www.grassley.senate.gov

Gray, G. (2007, October 21). Unmasking D. B. Cooper. *New York*. Retrieved from http://nymag.com

Green Book. (n.d.). CAIN (Conflict Archive on the Internet), University of Ulster. Retrieved from http://www.cain.ulst.ac.uk

Greenberg, A. (2013, January 14). Gunsmiths 3D-print high capacity ammo clips to thwart proposed gun laws. *Forbes*. Retrieved from http://www.forbes.com/

Greenberg, J. (1995, November 21). Rabin's killer says he acted for past generations of Jews. *The New York Times*. Retrieved from http://www.nytimes.com

Greenberg, J. (2000, March 1). Eichmann memoirs released to assist a libel defendant. *The New York Times*, p. A6.

Greenhouse, L. (1994, February 23). Death penalty is renounced by Blackmun. *The New York Times*. Retrieved from http://www.nytimes.com

Greenspan, A. (2007). *The age of turbulence: Adventures in a new world*. New York: Penguin Press.

Greenstone, M., & Looney, A. (2012, Spring). Paying too much for energy? The true costs of our energy choices. *Daedalus, 141*, 10–30.

Greenwald, G., MacAskill, E., & Poitras, L. (2013, June 11). Edward Snowden: The whistleblower behind the NSA surveillance revelations. *The Guardian*. Retrieved from http://www.theguardian.com

Greenwald, G., Poitras, L., & MacAskill, E. (2013, September 11). NSA shares raw intelligence including Americans' data with Israel. *The Guardian*. Retrieved from http://www.theguardian.com

Greiner, K., Singhal, A., & Hurlburt, S. (2007). "With an antenna we can stop the practice of female genital cutting": A participatory assessment of Ashreat Al Amal, an entertainment-education radio soap opera in Sudan. *Investigación y Desarrollo, 15*, 226–259. Retrieved from http://rcientificas.uninorte.edu.co

Griffith, M. [Marc], Griffith, M. [Michelle], Holland, G. B., Molina, G., & Paul, A. (Producers), & Tobias, M (Director). (2001). *The cost of cool: Youth, consumption, and the environment* [Motion picture documentary]. United States: Iron Image.

Gross, J. (1998). The emerging field of emotion regulation: An integrative review. *Review of General Psychology, 2*, 271–299.

Gross, S. R., & Ellsworth, P. C. (2003). Second thoughts: Americans' views on the death penalty at the turn of the century. In S. P. Garvey (Ed.), *Beyond repair? America's death penalty* (pp. 7–57). Durham, NC: Duke University Press.

Grow, G. (2012). How to write "official." IU Learning Systems Institute and Communication. Retrieved from http://uwf.edu/wbeatty/ism4113/writeofficial.html

Growing support for campaign against ISIS—and possible use of U.S. ground troops. (2015, February 24). Pew Research Center. Retrieved from http://www.people-press.org

Gruman, J. (2006). Quantifying people particles. *Good behavior*. Washington, DC: Center for the Advancement of Health, PI.

Guyer, P. E. (1998). *Kant's groundwork of the metaphysics of morals: Critical essays*. Lantham, MD: Rowman and Littlefield.

Hackett, G. (1995). Self-efficacy in career choice and development. In A. Bandura (Ed.), *Self-efficacy in changing societies* (pp. 232–258). New York: Cambridge University Press.

Hackett, G., & Betz, N. E. (1981). A self-efficacy approach to the career development of women. *Journal of Vocational Behavior, 18*, 326–339.

Haight, M. R. (1980). *A study of self-deception*. Atlantic Highlands, NJ: Humanities Press.

Hajjar, L. (2015, May 7). How the world's largest psychological association aided the CIA's torture program. *The Nation*. Retrieved from http://www.thenation.com/article/how-worlds-largest-psychological-association-aided-cias-torture-program/

Hakim, D. (2015, April 9). Sex education in Europe turns to urging more births. *The New York Times*, p. A1.

Halberstam, D. (1972). *The best and the brightest*. New York: Random House.

Halbfinger, D. M., & Kaplan, T. (2013, January 10). New York is moving quickly to enact tough curbs on guns. *The New York Times*, p. A1.

Hall, C. T. (1998, January 8). Company admits making high-nicotine tobacco: DNA Plant Technology says it worked 9 years on the project. *San Francisco Chronicle*. Retrieved from http://articles.mcall.com

Hall, J. (1995, January 30). FCC plan might pay PBS to air kid shows: Television; A marketplace 'baby-sitting' proposal could help commercial stations meet federal programming mandates, but children's TV advocates don't like the sound of it. *Los Angeles Times*. Retrieved from http://articles.latimes.com

Halloran, J. D., & Croll, P. (1972). Television programs in Great Britain: Content and control. In E. A. Rubinstein & G. A. Comstock (Eds.), *Television and Social Behavior: Vol. 1. Media content and control* (pp. 415–492). Washington, DC: U.S. Government Printing Office.

Hamilton, C. (2010a). *Requiem for a species: Why we resist the truth about climate change*. Abingdon: Earthscan.

Hamilton, C. (2010b, September 28). Think tanks, oil money and black ops. The Drum. Retrieved from ww.abc.net.au

Handguns for 18-Year-Olds? [Editorial]. (2010, November 26). *The New York Times*, p. A36.

Haney, C. (1997). Violence and the capital jury: Mechanisms of moral disengagement and the impulse to condemn to death. *Stanford Law Review, 49*, 1447–1486.

Haney, C. (2005). *Death by design: Capital punishment as social psychological system*. New York: Oxford University Press.

Haney, C., Banks, C., & Zimbardo, P. (1973). Interpersonal dynamics in a simulated prison. *International Journal of Criminology & Penology, 1*, 69–97.

Haney, C., Sontag, L., & Costanzo, S. (1994). Deciding to take a life: Capital juries, sentencing instructions, and the jurisprudence of death. *Journal of Social Issues, 50*, 149–176.

Hang, B., Sarker, A. H., Havel, C., Saha, S., Hazra, T. K., Schick, S., Jacob, P., Rehan, V. K., Chenna, A., Sharan, D., Sleiman, M., Destaillats, H., & Gundel, L. A. (2013). Thirdhand smoke causes DNA damage in human cells. *Mutagenesis, 28*(4), 381–391.

Haritos-Fatouros, M. (2003). *The psychological origins of institutionalized torture*. London: Routledge.

Harrabin, R. (2015, June 15). China "deserves more credit" for renewable energy effort. BBC. Retrieved from http://www.bbc.com

Harré, R., & Gillett, G. (1994). *The discursive mind*. Thousand Oaks, CA: Sage Publications.

Harris, W. D. (1971, October 5). [Letter to B. R. Leach, Painesveille]. Retrieved from http://www.deceitanddenial.org

Hartocollis, A. (2013, December 5). Vapors and emotions rise at hearing on e-cigarettes. *The New York Times*, p. A33.

Harvey, P. D. (2012, September 6). Sex and birth control. The Huffington Post. Retrieved from http://www.huffingtonpost.com

Hawkins, J. D., Catalano, R. F., Kosterman, R., Abbott, R., & Hill, K. G. (1999). Preventing adolescent health-risk behaviors by strengthening protection during childhood. *Archives of Pediatric and Adolescent Medicine, 153*, 226–234.

Hawkins, R. P., & Pingree, S. (1982). Television's influence on social reality. In D. Pearl, L. Bouthilet, & J. Lazarus (Eds.), *Television and behavior: Ten years of scientific progress and implications for the eighties* (Vol. 2, pp. 224–247). Rockville, MD: National Institute of Mental Health.

Hayhurst, E. (1925). Ethyl gasoline. *American Journal of Public Health, 15*, 239–240.

Healy, J. (2013a, September 11). Colorado lawmakers ousted in recall vote over gun law. *The New York Times*, p. A1.

Healy, J. (2013b, February 8). Some states push measures to repeal new U.S. gun laws. *The New York Times*, p. A16.

Heath, L. (1984). Impact of newspaper crime reports on fear of crime: Multimethodological investigation. *Journal of Personality and Social Psychology, 47*, 263–276.

Hedges, C., & Al-Arian, L. (2007, July 10). The other war: Iraq vets bear witness. *The Nation*. Retrieved from http://www.thenation.com

Heffernan, M. (2011). *Willful blindness: Why we ignore the obvious at our peril*. New York: Walker & Co.

Heinberg, R., & Lerch, D. (2010). *The post carbon reader: Managing the 21st century's sustainability crises*. Healdsburg, CA: Watershed Media.

Hemenway, D. (1998). More guns, less crime: Understanding crime and gun-control laws [Review of the book *Making a killing: The business of guns in America*, by T. Diaz]. *New England Journal of Medicine, 339*, 2029–2030.

Hendren, J. (1999, May 1). NRA and protesters face off in Denver. *The Washington Post*. Retrieved from http://www.washingtonpost.com

Hendrick, G. (1977, January 29). When television is a school for criminals. *TV Guide*, 4–10.

Henley, J., Younge, G., & Walsh, N. P. (2003, March 6). France, Russia and Germany harden stance. *The Guardian*. Retrieved from http://www.theguardian.com

Henning, P. J. (2014, December 16). Fallout for the S.E.C. and the Justice Dept. from the insider trading ruling. *The New York Times*. Retrieved from http://dealbook.nytimes.com

Henriques, D. B. (2011). *The wizard of lies: Bernie Madoff and the death of trust*. New York: Times Books/Henry Holt.

Herling, J. (1962). *The great price conspiracy: The story of the anti-trust violations in the electrical industry*. Washington, DC: Robert B. Luce.

Herrmann, T. (2012, June 20). Abortion proponents admit defeat at Rio UN conference. Life News. Retrieved from http://www.lifenews.com

Hersh, J. (2012, December 23). Wayne LaPierre: Schools with armed guards "the one thing that would keep people safe." The Huffington Post. Retrieved from http://www.huffingtonpost.com

Hersh, S. M. (2004, May 12). Torture at Abu Ghraib. *The New Yorker*.

Heston, C. (1997, December 7). Speech by National Rifle Association First Vice President Charlton Heston delivered at the Free Congress Foundation's 20th anniversary gala. Violence Policy Center. Retrieved from http://www.vpc.org

R-26   References

Heston, C. (1999, May 1). Speech to the NRA annual meeting in Colorado. The Land of the Free. Retrieved from http://www.thelandofthefree.net

Higgins, A. (2013, October 9). E.U. rejects tight limits on electronic cigarettes. *International Herald Tribune*, p. 17.

Hilburn, M. (2014, November 28). Children in Islamic State propaganda send powerful message. Voice of America. Retrieved from http://www.voanews.com

Hilsenrath, J. (2009, August 13). Cap-and-trade's unlikely critics: Its creators. *The Wall Street Journal*. Retrieved from http://online.wsj.com

Hilts, P. J. (1994, April 15). Tobacco chiefs say cigarettes aren't addictive. *The New York Times*. Retrieved from http://www.nytimes.com/

Hirayama, T. (1981). Non-smoking wives of heavy smokers have a higher risk of lung cancer: A study from Japan. *British Medical Journal (Clinical Research Edition), 282*, 183–185.

Hirth, A. C. (1936, April 14). Silicosis as an employer problem. Proceedings of National Conference on Silicosis and Similar Dust Diseases. National Archives, Record Group 100,7-0-4(1).

Hoffman, D. H., Carter, D. J., Lopez, C. R. V., Benzmiller, H. L., Guo, A. X., Latifi, S. Y., Craig, D. C., & Austin, S. (2015). Independent review relating to APA ethics guidelines, national security interrogations, and torture. Sidley Austin, LLP. Retrieved from http://www.apa.org/independent-review/APA-FINAL-Report-7.2.15.pdf

Hoffman, M. L. (2001). Toward a comprehensive empathy-based theory of prosocial moral development. In A. C. Bohart & D. J. Stipek (Eds.), *Constructive and destructive behavior: Implications for family, school, and society* (pp. 61–86). Washington, DC: American Psychological Association.

Hong, M. K., & Bero, L. A. (2002). How the tobacco industry responded to an influential study of the health effects of secondhand smoke. *British Medical Journal, 325*, 1413–1416.

Hooper, T. (2012, February 6). Santorum and Gingrich dismiss climate change, vow to dismantle the EPA. *Colorado Independent*. Retrieved from http://www.coloradoindependent.com

Hoover, K. (1994). Pro-smoking initiative on the ballot. *San Francisco Chronicle*, p.1.

Horn, A. (2012, November 2). Was Hurricane Sandy a sign of the "new normal"? Energy Tribune. Retrieved from http://www.energytribune.com

Hornblower, M. (1998, July 6). Have gun, will travel. *Time*. Retrieved from http://www.time.com

Hotel Employees and Restaurant Employees International Union. (1995, November 17). New study attacks the scientific basis for OSHA's proposed regulation of workplace smoking. University of California, San Francisco, Legacy Tobacco Documents Library. Retrieved from https://industrydocuments.library.ucsf.edu

House of Commons, Science and Technology Committee. (2011). *The reviews into the University of East Anglia's Climatic Research Unit's e-mails: First report of session 2010–11*. London: The Stationery Office.

Howe, N., & Jackson, R. (2007, February 10). Rising populations breed rising powers. *Financial Times*, p. 11.

Hoyt, J. L. (1970). Effect of media violence "justification" on aggression. *Journal of Broadcasting, 14*, 455–464.

Hubbard, B. (2014, November 15). Iraq and U.S. find some potential Sunni allies have already been lost. *The New York Times*. Retrieved from http://www.nytimes.com

Huesmann, L. R., Moise, J., Podolski, C. P., & Eron, L. D. (2003). Longitudinal relations between childhood exposure to media violence and adult aggression and violence: 1977–1992. *Developmental Psychology, 39*, 201–222.

Huggins, R. A. (2010). *Energy storage.* New York: Springer.

Humphery, K. (2010). *Excess: Anti-consumerism in the West.* Cambridge: Polity Press, 2010.

Hunt, K. (2013, January 30). Background checks take center stage at fractious Senate hearing. NBC. Retrieved from http://nbcpolitics.nbcnews.com

Hurdle, J. (2013, December 30). Philadelphia monsignor to be released on bail pending appeal in abuse case. *The New York Times.* Retrieved from http://www.nytimes.com

Hursthouse, R. (2012). Virtue ethics. In E. N. Zalta (Ed.), The Stanford encyclopedia of philosophy. Retrieved from http://plato.stanford.edu

Hurtado, P. (2015, April 23). The London Whale. Bloomberg QuickTake. Retrieved from http://www.bloombergview.com

Hymel, S., Schonert-Reichl, K. A., Bonanno, R. A., Vaillancourt, T., & Rocke Henderson, N. (2010). Bullying and morality: Understanding how good kids behave badly. In S. R. Jimerson, S. M. Swearer, & D. L. Espelage (Eds.), *Handbook of bullying in schools: An international perspective* (pp. 101–118). New York: Routledge.

ICLEI—Local Governments for Sustainability (2014, December 8). Launch of first global standard to measure greenhouse gas emissions from cities. [Press release]. Retrieved from http://www.iclei.org

Ideas and Consequences: Colin Powell on the decision to go to war. (2007, October). *The Atlantic.* Retrieved from http://www.theatlantic.com

Industrial Hygiene Foundation. (1946, November 30). Silicosis is not threat to workers' health. Science News Letter.

Ingle, G. W. (1969, May 8). [Letter to W. E. Nessell]. Chemical Industry Archives. Retrieved from http://www.chemicalindustryarchives.org

Institute for Communication Research. (1981, September). *Towards the social use of commercial television: Mexico's experience with the reinforcement of social values through TV soap operas.* Presented at the Annual Conference of the International Institute of Communications, Strasbourg, France. Mexico City: Institute for Communication Research.

Intergovernmental Panel on Climate Change. (2007). *Climate change 2007—The physical science basis: Contribution of Working Group I to the Fourth Assessment Report of the Intergovernmental Panel on Climate Change* [Solomon, S., D. Qin, M. Manning, Z. Chen, M. Marquis, K.B. Averyt, M. Tignor and H.L. Miller (Eds.)]. Cambridge, UK, and New York: Cambridge University Press.

Interview with Vice-President Dick Cheney. (2003, September 14). [Transcript]. *Meet the Press*, NBCNews. Retrieved from http://www.nbcnews.com

Iraq abuse 'ordered from the top.' (2004, June 15). BBCNews. Retrieved from http://news.bbc.co.uk

Irwin, W. (1983). Sidestream Research. UCSF Legacy Tobacco Documents Library, Brown & Williamson Collection, vad72d00. Retrieved from https://industrydocuments.library.ucsf.edu/tobacco/docs/ppfh0097

Ismael, J. (2006). Saving the baby: Dennett on autobiography, agency, and the self. *Philosophical Psychology, 19*, 345–360.

Ismael, J. T. (2007). *The situated self.* New York: Oxford University Press.

Ivie, R. L. (1980). Images of savagery in American justifications for war. *Communication Monographs, 47*, 270–294.

Jackson, D. (2015, August 3). Obama climate change plan affects 2016 race. *USA Today*. Retrieved from http://www.usatoday.com

Jah, F., Connolly, S., Barker, K., & Ryerson, W. (2014). Gender and reproductive outcomes: The effects of a radio serial drama in northern Nigeria. *International Journal of Population Research*. doi:10.1155/2014/326905

Janis, I. (1972). *Victims of groupthink: A psychology study of foreign policy decisions and fiascoes*. Boston: Houghton Mifflin.

Jehl, D. (2004, June 12). Files show Rumsfeld rejected some efforts to toughen prison rules. *The New York Times*, p. A10.

Jehl, D., & Sanger, D. E. (2004, June 2). Powell presses C.I.A. on faulty intelligence on Iraq arms. *The New York Times*. Retrieved from http://www.nytimes.com

Jennings, N. (2013, January 10). NRA "disappointed" by meeting with Biden. *The Washington Post*. Retrieved from http://www.washingtonpost.com

John, S. (2015, July 11). World Population Day 2015: Top 10 inspirational quotes from famous personalities. *International Business Times*. Retrieved from http://www.ibtimes.co.uk/world-population-day-2015-top-10-inspirational-quotes-famous-personalities-1510371

Johnson, B. (2011, December 5). Inhofe: Calling climate change "the greatest hoax ever" is "doing the Lord's work." Think Progress. Retrieved from http://thinkprogress.org

Johnson, J. (1974, March 11). Technical Task Group on Vinyl Chloride Research. Manufacturing Chemists Association.

Johnson, K. (2010, March 17). Feeling the heat, lawmakers push right of state. *The New York Times*, p. A1.

Johnson, K., & Kovaleski, S. F. (2012, December 13). Series of turning points kept mall toll lower than feared. *The New York Times*, p. A20.

Johnson, T. (2011, September 19). Muslims in the United States. Council on Foreign Relations. Retrieved from http://www.cfr.org

Johnson, T. (2012, December 19). CNN's confounding prediction: NRA's failed election spending will translate to congressional clout [Web log post]. Retrieved from http://mediamatters.org

Johnston, J., & Ettema, J. S. (1986). Using television to best advantage: Research for prosocial television. In J. Bryant & D. Zillmann (Eds.), *Perspectives on media effects* (pp. 143–164). Hillsdale, NJ: Erlbaum.

Jolly, D. (2011, November 2). Satirical magazine is firebombed in Paris. *The New York Times*. Retrieved from http://www.nytimes.com

Jolly, D. (2014, February 26). European Parliament approves tough rules on electronic cigarettes. *The New York Times*. Retrieved from http://www.nytimes.com

Jones, J. M. (2006, June 1). Two in three favor death penalty for convicted murderers. Gallup. Retrieved from http://www.gallup.com

Jones, J. M. (2013, October 29). U.S. death penalty support lowest in more than 40 years. Gallup. Retrieved from http://www.gallup.com

Jones, J. M. (2014, October 23). Americans' support for death penalty stable. Gallup. Retrieved from http://www.gallup.com

Jones, T. C. (2012). America, oil, and war in the Middle East. *Journal of American History*, *99*, 208–218.

Just, E. (1939, December 6). ["Dust Prevention in Tri-State Mines," in letter to Verne Zimmer]. National Archives, Record Group 100, 7-0-6-13.

Just, E. (1940, April 23). Proceedings, Tri-State Conference, National Archives, Record Group 100, 7-0-4(3), 13–19.

Juvenile delinquency: Hearings before the Subcommittee to Investigate Juvenile Delinquency, Part 10: Effects on young people of violence and crime portrayed on television. 87th Congress. (1992).

Kaczor, C. (2010, July). Did the church change its teaching on the death penalty? *Catholic Answers Magazine*, 21. Retrieved from http://www.catholic.com

Kane, J. (2012, January 25). Telenovelas provide platform for public health messages. *PBS NewsHour*. Retrieved from http://www.pbs.org

Kaplan, T. (2013, January 30). Gun rights backers, stung by Cuomo's law, push to undo it. *The New York Times*, p. A22.

Kaufman, L., & Zernike, K. (2012, February 11). Activists fight green projects, seeing U.N. plot. *The New York Times*, p. A1.

Kaysen, C., Miller, S. E., Malin, M. B., Nordhaus, W. D., & Steinbruner, J. D. (2002). *War with Iraq: Costs, consequences, and alternatives*. Cambridge, MA: American Academy of Arts and Sciences, Committee on International Security Studies.

Keefe, M. (2009, September 11). The truth about gun shows. American Rifleman. Retrieved from http://www.americanrifleman.org

Kelman, H. C. (1973). Violence without moral restraint: Reflections on the dehumanization of victims and victimizers. *Journal of Social Issues, 29*, 25–61.

Kelman, H. C., & Hamilton, V. L. (1989). *Crimes of obedience: Toward a social psychology of authority and responsibility*. New Haven, CT: Yale University Press.

Kenber, B. (2013, August 28). Nidal Hasan sentenced to death for Fort Hood shooting rampage. *The Washington Post*. Retrieved from http://www.washingtonpost.com

Kennedy, K. (Producer), & Spielberg, S. (Producer & Director). (2012). *Lincoln* [Motion picture]. United States: DreamWorks Pictures, 20th Century Fox, & Reliance Entertainment.

Keohane, R. O., & Nye, J. S. (1977). *Power and interdependence: World politics in transition*. Boston: Little, Brown.

Kepner, T. (2011, January 27). Pitcher spurns $12 million, to keep self-respect. *The New York Times*, p. A1.

Kessler, D. A., & Myers, M. L. (2015). It's time to regulate e-cigarettes. *The New York Times*, p. A27.

Kilham, W., & Mann, L. (1974). Level of destructive obedience as a function of transmitter and executant roles in the Milgram obedience paradigm. *Journal of Personality and Social Psychology, 29*, 692–702.

King, L. (2007, February 11). JP Morgan: If you "Google Madoff you will see the risks." Computerworld UK. Retrieved from http://www.computerworlduk.com

King, M. L., Jr. (1958). *Stride toward freedom: The Montgomery story*. New York: Harper.

Kinzer, S. (2006). *Overthrow: America's century of regime change from Hawaii to Iraq*. New York: Henry Holt.

Kipnis, D. (1974). The powerholders. In J. T. Tedeschi (Ed.), *Perspectives on social power* (pp. 82–122). Chicago: Aldine.

Kirkpatrick, D. D. (2014, November 23). Graft hobbles Iraq's military in fighting ISIS. *The New York Times*. Retrieved from http://www.nytimes.com

Kirschbaum, E. (2012, May 26). Germany sets new solar power record, institute says. Reuters. Retrieved from http://www.reuters.com

Klein, S. A. (2002). Libet's temporal anomalies: A reassessment of the data. *Consciousness and Cognition, 11*, 198–214; discussion 314–125.

Kleypas, J. A., Feely, R. A., Fabry, V. J., Langdon, C., Sabine, C. L., & Robbins, L. L. (2006). *Impacts of ocean acidification on coral reefs and other marine calcifiers: A guide for future research; Report of a workshop sponsored by NSF, NOAA, and the U.S. Geological Survey.* Retrieved from http://www.ucar.edu

Kloepfer, W. (1985). Tobacco Institute. Retrieved from: http://beta.industrydocuments.library.ucsf.edu/documentstore/z/m/k/k//zmkk0087/zmkk0087.pdf

Koblin, J. (2015, May 12). 'American Idol' prepares for its swan song. *The New York Times*, p. B1.

Kohlberg, L. (1984). *The psychology of moral development: The nature and validity of moral stages.* San Francisco: Harper & Row.

Kolankiewicz, L., & Beck, R. H. (2001). *Forsaking fundamentals: The environmental establishment abandons U.S. population stabilization.* Washington, DC: Center for Immigration Studies.

Kolbert, E. (1989, June 19). As vote on death penalty nears, Cuomo advocates life sentences. *The New York Times.* Retrieved from http://www.nytimes.com

Koronowski, R. (2013, June 13). Leave two-thirds of fossil fuels in the ground, says International Energy Agency. Climate Progress. Retrieved from http://thinkprogress.org

Kotlikoff, L. J., & Sachs, J. (1998, March/April). The personal security system: A framework for reforming social security. *Review*, pp. 11–13. Retrieved from https://research.stlouisfed.org

Kramer, A. E. (2012). Importing Russia's top gun. *The New York Times*, p. B1.

Kramer, M. (1990). The moral logic of Hizballah. In W. Reich (Ed.), *Origins of terrorism: Psychologies, ideologies, theologies, states of mind* (pp. 131–157). Cambridge, UK: Cambridge University Press.

Krauthammer, C. (2008, September 27). Congress rages, but the bailout is vital. *Record Searchlight.* Retrieved from http://www.redding.com

Kristof, N. (2003, June 10). Giving God a break. *The New York Times.* Retrieved from http://www.nytimes.com

Krugman, P. (2011, May 9). The unwisdom of elites. *The New York Times*, p. A23.

Krugman, P. (2014, April 17). Salvation gets cheap. *The New York Times.* Retrieved from http://www.nytimes.com

Krugman, P. R. (2009). *The return of depression economics and the crisis of 2008.* New York: W. W. Norton.

Kulish, N. (2012, October 28). Arrest of '70s rock star widens sexual abuse case tied to BBC. *The New York Times*, p. A1.

Kunkle, F. (2008, September 26). Last N.Y. suits against Va. dealers settled. *The Washington Post.* Retrieved from http://www.washingtonpost.com

Kuntz, T. (1995, September 24). Conversations/Paul Hill; From thought to deed: In the mind of a killer who says he served God. *The New York Times.* Retrieved from http://www.nytimes.com

Kwak, K., & Bandura, A. (1998). *Role of perceived self-efficacy and moral disengagement in antisocial conduct.* Unpublished manuscript, Osan College, Seoul.

Kydd, A. H., & Walter, B. F. (2006). The strategies of terrorism. *International Security*, *31*, 49–80.

Lacey, M. (2011, January 19). Arizona gun shows ignored red flags, New York investigators say. *The New York Times*, p. A9.

Lacey, M., & Herszenhorn, D. M. (2011, January 9). In attack's wake, political repercussions. *The New York Times*, p. A1.

Lakoff, G. (2002). *Moral politics: How liberals and conservatives think* (2nd ed.). Chicago: University of Chicago Press.

Lam, T. H., Ho, S. Y., Hedley, A. J., Mak, K. H., & Peto, R. (2001). Mortality and smoking in Hong Kong: Case-control study of all adult deaths in 1998. *British Medical Journal, 323*, 361–362.

Lamperti, J. (1996). Does capital punishment deter murder? Retrieved from https://math.dartmouth.edu

Lance Armstrong 'sold his soul' to doping, says former masseuse Emma O'Reilly. (2012, October 15). *The Telegraph.* Retrieved from http://www.telegraph.co.uk

Lance Armstrong comes face to face with whistleblower Emma O'Reilly. (2013, November 17). *The Guardian.* Retrieved from http://www.theguardian.com/

Landler, M. (2014). U.S. and China reach climate accord after months of talks. *The New York Times.* Retrieved from http://www.nytimes.com

Landrigan, P. J. (2000). Pediatric lead poisoning: Is there a threshold? *Public Health Reports, 115*, 530–531.

Langer, G. (2005, June 9). Poll: Support seen for Patriot Act. ABCNews. Retrieved from http://abcnews.go.com

Lantis, M. (1959). Alaskan Eskimo cultural values. *Polar Notes, 1*, 35–48.

Lanzetta, J. T., & Englis, B. G. (1989). Expectations of cooperation and competition and their effects on observers' vicarious emotional responses. *Journal of Personality and Social Psychology, 56*, 543–554.

LaPierre, W. (2012a, December 21). NRA press conference. Retrieved from http://home.nra.org

LaPierre, W. (2012b, April 14). Speech at annual meeting of the National Rifle Association, St. Louis. Retrieved from http://home.nra.org

Larsen, K. S., Coleman, D., Forbes, J., & Johnson, R. (1972). Is the subject's personality or the experimental situation a better predictor of a subject's willingness to administer shock to a victim? *Journal of Personality and Social Psychology, 22*, 287–295.

Larsen, O. N., Gray, L. N., & Fortis, J. G. (1968). Achieving goals through violence on television. In K. S. Larsen (Ed.), *Violence and the mass media* (pp. 97–111). New York: Harper & Row.

Latest news and developments in New York. (2015). Death Penalty Information Center. Retrieved from http://www.deathpenaltyinfo.org

Lattman, P. (2011, August 30). Latest trial set to begin in insider trading inquiry. *The New York Times*, p. B6.

Lattman, P. (2012, October 25). Ex-Goldman director to serve 2 years in insider case. *The New York Times*, p. B1.

Lattman, P., & Ahmed, A. (2011, May 11). A circle of tipsters who shared illicit secrets. *The New York Times.* Retrieved from http://dealbook.nytimes.com

Lattman, P., & Ahmed, A. (2012, June 15). Rajat Gupta convicted of insider trading. *The New York Times.* Retrieved from http://dealbook.nytimes.com

Lattman, P., & Protess, B. (2012, June 30). Peter Madoff says he didn't know about the fraud. *The New York Times*, p. B1.

Laub, Z., & Masters, J. (2014, August 8). Islamic State in Iraq and Syria. Council on Foreign Relations. Retrieved from http://www.cfr.org

Laughland, O. (2014, December 9). How the CIA tortured its detainees. *The Guardian.* Retrieved from http://www.theguardian.com

Law, S., & Singhal, A. (1999). Efficacy in letter-writing to an entertainment-education radio serial. *Gazette, 61*, 355–372.

Lazarus, R. S., & Folkman, S. (1984). *Stress, appraisal, and coping.* New York: Springer.

Leahy, E. (2007). *The shape of things to come: Why age structure matters to a safer, more equitable world.* Washington, DC: Population Action International.

Legacy Tobacco Documents Library, Brown & Williamson Collection. Bates no. 1200-1212. Retrieved from https://industrydocuments.library.ucsf.edu

Legislative Analyst's Office. (2014). California's annual costs to incarcerate an inmate in prison. Retrieved from http://www.lao.ca.gov

Lehrer, J. (2002, January 8). Interview with General Tommy Franks, January 8, 2002. *PBS NewsHour*. [Transcript]. Retrieved from http://www.pbs.org

Leibovich, M. (2004, June 4). George Tenet's 'slam-dunk' into the history books. *The Washington Post*. Retrieved from http://www.washingtonpost.com

Leiserowitz, A., Maibach, E. W., Roser-Renouf, C., Smith, N., & Dawson, E. (2013). Climategate, public opinion, and the loss of trust. *American Behavioral Scientist, 57*, 818–837.

Leiserowitz, A., Maibach, E., Roser-Renouf, C., Feinberg, G., & Rosenthal, S. (2014). *Climate change in the American mind: April, 2014*. Yale University and George Mason University. New Haven, CT: Yale Project on Climate Change Communication. Retrieved from http://environment.yale.edu

Lelyveld, J. (2001). All suicide bombers are not alike. *The New York Times Magazine*. Retrieved from http://www.nytimes.com

Leo Burnett. (1993, March 23). Project Brass: A plan of action for the ETS issue. University of California, San Francisco, Legacy Tobacco Documents Library, Philip Morris Collection. Bates No. 2023329411-2023329457. Retrieved from https://industrydocuments.library.ucsf.edu

Leon, M. (1980). Integration of intent and consequences information in children's moral judgments. In F. Wilkening, J. Becker, & T. Trabasso (Eds.), *Information integration by children* (pp. 71–97). Hillsdale, NJ: Erlbaum.

Lerner, M. J., & Miller, D. T. (1978). Just world research and the attribution process: Looking back and ahead. *Psychological Bulletin, 85*, 1030–1051.

Levi, P. (1987). *The drowned and the saved*. New York: Summit Books.

Levin, D. (2015, August 13). Study links polluted air in China to 1.6 million deaths a year. *The New York Times*. Retrieved from http://www.nytimes.com

Levine, G. (2006, March 7). Fastow tells of loss-hiding Enron "raptors." *Forbes*. Retrieved from http://www.forbes.com

Levine, J., Gussow, J. D., Hastings, D., & Eccher, A. (2003). Authors' financial relationships with the food and beverage industry and their published positions on the fat substitute olestra. *American Journal of Public Health, 93*(4), 664–669.

Levinson, R., & Link, W. (Producers), & Markowitz, R. (Director). (1977). *The storyteller* [Television motion picture]. United States: Fairmont/Foxcroft Productions, Universal Television.

Levitz, J. (2015, June 24). Boston Marathon bomber Dzokhar Tsarnaev sentenced to death, apologizes to victims. *The Wall Street Journal*. Retrieved from http://www.wsj.com

Levs, J., Payne, E., & Botelho, G. (2014, September 8). Oklahoma's botched lethal injection marks new front in battle over executions. CNN. Retrieved from http://www.cnn.com

Levy, R. I. (1969). On getting angry in the Society Islands. In W. Caudill & T.-Y. Lin (Eds.), *Mental Health Research in Asia and the Pacific* (pp. 358–380). Honolulu: East-West Center Press.

Lewandowsky, S., Gignac, G. E., & Vaughan, S. (2013). The pivotal role of perceived scientific consensus in acceptance of science. *Nature Climate Change, 3*, 399–404.

Lexchin, J., Bero, L. A., Djulbegovic, B., & Clark, O. (2003). Pharmaceutical industry sponsorship and research outcome and quality: Systematic review. *British Medical Journal, 326,* 1167–1170.

Leyens, J., Camino, L., Parke, R. D., & Berkowitz, L. (1975). The effects of movie violence on aggression in a field setting as a function of group dominance and cohesion. *Journal of Personality and Social Psychology, 32,* 346–360.

Libet, B. (1985). Unconscious cerebral initiative and the role of conscious will in voluntary action. *Behavioral and Brain Sciences, 8,* 529–539.

Libet, B. (1999). Do we have free will? *Journal of Consciousness Studies, 6,* 47–57.

Lichtblau, E., & Rich, M. (2012). N.R.A. envisions "a good guy with a gun" in every school. *The New York Times.* Retrieved from http://www.nytimes.com

Lieblich, J. (2003, January 31). Clergy leaders stand with Ryan on the death penalty. *Chicago Tribune.* Retrieved from http://articles.chicagotribune.com

Liebman, J. S., Fagan, J., & West, V. (2012). Error rates in capital cases, 1973–1995. In L. Vaughn (Ed.), *Contemporary moral arguments: Readings in ethical issues* (pp. 367–372). New York: Oxford University Press.

Lind, S. C. (1923, November 3). [Letter to Superintendent Fieldner, U.S. Bureau of Mines]. National Archives Record Group 70, 101869, File 725.

Linton, R. (1945). The Comanche. In A. Kardiner (Ed.), *The psychological frontiers of society* (pp. 47–80). New York: Columbia University Press.

Lipset, S. M. (1966). University students and politics in underdeveloped countries. *Comparative Education Review, 10,* 132–162.

Liptak, A. (2007, November 18). Does death penalty save lives? A new debate. *The New York Times,* p. 11.

Liptak, A. (2012, December 19). Supreme Court gun ruling doesn't block proposed controls, experts say. *The New York Times,* p. A32.

Liptak, A. (2013, April 15). Justices refuse case on gun law in New York. *The New York Times.* Retrieved from http://www.nytimes.com

Liptak, A. (2014, May 5). Justices turn away case about carrying guns in public. *The New York Times.* Retrieved from http://www.nytimes.com

Liptak, A. (2015, June 29). Supreme Court allows use of execution drug. *The New York Times.* Retrieved from http://www.nytimes.com

Lipton, E., & Lichtblau, E. (2010, July 15). Fund-raising before House vote draws scrutiny. *The New York Times.* Retrieved from http://www.nytimes.com

Lister, T. (2011, April 28). Osama bin Laden's escape: A tale of subterfuge and hard cash. CNN. Retrieved from http://www.cnn.com

Locke, E. A., & Latham, G. P. (1990). *A theory of goal setting & task performance.* Englewood Cliffs, NJ: Prentice-Hall.

LoGiurato, B. (2012, December 15). Rupert Murdoch: "When will politicians find courage to ban automatic weapons?" Business Insider. Retrieved from http://www.businessinsider.com

Lopatto, E. (2014, April 29). How many innocent people are sentenced to death? *Forbes.* Retrieved from http://www.forbes.com

Lovejoy, H. B. (1975, October 9). [Interoffice memo to J. M. Davis.] Chemical Industry Archives. Retrieved from http://www.chemicalindustryarchives.org

Lovett, I. (2013, January 22). Los Angeles cardinal hid abuse, files show. *The New York Times,* p. A16.

Lovett, I. (2014, February 12). Executions are suspended by governor in Washington. *The New York Times,* p. A12.

Lowe, W. (2011). The death penalty in the United States. Retrieved from http://www.wesleylowe.com/cp.html

Ludlow, L. (2001, October 7). Osama speaks: Inside the mind of a terrorist. SFGATE. Retrieved from http://www.sfgate.com

Ludwig, J., & Cook, P. J. (2003). *Evaluating gun policy: Effects on crime and violence.* Washington, DC: Brookings Institution Press.

Lumpkin, J. J. (2004, September 12). Rumsfeld: Beheadings worse than Abu Ghraib. Associated Press. Retrieved from http://www.boston.com

Luo, M. (2011, January 12). Sway of NRA blocks studies, scientists say. *The New York Times*, p. A1.

Luo, M., McIntire, M., & Palmer, G. (2013, April 17). Seeking gun or selling one, Web is a land of few rules. *The New York Times*. Retrieved from http://www.nytimes.com

Lutz, W. (1996). *The new doublespeak: Why no one knows what anyone's saying anymore.* New York: HarperCollins.

Lutz, W. D. (1987). Language, appearance, and reality: Doublespeak in 1984. In P. C. Boardman (Ed.), *The legacy of language: A tribute to Charlton Laird* (pp. 103–119). Reno: University of Nevada Press.

Lyall, S., & Turner, L. (2012, November 11). Complaint ignored for decades is heard at last in BBC abuse case. *The New York Times*, p. A16.

Lyman, R. (2013, August 19). Death row improvises, lacking lethal mix. *The New York Times*, p. A9.

Lyman, R. (2014, January 16). Ohio execution using untested drug cocktail renews the debate over lethal injections. *The New York Times*. Retrieved from http://www.nytimes.com

Lynch, B. S., & Bonnie, R. J. (Eds.) (1994). *Growing up tobacco free: Preventing nicotine addiction in children and youths.* Institute of Medicine, Washington, DC: National Academy Press.

MacAskill, E., & Norton-Taylor, R. (2003, September 26). 10 Ways to sex up a dossier. *The Guardian*. Retrieved from http://www.guardian.co.uk

MacGillis, A. (2009, August 12). In the Senate, small states wield outsize power. *The Washington Post*. Retrieved from http://www.washingtonpost.com

MacNab, B. R., & Worthley, R. (2008). Self-efficacy as an intrapersonal predictor for internal whistleblowing: A US and Canadian examination. *Journal of Business Ethics*, 79, 407–421.

Magill, B. (2014, September 24). Study: Natural gas reliance impediment to renewables. Climate Central. Retrieved from http://www.climatecentral.org

Magill, B. (2015a, January 8). EPA moves to count methane emissions from fracking. *Scientific American*. Retrieved from http://www.scientificamerican.com

Magill, B. (2015b, July 21). Recession caused U.S. emissions drop, study says. Climate Central. Retrieved from http://www.climatecentral.org

Maguire, D. C. (2012, June 27). Church abuse case. [Letter to the editor]. *The New York Times*. Retrieved from http://www.nytimes.com

Mahony, R. (2013, February 1). Historical evolution of dealing with the sexual abuse of minors. Retrieved from http://cardinalrogermahonyblogsla.blogspot.com

Maibach, E., Myers, T., & Leiserowitz, A. (2014). Climate scientists need to set the record straight: There is a scientific consensus that human-caused climate change is happening. *Earth's Future*, 2, 295–298.

Malloy, A., & Serfaty, S. (2015, August 3). Obama unveils major climate change proposal. CNN. Retrieved from http://www.cnn.com

Mann, C. C. (2007, May). The rise of big water. *Vanity Fair, 122*–142.

Manufacturing Chemists' Association (1960, October 5). Minutes of Meeting, Medical Advisory Committee. Offices of American Cyanamid Co., New York City. Retrieved from http://www.chemicalindustryarchives.org

March, J. G. (1982). Theories of choice and making decisions. *Society, 20,* 29–39.

Marder, J. (2012, August 8). Fracking: What is it, and is it safe? *PBS NewsHour*. Retrieved from http://www.pbs.org

Marine, C. (1990, March). Death's doorman. *San Francisco Examiner*, p. B5.

Mark, M. (2014, May 6). Missing Nigerian schoolgirls: Boko Haram claims responsibility for kidnapping. Alex Jones' Infowars.com. Retrieved from http://www.infowars.com

Markoe, L. (2014, September 25). Islamic scholars release open letter to Islamic State meticulously blasting its ideology. The Huffington Post. Retrieved from http://www.huffingtonpost.com

Markon, J. (2012, December 21). NRA's Wayne LaPierre: The force behind the nation's gun lobby. *The Washington Post*. Retrieved from http://www.washingtonpost.com

Markowitz, G., & Rosner, D. (2002). *Deceit and denial: The deadly politics of industrial pollution*. Berkeley: University of California Press.

Markowitz, G., & Rosner, D. (2008). Chronology. Retreived from http://www.deceitanddenial.org/docs/timeline.pdf

Martin, S. P., Smith, E. O., & Byrd, L. D. (1990). Effects of dominance rank on d-amphetamine-induced increases in aggression. *Pharmacology Biochemistry and Behavior, 37,* 493–496.

Martz, M., Powell, B., McCormick, J., Thomas, R., & Starr., M. (1986, December 1). True greed. *Newsweek*.

Maslach, C. (1982). *Burnout: The cost of caring*. Englewood Cliffs, NJ: Prentice Hall.

Mathiesen, K. (2014, May 6). Climate change: What are the worst impacts facing America? *The Guardian*. Retrieved from http://www.theguardian.com

Mattingly, P., & Hopkins, C. (2013, December 9). Glass-Steagall firewall could return if Volcker Rule disappoints. *Insurance Journal*. Retrieved from http://www.insurancejournal.com

Mauriello, T. (2011, December 6). $210 million settlement in Upper Big Branch mine explosion. *Pittsburgh Post-Gazette*. Retrieved from http://www.post-gazette.com

Mazza, E. (2014, September 2). Scalia once pushed death penalty for now-exonerated inmate Henry Lee McCollum. The Huffington Post. Retrieved from http://www.huffingtonpost.com

Mazzetti, M. (2014, October 14). C.I.A. study of covert aid fueled skepticism about helping Syrian rebels. *The New York Times*. Retrieved from http://www.nytimes.com

Mazzetti, M., & Apuzzo, M. (2014, December 12). C.I.A. director defends use of interrogation tactics, avoiding issue of torture. *The New York Times*, p. A1.

Mazzetti, M., Schmitt, E., & Landler, M. (2014, September 11). Struggling to gauge ISIS threat, even as U.S. prepares to act. *The New York Times*, p. A1.

McAlister, A., Ama, E., Barroso, C., Peters, R., & Kelder, S. (2000). Promoting tolerance and moral engagement through peer modeling. *Cultural Diversity and Ethnic Minority Psychology, 6,* 363–373.

McAlister, A., Bandura, A., & Owen, S. (2006). Mechanisms of moral disengagement in support of military force: The impact of September 11. *Journal of Social and Clinical Psychology, 25,* 141–166.

McAuliff, M., & Graves, L. (2011, October 9). War on the EPA: Republican bills would erase decades of protection. The Huffington Post. Retrieved from http://www.huffingtonpost.com

McAvoy, A. (2003, July 4). Japanese officials' remarks anger women. Associated Press. Retrieved from http://www.seattlepi.com

McCaolou, L. R. (2012). *Call of the mild: Learning to hunt my own dinner.* New York: Grand Central Publishing.

McDonald v. Chicago, 561 U.S. 742 (2010).

McDonald, F. (2013, June 12). Two-thirds of energy sector will have to be left undeveloped, Bonn conference told. *The Irish Times.* Retrieved from http://www.irishtimes.com

McFadden, R. D. (2009, November 6). Army doctor held in Ft. Hood rampage. *The New York Times,* p. A1.

McFadden, R. D. (2014, April 3). Charles Keating, key figure in crisis of savings and loans, is dead at 90. *The New York Times,* p. A24.

McGarvey, R. (1993). Resume fraud. *Training, 30,* 10–14.

McGinnis, J. M., & Foege, W. H. (1993). Actual causes of death in the United States. *Journal of the American Medical Association, 270,* 2207–2212.

McGuire, A. E. (2013, May 14). Why the pro-life movement must reject the death penalty for Kermit Gosnell. *The Washington Post.* Retrieved from http://www.washingtonpost.com

McHugo, G. J., Smith, C. A., & Lanzetta, J. T. (1982). The structure of self-reports of emotional responses to film segments. *Motivation and Emotion, 6,* 365–385.

McIntire, M. (2013, January 26). Selling a new generation on guns. *The New York Times.* Retrieved from http://www.nytimes.com

McIntyre, A. (2001). The Provisional Irish Republican Army and the morality of terrorism. *Democracy and Security, 7,* 289–294.

McKay, M.-J. (2002, October 11). Falwell sorry for bashing Muhammad. *60 Minutes.* Retrieved from http://www.cbsnews.com

McKenna, L. & Johnson, R. (2012, February 26). A look at the world's most powerful mercenary armies. Business Insider. Retrieved from http://www.businessinsider.com

McKinley, J. C., Jr. (2009, April 15). U.S. stymied as guns flow to Mexican cartels. *The New York Times,* p. A1.

McLaughlin, D. (n.d.) Silent Spring revisited. *FRONTLINE.* Retrieved from http://www.pbs.org

McLean, B., & P. Elkind (2006, July 5). The guiltiest guys in the room. CNN Money. Retrieved from http://money.cnn.com

McMahon, J. (2014, March 21). Stephen Chu solves utility companies' death spiral. *Forbes.* Retrieved from http://www.forbes.com

Mead, M. (1935). *Sex and temperament in three savage tribes.* New York: Morrow.

Meadows, M. S. (2010). *Tea time with terrorists: A motorcycle journey into the heart of Sri Lanka's civil war.* New York: Soft Skill Press.

Medina, J. (2013, March 14). Los Angeles Archdiocese to pay $10 million in abuse. *The New York Times,* p. A18.

Medina, J., & Lovett, I. (2013, February 4). Sexual abuse scandal grips and divides Hispanic parishioners in Los Angeles. *The New York Times,* p. A11.

Meier, B. (1998a, January 12). U.S. brings its first charges in the tobacco investigation. *The New York Times*, p. A17.

Meier, B. (1998b, January 15). Files of R. J. Reynolds Tobacco show efforts on youth. *The New York Times*, p. A10.

Meier, B. (1998c, February 23). Cigarette maker manipulated nicotine, its records suggest. *The New York Times*, p. A16.

Meier, B. (1998d, May 7). Philip Morris censored data about addiction. *The New York Times*, p. A14.

Meier, B. (2000, August 2). W.H.O. says files show tobacco companies fought anti-smoking efforts. *The New York Times*, p. A8.

Memos highlight importance of "younger adult smokers." (1998, January 15). *The Washington Post*. Retrieved from http://www.washingtonpost.com

MEMRI (Middle East Media Research Institute). (2015, January 7). Online jihad supporters celebrate attack on headquarters of French satirical weekly "Charlie Hebdo." Retrieved from http://www.memrijttm.org

Merton, R., & Barber, E. (2004). *The travels and adventures of serendipity*. Princeton, NJ: Princeton University Press.

Mesmer-Magnus, J., & Viswesvaran, C. (2005). Whistleblowing in organizations: An examination of correlates of whistleblowing intentions, actions, and retaliation. *Journal of Business Ethics, 62*, 277–297.

Meyer, T. P. (1972). Effects of viewing justified and unjustified real film violence on aggressive behavior. *Journal of Personality and Social Psychology, 23*, 21–29.

Meyerson, F. A. B. (1998). Population, carbon emissions, and global warming: The forgotten relationship at Kyoto. *Population and Development Review, 24*, 804–810.

Michel, L., & Herbeck, D. (2001). *American terrorist: Timothy McVeigh and the Oklahoma City bombing*. New York: Regan Books.

Midgley, M. (1978). *Beast and man: The roots of human nature*. Ithaca, NY: Cornell University Press.

Milgram, S. (1974). *Obedience to authority: An experimental view*. New York: Harper & Row.

Milgram, S., & Shotland, R. L. (1973). *Television and antisocial behavior: Field experiments*. New York: Academic Press.

Miller, R. E., Caul, W. F., & Mirsky, I. A. (1967). Communications of affect between feral and socially isolated monkeys. *Journal of Personality and Social Psychology, 7*, 231–239.

Miller, S. M. (1981). Predictability and human stress: Toward a clarification of evidence and theory. In L. Berkowitz (Ed.), *Advances in Experimental Social Psychology* (Vol. 14, pp. 203–256). New York: Academic Press.

Millhiser, R. (1970, January 6). Ralph Nader's federal suits barring smoking. University of California, San Francisco, Legacy Tobacco Documents Library. Retrieved from https://industrydocuments.library.ucsf.edu

Millman, J. (1992, November 10). Steady finger on the trigger. *Forbes*, 188.

Min, D. (2011, July 12). Why Wallison is wrong about the genesis of the U.S. housing crisis. Center for American Progress. Retrieved from https://www.americanprogress.org

Minegar, B. (2013, April 5). UN calls for worldwide death penalty moratorium. JURIST. Retrieved from http://jurist.org

Mir, A. M., & Shaikh, G. R. (2013). Islam and family planning: Changing perceptions of health care providers and medical faculty in Pakistan. *Global Health: Science and Practice, 1*, 228–236. Retrieved from http://www.ghspjournal.org

Moerk, E. (1995). Acquisition and transmission of pacifist mentalities in Sweden. *Peace and Conflict: Journal of Peace Psychology, 1*, 291–307.

Monahan, J. (2014). *Danger and disorder: Violence, guns and mental illness* [Video]. University of Virginia. Retrieved from https://www.youtube.com

Monin, B., & Miller, D. T. (2001). Moral credentials and the expression of prejudice. *Journal of Personality and Social Psychology, 81*, 33–43.

Moore, M. T. (2013, January 17). NRA criticized for ad about Obama's daughters. *USA Today.* Retrieved from http://www.usatoday.com

Moore, S., Lindes, D., Wolfe, S. M., & Douglas, C. (1993). *Contributing to death: The influence of tobacco money on the U.S. Congress; A report by Public Citizen's Health Research Group.* Washington, DC: Public Citizen's Health Research Group. University of California, San Francisco, Legacy Tobacco Documents Library, Bates no. 2058462252-2058462267. Retrieved from https://industrydocuments.library.ucsf.edu

Morgenson, G. (2013, December 15). Wake up the banking police. *The New York Times*, p. B1.

Morgenson, G. (2015a, January 11). Kicking Dodd-Frank in the teeth. *The New York Times*, p. B1.

Morgenson, G. (2015b, March 15). S.E.C. wants the sinners to own up. *The New York Times*, p. B1.

Morgenson, G., & Story, L. (2011, April 14). In financial crisis, no prosecution of top figures. *The New York Times.* Retrieved from http://www.nytimes.com

Morris, L. (2014, August 11). Iraqi president names Haider al-Abadi new prime minister, defying Maliki. *The Washington Post.* Retrieved from http://www.washingtonpost.com

Moseley, T. (2014, October 1). The enforcers of the death penalty. *The Atlantic.* Retrieved from http://www.theatlantic.com

Mowery, P. D., Babb, S., Hobart, R., Tworek, C., & McNeil, A. (2012). The impact of state preemption of local smoking restrictions on public health protections and changes in social norms. *Journal of Environmental and Public Health*, article ID 632629, 8 pages. Retrieved from http://www.hindawi.com

Moynihan, C., & Cohen, M. (2010, May 2). Bomb scare reveals another side of Times Square. *The New York Times.* Retrieved from http://www.nytimes.com

Mufson, S., & Marte, J. (2015, May 20). Five big banks agree to pay more than $5 billion to settle regulatory charges. *The Washington Post.* Retrieved from http://www.washingtonpost.com

Muller, E. (2012). 250 years of global warming: Berkeley Earth releases new analysis. Berkeley Earth.Surface Surface Temperature. Retrieved from http://static.berkeleyearth.org

Muller, R. (2012). *Energy for future presidents.* New York: W. W. Norton.

Murphy, D. (2011, December 22). Iraq war: Predictions made, and results. *The Christian Science Monitor.* Retrieved from http://www.csmonitor.com

Murray, S. (2005a, July 12). Liability shield for gunmakers near passage. *The Washington Post*, p. A1.

Murray, S. (2005b, July 30). Senate passes bill barring gun suits. *The Washington Post*, p. A8.

Muskal, M. (2013, January 28). Newtown families speak to Connecticut lawmakers about gun issues. *The Los Angeles Times.* Retrieved from http://articles.latimes.com

Muslims angered by Baptist criticism. (2002, June 13). CNN.com. Retrieved from http://edition.cnn.com

Mussen, P., & Eisenberg, N. (2001). Prosocial development in context. In A. C. Bohart & D. J. Stipek (Eds.), *Constructive and destructive behavior: Implications for family, school, and society* (pp. 103–126). Washington, DC: American Psychological Association.

Mynatt, C., & Herman, S. J. (1975). Responsibility attribution in groups and individuals: A direct test of the diffusion of responsibility hypothesis. *Journal of Personality and Social Psychology, 32,* 1111–1118.

1987: Bomb kills 11 at Enniskillen. (n.d.) BBC On This Day. http://news.bbc.co.uk

NAACP (2015, Spring). *Death row USA: A quarterly report by the Criminal Justice Project of the NAACP Legal Defense and Educational Fund, Inc.* Retrieved from http://www.naacpldf.org

Nagin, D., & Pepper, J. (2012). *Deterrence and the death penalty.* Washington, DC: National Academies Press.

Nagourney, A. (2011, January 12). In an ocean of firearms, Tucson is far away. *The New York Times,* p. A5.

Nagourney, A. (2012, December 19). Broad gun control efforts introduced in wake of shooting. *The New York Times,* p. A1.

Nahmias, E. A. (2002). When consciousness matters: A critical review of Daniel Wegner's *The illusion of conscious will. Philosophical Psychology, 15,* 527–541.

Nakashima, E. (2013, June 18). Officials: surveillance programs foiled more than 50 terrorist plots. *The Washington Post.* Retrieved from https://www.washingtonpost.com

Nathanson, S. (2012). An eye for an eye? In L. Vaughn (Ed.), *Contemporary moral arguments: Readings in ethical issues* (pp. 362–367). New York: Oxford University Press.

National Council of Teachers of English. (1999). NCTE Doublespeak Award. Retrieved from http://www.ncte.org

National Council of Teachers of English. (n.d.) Past recipients of the Doublespeak Award. Retrieved from http://www.ncte.org

National Council of Teachers of English. (n.d.) The Doublespeak Award. Retrieved from http://www.ncte.org/

National Shooting Sports Foundation. (2012, March 16). Hunting Heritage Trust/NSSF® study: Youth who hunt and shoot can positively influence peers. National Shooting Sports Foundation. Retrieved from http://www.nssf.org

Naylor, B. (2013, January 30). Giffords tells Senate panel on gun violence "We must do something." NPR. Retrieved from http://www.npr.org

Needleman, H. L., Gunnoe, C., Leviton, A., Reed, R., Peresie, H., Maher, C., & Barrett, P. (1979). Deficits in psychologic and classroom performance of children with elevated dentine lead levels. *New England Journal of Medicine, 13,* 689–695.

Nessell, W. E. (1967). M. D. Monsanto, AMCA Meeting, Ann Arbor, MI.

Nestle, M. (2002). *Food politics: How the food industry influences nutrition and health.* Berkeley: University of California Press.

Newport, F. (2011, October 13). In U.S., support for death penalty falls to 39-year low. Gallup. Retrieved from http://www.gallup.com

Newport, F. (2012, December 19). To stop shootings, Americans focus on police, mental health. Gallup. Retrieved from http://www.gallup.com

Nicholson, D. (2007, July 12). Populating and perishing. *Canberra Times,* p. B7.

Nisbett, R., & Ross, L. (1980). *Human inference: Strategies and shortcomings of social judgment.* Englewood Cliffs, NJ: Prentice Hall.

Nordhaus, W. D. (2009, March 10–12). *Climate change: Global risks, challenges, and decisions.* Paper presented at the Economic Issues in Designing a Global Agreement on Global Warming, Copenhagen, Denmark.

Norris, F. (2013, December 13). It's hard to summon sympathy for big banks. *The New York Times*, p. B1.

Novaco, R. W. (2013). Reducing anger-related offending. In L. Craig, L. Dixon, & T. Gannon (Eds.), *What works in offender rehabilitation: An evidence-based approach to assessment and treatment.* Chichester, UK: Wiley.

Novkov, J. (2013). *The Supreme Court and the presidency: Struggles for supremacy.* Washington, DC: CQ Press.

NRA representative compares I-594 to Nazi Germany. (2014, July 29). *NBC News.* Retrieved from http://www.nbcnews.com

O'Callaghan, S. (1998). *The informer.* London: Transworld Publishers Limited.

O'Keefe, E. (2013, January 29). NRA chief: Gun owners will resist new laws. *The Washington Post.* Retrieved from http://www.washingtonpost.com

O'Keefe, E., & Fahrenthold, D. (2013, January 30). Gabrielle Giffords speaks at hearing on gun violence. *The Washington Post.* Retrieved from http://www.washingtonpost.com

O'Neil, J. (2006, June 12). A warning on hazards of smoke secondhand. *The New York Times*, p. A14.

Obermann, M.-L. (2011). Moral disengagement among bystanders to school bullying. *Journal of School Violence, 10,* 239–257.

Office of the Surgeon General. (2014). The health consequences of smoking—50 years of progress. Atlanta: U.S. Department of Health and Human Services.

Oliner, S. P., & Oliner, P. M. (1988). *The altruistic personality: Rescuers of Jews in Nazi Europe.* New York: Free Press.

Olson, D. (2012, July 10). Faith-based organizations to make new commitments at London Family Planning Summit. Faith Street. Retrieved from http://www.faithstreet.com

Olson, E. (2001a, November 28). After U.S. objects, world fails to agree to curb smoking ads. *The New York Times*, p. A5.

Olson, E. (2001b, January 12). Big tobacco said to fight Swiss smoking laws. *The New York Times*, p. A8.

Olweus, D. (1991). Effects of nationwide campaign against bully-victim problems in Norwegian schools. In D. J. Pepler & K. H. Rubin (Eds.), *The development and treatment of childhood aggression* (pp. 411–448). Hillsdale, NJ: Erlbaum.

Olweus, D., & Limber, S. (2010). The Olweus bullying prevention program. In S. R. Jimerson, S. M. Swearer, & D. L. Espelage (Eds.), *International handbook of school bullying: An international perspective* (pp. 377–401). New York: Routledge.

Ordorica, R. (Ed.) (1997). *Handguns '98* (10th ed). Iola, WI: DBI Books.

Oskin, B. (2015, April 27). Fracking is not the cause of quakes. The real problem is wastewater. *The Washington Post.* Retrieved from http://www.washingtonpost.com

Osofsky, M., Bandura, A., & Zimbardo, P. (2005). The role of moral disengagement in the execution process. *Law and Human Behavior, 29,* 371–393.

Otterman, S. (2012). Priest puts blame on some victims of sexual abuse. *The New York Times*, p. A21.

Owen, R. (2010, March 11). Chief exorcist Father Gabriele Amorth says devil is in the Vatican. *The Telegraph.* Retrieved from http://www.telegraph.co.uk

Paciello, M., Fida, R., Tramontano, C., Lupinetti, M., & Caprara, G. V. (2008). Stability and change of moral disengagement and its impact on aggression and violence in late adolescence. *Child Development, 79,* 1288–1309.

Packer, G. (2002, December 12). The liberal quandary over Iraq. *The New York Times Magazine.* Retrieved from http://www.nytimes.com

Packer, H. L. (1968). *The limits of criminal sanction.* Stanford, CA: Stanford University Press.

Pages, R. (1991). Japan ETS exposure assessment study. University of California, San Francisco, Legacy Tobacco Documents Library. Bates No. 2023544456. Retrieved from http://legacy.library.ucsf.edu/tid/bqz91a00

Papa, M. J., Singhal, A., Law, S., Pant, S., Sood, S., Rogers, E. M., & Shefner-Rogers, C. L. (2000). Entertainment-education and social change: An analysis of parasocial interaction, social learning, collective efficacy, and paradoxical communication. *Journal of Communication, 50,* 31–55.

Papineu, D. (2007). Naturalism. In E. N. Zalta (Ed.), The Stanford Encyclopedia of Philosophy (Spring ed.). Retrieved from http://plato.stanford.edu

Parker, E. B., Schramm, W., & Lyle, J. (1961). *Television in the lives of our children: The facts about the effects of television based on studies of over 6,000 children.* Stanford, CA: Stanford University Press.

Parker, R. (2013, May 12). Pilotless planes, Pacific tensions. *The New York Times,* p. A21.

Parkinson, J., Zeleny, J., & Dwyer, D. (2014, September 22). Obama alerts leading supporters on Capitol Hill of ISIS airstrikes in Syria. *ABCNews.* Retrieved from http://abcnews.go.com

Pasha, S. (2006, April 10). Skilling comes out swinging. CNN Money. Retrieved from http://money.cnn.com

Pastorelli, C., Caprara, G. V., Barbaranelli, C., Rola, J., Rozsa, S., & Bandura, A. (2001). Structure of children's perceived self-efficacy: A cross-national study. *European Journal of Psychological Assessment, 17,* 87–97.

Pataki, G. (1996, August 30). Statement on anniversary of death penalty by Governor Pataki. ProCon.org. Retrieved from http://deathpenalty.procon.org

Patel, S. S. (2013, November 22). Banks and regulators clash on "regulatory fervor" and "pound of flesh" litigation. [Web log post]. MarketWatch, November 22, 2013. Retrieved from http://blogs.marketwatch.com

Patterson, G. (1986). Performance models for antisocial boys. *American Psychologist, 41,* 432–444.

Patterson, G. R. (1976). The aggressive child: Victim and architect of a coercive system. In E. J. Mash, L. A. Hamerlynck, & L. C. Handy (Eds.), *Behavior modification and families* (pp. 267–316). New York: Brunner/Mazel.

Patterson, G. R., & Bank, L. (1989). Some amplifying mechanisms for pathologic process in families. In M. Gunnar, & E. Thelen (Eds.), *Systems and development: The Minnesota Symposia on Child Psychology* (Vol. 22, pp. 167–210). Hillsdale, NJ: Erlbaum.

Paulson, H. M. Jr. (2014, June 21). The coming climate crash: Lessons for climate change in the 2008 recession. *The New York Times.* Retrieved from http://www.nytimes.com

Pavao, E. (2014). Slavery and the founding fathers. Retrieved from http://www.revolutionary-war.net/slavery-and-the-founding-fathers.html

Pavlo, W. (2011, December 21). Primary Global's James Fleishman gets 30 months in prison. *Forbes.* Retrieved from http://www.forbes.com

PCI Media Impact (2002). *Taru* [Radio serial drama]. Retrieved from http://mediaimpact.org

PCI Media Impact. (2009, September 1). Give a voice back to rural Hondurans. [Press release]. Retrieved from http://3blmedia.com

Pear, R. (2000, March 14). Clinton and Gore clash with N.R.A. official over gun control. *The New York Times*. Retrieved from http://www.nytimes.com

Pearce, F. (2013, July 15). Technology as our planet's last best hope. *The Guardian*. Retrieved from http://www.theguardian.com

Peltz, L. (2009). *The new investment superstars*. New York: Wiley.

Pérez-Peña, R., & Saulny, S. (2013, February 17). Gun advocates press for more inroads on campuses. *The New York Times*, p. A16.

Perlez, J. (2006, April 12). Forests in Southeast Asia fall to prosperity's ax. *The New York Times*, p. A1.

Pescosolido, B., Monahan, J., Link, B. G., Stueve, A., & Kikuzawa, S. (1999). The public's view of the competence, dangerousness, and need for legal coercion of persons with mental health problems. *American Journal of Public Health, 89*, 1339–1345.

Pettifor, T. (2012, October 17). Jimmy Savile scandal: Disgraced star was allowed to stay overnight at girls school run by Home Office. *The Mirror*. Retrieved from http://www.mirror.co.uk

Pew Research Center. (2012, December 20). After Newtown, modest change in opinion about gun control. Retrieved from http://www.people-press.org

Pew Research Center, Religion and Public Life. (2012, February 4). Scalia calls death penalty constitutional, not immoral. Retrieved from http://www.pewforum.org

Pflanz, M. (2013, September 12). Africa's population to double to 2.4 billion by 2050. *The Telegraph*. Retrieved from http://www.telegraph.co.uk

Philip Morris USA Inc. (1989). ETS Strategy. University of California, San Francisco, Legacy Tobacco Documents Library, Philip Morris Collection. Bates no. 2021159323- 2021159333. Retrieved from https://industrydocuments.library.ucsf.edu

Phillips, D. P. (1985). Natural experiments on the effects of mass media violence on fatal aggression: Strengths and weaknesses of a new approach. In L. Berkowitz (Ed.), *Advances in Experimental Social Psychology* (Vol. 19, pp. 207–250). New York: Academic Press.

Pilon, M. (2012, October 12). Armstrong aide talks of doping and price paid. *The New York Times*, p. A1.

Plumer, B. (2011). Getting ready for a wave of coal-plant shutdowns. *The Washington Post*. Retrieved from http://www.washingtonpost.com

Pogatchnik, S. (2012, May 2). Irish cardinal won't quit over abuse cover-up row. Associated Press. Retrieved from http://www.boston.com

Poindexter, D. O. (2004). A history of entertainment-education, 1958–2000. In A. Singhal, M. Cody, E. Rogers, & M. Sabido (Eds.), *Entertainment-education and social change: History, research, and practice* (pp. 21–37). Mahwah, NJ: Erlbaum.

Pokin, S. (2007, November 12). Pokin around: A real person, a real death. *St. Charles County Suburban Journals*, p. A4.

Poland seeks Iraqi oil stake. (2003, July 3). BBCNews. Retrieved from http://news.bbc.co.uk

Pollitt, K. (2007, April 8). Europeans do it better. *The Nation*. Retrieved from http://www.truth-out.org

Pool, B. (1991, May 9). Bill of Rights display opens to protests: Exhibit: Foes of smoking decry tobacco company's sponsorship of tour showing original copy of 10 constitutional amendments. *The Los Angeles Times*. Retrieved from http://articles.latimes.com

Pope John Paul II's statements on the death penalty. (2000, July 9). Retrieved from http://www.deathpenaltyinfo.org

Population Media Center (Producer) (2007). *Umuragi urukwiye* [Rwanda's brighter future]. [Radio serial drama]. Retrieved from https://www.populationmedia.org

Population Media Center (Producer). (2004). *Cesiri tono* [Fruits of perseverance]. [Radio serial drama]. Retrieved from https://www.populationmedia.org

Population Reference Bureau. 1875 Connecticut Ave., NW, Suite 520, Washington, DC 20009-5728.

Power, S. (2010, July 23). Senate halts effort to cap CO2 emissions. *The Wall Street Journal*. Retrieved from http://www.wsj.com

Powers, T. (1971). *Diana: The making of a terrorist*. Boston: Houghton Mifflin.

Preston, S. D., & de Waal, F. B. (2002). Empathy: Its ultimate and proximate bases. *Behavioral and Brain Sciences, 25*, 1–72.

Prial, D. (2014, December 10). Appeals court ruling strikes at insider trading cases. Fox Business. Retrieved from http://www.foxbusiness.com

Price, F. (Producer), & Graham, W. A. (Director). (1966). *The doomsday flight* [Motion picture]. United States: Universal Television.

Prins, N. (2014). *All the presidents' bankers*. New York: Nation Books.

PRNewswire (2012, October 4). ICLEI Releases first national standard for measuring a community's carbon footprint. Retrieved from http://www.prnewswire.com

Proctor, R. N. (2012). *Golden holocaust: Origins of the cigarette catastrophe and the case for abolition*. Berkeley: University of California Press.

Protess, B., & Silver-Greenberg, J. (2013a, November 19). In extracting deal from JPMorgan, U.S. aimed for bottom line. *The New York Times*. Retrieved from http://dealbook.nytimes.com

Protess, B., & Silver-Greenberg, J. (2013b, August 9). S.E.C. is said to press JPMorgan for an admission of wrongdoing. *The New York Times*, p. B1.

Protess, B., & Silver-Greenberg, J. (2014a, July 1). BNP admits guilt and agrees to pay $8.9 billion fine to U.S. *The New York Times*. Retrieved from http://www.nytimes.com

Protess, B., & Silver-Greenberg, J. (2014b, January 7). JPMorgan is penalized $2 billion over Madoff. *The New York Times*. Retrieved from http://www.nytimes.com

Protess, B., & Silver-Greenberg, J. (2014c, May 11). 2 Banking giants implore U.S. authorities to go easy. *The New York Times*. Retrieved from http://dealbook.nytimes.com

Pullella, P. (2011, October 27). Pope expresses shame for Christian violence in history. Reuters. Retrieved from http://www.reuters.com

Purdam, T. S. (2003). *A time of our choosing: America's war in Iraq*. New York: Henry Holt and Company.

Purdy, M., & Haughney, C. (2012, October 25). Parliament questions former BBC chief's role. *The New York Times*, p. A8.

Rabin, R. C. (2009, January 2). A new cigarette hazard: "Third-hand smoke." *The New York Times*. Retrieved from http://www.nytimes.com

Rabin, R. C. (2012, August 3). Big cigars offer way for smokers to save. *The New York Times*, p. A10.

Rachel Carson dies of cancer; "Silent Spring" author was 56. (1964, April 15). *The New York Times*. Retrieved from http://www.nytimes.com

Raghavan, A. (2013, May 19). Rajat Gupta's lust for zeros. *The New York Times Magazine*, p. 30.

Raines, H. (1987, November 15). Terrorism: With latest bomb, I.R.A. injures its own cause. *The New York Times*. Retrieved from http://www.nytimes.com

Ramdas, K. N. (2012, Summer). What's sex got to do with It? An inconvenient truth is hiding behind the current excitement about educating girls. *Stanford Social Innovation Review*. Retrieved from http://www.ssireview.org

Rand, A. (1966). *Capitalism, the unknown ideal*. New York: New American Library.

Ranieri, T. (2012, October 14). Lance Armstrong sued me for libel made my life a living hell. Examiner.com. Retrieved from http://www.examiner.com

Rankin, B. (2013, January 20). The insider: Whistleblower Emma O'Reilly on her astonishing time with sport's biggest drug cheat. *The Mirror*. Retrieved from http://www.mirror.co.uk

Rapoport, D. C. (1990). Sacred terror: A contemporary example from Islam. In W. Reich (Ed.), *Origins of terrorism: Psychologies, ideologies, theologies, states of mind* (pp. 103–130). Cambridge, UK: Cambridge University Press.

Rapoport, D. C., & Alexander, Y. (1982). *The morality of terrorism: Religious and secular justifications*. New York: Pergamon Press.

Ratzinger, J. (2004, July). Worthiness to receive Holy Communion: General principles. [Memo to Cardinal Theodore McCarrick]. Eternal Word Television Network. Retrieved from http://www.ewtn.com

Raush, H. L. (1965). Interaction sequences. *Journal of Personality and Social Psychology, 2*, 487–499.

Raush, H. L., Barry, W. A., Hertel, R. K., & Swain, M. A. (1974). *Communication, conflict, and marriage*. San Francisco: Jossey-Bass.

Raymond, N., & Stempel, J. (2014, March 12). Big fine imposed on ex-Goldman trader Tourre in SEC case. Reuters. Retrieved from http://www.reuters.com

Reagan, R. (1967, [April 20]). [Letter to Laurence Russell Walton]. Shapell Manuscript Foundation. Retrieved from http://www.shapell.org

Reed, S. (2014). European lawmakers try to spur market for carbon-emission credits. *The New York Times*. Retrieved from http://www.nytimes.com

Reich, W. (1990). *Origins of terrorism: Psychologies, ideologies, theologies, states of mind*. Cambridge, UK: Cambridge University Press.

Reiss, A. J. (1971). *The police and the public*. New Haven, CT: Yale University Press.

Religious Institute. (2012). Open letter to religious leaders on family planning. Retrieved from http://www.religiousinstitute.org

Reuters. (2014, March 4). China to "declare war" on pollution, premier says. Retrieved from http://www.reuters.com

Reuters. (2015, August 13). Fifteen U.S. states seek to block EPA carbon rule. *The New York Times*. Retrieved from http://www.nytimes.com

Richinick, M. (2015, February 15). Pennsylvania governor puts hold on death penalty. MSNBC. Retrieved from http://www.msnbc.com

Richtel, M. (2013, October 26). The e-cigarette industry, waiting to exhale. *The New York Times*. Retrieved from http://www.nytimes.com

Richtel, M. (2014a, March 5). E-cigarettes, by other names, lure young and worry experts. *The New York Times*, p. 1.

Richtel, M. (2014b, March 24). Selling a poison by the barrel: Liquid nicotine for e-cigarettes. *The New York Times*, p. A1.

Richtel, M. (2014c, May 4). Some e-cigarettes deliver a puff of carcinogens. *The New York Times*, p. A1.

Richtel, M. (2014d, April 27). Vaporland. *The New York Times*, p. B1.

Richter, E. D., Stein, Y., & Barnea, A. (2010, Spring). Incitement to genocide in the year in review 2009: With special emphasis on jihadist antisemitism and Iran's threats to destroy Israel. Genocide Prevention Now. Retrieved from http://www.genocidepreventionnow.org

Riley, M. W., Kahn, R. L., & Foner, A. (1994). *Age and structural lag: Society's failure to provide meaningful opportunities in work, family, and leisure*. New York: Wiley.

Rimer, S. (2000, December 17). Working death row: A special report; In the busiest death chamber, duty carries its own burdens. *The New York Times*, p. 1.

Risen, J. (2003, May 22). Prewar views of Iraq threat are under review by the C.I.A. *The New York Times*. Retrieved from http://www.nytimes.com

Risen, J. (2014). *Pay any price: Greed, power, and endless war*. New York: Houghton Mifflin Harcourt.

Risen, J. (2015a, July 10). Outside psychologists shielded U.S. torture program, report finds. *The New York Times*. Retrieved from http://www.nytimes.com

Risen, J. (2015b, August 7). Association bars psychologists from ties to U.S. national security interrogations. *The New York Times*, p. A11.

Roan, D., & Slater, M. (2015, January 26). Lance Armstrong: I'd change the man, not decision to cheat. BBC Sport. Retrieved from http://www.bbc.com/sport

Roberts, D., & Ackerman, S. (2013, June 15). US intelligence outlines checks it says validate surveillance. *The Guardian*. Retrieved from http://www.theguardian.com

Robinson, T., Wilde, M. L., Navracruz, L. C., Haydel, K. F., & Varady, A. (2001). Effects of reducing children's television and video game use on aggressive behavior: A randomized controlled trial. *Archives of Pediatrics and Adolescent Medicine*, *155*, 17–23.

Robinson, W. (2002, January 31). Scores of priests involved in sex abuse cases: Settlements kept scope of issue out of public eye. *The Boston Globe*. Retrieved from http://www.boston.com

Robles, F. (2012, July 19). Zimmerman: Trayvon's death was "God's plan." *Miami Herald*. Retrieved from http://www.miamiherald.com

Rogers, A. (2012, May 3). Catholic priests: Our lawyers told us not to report sex abuse. Business Insider. Retrieved from http://www.businessinsider.com

Rogers, E. M., & Kincaid, D. L. (1981). *Communication networks: Toward a new paradigm for research*. New York: Free Press.

Rogers, E., Vaughan, P. W., Swalehe, R. M., Rao, N., Svenkerud, P., & Sood, S. (1999). Effects of an entertainment-education radio soap opera on family planning behavior in Tanzania. *Studies in Family Planning*, *30*, 193–211.

Rohter, L. (2007, July 27). In the Amazon: Conservation or colonialism? *The New York Times*, p. A4.

Romero, S. (2012, May 17). Brazil's leader faces defining decision on bill relaxing protection of forests. *The New York Times*, p. A12.

Ronderos, M. T. (2001, March 3). In Latin America, Big Tobacco partners with money launderers, smugglers. *International Consortium of Investigative Journalists*. Retrieved from http://www.icij.org

Rorty, A. O. (1993). What it takes to be good. In G. Noam & T. E. Wren (Eds.), *The moral self* (pp. 28–55). Cambridge, MA: MIT Press.

Rose, D. (2008, December). Tortured reasoning. *Vanity Fair*. Retrieved from http://www.vanityfair.com

Rosenbaum, D. E. (1987, July 16). Iran-Contra hearings: Poindexter says he withheld Iran-contra link from Reagan; testimony gratifies president; admiral on stand. *The New York Times*, p. A1.

Rosenfeld, S. (2013, January 13). The suprising unknown history of the NRA. AlterNet. Retrieved from http://www.alternet.org

Rosenthal, E. (2012, April 15). Nigeria's population is soaring in preview of a global problem. *The New York Times*, p. A1.

Rosenthal, E., & Lehren, A. W. (2012a, August 9). Profits on carbon credits drive output of a harmful gas. *The New York Times*. Retrieved from http://www.nytimes.com

Rosenthal, E., & Lehren, A. W. (2012b, June 20). Relief in every window, but global worry too. *The New York Times*. Retrieved from http://www.nytimes.com

Roskies, A. (2006). Neuroscientific challenges to free will and responsibility. *Trends in Cognitive Sciences, 10*, 419–423.

Rosner, D., & Markowitz, G. (1991). *Deadly dust: Silicosis and the politics of occupational disease in twentieth-century America*. Princeton, NJ: Princeton University Press.

Rotella, C. (2011, August 11). Can Jeremy Grantham profit from ecological mayhem? *The New York Times*. Retrieved from http://www.nytimes.com

Rothwell, J. D. (1982). *Telling it like it isn't: Language misuse and malpractice*. Englewood Cliffs, NJ: Prentice-Hall.

Rowe, J. W., & Kahn, R. L. (1998). *Successful aging*. New York: Pantheon.

Rubin, A. J. (2015, May 6). French take step to vastly widen domestic spying. *The New York Times*, p. A1.

Rubin, R. (1994). Moral distancing and the use of information technologies: The seven temptations. In J. M. Kizza (Ed.), *Social and ethical issues of the computer revolution* (pp. 124–135). New York: McFarland.

Rubinstein, E. A., & Comstock, G. A. (1972). *Television and Social Behavior: Vol. 1. Media content and control*. Washington, DC: U.S. Government Printing Office.

Rudalevige, A. (2010, September 10). War powers and the White House. *The Washington Post*. Retrieved from http://www.washingtonpost.com

Rutenberg, J. (2007, July 12). Bush evokes Revolutionary War to bolster the U.S. cause in Iraq. *The New York Times*, p. A5.

Ryan, J. (2002, December 5). Uncle Sam lights the way for Big Tobacco. *San Francisco Chronicle*. Retrieved from http://articles.sun-sentinel.com

Ryerson, W. N. (1994). Population Communications International: Its role in family planning soap operas. *Population and Environment, 15*, 255–264.

Ryerson, W. N. (1995). Sixteen myths about population growth. *Focus, 5*, 22–37. Retrieved from http://www.mediamonitors.net

Ryerson, W. N. (1998). Political correctness and the population problem. *Wild Earth, 8*, 100–103.

Ryerson, W. N. (2010). Population: The multiplier of everything else. In W. Heinberg & D. Lerch (Eds.), *The post carbon reader: Managing the 21st century's sustainability crises* (pp. 153–174). Healdsburg, CA: Watershed Media.

Ryerson, W. N. (2015). Personal communication.

Saad, L. (2013, January 9). U.S. death penalty support stable at 63%. Gallup. Retrieved from http://www.gallup.com

Sabatino, P. (1986). Great American Smokeout. University of California, San Francisco, Legacy Tobacco Documents Library. Retrieved from http://legacy.library.ucsf.edu/ tid/vmh42e00;jsessionid=87CA596C85137DCBE0FADB4A83E17553.tobacco04

Sabin, P. (2013, September 8). Betting on the apocalypse. *The New York Times*. Retrieved from http://www.nytimes.com

Sackett, G. P. (1966). Monkeys reared in isolation with pictures as visual input: Evidence for an innate releasing mechanism. *Science, 154*, 1468–1473.

Salant, J. D. (2003, October 18). Presidential ecospeak. *The New York Times*. Retrieved from http://www.nytimes.com

Salant, J. D. (2013, January 13). Gun anger often fades as NRA plays waiting game: BGOV barometer. BloombergBusiness. Retrieved from http://www.bloomberg.com

Samuel, H. (2011, November 2). French satirical magazine petrol-bombed after caricature of Prophet Mohammed. *The Telegraph*. Retrieved from http://www.telegraph.co.uk

Samuels, B., & Glantz, S. A. (1991). The politics of local tobacco control. *Journal of the American Medical Association, 266*, 2110–2117.

Sanday, P. R. (1997). The socio-cultural context of rape: A cross-cultural study. In L. L. O'Toole & J. R. Schiffman (Eds.), *Gender violence: Interdisciplinary perspectives* (pp. 52–66). New York: New York University Press.

Sander, O. A. (1946). The pneumoconioses. *Industrial Medicine & Surgery, 15*, 528–530.

Sanger, D. E. (2002, January 30). Bush, focusing on terrorism, says secure U.S. is top priority. *The New York Times*. Retrieved from http://www.nytimes.com

Sankin, A. (2012, September 6). California spending more on prisons than colleges, report says. The Huffington Post. Retrieved from http://www.huffingtonpost.com

Sarat, A. (1995). Violence, representation, and responsibility in capital trials: The view from the jury. *Indiana Law Journal, 70*, 1103–1135.

Sarma, K. (2007). Defensive propaganda and IRA political control in Republican communities. *Studies in Conflict & Terrorism, 30*, 1073–1094.

Sarma, K. (2010). A psychosocial perspective on support for terrorism in the wake of attacks. In B. Brecher (Ed.), *The new order of war* (pp. 201–222). Amsterdam: Rodopi.

Savage, C. (2011, August 4). N.R.A. sues over rule that arms dealers at Mexican border report bulk rifle sales. *The New York Times*, p. A15.

Savage, C., & Risen, J. (2014, December 9). Senate report rejects claim on hunt for Bin Laden. *The New York Times*. Retrieved from http://www.nytimes.com

Savage, C., & Weisman, J. (2015, May 8). N.S.A. collection of bulk call data is ruled illegal. *The New York Times*, p. A1.

Sayare, S., & Clark, N. (2012, September 19). French magazine runs cartoons that mock Muhammad. *The New York Times*. Retrieved from http://www.nytimes.com

Schauer, F. F., & Sinnott-Armstrong, W. (1996). *The philosophy of law: Classic and contemporary readings with commentary*. Fort Worth: Harcourt Brace College Publishers.

Scheer, R., & Moss, D. (2012, September 14). Use it and lose it: The outsize effect of U.S. consumption on the environment. *Scientific American*. Retrieved from http://www.scientificamerican.com

Scheidegger, K. (2002, August 16). The death penalty Trojan horse. *Criminal Justice Legal Foundation*. Retrieved from http://www.cjlf.org

Scheidegger, K. S. (2005, September 23). Should states adopt moratoriums on executions? No. *CQ Researcher, 15*, 801. Retrieved from http://www.cjlf.org

Schmidt, M. S. (2013, January 17). Obama tells Senate that it's time to confirm A.T.F. director. *The New York Times*, p. A19.

Schmidt, M. S. (2014, September 25). F.B.I. confirms a sharp rise in mass shootings since 2000. *The New York Times*, p. A19.

Schmitt, E. (2003, February 28). Pentagon contradicts general on Iraq occupation force's size. *The New York Times*. Retrieved from http://www.nytimes.com

Schmitt, E. (2014, November 9). Obstacles limit targets and pace of strikes on ISIS. *The New York Times*. Retrieved from http://www.nytimes.com

Schmitt, E. (2015, February 17). U.S. intensifies effort to blunt ISIS' message. *The New York Times*, p. Al.

Schmitt, E., & Hubbard, B. (2015, July 21). ISIS leader takes steps to ensure group's survival. *The New York Times*, p. A1.

Schmitt, E., Mazzetti, M., Schmidt, M. S., & Shane, S. (2013, May 3). Boston plot said to have focused on July 4 attack. *The New York Times*, p. A1.

Schmitt, E., Sanger, D. E., & Savage, C. (2013, June 8). Administration says mining of data is crucial to fight terror. *The New York Times*, p. A1.

Schoichet, C. E., & Levs, J. (2015, January 21). Hebdo attack was years in the making. *CNN*. Retrieved from http://www.cnn.com

Schulberg, J. (2014, September 11). Obama's going to arm the Syrian rebels? He's already been doing it covertly for over a year. *New Republic*. Retrieved from http://www.newrepublic.com

Schulz, M., & Aitken, A. (2014, January 2). Extortionist Peter Macari threatens to blow up Qantas jet in historic 1971 'Doomsday Flight' demand for $500,000 cash. *Herald Sun*. Retrieved from http://www.heraldsun.com

Schwartz, F. (2015, January 1). Debate over U.S. government surveillance faces a deadline. *The Wall Street Journal*. Retrieved from http://www.wsj.com

Schwartz, J. (2014, May 15). Report says fewer bees perished over the winter, but the reason is a mystery. *The New York Times*. Retrieved from http://www.nytimes.com

Schwartz, J. (2015, March 16). The new optimism of Al Gore. *The New York Times*. Retrieved from http://www.nytimes.com

Schwarz, A. (2015, February 19). A bid for guns on campuses to deter rape. *The New York Times*, p. A1.

Scott, A. O. (2012, November 9). A president engaged in a great Civil War. *The New York Times*. Retrieved from http://www.nytimes.com

Scott, P. D. (2007). *The road to 9/11: Wealth, empire and the future of America*. Berkeley: University of California Press.

Scott, S. (1994). #188 Smoking and tobacco products. Local preemption. Statewide regulation. *California Journal*. Retrieved from http://calvoter.org

Searle, J. (2003). *Rationality in action*. Cambridge, MA: MIT Press.

Sears, R. R., Maccoby, E. E., & Levin, H. (1957). *Patterns of child rearing*. Evanston, IL: Row, Peterson.

Sedghi, A. (2015, June 24). Air pollution: Delhi is dirty, but how do other cities fare? *The Guardian*. Retrieved from http://www.theguardian.com

Seelye, K. Q. (1997, September 12). Heston asserts gun ownership is nation's highest right. *The New York Times*, p. A14.

Segal, D. (2015, June 21). The people v. the coal baron. *The New York Times*, p. B1.

Selinger, E. (2012, July 23). The philosophy of the technology of the gun. *The Atlantic*. Retrieved from http://www.theatlantic.com

Sellers, C. C. (2010). Cross-nationalizing the history of industrial hazard. *Medical History, 54, 315–340.*

Semple, K. (2014, October 16). At war against ISIS, Iraqi premier is facing battles closer to home. *The New York Times*. Retrieved from http://www.nytimes.com

Semple, K., & al-Jawoshy, O. (2014, October 8). ISIS militants shoot down Iraqi helicopter, killing 2. *The New York Times*. Retrieved from http://www.nytimes.com

Senate Hearings. (1962). Hearings before the Subcommittee to Investigate Juvenile Delinquency, Part 10: Effects on young people of violence and crime portrayed on television. 87th Congress.

Senate Select Committee on Intelligence. (2014). *Committee study of the Central Intelligence Agency's detention and interrogation program*. Washington, DC: U.S. Government Printing Office.

Sengupta, S. (2014a, November 17). Global number of youths is highest ever, U.N. reports. *The New York Times*, p. A6.

Sengupta, S. (2014b, September 17). A host of possible objections to extended airstrikes in Syria. *The New York Times*. Retrieved from http://www.nytimes.com

Sengupta, S. (2015, July 6). Global poverty drops sharply, with China making big strides, U.N. report says. *The New York Times*. Retrieved from http://www.nytimes.com

Serrano, R. A. (2004, June 9). Prison interrogators' gloves came off before Abu Ghraib. *Los Angeles Times*. Retrieved from http://articles.latimes.com

Shane, S. (2013a, May 22). Debate aside, drone strikes drop sharply. *The New York Times*, p. A1.

Shane, S. (2013b, May 5). A homemade style of terror: Jihadists push new tactics. *The New York Times*. Retrieved from http://www.nytimes.com

Shane, S. (2015, February 19). Faulted for avoiding 'Islamic' labels to describe terrorism, White House cites a strategic logic. *The New York Times*, p. A1.

Shane, S., & Hubbard, B. (2014, August 31). ISIS displaying a deft command of varied media. *The New York Times*, p. A1.

Shanker, T. (2002, July 12). Rumsfeld calls civilian deaths relatively low. *The New York Times*, p. A9.

Shanker, T. (2007, January 12). New strategy vindicates ex-army chief Shinseki. *The New York Times*. Retrieved from http://www.nytimes.com

Shapiro, A. (2008, July 17). Ashcroft defends actions on torture memos. *NPR*. Retrieved from http://www.npr.org

Shear, M. D. (2012, December 19). Obama vows fast action in new push for gun control. *The New York Times*. Retrieved from http://www.nytimes.com

Shear, M. D., & Davis, J. H. (2015, February 27). Move to ban a bullet adds to its appeal. *The New York Times*, p. A1.

Shenon, P. (2006, August 18). New limits set over marketing for cigarettes. *The New York Times*. Retrieved from http://www.nytimes.com

Sheppard, K. (2015, February 26). Jim Inhofe brings a snowball to the Senate floor to prove climate change is a "hoax." *The Huffington Post*. Retrieved from http://www.huffingtonpost.com

Shifrel, S., & McShane, L. (2010, October 5). Defiant Faisal Shahzad, Pakistani immigrant who tried to bomb Times Square, sentenced to life. *The Daily News*. Retrieved from http://www.nydailynews.com

Shiner, M. (2010, March 15). Jim Inhofe slams Al Gore on climate "hoax." *POLITICO*. Retrieved from http://www.politico.com

Shnayerson, M. (2007a, May). A convenient untruth. *Vanity Fair*. Retrieved from http://www.vanityfair.com

Shnayerson, M. (2007b, May). A funny thing happened on the way to the throne. *Vanity Fair*. Retrieved from http://www.vanityfair.com

Shulman, W. L. (2011). Criminal justice. In M. Shally-Jensen (Ed.), *Encyclopedia of contemporary American social issues* (Vol. 2, pp. 414–419). Santa Barbara, CA: ABC-CLIO.

Siddiqui, S. (2014, November 5). Voters in Washington State just approved universal background checks. The Huffington Post. Retrieved from http://www.huffingtonpost.com

Signorielli, N. (1985). *Role portrayal on television: An annotated bibliography of studies relating to women, minorities, aging, sexual behavior, health and handicaps*. Westport, CT: Greenwood Press.

Silbert, M. H. (1984). Delancey Street Foundation: Process of mutual restitution. In F. Reissman (Ed.), *Community Psychology Series* (Vol. 10, pp. 41–52). New York: Human Sciences Press.

Silver-Greenberg, J., & Protess, B. (2013, December 11). Criminal action is expected for JPMorgan in Madoff case. *The New York Times*. Retrieved from http://www.nytimes.com

Simon, J. L. (1998). *The ultimate resource 2* (Rev. ed.). Princeton, NJ: Princeton University Press.

Simone, S. (2009, April 22). Abu Ghraib head finds vindication in newly released memos. CNN. Retrieved from http://www.cnn.com

Singh, S., & Darroch, J. E. (2012). Adding it up: Costs and benefits of contraceptive services; Estimates for 2012. Retrieved from http://www.guttmacher.org

Singhal, A., & Rogers, E. M. (1999). *Entertainment-education: A communication strategy for social change*. Mahwah, NJ: Erlbaum.

Singhal, A., Cody, M., Rogers, E., & Sabido, M. (2003). *Entertainment-education and social change: History, research, and practice*. Mahwah, NJ: Erlbaum.

Skelton, G. (1985, February 17). Reagan appeals to public in battle to help contras. *Los Angeles Time*s. Retrieved from http://articles.latimes.com

Slavitt, J. (1992, January 17). The Legacy Tobacco Documents Library. Retrieved from https://industrydocuments.library.ucsf.edu/tobacco/docs/xfxj0045

Smith, G. (2012, March 12). Why I am leaving Goldman Sachs. *The New York Times*, p. A25.

Smith, M. (2005, May 1). Blair planned Iraq war from start. *The Sunday Times*. Retrieved from http://www.thesundaytimes.co.uk

Smith, M. (2014, April 13). "Modest hope" to slow warming but no "free lunch," U.N. warns. *CNN*. Retrieved from http://www.cnn.com

Smith, M. B. (2002). The metaphor (and fact) of war. *Peace and Conflict: Journal of Peace Psychology, 8*, 249–258.

Smith, R. J., & White, J. (2004, June 12). General granted latitude at prison. *The Washington Post*. Retrieved from http://www.washingtonpost.com

Smoking biggest killer in France. (2004, January 4). *Medical News Today*. Retrieved from www.medicalnewstoday.com

Snyder, M. (1980). Seek, and ye shall find: Testing hypotheses about other people. In E. T. Higgins, C. P. Herman, & M. P. Zanna (Eds.), *Social cognition: The Ontario Symposium on Personality and Social Psychology* (pp. 105–130). Hillsdale, NJ: Erlbaum.

Snyder, M., & Campbell, B. H. (1982). Self-monitoring: The self in action. In J. Suls (Ed.), *Psychological perspectives on the self* (pp. 185–207). Hillsdale, NJ: Erlbaum.

Sokolove, M. (2014, July 20). The trials of Graham Spanier, Penn State's ousted president. *The New York Times Magazine*, p. MM24.

Somaiya, R. (2014, January 5). Banished for questioning the gospel of guns. *The New York Times*, p. A1.

Sperry, R. (1993). The impact and promise of the cognitive revolution. *American Psychologist, 48*, 878–885.

Spiegel, P. (2002, February 5). Andersen's chief shifts blame in Enron debacle. FT.com. Retrieved from http://www.ft.com

Spielman, P. J. (2012, March 27). Capital punishment: U.S. ranks 5th on global execution scale, Amnesty International reports. *The Huffington Post*. Retrieved from http://www.huffingtonpost.com

Spitzer, R. J. (1995). *The politics of gun control*. Chatham, NJ: Chatham House.

Spitzer, R. J. (2014). *The politics of gun control* (6th ed.). Boulder: Paradigm Publishers.

Sprinzak, E. (1990). The psychopolitical formation of extreme left terrorism in a democracy: The case of the Weathermen. In W. Reich (Ed.), *Origins of terrorism: Psychologies, ideologies, theologies, states of mind* (pp. 65–85). Cambridge, UK: Cambridge University Press.

Sprinzak, E., & Karmon, E. (2007, June 17). Why so little? The Palestinian terrorist organizations and unconventional terrorism. *Herzliya*. Retrieved from http://www.ict.org

Spyer, J., & al-Tamimi, A. (2014, May 27). Syria's ISIS crucifying opponents, justifying horror with Quran passages. *Middle East Forum*. Retrieved from http://www.meforum.org

St. Augustine and St. Thomas in favor of the death penalty. (2011). Retrieved from http://www.traditioninaction.org

Stajkovic, A. D., Lee, D. S., & Nyberg, A. J. (2009). Collective efficacy, group potency, and group performance: Meta-analyses of their relationships, and test of a mediation model. *Journal of Applied Psychology, 94*, 814–828.

Stalinsky, S. (2004, May 13). Kingdom comes to North America. *National Review*. Retrieved from http://www.nationalreview.com

Stall, B. (1994, August 3). California elections / Governor: Wilson, Brown escalate battle over rape ad. *Los Angeles Times*. Retrieved from http://articles.latimes.com

Steinhauer, J. (2013a, March 13). Congressional committees make some gun-rights provisions permanent. *The New York Times*. Retrieved from http://www.nytimes.com

Steinhauer, J. (2013b, March 13). Senate panel approves two gun control bills. *The New York Times*, p. A16.

Steinhauer, J. (2013c, April 4). Upstart group pushes harder than the N.R.A. *The New York Times*, p. A1.

Steinhauer, J. (2015, Janurary 3). Fight on guns is being taken to state ballots. *The New York Times*, p. A1.

Steuter, E., & Wills, D. (2009). Discourses of dehumanization: Enemy construction and the Canadian media complicity in the framing of the war on terror. *Global Media Journal: Canadian Edition, 2*, 7–24.

Stewart, J. B. (1991). *Den of thieves*. New York: Simon & Schuster.

Stewart, J. B. (2011, October 22). Volcker Rule, once simple, now boggles. *The New York Times*, p. B1.

Stiff, E. (1982, November 8). Letter from the editor: Officials know how to obfuscate. *Evening Independent*. Retrieved from https://news.google.com

Stiglitz, J. (2009, September 13). The great GDP swindle. *The Guardian*. Retrieved from http://www.theguardian.com

Stiglitz, J., Sen, A., & Fitoussi, J.-P. (2015, September). *Report by the Commission on the Measurement of Economic Performance and Social Progress*. Paris: Institut National de la Statistique et des Études Économiques.

Stinson, J. (2007, August 16). Euro-babies go from bust to boom. *USAToday*. Retrieved from http://usatoday30.usatoday.com

Stolberg, S. G., & Kantor, J. (2013, April 14). Shy no more, N.R.A.'s top gun sticks to cause. *The New York Times*, p. A1.

Story, L., & Morgenson, G. (2011a, May 12). Naming culprits in the financial crisis. *The New York Times*. Retrieved from http://www.nytimes.com

Story, L., & Morgenson, G. (2011b, May 31). S.E.C. case stands out because it stands alone. *The New York Times*. Retrieved from http://www.nytimes.com

Strauss, B. H. (2015, July 9). How 2°C of warming could reshape the U.S. Climate Central. Retrieved from http://www.climatecentral.org

Strauss, B. H., Ziemlinski, R., Weiss, J. L., & Overpeck, J. T. (2012, March 14). Tidally adjusted estimates of topographic vulnerability to sea level rise and flooding for the contiguous United States. *Environmental Research Letters*, 7. Retrieved from http://iopscience.iop.org

Streck, M., & Wiechmann, J. (2008, March 17). Lynndie England: "Rumsfeld knew." *Stern*. Retrieved from http://www.stern.de

Strzelczyk, C., & Rothschild, R. (2009, October 28). UN Agenda 21—Coming to a neighborhood near you. American Thinker. Retrieved from http://www.americanthinker.com

Sullivan, A. (2005, January 23). Atrocities in plain sight. *The New York Times*. Retrieved from http://www.nytimes.com

Sum, A., Khatiwada, I., McLaughlin, J., & Palma, S. (2009, October). *The consequences of dropping out of high school: Joblessness and jailing for high school dropouts and the high cost for taxpayers*. Boston: Center for Labor Market Studies Publications, Northeastern University. Retrieved from http://www.northeastern.edu

Swanson, J. W. (2011). Explaining rare acts of violence: The limits of evidence from population research. *Psychiatric Services*, 62, 1369–1371.

Swiss Armed Forces. (n.d.). Retrieved from www.vtg.admin.ch

Tabuchi, H., Belson, K., & Onishi, N. (2011, March 16). Dearth of candor from Japan's leadership. *The New York Times*. Retrieved from http://www.nytimes.com

Taibbi, M. (2010, April 5). The great American bubble machine. *Rolling Stone*. Retrieved from http://www.rollingstone.com

Taibbi, M. (2013, April 25). Everything is rigged: The biggest price-fixing scandal ever. *Rolling Stone*. Retrieved from http://www.rollingstone.com

Tavernise, S. (2011, May 20). Report faults mine owner for explosion that killed 29. *The New York Times*, p. A11.

Tavernise, S. (2013a, September 6). Rise is seen in students who use e-cigarettes. *The New York Times*, p. A12.

Tavernise, S. (2013b, December 13). Tobacco industry tactics limit poorer nations' smoking laws. *The New York Times*, p. A1.

Tavernise, S. (2015a, March 19). New global fund to help countries defend smoking laws. *The New York Times*, p. A4.

Tavernise, S. (2015b, April 17). Teenagers pick up e-cigarettes as old-school smoking declines. *The New York Times*, p. A1.

Taylor, A. (2013). Capital punishment and public safety. Retrieved from http://ethikapolitika.org

Ten most harmful books of the 19th and 20th centuries. (2005, May 31). *Human Events*. Retrieved from http://humanevents.com

Thaker, J. (2014). *Climate change in the Indian mind: Role of collective efficacy in climate change adaptation*. (Doctoral dissertation). Retrieved from http://digilib.gmu.edu

Thamel, P. (2012, July 23). Sanctions decimate the Nittany Lions now and for years to come. *The New York Times*. Retrieved from http://www.nytimes.com/

The Death Penalty in the United States. http://www.wesleylowe.com/cp.html

Thibodeau, P., & Boroditsky, L. (2011, February). Metaphors we think with: The role of metaphor in reasoning. *PloS One*. Retrieved from http://www.plosone.org

Thomas, A. (Writer & director). (1982). Frank Terpil: Confessions of a dangerous man. [Television series episode]. [Transcript]. In D. Fanning (Producer), *World*. Boston: WGBH Educational Foundation.

Thomas, M. H., & Drabman, R. S. (1975). Toleration of real life aggression as a function of exposure to televised violence and age of subject. *Merrill-Palmer Quarterly of Behavior and Development, 21*, 227–232.

Thomas, M. H., Horton, R. W., Lippincott, E. C., & Drabman, R. S. (1977). Desensitization to portrayals of real-life aggression as function of exposure to television violence. *Journal of Personality and Social Psychology Today, 35*, 450–458.

Thornberg, R., & Jungert, T. (2013). Bystander behavior in bullying situations: Basic moral sensitivity, moral disengagement and defender self-efficacy. *Journal of Adolesence, 36*, 475–483.

Thornton, M. (1983, September 22). Terpil reported paid for story. *The Washington Post*. Retrieved from http://www.washingtonpost.com

Thornton, R. (1977, January 26). Some "benefits" of smoking. BAT Group Research and Development Centre, publication RD1461, unclassified. University of California, San Francisco, Legacy Tobacco Documents Library, Brown & Williamson Collection. File No. 1223.01. Retrieved from https://industrydocuments.library.ucsf.edu

Tilker, H. A. (1970). Socially responsible behavior as a function of observer responsibility and victim feedback. *Journal of Personality and Social Psychology, 14*, 95–100.

Tittle, C. R. (1977). Sanction fear and the maintenance of social order. *Oxford Journal, 55*, 579–596.

Toch, H. (1992). The anatomy of violence. In *Violent men: An inquiry into the psychology of violence* (Rev. ed., pp. 179–215). Washington, DC: American Psychological Association.

Tollefsen, C. O. (2011, September 16). Capital punishment, sanctity of life, and human dignity. Public Discourse. Retrieved from http://www.thepublicdiscourse.com

Top 15 counties by execution since 1976. (2013, January 1). Death Penalty Information Center. Retrieved from http://www.deathpenaltyinfo.org

Totenberg, N. (2015, June 30). Supreme Court concludes term with death penalty ruling, looks ahead. *NPR*. Retrieved from http://www.npr.org

Trotta, D. (2013, March 14). Iraq war cost U.S. more than $2 trillion: Study. Reuters. Retrieved from http://www.reuters.com

Tseng, N. (2014, January 8). JPMorgan could have ratted out Madoff but didn't. *Fortune*. Retrieved from http://fortune.com

Turiel, E. M. (1983). *The development of social knowledge: Morality and convention*. Cambridge: Cambridge University Press.

Turnbull, C. M. (1961). *The forest people*. New York: Simon & Schuster.

Tyler, P. E. (2004, February 5). Blair tells Commons that results in Iraq are more important than faulty intelligence. *The New York Times*. Retrieved from http://www.nytimes.com

U. S. Environmental Protection Agency (1993, January 7). EPA designates passive smoking a "Class A" or known human carcinogen. *Press release*. Retrieved from http://www2.epa.gov

U.S. Army Corps of Engineers (1996, September 3). *Safety and health requirements manual*. Edited by R. H. Griffin. Washington, DC: U.S. Government Printing Office.

U.S. Census Bureau (2015a, July). International data base: World population: 1950–2050. Washington, DC: U.S. *Census Bureau*. Retrieved from https://www.census.gov

U.S. Census Bureau (2015b, March 3). New Census Bureau report analyzes U.S. population projections. Washington, DC: U.S. *Census Bureau*. Retrieved from https://www.census.gov

U.S. Department of Labor, Division of Labor Standards (1937, February 3). National Silicosis Conference: Summary Reports Submitted to the Secretary of Labor by Conference Committees. Bulletin no. 13. Washington, DC: U.S. Government Printing Office. Retrieved from http://babel.hathitrust.org

U.S. Department of Labor, Division of Labor Standards (1938). National Silicosis Conference, Report on Medical Control. Bulletin No. 21, Part 1. Washington, DC: Government Printing Office.

U.S. Environmental Protection Agency. (2008). Global greenhouse gas emissions data. Retrieved from http://www.epa.gov

U.S. Public Health Service (1925). *Conference to determine whether or not there is a public health question in the manufacture, distribution or use of tetraethyl lead gasoline* (Public Health Bulletin No. 158). Washington, DC: U.S. Government Printing Office.

U.S. Securities and Exchange Commission (2013, September 29). JPMorgan Chase agrees to pay $200 million and admits wrongdoing to settle SEC charges [Press release]. Retrieved from http://www.sec.gov

Uchitelle, L. (2010, July 11). Volcker pushes for reform, regretting past silence. *The New York Times*, p. B1.

Uhlmann, D. M. (2013, December 14). Prosecution deferred, justice denied. *The New York Times*, p. A23.

United Nations Population Fund (2014). International Conference on Population and Development. Retrieved from http://www.unfpa.org

Upton, J. (2015, August 4). Obama just created a carbon cap-and-trade program. *Climate Central*. Retrieved from http://www.climatecentral.org

Urbina, I. (2010, February 24). Fearing limits, states weaken gun regulation. *The New York Times*, p. A1.

Urofsky, M. I. (1988). *A march of liberty: A constitutional history of the United States*. New York: Knopf.

Valls, A. (2010). Can terrorism be justified? In L. Vaughn (Ed.), *Contemporary moral arguments: Readings in ethical issues* (pp. 446–456). New York: Oxford University Press.

Van Den Haag, E. (1968). On deterrence and the death penalty. *Ethics, 78,* 280–288.

Van Den Haag, E. (1986). The ultimate punishment: A defense. *Harvard Law Review,* *99,* 1662–1669.

Vidmar, N., & Ellsworth, P. (1974). Public opinion and the death penalty. *Stanford Law Review, 26,* 1245–1270.

Violence Policy Center. (2015, February 12). Concealed carry killers. Retrieved from http://concealedcarrykillers.org

Wainwright, O. (2014, September 16). Inside Beijing's airpocalypse—a city made 'almost uninhabitable' by pollution. *The Guardian.* Retrieved from http://www.theguardian.com

Wakin, D. J., & Donadio, R. (2010, April 3). Vatican priest likens criticism over abuse to anti-Semitism. *The New York Times,* p. A1.

Waldman, M. (2014). *The second amendment: A biography.* New York: Simon & Schuster.

Wallack, L., Dorfman, L., Jernigan, D., & Themba, M. (1993). *Media advocacy and public health: Power for prevention.* Newbury Park, CA: Sage Publications.

Walsh, D., & Caldwell, L. A. (2014, September 23). Most positive reaction to Syrian airstrikes comes from Obama's critics. *CNN.* Retrieved from http://www.cnn.com

Walter, K. M., Zimov, S. A., Chanton, J. P., Verbyla, D., & Chapin III, F. S. (2006). Methane bubbling from Siberian thaw lakes as a positive feedback to climate warming. *Nature, 443,* 71–75.

Walzer, M. (2010). Terrorism: A critique of excuses. In L. Vaughn (Ed.), *Contemporary moral arguments: Readings in ethical issues* (pp. 440–446). New York: Oxford University Press.

Wang, H. L. (2013, May 15). Immigrants to be largest driver of U.S. population growth. *NPR.* Retrieved from http://www.npr.org

Warner, D. (2012a, May 23). Senior priest testifies at sex abuse trial. Reuters. Retrieved from http://www.reuters.com

Warner, D. (2012b, May 24). Senior US priest defends response to child abuse complaint. *Reuters.* Retrieved from http://www.reuters.com

Weber, B. (2010, September 9). David Dortort, 'Bonanza' creator, dies at 93. *The New York Times,* p. A28.

Wegner, D. (2002). *The illusion of conscious will.* Cambridge, MA: MIT Press.

Wegner, D. (2004). Précis of *The illusion of conscious will. Behavioral and Brain Sciences, 27,* 649–659.

Wegner, D. M. (1989). *White bears and other unwanted thoughts: Suppression, obsession, and the psychology of mental control.* New York: Viking.

Weidlein, E. (1935, March 21). [Cover letter to W. Hazard, Mellon Institute, and plan for study of dust problems]. National Archives, Record Group 90, State Boards of Health (0875-96-49), Pittsburgh, PA.

Weintraub, S. (2001). *Silent night: The story of the World War I Christmas truce.* New York: Free Press.

Weir, D. (1987). *The Bhopal syndrome.* San Francisco: Sierra Club Books.

Weitz, R., & Neal, S. R. (2007). Preventing terrorist best practices from going mass market: A case study of suicide attacks "crossing the chasm." In S. S. Costigan & D. Gold (Eds.), *Terrornomics* (pp. 129–144). Aldershot, UK: Ashgate.

Wells, J. (1981, July 24). Re: Smoking and health—Tim Finnegan. University of California, San Francisco, Legacy Tobacco Documents Library, Brown & Williamson Collection. Bates no. 1825-1901. Retrieved from https://industrydocuments.library.ucsf.edu

Wells, W. D. (1971). *Television and aggression: Replication of an experimental field study.* Unpublished manuscript, University of Chicago.

Wenk, E., Jr. (1979). Political limits in steering technology: Pathologies of the short run. *Technology in Society, 1,* 27–36.

Westoff, C. F., & Rodríguez, G. (1995). The mass media and family planning in Kenya. *International Family Planning Perspectives, 21,* 26–31, 36.

Wetzel, D. (2011, November 5). Penn State's insufficient action amid child sex allegations stunning. Yahoo Sports. Retrieved from http://sports.yahoo.com

Wexler, N. (2006). Successful resume fraud: Conjectures on the origins of amorality in the workplace. *Journal of Human Values, 12,* 137–152.

Weyler, R. (2013, May 6). Population and ecology [Web log post]. *Greenpeace.* Retrieved from http://www.greenpeace.org

WFAA Staff. (2013, January 18). Armstrong interview leaves much to be desired. *WFAA.* Retrieved from http://www.wfaa.com

What is a euphemism? (n.d.). Retrieved from http:/www.vizettes.com

Wheeler, R. (1977a, August 24). [Letter to T. R. Torkelson]. Manufacturing Chemists' Association Papers.

Wheeler, R.N. (1977b). Union Carbide. Comments on Equitable Environmental Health report of epidemiology study of polyvinyl chloride workers. Manufacturing Chemists' Association; August 24.

Whitaker, B. (2003, February 11). Bin Laden offers tips to defend Iraq. *The Guardian.* Retrieved from http://www.theguardian.com

White, G. (1998). Recasting Janis's groupthink decision fiascoes. *Organizational Behavior and Human Decision Processes, 73,* 185–209.

White, J., & Higham, S. (2004, July 23). Abuses an aberration, report says, 94 cases confirmed or called possible—individuals blamed. *The Washington Post.* Retrieved from http://www.washingtonpost.com

White, J., Bandura, A., & Bero, L. (2009). Moral disengagement in the corporate world. *Accountability in Research, 16,* 41–74.

Whiting, J. W. M. (1941). *Becoming a Kwoma.* New Haven: Yale University Press.

Whitney, C. R. (2012, July 25). A way out of the gun stalemate. *The New York Times,* p. A25.

Who pays for cap and trade? (2009, March 9). *The Wall Street Journal.* Retrieved from http://online.wsj.com

Williams, T. M. (1986). *The impact of television: A natural experiment in three communities.* New York: Academic Press.

Wilson, E. (1998). *Consilience: The unity of knowledge.* New York: Knopf.

Winfield, N. (2007, September 7). Pope urges young people to care for planet. *Napa Valley Register.* Retrieved from http://napavalleyregister.com

Winfield, N. (2014, February 5). Pope pressured to act on abuse after UN rebuke. Associated Press. Retrieved from http://bigstory.ap.org/

Wing, N. (2013, January 21). Mitch McConnell gun control email: You're "literally surrounded," they're "coming for your guns." *The Huffington Post.* Retrieved from http://www.huffingtonpost.com

Winkler, A. (2011, September 9). Did the Wild West have more gun control than we do today? The Huffington Post. Retrieved from http://www.huffingtonpost.com

Wistrich, R. S. (2010). *A lethal obsession: Antisemitism from antiquity to the global jihad.* New York: Random House.

Wolfe, T. (1996). Sorry, but your soul just died. *Forbes, 158,* 210.

Wolfowitz: WMD chosen as reason for Iraq War for 'bureaucratic reasons.' (2003, May 30). [Transcript]. CNN. Retrieved from http://www.cnn.com

Wong, C. H. (2015, March 10). China sets timeline for first change to retirement age since 1950s. *The Wall Street Journal*. Retrieved from http://blogs.wsj.com

Wood, D. (2014, March 20). A warrior's moral dilemma. *The Huffington Post*. Retrieved from http://projects.huffingtonpost.com

Wood, G. S. (2009). *Empire of liberty: A history of the early Republic, 1789–1815.* Oxford, UK: Oxford University Press.

World Health Organization. (2014, February). Female genital mutilation. Fact sheet no. 241. Retrieved from http://www.who.int

Wormser, F. (1945a, January). Preliminary report of investigation of "Time" article "Paint eaters." *Lead Hygiene and Safety Bulletin, 40.*

Wormser, F. (1945b). *A safety and hygiene program for the Lead Industries Association.* LIA Executive Committee Meeting, Exhibit D. Lead Industry Association Papers.

Wright, G. (1949). Disability evaluation in industrial pulmonary disease. *Journal of the American Medical Association, 141,* 1218–1222.

Wyatt, E. (2012, February 24). Settlements without admissions get scrutiny. *The New York Times.* Retrieved from http://www.nytimes.com

Wyatt, E., & Protess, B. (2011, May 12). Foes revise plan to curb new agency. *The New York Times,* p. B1.

Yaccino, S. (2012, April 12). N.R.A. official attacks Florida shooting coverage. *The New York Times,* p. A15.

Yaccino, S. (2013, May 31). Illinois lawmakers race for compromise on guns. *The New York Times,* p. A12.

Yaccino, S., & Davey, M. (2012, October 22). Three killed in shooting at spa in Wisconsin. *The New York Times,* p. A13.

Yardley, J., & Schwartz, J. (2002, January 15). Enron's collapse: The law firm; Legal counsel in many ways mirrors client. *The New York Times.* Retrieved from http://www.nytimes.com

Yardley, J., Y Goodstein, L. (2015, June 18). Pope Francis, in sweeping encyclical, calls for swift action on climate change. *The New York Times.* Retrieved from http://www.nytimes.com

Yardley, W. (2011, November 23). Oregon governor says he will not allow executions. *The New York Times,* p. A14.

Yeaman, A. (1963, July 3). Outgoing cable (regarding disclosure of research on nicotine to surgeon general's committee). University of California, San Francisco.

Yeginsu, C. (2014, September 16). ISIS draws a steady stream of recruits from Turkey. *The New York Times,* p. A1.

Yoo, J. (2003, March 14). [Memo for William J. Haynes II]. Retrieved from https://www.aclu.org

Yoo, J. (2004, May 26). Terrorists have no Geneva rights. *The Wall Street Journal.* Retrieved from http://www.wsj.com

York, A. C., & Skeyhill, T. J. (1928). *Sergeant York: His own life story and war diary.* Garden City, NY: Doubleday Doran.

Young, R. L. (2004). Guilty until proven innocent: Conviction orientation, racial attitudes, and support for capital punishment. *Deviant Behavior, 25,* 151–167.

Zaelke, D. J., & Ramanathan, V. (2012, December 7). Going beyond carbon dioxide. *The New York Times,* p. A39.

Zane, M. (1981, December 8). Court rejects girl's rape suit that blames TV. *San Francisco Chronicle*, p. 6.

Zernike, K. (2004, May 12). Prison guard calls abuse routine and sometimes amusing. *The New York Times*, p. N16.

Zernike, K. (2006, February 12). Violent crime rising sharply in some cities. *The New York Times*. Retrieved from http://www.nytimes.com

Zernike, K., & Kaufman, M. T. (2011, May 2). The most wanted face of terrorism. *The New York Times*. Retrieved from http://www.nytimes.com

Zganjar, L. (1998, March 12). Forgotten hero of My Lai to be honored after 30 years. Associated Press. *San Francisco Chronicle*, p. A9.

Zha, W., & Nicola, S. (2015, April 15). German solar records may keep traders busy on weekends. BloombergBusiness. Retrieved from http://www.bloomberg.com

Zielinski, B. (2011, March 3). Who is to blame for borrowers taking loans they can't afford? Problem Bank List. Retrieved from http://problembanklist.com

Zillmann, D. (1988). Cognition-excitation interdependences in aggressive behavior. *Aggressive Behavior, 14*, 51–64.

Zillmann, D., & Bryant, J. (1984). Effects of massive exposure to pornography. In N. M. Malamuth & E. Donnerstein (Eds.), *Pornography and sexual aggression* (pp. 115–138). New York: Academic Press.

Zimbardo, P. (1969). The human choice: Individuation, reason, and order versus deindividuation, impulse, and chaos. In W. J. Arnold & D. Levine (Eds.), *Nebraska Symposium on Motivation* (pp. 237–309). Lincoln: University of Nebraska Press.

Zimbardo, P. (2007). *The Lucifer effect: Understanding how good people turn evil*. New York: Random House.

Zimring, F. E., & Hawkins, G. J. (1973). *Deterrence: The legal threat in crime control*. Chicago: University of Chicago Press.

Zmirak, J. (2013, May 15). When justice demands the hangman. First Things. Retrieved from http://www.firstthings.com

NAME INDEX

SUBJECT INDEX